CONSTITUTIONAL REFORM

CONSTITUTIONAL REFORM
The Labour Government's Constitutional Reform Agenda

EDITED BY
ROBERT BLACKBURN
AND
RAYMOND PLANT

LONGMAN
London and New York

Addison Wesley Longman Limited
Edinburgh Gate
Harlow
Essex   CM20 2JE
United Kingdom
and Associated Companies throughout the world.

First published 1999

ISBN 0-582-36999-1   Ppr

Visit Addison Wesley Longman on the world wide web at http://www.awl-he.com

British Library Cataloguing-in-Publication Data

A catalogue record for this book is available from the British Library

Set by 35 in 10/12 pt Plantin
Produced by Addison Wesley Longman Singapore (Pte) Ltd.,
Printed in Singapore

CONTENTS

ACKNOWLEDGEMENTS

We are indebted to the following for permission to reproduce copyright material:

The Conservative Party for extracts from *THE CONSERVATIVE PARTY GENERAL ELECTION MANIFESTO* 1997; The Labour Party for extracts from *THE LABOUR PARTY GENERAL ELECTION MANIFESTO* 1997 & *LABOUR POLICY COMMISSION, A NEW AGENDA FOR DEMOCRACY: LABOUR'S PROPOSALS FOR CONSTITUTIONAL REFORM* 1993; The Labour Party/Liberal Democrats Federal Party for extracts from the *Joint Labour Party–Liberal Democrats CONSULTATIVE COMMITTEE REPORT ON CONSTITUTIONAL REFORM* 1997; The Liberal Democrats Federal Party for extracts from the *LIBERAL DEMOCRAT GENERAL ELECTION MANIFESTO* 1997.

THE CONTRIBUTORS

Robert Blackburn is Professor of Constitutional Law at King's College, University of London. His research interests include government affairs and parliamentary practice, on which he has lectured widely in the UK and abroad. He has conducted policy work for think-tanks and official bodies on many occasions, including the Institute for Public Policy Research as a member of its working group on a written constitution for the UK (1990–91), the Constitution Unit as an adviser on parliamentary reform (1995–96), the Bar Council as a member of its Law Reform Committee on the Human Rights Bill (1997–98), the Council of Europe as its UK legal consultant on the domestic impact of the European Convention on Human Rights (1993–99), and the House of Commons Home Affairs Committee as an expert witness on electoral law reform (1997–98). His affiliations include the Study of Parliament Group of which he was appointed Academic Secretary in 1996, the British Institute of Human Rights of which was appointed a Governor in 1990, and the Royal Historical Society of which he he was elected a Fellow in 1986. Recent books include *The Electoral System in Britain* (London: Macmillan, 1995), *Towards a Constitutional Bill of Rights for the United Kingdom* (London: Pinter, 1999), and a title in Halsbury's Laws of England on *The Crown and the Royal Family* (London: Butterworths, 1998).

Raymond Plant is the Master of St Catherine's College, University of Oxford, prior to which he was Professor of Political Science at Southampton University. He has written widely in the field of political theory, and has given the Stanton lectures at Cambridge University, the Sarum Lectures at Oxford, the Ferguson Lectures at Manchester University and the Scott Holland Lectures at Manchester Cathedral. He currently serves as President of both the National Council of Voluntary Organisations and the Association of Learned Societies in the Social Sciences, and has been an executive member of the Fabian Society since 1990. He is a life peer (Lord Plant of Highfield) in the House of Lords where he takes the Labour whip and is a member of the European Communities Sub-Committee on Law and Institutions. In

1990–93 he chaired Labour's National Executive Committee Working Party on Electoral Systems. His books include *Community and Ideology* (London: Routledge and Kegan Paul, 1974), *Hegel* (London: Allen and Unwin, 1983), *Philosophy, Politics and Citizenship* (with A Vincent, Oxford: Basil Blackwell, 1983), *Conservative Capitalism in Britain and the United States* (with K Hoover, London: Routledge, 1988) and *Modern Political Thought* (Oxford: Basil Blackwell, 1991).

Patrick Birkinshaw has been Director of the Institute of European Public Law at Hull University since 1992, and has been a Professor in the Law School at that University since 1990. Author of many books and articles including *Grievances, Remedies and the State* (London: Sweet & Maxwell, 2nd edn, 1995) and *Freedom of Information: The Law, the Practice and the Ideal* (London: Butterworths, 2nd edn, 1996), he has been Dean of the Law School at Hull University since 1997.

Kevin Boyle is the Director of the Human Rights Centre and Professor of Law at Essex University. His career has included periods as a law teacher in Queen's University Belfast and University College Galway where he was Dean of the Faculty of Law from 1978–86. He has had a long-term collaboration with Professor Tom Hadden in research and writing on the legal and political dimensions of the conflict in Northern Ireland. Their last book was *Northern Ireland: The Choice* (London: Penguin, 1994).

Rodney Brazier is a Professor of Law at the University of Manchester. His main research interests lie in constitutional law and practice, and in constitutional reform. His principal publications include *Constitutional Practice* (Oxford: Clarendon Press, 2nd edn, 1994), *Constitutional Reform* (Oxford University Press, 2nd edn, 1998), *Constitutional Texts* (Oxford University Press, 1990), *Constitutional and Administrative Law* (London: Penguin, 8th edn, 1998) and *Ministers of the Crown* (Oxford: Clarendon Press, 1997).

Katy Donnelly is a Consultant on Economic Regeneration with Martin Caldwell Associates. After graduating with a First in Politics from Queen Mary and Westfield College, London, she worked as a volunteer for Charter 88 and conducted research at Sheffield University on the constitutional role of the National Audit Office. In 1995–97 she was Research Officer at the Constitution Unit (an independent inquiry into the implementation of constitutional reform, directed by Robert Hazell), where she co-authored the Unit's reports on *Delivering Constitutional Reform* (with Nicole Smith, 1996) and *Regional Government in England* (with Paul McQuail, 1996).

Gavin Drewry is Professor of Public Administration and Director of the Centre for Political Studies at Royal Holloway, University of London. He has written extensively, and lectured to both UK and overseas audiences, on aspects of public service and parliamentary reform. His most recent book (co-edited with Dawn Oliver) is *The Law and Parliament* (London: Butterworths, 1998). Professor Drewry is Chairman of the Study of Parliament Group, a member of the Advisory Council of the Civil Service College, Deputy Editor of the *Statute Law Review*, and he serves on the Editorial Committee of *Public Law*.

Tom Hadden, after graduating and completing his doctorate at Cambridge, taught at the University of Kent. In 1969 he took up a lectureship at the Queen's University of Belfast, where he is now a part-time Professor of Law. From 1985 to 1990 he was a member of the Standing Advisory Commission for Human Rights for Northern Ireland. He was the founding editor of *Fortnight: An Independent Review* for Northern Ireland and remains an active member of its editorial committee. With Kevin Boyle, he has written a number of influential books on Northern Ireland including *Northern Ireland – The Choice* (London: Penguin, 1994).

Carol Harlow is Professor of Public Law at the London School of Economics, specialising in the constitutional and administrative law of the UK and European Union. She is the author of numerous articles and books, including *Law and Administration* (with Richard Rawlings, London: Weidenfeld and Nicolson, 2nd edn, 1997), *Pressure Through Law* (with Richard Rawlings, London: Routledge, 1992) and, as co-editor (with Paul Craig), *The European Lawmaking Process* (The Hague: Kluwer, 1998).

Alastair Hudson is a Barrister and a Lecturer in Law at Queen Mary and Westfield College, University of London. His published works include a book on *The Law on Homelessness* (London: Sweet & Maxwell, 1997), which draws upon his experience of legal practice in this area, *The Law on Financial Derivatives* (London: Sweet and Maxwell, 2nd edn 1998), and contributions to *Palmer's Company Law*. He was the Labour Party candidate for Beaconsfield at the 1997 general election, prior to which he was an opposition Special Adviser on legal affairs. He was the author of the original draft of Labour's policy document on *Access to Justice* (1995).

Graham Leicester is Director of the Scottish Council Foundation, promoting independent thinking in public policy. Formerly he spent 11 years as a member of HM Diplomatic Service, specialising in European Union affairs. In 1995–97 he worked as Research Fellow at the Constitution Unit, working on devolution, and he was the principal author of the Unit's report on *Scotland's Parliament: Fundamentals for a New Scotland Act* (1996).

Martin Linton MP was elected to the House of Commons at the 1997 general election for Battersea, and is an active member of the Home Affairs Committee. As a writer he has specialised in political and constitutional affairs, formerly working as a journalist with *The Guardian* newspaper. His published works include *Money and Votes* (for the Institute for Public Policy Research, 1994) and, most recently, *Making Votes Count* (co-authored with Mary Southcott, 1998).

Ian Loveland is a graduate of the Universities of Warwick, London and Oxford, and between 1988–91 was a Fellow of Nuffield College, Oxford. After a period as Lecturer in Law at Queen Mary College, London, he was appointed Professor of Law at Brunel University in 1996. He is the author and editor of numerous works on British and comparative public law, including *Constitutional Law: A Critical Introduction* (London: Butterworths, 1996), *A Special Relationship? American Influences on Public Law in the United Kingdom* (ed, Oxford University Press, 1995), and *Importing the First Amendment: Freedom of Speech and Expression in Britain, Europe and the USA* (ed, Oxford: Richard Hart, 1998).

Paul McQuail, a former Deputy Secretary in the Department of the Environment, worked as a Research Associate for the Constitution Unit in the preparation of its reports between 1995–97 on devolution to the English regions.

Richard Norton-Taylor is a writer and journalist specialising in official secrecy, behind-the-scenes decision-making in government, and the security and intelligence services. He has worked for *The Guardian* since 1975 and appears regularly as a commentator on TV and radio news and current affairs programmes. His numerous books include *Blacklist: The Inside Story of Political Vetting* (with Mark Holingsworth, Hogarth Press, 1988); *In Defence of the Realm: The Case for Accountable Security and Intelligence Services* (Civil Liberties Trust, 1990); *Truth is a Difficult Concept: Inside the Scott Inquiry* (Fourth Estate, Guardian Book, 1995); and *Knee Deep in Dishonour: The Scott Report and its Aftermath* (London: Victor Gollancz, 1996). He won the Freedom of Information Campaign Award in 1986, and again in 1994 for his play, *Half the Picture*, based on the Scott arms-to-Iraq inquiry. In 1996 he edited a stage play on the 1945 Nuremberg war crimes trial.

Alan Parkin has published various articles on public law and health law. He is a Lecturer in the Law School at Hull University and is the Academic Director of the School.

Michael Ryle served in the Clerk's Department, House of Commons, from 1951 to 1989, retiring as Clerk of Committees. He was a founder member of the Study of Parliament Group; and a Council member of the Hansard Society, serving on its Commission on the Legislative Process, 1991–93, as Secretary. Since 1989, he has lectured, broadcast and written on parliamentary topics, and advised several Parliaments in Eastern Europe and the former

Soviet Union on their practices and procedures. He chaired the Liberal Democrat Working Group on Reform of the House of Commons, whose proposals were published as *A Parliament for the People* (Liberal Democrats, Policy Paper 20, 1996). He has edited and contributed to a number of books on Parliament, and is the author (with J A G Griffith) of *Parliament: Functions, Practice and Procedures* (London: Sweet & Maxwell, 1989).

Nicole Smith was Assistant Director of the Constitution Unit between 1995–97 and prepared several of the Unit's reports, including *Delivering Constitutional Reform* (with Katy Donnelly, 1996), *Reform of the House of Lords* (1996) and *Human Rights Legislation* (1996). She has also worked for the Home Office and in the voluntary sector as a campaigner for civil rights.

Sarah Spencer is the Director of the Human Rights Programme at the Institute for Public Policy Research, the centre-left think-tank. She was formerly General Secretary of the National Council for Civil Liberties (1985–89) and Director of the human rights education and research charity, the Cobden Trust (1984–85). She is a member of the Home Secretary's Taskforce on Implementation of the Human Rights Act, and of the ESRC Advisory Board on Transnational Communities. Her recent publications include *A Human Rights Commission: The Options for Britain and Northern Ireland* (with Ian Bynoe, 1998); *Migrants, Refugees and the Boundaries of Citizenship* (1995); *Strangers and Citizens: A Positive Approach to Migrants and Refugees* (ed, 1994); *Immigration as an Economic Asset: the German Experience* (ed, 1994); *Accountable Policing* (co-ed, 1993); and *A British Bill of Rights* (co-author, 1990).

John Wadham is a Solicitor and the Director of Liberty (National Council for Civil Liberties). He has acted for large numbers of applicants in cases before the Commission and Court of Human Rights. He is the editor of *Your Rights: The Liberty Guide*; the civil liberties section of *The Penguin Guide to the Law*; the case reports for *The European Rights Law Review*; and *Blackstone's Guide to the Human Rights Act 1998*. He has contributed to many other publications and written many articles on human rights and civil liberties. He also appears as a spokesperson on human rights issues in the media and is a regular speaker at conferences and on training courses.

INTRODUCTION

Professor Robert Blackburn (King's College, London)
and Professor Raymond Plant (Oxford University)

This book contains a collection of individual commentaries upon the Labour government's ambitious plans and objectives in the field of constitutional reform. Labour's agenda in this area of public policy, as presented in their published statements and reports in recent years,[1] is wider than that of any political party taking office this century. Indeed, taken as a whole, the parameters and range of subjects affected cover virtually the entire terrain of our constitutional structure. Devolution and regional government, the modernisation of both chambers in the Westminster Parliament, a rolling programme of human rights reform beginning with a Human Rights Act, a forthcoming statute on freedom of information – these measures and many more which are described within Labour's policy documentation leading up to its 1997 election victory extend across the length and breadth of our political and legal systems in the UK.

As co-editors of this work, our aim has been to produce a constructive offering on how the underlying objectives of the Labour Party with respect to constitutional reform, which to a large extent are now shared with Liberal Democrats and across the centre-left of politics, might be best achieved. Individual political and legal writers, known to be broadly supportive of the general case for reform, were invited to write on some specific subject within their own area of work. They were asked to examine Labour's stated policy objectives and to offer ideas and practical suggestions on how these might be put into practice.

Labour's policy programme in constitutional as well as social and economic affairs has undergone a revolution since 1987. The comprehensive policy review launched by Neil Kinnock as Labour leader, in the aftermath of the party's election defeat that year, left virtually no aspect of policy unexplored or untouched. Its final report published in 1989, *Meet the Challenge: Make the Change*, placed the constitution at the forefront of the party's programme for government, as had never been the case before. 'Central to

---

[1] For extracts from constitutional reform policy documents, see the Appendices 1–3 below.

Labour's purpose in government', the party's 1992 election manifesto was to say, 'is our commitment to radical constitutional reform.' Over the next two years, the strong personal backing that John Smith gave as Labour leader served to galvanise the party's constitutional programme still further. The speeches of John Smith at that time still stand as providing some of the most potent rhetoric ever delivered on the subject of reform.[2] Smith established a new policy commission on the constitution, under Tony Blair's convenorship as the party's then home affairs spokesperson, which produced a major policy statement in 1993, *A New Agenda for Democracy: Labour's Programme for Constitutional Reform*, subsequently endorsed by the party conference. This report embraced a wide range of radical new ideas and goals, and still forms the most authoritative document on contemporary Labour ideology on the subject. The pre-election policy statements published in 1996–97, including *New Labour New Britain: Labour's Contract for a New Britain* and *Because Britain Deserves Better: Labour Election Manifesto*, wisely restricted Labour's attention to what was achievable within a single term of government and how best to present those items to the electorate.

Labour's agenda, then, must be viewed as containing an array of policy items which are at very different stages of readiness for being put into effect. They range from imminent parliamentary enactment to indefinite postponement pending completion of the present parliamentary term. Some constitutional measures have been subject to painstaking planning and political consultation in advance of the 1997 general election. The Scotland Bill is a leading case in point (see Chapter 12), for which much of the preparatory work involved had been carried out in advance by the Scottish Constitutional Convention. The Human Rights Bill, being the other major constitutional measure being carried through this 1997–98 session, was the subject of an extensive Opposition consultation exercise, analogous to a Green Paper, during the winter months prior to the 1997 election. Other long-standing policy commitments too, such as open government and statutory rights of access to official information, have been the subject of a great deal of advance thought prior to the legislation anticipated in the next parliamentary session (see Chapter 8).

The greater part of Labour's constitutional programme, however, represents the identification of some problem or the expression of a social or political principle, which as yet lacks any detailed form of solution. A process of review, consultation or inquiry is now or will shortly be underway with regard to many policy commitments targeted by the Cabinet for implementation during the life of the present Parliament, including some contained in *New Labour New Britain: Labour's Contract for a New Britain*, comprising pledges that Tony Blair has personally put forward as measures upon which the success or otherwise of his tenure in office should be judged at the next

---

[2] See eg his speech on *A Citizens' Democracy* (London: Charter 88, 1993).

election. During the early months of 1998, for example, several inquiries have been in progress with respect to elections, including the Jenkins Commission on the voting system (see Chapter 3), the Neill Committee into the funding of political parties (see Chapter 2), and the Howarth Committee on electoral law and administration (see Chapter 4). The creation of a Select Committee on the Modernisation of the House of Commons was one of the first government-prompted acts of the new Parliament (see Chapter 5). An independent inquiry on the future of the House of Lords has been suggested as part of the scheme whereby hereditary peers are to be removed from the Second Chamber within the next year or so (see Chapter 1).

For many, a significant number of Labour's objectives are further removed but not forgotten. Some, because of the sheer preparatory work involved must await a second term of office; others must be conditional upon the digestion of earlier measures taking effect successfully over the next few years. Reforms of this nature include a permanent reconstruction of the House of Lords (see Chapter 1), the preparation of a homegrown Bill of Rights (see Chapter 17), the issue of English regional government (see Chapter 13), and a new Ministry of Justice (see Chapters 16 and 20). It is with respect to this class of policy objectives in particular, that those with a vision of the long-term modernisation of the British constitution must be most apprehensive. For the reality is that reforms of a constitutional nature rarely operate to the administrative advantage of our rulers, meaning both our political leaders in Cabinet and their official advisers in Whitehall. Constitutions are about the institution and regulation of the checks and balances controlling government. They diffuse political power to other democratic agencies and render the exercise of official decision-making more closely accountable to those to whom they apply. The fear is, therefore, that the prioritisation of constitutional reform may suffer the longer the party is in power. The accomplishment of Labour's second-stage or longer-term objectives will depend upon considerable strength of purpose on the part of the Labour Cabinet and of key figures within it including the Prime Minister personally.

The Labour leadership's determination to push ahead with its programme of constitutional reform in its first year of office has been impressive, even spectacular. That the new government 'hit the ground running' became a political observation so commonplace that it became trite to continue saying so. The strength of leadership and sheer level of activity performed by the Prime Minister and his Cabinet colleagues with whom he shares responsibility for constitutional reform (the Lord Chancellor, the Home Secretary, and the Scottish, Welsh and Northern Ireland Secretaries of State) have left all but the most cynical on the Left with a real sense that this is an administration more, not less, radical in its commitment to modernisation and change. With an overall House of Commons majority of 177 MPs behind him, the Prime Minister is clearly in no mood for delay.

The Prime Minister's Cabinet committee structure has given an unprecedented level of emphasis to matters of constitutional reform. Tony Blair himself chairs the most important Cabinet committee on the subject, the Ministerial Committee on Constitutional Reform Policy (terms of reference: To consider strategic issues relating to the government's constitutional reform policies). There are separate Ministerial Committees on Northern Ireland, on the Intelligence Services, on Local Government, and on Devolution to Scotland and Wales and the English Regions (terms of reference: To consider policy and other issues arising from the government's policies for devolution to Scotland and Wales and the regions of England and to promote and oversee progress of the relevant legislation through Parliament and its subsequent implementation). Under the Committee on Constitutional Reform Policy and reporting to it, the Prime Minister has created special Ministerial Sub-Committees under the chairmanship of the Lord Chancellor, Lord Irvine, on Incorporation of the European Convention on Human Rights, and on House of Lords' Reform (terms of reference: To consider policy and other issues arising from the government's plans for reform of the House of Lords and to make recommendations).

No less important to securing the lasting effects of reform has been the Prime Minister's commitment to embrace procedures for reaching agreement across party lines, wherever possible. Prior to the 1997 general election, Labour had already successfully engaged in cross-party negotiation and agreement on Scottish devolution (the Scottish Constitutional Convention, established in 1989). A broad spectrum of constitutional reforms designed for early implementation were discussed and agreed in the Report of the Joint Consultative Committee on Constitutional Reform, co-chaired by Robin Cook and Robert Maclennan, in March 1997. Once in office, notwithstanding the scale of Labour's electoral victory, Tony Blair proceeded to establish a formal channel for ongoing inter-party links with Liberal Democrats by creating a Joint Consultative Committee which meets at 10 Downing Street and conferring upon it the status of Cabinet Committee (terms of reference: To consider policy issues of joint interest to the government and the Liberal Democrats). In practice, the policy areas that will dominate the agenda of the Joint Consultative Committee will be those relating to constitutional reform.

This book is offered as a contribution towards the ongoing process of political debate and policy analysis over the details of pending and outstanding items on Labour's constitutional agenda. This collaborative project was only made possible by the willing participation of the many contributors to this work, to whom we express our many thanks. Whilst all the contributors share a centre-left outlook and are broadly supportive of Labour's programme of constitutional reform, their collaboration in this venture should not be taken as necessarily signifying their membership or endorsement of Labour; neither are any views expressed in any individual chapter to be construed as being necessarily shared by the authors of other chapters.

July 1998

NOTE

Editing a large collected work such as this, on a wide range of subjects
are very much alive politically and 'on the move', has posed some difficulties
as to the timing of authorship and publication. Actual implementation of some
major reforms enacted in the 1997–98 parliamentary session are still awaited
or else are still in their early infancy. At proof stage in September 1998, two
major reports, from the Jenkins Commission and Neill Committee, had not
yet been published, and the legislative programme of constitutional reforms
for the new session beginning November 1998, widely expected to affect the
House of Lords and freedom of information, had still not been confirmed.

In particular, it should be noted by readers that some of the legislative
measures referred to in this work as Acts had not yet actually reached the
statute book by proof stage, though they seem certain to do so imminently.
These include the Human Rights Act and the European Parliamentary
Elections Act. It is conceivable but unlikely, therefore, that these measures
either fail or are subject to some last-minute amendment in their section
arrangement.

R.B.
R.P.

PART I

PARLIAMENT

CHAPTER 1

THE HOUSE OF LORDS

Professor Robert Blackburn (King's College, London)

'Constitutional reforms will include those leading to the replacement of the House of Lords with a new elected chamber which will have the power to delay, for the lifetime of a Parliament, changes to designated legislation reducing individual or constitutional rights.'

(Labour Party, General Election Manifesto, 1992)

'We will remove the right of hereditary peers to sit and vote in the House of Lords as a first step towards a more democratic and representative chamber. We will consult widely on the further reforms necessary.'

(Labour Party, General Election Manifesto, 1997)

'The onus is on the government, if it wants to make change, to think more deeply, to consult widely, to come out, if it can, with a better alternative, and then to carry that alternative through Parliament . . . The whole process, if it is done, must be done in one step, not in a half-baked way that destroys the independence of the present House, while leaving its future hanging indefinitely in the air – to the immense advantage of the Executive and the further diminution of Parliament.'

(William Hague MP, Conservative leader, 1998)

LABOUR POLICY ON THE HOUSE OF LORDS

Upon his appointment as Labour leader in 1994, Tony Blair singled out House of Lords reform for his most high profile and strongest criticisms of the constitutional status quo then presided over by John Major's Conservative government. In a series of speeches down to and during the 1997 general election campaign, Mr Blair delivered some of the fiercest attacks ever by a Labour leader on the hereditary element in the House of Lords. Most peers were 'just Tory voting fodder', he declared, some of them there simply because their ancestor was the mistress of a monarch. 'Perhaps the least defensible part of the British constitution is the power wielded by hereditary

9

peers in the House of Lords', he said in his John Smith Memorial Lecture in 1996. 'It is in principle wrong and absurd that people should wield power on the basis of birth not merit or election.'

The Labour Party's 1996–97 policy documents proceeded to give House of Lords reform top billing in its sections on constitutional reform. The need to modernise the Second Chamber was mentioned as the first item in the sections devoted to the constitution in both the 1997 election manifesto and in the preceding 'contract for a new Britain' policy document endorsed in a postal vote of all Labour members in 1996. Whilst firmly rooted in a sincere belief that the Second Chamber must be reformed, Labour's spin-doctors will not have been slow to realise that there were wider benefits to be gained from hammering home this message about the anachronism of the hereditary peerage in the Lords. For the reasoning and sentiments supporting Tony Blair's rhetoric in favour of removing hereditary peers from Britain's parliamentary legislature were incontrovertible to the minds of the overwhelming majority of the public, and even to many Conservatives. The Conservative leadership's continued defence of the hereditary element in the Lords – of whom at the time of the election 323 were Conservatives, compared to 14 Labour and 23 Liberal Democrats[1] – was seen by many voters as further evidence of a tawdry and self-interested approach to parliamentary affairs. Consequently, Labour's arguments for Lords' reform helped lend popular credence to their political modernisation and constitutional reform agenda more generally, which otherwise included many individual items the benefits for which were more open to public controversy and reservation.

However, even from a Labour perspective, the electioneering capital that could be made out of pillorying hereditary peers and the Conservatives' association with them in debates on the constitution, barely served to disguise the fact that the Labour Party had made remarkably little progress in its own internal policy-making on what the permanent basis for the future membership, role and working of the Second Chamber should be, post-removal of the hereditary peers. 'As an initial, self-contained reform, not dependent on further reform in the future, the right of hereditary peers to sit and vote in the House of Lords will be ended by statute', read the 1997 manifesto. But the question which then naturally arises, of course, is by what system of arrangement should future members of the Second Chamber be chosen, particularly bearing in mind that the case for reforming the Prime Minister's patronage over appointing life peers is almost as blatant as the case for removing hereditary peers. Indeed, the most effective rhetoric launched in riposte by Conservatives against Labour's plans for Lords' reform has been the allegation that Tony Blair is planning to convert the Second Chamber into a super-quango 'stuffed with his own placemen'.[2]

---

[1] For more recent statistics, see Table 1.1.

[2] In 1998, Lord Cranborne as Conservative leader in the House of Lords publicly set out six tests which he believed any reform of the Lords should meet, and one of these gave particular emphasis to the need to restrict the Prime Minister's powers of patronage in appointing peers.

Labour's pre-election policy documents failed to provide any real political lead or coherent vision on what the long-term future of the parliamentary Second Chamber should be. Indeed, they displayed a singular lack of detailed consideration altogether. This seems to be explicable from the fact that, prior to the 1997 election, a decision emerged – one suspects taken more by default than by design – simply to refer the matter of Second Chamber reform to an independent inquiry. The form of inquiry the Labour leadership advocated in its 1997 policy documents was a Joint Committee of both Houses of Parliament (see pp 479, 492 below).

On the composition of the House, Labour's 1997 election manifesto read that the removal of hereditary peers was to be regarded as 'the first stage in a process of reform to make the House of Lords more democratic and representative . . . The system of appointment of life peers to the House of Lords will be reviewed'. In other words, the Labour government aims to remove the hereditary peerage in advance of any thought-out and widely approved scheme being prepared by the party on the future composition and membership of the Second Chamber.

In the first half of the 1990s, Labour policy seemed unequivocal on the principle that the reformed Second Chamber should be composed through some method of direct popular elections. A firm commitment to replacing the House of Lords with an elected Chamber was contained in Labour's 1991 statement *Opportunity Britain*, in the party's 1992 election manifesto, and in the 1993 comprehensive constitutional reform package *A New Agenda for Democracy: Labour's Proposals for Constitutional Reform* (see Appendix 1). The last of these three documents, prepared during Tony Blair's tenure as home affairs spokesperson of the party, declared that the Lords 'must be made democratically acceptable. We therefore propose replacing the House of Lords with *an elected second chamber*'.[3] When the subject was dealt with in Tony Blair's conference speech in 1995, he again spoke of removal of the hereditary peerage as a first step towards a '*proper directly elected second chamber*'.[4] But then in 1996–97, in the Labour leadership's policy papers, articles and speeches, this prior level of public commitment to the principle of popular elections as a means of composing the Second Chamber went into some decline. The 1996 'contract for a new Britain' paper and the 1997 general election manifesto failed to repeat the earlier express pledge on elections. Instead, the two documents spoke of developing some method of composition

---

These were that: (1) A substantial independent element must remain; (2) The reformed chamber must be better at scrutinising and revising legislation than the present one; (3) The Prime Minister's powers of patronage must not be increased; (4) Members must be drawn from all parts of the UK; (5) Reform must be considered in the context of its effects on Parliament as a whole; (6) The supreme authority of the House of Commons must remain intact. This approach has the endorsement of William Hague, the Conservative leader of the Opposition (see eg W Hague, 'Change and Tradition: Thinking Creatively about the Constitution', speech to the Centre for Policy Studies, 24 February 1998).

[3] At p 35; my italics (Appendix 1, p 456).

[4] My italics.

that was 'democratically acceptable', in effect opening up the range of options – including an elaboration on new nomination procedures – even wider than before, and referred to the need for some committee of inquiry to 'consult widely' and conduct a 'wide-ranging review'.

On what the future functions and working of the Second Chamber should entail, current Labour policy is even more undeveloped. The 1997 manifesto simply said, 'The legislative powers of the House of Lords will remain unaltered. Its function will remain that of a revising chamber.' This rather flat and negative description of the work of the Lords was surprising, considering that Labour was proposing to reform the Second Chamber. Some positive mention of the constitutional value of the House would not have been inappropriate, such as some reference to its universally praised Committee work in the field of European law-making, even if no new functions were to be added. The 1997 manifesto also raised the suspicion among supporters of reform that the Labour leadership in its preparation for office had become less genuinely interested in establishing a new parliamentary chamber to replace the House of Lords, born perhaps out of a realisation that almost any reform involving a redefinition of its functions and powers would represent a greater inconvenience to the government over the status quo.

By contrast the earlier 1992 election manifesto, whilst also envisaging some form of commission to review the position of the Lords, spoke of the 'substantial part' a reformed Second Chamber could play in extending British democracy. It envisaged extending the functions and business of the Second Chamber to include a special role in reflecting the 'interests and aspirations of the regions and nations of Britain', the creation of a system of Second Chamber Standing Committees for closer examination of certain types of government policy and legislation, and an 'essential element in the protection and promotion of fundamental rights'. The 1992 election manifesto was altogether a more confident and focused statement of principle than its successor in 1997. It clearly affirmed what should be the central objective of Labour policy on House of Lords' reform, namely 'an elected second chamber with a specific and precisely defined constitutional role'.[5]

STAGE ONE REFORM: REMOVING THE HEREDITARY PEERS

Labour's post-1996 statements on the future of the Second Chamber have been couched in terms of a 'first stage' of reform designed to remove the hereditary peers, followed by a 'second stage' of reform concluding matters relating to the composition and operation of the Chamber on a permanent basis. In the short term, Labour's plans are to remove the hereditary peers early within the lifetime of this Parliament, and only then will an independent inquiry be set up to commence work leading to recommendations on the

[5] At p 25.

future structure and functions of the House. This means that there will necessarily be a substantial interim period between completion of the first and second stages of House of Lords' reform.

The new Labour government's crowded constitutional reform programme did not permit a Bill for removing the hereditary peers to be introduced in the first annual parliamentary session of the incoming Blair administration. Whilst not included in the Queen's Speech for 1997–98, however, it is now widely expected in the subsequent legislative programme for 1998–99. From a legal perspective, the drafting of the reform measure will be straightforward. The Bill in question will require only two short sections to be drafted by parliamentary counsel. The first section should provide that any holder by succession of an hereditary peerage shall not 'in right of that peerage' sit or vote in the House of Lords and shall no longer receive a writ of summons. The second section should clarify their position with regard to the parliamentary franchise and election as a member of the House of Commons, providing that such persons shall no longer by virtue only of their hereditary peerage be disqualified from voting at elections to the House of Commons or being elected as an MP.

But while the legal side of this first stage of reform is easy, yet its political implementation could still prove a parliamentary battlefield and a public relations disaster if handled badly. A relatively smooth passage through the Commons is assured by Labour's huge numerical supremacy over the Conservatives, 418 MPs to 165 respectively. This advantage in the Commons is further reinforced by Labour's working agreement with the Liberal Democrats over reform, thereby adding 46 Liberal Democrat MPs to their side of the voting lobby and neutralising a secondary source of opposition and disruption as the legislation passes through the Chamber. However, by contrast the Conservatives hold a strong majority in the House of Lords, with 472 peers taking the Conservative whip compared to 157 Labour and 66 Liberal Democrat. Of the remaining 324 crossbench peers, whose votes will be very important, although they are in theory independent, most in practice tend to vote in support of Conservative interests, and, so far as this particular issue is concerned, 204 crossbenchers are hereditary peers and will therefore have a close personal vested interest in the government's proposals to remove them and replace them with some other scheme of composition. A breakdown of the party strengths in the House of Lords is shown in Table 1.1[6] (see p 14).

A strong majority in the House of Lords, therefore, could choose to mount an effective or troublesome opposition to the measure. The fact that Labour has yet to propose a convincing detailed scheme for replacing the existing method(s) of composing the Second Chamber is to some extent playing into the hands of Conservatives, whose leaders in both Houses have made it clear that they would much prefer to keep the Tory-dominated Lords as it stands, and who now have a vested interest in causing the Labour government they

---

[6] As at 13 June 1998: House of Lords information office.

Table 1.1 Party strengths in the House of Lords

Party	Life peers	Hereditary peers	Total
Conservative	159	303	472
Labour	140	17	157
Liberal Democrat	42	24	66
Crossbench	118	204	322
Other	8	83	91
Total	477	631	1,108

Notes:
(a) There are also 26 bishops who are independent and sit separately.
(b) Figures for hereditary peers exclude those on leave of absence or without writs of summons.

oppose the maximum political embarrassment and parliamentary inconvenience possible. If so, it is probable that they will raise a constitutional objection that before they are prepared to approve any fundamental alteration in the present composition of the House, they wish to know and in principle approve the details of the government's intentions for the long-term or permanent form of membership of the Second Chamber.[7] They might seek to argue that, despite the conventional principle known as the 'Salisbury doctrine', according to which the Upper House should not reject a government Bill whose policy it enshrines was included in the prior election manifesto of the government, over this issue a more fundamental principle going to the heart of parliamentary agreement to a measure of major constitutional significance takes precedence. Alternatively, drawing short of outright rejection of the Bill, it is widely viewed as permissible within the Salisbury doctrine that the Lords may effect major amendments to the legislation on such constitutional grounds.[8]

Furthermore, it has to be admitted that there is some cogency to this constitutional view. It was on precisely such grounds that the House of Lords – comprising a coalition of Labour, Liberal Democrat, crossbench and some dissident Conservative peers – rejected the Thatcher government's original proposals contained in the Local Government (Interim Provisions) Bill 1984 which sought to cancel elections to the Greater London Council (which was Labour controlled) and substitute in the GLC's place a nominated body (which would be Conservative approved), in advance of Parliament's agree-

---

[7] In his speech to the Centre for Policy Studies on 24 February 1998, William Hague stated that, 'The whole process, if it is done, must be done in one step, not in a half-baked way that destroys the independence of the present House, while leaving its future hanging indefinitely in the air – to the immense advantage of the Executive and the future diminution of Parliament.'
[8] See pp 225–6.

ment to the abolition of the GLC itself, which had been a prominent policy in the Conservatives' 1983 general election manifesto. An associated line of attack levelled at the Blair Cabinet by reactionary opponents to removal of hereditary peers is almost certain to be that, far from being the politically upright and selfless leaders they have often held themselves out to be, their prime motivation in what will be described as a hurried and precipitative 'first stage' of reform is simply to remove a tranche of 303 Conservative members in the parliamentary Second Chamber.

If the reform Bill is rejected by the House of Lords, or subject to some major amendment qualifying the hereditary peerage's removal, then the Labour government could of course decide simply to ignore the verdict of peers and proceed a year later, in the following parliamentary session, to enact the legislation without the consent of the Lords under the provisions of the Parliament Acts 1911–49. This would follow the earlier precedents of the Attlee government, when it chose to enact the 1949 Parliament Act itself, following rejection of it by the House of Lords; and, more recently over a different field of public policy, John Major's Conservative administration in passing the War Crimes Act 1991. However, such a course of action by the Labour government might work against the best interests of long-term reform, as it could serve to further antagonise and divide political opinion over reform of the House of Lords, and prejudice the prospects for some measure of all-party agreement over a permanent basis for the future structure and working of the Second Chamber.

Labour's strategy towards Second Chamber reform would have benefitted very substantially from having commenced its detailed party policy deliberations in 1997, straightaway following its election victory.[9] The preparatory

---

[9] The original version of this chapter was prepared in mid-1997 when this advice was most apposite. The only Labour policy initiative of any kind in the 18 months since Labour took office has been the creation by the Prime Minister Tony Blair of a Ministerial Sub-Committee on the House of Lords. This body met for the first time on 13 January 1998 and conducts its proceedings in secret. Its terms of reference are 'to consider policy and other issues arising from the Government's plans for reform of the House of Lords' and it is to make recommendations to the Ministerial Committee on Constitutional Reform Policy which is chaired by the Prime Minister.

The membership of the Sub-Committee, as it existed down to the July 1998 government reshuffle, comprised the Lord Chancellor as chairman (Lord Irvine); the Home Secretary (Jack Straw); the Leader of the House of Lords (then Lord Richard); the Leader of the House of Commons and President of the Privy Council (then Ann Taylor); the Chief Whip in the House of Lords (Lord Carter); the Chief Whip in the House of Commons (then Nick Brown); and the Minister without Portfolio (then Peter Mandelson). It has therefore been a very small body, even by Cabinet committee standards, with its personnel having the appearance of a task force entrusted with party political strategy rather than constitutional policy analysis.

Following the meeting of the Sub-Committee on 13 January 1998, it was stated that no conclusions on the substance of Labour's long-term aims for reforming the Lords had been reached. Instead, members of the Sub-Committee suggested to the press that the full range of options remained open, and that removal of the hereditary peerage from the Chamber would go ahead, after which an inquiry and consultation period would be established to determine wider reform either before or after the next general election. *(continued over)*

advice necessary to gain widespread political agreement to a sound scheme of permanent reconstitution of the Lords cannot come from within the civil service alone, and clearly requires at least one specialist commission external to Parliament to examine and report on the comparative options available for Westminster, together with provisional recommendations. This could be a Royal Commission, though such bodies have a reputation for being dilatory in their proceedings and in the past have proved mixed in the success with which their recommendations have been implemented (see further, p 215). The preparatory work involved in leading to a permanent basis of reform must also surely include the participation of a policy sub-committee of the Labour's Party's ruling National Executive Committee. As yet, the Labour movement as a whole has had minimal involvement in front-bench policy on the House of Lords, certainly by contrast to other major constitutional reforms including devolution to Scotland and Wales and even electoral reform.

Whatever approach the Labour Cabinet adopts in its preparation for second-stage reform (and whether it includes or circumvents the party membership in the process), some authoritative Labour government statement on the future direction of the House of Lords is necessary as an accompaniment to the Bill seeking to implement the first-stage reform of removing hereditary peers. This document, which might take the form of a white paper, similar to the nature of the document issued by the Wilson government to accompany its unsuccessful Parliament Bill in 1968–69 (see p 24), should as a minimum set the parameters within which the next steps of reform will take place and it should indicate the methodology it proposes to adopt in proceeding with stage-two reform. Thus, it should powerfully endorse as a general principle the indefensible and anachronistic nature of the House of Lords' present form of memberhsip. A detailed breakdown of present composition of the Lords shows that almost two-thirds of its present membership are hereditary peers (see Table 1.2,[10] p 17). Clearly, it is no longer acceptable for this aristocratic, hereditary method of appointment to continue to operate to any political effect within the British legislature. Some historical comment might be given on the failure of successive British governments to tackle House of Lords reform, following the clear statement of purpose laid down in the preamble to the Parliament Act 1911 that 'It is intended to substitute for the House of Lords as it at present exists a Second Chamber constituted on a popular instead of hereditary basis'. The feasibility of any hereditary element remaining in the twenty-first century Parliament should be firmly ruled out, in the manner of an empirical and detached elucidation of the issues, whilst

---

Meanwhile by contrast, in June 1998 the Conservative leader William Hague began setting up a Constitutional Commission on the House of Lords. Its membership is to include some independent (ie non-Conservative) members, and as a forum will explore all options for reform (as well as retention of the hereditary element): see *The Guardian*, 14 July 1998. Since Labour–Conservative co-operation over House of Lords' reform appears non-existent at present, this Commission will become a party political tool for the Conservative Opposition with which to challenge the Labour government's reforming legislation.

[10] As at 13 June 1998: House of Lords information office.

Table 1.2 Composition of the House of Lords by peerage type

Archbishop and bishops	26
Peers by succession	750 (16 women)
Hereditary peers of first creation	9
Life peers under the Appellate Jurisdiction Act 1876	26
Life peers under the Life Peerages Act 1958	459 (91 women)
Total	1,270

Notes:
(a) 11 persons inheriting peerages have disclaimed them for life (two of these now sit in the House by virtue of other titles).
(b) 134 peers are on leave of absence (67) or without writs of summons (69 including two minors).

avoiding repetition of the tone and rhetoric used by Labour in its pre-1997 election literature, such as the party's 'Tory Lords A-Leaping' propaganda pamphlet, berating particular hereditary peerages and individual title-holders on a personal basis.

Not only must hereditary peers by succession be removed from voting, but it is important as a further matter of principle that their attendance or any other form of membership of the House is ended or phased out within a short time-frame. This may be sad for hereditary members, many of whom will have formed a sentimental attachment to the Palace of Westminster and its facilities. However, any new form of democratic composition must be allowed firmly to establish itself. To do so effectively, a clearly presented public impression of a modern and relevant system of parliamentary membership will be essential. In any event, any new method of composition will allow for the possibility of politically active and able hereditary peers becoming party nominees or candidates under whatever scheme of membership is decided upon. The desirability of establishing some new system which avoids a permanent political bias in favour of one party, and also which sets some numerical limit upon the size of the Chamber, are, whilst closely associated to Labour's first-stage reform, conceptually distinct from the issue of hereditary membership and would be best addressed during the second-stage reform process.

It will be important that the government in its documents and statements accompanying the legislation removing the hereditary peerage clearly addresses the timescale of reform generally, and the tenure of the post-hereditary interim arrangements in particular, in order to sustain the political momentum towards completion of Labour's long-term objectives. Already, the delay that has taken place since the 1997 election in commencing the preparatory work involved in moving towards a permanent basis of reform is unfortunate in many respects, two of which, already mentioned, being that the Prime Minister's patronage exercised under the Crown prerogative will become the sole basis for membership of the House of Lords, and that the absence of a credible political vision for the future of the Chamber has strengthened political opposition to Labour's plans over stage-one reform. Even if some form of new code of practice is adopted, declaring new procedures under which the power of the Prime Minister to create members of the House of Lords will be exercised (perhaps enlarging on the present custom whereby leaders of the other parties may nominate peers in proportion to their parliamentary strength in the House of Commons), critics will still be able to make much of the political fact that whilst the royal prerogative continues to remain as the legal basis for appointing members of the House of Lords the Prime Minister will ultimately be in a position to control the whole process. But the greatest danger in allowing this interim period to endure beyond the minimum time possible is that if Labour fails to act promptly, or for any reason of its own chooses to prolong second-stage reform, the interim Chamber which is left behind after removal of the hereditary peerage will then operate well into the twenty-first century, and – if the party fails to win a second term of office – stands the danger of taking root as the long-term basis of reform itself. Whatever interim arrangements emerge after removal of the hereditary peers should therefore be regarded as strictly temporary.

Some ideas on what should happen provisionally until a permanent basis of composition for the Second Chamber in the future is established, were agreed between the Labour leadership and the Liberal Democrats in March 1997 and laid out in the Report of the Joint Consultative Committee on Constitutional Reform (see Appendix 2, p 479). The most important propositions agreed, later also reiterated in Labour's 1997 election manifesto, were, first, that no one political party should seek a majority in the House of Lords, and, secondly, that an attempt should be made to fill the membership of the House of Lords in such a way as to reflect the proportion of votes received by each party in the previous general election. Further points were agreed, one affecting the continuation of the present crossbench or non-party membership in the House of Lords, now amounting to about one-fifth of the size of the House. 'An open and legitimate mechanism for appointing cross-bench peers should be developed', said the document, 'and the cross-benchers should be consulted about the mode of replenishing their members.' It was also recognised that there were some hereditary peers who should continue to be members, by virtue of their own individual qualification and past distinguished contribution to the work of the House. Finally, it was agreed that there should be some new procedure established whereby life peers might voluntarily retire.

These interim procedures are sensible enough for their immediate purpose; but they are no substitute for Labour proceeding at the earliest opportunity to settle a comprehensive, more detailed long-term strategy for the long-term composition of the reformed House. Indeed, there is a danger that in developing a system of sophisticated rules and principles based around the Prime Minister's power of appointment of life peers, attention will be distracted from the real issue of settling a permanent basis for reform. Those who oppose a strengthened Second Chamber will be able to argue that these interim arrangements have become constitutionally acceptable in their own right. For the converse reason, there are those today who believe Labour's two-stage process of Lords' reform is flawed precisely because the hereditary peerage represents the greatest head of steam driving the process of reform altogether. In other words, by removing hereditary peers for immediate polit-ical purposes in advance of establishing a firm foundation for long-term reform, the Labour leadership may be destroying the goose that lays the golden egg of a modernised Second Chamber for our 21st century Parliament.

STAGE TWO REFORM: ROLE AND FUNCTIONS OF THE REFORMED SECOND CHAMBER

Before any final questions relating to the permanent form of composition and membership of the Second Chamber can be satisfactorily addressed, it is necessary to examine the more politically complex issue of what the precise functions, business and powers of a reformed Second Chamber will be. One chooses members of any organisation, or sets up the scheme of arrangement which produces those members, according to whatever qualities one is look-ing for in such persons, so as to maximise the effectiveness of that body at work. In the case of the House of Lords, this logical approach to the whole question of reform has largely been obscured by media sensationalism and public fascination with the idiosyncrasies and quirkiness of the present Cham-ber, especially its hereditary peers, enrobed bishops, and geriatric former Cabinet ministers. Nonetheless, any inquiry or recommendations on reform-ing the House of Lords must commence with settling the role and powers it is to perform for the constitution of the new century.

This task is best undertaken, first, with an understanding of how Second Chambers operate generally in comparative legislatures among the other modern political democracies of the world; secondly, with an appreciation of the state of the unreformed House of Lords within Britain's parliamentary system between 1911–97; thirdly, by identifying the actual and most valuable work and functions conducted in practice by the House of Lords today; and, finally, by integrating any enhanced or new parliamentary functions for the reformed Second Chamber within the overall context and pattern of con-stitutional reform now being embarked upon by the Labour government in consultation with other political parties.

Second Chambers abroad

So first, how is the need for a Second Chamber commonly interpreted else-where, especially in the European Union, the Commonwealth and United States? Among the advanced democracies of the world, bicameral legislatures have proved to be the norm. A Senate, Upper House, or Second Chamber exists in the great majority of political constitutions today, operating along-side a House of Representatives or Assembly which deals with legislation and political accountability for the day-to-day governmental administration of the country.

In those countries which possess a federal or confederate system of govern-ment, such as the USA, Germany, Canada and Australia, one special func-tion of the Second Chamber is commonly to represent and protect the interests of the constituent states of the federation or confederation; to act as a watch-dog and protector of the distribution of power between the federal and state governments. In countries which are unitary states, such as France, Ireland and the UK, Second Chambers are still generally thought necessary or desir-able for a number of different reasons. Second Chambers often perform a special role with respect to the constitutional affairs of the state and any special legislative processes whereby its country's constitutional law is made or amended. All advanced countries in the world today, with the exceptions of the UK, Israel and New Zealand, possess a written constitution, the great majority of which give rise to a formal distinction between legislative meas-ures of an ordinary or administrative character and those designed to effect a change to the constitutional law of the state, often including matters relating to the protection of human rights. Such constitutions frequently contain articles laying down special legislative procedures for amending constitu-tional law involving the Second Chamber possessing a power of rejection or extended delay.

Other reasons for Second Chambers operating around the world today concern pragmatic advantages which support the work of the lower House. An important part of perceived advantages in complementing or supplement-ing the work of a Lower House flows from the more independent-minded and politically detached brand of partisanship which is promoted in Upper Houses. Their membership is also often more expert and experienced than average members in the Lower House, and may be more representative of special interests in the community. A Second Chamber therefore permits a second look at legislative proposals or government policies of national import-ance, which may be particularly useful if the Lower House is overburdened or for some temporary reason failing to scrutinise and carry out its parliamentary function as constitutionally appropriate. This may be the case, for example, if a measure has been pushed through the Lower House in a precipitative, rushed and ill-considered manner, which may be more likely when there is a large majority for one political party in the Lower House facing an ineffective or demoralised opposition. Or it may also be the case when a decision in the

Lower House has been narrowly reached in circumstances of deep political controversy, where some period of further reflection with reference to the basic principles of the state as well as public opinion might best serve the national interest. Even without a power of veto, a power of delay over legislative measures or government decisions may be valued within the constitutional arrangements of a country, to allow time for further reflection by ministers and parliamentarians alike, as well as in public opinion and among the electorate. Thus, in addition to any special role over matters of special importance in the state such as constitutional change or foreign affairs, Second Chambers serve to supplement the general work of the Lower House and inject a more detached brand of political partisanship into the legislative process.

1911–97: Britain's unreformed Second Chamber

Currently, there is no formal document which prescribes the proper functions of the House of Lords. One may speak accurately of the business it transacts and carries out in practice, and there exists in literary works such as Erskine May's, *Parliamentary Practice* (1985) authoritative descriptions of its work together with the procedures which regulate its affairs. But there is nothing written down in the form of an official statement which sets out the political raison d'être and constitutional functions specific to the House of Lords.

Historically, the British Second Chamber inherited a common parliamentary workload to that of the House of Commons, with a few specific tasks falling to one or other Chamber, notably the judicial appellate jurisdiction of the Lords and the political control of national finance by the Commons. However, the Parliament Acts 1911–49 sought to curtail the Second Chamber's role as an essential component in government and legislative decision-making by taking away its earlier authority to reject government public Bills of which it disapproved. Whilst its powers over money Bills (which had caused the crisis between the two Houses following the Lords' rejection of Lloyd George's 1909 Budget) were rightly removed by substituting a power of delay of one month only, the Parliament Acts also took the opportunity to minimise the Second Chamber's power over all other Bills indiscriminately (with just one exception, discussed at p 32 below), permitting the House to delay such measures for two years (under the 1911 Act), then further reduced to one year (under the later 1949 Act). Over the period since 1911, the Second Chamber's diminution of political influence has continued to be eroded by its archaic form of membership – dominated by hereditary peers – being left in a wholly untenable, undemocratic state. This state of affairs has then been compounded by the arrogance with which party majorities in the House of Commons have regularly regarded decisions of the Second Chamber which conflicted with its own. The authority of the House of Lords in this respect reached its lowest ebb in 1991, when the then government –

21

and one of the Conservative Party which has traditionally championed the role of the House of Lords – chose simply to overrule the Second Chamber's carefully considered rejection of the War Crimes Bill and proceed to enact the legislation without peers' consent under the terms of the Parliament Acts. Behind the ceremonial facade at Westminster now lies a parliamentary process which has been described by many commentators as one of 'disguised unicameralism'. As the LSE economics professor Lord Desai wrote in 1997 in his Fabian Society pamphlet on the subject, *Destiny Not Defeat: Reforming the Lords*, 'the House of Lords is a fig leaf for what is effectively a unicameral system'.[11]

The principal reason behind the remarkable failure of successive generations of politicians to reconstruct the House of Lords following the 1911 Parliament Act might simply be attributed to their failure to agree upon a coherent and distinctive vision of what is, or should be, the constitutional purpose and parliamentary functions of the Second Chamber in the modern British state. Clearly, the House of Lords' former position down to 1832 as an equal or superior partner with the Commons, based upon its representation of the aristocracy as one of the three estates of the realm balancing the social elements of the country in its legislature, had become an anachronism by the end of the 19th century. With the progressive extensions of the franchise down to 1918 and acceptance of the principle of popular democracy across the political parties, the House of Commons as the elected Chamber assumed an increasingly exclusive position as both the seat of the government and the sovereign source of legislative power. The challenge for our politicians in the years following the Parliament Act 1911 was to forge a new constitutional settlement, in which Parliament could embrace the advent of democratic ideals, and develop new and modern forms of constitutional checks and balance suitable for the very different era of big interventionist government.

But more accurately, what has served to stymie reform more than any other factor has been the evolution and self-perpetuation of what Lord Hailsham has described as 'elective dictatorship' in Britain. Despite widespread public interest in House of Lords' reform and numerous well-thought through proposals for change, successive generations of political leaders of all persuasions have shrunk from the task of redefining the role and powers of the Second Chamber and resolving matters relating to its composition. It has proved more politically convenient for those holding the reins of power in government and the House of Commons to allow the matter of Lords' reform to remain in abeyance, for virtually any measure of reconstruction even if limited only to matters of composition would serve to enhance its authority. This inertia towards reform of the House of Lords is just part of a wider resistance that has been displayed by party majorities in Britain towards constitutional reform generally, particularly with respect to any suggestions

---

[11] At p 2.

Figure 1.1 The Bryce Commission on the functions appropriate to a Second Chamber, 1918

---

(1)   The examination and revision of Bills brought from the House of Commons, a function which has become more needed since, on many occasions, during the last thirty years, the House of Commons has been obliged to act under special rules limiting debate.

(2)   The initiation of Bills dealing with subjects of a comparatively non-controversial character which may have an easier passage through the House of Commons if they have been fully discussed and put into a well-considered shape before being submitted to it.

(3)   The interposition of so much delay (and no more) in the passing of a Bill into law as may be needed to enable the opinion of the nation to be adequately expressed upon it. This would be specially needed as regards Bills which affect the fundamentals of the Constitution or introduce new principles of legislation, or which raise issues whereon the opinion of the country may appear to be almost equally divided.

(4)   Full and free discussion of large and important questions, such as those of foreign policy, at moments when the House of Commons may happen to be so much occupied that it cannot find sufficient time for them. Such discussions may often be all the more useful if conducted in an Assembly whose debates and divisions do not involve the fate of the Executive Government.

---

for reconstructing the doctrine of the 'Crown in Parliament' which is the foundation of Britain's constitutional arrangements, promoting the ability of the party majorities in the House of Commons to exercise absolute power as and when they choose to do so. An essential feature of most constitutional innovations is that they usually tend to restrict or provide some new form of inconvenience to rulers in government, limiting their freedom of action or representing a devolution or diffusion of power so that they stand to lose some measure of absolute control.

British political history shows that instead of embarking on any serious renewal of the post-1911 Second Chamber, our political elite has displayed either vacillation or a clear preference to keep things as they were. The most promising independent official inquiry into the subject was the Conference on Reform of the Second Chamber set up by David Lloyd George as Prime Minister in 1917, which included 34 well-qualified national figures among them senior parliamentarians, lawyers and professors, chaired by Viscount Bryce, which reported the following year (see Figure 1.1 and p 41). But for lack of political will, and also in part through being eclipsed by parliamentary attention being focused on the Representation of the People Act 1918, the report did not lead to any changes.[12]

Even when proposed measures of reform were later forthcoming from Labour and Conservative governments, they increasingly tended to reflect a desire to maintain the supremacy of the House of Commons over all matters and to formalise further the subordination of the Lords to the decisions of the Lower House. The initiative of the Labour government under Clement Attlee after the war produced a preliminary agreement between the parties on proposals simply modifying the hereditary element and Conservative domination of the Chamber. These all-party talks eventually collapsed, and the Parliament Act 1949 – enacted unilaterally by the Labour-controlled House of Commons – brought about a still weaker Second Chamber with a further restricted power of delay over government legislation.[13] The Conservative administration under Harold Macmillan enacted the Life Peerages Act 1958, conferring upon the Crown the power to grant peerages (and therefore membership of the House of Lords) for the duration of the recipient's life whereas previously all peerages were automatically hereditary. This ostensibly modernising measure was in fact deeply reactionary: it served both to prolong the enfeeblement of the Second Chamber by deflecting rising criticism of the continuing appointment of hereditary peers and to strengthen the premier's powers of political patronage.

The last major initiative on reform, undertaken by Harold Wilson's Labour administration 1968–69, produced a White Paper and Parliament (No 2) Bill which in the event was withdrawn.[14] The effect of the Wilson government's Bill would have been to cause the political composition of the Lords to mirror that in the Commons (see pp 41–2) and to duplicate the general nature of non-financial parliamentary business in the Commons to be carried out by the Lords whilst further restricting the Lords' capacity to hold up legislation in the event that they failed to agree to six months (being therefore circumventable within the timeframe of a single annual parliamentary session).

What is most remarkable about the 1968 White Paper's account of the functions of the Lords (see Figure 1.2) is that it attributed no political responsibilities to the Second Chamber which were distinctive to the Lords alone. The policy of the Labour Cabinet at that time, including that of Richard Crossman who as Leader of the House presented the government's Bill to the Commons, sought to maintain the Second Chamber's minimal political influence and offset any increase in its authority arising from the removal of the hereditary peers by reducing still further its power of delay over government Bills. The White Paper referred to the House of Lords' role as being one which was generally 'complementary to but not rivalling that of

[12] *The Reform of the Second Chamber*, Cd 9038 (1918), para 6.
[13] See p 36.
[14] *House of Lords Reform*, Cmnd 3799 (1968), para 8.

Figure 1.2 The Wilson government's White Paper on the functions of the House of Lords, 1968

(A) The provision of a forum for full and free debate on matters of public interest;

(B) The revision of public bills brought from the House of Commons;

(C) The initiation of public legislation, including in particular those government bills which are less controversial in party political terms and private members' bills;

(D) The consideration of subordinate legislation;

(E) The scrutiny of the activities of the executive; and

(F) The scrutiny of private legislation.

---

the Commons'. Richard Crossman was also the editor of a reprinted version of Walter Bagehot's *The English Constitution* (1867) from whom he drew theoretical backing for the minimalist role being advocated for the Second Chamber. In Bagehot's well-known phrase, that 'leisured legislature', the House of Lords, was a 'useful if not quite necessary' component of Parliament. More deeply embedded within Labour's attitude, both in 1969 as in 1948, was the antagonism felt by many of its members, particularly on the Left, towards an institution so closely associated with wealth, privilege, and an outdated hereditary aristocracy.

The Wilson government's reform initiative lacked any real constitutional originality and generated little political enthusiasm, even among those who were prepared to vote for the Parliament (No 2) Bill. Even with the support of the government and opposition front benches and majority cross-party support in both Houses, the Labour government eventually withdrew the measure on the grounds of it taking up too much parliamentary time when confronted by a minority of voluble and principled opponents who saw the Bill as deeply negative.

The actual working of the Chamber today

The task ahead is one of redefinition and restatement of the Second Chamber's role in the British Parliament. This requires, first, an accurate assessment of de facto developments over the past 20 or so years, in which the length of time devoted by peers to business of the House has substantially

Table 1.3a   Government Bills brought from the Commons

Sessions	Total number of Bills	Number of Bills amended by Lords	Number of amendments made by Lords
1970–73	79	31	2,366
1974–77	68	49	1,859
1979–82	82	39	2,231
1983–86	69	43	4,137
1987–90	61	38	5,181
1992–95	46	24	3,664

Note:
Figures exclude money and supply Bills.

Table 1.3b   Government Bills introduced into the House of Lords

Sessions	Total number of Bills	Number of Bills amended by Lords	Number of amendments made by Lords
1970–73	39	29	488
1974–77	58	38	1,594
1979–82	33	20	1,604
1983–86	42	28	1,373
1987–90	29	18	2,687
1992–95	29	22	1,812

Note:
Figures exclude consolidation Bills[15].

increased and the work of the House of Lords in several important different respects has become more proactive.

Thus, any political calculation of the future role and powers of the House of Lords must commence by identifying the principal spheres of parliamentary business which the chamber successfully performs today. The most important of these is generally accepted to be its legislative work, particularly the revision of Bills brought from the House of Commons. Both Houses in

---

[15] *Source*: Donald Shell, *The House of Lords*, p 144, and information supplied by the House of Lords Clerk of Committees. Statistics are drawn from only the first three sessions in each successive Parliament (to avoid any distorted comparisons where later sessions were cut short by an early election).

fact perform a 'revisionary' or 'reviewing' role with respect to government Bills, since the preparation and drafting of statutory measures takes place within government departments prior to a parliamentary first reading. Government Bills as a whole only very rarely fail actually to be approved in the Commons, because of the government's majority in that place. Because of that same majority which supports the government, and the greater political partisanship of proceedings in Commons standing committees, the Second Chamber offers a far more detached form of detailed legislative scrutiny with which to buttress and support the institutional work of the House of Commons. In any empirical study of its legislative work as conducted over the past 20 years, the Second Chamber is shown up as being at least twice as successful as the Commons in improving the quality of legislation through debating and securing agreement to amendments.[16] The great majority of such amendments deal with drafting and technical matters, although significant points of social principle are not infrequently raised and won.

Given the present state of the Lords, with its composition and appearance lacking democratic credibility, in the past it has been regarded as politically unpalatable to lay too much emphasis upon the importance of the work it performs, including its superior quality of legislative scrutiny over that conducted in the Commons. However, many independent studies have concluded that the Second Chamber, de facto, happens to be the best scrutinising body we possess within the whole legislative process. Professor John Griffith has supported this view, writing in his research monograph on *Parliamentary Scrutiny of Government Bills*:[17]

'What is clear is that, with pressures as they are and with the House of Commons and government departments functioning as they do, legislation sometimes leaves the Commons in a state unfit to be let loose on the public. Some kind of reviewing is necessary. And the House of Lords is presently the best reviewing body we have.'

The distinctive revisionary role it today performs with respect to government Bills – in theory subordinate to but in practice a near essential concomitant with the scrutiny conducted in the Lower House – will be strengthened by the future changes soon to be made in the membership of the Upper House. A democratically acceptable form of membership will endow its legislative work with greater authority, possibly generating a greater use of Standing Committees (including Special Standing Commitees) as suggested in Labour's 1989 policy review and in the most recent general review[18] conducted by the House of Lords of its own work.[19]

[16] See eg J A G Griffith, *Parliamentary Scrutiny of Government Bills* (London: George Allen Unwin, 1974), Ch 4; J A G Griffith and M Ryle, *Parliament: Functions, Practice and Procedures* (London: Sweet & Maxwell, 1989); Donald Shell, *The House of Lords* (Hemel Hempstead: Harvester Wheatsheaf, 2nd edn, 1992).
[17] At p 231.
[18] *Meet the Challenge: Make the Change*, p 56.
[19] Report by the Group on the Working of the House, HL [1987–88] pp 9 f.

There are other associated but distinct functions within the area of law-making. The importance of private legislation has diminished over the course of this century, but about 30 private Bills are presented to Parliament each year, over which the Lords devotes a similar degree of attention to that of the Commons (and enjoys equal powers, the Parliament Acts only applying to public legislation). Also, the Second Chamber has proved a valuable forum for introducing private members' Bills. Though only a few such Bills (about 15 per cent of those introduced) are successful in terms of reaching the statute book (similar to those introduced by MPs in the Commons), in the Lords they have often performed a uniquely valuable role in drawing public attention to some issue of public policy for which the government or Commons has little time. Serious debate on the need for a Human Rights Bill, for example, was first initiated in 1976 by Lord Wade in the Upper House, since when five revised versions of such Bills were considered and passed by peers, serving as blueprints leading up to the government's own Human Rights Act in 1998.

Meanwhile, parliamentary control of subordinate legislation has become a matter of ever-growing importance over the course of this century (in 1918, a function not even mentioned by the Bryce Commission). The theory has been that such legislation covers governmental subject-matter of a purely administrative nature, but increasingly such measures are used to enshrine significant matters of social or political principle (to take two obvious examples, the Hong Kong (British Nationality) Order 1986 or the Income Support (General) Regulations 1987). A Joint Committee on Statutory Instruments (comprising equal members from each House) scrutinises instruments before they are laid before Parliament, but within the narrow remit of ensuring that delegated powers are exercised within the confines of their parent Act. The actual 'merits' of any particular measure are a matter for each House to scrutinise and decide. Between 1,000–2,000 statutory instruments are enacted each year, most involving a single 'laying' procedure in each House (either 'affirmative' requiring a positive vote or, far more commonly, 'negative' whereunder the measure will take effect unless voted down in either House). As with private Bills, the Lords enjoys equal powers with the Commons over statutory instruments, and in some respects its forms of scrutiny are more effective than the Lower House. Whereas scrutiny in the Commons tends to take place within Standing Committees, the Lords conducts its work in the Chamber itself, thereby requiring government ministers to give a clarification and explanation of the proposed measures, with a full record of the debate appearing the following day in Hansard. The recent creation of a House of Lords Select Committee on the Scrutiny of Delegated Powers has further strengthened the work of the Second Chamber with respect to a particular aspect of the process of delegated legislation. Set up in 1992, with its terms of reference being to report on whether the provisions of any Bill inappropriately delegate legislative power or whether they subject the exercise of legislative power to an inappropriate degree of parliamentary scrutiny, this

Committee is widely acclaimed to have proved highly successful, in practice it has secured necessary amendments to a number of Bills seeking to grant wide law-making powers to government ministers. In one case in 1995, an excessively wide delegated power under the Community Care (Direct Payments) Bill was withdrawn altogether. The Committee has established itself sufficiently such that it is now routinely consulted by government departments in the preparation of primary legislation.

Some comment is warranted on a supposed function of the Second Chamber with respect to the introduction of government Bills of a non-controversial character. Both the Bryce Commission and 1968 White Paper included this as a distinct line of parliamentary business (see Figures 1.1 and 1.2 above). In reality, this is not a function as such at all. It is merely a reflection of an obvious procedure of administrative convenience. Some Bills have to be introduced there first, otherwise the Lords would have no legislative work at all in the first few months of each annual session. The government's choice of which Bills are to be introduced in the Lords will be determined not only by their level of controversiality but by the parliamentary advantage of having secured the Lords' approval (with any amendments) in advance of the Bill reaching the Commons. For example, the Human Rights Act – originally presented as a Bill into the House of Lords in the 1997–98 session – is hardly non-controversial. But, given the fact that a great many senior lawyers and judges happen to be members of the House of Lords, and that the Lords has already considered and passed numerous Bills to incorporate the European Convention on Human Rights into UK law over the past 20 years, it is particularly appropriate for this particular Bill to start its legislative progress in the Second Chamber. Any meaningful definition of the functions and role of the Second Chamber, therefore, would do well to avoid reiteration of this analytical confusion.

Among all its evolving work and functions since the 1970s, several other important developments should be emphasised. It has de facto been the forum for specialist consideration of major legal reforms. For this reason, most major Bills affecting the legal system and matters of civil or criminal justice have been commenced in the Lords, where the Lord Chancellor (the British equivalent of a minister of justice) sits. The widely-regretted abolition of the Commons Science and Technology Committee in 1979 was met by the House of Lords the following year, filling the gap and establishing its own Select Committee on the subject, which now operates with a wide-ranging remit across government departments and has produced numerous valuable advisory reports on matters ranging from medical research and the use of antibiotics in the National Health Service to the 'greenhouse effect'. However, it is the House of Lords' contribution as part of the Westminster Parliament's scrutiny of EC law-making that represents its most important (and time-consuming) development. In the early 1970s, each House set up a Select Committee to examine European affairs, the Lords' Select Committee on the European Communities being required 'to consider Community proposals whether in draft or otherwise, to obtain all necessary information about them, and to make reports on those which, in the opinion of the Committee, raise important questions of policy or principle, and on other questions to which the Committee considers that the special attention of the House should be drawn'. Six sub-committees were subsequently established on a wide range of European matters including economic affairs, energy, the environment, agriculture, and social affairs, with sub-committee E (chaired by a Law Lord, currently Lord Hoffmann) having the important role of examining the legal implications of European proposals. The quality of the reports which have been produced by the Lords' Select Committee have been such that they are now widely regarded across the European Union, including at Brussels, as the most valuable source of scrutiny of European affairs in existence. A recent in-depth study of the subject by Dr Adam Cygan points to one such instance. The Select Committee's Report on Fraud and Mismanagement in the Community's Finances in 1994, he observed, 'was acknowledged as a highly valued inquiry among the Commission and the other Member States. It articulated in a non-partisan way the concerns which the government had held for many years, but which the government had not been successful in putting across primarily because it was viewed by other Member States as another complaint by a "Eurosceptic" government.'[20]

Constitutional affairs, human rights and international relations

Alongside a realistic account of how the actual working of the House of Lords has evolved in recent decades, the most significant element in the redefinition of the role of a reconstituted Second Chamber will be an accurate assessment of what new or enhanced functions it will acquire in the foreseeable future. What is important to appreciate is that Labour's overall constitutional reform programme contains individual policies which carry major implications for the parliamentary process, and will of necessity involve new procedures to be developed in which a reconstituted Second Chamber is very likely to have an essential role to play. The general areas of governmental activity which will become more closely subject to parliamentary control are with respect to human rights, constitutional law, and foreign affairs.

Labour policy documents over the past ten years have often proposed that the Second Chamber should have an elevated role to play with respect to the protection of human rights. The 1989 policy review document *Meet the Challenge: Make the Change* specifically included in its constitutional recommendations that the House of Lords should take on a special function in protecting human rights and be vested with extended legislative powers of delay over government Bills affecting basic rights and freedoms (see p 38

---

[20] *The Role of the UK Parliament in the Law-Making Process of the European Union* (London: Kluwer, 1998) p 214. See also T St J Bates, 'Select Committees in the House of Lords', in Gavin Drewry (ed), *The New Select Committees* (Oxford University Press, 1985).

below). The same view was reiterated by the Plant Commission on Electoral Systems in 1993 when considering a method of future composition for the Lords. The Second Chamber 'will have a specific concern with the protection of civil liberties', stated the Plant Report. Now in office, the Labour leadership has already fulfilled the first objective of its human rights reform programme by incorporating the European Convention on Human Rights (ECHR) into UK law. The Human Rights Act 1998 enshrines the concept of positive rights in our law which are actionable against public authorities. The constitutional and legal significance of the Act is very great indeed. Although the ECHR principles in law will have interpretative status only, they will come to form a corpus of fundamental moral principles against which all future executive and legislative acts of the government will be viewed, not simply judicially within the courts of law but politically within the parliamentary process. Furthermore, under s 4 of the 1998 Act, British courts may now issue a 'declaration of incompatibility' where legislation is held to be in violation of human rights, which will then oblige the government to initiate statutory reform to carry out the determination of the court. As discussed in Chapter 18, there is now a consensus of opinion supporting closer parliamentary scrutiny of all future legislative proposals for compliance with the ECHR in order to minimise the possibility of Bills and subordinate legislation falling foul of its human rights standards both before the European Court of Human Rights at Strasbourg and before our own domestic courts.

There are several advantages and benefits which the Second Chamber can bring to this scrutiny process. Perhaps the most important of these is the more independent and politically-detached process by which it can conduct its work, compared to MPs in the Commons, which is especially useful in the case of legislation upon which the Commons has divided along party lines. The Official Secrets Act and Prevention of Terrorism (Temporary Provisions) Act are obvious examples of such partisanship working against the best interests of expert scrutiny for compliance with the ECHR. Another advantage is the greater degree of legal specialisation to be found among the membership of the House of Lords, not only at present but as the Chamber can expect to be composed by whatever future method comes to be adopted as part of Labour's 'second stage' of Lords' reform (see p 44 below).

There is a further aspect to Labour's human rights reform programme which in the long term is likely to prove of even greater significance to the future role of the Second Chamber. Labour's policy programme indicates that incorporation of the ECHR is just a 'first step' towards a constitutional Bill of Rights for the United Kingdom. Its 1993 constitutional policy paper, *A New Agenda for Democracy*, prepared for the National Executive Committee by the then home affairs spokesperson, Tony Blair, and endorsed by the party conference, believed that:[21]

---

[21] At p 31. See Appendix 1. More generally see Robert Blackburn, *Towards a Constitutional Bill of Rights for the United Kingdom* (London: Pinter, 1999).

'The incorporation of the European Convention on Human Rights is a necessary first step, but it is not a substitute for our own written Bill of Rights . . . There is a good case for drafting our own Bill of Rights . . . We therefore propose the establishment of an all-party commission that will be charged with drafting the Bill of Rights and considering a suitable method of entrenchment.'

This policy objective, discussed in Chapter 17, cannot be implemented within the lifetime of the present Parliament and will follow only after the incorporation of the ECHR has been allowed time to become fully integrated into our legal and parliamentary system. But once this necessary interval of time has elapsed, the case for establishing our own indigenous Bill of Rights will become very strong indeed. This development, when it occurs, will signify an important change in our future legislative process in that the Bill of Rights is likely to adopt for itself some suitable measure of entrenchment, possibly akin to that which operates under the Canadian Bill of Rights. The point here is that an entrenched or partially entrenched Bill of Rights can be expected to involve the Second Chamber in some special legislative process for the future amendment of or passage of emergency derogating measures from the Bill of Rights. As is common in other countries' Parliaments, the Second Chamber should possess greater powers than those it possesses over ordinary legislation.

This should be part of a general re-definition of the role of the Second Chamber which emphasises its work with respect to constitutional matters generally. Ideological ancestry already exists for the proposition that the Second Chamber has a special role to perform in the field of constitutional legislation, even if previous Labour governments down to the Wilson and Callaghan administrations have done little to encourage the idea. The Bryce Commission (see Figure 1.1 above) clearly identified constitutional legislation as a subject for special consideration by a reformed Second Chamber, even if – understandably, for it was only a few years following the Parliament Act 1911 – it did not actually recommend restoring any part of its earlier legislative powers. In fact, the Lords has always retained a legislative veto over one fundamental matter of British constitutionalism. This is the suspension of general elections and prolongation of any existing Parliament beyond the present five-year maximum duration.[22] Over any item of legislation seeking to prolong the life of Parliament – and therefore the government and its party majority in the Commons – the Lords has retained a power of absolute veto, notwithstanding the application of the Parliament Acts to statutes of any other character. Few parliamentary reformers will be unaware of the empirical fact, already explained (pp 19–21), that Second Chambers around the world are normally vested with express functions and powers in relation to constitutional matters. It is only Britain's eccentricity of lacking a written constitution for the modern era that has obviated the need for parliamentary

---

[22] Parliament Act 1911, s 2(1).

distinctions in its legislative processes and scrutiny procedures to be drawn between ordinary and constitutional law.

The final area in which foreseeable developments are likely to involve some new parliamentary procedures suitable for Second Chamber involvement is foreign affairs. As part of its constitutional reform programme published in 1993, the Labour Party singled out treaty-making and military involvement of UK forces overseas as matters requiring new formal rules for securing proper parliamentary scrutiny and approval. Currently, almost the whole terrain of foreign policy in the UK is carried on by the government under the common law authority of the royal prerogative, thereby avoiding the need to secure any formal approval to its diplomatic agreements and executive decisions. As the Labour document complained, 'Treaty after treaty is concluded without the formal consent of Parliament. Indeed, foreign policy as a whole is an area virtually free from democratic control and accountability.'[23] Even the two major international human rights treaties to which the UK became a party in 1951 and 1976, the European Convention on Human Rights and United Nations International Covenant on Civil and Political Rights, were both ratified by the Crown without any parliamentary scrutiny. In 1995, the Major government's ratification of Protocol 11 to the European Convention on Human Rights in 1996 was not even announced in Parliament. As Professor Francis Jacobs (now Advocate General at the European Court of Justice) has observed, 'By a strange legal anachronism, some States, notably the United Kingdom, still seem to consider that treaties are matters for governments alone.'[24] The UK now has the only Parliament in the European Union that lacks any formal mechanism for securing scrutiny and approval to treaties and other major foreign policy decisions. The 1924 Ponsonby 'rule' – now a Foreign Office circular – is clearly inadequate as a basis for effective scrutiny. It involves the voluntary practice of governments laying treaties signed by the UK before Parliament as Command Papers after their entry into force, and in the case of treaties requiring legal ratification a copy being placed on the Table of the House 21 days beforehand.

Whether statutory reform and/or parliamentary self-regulation by way of Standing Orders proves to be the way forward for enlarging the UK Parliament's involvement in treaty-making and foreign affairs, a reconstituted Second Chamber could well have a distinctive role to play, independently and/or jointly with the work of the House of Commons. It is worth recalling that foreign affairs was a subject upon which the Report of the Bryce Commission believed the Second Chamber should pay some special attention (see p 23 above). If reform of the Crown prerogative of treaty-making involves the legal requirement for an affirmative resolution, then the formal consent of the House of Lords as well as the House of Commons will be required. A chief objective of the reform will be greater scrutiny, debate and openness in

[23] See Labour Party, *A New Agenda for Democracy* (1993) p. 33: Appendix 1.
[24] Quoted in HL Deb, 28 February 1996, col 1531.

the treaty-making process, and from a parliamentary perspective this will involve the establishment of one or more specialist committees – either Joint between the two Houses or each creating its own – which will prepare a report on matters which should be brought to the attention of the House. A 'scrutiny reserve' stipulation will become necessary, similar to the work of the Select Committees which examine draft legislative proposals of the European Union, to ensure that treaties are not ratified prior to Parliament having completed its work.

The purpose of Parliament as a whole is to act as the constitutional watchdog of the executive and its legislative measures. Parliament serves as the sounding-board of the nation and seeks to represent local, regional and national opinion in all its proceedings. But whilst the House of Commons, with the Prime Minister and up to 95 of his ministers among its membership, is inevitably more government-focused and more suitable for transacting certain kinds of administrative business, such as financial matters, there is a good case today that certain types of business and function should now be formally attributed to the Second Chamber. The Labour government should embrace the concept of some form of division of business between the two Houses of Parliament, and recognise that some such division already exists or is emerging in practice. This, then, should be reflected in the theory and practice of Parliament and in the powers and regulation controlling the relationship between the two Houses.

An accurate statement of the present and foreseeable role and functions of the House of Lords might be given as follows in Figure 1.3:

Figure 1.3 A re-statement of the role and functions for a reformed House of Lords

---

1 *Public Bills*
The revision and approval of public legislation.

2 *Other primary legislation*
The revision and approval of other forms of primary legislation including local and personal Acts, Private Acts, Measures of the Church Assembly and General Synod of the Church of England.

3 *Delegated legislation*
The scrutiny and approval of subordinate legislation subject to parliamentary proceedings.

4 *Parliamentary debate*
Full and free debate on matters of national and regional importance.

continued . . .

... *continued*

5   *Government policy and administration*
Scrutiny of public policy and administration by way of Questions and Select Committee inquiries.

6   *European Union law*
Scrutiny and advisory reports on prospective law-making by the institutions of the European Union.

7   *European Union policy and administration*
Debate and advisory reports on European Union affairs raising questions of national or regional importance.

8   *Treaties*
The scrutiny and debate of treaty negotiations conducted by the government, and the ratification of treaty provisions of the European Union.

9   *International conflict*
The examination and approval of executive acts determining military intervention by the armed forces and the recognition of foreign states.

10   *International human rights*
Inquiries into domestic compliance with international human rights law treaties.

11   *The Bill of Rights*
The approval of amendments to, and derogations from, the Bill of Rights.

12   *The constitution*
The approval of legislation affecting the Crown, Parliament and structure of the UK which is designated as a Constitutional Act.

Note:
The above assumes future implementation of Labour's policy objectives of:
(a)   a Scottish Parliament and Welsh Assembly;
(b)   a homegrown Bill of Rights;
(c)   greater parliamentary involvement in the treaty process; and
(d)   parliamentary ratification of executive action in going to war.
It assumes also a special legislative procedure being introduced in the future under which the Second Chamber would possess a power of veto or extended delay with respect to amendments to the Bill of Rights and a defined category of Constitutional Acts covering legislation designated as being of first-class constitutional importance (such as the status of the Crown, the relationship between the two Houses of Parliament, and the regional structure of the UK).

The powers of the Second Chamber

The performance of these enhanced functions of the Second Chamber can only be carried out effectively if, at the same time, a new regime governing its powers of delay or veto over certain classes of legislation and executive decision-making is put into place. If, as I have suggested, a process of re-defining and establishing the functions of the Second Chamber is central to the whole direction of its future reform, then the question of precisely what new powers the reformed Chamber should possess is crucial to the degree of success or otherwise with which it can be expected to carry out its future par-liamentary work. The point at which a reformed Chamber takes on extended functions of scrutiny and agreement will be the time to rationalise its powers as currently regulated under the Parliament Acts 1911–49.

Until 1911, the consent of the House of Lords was required to all legisla-tion. The Second Chamber's legislative powers therefore were similar to those of the House of Commons, except with respect to financial legislation which had to be introduced first into the Commons and could only be rejected, not amended, by the Lords. It was the Lords' rejection of Lloyd George's 'people's budget' in 1909 that provided the political trigger for the 1911 reform. The only distinction of a general legislative character which is drawn by the Parliament Acts is between Money Bills and other Bills. Money Bills (defined at length in the Act,[25] but principally concerned with taxation and financial expenditure) are effectively taken away altogether from the power of the Chamber by providing that it has one month in which to agree to such a Bill, in default of which it can be sent up to the Sovereign for the royal assent. All other types of public Bill are dealt with as one species of legislation in s 2 of the 1911 Act, the effect of which was to transform the earlier power of veto of the Second Chamber to one of a power of delay only, for a term initially of two years under the 1911 Act, then reduced further to one year under the the 1949 Act (which was enacted without the Second Chamber's consent under the 1911 Act itself, a process probably unlawful though never actually challenged in the courts).[26] As mentioned above (p 32),

---

[25] s 1(2)–(3).

[26] The tortuously drafted provision in s 2(1) is as follows: 'If any Public Bill (other than a Money Bill or a Bill containing any provision to extend the maximum duration of Parliament beyond five years) is passed by the House of Commons [in two successive sessions] (whether of the same Parliament or not), and, having been sent up to the House of Lords at least one month before the end of the session, is rejected by the House of Lords in each of those sessions, that Bill shall, on its rejection [for the second time] by the House of Lords, unless the House of Commons direct to the contrary, be presented to His Majesty and become an Act of Parliament on the Royal Assent being signified thereto, notwithstanding that the House of Lords have not consented to the Bill: Provided that this provision shall not take effect unless [one year has elapsed] between the date of the second reading in the first of those sessions of the Bill in the House of Commons and the date on which it passes the House of Commons [in the second of those sessions].' On the question whether the Parliament Act 1949 Act is a valid Act, see Owen Hood Phillips, *Reform of the Constitution* (London: Chatto & Windus, 1970) p 91.

the only exception to this restriction is in the case of Bills to extend the duration of Parliament, where the Second Chamber retains a power of veto.

It is worth reminding ourselves that the Parliament Act 1911 was expressly enacted as a temporary, interim measure pending a permanent basis for reform being installed. As a piece of legislation it had the immediate, specific objective of overriding the political opposition in the Tory-dominated House of Lords to the social reform programme of the then Liberal government.[27] The preamble to the 1911 Act made it clear that its purpose was simply to restrict the powers of the Lords for the time being, pending a permanent basis for reform being agreed and implemented. After setting out its intention to substitute a popularly composed Second Chamber for the existing hereditary House of Lords (see p 16), the Act declared that, 'Provision will require hereafter to be made by Parliament in a measure effecting such substitution for limiting and defining the powers of the new Second Chamber.' Clearly the powers of the Second Chamber over Bills of a financial and administrative nature should be of a lower order than those of the House of Commons. The real question, which the expedient of the 1911 Act deferred, was in respect of which types of business (apart from those of a financial and purely administrative nature) should the Second Chamber retain its power of veto or possess an extended power of delay.

The Parliament Acts are rooted in their own historical sets of circumstances and as the basis for bicameralism in the modern state have proved unfortunate. As a temporary expedient, the 1911 Act soon became crystallised into a permanent anachronism promoting the ascendancy of the House of Commons, or more precisely the ruling party of the day, over all matters of government business. When the Act was passed, the nature and scale of government was very different to that which it had become following the cessation of the Second World War. Over the period since, government activity has become ever more interventionist and public regulation now dominates most aspects of our private and working lives. In 1911, the civil service had barely developed beyond ministerial secretariats and measures of government legislation numbered only around 15 short Bills each year (compared with today's average of around 40 lengthy statutes). The phenomenon of delegated legislation in 1911 barely existed, and was not even provided for in the Parliament Acts, whereas nowadays around 1,500 statutory instruments are passed every year. This explains the curious anomaly why today the House of Lords possesses an absolute veto over the smallest minutiae of administrative procedure contained in a statutory instrument, yet over major Bills of first rate constitutional importance, such as those giving domestic legal effect to the European treaties, establishing the new Scottish Parliament, or

---

[27] For a lively study of this episode, see Roy (now Lord) Jenkins, *Mr. Balfour's Poodle: An Account of the Struggle between the House of Lords and the Government of Mr. Asquith* (London: William Heinemann, 1954).

implementing major parliamentary reform itself, it possesses no special legislative powers beyond a 12-month period of delay.

Our conclusion must be that the Parliament Acts ceased some time ago to represent an appropriate constitutional balance between the two Houses of Parliament. A rationalisation of the powers of the House of Lords is necessary which distinguishes between legislation of differing kinds. Public general Bills and other forms of primary legislation would fall into one category, over which the Second Chamber might exercise a short delaying power of one year or possibly its pre-1949 position of two years. A similar power should exist over statutory instruments, being subject to a one-stage parliamentary process not capable of amendment, though some special procedure might be adopted in the case of human rights legislation enacted by way of remedial orders under the Human Rights Act (see Chapter 18). Bills dealing with matters of fundamental importance to the structure of the state (such as the status of the Crown, the relationship between the two Houses of Parliament, and the structure of the UK) and amendments to a future Bill of Rights should be placed in a special category for which the Second Chamber has a veto or extended power of delay. Some of Labour's policy documents over the past decade have pointed clearly in this direction. In 1989, *Meet the Challenge: Make the Change* (Labour's Policy Review for the 1990s) recommended that:[28]

'The new Second Chamber should have new delaying powers over measures affecting fundamental rights. It will possess the power to delay repeal of legislation affecting fundamental rights for the whole life of a Parliament – thus providing an opportunity for the electorate to determine whether or not the government which proposes such measures should remain in office. The extra delaying power will apply to all items of legislation specifically designated as concerning fundamental rights and all legislation establishing the national and regional assemblies. The second chamber will also possess the absolute right of veto on any proposal to extend the life of Parliament beyond the constitutional maximum of five years.'

If the Westminster Parliament of the 21st century is to be a genuinely bicameral system structured upon a complementary division of functions, with the Second Chamber taking on a more developed role as suggested in this chapter, then a significant extension of its powers will be involved. Perhaps the greatest factor involved will arise as a necessary implication of other changes on Labour's constitutional reform agenda. A distinctive category of constitutional legislation is already beginning to emerge – such as the law governing the relationship between the Scottish Parliament and Westminster, and in the future the relationship between ordinary law and a homegrown Bill of Rights – with respect to which it would seem natural for the Upper House, the reformed House of Lords, to possess special functions and powers.

---

[28] At p 56.

STAGE TWO REFORM: MEMBERSHIP OF THE REFORMED SECOND CHAMBER

Method of composition

A multitude of different schemes for composing the Upper House have been put forward in numerous reports, political studies and draft legislation on the subject since the end of the 19th century.[29] This proliferation of views and alternatives has, if anything, fed further confusion rather than produce greater clarity or cross-party consensus on the matter.

Equally, the policy of the Labour Party on composing the Lords has been erratic and contradictory when looked at over a period of time. In 1968–69 the Wilson government tried and failed to combine removing hereditary peers with otherwise consolidating the Lords as an appointed chamber carrying out existing functions with weaker powers (see pp 24–5 and below). At the 1977 party conference a policy of outright unicameral abolition of the Chamber was endorsed by 6 million votes to 91,000 (and later included in the party's 1983 election manifesto). Then in 1989, following the comprehensive policy review concluded in *Meet the Challenge: Make the Change*, opinion within the Labour Party moved sharply towards a directly elected Second Chamber with extended powers (see p 11). The policy of an elected Chamber was subsequently included in its 1992 election manifesto, and elaborated upon further in Labour's comprehensive constitutional reform *A New Agenda for Democracy* in 1993. However, as mentioned earlier, the pre-election policy documents of 1996–97 failed to include a reference to elections, instead suggesting that the whole matter of long-term reform should be referred to a joint committee of both Houses to consider.

As is evident from experience abroad (see Table 1.4 below) and the conclusions of earlier inquiries and reports in this country, some of which are outlined below, there are essentially three avenues down which reform of the composition of the new Chamber can proceed.

Option One: Appointment

Members could be appointed by a designated official or body, including as at present by the Crown on the advice of the Prime Minister, or else by some new commission specially created for the purpose. This would in effect be tantamount to a continuation of the present system, after removing any element of hereditary membership. It would be the minimalist way forward, perpetuating the interim basis of membership pending the outcome of the Joint Parliamentary Committee inquiry proposed by Labour (see p 10 above) and any preceding Royal Commission. It is the system most capable of being

---

[29] See House of Lords Library, *Proposals for Reform of the Composition and Powers of the House of Lords, 1968–96* (1996); Constitution Unit, *Reform of the House of Lords* (1996); Robert Blackburn, 'House of Lords Reform', *Public Law* (1988) 187.

manipulated in order to achieve other desired political objects, for example particular quotas of party politicians or experts.

Option Two: Indirect elections

A different approach would be to install a system of indirect elections, whereby an electoral college or class of designated officials or bodies selected a quota of representatives. This system can be effective if a particular type of political or social representation is desired in the Second Chamber, particularly geographical representation. Thus, the French Senate is composed of individuals put forward through selection by an electoral college comprising a large number of local and regional officials. The German Bundesrat has members who are delegates of the state governments. Clearly, a connection could be drawn here between the composition of the Second Chamber and the Scottish Parliament, Welsh Assembly and proposed regional assemblies for England (see Chapters 12–13). Labour's policy review document in 1989 expressed the view that, whilst 'We intend that members of the new Second Chamber should particularly reflect the interests and aspirations of the regions and nations of Britain . . . We do not, however, propose direct links between members of the national and regional assemblies and members of the Upper House.'[30]

Few today support the idea of a functional or vocational Chamber, whereby designated professions and occupations form electoral colleges, each returning a prescribed number of representatives. However, to some extent such a scheme would be consistent with the claims of those who defend the status quo on grounds of the expertise of different disciplines it happens to possess, for instance in law (the Law Lords and former holders of judicial office), the church (26 of the Anglican bishops) and big business (an influential criterion in past appointments).

Option Three: Direct election

The third (and most straightforward) option is simply to elect members of the House. Most people regard this as the presumptive way forward, and certainly opinion polls indicate a distinct popular preference for this method of composing a reformed Second Chamber (and one which is particularly strong among Labour members).[31] This means that those who believe that there exist strong reasons why members of the Upper House should not be held directly accountable to the electorate must make out their case to the contrary. However, it is true that not all bicameral legislatures have elected Second Chambers.

---

[30] At p 55.

[31] MORI's State of the Nation 1996 poll indicated 55 per cent support for House of Lords' reform (with 27 per cent for the status quo, others don't know) of which 25 per cent backed elections, 15 per cent unicameral abolition, and 15 per cent simply removing hereditary peers. An *Observer* survey of new Labour MPs, published 11 May 1997, indicated 95 per cent support for replacing the House of Lords with an elected Second Chamber.

Of those that do, the United States elects 100 Senators and Australia 76 Senators, in both cases for six-year terms of office (see Table 1.4 below).

A decision on which electoral system would be most appropriate to the Second Chamber must take into account a number of factors, among them the method already employed in the House of Commons (a subject under review by the Jenkins Commission: see Chapter 3), the number of members to be elected, and the Chamber's precise functions. The adoption of large, regional constituencies would be natural, not only because the new Second Chamber is almost certain to include at least some element of regional representation, but also because the Commons is already based on small constituencies and likely to remain so. Lord Plant's Commission recommended a List System operating upon 12 constituencies and an electoral quota of 135,000, which would create a membership of 322. The single transferable vote (STV) would be another proportional system and one with the added advantage of allowing voters to distinguish between individual candidates put up by the same party. Furthermore, if as is common abroad, a rotating system of membership was adopted, protecting the Chamber from electoral volatility and providing an element of continuity, the same 12 regional constituencies proposed by the Plant Report could be used to implement STV on the basis of seven members being returned for six-year terms of office at elections held every two years (making a total membership of 252).

Support for one or other of these options – or a combination among them – can be gleaned from the reports of earlier inquiries into House of Lords' reform. The Conference on Reform of the Second Chamber, set up by the Liberal Prime Minister Lloyd George and chaired by Viscount Bryce (see p 23), examined in detail various methods of composition, including – nomination by the Crown; direct popular elections, using large constituencies; election by local authorities, grouped into large districts; selection by a Joint Standing Committee of both Houses of Parliament; and election by the House of Commons, either as a whole or divided into groups. Its final recommendation was that the Second Chamber should consist of around 340 members, retaining among them the Lord Chancellor and the Law Lords. Three-quarters of these (246 members) would be chosen by panels of MPs, grouped according to the geographical areas of the country they represented. One-quarter (81 members) would be selected by a Joint Standing Committee of both Houses. Members would serve for 12-year terms of office, with one-third retiring every four years.

The conclusions of Harold Wilson's Labour government in its White Paper on House of Lords Reform and Parliament (No 2) Bill 1969 made no such wide-ranging inquiry. As with the Attlee government's views in 1948,[32]

---

[32] See also *Agreed Statement on the Conclusion of the Conference of Party Leaders*, Cmnd 7380 (1948). This preliminary agreement, prior to the collapse of the all-party talks, included the principles that, 'The Second Chamber should be complementary to and not a rival to the Lower House, and, with this end in view, the reform of the House of Lords should be based

it rejected direct elections upon the basis that a democratised Second Chamber would become a rival to the House of Commons and serve to violate our parliamentary system by which the government stands and falls in the Commons. This is consistent with the Wilson government's minimalist view of the Second Chamber's role generally and its failure to countenance any division of function between the two Chambers. Schemes of indirect election, such as the three put forward by consideration by the Bryce Commission, received no serious consideration at all. What was proposed instead was simply to continue utilising the existing system of nomination by the Crown. Basically, the hereditary peerage would have its voting rights taken away, but could attend and speak in the Chamber. Voting members, numbering around 230, would be the existing and newly appointed life peers (and hereditary peers of first creation). Members would lose their voting rights on attaining the age of 72 years.

Meanwhile, opinion within the Conservative Party throughout its period of opposition in the 1970s proceeded to move towards a strengthening of the Second Chamber's membership. The former Lord Chancellor, Lord Hailsham, gave his public endorsement to radical reform, writing, 'The present House of Lords is doomed, and there is therefore no longer any point in arguing whether or not it should be retained. The only question is, with what to replace it and when. To my mind there is no alternative to an elected chamber.'[33] In 1978, a Conservative Review Committee on the future of the Lords, chaired by the former Prime Minister, Lord Home, was appointed by Margaret Thatcher. It recommended a House of 430 members, composed through a mixture of election and appointment. One-third would be appointed by the Crown on the advice of the Prime Minister as at present, but the Prime Minister would be obliged to consult and take note of the recommendations of a Committee of Privy Counsellors comprising senior representatives of the main political parties. The majority of members, two-thirds, would then be directly elected under a scheme of proportional representation, serving nine-year terms of office.[34] Shortly after the Conservatives took office in 1979, two discussion documents were produced by their Parliamentary Constitutional Committee, one of which again backed the Home Committee's recommendations for two-thirds of the Chamber to be directly elected.[35]

The most recent inquiry into the composition of the Second Chamber was conducted as part of the Labour NEC Working Party on Electoral Systems, chaired by Raymond Plant. Its report, published in 1993, endorsed the party's

---

on a modification of its existing constitution as opposed to the establishment of a Second Chamber of a completely new type based on some system of election . . . Members of the Second Chamber should be styled "Lords of Parliament" and would be appointed on grounds of personal distinction or public service . . . Some remuneration would be payable to members of the Second Chamber.'

[33] *The Dilemma of Democracy* (London: William Collins, 1978) p 152.

[34] Conservative Review Committee, *The House of Lords* (1978).

[35] Conservative Parliamentary Constitutional Committee, *Reform of the House of Lords: Discussion Documents* (1980).

Table 1.4 Foreign Second Chambers

Country	Name of Upper House	Federal or unitary	Number of members	Term of office	Method of composition
USA	Senate	Federal	100	6 years	Direct popular election
One-third elected every 2 years; each state returns 2 members					
France	Senate	Unitary	321	9 years	Indirect election
One-third elected every 3 years by an electoral college comprising 145,000 local and regional officials					
Germany	Bundesrat	Federal	79	Floating	Indirect election
Members are delegates selected by the Länder (state governments)					
Australia	Senate	Federal	76	6 years	Direct popular election
One-half are elected every three years; each state returns 12 members by single transferable vote.					
Canada	Senate	Federal	104	Life (retire at 75)	Appointment
Vacancies are filled by persons appointed by the Governor General acting on the advice of the Prime Minister; a quota of numbers from each province applies and each Senator must reside and own property in the province she or he represents.					

commitment at that time to establish direct popular election, and proceeded to consider which system of election would be most suitable for the Second Chamber. It recommended the adoption of a party List System, operating on 12 regional constituencies as follows: East Anglia (1.6 million), East Midlands (3.1 million), Greater London (4.9 million), North West (4.8 million), Northern (2.4 million), South East (8 million), South West (3.6 million), West Midlands (4 million), Yorks and Humberside (3.8 million), Scotland (3.9 million), Wales (2.2 million) and Northern Ireland (1.1 million). Each region would return a number of members based upon its size of population divided by an electoral quota (set at 135,000) which initially would create a membership of 322.

My own preference is clearly on the side of direct elections. The democratic arguments in favour of elections are very strong indeed, and those against – particularly in support of the continuation of some system of appointment – rather weak. Politicians working on our behalf, serving as watchdogs of the executive and scrutineers of good government and legislation, should be accountable directly to those they represent. Most of the arguments in favour of the status quo, or those which seek to avoid elections on any basis upon the ground that some other body or person is better equipped than ourselves to choose who should be working in the Second Chamber, are somewhat specious and patronising. The 'expertise' argument – that the Upper House requires persons of a special level of ability and knowledge to be selected – is palpably misleading to anyone who regularly sits in on debates in the House of Lords today. Certainly there are some highly able peers conducting legislative and committee work, but they represent a minority in the House and even then they attend only on a part-time or spasmodic basis. The fact is that the great majority of life peers who have been appointed at the personal selection of Conservative and Labour leaders over the past 20 years have been persons retired from politics or are not actively engaged in practical politics at all. The converse argument of those who oppose elections, namely that persons of the calibre required for the particular work of the Second Chamber will not be forthcoming through any system of elections, is also misleading. It will be for the political parties to select suitably qualified persons prepared to stand as candidates and undertake a working career in Parliament.

This last point raises the important question of the terms and conditions upon which individuals are chosen to be members of Parliament. The principle that members of the Second Chamber should be paid a salary and given proper office facilities will be an essential part of the process by which the Second Chamber is modernised. Membership should be a proper form of employment, not an honorary position, though as with MPs in the past there might be no constitutional objection to them carrying on other careers so long as there was no serious conflict of interest.

This means that there must be an end to the confusion of purpose for which life peerages have been awarded since 1958. Either a person is being nominated as a peer by a political party leader for a seat in the House of Lords because he has some special contribution which he will make to the working of the House, and is prepared to attend and participate in its business; or, if the sole or principal purpose for which a person is being given a top honour is as a form of reward or personal recognition, then that person should receive a knighthood or medal and not a peerage entitling him to a seat in the legislature.

Future membership of the Second Chamber dependent upon or attached to the award of a title under the honours system should be abolished as part of Labour's first-stage process of reform.[36] If a former senior politician relinquishing his seat in the Commons is in effect choosing to retire from political life, then it is unlikely he or she should be thought suitable to perform a useful role in the Second Chamber. Retiring politicians often accept peerages

[36] See Robert Blackburn, 'Citizenship and the Honours System', in Blackburn (ed), *Rights of Citizenship* (London: Mansell, 1993) Ch 15.

at present for sentimental (and possibly commercial) reasons because it enables them to continue personal acquaintances at Westminster and use its facilities. But an active contribution to the life of the Second Chamber must become the litmus test for membership in the future. Former ministers will find other platforms, public and private, from which they can offer advice and continue to contribute to political debate. Honorary membership to the facilities of Westminster Palace might also be a possibility to be considered in special circumstances, such as lengthy service in either House or former holders of one of a specified range of public offices. Clarification of the line to be drawn between the future award of honours, and how the future membership of the House of Lords is to be determined, will be conducive to the whole anachronistic concept of a peerage becoming obsolete altogether.

CONCLUSION

The lessons of our political history are clear: to stand any realistic prospect of success, a major constitutional measure such as the legislation involved in putting into effect the second-stage of Labour's House of Lords reform programme, following removal of the hereditary peerage, will require detailed advance planning and agreement within the party (or parties) supporting reform, followed by strong leadership from the government of the day. By the same token House of Lords' reform will involve an element of political self-sacrifice on the part of the Labour Cabinet, rare in modern politics, since reforming the Lords in a manner that genuinely strengthens its role, powers and composition will create a more efficient mechanism for scrutiny and influence over the executive. A similar level of political drive and commitment to that which Tony Blair's administration has displayed in establishing the new Scottish Parliament at Edinburgh will be necessary to create a new Second Chamber at Westminster.

Finally, on one presentational aspect that will be of particular interest to Labour's communications advisers, should the reformed House of Lords be re-titled and called by a different name? This seems hardly worthwhile to me, particularly since all the alternatives that have been canvassed – including 'Senate', 'Council of State' or simply 'Second Chamber' – equally suffer from some negative attribute, be it foreign connotations or blandness. I would suggest that the Chamber itself continues to be referred to as the 'House of Lords' – which on reflection is no worse than the 'House of Commons' in its historical overtones. In any event, as is the case with other bicameral Parliaments around the world, the Lords will routinely be spoken of co-terminously as the Second Chamber or Upper House. The more important point is that its members are no longer spoken of as 'Lords'. Members of the House of Lords should retain their proper names and be regarded for all purposes as working Members of Parliament, abbreviated where necessary either to MP in common with members of the House of Commons, or else MP(L) or MHL which should give rise to no greater problems than the way members of the European Parliament (MEP) or Scottish Parliament (MSP) are at present described with respect to their assemblies.

Further reading

Constitution Unit (Nicole Smith), *Reform of the House of Lords* (London, 1996)

Lord Desai and Lord Kilmarnock, *Destiny Not Defeat: Reforming the House of Lords* (London: Fabian Society Discussion Document 29, 1997)

Lord Carnarvon et al, *Second Chamber: Some Remarks on Reforming the House of Lords* (London: Douglas Slater, 1995)

Institute for Public Policy Research (Jeremy Mitchell and Anne Davies), *Reforming the Lords* (London, 1993)

Donald Shell, *The House of Lords* (Hemel Hempstead: Harvester Wheatsheaf, 2nd edn, 1992)

Donald Shell and David Beamish (eds), *The House of Lords at Work* (Oxford: Clarendon Press, 1993)

CHAPTER 2

THE FUNDING OF POLITICAL PARTIES

Martin Linton MP (Commons Home Affairs Committee)

Of all the constitutional issues that were debated in the run-up to the last election, none received as much media attention as the funding of political parties. It was kept in the public eye by a seemingly never-ending series of scandals involving either payments to individual MPs or donations to the Conservative Party. John Major tackled the first of these issues when he set up the Committee on Standards in Public Life and appointed Lord Nolan to be its chairman in October 1994. But he drew its terms of reference tightly around the conduct of MPs and steadfastly refused to allow Lord Nolan to look at what many would see as the more serious issue of how parties raise their income.

When the election finally came in 1997, the issue of sleaze dominated the campaign and played no small part in the Conservatives' defeat. The new Labour government elected on 1 May came with an overwhelming mandate to tackle sleaze but with only two specific pledges – to ban donations from overseas and to oblige parties to disclose donations above £5,000.[1] Beyond that its manifesto undertook simply to refer the whole issue to the Nolan Committee. It did not repeat any of the Labour Party's earlier policy positions in favour of national spending limits, shareholder ballots or indeed state funding, beyond saying that the whole subject was to be reviewed by Lord Nolan and his colleagues before the government took any decisions.

This meant that on party funding, unlike some of the other areas of constitutional reform where it already had a detailed blueprint, the Government was writing on something very close to a blank sheet of paper. The UK had very little legislation on party funding, at least by the standards of developed democracies, and it was almost a misnomer to call it constitutional *reform*. If reform implies a redrawing of existing rules, then the government was not so much in the business of constitutional reform as of constitutional innovation. It had an opportunity to conceive and create an approach to the funding of political parties from first principles.

---

[1] See Appendix 3.

The most basic principle is that democracy should treat people as political equals. That does not just mean that they should all have a vote and that their votes should count the same, but that they should have the same access to information on which to make their decision. And that means, looking at it from the other side of the fence, that candidates and political parties should have the same access to voters through advertising, broadcasting and the press, the same resources to spend in elections and the same claim on public resources.

Behind this lies the principle that political power should be insulated from economic power. Separation of wealth from power is the essence of a democratic system. If wealth is able to buy power, then even a system that is perfectly democratic in form will not be democratic in effect. It will be a plutocracy.

The existence of political parties is hardly acknowledged in our constitution and goes almost unmentioned in legislation. Parties are treated as private organisations. They are indeed legally private, but they have acquired a public function in our political system. They are the link between candidates standing for Parliament and governments holding office. Candidates' election spending has been regulated since 1883. They must publish their accounts, declare the source of donations and restrict their spending to a limit set by Parliament.[2] MPs, too, must declare their interests and their income.[3] Governments are open to public scrutiny. But the link between them, the political parties, have been left unregulated, unaccountable and opaque. That is why they are the part of the political system that is most vulnerable to corruption.

While parties are private organisations, that does not mean that the state has no business regulating their activities. They are in the same relationship as the football clubs are in to the Football Association. The clubs are private, but they accept the right of the FA to set the rules, to inspect the pitch and to appoint the referee and linesmen. Just as the clubs are entitled to play the game in any way they wish that is within the rules, so the parties have an absolute right to determine their policies and strategies in an election, but how much money they raise and spend is a different matter. Rules on party funding and on election spending are essential if we are to ensure that elections are fought on a level playing field.

There are five main ways in which party funding and election spending can be regulated. They are:

(1) Donations limits (on size and/or source).
(2) Election spending limits (on candidates and/or parties).
(3) Disclosure (of individual and/or corporate donors).
(4) Tax breaks (rebates and/or check-offs).
(5) State aid (in cash and/or in kind).

---

[2] See Robert Blackburn, *The Electoral System in Britain* (London: Macmillan, 1995), pp 282 ff.
[3] See J A G Griffith and Michael Ryle, *Parliament: Functions, Practice and Procedures* (London: Sweet & Maxwell, 1989), pp 55 ff.

These are not alternatives. They are usually applied in combination. The most common form of regulation is disclosure which is a legal requirement in every Western democracy apart from the UK. Disclosure levels vary widely from £40 in Canada and £60 in the USA, to £1,700 in Italy, £3,000 for individuals and £5,000 for companies in France and £7,000 in Germany.[4] State aid is given to parties in almost every Western democracy, including Australia, Austria, Canada, France, Germany, Greece, Portugal, Spain, Sweden and the USA. The only notable exceptions are Belgium and the Netherlands where funding is given to party research institutes instead and Italy where it was recently abolished. Tax concessions are given on donations to political parties in several countries, including Germany, Canada, the Netherlands and France. The USA uses a tax check-off system. Election spending limits are used in Canada and the USA, although they have been rendered ineffective in the USA by a series of Supreme Court decisions. Donations limits are the least common. Quebec limits donations to individuals who may give no more than $3,000 a year (£1,200). The USA also limits donations but there are many loopholes for those who wish to get round them. France bans donations from companies and Germany bans donations from trade unions. Every other Western democracy has adopted a ban on overseas donations. The UK is the only country that has yet to apply any of these five forms of regulation in anything more than a partial way. The position can be quickly summarised:

Donations limits:
- There are no limits on the size of donations.
- There are no limits on the source of donations, except that trade unions and employers' associations can only give donations to political parties if they hold a ballot every ten years to establish a political fund and, if one is set up, give their members the right to contract out (Trade Union Act 1984, now the Trade Union and Labour Relations (Consolidation) Act 1992).

Spending limits:
- Spending to promote a party is unlimited.
- Spending to promote a named candidate is limited to about £8,000 depending on the size and the electorate of a constituency (Representation of the People Act 1983) after the declaration of a candidacy.

Disclosure:
- Individual donations do not have to be disclosed.
- Company donations over £200 must be disclosed in the directors' reports (Companies Act 1967, as amended by the Companies Act 1985).

---

[4] Canadian $100; US$100; LIT5 million; FF30,000 and FF50,000; DM20,000.

Tax breaks:
- Donations are not exempt from income tax.
- Bequests of up to £1,000 are exempt from capital transfer tax.

State aid:
- There is no state aid to the parties in cash.
- Candidates receive a free postal delivery and free hire of public halls (Representation of the People Act 1918). Parties receive free radio and television broadcasts on BBC and ITV (Television Act 1954, as amended by the Broadcasting Act 1990). Opposition parties receive aid for parliamentary duties.

A NEW APPROACH

New laws on party funding have been introduced in many countries in the wake of financial or political scandals. Usually the party tainted by sleaze has been defeated and replaced by the party that campaigned against sleaze. The most obvious example is the post-Watergate reform of party funding in the USA, which produced a series of tough party funding laws that were subsequently undermined by rulings of the Supreme Court. In the UK the election of a new Labour government created an opportunity not only to stop the sleaze but to put laws in place that would establish a new framework for the financing of politics.

Everything that has happened since the election of 1 May 1997 has made a radical reform of the system even more certain. In October the Prime Minister appointed Sir Patrick (now Lord) Neill, a lawyer, to succeed Lord Nolan as chairman of the Committee on Standards in Public Life and extended its terms of reference to include the funding of political parties. In November it emerged that the Labour Party had accepted a donation of £1 million before the election from the head of Formula One motor racing, Bernie Ecclestone, who was also the beneficiary of a government proposal to phase the application of a tobacco sponsorship ban on the motor racing industry.

After consulting Lord Neill, the Labour Party was advised to return the donation 'for fear that it might give the impression of a conflict of interest'. It promptly followed that advice. The episode was acutely embarrassing for the Labour Party, but the paradoxical result was that it confirmed the Prime Minister in his determination to press ahead with radical reforms of party funding. *The Times* headline summed it up: 'Labour cash row hastens funding law.'

The importance of the Ecclestone affair was not that the Labour Party had acted wrongly in accepting the donation, nor that it had been influenced by the donation, but that it illuminated a fundamental problem about business funding – that business people with enough money to make donations of

£1 million are likely to be affected by government decisions, beneficially or adversely, sooner or later, and that therefore accepting £million donations is likely to create a conflict of interest which will compromise the integrity of a governing party. As I said in oral evidence to the Neill Committee:

> 'The danger is not that there will be corrupt deals behind closed doors. It is that parties will feel beholden to their major donors, nervous of offending them, anxious not to jeopardise the possibility of another large donation. The very fact of having received large sums of money will, regardless of the donor's motives or intentions, restrict the parties' freedom of action.'

Faced with a crisis, the Prime Minister's response was to appear on national television, to apologise for his handling of the affair and to vow that he would learn from his mistakes. The following day he wrote an article for *The Times* in which he proposed a number of new options for the Neill Committee to consider that were far more radical than anything he had suggested before. There was a 'powerful case' for national limits on election spending, he said. The government should be ready to 'limit individual and company donations to a modest amount', even to consider 'whether there should be business funding at all'. He said the Labour Party 'stood ready to publish names and amounts' of donations. It was happy, too, to publish a list of all those who had made donations during the past five years, provided other parties did the same, and if Lord Neill decided it was right, they would offer legislative backing for retrospective disclosure. He was still 'instinctively cautious' about state funding, but the UK already had state funding by the backdoor – through the so-called 'Short money', the election freepost and free TV time.[5] The government would 'be ready to consider any proposals Lord Neill has for state funding'.

When the Neill Committee published its consultation document in December 1997,[6] some of the more radical ideas thrown up in the wake of the Ecclestone affair had already been added to the list of issues to be considered. The document asked whether there was a case 'for limiting the amount which an individual or a corporation may give', whether shareholders 'should have to give consent to company political donations', whether there was a case for limiting national campaign expenditure and whether additional controls were needed on the use of newspaper advertisements and billboard sites. It also contained a section on the honours system which pointed out that the sale of honours was abused for party fund-raising from the 17th century until the 1920s and asked whether 'additional arrangements' would be necessary to prevent abuses now.

Before reporting in 1998, the Neill Committee looked at all the options for reform that emerged under each of the following headings.

---

[5] See Blackburn, *The Electoral System in Britain*, pp 336–38; and further p 63 below.
[6] Committee on Standards in Public Life, *Issues and Questions: The Funding of Political Parties* (1997).

DONATION LIMITS

Limited by size

It is difficult to limit the size of donations. In the USA there is an official limit of $25,000 (£15,000) but it is easily evaded by giving money to Political Action Committees. In Quebec there is a limit of $3,000 and although there are attempts at evasion, it seems to work reasonably well.

Limited by source

It is more common to limit the source of donations. Most countries ban overseas donations and donations that are anonymous or of uncertain ethical standing. Some countries ban or limit corporate donations from companies and trade unions. A ban on overseas donations has already been promised. There will have to be some exceptions, such as registered overseas voters and parliamentary groups in the European Parliament who distribute funds to their member parties. A set of possible exceptions were set out in an internal Labour Party Policy Paper, *Donations to the Labour Party*, passed by the National Executive in 1994 to determine the party's own rules for accepting or rejecting donations. It said the presumption would be that foreign sourced donations were an unacceptable attempt to influence the British political process. For such donations to be deemed legitimate, the following guidelines would apply:

Individual donations
Donations may be accepted only from individuals who are normally resident in the UK or who are entitled to vote in UK general elections on a simple 'can't vote–can't give' principle.

Companies incorporated outside the UK
No political donation shall be accepted from an overseas company controlled by a company incorporated in the UK. Donations may be accepted from companies incorporated outside the UK but within the European Union, subject to annual limits determined by the location of their ultimate control, but donations shall only be accepted from one company in any one group. Donations shall not be accepted from any company incorporated outside the European Union.

Unincorporated bodies outside the UK
Donations may be accepted from unincorporated bodies outside the UK but within the European Union, subject to annual limits. No donations shall be accepted from unincorporated bodies outside the European Union.

Ethical considerations

The 1994 Policy Paper was intended to provide a voluntary framework for the Labour Party's own internal decisions on donations 'pending the enactment of appropriate legislation'. The government will presumably want to write similar safeguards into the law it introduces. It said:

'The Labour Party may decide not to accept a donation offered for whatever reason. The Labour Party will in any event not accept donations from companies the activities of which are inconsistent with the principles of the Labour Party...

Whilst they seek to establish openness, they also recognise that political donations are an important feature of political life and any monitoring procedures should not be such as to discourage would-be donors. Openness and accountability involve a duty to maintain records and to report or make available their contents. The effort involved in complying with these guidelines must be proportionate to the benefits of disclosure and the limit on non-disclosable donations is designed to provide this balance.'

Company donations

One proposal that is also likely to feature in a Bill is a requirement that companies should submit a proposal to make a political donation to its shareholders in a ballot before the annual meeting. This is unlikely to run into opposition from the majority of companies. Only one company in 16 gives money to a political party and the trend, if there is one, is away from corporate involvement in politics. There is also an increasing recognition among pensions and insurance companies that many of their policy holders have political or ethical objections to having their money invested in companies that make political donations. There are also a few companies that have already held shareholder ballots, such as Marks & Spencer and the Rank Organisation.

Running alongside this is likely to be a proposal to allow shareholders the right to opt out of their part of a political donation. That would be difficult for Conservatives to oppose since it closely mirrors the provisions of the Trade Union Act 1984, a Conservative measure, which introduced the same measures for trade unions and employers' associations.

A Labour Party policy document, *Charter for Political Funding*, published in April 1994, expanded the party's proposal for shareholder ballots. It proposed that:

(1)   Companies wishing to make political donations would, with some limited exceptions, only be able to do so from a political fund established for that purpose.

(2)   The political fund would receive monies from amounts appropriated by the directors for distribution to shareholders by way of dividend.

(3)   Shareholders would have the right to contract out from the political contribution and would receive an enhanced dividend. Certain shareholders,

eg those holding shares collectively for the benefit of others, would be required by law to contract out.

(4) The tax credit in respect of any political donation would not be reclaimable by the recipient.

It also stipulated that:

'only companies incorporated in the United Kingdom with limited liability may have political funds. No company which is a subsidiary or associated company (as defined by the Companies Act and the Income Taxes Act) of another company, or which is otherwise controlled by another company, shall have a political fund. No company which is a subsidiary of, or associated with, or otherwise controlled by, another company, shall have a political fund.'

The policy document went on to exclude pension funds and unit trusts:

'Certain categories of shareholder shall be deemed to contract out from contributing to the political fund and it shall be the responsibility of the directors of the company to identify such shareholders. This provision will apply to:
i) any shareholding of a unit trust, pension fund, life fund or any other collective or aggregated investment arrangement;
ii) any shareholding with a registered address outside the UK or where the directors might reasonably be aware that the shareholding is held on behalf of a shareholder not resident in the UK.'

It also set donation limits on certain types of European companies:

(a) a company incorporated in the UK which is a subsidiary or associated company of, or which is otherwise controlled by, another company which is incorporated in the European Union (other than the UK) – £20,000;

(b) a company incorporated in the UK which is a subsidiary or associated company of, or which is otherwise controlled by, another company which is incorporated outside the European Union – £10,000;

(c) a company incorporated in and controlled from within the European Union (other than the UK) – £10,000;

(d) a company incorporated in the European Union (other than the UK) but controlled from outside the European Union – £5,000.

SPENDING LIMITS

Parties

The most glaring anomaly of the UK's existing legislation is that it applies election spending limits to candidates but not to parties. This is a hangover from the Corrupt and Illegal Practices Prevention Act 1883 which referred only to expenses incurred 'by a candidate . . . or his election agent' and took no account of political parties which played little part in election campaigns in those days. This has led to the situation where a leaflet published by a candidate or promoting a candidate is an election expense, but a leaflet published by a party, so long as it does not name a candidate, is not. For instance, a poster urging people to 'Vote Bloggs, Conservative' is an election expense, but a poster urging people to 'Vote Conservative' is probably not. Thus the UK has a law that controls the cost of elections at constituency level as strictly as anywhere in the world, but this is completely undermined by the fact that it leaves a free-for-all in national campaign spending.

Although the Neill Committee dealt with the issue of national spending limits in its report, the government was forced to anticipate its decision because of the need to pass a European Parliamentary Elections Bill to change the voting system in time for the European Parliament elections of June 1999. Since the only spending limit in UK law is based on candidates in constituencies and the Regional List voting system under which the European elections will be fought will not have single-member constituencies, the Bill published in November 1997 provided for limits to be set on election spending by national parties for the first time. This was not even in the main Bill but in an obscure Schedule entitled 'Minor and Consequential Amendments to Schedule 1 to the European Parliamentary Elections Act 1978'.

The simplest way in which to introduce national spending limits would be to make the limits on constituency campaign spending apply to any election expense where the party and not just the candidate is named. There would have to be a consequential increase in constituency spending limits. Alternatively it could set an expenditure limit for the national campaign – the Labour Party suggested £10 million in 1994 and £15 million in its evidence to the Neill Committee in 1997.

Candidates

Limits on candidate spending is the one area where the UK has had tough legislation. Spending limits were first set in 1883 and have been revised upwards at regular intervals, but remain low enough to act as a real constraint on local campaign spending. But three things have happened to make these limits less effective. First, the parties' national election campaigns have become far more important and the candidates' local campaigns have dwindled into what Dr David Butler aptly described as 'a sideshow'. Secondly, judicial rulings have widened the loophole even further. A case in 1952, *R v Tronoh Mines*[7] established that advertisements need not count as an election expense if they did not mention the name of a candidate. A further legal precedent was established in the 1974 election when the High Court did not step in to

---

[7] [1952] 1 All ER 697.

prevent the Liberal Party placing advertisements in newspapers during an election campaign. Thirdly, there has been a trend for the electoral returning officers to ignore the cost of phone calls for telephone canvassing and mailshots. There has also been a trend in by-elections for parties to find ways of exceeding the limit, for instance by sending full-time agents from other constituencies or regional offices to work as unpaid volunteers in by-elections while they remain on the payroll of the party.

A new threat to candidate spending controls has appeared in the form of a finding of the European Court of Human Rights in a case brought by Phyllis Bowman, national director of the Society for the Protection of the Unborn Child. Having been prosecuted for making an illegal election expense in the form of a leaflet attacking Alice Mahon, Labour MP for Halifax, she referred the case to the European Court of Human Rights as an infringement of Article 10 of the European Convention on Human Rights which guarantees freedom of speech. The European Court ruled in her favour in February 1998 in a judgment that seems to invalidate the UK's existing candidate spending limits on candidates and therefore rule out the extension of spending limits to political parties.[8] However, on closer inspection the judgment, by 14 votes to six, is not as far-reaching as it appears. It says the Court was not satisfied that it was necessary to limit Mrs Bowman's right to issue a leaflet attacking Mrs Mahon 'particularly in view of the fact that there were no restrictions placed . . . upon political parties . . . to advertise at national or regional level'. In other words, the judgment does not state that it would be wrong to have spending controls at both local and national level, only that it is wrong to have spending controls on candidates but not on parties. If the anomaly is removed, the law might not be considered to conflict with the European Convention on Human Rights.

DISCLOSURE

Individuals

In its evidence to the House of Commons Home Affairs Committee inquiry into party funding in 1993[9] the Labour Party committed itself to the principle that a political party should disclose in its annual accounts all donations from a single source amounting to more than £5,000 over a calendar year. That was applied by the party to its own donations from the calendar year 1995 and a list of donors was appended to the 1995 annual accounts reported to the 1996 conference.

---

[8] *Bowman v United Kingdom* (1998).
[9] Home Affairs Committee, *Funding of Political Parties*, HC [1993–94] 301 (Report) and 726 (Minutes and Memoranda of Evidence).

According to an internal policy paper passed by the National Executive in 1994 and setting out the party's own rules for donations to the Labour Party, the purposes of disclosure are:

(1)   to ensure the legitimacy of political giving and
(2)   to demonstrate openness.

In addition to publishing comprehensive annual accounts covering both its income and expenditure, the party now undertakes:

(1)   to disclose in its annual report the name of each donor giving, with effect from 1 January 1995, in the aggregate in excess of £5,000 in any one calendar year;
(2)   not to accept foreign-sourced donations which do not meet the criteria for acceptance set out in these guidelines; and
(3)   to recommend that Labour MPs, MEPs, Councillors and those working on their behalf to apply these same standards of disclosure.

Giving evidence to the same Home Affairs Committee inquiry the chairman of the Conservative Party, Sir Norman Fowler, rejected the case for disclosing the names of donors on the grounds that privacy was a fundamental right for donors to political parties 'as for donors to any other charitable organisations'. However, William Hague reversed this policy in his first speech at Conservative Central Office after taking over as Conservative party leader in July 1997. He promised that the party would ban foreign donations and disclose the source of donations above a given level, later identified as £5,000.

Soon after starting his inquiry Lord Neill commented that a £5,000 limit struck him as rather high in comparison with the Canadian limit of $200. 'I am keeping an open mind,' he told the BBC, 'but £1,000 might be a more reasonable limit.' Another issue is whether the precise amount of the donation should be declared, as is the case in most other countries, or whether donations should be declared in bands, such as £5,000 to £10,000 and £10,000 to £20,000, as suggested by the Conservative Party.

The experience of countries with a low disclosure limit is that the number of donors becomes unwieldy. The annual report of the Canadian New Democratic Party lists 76,589 names of donors who give more than $100 (£40). It includes several pages of Smiths and practically the entire membership of the party. On the other hand, German parties have an appendix of only one or two pages of donors who give more than DM20,000 (£8,000).

In practice banding systems simply mean that donors who would have given £10,000 give £9,999 and donors who would have given £50,000 will give £49,999. The media assume that donors give up to the limit of their band and they are usually right. So nobody is fooled.

TAX BREAKS

Rebates

The Neill Committee raised the question of whether donations or subscriptions to political parties should be encouraged by allowing them to attract tax relief. Some taxpayers will express horror at the idea of tax concessions to political parties, but it is common practice in other democracies and the precedent has already been set in this country through the tax exemption of bequests to political parties, introduced with little controversy by the last Labour government. The rationale for such tax concessions is the same as the rationale for special tax treatment of charities. Charities carry out functions that are better carried out by a voluntary organisation than by the state, but would probably need to be carried out by the state if the voluntary organisation did not exist. Although political parties can hardly be described as charitable, they do perform a function that is both necessary to the function of the political system but has to be performed by a voluntary organisation. Tax exemption is a way in which the state can acknowledge the importance of political parties without compromising their independence.

Tax exemption is usually achieved by making the sum paid allowable against income tax, but this means that the value of exemption varies with the marginal tax rate at which tax is being paid. A £100 tax exemption would be worth £40 to a higher rate taxpayer, £23 to a standard rate payer, £10 to a lower rate payer and nothing to a non-taxpayer. In order to make the value of the tax exemption equal to all voters, the Canadians use a system of tax credits. On a donation of £300 everyone gets a tax repayment of two-thirds, on the next £400 a repayment of half and on the next £300 a repayment of one-third. Thus if they make a donation of £1,000, they get £500 back. But if they make a donation of £10,000, they still get only £500 back. This has the effect of encouraging small donors to give money and it also encourages political parties to raise their funds in the form of small donations from many individuals rather than in the form of large donations from a few individuals. It has helped all the main parties in Canada build up a huge donor base through direct mail fund-raising and wean themselves off corporate funding from companies and trade unions which used to be their only source of funding.

One of the main objections to state funding of political parties is that individual taxpayers do not want to see their money paid to a party to which they may have a rooted objection. The tax check-off system used in the USA allows taxpayers to give their authority for a small part of their tax revenues to be used for state funding to political parties and allows them to nominate the party to which it can be paid. For instance, they can tick a box on their tax form to direct $1 of their tax liability to the Democrats. The parties can only draw money from the pool to the extent that taxpayers have earmarked funds for them. They are entitled to funds according to a formula set down in the law, but if there isn't enough money in the pool, they don't get it. It's a new concept, not a hypothecated tax, but hypothecated tax revenue.

STATE AID

In cash

State funding is hugely unpopular with the public.[10] Tony Blair has said he is 'instinctively cautious' about it. Lord Neill said he had 'quite an inclination to think that it is rather good that political parties raise their own money'. But it is difficult to see how the parties can be weaned off dependence on £million donations from wealthy business people without replacing that income with state funding of some kind. State funding was in the brief of the Neill Committee and Tony Blair said he would introduce it if the committee recommended it. They therefore had to weigh up the arguments for and against state funding. They are:

Democracy has to be paid for
In the 19th century many politicians regarded the unpaid status of MPs as a useful bulwark against change. Some openly opposed the payment of MPs because it would bring 'radicals and socialists' into the Commons. It was only after the influx of Labour MPs in 1906 that MPs finally won the right to be paid in 1911. Until 1918 MPs also had to pay for the upkeep of the electoral register and the expenses of the returning officer, a ruinous cost for the infant Labour Party. Since then Labour governments have introduced every step towards the funding of our democratic system: MPs' travel expenses in 1924, MPs' pensions in 1965, MPs' secretarial costs in 1969, councillors' allowances in 1969, the funding for opposition parties in Parliament in 1975. The last Labour government wanted to introduce state funding in 1977, but as a minority government it was obliged to drop it.

Parties are an essential part of our democratic system
Parties are private organisations, but the voters have given them a key role in our system of government. Gradually over the last century they have thrown out all the independents and replaced them with party candidates. Nowadays there are just a few rural councils and exceptional cases like Tatton where people vote for independents. Elsewhere they prefer party candidates because independents are unknown quantities whereas they have at least some idea how candidates with party labels will vote.

But if the voters want party labels in order to make sense of their democratic choice, then it can be argued that they should be prepared to pay at

[10] Should public money be used to finance political parties? Yes 13 per cent, No 79 per cent, ICM, June 1993.

least some of the costs that parties incur, not in advocating their policies, but in fulfilling the minimum requirements of the democratic process: the selection of candidates, the preparation of manifestos, the printing of election addresses.

Britain is almost the only advanced democracy without state funding

Internationally, Britain has become the odd man out. As pointed out earlier, state funding is already the practice in most other European countries. State funding has been introduced in these countries in the last 30 years because there was not enough money to fund the parties adequately from private sources and they faced a choice between a 'slum' democracy, where political parties are poorly staffed, poorly researched and unprepared for the task of running the country, or a 'sleaze' democracy, where the parties are forced into an unhealthy reliance on private funding which will sooner or later compromise their integrity.

That danger has been recognised by parties of both left and right. In Germany it was the Christian Democrats who introduced the first state funding regime in 1967. They were followed by Sweden and Denmark in 1969, the Netherlands in 1972, the USA after Watergate in the early 1970s, Italy and Canada in 1974, Greece in 1984, Spain in 1987, France and Portugal in 1988. Britain would have done so in 1977 had it not been for the opposition of the Conservative Party under Mrs Thatcher. She had accepted state funding for opposition parties in Parliament in 1975, the so-called 'Short money', but opposed state funding for other parties.

The Conservatives opposed state funding for partisan reasons

Unlike the other European countries, where state funding was introduced with bipartisan support, the Conservatives took a partisan view. The party chairman before Mrs Thatcher became leader, Lord Thorneycroft, had said he might accept state funds because the party was heavily in debt. But Mrs Thatcher's party treasurer, Lord McAlpine, adopted a strategy of opposing state funding on the grounds that, however badly off the Conservatives might be, Labour would be even worse off.

This beggar-my-neighbour strategy helped the Conservatives to outspend the Labour Party at the next five elections, but it had dire consequences for British politics. As it became progressively more difficult for the Conservatives to raise donations from British industry, they were forced into more and more desperate measures to attract funds. Department of Trade and Industry ministers leant on companies to give money to the Tory party. Honours were given liberally to companies that had made donations. And in 1989 the party launched a fund-raising initiative in Hong Kong. Companies were bombarded with begging letters from Central Office. Ministers visiting Hong Kong on official business were expected to attend fund-raising dinners with representatives from the business community. John Major also gave fund-raising dinners at 10 Downing Street.

The UK already gives state funding to overseas parties

Ironically the last Conservative government, while always denouncing state funding in this country, set up the Westminster Foundation for Democracy to give British taxpayers' money to political parties in other countries. As an offshoot of the Foreign and Commonwealth Office it was allocated a budget of £2.5 million in 1997 to help amongst other things, democratic political parties in Eastern Europe and the Third World. All the main British parties are represented on the board of the Foundation and they nominate the political parties in other countries to whom financial assistance should be given. Indeed a part of the financial assistance may be spent in the research departments of the sponsoring party in this country.

These dual standards follow a great British tradition of applying constitutional innovations to other countries but not to our own. After the Second World War the British administration in the occupied zone in Germany helped to introduce a new voting system, the additional member system, and a new trade union structure, based on 16 industrial unions. It helped the founders of the new German state to establish a written constitution which laid down that political parties should be 'democratic in their internal structure and account publicly for the sources of their funds'. It also set up a political education service, the *Heimatdienst*, as a bulwark against the re-emergence of fascism. It was the success of the *Heimatdienst* that led to the political funding, first of political education and then of political parties.

Consideration of how many of Britain's postwar problems have derived from the unfairness of the electoral system, the chaotic structure of the trade union movement, the lack of a written constitution, the undemocratic structure of political parties, their refusal to publish accounts showing their sources of income, the lack of political education and the absence of state funding, provides an understanding as to just how perverse is the British attitude to nation-building. It was not only in the colonial era but even in the postwar era that the British have had to watch their constitutional innovations, like their inventions, help the rest of the world to thrive and prosper while the 'old country' wallows in its conservative traditions.

Although the Labour Party has no current commitment to state funding, it has supported the idea at previous elections. It won the February 1974 election on a manifesto that included public contributions to political parties. It introduced state funding of opposition parliamentary parties in 1975 and set up a committee of inquiry, the Houghton Committee, which recommended public funding through the partial reimbursement of candidates' expenses and annual grants to political parties in August 1976.[11]

---

[11] *Report of the Committee on Financial Aid to Political Parties*, Cmd 6601 (1976).

More recently, the Labour Party argued in favour of state funding in its evidence to the Home Affairs Select Committee in May 1993:

> 'The Labour party submits that every democracy requires continuously functioning political parties and not just at election times. This is recognised in many European countries, and on a very generous scale in countries such as Germany and Sweden. To ensure political parties have a reasonable degree of support in the country, they must function properly, and it is in the public interest that public funds should be provided to do so. This is not to replace funds from individual and institutional supporters, but to supplement these resources, although it may have the effect of diluting dependence on their existing support. The primary aim is to ensure at least at the minimum level that political parties can function through the electoral cycle.'[12]

It specifically endorsed the recommendation of the Houghton Committee that 50 per cent of candidates' election expenses (up to the legal limit) should be reimbursed and that national expenditure should be limited. This should apply to all parties that crossed a threshold of 5 per cent of the national vote. It also called for all parties to publish full accounts: 'All political parties should produce annual accounts which should be independently audited and which should show all the main items of income and expenditure in all their funds, and also show assets and liabilities and surpluses/deficits and how those are funded.'[13]

The Liberal Democrats also argued in favour of state aid, spending limits and audited accounts in their evidence in June 1993:

> 'Political parties are integral to the democratic process and most of their activities are closely regulated by statute. It is right that the state should therefore make funding available to ensure fair competition between them and to reduce their financial dependence upon sectional interests. At present there is no such fair competition and both the Conservative and Labour Parties continue to rely on finance from corporate interests to an unhealthy degree. It is now seventeen years since the Houghton Committee recommended a "modest injection of state aid" into the United Kingdom's political parties. The time for such action is now.
>
> The introduction of state funding should go hand in hand with curbs on the national expenditure of parties in elections, in much the same way as those that apply at constituency level. Furthermore, acceptance of such funds should be conditional upon the parties' publication of full audited accounts showing the sources and application of all their funding.'

It would be a mistake, however, to overlook the real difficulties that would stand in the way of a government that wanted to introduce state funding. The opinion polls show that a majority of the public support almost every aspect of Labour's constitutional reforms, including a Bill of Rights, a

---

[12] Chapter 3.10, 'Grants to Organisation Expenses'.
[13] Labour Party Proposals, 2.9, point 1.

written constitution, devolution and a referendum on the voting system, but there is a majority against state funding of political parties. Similarly, there is a strong majority in favour of almost every other proposal outlined above, including disclosure, a ban on overseas donations, a limit on national spending, but not for the use of public money to finance political parties.

The inclusion of state funding in a package of proposals to reform the funding of parties and elections would immediately turn a popular measure into a controversial one and give the Conservatives a cause to campaign on. It is ironic that the British public has become more opposed to state funding as a result of sleaze, even though the sleaze was caused, or at least aggravated, by the refusal of political parties to agree to a system of state funding in the first place. Sleaze is why we need state funding, but it is also why people oppose it. But there is no point in the parties' complaining that the public is being irrational. It is up to them to regain the public's trust. Political parties cannot simply award themselves state funding out of taxpayers' money without first convincing the public that it is in their interest.

In kind

Although the parties receive no direct state aid in cash, they receive at least four forms of aid in kind:

(1)   The benefit of a free mail delivery service during the election for which the Royal Mail was paid approximately £12 million by the Treasury.
(2)   The right to free hire of halls in any public building during the election.
(3)   The right of free security at party conferences, which other organisations have to pay for. That is worth more than £2 million a year to the governing party.
(4)   An entitlement to party election broadcasts which, if paid for as television and radio advertising, would be worth well over £10 million.

The value of this aid in kind is far more than the party headquarters spend in cash during an election campaign. Opinion polls show that voters are opposed, by an overwhelming margin, to state aid in cash being given to the parties. But there is no evidence that voters are opposed to aid in kind. They have never objected to paying for free post, free hire or free broadcasting which goes to all parties. What voters seem to dislike is their money going to pay for party propaganda that they may disagree with, or they may simply not like to see their cash in the parties' pockets. Whatever the rationale, it may make more sense to respect this distinction in voters' minds between paying for the medium, which can be done by the taxpayer, though on the basis of aid in kind, and paying for the message, which must be left to the parties themselves.

In a pamphlet published by the Institute for Public Policy Research in 1994,[14] a number of recommendations for direct assistance to parties in elections, which could help solve the problem without raising the issue of state aid in cash, were put forward. They included:

(1) The number of free postal deliveries for each candidate should be increased from one to two.

(2) There should be a black-out period in which political advertisements cannot be displayed during the first four days after the date of the election is announced and the eve of poll and polling day.

(3) A committee should be established on the same basis as the Committee on Party Political Broadcasting to allocate adequate hoarding space to the parties on the day an election is called.

(4) The cost of poster space should be met from public funds in the same way as party election broadcasts.

(5) Parties should be given the right during an election campaign to display small posters in any public place.

(6) A similar committee to that referred to in (3) above should allocate party election advertisements to the parties on the same basis and the parties should be free to place them as they wish.

(7) The committee should have reserve powers to oblige newspapers to accept advertisements, to protect the legal position of editors and publishers and to ensure copy deadlines are no earlier than for other advertisers.

(8) Political parties which qualify for party political broadcasts and party election broadcasts should also be given a contribution towards production costs.

A number of these proposals were included in *Issues and Questions*, the Neill Committee's consultation document.[15] For instance, the Committee asked for comments on the suggestion that available hoarding space should be allocated to the parties at the start of an election and paid for out of public funds. The same could be done for press advertising with the parties free to place a given amount of advertising in the newspapers or magazines of their choice. The freepost, which pays for one free delivery to each voter, could be extended to two. The display of small posters in public places, currently allowed in some areas but not in others, should be a right given to all parties during the election. But equally there should be some protection for the voter against over-exposure. This will be achieved primarily by imposing a limit on all election spending, national and local, but that could usefully be supplemented by a black-out period when no election advertising is allowed, both in the first four days and on the last day of the campaign. The black-out

---

[14] Martin Linton, *Money and Votes* (London: Institute for Public Policy Research, 1994).
[15] Note 6 above; and see the Committee's forthcoming Report on the subject (1998).

period will also reduce the advantage of the governing party in being able to choose the date of the election.

Lord Neill stated before his report was published that an Electoral Commission would be needed to ensure fairness in elections and that this body could take the responsibility of enforcing the spending limits, setting their level and defining election expenses. But it should have as much independence from parliamentary pressure as the Boundary Commissions. Most countries have an Electoral Commission that is at arm's length from the politicians; sets, defines and polices the parties' expenditure limits and is responsible for supervising elections.[16]

The problem with aid in kind is that it can only be given for specified forms of election spending. Election campaigning is changing so rapidly that any aid in kind granted today may rapidly become out of date, just as the free hire of elementary school halls, first granted in 1918, is now of little value. Aid in kind may simply become a subsidy for old-fashioned forms of campaigning. It would certainly be more logical to give the parties an equivalent sum in cash so that they can decide on the best medium for their message.

In *Money and Votes*, however, I argued that the public was not ready to accept direct state aid:

> 'The public may still be unwilling . . . to cross the Rubicon of paying state aid in cash direct to political parties. This is understandable at a time when public respect for the political parties is low. Other countries have usually introduced state aid at a time when public confidence in the integrity of political parties was high rather than low. In Sweden state aid was given to the parties' youth organisations and adult education programmes long before it was given to the political parties themselves. Arguably it was only because of the work that the parties were already doing in these areas that there was a sufficiently positive attitude to political parties for it to be politically acceptable to introduce state aid.'[17]

There would seem to be no reason to change that judgment yet.

Further reading

Committee on Standards in Public Life, *The Funding of Political Parties in the United Kingdom* (Cm 4057, 1998)

Martin Linton, *Money and Votes* (Institute for Public Policy Research, 1994)

Robert Blackburn, *The Electoral System in Britain* (London: Macmillan, 1995), especially Ch 7

K D Ewing, *The Funding of Political Parties in Britain* (Cambridge University Press, 1987)

---

[16] For further discussion, see Ch 4 below.

[17] At p 112.

CHAPTER 3

PROPORTIONAL REPRESENTATION

Professor Raymond Plant (Oxford University)

PROPOSALS FOR ELECTORAL REFORM

The agenda on electoral reform has moved ahead very quickly and very effectively and the aim of this chapter is to shed some light on the recent history of the debate within the Labour Party about changes in the voting system which in turn will, I hope, illuminate the current state of the argument.

After the 1987 election defeat the Labour Party developed various policy reviews and as the result of these decided as a matter of policy that a future Labour government should set up a Parliament in Scotland, an Assembly in Wales, abolish the House of Lords and replace it with a small elected Second Chamber, create a new strategic authority for London, and create assemblies in the regions of England. Given these policies, it was important that the party considered the appropriate electoral system to be used for elections to these new bodies. In addition, the party had developed a more positive attitude to Europe and one issue on the European agenda was the electoral system for the European Parliament for which Britain used First Past the Post (except in Northern Ireland) unlike all the other countries in the European Union.[1] In 1990 the Labour Party Conference voted in favour of a proposal from the National Executive Committee of the party to establish a Working Party to consider these matters. At the same time Conference voted to include the electoral system for the House of Commons as part of the remit of this Working Party. This addition to the agenda of the Working Party was made in the face of opposition from the National Executive.

There seem to have been several reasons for the move. The first was undoubtedly the one of logical and political consistency: that it would not make sense to make recommendations for elections to new devolved bodies without considering the impact of any such recommendations on the House of Commons. Secondly, there was also the view that Labour had lost three

---

[1] Proportional representation by way of party lists is to be introduced into UK law for elections to the European Parliament (European Parliamentary Elections Bill 1998).

successive elections under First Past the Post and had never in its history won two full terms under that electoral system. In addition there was the view that successive Thatcher governments had pursued radical and unpopular policies bolstered by large majorities in the House of Commons based upon a percentage of the vote in the low forties and that this exercise of power lacked a degree of legitimacy. So undoubtedly delegates to the Conference were swayed by these sorts of considerations.

I was asked to chair what was quite a large Electoral Systems Working Party composed mainly, but not exclusively, of MPs representing views across the range of opinion within the party.[2] It was also made clear that we should not produce any final recommendations about the electoral system for the House of Commons until after the 1992 election. It was thought quite correctly that to have a debate about any such recommendations just prior to an election would be divisive given the range of opinion in the party and that if the recommendations were in favour of changing the system, it might look like a confession of weakness on the part of the party betraying a conviction that it could not win under First Past the Post. The fact was that the 1992 election was to be won or lost under First Past the Post, and there seemed to be little to be gained by the Working Party making recommendations for change just prior to the election. Nevertheless the Party Manifesto in 1992 highlighted the existence of the Working Party by arguing that if Labour won the election, then the Working Party's status would be upgraded (probably to a Royal Commission) and that other parties would be invited to join in its work.

ELECTORAL SYSTEMS WORKING PARTY

Although the Working Party was asked not to report on the House of Commons until after the election, it was asked to produce recommendations about the Scottish Parliament before the election. Given that the Labour Party had made the establishment of a Parliament a high priority for its legislative programme, it was felt that to enter the election without an agreement about the electoral system would put the party at a disadvantage over this proposal. This was so for two reasons. In the first place it might have looked as if the proposal for a Scottish Parliament was half-baked if the party did not have an agreed view about its electoral system. Secondly, it was argued that if voters in Scotland thought that elections under First Past the Post were a possibility, then this might make the proposed Parliament very unattractive to voters since the strength of the Labour Party in Scotland

---

[2] Membership of the committee was Raymond Plant (chair), Graham Allen, Hilary Armstrong, Margaret Beckett, Tom Burlison, Judith Church, Alistair Darling, John Evans, Bryan Gould, Patricia Hollis, Ken Hopkins, Geoff Hoon, Ben Pimlott, Jeff Rooker, Richard Rosser, Gary Titley, Reg Underhill (until his death in 1993), Larry Whitty, Joyce Gould, Jack McConnell, Tim Lamport (secretary).

might make it look as though almost a one party state was being proposed if the Parliament were to be elected under First Past the Post. The Working Party worked hard on the electoral system for the Parliament and had a constant dialogue with the executive of the Scottish Party and finally recommended an additional member system for the Scottish Parliament. This proposal was accepted by the National Executive Committee before the election and after the election was lost formed the basis of Labour's attitude to the deliberations on the Scottish Constitutional Convention as regards the issue of the electoral system for a future version of the Parliament.

In the election of 1997, the Labour Party went into the election with the proposal for a Scottish Parliament with an electoral system based essentially on what the Working Party had proposed in the run up to the 1992 election and this electoral system will be established once the legislation has passed through both Houses of Parliament.

In addition to developing ideas about the electoral system for the Scottish Parliament the Working Party produced a large-scale document called *Democracy, Representation and Elections*,[3] which sought to produce a reasonably comprehensive analysis of the strengths and weaknesses of different electoral systems against the background of a range of criteria that it might be thought an electoral system ought to satisfy. While this document did not make recommendations it drew a number of distinctions which were important then and have become rather commonplace in the debate since. It drew a distinction between different sorts of representation, particularly between microcosmic views of representation in which an elected assembly is supposed to be a kind of microcosm of society representing, as far as possible, the range of political interests within society; and what we called the principal/agent view of representation in which a representative under a majoritarian electoral system would claim to have the legitimacy to speak for the whole of a constituency even though large numbers may have voted against that person. Microcosmic representation implied a commitment to proportionality; the principal/agent view a commitment to a majoritarian electoral system, although not necessarily First Past the Post. Such a view of representation would also be compatible with the Alternative Vote, the Supplementary Vote or a Second Ballot procedure as in France.

The Working Party argued also that different views about the nature of representation and their associated electoral systems might fit the different roles which institutions might play. We thought that there was a distinction to be drawn between legislative and deliberative institutions. Legislative institutions have the duty to initiate and produce legislative outcomes. Deliberative bodies might play more of a role in ensuring the accountability of public

---

[3] Interim Report of the National Executive Committee Working Party on Electoral Systems (Labour Party, 1991). On different models of proportional representation electoral systems, see the Report, Section 1, Ch 2; and Robert Blackburn, *The Electoral System in Britain* (London: Macmillan, 1995), Ch 8.

bodies and monitoring the expenditure and the priorities embodied in such expenditure. Of course, such distinctions are not hard and fast. Regional assemblies under Labour's plans were clearly at the deliberative end and the House of Commons at the legislative end of the spectrum. The Second Chamber to replace the House of Lords would be more hybrid; the European Parliament would be towards the deliberative end (with aspirations to move towards the legislative), while the Scottish Parliament was nearer the legislative, but without the full powers of the Commons. It was argued that deliberative bodies and microcosmic views of representation went well together. The question of how far legislative bodies which required that outcomes were clearly and effectively arrived at, might be compatible with other than majoritarian electoral systems and principal/agent views of representation was much more controversial.

The Working Party was able to agree that First Past the Post tended to produce strong single party government, but was much more divided about whether strong government was the same as effective government. For those members of the Working Party who took this latter view, as I did, two examples weighed heavily. The first was the catastrophic, and as it turned out, colossally expensive legislation on the poll tax. This appeared to be a very clear exercise in strong single party government supported by a large majority in the House of Commons produced on a minority of First Past the Post votes, but it could be doubted that strong as it was, it was hardly effective government. At the same time Germany was responding well to the monumental task of reunification under a coalition government produced by a proportional electoral system set within a federal structure in which the Länder often had coalitions which were of quite a different complexion from the Federal Government. Yet the Federal Government was able to deal effectively and decisively with the pressures of reunification. So in our view there was no easy equation of strong with effective government. Effective government usually means securing widespread consent for what is being done because reform will then last, this is not the same as strong single party government and indeed might be impeded by strong government.

Be that as it may, the upshot of the Working Party's Interim Report was that there is no perfect electoral system. Electoral systems involve different understandings of the nature of representation and these different types of representation might be more suitable for one sort of institution rather than another. So it was quite possible to envisage different systems being used to elect representatives to different institutions. Some ridicule was heaped on this idea at the time, but the Working Party saw the logic of the position and indeed this approach has become embodied in the legislation of the new Labour government in that the electoral systems for the Scottish Parliament and Welsh Assembly will be different from that used for European Parliament elections, which in turn are different from First Past the Post.

Following the 1992 election the Working Party decided to produce a report which could go to the Conference in 1993 and this is indeed what happened, nevertheless it is worth recounting a little of the history of this process since it does shed some light on the current situation, particularly in relation to the proposed referendum on the electoral system for the House of Commons.

LABOUR'S COMMITMENT TO ELECTORAL REFORM

After the election defeat John Smith succeeded Neil Kinnock as Leader with Tony Blair as Shadow Home Secretary and Gordon Brown as Shadow Chancellor. They were convinced by the experience of the election defeat that the process of modernisation of the Labour Party should be speeded up and in particular the introduction of One Member One Vote (OMOV) and that a commitment to change the electoral system was almost a way of not facing up to the need to change the party more quickly than Kinnock had done. This led John Smith as Leader with the apparent agreement of Margaret Beckett, a member of the Working Party and Deputy Leader of the Party, to argue that it would be a mistake for the Working Party to arrive at a recommendation to change the electoral system for the House of Commons since this would be a diversion from the task of policy and organisational modernisation. This posed a real difficulty since it had become clear from straw polls in the Working Party that there was a majority against retaining First Past the Post. There was not, so it seemed, majority agreement on what should replace it, although at this stage I believed that there was a majority in favour of an additional member system. I argued with John Smith in a room at the back of the stage at the 1992 Conference that the Working Party should be allowed to make recommendations on the House of Commons rather than arriving at conclusions of BBC-like impartiality without making recommendations. We had already produced one document of this sort, 'Democracy, Representation and Elections', and we would look silly if we produced another. In addition, as I have said, I believed that there was a majority in the Working Party in favour of change and I was keen that this majority should have a right to express its opinion.

I recognised John Smith's political difficulties with this and did make the suggestion that if we did recommend change and he was uncomfortable and unpersuaded by that, he might like to consider the possibility of a referendum particularly since New Zealand was in the middle of holding such an exercise and that lessons might be learned from that. At a lecture[4] to Charter 88 soon after these discussions those who were present detected some degree of interest in a referendum when the issue was raised from the floor.

---

[4] John Smith's lecture, on 1 March 1993, was entitled 'A Citizens' Democracy' (Charter 88, 1993).

The Working Party duly reported[5] with detailed recommendations on the Second Chamber, the European Parliament and the House of Commons, having already made proposals in respect of Scotland which had been accepted before the 1992 election.

The proposal for the House of Commons came as something of a surprise to members of the Working Party, or at least it did to me. As I have already said, there seemed to me to be a small majority in favour of an additional member system but between these straw polls and the final meeting of the Working Party at which final recommendations were made some changes came about in the intimated voting intentions of certain members of the Working Party. First Past the Post did not command a majority. Equally, the Working Party's version of an additional or mixed member system, devised by Jeff Rooker also failed to secure a majority of the votes. The only alternative to First Past the Post that did command a majority was the Supplementary Vote (which retains existing constituencies and under which voters are allowed to indicate their first and second preference votes). The Supplementary Vote (SV) had been put to us impressively and forcefully by Dale Campbell Savours MP and this was the final recommendation of the Committee in respect of the Commons. The Report then went to the Executive Committee and I was invited to make a presentation on it prior to discussion. Following my presentation, John Smith read out a carefully prepared statement which was being simultaneously released to the press in which he said that he was not convinced by our recommendations and that the issue of the electoral system for the House of Commons should be put to a referendum. This was pretty controversial since at the time the Leadership was also resisting a referendum on the future of European integration in the light of the Maastricht Treaty.

In the spring of 1994 John Smith tragically died at the height of his political powers. Nevertheless the commitment to a referendum which had seemed so personal to him has been retained by the Labour leadership. There were two opportunities to abandon the commitment. The first was in the leadership elections following John Smith's death when the candidates could have resiled from the commitment on the ground that it had been John Smith's own response to a particular problem which they would handle in a different way. None of the candidates took this view despite the hostility or scepticism of all of them towards electoral reform for the Commons. The second possibility was just before the Party Conference in 1995 when it seemed that there was a concerted effort by some members of the Shadow Cabinet to drop the commitment. This was however successfully resisted, partly within the Labour Party and by some newspaper campaigning.

I think that it would probably be true to say that Tony Blair himself saw the debate about electoral reform for the House of Commons as a distraction

---

[5] Report of the National Executive Committee Working Party on Electoral Systems (Labour Party, 1993).

from the task of modernising the Labour Party. Part of Blair's project for the Labour Party has been to make it internally more pluralistic and to widen its value basis to appeal to a wider cross-section of the electorate. In some ways he may have believed that a preoccupation with electoral reform could have stood in direct opposition to this, namely a concern to secure an electoral system under which older and unreformed Labour would be able to do well even though it would mean coalition government. Electoral reform therefore could almost be seen as providing an incentive not to modernise, but to seek an electoral system under which Labour could gain at least a share of power on its less radically modernised policies and values. Given that Blair took the view that the party needed to change and develop its basic values and policies, it is easy to see why this was a distraction. Indeed there has been some post-election confirmation of this view when some Labour politicians who are less than happy with Labour's policy stance now seem more interested in electoral reform because they take the view that Labour has had to pay too high an ideological price to win under First Past the Post. A changed electoral system might allow for the possibility of a party in Parliament which was to the left of the current centre of political gravity in the Labour Party. Blair was, however, more interested in intra-party pluralism within the Labour Party to allow it to win under First Past the Post as opposed to inter-party pluralism which a PR electoral system would have required in terms of coalition building. This is not to say that he is uninterested in institutional pluralism since we have had devolution and the Liberal Democrats have been invited onto the Joint Consultative Committee concerned with policy issues of joint interest to the government and themselves including constitutional reform,[6] but I think that he probably feels content in his creation of an internally pluralistic Labour Party able to reach out widely across the electorate which a preoccupation with a change in the electoral system might have impeded.

Nevertheless, despite what I suspect were Tony Blair's own reservations about the importance of electoral reform for the Commons (I am not being coy about this as I have never talked to Tony Blair as leader of the party and as Prime Minister about electoral reform), the referendum survived as a commitment. However, little or no work was done to develop the idea following Tony Blair's accession to the Leadership, but it resurfaced as an item of policy in the Joint Consultative Committee of Labour and the Liberal Democrats on constitutional reform[7] which was set up to see whether a common approach to constitutional reform could be agreed before the election. Although there was not a very extensive discussion of the proposed referendum, nevertheless two points were agreed which have assumed subsequent importance. The first is that the referendum would be a choice between First Past the Post and just one other alternative. There was full agreement

---

[6] See Introduction, p 4 above.
[7] See Appendix 2 below.

that a multi-choice referendum should be avoided partly because it might well be very difficult to secure a non-controversial interpretation of the result. If, for example, the referendum presented a choice between First Past the Post and two or three other systems, then it is possible that if the counting were to be on a First Past the Post basis it might be quite likely that there would be a majority in favour of First Past the Post, while at the same time the aggregate votes of those voting for the alternatives and thus against First Past the Post might well be larger than those cast for First Past the Post. Given that the referendum was to be on the electoral system, it seemed important to avoid controversies of this sort and this could only be done by having a straight choice between First Past the Post and an agreed alternative. The problem then moved to how to secure an agreed alternative. The Joint Committee agreed that this alternative should embody a principle of proportionality, but beyond that it did not make a recommendation. It did however agree that a commission should be set up to recommend an agreed alternative which it would be hoped Parliament would embody in a referendum Act on the voting system for the House of Commons.

Following the 1997 election, the Independent Commission on the Voting System was set up with Lord Jenkins of Hillhead as the chairman,[8] and with terms of reference which required it to consider broadly proportional voting systems, but also voting systems which would respect the link between an MP and the constituency. Its precise terms of reference, as announced by the government on 1 December 1997, were that:

'The Commission shall be free to consider and recommend any appropriate system or combination of systems in recommending an alternative to the present system for Parliamentary elections to be put before the people in the Government's referendum. The Commission shall observe the requirement for broad proportionality, the need for stable government, an extension of voter choice and the maintenance of a link between MPs and geographical constituencies.'

VOTING REFORM: PRACTICAL CONSIDERATIONS

Reforming our existing method of electing MPs to the House of Commons will take place within the context of the devolution programme having been agreed and with the Scottish Parliament and Welsh Assembly on the horizon each to be elected by an additional member electoral system which in Scotland at least is most likely to require coalition. At the same time, the electoral system for the European Parliament has been changed for the next elections from First Past the Post to a regional list system. Hence the political institutions of the UK will have become more devolved and more pluralistic.

---

[8] The full membership of the Commission was: Lord Jenkins of Hillhead (chair), Lord Alexander of Weedon, Lady Gould of Potternewton, Sir John Chilcot and David Lipsey.

This could lead to certain consequences in the thinking of members of the Commission. It might of course be argued first of all that if the House of Commons were to be elected by a broadly proportional electoral system, and after all broad proportionality is one of the criteria for the Commission to work with, then it should be on a par with the Scottish Parliament and the Welsh Assembly and thus be a version of an additional or mixed member system. It is highly unlikely that a Labour government would be receptive to the idea of legislating in favour of a single transferable vote (STV) in multi-member constituencies as the alternative voting system to be presented in a referendum Act. The Working Party rehearsed the reasons for this in its document, *Democracy, Representation and Elections*, but the main political objection to STV turns on the role of parties in a representative democracy. It seems to be true that STV has the potential to weaken parties because the possibility of intra-party division is built into an electoral system in which candidates from the same party in multi-member seats have to compete against each other for high or first preference votes, as well as against the opposition. Hence issues such as Europe might well lead to intolerable internal party pressures during elections in which candidates with differing views in the same party would seek to exploit their differences to secure higher numbers of first preference votes. Given the experience that the Labour Party had of internal disputes in the 1980s, it seems very unlikely that a Labour government would wish to present an alternative to First Past the Post which created in effect incentives to differentiation within parties. The same would probably be true of the Conservative Party in relation to Europe. Equally, the issue of the constituency link would become problematic in multi-member seats since the norm would have to be five if the greatest degree of proportionality were to be achieved, which would then give constituency electorates of say 350,000 people and would result in a considerable watering down of the constituency link. At the same time different members from different parties might claim to represent the same sort of area within the constituency, or the same set of interests across the constituency and the idea that an MP can speak on behalf of his or her constituents would become very controversial. There are also problems with multi-member constituencies in sparsely populated areas. On the one hand, the larger the number of members, the greater the degree of proportionality, but to secure constituencies large enough to secure multi-members in sparsely populated areas could well mean constituencies of vast geographical size and perhaps with very little sense of their representing some kind of natural geographical community which has been important historically in the British view of representation.

At the same time it can be taken for granted that any reform involving a purely national or regional list will fail to command any widespread body of support across the political spectrum. This would potentially cut the link altogether between members of Parliament and their constituencies. It would also immeasurably strengthen the power of parties since they would order the lists. Even if it were to be accepted that lists could be varied by the elector (which is not going to be allowed in respect of the European elections), given the size of regional lists and the number of candidates, it is difficult to see how such a power could be anything other than arbitrary. It may be argued that democracy is based not just upon choice, but also on some capacity for deliberation. In a list election, it might be argued that electors will have deliberated about parties and have arrived at a view of which party they wish to support, but that empowering them to change the ordering of the list for the party which they support would be to give the voter an arbitrary and relatively uninformed capacity for choice. Neither regional or national lists are feasible for the House of Commons because the distance between the elector and the representative would become too great in a Parliament of the present size.

THE ADDITIONAL MEMBER APPROACH

So, in view of the issues over STV, despite the fact that it is still supported as the favoured option by the Liberal Democrats, and given the fatal objections to national or regional lists as the sole method of election for the House of Commons, the additional member system (AMS) becomes the most appropriate option for reform if we are seeking an electoral system which embodies broad proportionality.

However, even AMS (which is what I think a large number of reformers are hoping for) is not without difficulty. The first is numbers. If it were to be assumed that broad proportionality might require 150 additional members distributed around the regions, then if the size of the Commons is not to grow to absurd proportions for the population of the UK, it would be necessary to reduce the constituency members by about the same number as the additional members. Indeed this reduction would be necessary in any case to make the 150 additional members count in terms of proportionality. If there were still to be over 650 constituency seats, there would have to even more than 150 members to create proportionality out of such large numbers. Hence there would have to be a reduction in the number of constituency seats and a corresponding increase in the size of the electorates voting in such seats. This would create quite large-scale uncertainties for existing MPs and might be very difficult to get through the House of Commons. So an additional member system would have a clear effect on the constituency link. It would still be retained, but constituencies would have to grow in size, although not by that much, but the process of achieving this rationalisation would be very difficult.

However, there is a second problem in relation to a constituency link and that is posed by the additional members themselves. On the assumption that there would be a parliament of 500 constituency and 150 additional members, how would additional members who would be elected on a regional basis relate to constituency MPs? How different would the role, the duties and the workload be? It might be argued, for example, that regionally elected MPs would not carry the caseload of a constituency MP and might therefore have much more time to nurse a seat to which that regional MP might aspire at the next election, thus placing at a disadvantage the current constituency representative from another party.

Also fairly crucial would be the method of election of the additional members and whether there should be a threshold before which a party should become eligible to secure representation on the list. A threshold could either be a constituency test, namely winning a constituency before becoming eligible for a top up, or it could be a test in terms of the percentage of the vote or a combination of both. The problem with the constituency test, which might otherwise seem to be a very plausible one, is why winning a seat, let us say, in the south west region should allow a party to have access to top up seats in the west of Scotland. On the other hand, if a party had to win a seat in each region to share in the top up in that region, this would set the threshold too high for a reasonable recognition of pluralism. The percentage of the vote test is rather arbitrary and the level at which it is set will always appear controversial to those who fall under it. As already noted, pure list systems of election can be seen to strengthen the powers of the parties in terms of ordering the list so that a voter is essentially required to vote for a party rather than the individual. So if regional lists were to be compiled by parties with people being elected off the list in proportion to the party's overall vote in both the constituency and the list section in that region, then this would mean that there were members of the House of Commons who had not stood as individuals in front of the electorate. This would be a very radical change indeed in terms of ideas about representation.

There are perhaps two ways in which this problem could be ameliorated, but in each case not without difficulty. The first would be not to have a list of candidates in a region at all. Rather constituencies would be regarded as belonging to a region and all candidates in the election would stand in a constituency. The additional members would then be drawn from the best losers in these constituencies in the numbers necessary to create a more proportional outcome than in the constituency elections alone. This would have the advantage that all members would then have stood for election but with some getting into Parliament as the best losers (who might in fact have polled more votes, or a greater proportion of the votes than some of the direct winners under First Past the Post). So who actually would get elected on this view would be in the hands of the electors entirely and there would be no separate party list.

There is quite a lot of logic in this position. It does however suffer from a major flaw in that while it is quite a plausible way of resolving the problem of avoiding a party list, nevertheless, it would probably be subjected to a good deal of ridicule, that people who actually lose elections then end up being elected. One can imagine tabloid headlines of the sort 'A Parliament of Losers!'.

The alternative would be to require candidates to stand in constituencies if their name is to go on the party list for which a separate vote would be cast. On this basis the party list would be fixed by the number of constituencies in the region, all of those on the list would have been selected by the party in constituencies and the list would just be an aggregate of those names. There would still have to be an ordering, however, in that the top up from the list would not exhaust all the names on the list. Those who get elected in constituencies are removed from the list, if there are still seats to fill to ensure proportionality arising out of the votes cast in the constituency and on the list, then unsuccessful candidates in the constituencies and whose names are on the list would be selected in the order fixed by the party when the list was compiled. This is probably a more plausible political solution than the logic-ally more attractive 'best loser' approach. It does constrain party power to an extent in that all candidates on the list would have to have been selected by constituencies in the way they are selected at present. Those names go on the list and have to be ordered by the party. Nevertheless it would appear obvious that some are only on the list in a formal way since they are bound to be elected in the constituency, so the party ordering only becomes relevant for those in marginal or hopeless seats rather than over the list as a whole. It also mitigates the best loser problem in that there would be a vote for the list although not for individual members on it and thus those elected from the list would have faced the electorate in a constituency which they had indeed lost, but were then elected from a list for which a separate ballot had been cast on a party basis, so the list member could claim greater legitimacy through this procedure than by a pure best loser method.

This additional member approach is certainly a strong possibility if polit-ical and popular opinion during the run-up to the promised referendum on the issue puts a great deal of weight on proportionality. It is not inconceiv-able however that there could be a more complex, perhaps more political approach, which could appeal to the Commission. This view might take up the following line of argument, although I have not heard it deployed as yet in this way. By the time the issues raised by the Jenkins Commission are to be legislated upon there will be substantial progress towards devolution with representative bodies in Wales, Scotland and London being elected by a form of proportional representation, with the possible development of de-volved regional assemblies in England to follow as appropriate. It could be argued in this context that to move towards a proportional system of election for the House of Commons would be too risky in these new and untried circumstances. A PR system for the House of Commons would be very likely to lead to a coalition government, let us say, of Labour and the Liberal Democrats in the first instance. This government will have responsibility for at the least macro economic policy, foreign affairs, defence and social secur-ity, and indeed will have more or less full parliamentary powers in relation to nations and regions other than Scotland. Scotland and Wales will elect a Parliament and an Assembly and London will elect an assembly by PR and therefore the administrations of these bodies are likely to be coalitions as well. These coalitions may have a rather different complexion from that at Westminster – it is not impossible to imagine in the future a Liberal Democrat/SNP coalition in Scotland. It is obviously extremely unlikely at the moment, but constitutional changes are not just for the medium term. How would one sort of coalition in London relate to another sort of coalition in Edinburgh, when one coalition partner is the same but part of a radically different administration?

Now, it will be argued in response to this that this happens all the time in a country like Germany with an additional member electoral system at both the federal and the Länder level. The CDU/CSU/FDP coalition in Bonn has to deal with a full spectrum of coalitions around the Länder and manages perfectly well. Nevertheless the Federal Republic of Germany is what its name suggests, namely a federal system. Despite the degree of devolution and despite the fact that some political commentators see our present arrangements as a significant step on the road to federalism, the UK is not and in the medium term will not be a federal state and therefore one cannot assume that what works in Germany in terms of cross-cutting coalitions at different levels will in fact apply in the UK.

If these points are discomforting, then to pursue the line of argument, it might suggest that there is a case for single party government at the centre of this devolved structure to have a clear strategic centre to the state, or that at the very least the move to an additional member system of proportional representation should be postponed until such time as the way devolution is working out becomes much clearer. It might still be argued, however, that even if one accepted these arguments, there is still a strong case for the reform of the electoral system for the House of Commons. It might be argued that as people become used to proportional representation for devolved bodies the unfairness of First Past the Post in relation to UK elections will become more obvious. So, for example, the likely representation of the Conservative Party in the Scottish Parliament while having no Westminster seats, will throw into relief the contrast in these two methods of election, which in the view of critics is likely to make the case for First Past the Post unsustainable. So the argument might continue, while there is a case for having an electoral system which would be likely to lead to single party government at Westminster, there will be a need to move towards a more legitimate majoritarian system than First Past the Post, namely either the Alternative Vote (AV) or the Supplementary Vote (SV). These are more pluralistic in that they allow more preferences to be expressed and carry weight (all preferences expressed in the case of the AV; two preferences in the case of the SV) while at the same time maintaining the constituency link unchanged and possibly leading under present conditions to single party government.

At this stage in the argument the critic will also point out that neither system embodies a principle of proportionality and indeed in certain circumstances can be less proportional in its outcome than First Past the Post. So while the constituency base is kept and single party government is secured as the likely outcome, each of which are desideratum on the point of view we are discussing, both are secured at the cost of proportionality. The defender of the majoritarian position will not be too discomforted by this because as I have explained part of the aim is to argue that a majoritarian system is required at the centre since there is to be PR in devolved bodies in the nations and the regions. To move to AV or SV would on this view make the majoritarian basis of the centre more legitimate than First Past the Post so that the centre would be less susceptible to the unfairness argument which could be levelled against First Past the Post, but it would leave the way open as the country got used to devolution and coalition to add additional members to a basically AV or SV constituency voting system. So AV or SV 'plus' could be introduced at a later date once the system had shaken down and the rough edges of the relationship between central and devolved bodies had been smoothed out. Essentially this would be an additional member system with single member constituencies elected by AV or SV with top up members to increase proportionality being added, say, after debate in the next Parliament. So there could be what might be seen as a strengthening of the legitimacy of the voting system at the centre, making it more responsive to pluralism if not to proportionality, with the option of extending its proportionality at a later date following a sense of how the relations between the Westminster government and devolved bodies works out. This might also be seen as administratively attractive in terms of timetable in that AV or SV could be introduced for the next election since it does not include changes in electoral boundaries with the question of adding a proportional top up being left over to a future Parliament in the light of the experience of proportional representation in the bodies that will use it and the relations of those bodies to Westminster.

AV AND SV VOTING SYSTEMS: STRENGTHS AND WEAKNESSES

So is there anything much to choose between AV and SV? The SV was recommended by the Electoral Systems Working Party and the central reason why it was chosen over AV is still very salient. Under the AV the elector has a right to order his or her preferences for all candidates, however many candidates there are (and sometimes there are quite a few!). All these preferences, even the lowest or weakest ones will count in that the second preferences and so on of eliminated first preference candidates are redistributed in the count until such time as the successful candidate has 51 per cent of the vote. So weak preferences still have a role to play. This is both a strength and a weakness, but in the view of the Electoral Systems Working Party, its weaknesses outweighed its strengths in that while it did leave successful candidates with 51 per cent of the vote and might be thought therefore to be an improvement in legitimacy on First Past the Post, nevertheless it achieves this by bringing into play all preferences however weak and indeed arbitrary. Under the SV however, while only some of those elected will have 51 per cent of the vote, only the first two preferences are allowed to be revealed and to count in the final determination. It can be plausibly argued that it is perfectly legitimate to count the first two preferences since these will be held reasonably strongly and that this incorporates a degree of serious pluralism in the electoral system; the AV, by allowing all preferences to be revealed is taking cognisance of weak and arbitrary preferences. It could therefore be argued that while SV does not strengthen the legitimacy of the centre by getting all of those elected over the 50 per cent hurdle, nevertheless it does embody a fair and rational degree of pluralism which is an improvement on First Past the Post and it only counts very strong preferences. In the view of the SV supporter the legitimacy of the over 50 per cent principle behind the AV is spurious in that the hurdle can only be crossed by allowing some kind of value to very weak preferences. Consequently if one were to go down this path of trying to improve the legitimacy of the electoral system for the House of Commons against the background of devolution to PR elected bodies, then SV (or as I have said possibly AV) could provide a reasonable basis for reform, particularly if a top up to increase proportionality could be added at a future point.

CONCLUSION

So the future shape of the debate will be heavily influenced during the course of 1999 by the Jenkins Commission report, due at the end of 1998, and the plausibility and practicability of its recommendations will be the decisive factor in whether or not there is finally some change at Westminster. We have got to this threshold of reform a lot faster than many people might have thought possible, but the difficulty of mobilising those who wish to see reform around only one option for reform to be placed before the people in a referendum will become critical and it would be a very grave mistake to underestimate the difficulties in getting all the reformers aligned behind an alternative. It will be very important for the Jenkins Commission to make the basis of its recommendations absolutely clear, particularly when they apply to the Commission's own view about what is politically practicable as opposed to following through issues of the pure logic and mathematics of different electoral systems.[9]

---

[9] See the forthcoming Report of the Independent Commission on the Voting System (1998).

Further reading

Report of the Independent Commission on the Voting System (the Jenkins Report) (London: HMSO, 1998)

Reports of the National Executive Committee Working Party on Electoral Systems (The Plant Report) (Labour Party, 1991–93)

Martin Linton and Mary Southcott, *Making Votes Count: The Case for Electoral Reform* (London: Profile Books, 1998)

Robert Blackburn, *The Electoral System in Britain* (London: Macmillan, 1995), especially Ch 8

Patrick Dunleavy, Helen Margetts, Brendan O'Duffy and Stuart Weir, *Making Votes Count: Replaying the 1990s General Elections Under Alternative Electoral Systems* (Essex: Democratic Audit, 1997)

CHAPTER 4

ELECTORAL LAW AND ADMINISTRATION

Professor Robert Blackburn (King's College, London)

'The Labour Party is committed to examining all aspects of electoral law and administration and to ensuring that citizens are aware of their voting rights and responsibilities.'

(Labour Party, *A New Agenda for Democracy*, 1993)

Political attention on modernising the electoral system has tended to focus principally on proportional representation and the financial affairs of the political parties. What has received far less analysis and commentary generally, including in terms of reform proposals, is the separate and in some respects equally important subject of electoral law and administration.[1] It is now widely believed that many features in the way we organise and regulate elections and electioneering in Britain are out of date and have failed to keep pace with the rapidly developing social and technological changes of the late 20th century. In recognition of this, the Labour Party in its 1993 constitutional reform proposals committed itself to an in-depth review of all aspects of the subject. Now in government, the party leadership is equipped to carry out that pledge. At the start of 1998, Labour's Home Office Minister George Howarth set up a Ministerial Working Party into electoral law and administration.[2] Whilst a Home Office review of this kind is routine after every general election, it is anticipated that this inquiry will prove more radical and wide-ranging than others before it. Meanwhile, in the House of Commons, the

---

[1] This chapter draws upon the author's earlier work on general elections, especially R Blackburn, *The Electoral System in Britain* (London: Macmillan, 1995).

[2] In a press release announcing the Home Office Working Party on Electoral Procedures on 20 January 1998, George Howarth said, 'As chairman of this working party, I am determined that we make recommendations for change which will have a positive impact on people's experience of participating in the democratic process. This review will contribute to the Government's drive towards democratic renewal.' The terms of reference of the Working Party are drawn very widely, being to 'examine and review current electoral arrangements, including legislation where relevant, in the light of the recent general election', and are primarily concerned with parliamentary elections. Recommendations of the Working Party will be presented to the Home Secretary.

Home Affairs Committee has started conducting its own examination of election law and administration during the first session of the new Parliament.[3]

The reform issues involved are of a very different character to those raised by the voting system (as examined by the Jenkins Commission[4]) or by the financial affairs of the political parties (as inquired into by the Neill Committee[5]). This is because the subject by comparison is relatively depoliticised, being concerned principally with matters of efficiency and fairness in the administration of elections and in the conduct of electioneering. That is not to say that some subjects of election law reform are non-controversial. They are: for example, the timing of general elections and proposal for fixed-term Parliaments (which to some extent is associated with the issue of proportional representation since this would be more conducive to 'hung parliaments' which in turn would cause problems of legitimacy as to when the incumbent Prime Minister is entitled to call an early second election). But others are less so: for example, the case for an Electoral Commission or the rules relating to the franchise and parliamentary candidature.

Whereas all political parties might be expected to concur about the desirability of any administrative proposal that served to improve the conduct of elections and electioneering, in a way that was equally advantageous to all political parties, it has in fact been the Labour Party which has most prominently backed the case for a major overhaul of our system of electoral law and administration. Against this background, therefore, and within the context of Labour's overall modernisation programme, I will now turn to a number of reform issues contained within the very wide subject-matter concerned. The topics selected focus primarily on elections to the House of Commons, and represent areas where the case for change is strongest and where political acceptance of the desirability or need for legislative and administrative action now already exists or is most likely to be forthcoming.

A FIXED FOUR-YEAR TERM BETWEEN ELECTIONS?

Under existing electoral law, the date of the next general election remains unknown to British voters and opposition parties alike, until it is announced by the Prime Minister approximately five weeks before polling is due to take place.[6] All the statute book has to say is that no Parliament should exceed

---

[3] The author gave oral evidence based upon this chapter to the Committee on 2 June 1998. See its forthcoming report, Home Affairs Committee, *Electoral Law and Administration*, HC [1997–98] 768.

[4] See Report of the Independent Commission on the Voting System, 1998; and Chapter 4 above.

[5] See Report of the Committee on Standards in Public Life, *The Funding of Political Parties in the United Kingdom*, 1998; and Chapter 2 above.

[6] For a full account of the law and practice on general election timing, see R Blackburn, *The Meeting of Parliament* (Aldershot: Dartmouth, 1990), and R Blackburn, *The Electoral System in Britain*, Ch 2.

five years in duration (by the Septennial Act 1715, as amended by s 7 of the Parliament Act 1911) and if it does, it will automatically terminate. Even then, there is no statutory requirement for a new Parliament to be called and a general election held for a further three years (under the Triennial Act 1694 still in force). This means that in strict legal theory general elections only need to be held once in every eight years.

The legality of electoral timing otherwise is a matter purely for the royal prerogative. The Queen carries out the legal ceremonies involved in dissolving Parliament and causing election writs to be issued to constituency returning officers simply whenever the Prime Minister requests her so to do. So long as the Prime Minister retains his majority in the House of Commons (or if a minority administration, can ward off any no confidence motion), he is free to call a general election whenever he likes. No law or convention exists to require the Prime Minister to obtain the consent of MPs to a dissolution, nor even to oblige him to consult or notify them in the House of Commons. The general election date is cursorily announced to the world in the form of a Press Notice issued direct to the media by the Prime Minister's staff at 10 Downing Street.[7]

And, as everybody knows, a Prime Minister sets an election date at the time when he thinks he is most likely to win it.[8] Conversely, he will avoid such times as he is likely to lose it. The anachronistic state of the law on electoral timing adversely affects the fairness of the election process as a whole. It gives the party in government a tremendous tactical advantage over the opposition parties, and of all the possible flaws to be found in our electoral law and administration, this perhaps above all other matters does most harm to the integrity of the electioneering contest. More generally, it serves to feed the existing sense of public cynicism about the motivation of its political leaders.

In his 1991 party leader's conference speech, Neil Kinnock promised that an incoming Labour government would establish fixed intervals between general elections, so as to do away with the unfair advantage possessed by a Prime Minister to control the election date. The 1992 Labour election manifesto subsequently read:[9]

'The general election was called only after months of on-again, off-again dithering which damaged our economy and weakened our democracy. No government with a majority should be allowed to put the interests of party above country as the Conservatives have done. Although an early election will sometimes be necessary, we will introduce as a general rule a fixed parliamentary term.'

---

[7] For an account and criticism of this procedure, see R Blackburn, *The Electoral System in Britain*, pp 33–37; R Blackburn, 'Hail to the Chief', *The Guardian*, 18 March 1997.
[8] For historical and political observations on this fact, see R Blackburn, *The Electoral System in Britain*, pp 28–32 and 50–57.
[9] Labour's Election Manifesto 1992, p 25.

Though Labour's policy documents have been quiet on the matter since, it has become firmly established as a Liberal Democrat commitment.[10] Furthermore, since the 1997 election the rationale for the existing system has become ever more tenuous. Even the purported justification that the prerogative of dissolution permits the government some mechanism whereby it may test electoral opinion on some major item of public policy has now evaporated with the government's clear espousal of the institution of referendums in the politics of the 1990s. In the creation of the new Scottish Parliament, a fixed four-year term applies[11] and there was never any question of utilising the prerogative or an Order in Council as the basis for its election timing.

The construction of a fixed term for the Westminster Parliament raises more complex issues than at first meet the eye. One important detail to be settled at the outset is the most appropriate length of the fixed interval between elections. Elsewhere in the world, the tenure of members of legislatures or of positions in government office tend to vary between two and seven years. In the USA, members of the House of Representatives (the lower House in Congress) are elected every two years, the President holds office for four years, and members of the Senate (the second chamber of Congress) serve for six-year terms. The Parliaments of both Australia and New Zealand operate three-year terms between elections. French law operates at the maximum end, with the French President being elected every seventh year, members of the French second chamber (the Senate) being elected for nine-year terms, and National Assembly elections being every fifth year. In Sweden, members of the Rikstag serve for three-year terms. But the majority of European countries, including Denmark, the Netherlands, Germany, Norway, Portugal and Austria, all regulate the intervals between their parliamentary elections at the period of four years.

In the UK, there can be little doubt that the period between general elections should be four years. The proposal for fixed-term Parliament as a whole should fit as closely as possible into existing constitutional expectations, and the idea that four years is about the right length of time between elections is very prevalent. It was the period expressly approved of as being normal in practice, when the Parliament Act set the period of five years as a maximum.[12] In an ideal democracy it may be that there should be elections as frequently as possible – even annually as supported by the Chartists in the 18th century – but a government must be allowed a sufficient period of time in which to put its programme of public policies into effect before submitting

---

[10] See eg Liberal Democrats, *Here We Stand: Proposals for Modernising Britain's Democracy* (1993) p 15.

[11] See clauses 2 and 3, Scotland Bill [1997–98] 104.

[12] On the parliamentary context of the 1911 amendment to the earlier Septennial Act, see R Blackburn, *The Meeting of Parliament*, p 22.

its record of achievement, or otherwise, to the voters. Three full legislative sessions, and certainly four, is sufficient for this purpose.

A second important detail must be to lay down clearly the circumstances in which an earlier election might be permitted within the four-year period. It is important that there is some such safety valve, as is common in fixed term arrangements in other countries, to provide for those exceptional situations where, for example, the government loses the confidence of the House of Commons, and no new government can be constructed from the composition of the House as it stands. Essentially, the new legislation should provide for the House of Commons to be able to control whether there should be either a fresh general election, or whether there should simply be a change of Prime Minister and government. The trigger for any such process should be a no confidence motion in the House of Commons, consisting either of an opposition motion of no confidence in the government or Prime Minister being passed, or a government motion seeking the formal confidence of the House being put forward and lost. If any such motion is expressed towards the government as a whole, then there should be a general election; but if the motion is expressed towards the Prime Minister, then he should resign office. If it transpires, following a prime ministerial resignation, whether voluntary or through a no confidence vote, that no Prime Minister is appointed within a prescribed period of time (say, 20 days), for example because no alternative party leader feels able to form a new government, then again there should be a general election.

It is appropriate that the process of confidence motions is adopted as the only procedure for an early general election, because any other form of Commons' resolution, such as a vote on dissolution itself, would allow the government to remain in full control of electoral timing. Little would change if dissolution was simply put to the vote or confirmed by the Commons, as has been suggested by some, because assuming the Prime Minister took the usual care through the whips to ensure the loyalty of his or her own party backbenchers, the government's majority in the House could be relied upon to support the Prime Minister's decision on the timing of the election whenever he or she chose to put the motion before the House. A simple confirmation vote does have one advantage, however, over existing arrangements, in that before putting forward his or her motion, the Prime Minister would be obliged to take soundings of backbenchers and Cabinet colleagues to ensure the party voted together. But it is only under a fixed term arrangement subject to no confidence motions as proposed that one could realistically hope to keep early dissolutions free from political manipulation by the government, and ensure electoral timing was determined by reasons of genuine constitutional need, as opposed to purely party political advantage.[13]

---

[13] For a draft Bill to implement what is proposed, see R Blackburn, *The Electoral System in Britain*, p 65.

HOW SECRET IS THE BALLOT?

It is a basic constitutional principle that everyone should be able to exercise their right to vote in conditions of secrecy. There are three associated aspects to this principle which need to be distinguished and borne in mind when examining current electoral law on the secrecy of the ballot. First, there must be conditions of secrecy at the polling station such that no one may observe or seek to influence voters. Secondly, legal and administrative procedures should prevent ballot papers being matched with other documentation to discover how persons voted. Thirdly, the information of how people choose to cast their vote should not be recorded in any form without the express knowledge and permission of the voters concerned.

British electoral law on the secrecy of the ballot is to be found in the Representation of the People Act 1983. The Act specifies that 'votes at the poll shall be given by ballot', and lays down a wide range of stipulations for maintaining the secrecy of how electors have voted.[14] All officials and other persons allowed to attend the polling station are required to 'maintain and aid in maintaining the secrecy of voting'. Detailed requirements prohibit any interference with voters or attempts being made to discover for which candidate he or she voted for, and regulations specify who is and is not permitted to be present inside the polling station. The rigour of our legal theory behind the secret ballot might even be regarded as excessive in certain respects: for example, if a person voting wishes to identify himself and write his name or initials on his ballot paper, the effect of this will be to invalidate his vote altogether.

This great stress in the 1983 Act on the secrecy of the ballot stands at some odds with the obvious flaw in the modern British practice of ballot voting. Casting one's vote in the polling booth in circumstances of privacy is to be sharply distinguished from the equally important matter of maintaining the secrecy of how each citizen actually voted. In this second respect, there is and never has been a secret ballot in Britain, because the way in which individual citizens vote can be traced from each ballot paper used. Every ballot paper given to the citizen who is voting contains a serial number on it, which is also printed on the counterfoil retained by electoral officials. Before a ballot paper is handed to the citizen, he is asked for his name and address (or preferably to show the clerk his official poll card which shows his name, address and electoral registration number on it). The polling clerk then traces the person in the copy of the electoral register that he has on the table in front of him, and ticks the voter's name off the list. The clerk then tears one of the ballot papers out of the book of papers printed for the purpose, hands it to the voter and directs him or her to the private booth. And then the clerk writes the electoral registration number of the voter on the counterfoil to the ballot paper just issued.

---

[14] See especially Representation of the People Act 1983, s 66 and Election Rules, rr 55, 57.

This means that after the election documentary information is in existence which will disclose who voted for which particular party in the constituency. The count by the returning officer's officials leaves all votes for each candidate in separate bundles, which are then placed in paper sacks with special labels and seals supplied by The Stationery Office and forwarded to the Clerk of the Crown in London. It is possible for the serial numbers of these ballot papers to be matched against those retained on the counterfoil stubs which disclose the electoral registration number – and therefore the name and address of citizens and how they voted – which are similarly forwarded to the Clerk of the Crown in London. Copies of electoral registers are already available on computerised disk, and in the future computerised counting of ballot papers by means of electronic vote counting machines is likely to replace manual counting of votes. If computers now in existence are able to read numbers on stacks of papers, then the technology for speedy cross-referencing and making such political inquiries is already with us. It seems that computerised matching and print-outs of entire lists of voters for each party is now perfectly possible. It may or may not be far-fetched to conjecture that at some point in the future an oppressive government or its over-zealous officials might surreptitiously wish to find out the name and address of all 'dissidents' who voted against them at a general election, but if so the bundles of ballot papers and counterfoil stubs retained by the Clerk of the Crown are available for analysis to produce the necessary information. Of course the law prohibits such inquiries, but the practical reality is that compliance with and enforcement of the law ultimately depends upon the various interested agencies of government themselves.

The ostensible argument for putting the voter's electoral registration number on the counterfoils of ballot papers is said to be that it facilitates investigations into alleged electoral offences, such as multiple voting and impersonation, so as to decide whether a fresh election needs to be ordered by the Election Court. However, vote-tracing hardly helps in the detection and prevention of any offence in itself, for there is no way that the identity of the impersonator can be discovered from the ballot paper. Investigations of such electoral fraud, involving voters finding out when they arrive at the polling station that their name has already been ticked off the electoral register by the clerk, can rely upon the evidence of the polling clerk that a ballot paper has indeed already been handed to some impersonator – tracing the ballot paper itself is not necessary.

The case for recording voters' registration numbers on the ballot counterfoils therefore is a weak one and cannot outweigh a growing public concern at the risk to the secrecy of the ballot. The regulations contained in the Representation of the People Act 1983 limiting the legal circumstances in which the information may be retrieved may be sufficient as rules themselves, but guaranteeing actual compliance with the rules in the real world raises more complex questions: for whilst the information to discover how individual citizens voted continues to be stored, the potential for their misuse remains.

The practice of writing voters' electoral registration numbers – or entering any other note which might disclose a voter's personal identity – on the counter-foils of ballot papers should be expressly abolished by law.[15]

As part of this reform, two new measures are desirable to help strengthen existing practices designed to combat the potential for voter impersonation. First, as suggested above, citizens should be eligible to vote in only one constituency, being their main place of residence. This would remove the ease with which dual or multiple voting could take place as a result of dual or multiple electoral registration being permitted under existing law. Secondly, voters throughout the UK, as is already the case in Northern Ireland, should be required as a matter of course to produce formal identification to the polling clerk – being one of a list of specified documents, for example passport, birth or marriage certificate, driving licence or National Health Service card – before being ticked off on the electoral register and given a ballot paper.

SHOULD COMPLETING A BALLOT PAPER BE A LEGAL REQUIREMENT?

The question whether voting should be made compulsory in the UK has never been seriously considered by past government or parliamentary inquiries into election law.[16] It was one of the large number of issues identified for inquiry in 1982–83 by the House of Commons Home Affairs Committee, but in the event it was not examined in any depth in its discussions and was not even mentioned in its final Report. A significant shift in opinion, however, now seems to be taking place on the subject. Many Labour members have been advocating compulsory voting in recent years, including some who are now members of the Labour government.[17] Labour's 1993 policy document, *A New Agenda for Democracy: Labour's Proposals for Constitutional Reform*, included a reference to the need for citizens to be made more aware of 'their voting rights and *responsibilities*'.[18] Meanwhile, public opinion polls would seem to indicate that a majority of people in the UK actively support such a change in election law.[19]

Whether or not the moral duty to vote should be crystallised into law confronts traditional British feelings about encroaching upon a citizen's 'right to be left alone'. But the introduction of a legal duty to vote would merely

[15] For further discussion see Electoral Reform Society/Liberty Working Party Report, *Ballot Secrecy* (1996).
[16] However, shortly after the original draft of this chapter was prepared, the House of Commons Home Affairs Committee considered the proposal at some length: see note 3 above.
[17] For example Peter Hain MP in his book, *Ayes to the Left* (London: Lawrence and Wishart, 1995).
[18] At p 39; author's italics. Appendix 1
[19] A poll commissioned by the Rowntree Reform Trust in 1991 indicated that a majority of people in the UK support compulsory voting. The result was 49 per cent for, 42 per cent against, and 9 per cent 'don't knows'.

be consistent with the legal compulsion in the first place to register one's name and address as a voter at the local Town Hall. Several countries abroad have introduced compulsory voting, including Australia, Belgium, Greece, Luxembourg and Italy, and the obvious result is a far higher turnout of the electorate (even if 100 per cent is never in practice attainable), and therefore a more comprehensive expression of public opinion at the polls. The turnout of voters at general elections in Britain since 1945 has been as follows:

Table 4.1 Turnout of voters: general elections

Year	%
1945	72.8
1950	83.9
1951	82.6
1955	76.8
1959	78.7
1964	77.1
1966	75.8
1970	72.0
1974 (February)	78.8
1974 (October)	72.8
1979	76.0
1983	72.7
1987	75.3
1992	77.7
1997	71.5

The traditional British view on compulsory voting has been that politics is an essentially voluntary exercise and people should be left alone to decide for themselves how and whether to vote. Some also believe that it is no bad thing if the country as a whole is relatively depoliticised, and this is simply reflected in a number of citizens not being sufficiently interested in turning up at the polling station to vote on election day. Some have said that compulsory voting is only needed in countries with a weak political culture or fragile national identity. The (then) Liberal Party argued, in giving evidence to the Home Affairs Select Committee in 1982, that compulsory voting produces an undesirable 'donkey vote',[20] presumably meaning that groups of politically mindless UK voters would be forced into the polling booths. A final reservation has been the alleged impracticality of enforcing such an obligation, a factor that has troubled some election administrators such as officials in

---

[20] Home Affairs Committee, *Representation of the People Acts*, HC [1992–93] 32-II, p 106.

Rochdale (who spoke of 'severe enforcement problems and there would be the problems created by electors who could not vote on account of sickness'[21]) in giving evidence to the Home Affairs Committee in 1982.

These arguments when looked at closely are rather weak. There are very few practical problems of compulsory voting in Australia. Easier voting arrangements, such as greater use of postal voting or (as in Australia) centres in each constituency where voters from other constituencies might vote, would alleviate any hardship on voters with physical disability or with travel commitments, and for the ordinary voter a walk to the local ballot station is hardly a taxing exercise. The 'donkey vote' argument is highly suspect if it assumes that people who choose not to vote are on the whole likely to be any weaker in their mental faculties than many people who do vote. Neither is any draconian enforcement of compulsory voting any more likely than prosecutions at present for householders failing to complete and return the annual forms requiring details of all persons resident in the home sent out each year by the electoral registration officer, for which there were just three prosecutions in 1979, one in 1980, and four in 1981.

On the other hand, there are good reasons of principle and practice supporting the idea of compulsory voting. First, few would disagree with the proposition that individuals are under some degree of moral obligation to participate in the operation of the democracy to which they belong. Citizenship involves responsibilities as well as rights, and compulsory completion of ballot forms would simply be consistent with the notion of a social or moral duty to vote. Such a duty, of course, falls short of being compelled to vote positively for persons of whom one disapproves, which could conceivably include all persons named on the ballot paper. An important detail of any legislative provision on compulsory voting, therefore, will be to expressly provide for those electors who consciously wish to abstain and vote for none of the candidates. All ballot papers, therefore, would need to contain a box in addition to the names of the candidates (and, where applicable, parties) against which the voter could signify an abstention.

Secondly, there is reason to suppose that a duty to vote would tend towards a better informed electorate as a whole. Compulsory voting would transform the work of party workers and canvassers away from 'getting out the vote' (in other words, persuading people to go to the polling station) and allow them to concentrate more on talking with voters about the issues and policies that are represented by their party. At present, local party electioneering concentrates almost entirely on canvassers identifying where their party's support is the greatest, so that their colleagues acting as 'tellers' waiting outside ballot stations on polling day can try to calculate which of their supporters have voted, and then instruct other party colleagues to call at non-voters' homes to try to persuade them to vote. If everyone knows that they are obliged to fill in a ballot paper and vote, some may prove more

---

[21] ibid, p 244.

diligent in finding out more about what the parties and candidates stand for and what their policies are. Compulsory voting would be a new factor helping promote greater participation and awareness of what elections are about.

A related, final detail is whether general elections should be held on a Sunday or date declared to be a public holiday, as is the case in many other countries including France and Germany, instead of on a normal weekday (generally Thursday) as is customary at present in the UK. If this concomitant change to our system of elections was made, there would be even less reason why UK citizens would be inconvenienced in any way by being required by law to express their opinion on who should be representing them as an MP and in government over the lifetime of the new Parliament.

UNJUSTIFIABLE RESTRICTIONS ON PARLIAMENTARY CANDIDATURE

There are good arguments for suggesting that the state of British election law on parliamentary candidature should be codified.[22] Currently, it exists in the form of numerous, diverse disqualifications laid down in a series of ancient common law principles and statutes harking back to the Middle Ages. Two particular present forms of disqualification are in need of reform, being the age limit for candidature, and the disqualification of Christian priests, and these are discussed below. Also discussed below is the question whether candidates today should still be required to deposit a sum of money before having their nomination accepted.

The age limit for candidature

The Labour Party view expressed in *A New Agenda for Democracy: Labour's Proposals for Constitutional Reform* (1993) was unequivocal that the age for parliamentary candidature, currently 21 years, should be similar to that for voting, which is 18 years. 'There is no justification for the continued discrepancy between the age of nomination and voting rights. We believe that it is right that the age of nomination which at present stands at 21 should be reduced to the age of 18.' Ironically, however, it was a Labour administration which created the anomaly in the first place. In the late 1960s the Wilson government granted full citizenship to all persons at the age of 18, under s 1 of the Family Law Reform Act 1969. Persons at 18 were now to be entitled to equal civil rights as with any other adult, including freedom from restrictions on property ownership, the right to marry, the right to bring legal actions, and the enjoyment of a host of other basic rights of citizenship. It excluded voting, but separately in the same year a Representation of the

---

[22] For a detailed account, see R Blackburn, *The Electoral System in Britain*, pp 158 ff.

People Act was passed lowering the right to vote from 21 to 18 years. No consideration at that time, either in Cabinet or Parliament, was given to similarly lowering the age at which one had the right to stand for election to Parliament.[23]

So there remains today this inconsistency in our election law, between being an elector at 18 but not being electable until 21. At one end of the political process – the exercise of the vote – the age of maturity is set at 18 but at the other receiving end – parliamentary candidature – a different level of maturity is prescribed. Arguments for this discrepancy might include that 18 year olds are too immature and inexperienced actually to be working at Westminster and representing the nation, as opposed to expressing a political opinion through the vote. Some would say there is no reason why voting and candidature ages should automatically be identical, and it is true that some other countries have disparate ages. In the USA voting is at 18, but candidature to the House of Representatives is limited to 25 year olds (30 years in the case of their Second Chamber, the Senate). In France voting is at 18, but you must be 23 before standing for election to the National Assembly and 35 years for their Senate. On the other hand, it is precisely upon the principle that adults should assume equal civil responsibilites at the same time, and that only the electorate can pass any further judgment on a candidate's suitability for political office, that many other countries including Australia, Canada and Germany make 18 years the age for both voting and candidature.

Some will also argue that reducing the age for candidature will make negligible difference in the number of candidates coming forward, and so it is not worth the bother of drawing up the necessary legislation or amending clause in the next Representation of the People Act. It is again true that in practice few persons between 18 and 20 years of age will wish to start a professional political career so young, and it is very rare for a local party association to wish to select someone at that age as their official candidate, especially as there is always stiff competition from experienced party members and campaigners, and former MPs defeated at the last election looking for a new constituency. Nonetheless the law governing our democracy should reflect points of rational principle, not anachronisms that Parliament has overlooked to debate, or finds inconvenient to find time to consider. Even if only one person is blocked from becoming a parliamentary candidate, in the absence of a sound constitutional basis it is an unjustificable restriction upon the electoral process. Over the past 25 years there have been many parliamentary candidates in their early 20s, mainly beginning their political careers in unwinnable seats for their parties, but also some who have won and been elected to the House of Commons.

The signs are that there is in fact strong cross-party support for this reform. Many Labour MPs support the idea; the Liberal Democrats have included it in their election manifestos; and in 1985 a group of Conservative

---

[23] See R Blackburn, *The Electoral System in Britain*, p 168.

backbenchers tabled a Members of Parliament (Minimum Age) Bill on the matter. The 21 age restriction upon candidature should be reduced to 18 years, consistent with the right to vote, at the earliest opportunity. After a person has reached adulthood at 18 for virtually all other civil purposes, he or she should be free to offer himself or herself for election to Parliament, and the law should not restrict the choice of local voters to decide for themselves on the suitability of the particular candidate, and whether or not he or she is the best person to be representing them.

Religious discrimination

One rather different form of disqualification from parliamentary candidature may also today lead to an injustice. This is with respect to the right of a present or former minister of religion to enter a political career.

For anyone seeking a simple answer to the question 'Can a priest stand for Parliament?', reading the legal sources on the subject requires burrowing away in collections of parliamentary statutes to find at least nine separate legislative acts on the subject stretching back to the 16th century.[24] The short answer is that some priests are disqualified, and others are not; and some priests can relinquish their ministry to become an MP, but others are unable to do so. The following generalisations apply.

(1) Only certain Christian priests are disqualified whereas ministers of all other religious faiths, such as Judaism, Islam and Buddhism, are eligible.
(2) All episcopally ordained priests of the Anglican Church are disqualified, but not in Wales.
(3) All Roman Catholic priests are disqualified.
(4) Nonconformist clergy (being priests not ordained episcopally, in other words not made a priest by a bishop) are not disqualified but they are in Scotland.

The reasons for the discriminatory principles applying here between and across different faiths are ones derived purely from our ancient history and have no political justification today.

Furthermore, currently, it is only priests of the Established Church of England who are able in law to resign their ministry in order to become a parliamentary candidate. All other ordained priests are disqualified by British law for life and it makes no difference that they might have given up working as a priest, or lost their faith, or even become a member of some completely different faith, such as Buddhism; they can never be MPs. Into this wide group of former Christian priests who are treated differently from those in the Church of England are those who have ever practised as ministers of the

---

[24] For a full account, see R Blackburn, *The Electoral System in Britain*, pp 185–97.

Church of Scotland or ever been ordained into the Roman Catholic Church. Bruce Kent, the former Roman Catholic priest who resigned his ministry to lobby for nuclear disarmament and enter politics, stood as a parliamentary candidate at the 1992 general election for the constituency of Oxford West and Abingdon (comfortably won, in the event, by the Conservative candidate). In fact, under present electoral law, Mr Kent was disqualified for life from ever becoming an MP. If he had won the constituency election, he would have been unable to take up his seat at Westminster. The situation would have been analogous to the position of Tony Benn MP in the 1960s, who found himself disqualified from membership of the Commons for life by virtue of succeeding to his father's hereditary peerage in 1960, until the Peerage Act 1963 was passed permitting him to renounce his hereditary title.

Many people will believe that there are one or more good reasons why, as a general principle, it is preferable that active ministers of religion do not stand as parliamentary candidates. But it is important to emphasise that this does not mean automatically that the state should ban them by law from doing so. The original reasons for the ancient clergy disqualification statutes have long since ceased to exist. Roman Catholic priests are no longer seen as potential subversives, and the Anglican clergy no longer represent a fourth estate of the realm. Still less should the state use the law of the country to disqualify clergy in such an inconsistent and illogical fashion, so that the Reverend Ian Paisley could be an MP by virtue of being a Nonconformist but other priests who are Anglicans or Roman Catholics are subject to legal prohibition. Perhaps most objectionable of all is that only Anglican religious ministers can choose one profession or the other, and relinquish religious office for a new career as an MP, but all other ordained priests cannot do so.

One simple reform that would be a definite improvement would be simply to extend the terms of the Clergy Disabilities Act 1870 to cover all disqualified priests. But more generally it is wrong for the state today to be regulating a matter that should more properly be for internal Church discipline to decide. The objections to priests standing for Parliament are canonical ones, not constitutional, and it should be ecclesiastical law, not the state, that imposes disqualifications upon the individual's political liberties. It is for the individual Churches concerned to decide whether or not to impose restrictions as a matter of religious ethics, or incompatibility of the two professions, as a necessary condition of the priest's particular work. And just as a civil servant can resign to go into politics so too should a minister of religion be free to do so. Ultimately the question of the individual's suitability for politics should be left to the local electorate to decide, and it is fundamental that there should be as few restrictions as possible upon the right of the voters freely to decide whom they wish to represent them. There are basic principles of political liberty involved here, about which British public policy as enshrined in its law is muddled and which the government and Parliament seem reluctant to confront and prefer to ignore. In recent times, there has been growing support within the Anglican Church for reform of clergy disqualification. In 1982, its General Synod carried a motion that 'this Synod believes that clergymen of the Church of England should be free like other citizens to take their seats as elected Members of Parliament'. It is time for the clergy disqualification legislation simply to be repealed.

The financial deposit

Parliamentary candidates cannot be validly nominated unless the sum of £500 is deposited by them or on their behalf with the returning officer during the time for delivery of nomination papers. The money may be handed over in cash, or by banker's draft, or any other manner acceptable to the returning officer. This £500 will be returned to the candidate after the general election if he or she managed to collect at least 5 per cent of the total votes cast in the constituency, but if the candidate polls less than 5 per cent then he or she loses the money which then goes to the Treasury. There exists a serious issue today in our electoral law whether this requirement of a financial deposit is consistent with the democratic right of every citizen to stand for election if he or she wishes regardless of financial status.

From a comparative perspective, the present deposit system – and the desire in some quarters to push the sum of money involved even higher – is an extraordinary state of affairs. Only four other states in Europe (France, Ireland, Greece and the Netherlands) and none in the USA have deposit systems at all, and even in those four states the sums required are far lower than the £500 at present demanded of a parliamentary candidate in Britain.

Prior to 1918 candidates had been nominated without any need to deposit sums of money with the returning officer. The Home Office's invention of the deposit in 1918 was barely mentioned, let alone properly discussed, during the otherwise very lengthy debates on the parliamentary passage of the Representation of the People Act, but a tacit acceptance seems to have existed at the time that some capital requirement was a good idea in order to keep out unsuitable candidates. Undoubtedly, there were many within the political establishment at that time who regarded the fledgling Labour Party and its trade union and working class candidates (who would be hit hardest by the requirement of a deposit) as less than top-class parliamentary material and a potential threat to the good government of the country. This same idea of the deposit being a tool for keeping out 'unsuitable' candidates is still inherent in our law today and is democratically indefensible.

Those who justify the deposit today seek to put off candidates indiscriminately upon the basis that they have no serious chance of winning. As Sir Leon Brittan said, when defending the Representation of the People Bill as Home Secretary in 1985, 'The deposit is a perfectly respectable parliamentary barrier founded in principle. The deposit is founded in principle because the essence of election to Parliament is the contest between people who have serious aspirations to represent a constituency'.[25] However, surely it is essential to draw a distinction between (a) joke candidates who by their own admission are out to make mischief for one or more of the other candidates or who are otherwise seeking publicity for some selfish reason; and (b) serious candidates who may stand no realistic chance of winning but who legitimately seek to draw attention to their views, contribute to political debate and display what level of popular support they happen to possess. The latter have every right to engage in the democratic process of electioneering as candidates and our election law should seek to promote and facilitate that right, not obstruct it.

One of the most important objections to the deposit is that it financially penalises serious minority parties and independents, who are least able to afford to put forward sizeable sums of capital, especially when added to their expenses in financing their election campaign, such as printing election addresses and posters. At the 1992 general election, for example, the Green Party fielded 253 candidates, which necessitated a capital investment of £126,500, and every single candidate lost their deposit by polling below 5 per cent of the local votes, though 170,047 electors across the country voted for the party. Were the Greens not serious candidates therefore? Did they detract from the seriousness of the general election? On virtually any democratic interpretation of their involvement that can be made, they should be regarded as having constructively participated in the election debate by directly putting serious environmental issues across to the voting public (and indirectly, having legitimately put pressure on the main parties to help make the issues they were drawing attention to a higher priority within those parties' policy programmes).

Conversely, defenders of the deposit tend to exaggerate the negative impact of minority or fringe candidates. How many of us can ever remember actually being seriously misled or confused by a candidate such as Screaming Lord Sutch? No doubt many people see some of the fringe parties apart from the Greens, notably the Communist Party and the British National Party, as extremist groups on the Left and Right who should be excluded from the political process altogether. But this may be short-sighted: by obstructing such groups from participation in the electoral process, extremist politics may be fed by a legitimate sense of grievance and be driven in the direction of extra-parliamentary tactics.

Clearly, some form of support for an individual's candidature should apply. Parliamentary candidates have rights, privileges and advantages conferred upon them (such as the right to free postage of election addresses, the right to free use of publicly maintained buildings for public meetings, the right to veto broadcast transmission of material relating to the constituency election and in addition considerable publicity) and an unrestricted exercise

---

[25] HC Deb, 10 December 1984, col 789.

of the freedom to stand for election can therefore be open to abuse, for example by businessmen seeking free advertising for their companies' products. But the way to resolve that problem is not by penalising all candidates who do not belong to the major parties, but by establishing some procedures indicating that the candidate has some measure of political backing.

The requirement of a financial deposit should be abolished and replaced by a new form of requirement involving a candidate being nominated by a much larger prescribed number of local electors nominating him or her. An appropriate number of such nominators would be 200. Each person putting their name to the nomination should be required to sign the paper, and add in a clear, legible form their full name and electoral registration number. The statutory provision should permit the list of nominations to be drawn up at any time within one year prior to the election date, so that proper care and consideration can be given to the matter (and avoid a rush in the six days following the Royal Proclamation). The lists of nominators for each candidate should be displayed in a public place, and published in at least one local newspaper. The fact that a nominator's electoral registration number must be stated would avoid petition-like gatherings of names for frivolous candidates in town centres, since the person approached would need to have time to find out his electoral number and this would ensure a period of serious reflection. On the other hand established parties, whether one of the three major parties or a smaller organisation like the Green Party, would have no difficulty in arranging for a sufficient number of local party members to sign the nomination papers.

Finally, the predictable objections to replacing the financial deposit with such an extended nomination system should be answered. In the Conservative government's White Paper prior to the Representation of the People Act 1985, it was suggested,[26]

'A requirement of this kind would greatly increase the work of the acting returning officer, who would have to check the signatures on each nomination paper against the electoral register in the busy period before nominations close, and it would increase the risk of a nomination being held invalid on purely technical grounds. But the main objection, in the Government's view, is that a candidate's ability to produce signatures is no test of the number of votes he or she will receive in the Election.'

There are three points here to answer therefore. First, it is said this 'would greatly increase the work of the acting returning officer'. To use the word 'greatly' here is a serious exaggeration. It has been calculated that it would take one minute on average to check each signature. In other words, all the nomination lists could be checked within one working day by a competent official, and even if in the planning of resources allowance was made for

[26] *Representation of the People Acts*, Cmnd 9140 (1984) p 21.

an extra working day to deal with exceptional cases where an allegation of impersonation needed to be investigated, the total work involved would still only be two working days for one official, at a total cost of around £200. Secondly, it is asserted that a nomination procedure as proposed 'would increase the risk of a nomination being held invalid on purely technical grounds'. This too is a very weak argument. Good planning by the candidates' organisations would always ensure that there was a small number of signatories in excess of the 200 required, say 225, so that in the unlikely event that one or two of their supporters proving ineligible (for example, not actually being registered on the electoral roll) there would still be the statutory number required. The third objection stated is that, 'a candidate's ability to produce signatures is no test of the number of votes he or she will receive'. This, as the political editor of the *New Statesman* commented at the time, is '. . . the worst argument of all. The point of setting any hurdles is not – or should not be – to block serious minority candidates, but to block frivolous ones.' Certainly persons nominating a candidate would not necessarily be undertaking to vote for him or her personally (though in the majority of cases they will in fact do so). But this misses the whole point of the nomination procedure: what is being suggested is a legal requirement for the judgment of a substantial number of local electors to be expressed on the suitability of the candidate to participate at the election.

This would replace the present insidious barrier existing at present in our electoral law that penalises or blocks serious parties and candidates from participating in the democratic process, whilst still allowing affluent individuals who can afford to lose £500, however frivolous, regardless of whether or not there is any substantial support for his or her nomination.

REFORM ISSUES AFFECTING THE FRANCHISE AND REGISTRATION

The expatriate vote

During the 1980s the Conservative government brought forward legislation granting successive extensions of the franchise to British nationals who were no longer resident in the UK. Some claimed that this had the effect of maximising the Conservative Party vote, on the assumption that the relatively affluent tend to vote Conservative and that persons living abroad tend to be relatively affluent. True or false, the Representation of the People Act 1985 allowed persons to continue voting in the constituency where they were last resident for a period of up to five years' absence. This was then taken much further by the Representation of the People Act 1989, which permitted such voting in UK elections for a period of up to 20 years' absence.

This means that an expatriate living hundreds or thousands of miles away, for the duration of up to a period exceeding a whole generation, carrying memories of British politics in the past and with little or no personal know-ledge of contemporary issues in the constituency where he or she used to live, can influence the election of the government of a country to which he or she is not subject and to whom he or she may be paying no taxes. Indeed many such persons may have left the country specifically to avoid paying taxes here, yet now since 1989 have been rewarded with a vote in the coun-try's affairs. Each parliamentary constituency's registration officer at present compiles a list of overseas electors, to whom letters are sent each year re-minding the voter of the need to make an overseas elector's declaration in order to remain on the register. This declaration confirms the person's Brit-ish citizenship and non-residence, and gives the date of his or her last resi-dence in the UK. The overseas voter can then vote in that constituency in which he last resided at some time within the last 20 years, and may use a proxy for the purpose who may not live in the constituency at all.

This extension of voting rights flouts two traditional principles of the British electoral system, namely that the basis of the parliamentary system is the representation of constituencies, and that the basis of the right to vote is one of residency in a constituency. It was largely for these reasons that the Home Affairs Select Committee of the House of Commons in its Report in 1983 unanimously rejected the introduction of giving all expatriates the right to vote, recommending instead that it be restricted to British citizens working or living within the European Community.[27]

Government and related personnel working overseas, such as members of the armed forces and Embassy officials, have always had the right to vote, however long the absence from home, and special arrangements are made for them. But for other overseas voters, some modification of the law is neces-sary. It is estimated that some three million persons are now eligible as over-seas voters, though in 1992 and 1997 the number of such persons actually wanting to vote was below 40,000.[28] Only a small proportion of expatriates, therefore, appear actually to desire still to be involved in the political affairs of the country they have left behind.

One approach is simply to reduce the period of absence from the constitu-ency down from 20 years, perhaps to five years as in the original 1985 Act conferring the right to vote upon non-resident British citizens. Two better approaches, aimed at citizens working temporarily abroad, would be either (1) to abolish this novel extension of the 1980s altogether but reserve a right to vote to those persons overseas who owned a house in the UK and lived in it for part of the year, or preferably (2) to revert to the five-year period of the 1985 Act but at the same time make the right to vote dependent upon a genuine intention to return to this country. Such an intention is expressed in a person's choice of domicile, which is a legal concept used mainly in family law, and is also of some significance for inland revenue tax purposes.

---

[27] HC [1982–83] 32–1, pp xiv–xix.
[28] 1992 Electoral Statistics (Series EL No 19) p 1; and House of Commons library.

Domicile, therefore, should become a principal factor in a British citizen's eligibility to vote. British citizens abroad should be permitted to vote for only such length of time, up to a maximum of five years, that they declare their domicile to be in the UK and thus retain a firm root in its body of citizenship.

A rolling electoral register?

Within Great Britain there is no required duration for which the citizen must have lived in a constituency in order to be qualified to vote there. A person must simply have been living in the locality on a 'qualifying date' (which is 10 October). In Northern Ireland, however, a requirement for three months' residency applies (and there is a separate qualifying date, 15 September). Residency is established by forms being sent out to the occupier of each household in the UK from the electoral registration officer for each constituency several weeks before the qualifying date.

Persons who are otherwise legally qualified to vote[29] may only be permitted to do so if their name has been accurately entered on the electoral register in the constituency where he or she has been living and wishes to vote. The quality and efficiency with which the electoral register is drawn up, therefore, is crucial to the operation of our electoral system. The legal responsibility for this important administrative task in each constituency is that of electoral registration officers appointed by the local authority. The duties and powers of electoral registration officers are laid down by the Representation of the People Act 1983 which requires them 'to prepare and publish in each year a register of parliamentary electors for each constituency or part of a constituency in the area for which he acts'. The names of people who are resident in the constituency on the statutory qualifying date must be entered on the register, which then becomes operable on the following 16 February for the purposes of any general election held during the next 12 months.

At the 1997 general election, there were 44,204,000 names entered on the electoral register, accounting for 95.2 per cent of the resident adult population in the preceding mid-year.[30] This was an increase of 479,000 electors over the situation in 1992 and represents a considerable improvement over the early 1980s when the House of Commons Home Affairs Committee last inquired into electoral registration and found a discrepancy between eligible and registered voters standing at 9 per cent, rightly described in its report as 'an alarming degree of inexactitude'. Sustained efforts at increasing the numbers and accuracy on the register have been made by registration officers in recent years, including more advertising and greater door-to-door efforts to ensure the return of the annual request sent out to all householders for information on the persons resident in their home.

---

[29] For the qualifications, see R Blackburn, *The Electoral System in Britain*, pp 72 ff.
[30] 1997 Electoral Statistics, ONS.

To sustain and further improve the quality of voter registration in this country, a radical overhaul of its basic system of administration is needed, particularly now that virtually all electoral registration offices are installed with computers. Earlier administrative practices connected with the laborious manual paperwork involved have made the present annual method of voter registration an anachronism. Today a citizen's right to vote should be founded not upon an arbitrary annual anniversary as at present, but upon the date on which he or she files a claim of eligibility to vote in a particular constituency. In other words, electoral registration should become a 'rolling' exercise, being constantly updated, with the annual issue and return of forms to householders being just one method of verification and accuracy of the register. Such a proposal was endorsed by Labour policy documents in 1993, both in *A New Agenda for Democracy: Labour's Proposals for Constitutional Reform* and in the Report of the Working Party on Electoral Systems chaired by Lord Plant.[31]

Legislation will be needed to implement this new system of voter registration which could usefully adopt some of the drafting contained in the Representation of the People (Amendment) Bill which was presented to Parliament by Harry Barnes in 1993.[32] Statutory provisions should create the requirement for a rolling register and then proceed to modify the registration officers' duty so that he or she is to take all reasonable steps to ensure that the rolling register is accurate at all times. Persons moving into a new constituency should be placed under a legal requirement to notify the registration officer within three weeks of taking up residence there. Provision should also be made for voters left off the register by accident. It very often happens at present that voters do not realise that their name is missing from the electoral register until the general election is called and they do not receive a official poll card telling them where to vote. Under a rolling register system, provision should be made so that such persons can in fact vote assuming they are otherwise legally qualified to do so at the time the general election is called. The new legislation should require returning officers to publish the electoral register, and send out the official poll cards to all voters, within two days of the dissolution of Parliament, and local advertising and notices in the national and local press should then inform the public that all qualified persons failing to appear on the register or receive poll cards should apply to their registration office immediately to be entered on the electoral roll and be permitted to vote.

Co-ordination and supervision of the new system of voter registration will be desirable, and would best be entrusted to a new national agency set up for this and other electoral purposes, an Electoral Commission as envisaged and proposed below.

---

[31] Respectively, p 39; Labour Party, *Report of the Working Party on Electoral Systems* (Third Report, 1993) pp 48–49.

[32] HC [1992–93] 17, debated HC Deb, 12 February 1993, col 1207.

An end to multiple registration?

It is fundamental that each voter should only have one vote at a general election. However, the situation regularly arises today that a voter is treated as being 'resident' in more than one parliamentary constituency, and therefore has his or her name entered more than once on the electoral register. To cover such situations s 1 of the Representation of the People Act 1983 precludes double voting by providing that, 'A person is not entitled to vote as an elector . . . in more than one constituency.'

It was the decision in the case of *Fox v Stirk and Bristol Electoral Registration Officer* which confirmed that persons could be treated as being resident in two places for voting purposes. On the facts of that particular case, the court held that university students were eligible for registration and voting both in the constituency where they lived during university term-time and in the constituency where their parents lived and they returned during the university vacation. Lord Denning, then Master of the Rolls, decided that, 'A person may properly be said to be "resident" in a place when his stay there has a considerable degree of permanence'. He then went on to lay down three general principles on the meaning of 'residence' under the Representation of the People Acts, as follows:[33]

'The first principle is that a man can have two residences. He can have a flat in London and a house in the country. He is resident in both. The second principle is that temporary presence at an address does not make a man resident there. A guest who comes for the weekend is not resident. The third principle is that temporary absence does not deprive a person of his residence.'

Currently, this means that a person 'resident' in more than one constituency has a choice of where to vote. Dual or multiple registration – and thereby a choice of constituency at general elections – applies most commonly to our more affluent citizens by virtue of their ownership of two or more houses. Such persons may travel to (or apply for a postal vote at) the constituency rather than vote in the one where they spend most of their time. Furthermore, persons registered in two or more constituencies may prefer to cast their vote in the constituency which is more marginal and therefore where their vote is more likely to prove of political impact to the result.

It would be preferable to remove this element of electoral chicanery which has systematically favoured the better-off. The principal solution required is that persons who live at two locations or who own properties in different constituencies should be required to nominate a 'main residence' for voting purposes. This process of nomination might be guided by a set of criteria, laid down either in the Representation of the People Act or in some code of practice drawn up under its authority, and would prove no more administratively

---

[33] *Fox v Stirk and Bristol Electoral Registration Officer* [1970] 2 QB 463 at p 475.

difficult to enforce than that which is required at present for capital gains tax purposes. Our electoral law would thereby be amended so that every elector is treated, for the purposes of the right to vote at parliamentary elections, as resident at his main residence only.

OPTIONS FOR A UK ELECTORAL COMMISSION

The largest issue of reform facing electoral administration generally is that of an Electoral Commission. Since the 1980s there has been a growing body of support for the idea of a single Commission, independent of government, to whom would be given a range of responsibilities with respect to electoral affairs. Such commissions operate successfully in many of the major western democracies: indeed, they are widely perceived in those countries as being essential bulwarks of the democratic process. The Federal Election Commission in the USA is the best known example of such a body, and as British electioneering practices and legal regulation of political parties' finances moves closer towards those that apply in the USA, the case for some such similar body will become even stronger.[34]

The Labour Party gave its clear endorsement to the principle of an Electoral Commission in its 1993 policy report, *A New Agenda for Democracy: Labour's Proposals for Constitutional Reform*. Stating that it 'fully supported' an independent Electoral Commission, it envisaged that it would be 'directly and solely responsible for all aspects of electoral administration and for ensuring freedom and fairness in all aspects of our electoral system.' Similarly, the Plant Report 1993 also advocated the desirability of such a body, arguing that, 'The case for such an electoral commission is that it would provide continuity, a permanent expertise on electoral matters, and ensure that good practice was being followed throughout the country by electoral registration officers and returning officers.'[35]

The desirability of an Electoral Commission is closely associated with other reforms of electoral law and political finance that will need or would greatly benefit from the support of an independent electoral agency. In other words, as things stand an Electoral Commission is desirable, if not actually essential, and could perform a number of valuable functions which already exist (such as boundary review) or might help streamline the national supervision of electoral administration (such as the issue of codes of practice or appointment of returning officers). However, if the case for other reforms is accepted, then new functions arise, making an Electoral Commission virtually essential. These reforms include, for example, the statutory regulation of political finance, including accounting, prohibited donations, expenditure

---

[34] See D Butler, King-Hall Paper No 5, *The Case for an Electoral Commission*, 1998.
[35] At p 39.

limits and funding; and measures to improve the quality of political information to electors, including further regulation of media coverage, opinion polls, political advertising, election broadcasts.

The functions of the Electoral Commission might become, therefore:

(1) *Constituency review* The Commission might replace and unify the existing four Boundary Commissions, operating under newly revised rules,[36] and have a duty to keep the boundaries and numbers of constituencies under review for the purposes of elections to the House of Commons, any reformed House of Lords, the European Parliament, the Scottish Parliament, Welsh Assembly and local authorities.

(2) *Electoral officials* The Commission might have a duty to supervise and keep under review electoral administration generally, including responsibilities to appoint returning officers and prepare codes of practice for the conduct of electoral registration and work of returning officers.

(3) *Political campaigning* The Commission might have the duty to keep under continuous review developments in the fields of political campaigning and electioneering, including matters relating to the media (including arrangements for party political broadcasts) and party propaganda (including advertisements).

(4) *Official inquiries and reports* The Commission might serve as an expert advisory body for government ministers and parliamentary committees, undertaking inquiries into specific problems that arise and offering policy reform advice as requested enabling our election law and administration to keep apace with new electoral, political and technological developments.

(5) *Complaints of electoral malpractice* The Commission might have the powers to investigate allegations of electoral malpractice, to assist persons in making complaints, and to institute legal proceedings in its own name for alleged breaches of election law. It could also have a limited adjudicatory role in the enforcement of a range of certain matters of electoral law and administration including disputes relating to names and descriptions on ballot papers.

(6) *Regulation of political parties* The Commission might be charged with responsibility for the registration of political parties, for the purposes of parties nominated at elections, for receiving accounts on income and expenditure (both annually and in relation to election campaigns where a maximum expenditure limit applies), and for administering new funding arrangements by reference to the legislation establishing the scheme.

---

[36] For an account of the rules for redistribution of seats and suggestions on how they might be revised, see R Blackburn, *The Electoral System in Britain*, pp 142–157.

(7) *Referendum campaigns* With referendums being held on a more regular basis, the Commission might be given the duty to supervise arrangements concerning the policy and question to be put to the electorate, special matters relating to political campaigning on the particular issue in question, and administrative arrangements for the count.

(8) *Public information* The Commission could perform a valuable role in promoting information, education and greater public awareness generally about elections. It could become the official depository of electoral statistics, act as a clearing house for all official electoral literature, and initiate learning and research programmes on electoral and related subjects.

Once instituted, the work of the Electoral Commission could be phased in. An initial range of responsibilities could be given to it, with later functions emerging in due course, such as acting in an 'amicus curiae' role before the Election Court and performing a limited adjudicatory role in such matters as misleading names or party descriptions on candidature nomination papers.

How might the membership of this important new public body be constructed? The determining factors in this will be (1) the volume of responsibilities it is required to perform, and (2) the level of resources the government and Parliament is prepared to commit to the project. The initial work involved might be deemed sufficiently limited to simply require a single Commissioner, backed by a high-calibre team of officials. Ideally in the long term, however, particularly if the full range of functions identified above is adopted, the organisation might comprise several Commissioners, each receiving salaries and office and administrative facilities appropriate to the full or part-time performance of their responsibilities. The organisation would benefit from having not only a national headquarters but also a number of regional and local offices. Commissioners could be nominated by the Prime Minister or Home Secretary, and approved by Parliament. They should be given some limited security of tenure, to protect their impartiality and independence from political interference, in the form of fixed five-year appointments. These fixed appointments could be renewable for a second term, and otherwise the Commission could only leave office by way of removal for misconduct or incapacity or else by resignation or attaining a retirement age of 65 years. The Speaker of the House of Commons should not be the ex officio Chairman of the Electoral Commission, in the same way as she is at present in the case of the Boundary Commissions. Indeed, the disadvantages of the Speaker continuing as chairman in the work of constituency review has already come to outweigh any purported advantages. The chairman of the new Electoral Commission should simply be appointed by the Commission itself from amongst its members.

As with the two UK members of the European Commission at present appointed by the Prime Minister, a convention should arise that the Leader of the Opposition might nominate one of every two persons invited to serve. This analogy with the European Commission is a worthwhile one in one further respect also. For in the same way that for example Roy Jenkins and Leon Brittan, both former Home Secretaries for Labour and Conservatives respectively, gave up their work as MPs to serve as members of the European Commission, so experience of political life in the composition of the Electoral Commission should certainly not be a bar to persons appointed, in the way that it is at present in the selection of persons to serve on the Boundary Commissions. To the contrary, knowledge and experience of political affairs would be an asset on the Commission, although of course there must be a prohibition that Commissioners could not at the same time be members of or candidates for election to Parliament, the European Parliament or local authorities.

To facilitate the political independence of the Commission, members should be in charge of their own budget and permitted to recruit their own staff. A long-running complaint about the Boundary Commissions' work in the past has been that they have been insufficiently independent from the Home Office, and that the administrative process of the Commissions are too influenced by informal direction from the government. In the view of some critics, this is facilitated precisely because of the interchange of administrative staff between the Home Office and the Boundary Commissions. Clearly the Home Secretary at present is in a somewhat ambivalent position within the House of Commons in that it falls to him to present the Commissions' recommendations to the House, and although the work is not presented as that of his department, he or she generally explains and defends their conclusions. An important incidental detail in promoting the independence of the Electoral Commission's work from government, and in promoting the Commission as an independent impartial agency established for the purpose of making recommendations to the House of Commons, will be to strengthen existing parliamentary scrutiny procedures with respect to changes in constituency boundaries and draft electoral law reform emanating from the work of the Electoral Commission.

The field of public administration and political activity covered by election law is vast and will shortly become even more heavily regulated. New legislation will be brought forward by the government to put into effect recommendations of the Neill Committee on the funding of political parties. The Registration of Political Parties Bill is already set to help resolve the serious problems caused by mischievous candidates adopting misleading party descriptions on ballot papers in the constituencies where they seek to stand. The range of election law and administration topics selected in this memorandum have concentrated on those which carry the widest level of support. For the future, there are important policy matters to be addressed which the new Labour government and the Home Affairs Committee may wish to start considering, even if legislation on the matter is unlikely to be adopted in present circumstances. They concern, for example, statutory controls over the publication of public opinion polls during the period of the election campaign (limited, perhaps, to a specified number of days before polling), and statutory guidelines on the content and factual accuracy of political advertisements.

The review of our election law and administration needs to be a continuous, ongoing exercise, not least because of the now rapidly changing social and technological environment in which elections and electioneering are conducted. Whilst the current home office inquiry being conducted by the Home Office Minister George Howarth is welcome, one-off inquiries every four or five years are no longer any substitute for what is now required: that is, an independent permanent Electoral Commission whose most valuable work will be to monitor new developments affecting elections and electioneering as they happen, to offer expert advice as and when it is asked for or needed, to issue authoritative administrative regulations and codes of practice for parties and election administrators, and to bring forward proposals for the government and Parliament on improvements in our election law, free from any taint of bias or favour as between the political parties.

Further reading

Robert Blackburn, *The Electoral System in Britain* (London: Macmillan, 1995)

Labour Party, *Report of the Working Party on Electoral Systems* (The Plant Report) (Third Report, 1993), section 2

House of Commons Home Affairs Committee, *Electoral Law and Administration*, HC [1997–98] 768

Richard Rawlings, *Law and the Electoral Process* (London: Sweet & Maxwell, 1988)

Hansard Society Commission on Election Campaigns, *Agenda for Change* (London: Hansard Society, 1991)

David Butler, King-Hall Paper No 5: *The Case for an Electoral Commission* (London: Hansard Society, 1998)

CHAPTER 5

HOUSE OF COMMONS PROCEDURES

Michael Ryle (formerly Clerk of Committees, House of Commons)

A Labour government with a majority over all parties of 179; 418 Labour members in the House of Commons; some 330 backbenchers (including PPSs) on the government side; 242 members who are new to Parliament; 120 women members (double the number before the election) – the very statistics create a new momentum. After the general election of 1 May 1997, there have been and will continue to be many changes in British politics, and the way the House of Commons conducts its business will be no exception.

A massive government majority, with a corresponding increase in the number of backbenchers on the government side and a reduction in the numbers of opposition backbenchers, creates many challenges for the government and opposition parties alike, and not least in the way the two sides behave in the House of Commons. The practices and procedures of the House have to be reconsidered, particularly in respect of the arrangement of business and the use and composition of committees.

Two other factors will also stimulate change: the significant increase in the strength of the Liberal Democrats as the third party in the Commons, and the fact that so many of the backbench members are new to Parliament. Indeed, on the government side, quite a number of these new members had stood for Parliament with no expectation of winning and therefore, in many cases, came with different backgrounds and experience compared with candidates who had more realistic political ambitions. These new members – especially, perhaps, the women – arrived with new ideas of the functions of Parliament and a different understanding of the role that MPs have to play. They brought a breath of fresh air to Westminster.

This then is the challenge. In this chapter I examine some of the changes that have been proposed in the past and, against this background, the reforms of the House of Commons to which the new Labour government is committed.

THE PRESSURES FOR REFORM

One man's reform is another man's phobia, and 'reform of the House of Commons' has meant different things to different people. For some (myself included) it has primarily meant improvements in the procedures and methods for scrutinising legislation and calling ministers to account for their policies and actions, and these are the areas of reform on which this chapter concentrates. Others, however, have been more concerned with the electoral processes and the qualifications and qualities of MPs. For others the conditions of work of MPs are important. And some people wish to modernise the image of Parliament by abolishing what they see as outmoded ceremonies and rituals and by symbolic changes (such as converting the rifle range into a crèche – whether the children would be happy in a somewhat remote and gloomy basement is another question).

All these themes overlap, and are sometimes complementary and sometimes in conflict. But, as we shall see, these various strands of thinking have come together to form a strong, growing and now voracious demand for reform of the House of Commons.

Parliamentary reform is no new fad. Ever since the House of Commons became established over 700 years ago, it has changed and continues to change. Over the past 50 years, there have been many significant advances in the way the House conducts its business and in particular in the ability of the Commons to fulfil its central scrutiny functions. These include the establishment of opposition days, the increasing willingness of backbench members to take an independent line and to dissent in the division lobbies, the expansion and strengthening of the committee systems, the creation of the departmental select committees to review policies, and the opening up of Parliament to the public, especially through the televising of its proceedings.

These developments have greatly strengthened the influence of the House and its members over the government, made Parliament much more interesting and significant to the ordinary citizen, and thus made the House of Commons more effective than it has been at any previous time in this century.[1]

In view of these real advances, it may seem surprising that Parliament – particularly the House of Commons and its members – now appears to be held in such low public esteem. This is partly because of widespread public misconception of the role of Parliament, which mistakenly regards the House as a law-making and decision-taking body and therefore to be blamed for the failures of the government. The poor repute of Parliament has also been irresponsibly fuelled by its constant denigration by the media, together with an almost complete failure by the press today to report its proceedings properly and constant harking on allegations of 'sleaze'. However well-justified

---

[1] I set out this argument more fully in Michael Ryle, 'The Changing Commons', *Parliamentary Affairs* (1994) Vol 47, No 4, pp 647–668.

in some cases, this does nothing to encourage people to think positively about the achievement of Parliament.

Nevertheless it must be accepted that an underlying cause of the fall in the public standing of the House of Commons is because the welcome increase in public awareness of Parliament – its greater newsworthiness – has also highlighted serious weaknesses in the ways the House conducts its business. To this extent the low esteem of Parliament is justified and has stimulated demand – by many members themselves as much as by the wider public – for reform of the House of Commons.

VARIOUS PROPOSALS FOR REFORM

The nature of proposed reforms of the House of Commons has changed significantly in the last two decades. Pressure for procedural reform, which could be implemented by the House itself, was the dominant theme in the 1960s, and was clearly articulated by a number of academic critics, led by Bernard Crick in his seminal book, *Reform of Parliament* (1964) and by the Study of Parliament Group. This movement reached its zenith with the appointment of departmental Select Committees in 1979.

Despite this success, disillusion began to set in about the value of internal procedural changes and the case for procedural reform waned in favour of arguments for wider constitutional changes. Again the advocates of this approach came mainly from the academic world. However, when it became clear that little progress was likely on this front under a Conservative government, attention turned back to more traditional procedural reform.

In the last five years, a number of studies have argued for specific changes in the way the House conducts its business, particularly for reform of the legislative process and for improvements in the support services provided for members. As these studies have provided the springboard for the actual reforms now being advanced by the new Labour government, it is worth summarising their main conclusions and recommendations.

Hansard Society Commission on the legislative process and other external studies

Significant progress has been made since 1979 in strengthening the oversight role of Parliament through the select committee system, but, until recently, the central legislative function of Parliament had been largely ignored. Despite several attempts over the years by the Procedure Committee – particularly by advocating more use of Special Standing Committees and limited timetabling of proceedings on Bills – surprisingly few changes of any importance have been made in public Bill procedures since 1945. In 1991, therefore, the Hansard

Society decided to appoint a Commission on the Legislative Process (chaired by Lord Rippon), which published its report, *Making the Law*, in 1993.[2]

The Report was lengthy and detailed, and based on evidence published with the Report. The Commission concentrated on looking at legislation from the point of view of users and outside experience, not just from a parliamentary perspective. It also looked at the legislative process as a whole and emphasised how all the stages must be considered together.

The Commission's conclusions start with the need for much more systematic consultation on proposed legislation, including the publication of more Bills in draft, and less hasty drafting to secure the best possible preparation of Bills before their introduction to Parliament.

The Commission's findings on the scrutiny of Bills and procedures in the Commons included:

(1) the need for the House to play a more positive role in pre-legislative scrutiny of proposed legislation;
(2) the need for more effective techniques for detailed examination of Bills in committee, including hearing of evidence;
(3) the need for committees on Bills to pay more attention to the practicalities of legislation as well as the policy;
(4) the undesirability of rushed legislation; and
(5) the desirability of systematic examination by the departmental or other Select Committees of how Acts have worked in practice.

The Commission was particularly critical of the way the House fails to examine delegated legislation effectively. It made detailed recommendations to remedy all these matters.

The Commission was also concerned to ensure ready public access to statute law, and urged the speedy completion of a Statute Law Database, cheaper publication of legislative documents and more use of explanatory material.

The effective preparation, drafting and parliamentary scrutiny of legislation depends entirely on proper planning of the legislative programme and on effective timetabling of debates on Bills in the Commons. Without adequate time being made available, consultation on Bills may be curtailed, drafting may be too hurried and Bills may not receive adequate examination in the two Houses of Parliament. And without assurance that their Bills would eventually be approved without unreasonable delay, governments would be very reluctant to agree to improved scrutiny procedures – particularly the hearing of evidence – because of the opportunities these would provide for filibustering.

The Commission therefore recommended that the government should move towards the adoption of a two-year legislative programme for major Bills so that the consultation and drafting processes could begin earlier. It also

---

[2] I declare an interest as a member of, and Secretary to, the Commission.

recommended that, if a Bill requires more time in Parliament and is not urgent, it should be possible to carry that Bill over to a second session to complete its consideration.

The Commission also proposed that the House should adopt systematic timetabling of all legislation at all stages. To implement this it suggested that, instead of using government imposed guillotines, a Legislative Steering Committee, comprising representatives of all parties and backbenchers and chaired by the Speaker, should be appointed to agree the legislative calendar for the main Bills of each session, and that, within the total times so allotted, detailed timetables should be drawn up for all Bills by a Business Committee set up for each Bill.

Another advocate of reform was Greg Power, the Political and Parliamentary Officer of Charter 88, in the paper he wrote for that body in 1996 entitled *Reinventing Westminster: The MPs role and reform of the House of Commons*. He believed that the House of Commons fails to hold the executive to account because members are not able to have much influence on the policy process or the scrutiny of ministers; the majority of members are thus left without a meaningful role in Parliament. He concentrated on proposals designed to provide a new role for MPs, including enlarging the membership of departmental Select Committees so that they involve every backbench MP. The enlarged committees would combine the roles of the present Select Committees and Standing Committees. Each committee would have over 30 members, so they would work through sub-committees for much of their business.

Power proposed that all Bills should be committed to Special Standing Committees, whose members should be drawn from those on the new departmental committees, to hear evidence before voting on amendments and the clauses of the Bill. He also advocated the timetabling of all Bills in the Commons and the ability to carry over Bills from one parliamentary session to the next. Finally, all MPs should be given a broad-based job description, including guidance on standards and conduct.

Other outside authorities, particularly academic members of the Study of Parliament Group, have drawn attention to the need for reforms in other areas, including the facilities available to members, the need for improved research and information services, the growing problem of the accountability of government agencies and the role of Parliament in relation to European legislation and developments in the European Union.

The Procedure Committee

Turning to reform proposals emanating from the House itself, over the years the House of Commons Procedure Committee has worked indefatigably, especially under the chairmanship for the last 14 years of Sir Peter Emery, to improve parliamentary processes and procedures in ways that would command support from all parts of the House. Sometimes it has succeeded, especially when changes were broadly agreed or on minor matters. On more important matters it has often taken the initiative, but here its success rate has been lower; on a number of important questions it took a lead ahead of both the government and the Opposition, for example in its frequent advocacy of greater use of Special Standing Committees and for new procedures for timetabling controversial Bills.

However, even when its recommendations have not been accepted, the Committee has prepared a valuable menu for procedural reform which could be taken up and reconsidered by any new government. It is therefore interesting to look at the main recommendations made by the Committee in the last Parliament that were not implemented by the government of the day. These were handily summarised in the Fourth Report of the Committee at the end of the 1996–97 session.

The Committee was particularly disappointed that its recommendations on three matters had not been accepted: reform of budgetary procedures; Prime Minister's Questions; and the scrutiny of delegated legislation. There is not the space here to set out the detailed recommendations of the Procedure Committee on all these matters but they should certainly be carefully reconsidered by another committee in the new Parliament. And another major subject, on which the Committee reported at the end of the last Parliament, was that of how the House could best consider and debate European Union legislation and other documents which have been submitted to the Council of Ministers and other important European policy proposals. This still awaits a full debate.

ATTITUDES OF THE POLITICAL PARTIES AND THEIR PROPOSALS FOR REFORM BEFORE THE GENERAL ELECTION

The Conservative Party

The Conservative government had, during a long period in power, agreed to a number of important changes in the practices and procedures of the House of Commons. The creation of the departmental select committees in 1979 was the most important change in this century in the way the House performs its functions. The research and information services have been steadily expanded and improved. Members' office allowances have been increased (sometimes against the advice of the government) so enabling members to employ more research assistants. A start has been made in applying computerised information technology to the work of members and the departments of the House, and *Hansard* and other parliamentary publications are now available on the Internet. More information about the work of the House has been published for both members and the public, and educational services for schools have been further developed.

On the procedural side, significant changes were agreed following the report of the Jopling Committee on the sitting arrangements of the House. The Northern Ireland Affairs Committee was added to the list of departmental Select Committees. The role of the Scottish Grand Committee was expanded to include questions to Scottish ministers, ministerial statements, debates on delegated legislation, adjournment debates and short debates; the Committee could sit in Scotland. Similar powers and functions were given to the Welsh Grand Committee and to a newly created Northern Ireland Grand Committee.

Another reform introduced by the Conservative government was some expansion of the opportunities to debate European legislation in committees and improvements in the procedures of these committees, including questions to ministers before the documents are debated.

Unfortunately no equivalent progress was made in the procedures for scrutiny of delegated legislation, but a way ahead may be indicated by the successful application of procedures for examination of deregulation orders under the Deregulation and Contracting Out Act 1994, which have enabled members to secure significant amendments to the proposed orders and, on at least one occasion, the negation of a draft order.[3] In my view, the procedures developed for scrutiny of deregulation orders could also be effectively applied to other major instruments of delegated legislation.[4]

The Conservative government committed itself to two important reforms designed to make statute law more intelligible to the user. The first was the creation of a Statute Law Database so that the statute book could readily be consulted on computer, although regrettably this project has been long delayed.[5] The second was a remarkable undertaking to rewrite the entire body of direct tax law (at present some 6,000 pages) in plain English and in a radically clearer and more user-friendly form. Procedures for the parliamentary scrutiny of this massive exercise were devised by a working party of the Tax Law Review Committee, endorsed by the Procedure Committee and accepted by the government.

The practices and procedure of the Commons were highly germane to the reports of two distinguished judges – Sir Richard Scott and Lord Nolan – appointed, in the final years of the Conservative government, to inquire into serious allegations regarding the conduct of ministers or MPs in the course of their parliamentary duties and into the wider issues thrown up by such allegations. The stories are all too familiar and need not be rehearsed again

---

[3] Twelfth Report of the Deregulation Committee, Session 1996–97 (HC 387), relating to the Proposal for the Deregulation (Civil Aviation Act 1982) Order 1997.

[4] See Michael Ryle, 'The Deregulation and Contracting Out Bill 1994 – A Blueprint for Reform of the Legislative Process?', *Statute Law Review* (1994) Vol 15, No 3, pp 170–181.

[5] For details of the proposal, see the report of the Hansard Society Commission, *Making the Law* (1993) paras 441–5 and 454–6.

here, but certain findings will have to be carefully considered by the Labour government.

Although both inquiries were ordered on the direct authority of the Prime Minister – and it remains to John Major's credit that he was prepared to grasp the nettle to this extent – the government's responses (and that of Conservative MPs) to the two Reports were markedly different.

The government's response to the Scott Report, on the sale of arms to Iraq and related issues, was, as far as possible, to avoid accepting that ministers had done anything wrong (in defiance of Sir Richard's conclusions) or that any significant changes were needed in the procedures for securing the accountability of ministers to Parliament. On the latter aspect, the Public Services Committee of the House, in its Second Report of Session 1995–96 on Ministerial Accountability and Responsibility, made specific recommendations on the giving or withholding by ministers and civil servants of information for members, the powers and procedures of select committees, and other matters designed to make the House more effective in calling ministers to account. The Committee also recommended that the House should pass a resolution on accountability. Just before Parliament was dissolved, such a resolution was agreed to on a government motion, but that was about as far as it was prepared to go.

The government's response to the Nolan Report was more positive. First of all, following a detailed review by a Select Committee of the Nolan Committee's recommendations, it agreed to a number of important changes, including the adoption of a code of conduct, new rules on the acceptance of payments for lobbying and other parliamentary activities and on employment agreements, the appointment of the Parliamentary Commissioner for Standards and the setting up of the new Committee on Standards and Privileges. Tighter rules on registration of interests were accepted and, against the advice of ministers and despite considerable opposition from many Conservative backbenchers in the division lobbies, the rules now require disclosure, in many circumstances, of the actual remuneration received by members from outside sources.

Summing up the Conservative achievements and approach, it will be seen that, during its long period in power, the last government did bring about a number of major reforms of House of Commons procedure. However, its attitude in recent years was generally negative, particularly on the legislative processes, despite regular prodding by the Procedure Committee. It is not surprising that the more wide-ranging and radical recommendations of the Hansard Society Commission were almost totally ignored, although, towards the end of the 1996–97 Parliament, the government did agree to certain changes recommended by the Commission: the preparation of the legislative programme for each session would be completed slightly earlier, more Bills were to be first published in draft form and the Queen's Speech would include provisional plans for legislation in the session after the one being opened.

It may be that the extended arguments over the Jopling reforms of business management and sitting hours[6] blunted ministers' interest in further changes, or it may be that at the end of a long period of office, with a strong radical policy content, interest in the mechanics of procedure inevitably waned. However, for reformers, this was particularly disappointing.

Public concern about Parliament has been deep and widespread and a change of heart and of attitudes is required on the part of ministers, the Opposition and of Parliament itself if things are to be put right. The Conservative Party, in its last years in power, gave no indication of any such change. Its manifesto for the general election was largely silent on further reform of Parliament. Anxious reformers had to look elsewhere.

The Labour Party

The Labour Party was, for a long time, surprisingly uncommitted to reform of the practices and procedures of the House, although a number of its back-benchers had been outspoken advocates of change. Its general approach was reformist, but there was little attention to specifics or practicalities. Too often would-be reformers in the Labour Party would speak of the need to strengthen the legislature against the executive, or to improve the ways Parliament could call ministers to account, or call for the modernisation of the House of Commons without giving any indication of how these desirable aims should be achieved. Parliamentary reform requires explicit changes in procedures and in the ways the House operates, and up till the election the Labour Party showed little sign that it had thought about these difficult questions.

The main exception was contained in a speech, entitled *New Politics, New Parliament*, given by Ann Taylor (then the Shadow Leader of the House of Commons) to a Charter 88 seminar on 14 May 1996. Elaborating earlier outline proposals, including those published by a party commission on constitutional reform, and starting from the propositions that Parliament no longer held ministers properly to account and that legislation was not given the scrutiny it requires, she indicated the main lines of the reforms she believed were needed.

These included reform of Question Time, including the adoption of a half-hour period each week for Prime Minister's Questions. On legislation, her thinking was on much the same lines as that of the Hansard Society Commission and included, as a range of options, more pre-legislation consultation and parliamentary scrutiny, publication of draft Bills, First Reading Committees to take evidence on some Bills, and more use of Second Reading Committees and of Special Standing Committees. She also favoured the carry-over of some Bills into a second session. To achieve essential

---

[6] See the Sittings of the House Select Committee Report HC [1991–92] 20, Parts I–IV.

improvements in the scrutiny of delegated legislation, she favoured extended opportunities for debate in Standing Committees along the lines of the procedures now employed for European documents. She referred to the need for more audit of existing legislation but did not say how this should be done. On one matter which is key to improved legislative scrutiny – timetabling or programming – Ann Taylor had, at that stage, no proposals for replacing the old guillotine procedures.

Turning to accountability, Ann Taylor made specific proposals for strengthening the role and standing of Select Committees: extra opportunities for debating their reports; requiring certain public appointments to be subject to ratification by the appropriate committee; and requiring every agency and national quango to report annually to the relevant committee. Accountability would also be better enforced if Parliament was not in recess during so much of the summer, and she set out a number of possibilities – without committing the party to any one – for revising the parliamentary year to make better use of the time available.

Finally, to redress the imbalance of support between the government and the Opposition and hence strengthen the Opposition in its constitutional role as an alternative party of government, Ann Taylor also proposed that a limited number of civil servants should be seconded for up to two years at a time to the offices of senior opposition frontbenchers.

It is worth noting that Ann Taylor made at this time, before the general election, no proposals on a number of important matters. As well as legislative timetabling, these included scrutiny or control of taxation and expenditure, the Commons handling of European Union legislation, working facilities for members and staff, the application of information technology, the pay and allowances of members, and the whole wide issue of the access of the public to Parliament including easier and cheaper access to information about business before the House.

General election manifestos are generally – probably wisely – not over-specific on the details of the party's proposals, and as far as reform of the practices and procedures of the Commons was concerned, the Labour manifesto for the 1997 election was no exception. It added little to the outline of reforms set out by Ann Taylor, except to commit a Labour government to overhauling the process for scrutinising European legislation, but it did confirm that a special committee would be established to review and modernise Commons procedures.

The Liberal Democrat Party

The Liberal Democrats have long advocated a broad package of constitutional reform, including reform of the House of Commons.[7] In 1996,

---

[7] See particularly, *Here We Stand* (1993).

however, the party went much further than any of the other parties and published many detailed and specific proposals for Commons reform in a Policy Paper, *A Parliament for the People*, which was adopted at the party conference that year.[8] The paper covered nearly all aspects of the practices, procedures and workings of the House of Commons. Its conclusions and recommendations were specific and, it was claimed, workable; they might well be acceptable to most members of all parties in the House, and could be adopted without the need to wait for wider constitutional change.

The paper described certain broad purposes, derived from traditional liberal themes – to open up government, to reduce secrecy and to give the people better access to Parliament. The proposals were designed to enable the public to make a direct contribution, in the House of Commons itself, to policy-making, legislation and scrutiny of the government, and they heeded the interests of minorities and individuals. It would be essential to enable Members to make the best use of their time to deal with increasingly voluminous and complex business; and this would require much more use of committees, more systematic organisation and programming of business, and the provision of adequate staff and technical resources for members.

The paper contained over 70 recommendations. On legislation, the Liberal Democrats followed closely the findings and proposals of the Hansard Society Commission, recommending reforms designed to achieve more and better pre-legislative consultation, preparation and drafting; improved scrutiny in Parliament requiring particularly the hearing of evidence on how Bills would or should work; timetabling by an all-party body of all legislation at all stages in the Commons; and systematic post-legislative review of all legislation to see how well the Acts have worked.

The Liberal Democrats are committed to constitutional changes and the paper recommended that particularly careful scrutiny should be given to constitutional Bills, with prior examination in many cases by a pre-legislative committee. The main issues of principle in such legislation should continue to be debated in committee of the whole House, but the more detailed clauses should be sent to smaller committees, with powers to hear evidence on how the Bill would work.

The Liberal Democrats would do away with annual parliamentary sessions, which would enable the adoption of two-year legislative programmes for long or complex Bills, so allowing more time for consultation, drafting and more stringent parliamentary scrutiny.

The paper supported the case for specific reforms of the ways in which secondary legislation is conducted, including systematic and monitored consultation on major items, as is now done for deregulation orders; improved arrangements for debates on statutory instruments which the Opposition parties or backbenchers wish to debate; the hearing of evidence on important or

---

[8] Again I declare an interest, as I was the Chair of the Working Group which prepared this Policy Paper.

controversial delegated legislation; and the application, to the more important statutory instruments, of the procedures for parliamentary scrutiny that
are now used for deregulation orders.

The Liberal Democrats were concerned to enhance and protect the rights
of backbenchers in initiating legislation. They would again apply timetabling
to ensure that, provided there had been adequate discussion, votes would be
allowed on all stages of Private Members' Bills, so preventing minorities from
frustrating the wishes of the majority by delaying tactics. There would also be
opportunities for the House to debate Bills prepared by Select Committees
and for backbenchers to introduce Bills initiated by citizens' petitions.

Finally, on legislation, the Liberal Democrats would seek to enable the House
to examine legislation proposed by the European Commission before it is
presented to the Council of Ministers, and would generally improve arrangements for parliamentary debate of European Union policies and proposals.[9]

Under the heading of 'Money Matters', the Liberal Democrat Policy
Paper made some radical proposals about the financial business of the House.
It recommended:

(1) a more even spread of financial business through the year;

(2) the introduction of a Tax Management Bill to permit more thorough
     scrutiny of complex fiscal legislation;

(3) consideration, on the Budget, of the balance between expenditure and
     taxation, concluding with votes on the levels of government borrowing
     and taxation and on the planned totals of all government expenditure;

(4) following reviews by departmental Select Committees, further short
     debates and votes on the planned total expenditure on each of the
     separate major services (with amendments being permitted to transfer
     money from one service to another, so enabling the House to consider
     and vote on expenditure options within the fixed total);

(5) requiring departmental Select Committees to report annually on the
     details of departments' spending programmes and particularly on the
     government's plans for major additional expenditure;

(6) specific sanction to be sought in the annual Appropriation Bill for
     major capital and development projects, with debates and votes on
     items selected by the Opposition parties and backbenchers;

(7) an increase in the number of Estimates days;

(8) an annual debate to inform the public how their money is being spent;

(9) placing public expenditure by all quangos and government agencies
     under the jurisdiction of the National Audit Office and the Public
     Accounts Committee; and

(10) repealing the old rules that can prevent members (other than minis-
     ters) from moving amendments to increase expenditure or taxation.

[9] See also Liberal Democrat Policy Paper, *Meeting the European Challenge* (1996).

Liberal Democrats are concerned to improve scrutiny of the executive in other ways. Their Policy Paper included some radical proposals to strengthen the Commons' ability to call ministers to account, including:

(1) a significant reduction in the number of ministers in the Commons;

(2) transfer to the House of Commons of certain royal prerogative powers, including the appointment of a Prime Minister and the ratification of international treaties;

(3) fixed-term Parliaments, except after a constructive vote of no confidence, when a majority of the House vote in favour of an alternative government;

(4) more time for debating major policy changes that do not involve legislation;

(5) more short debates on topical issues of current concern;

(6) more opportunities to debate important reports of Select Committees;

(7) debates in committees on matters of concern to particular regions;

(8) a fundamental restructuring of Prime Minister's Questions, concentrating on questions on specific matters;

(9) weekly opportunities for mini-debates, to be answered by the Prime Minister, on topics selected by ballot;

(10) more topical questions to other ministers;

(11) preparation by the Procedure Committee of guidelines relating to ministerial refusals to answer certain questions and monitoring of such refusals by the Committee;

(12) audit of the staff and other resources required by each Select Committee, and provision of extra resources where required;

(13) experimental use of rapporteurs by some committees; and

(14) consideration by the Procedure Committee of additional payments for the chairs and other key members of committees.

The Liberal Democrat Policy Paper also contained a number of specific proposals relating to the machinery and operation of the House of Commons, including systematic programming and timetabling of business on the basis of proposals made by a Business Steering Committee, chaired by the Speaker, comprising representatives of all the larger parties (proportionate to their numbers in the House) and of backbenchers; more use of morning sittings and of debates in committees; improved presentation of the Order Paper and other papers; re-examination of the feasibility of electronic voting; preparation of fuller guidance for new members on the organisation, practices and procedures of the House; and support for the Speaker in seeking to eliminate unnecessarily partisan behaviour, disruptive or insulting language and time wasting. The paper also proposed improvements in the design and accommodation of the Palace of Westminster to ease the working life of members and to make Parliament more welcoming and accessible to the public.

The Liberal Democrat Policy Paper then turned to services for members, including their remuneration. Increasingly the job of a member was becoming full-time and the salaries of MPs did not adequately reflect this and should again be reviewed. A new pay regime should be designed that prohibited Members from receiving substantial outside incomes. The paper warmly welcomed the decision to implement, with some modifications, the major recommendations of the Nolan Committee, which should be carefully monitored.

Research and information services and other staffing should be audited and, where shown to be needed, further expanded. Free and widespread provision of information is essential for the effective working of any Parliament, and the Liberal Democrats proposed that the principles of the Public Information Act they advocate should equally apply to the access by MPs to official information, with special procedures being invoked to enable the House to consider any refusal by a minister to supply information covered by the general right of access.

Services for the public were also important (it is an area neglected by most critics) and the paper made specific proposals for a number of reforms, particularly concerned with provision of information, including considerable reductions in the prices of parliamentary papers and the provision, free of charge to those attending the House or committees, of all the working documents relevant to the business before them.

The Liberal Democrats also looked at possible longer-term reforms, but nevertheless concluded that the reforms of the House of Commons set out in their paper could start immediately. All that was missing was the willingness of the ministers then in office, and of members, to make that start.

The Liberal Democrat manifesto for the general election repeated the party's commitment to a number of constitutional changes which would considerably affect the way the House of Commons works. On the immediate question of the reform of the House itself, however, it added nothing to the Policy Paper, *A Parliament for the People*, except to specify that the fixed term for a Parliament would be four years and that Liberal Democrats wished to reduce the number of MPs by 200.

COMING UP TO THE ELECTION: THE LABOUR–LIBERAL DEMOCRAT JOINT CONSULTATIVE COMMITTEE ON CONSTITUTIONAL REFORM

It can now be seen that the state of play on reform of the House of Commons as the general election loomed was that a wide range of ideas had been canvassed or advocated by various non-party bodies. However, whatever the contribution of outside bodies to thinking on parliamentary reform, the attitudes and policies of the political parties would be the crucial factor. These are simply summarised. The Conservative government had done quite a lot over the years but had shown little interest in further reform. The Labour Party had indicated the directions it wished to take, but had not spelt out its proposals in any detail. The Liberal Democrats had committed themselves to a detailed package of specific reforms, but were unlikely to secure the power to implement them on their own.

As it happened the opportunity for a joint-party approach was speedily created. In October 1996 Labour and the Liberal Democrats agreed to form a Joint Consultative Committee to examine the current proposals of the two parties for constitutional reform and to see if they could reach agreement on a programme. Reform of Parliament was one part of this review.

The Joint Committee was closely advised and assisted at every stage by the Constitution Unit. The Unit, an independent and expert organisation with Robert Hazell as Director, backed by skilled staff with civil service backgrounds, had been set up in April 1995 to conduct an independent inquiry into the implementation of constitutional reform. This included parliamentary reform. The main contribution of the Unit lay not in the origination of new proposals, but in drawing together the reforms proposed by other bodies and the political parties and advising on how these changes – whatever the view of their merits – could best be implemented if the government in power so intended. The main study of parliamentary reform was published in the Unit's report, *Delivering Constitutional Reform*, which dealt with the various procedures that the House of Commons could use for the passage of controversial constitutional Bills and on how such procedural changes could best be adopted.[10] The work of the Unit was to prove of great value in the next stage of this story.

The Joint Consultative Committee reported, in agreement, early in 1997. The full text of the report is set out in Appendix 2. The Committee saw reform of Parliament as key to the wider modernisation of the country's system of government. The House of Commons no longer held ministers to account and legislation was not given the scrutiny it requires. 'Both the Labour and Liberal Democrat parties are convinced of the need to re-establish confidence in the political process, politicians and Parliament itself.'

The Committee did not agree a raft of detailed proposals like those of the Liberal Democrats, but, drawing on them and the recommendations of the Procedure Committee and the Hansard Society Commission, it set out the priorities for modernising the House of Commons as follows:

(1) to programme parliamentary business;
(2) to improve the quality of legislation by better pre-legislative consultation and improved mechanisms for parliamentary scrutiny;
(3) to change Prime Minister's Question Time;

---

[10] For more details, see Katy Donnelly, 'Parliamentary Reform: Paving the Way for Constitutional Change', *Parliamentary Affairs* (1997) Vol 50, No 2, pp 246–262, and Chapter 10 on implementing constitutional reform in this book.

(4) to overhaul the process for scrutinising European legislation;

(5) to strengthen the ability of MPs to make the government answerable for its actions; and

(6) to enhance the role of Select Committees in ensuring the accountability of departments. (For details, see Appendix 2.)

The Joint Consultative Committee emphasised that no one political party should dictate changes to parliamentary procedure; Parliament must own the process. It therefore agreed that early in the new Parliament a special Select Committee on Modernising the House of Commons should be established, and that both the Leader and Shadow Leader of the House should be on the Committee. The Committee should consult outside advisers as appropriate and canvass the views of MPs, and other interested people. It was hoped that the Committee would report swiftly on the priority issues, especially legislation, so that it would be possible to implement its first recommendations early in the new Parliament.

As they prepared for the general election and the new Parliament, much preliminary work had therefore been done by the two opposition parties. A general approach had been agreed, although many details remained to be thrashed out and laid before the House. The foundations for quite fundamental procedural reform had been laid. Whether the building was to be erected depended on the result of the election.

THE PROPOSALS AND ACTIONS OF THE LABOUR GOVERNMENT

So we return to the point from which we started – a new government with a massive majority and a new challenge for the House of Commons. What have the Labour government done so far to reform the practices and procedures of the House and what do they now plan to do?

Prime Minister's Questions

The government acted speedily on one matter – perhaps too speedily for those who thought there should have been more consultation, and at least an attempt to reach agreement between the parties – on the changes to Prime Minister's Question Time. Almost as soon as the House met the government announced (it could be done by ministerial fiat as it did not require any change in the Standing Orders) that the 15 minutes allotted twice a week for questions to the Prime Minister would be replaced by a half-hour period every Wednesday. At first this met strong objection from the Conservative Opposition, partly because of the lack of consultation (which appeared insensitive and unnecessary, although the convenience of making this change at the very beginning of the session must be accepted) and partly because, as first presented, it appeared that the conventional rights of the Leader of the Opposition to ask some six questions a week (three on both Tuesdays and Thursdays) had been halved. However this objection was rapidly countered by the Speaker who has been allowing the Leader of the Opposition to ask up to five supplementary questions every Wednesday.

It is too early to reach a firm conclusion on the merits of the new system in contrast with the old. Questions are still mainly 'open', although the welcome abolition of the need for the Prime Minister to repeat his standard answer to the questions on the Order Paper about his engagements leaves a little more time for other questions. It may also help backbenchers to see the advantages of giving notice of a specific question of substance so they can get two answers – to the original question and to a supplementary – instead of only one. Allowing the Leader of the Opposition five thrusts at the Prime Minister may also enable him to fire off questions on more than one topic, although William Hague has scarcely taken advantage of this possibility.

We shall have to see, but limited experience so far suggests that spreading questions to the Prime Minister over 30 minutes has made it possible to probe certain matters, especially those chosen by the Opposition, in rather greater depth than under the old system. The random leaping from one subject to another remains disconcerting, but again this may change with time.

Select Committee on the Modernisation of the House of Commons

The second action of the Labour government was crucial and not long delayed. After a general debate on modernisation of procedure on 22 May 1997, the promised Select Committee on the Modernisation of the House of Commons was appointed on 4 June. Ann Taylor, then Leader of the House, had emphasised in the debate her desire to get away from the adoption of rigid positions by both government and opposition and to move towards closer agreement on matters, such as the procedures of the House, which affected all members. This approach was manifested in the composition of the Committee. It consisted of 15 members – nine Labour, four Conservative, two Liberal Democrat – and included Ann Taylor (in the chair), Alastair Goodlad (the then Shadow Leader of the House) and a good blend of experience (with the former Chairman of the Procedure Committee) and fresh minds (two new members).

The appointment of the Leader of the House herself to the chair was novel and significant. For many years governments have tended to leave it to Procedure Committees to recommend changes, giving little lead themselves, and have stood back from the conduct of the Committee, with no ministers being appointed. This time – like many other things in the new political world – it was different. The new government wished to follow the precedent of 1945–46 when the incoming Labour government came to power with a number of procedural changes (particularly for the much greater use of

Standing Committees on Bills) already firmly decided. These only needed to be presented to a Procedure Committee for checking and fine tuning before the necessary Standing Orders were moved in the House – a speedy process with no long drawn-out haggling or discussions.

To assist a rapid decision, Ann Taylor, considerably influenced, I believe, by her experience as Shadow Leader of the House on the post-Nolan Select Committee on Standards in Public Life, which was chaired by the Leader of the House (and perhaps by her contrary experience of the lengthy dealings needed to secure agreement on implementing the Jopling Report) decided that she should chair the Committee herself. Backed by a sound majority on the Committee and by a massive majority in the House, this would almost certainly ensure that whatever the government wanted – give or take a few details – would receive the approval of the Committee and the speedy endorsement of the House.

Thus it appeared that at this stage the government clearly meant business and would press on with early reforms, at least of the legislative processes. The latter appeared especially urgent as new procedures should be in place to handle the controversial and in some cases complex constitutional legislation to which the government was committed.

The two debates of 22 May and 4 June were well attended and evidenced considerable agreement on the way ahead, particularly on legislation. The Opposition frontbench had reservations on three matters – possible changes in the procedures for timetabling legislation, procedures for scrutiny of constitutional Bills, and Prime Minister's Question Time – but broadly welcomed the early review of the practices and procedures of the House. And the backbench members who spoke were constructive and encouraging about the prospects of reform.

The government's proposals

The government's detailed proposals were therefore eagerly awaited. When these came, in the form of a memorandum from Ann Taylor to the Committee,[11] they were somewhat disappointing for those who were anxious to discover exactly what changes the government proposed to make to the practices and procedures of the House. Surprisingly, on many important aspects, the government appeared not to have decided how their various objectives for reform should, in practice, be achieved. No doubt (particularly after the failure to consult over the changes to Prime Minister's Questions) the Leader of the House wanted to show an open mind and to leave many options for later discussions, or decision by the Committee. However, it might have concentrated the minds of the Committee and speeded its deliberations if

---

[11] First Report of the Select Committee on the Modernisation of the House of Commons, HC [1997–98] 190, Appendix 1.

the government had tabled detailed and carefully worked-out proposals and invited the Committee's reactions.

The memorandum started by stating that the government regards a vital and effective House of Commons as central to the revival of confidence in politics and public life. After a number of recent reviews of aspects of procedure, the time had come to draw the threads together and embark on a significant programme of change. The government asked the Committee to give particular attention to the handling of legislative proposals, the means by which the House holds ministers to account, the impact of the House's procedures and practices on the working lives of members, and the style and form of proceedings. The memorandum dealt only with the first of these issues – legislation – because it was the most urgent, but the government's views on other matters would be submitted in due course.

The government's need to obtain Parliament's approval of its proposed legislation need not be incompatible with its proper scrutiny, and the government accepted that procedures could be developed, and applied on a case-to-case basis – Bills differ and there should not be a blueprint for handling all Bills – which would, overall, improve the scrutiny of legislation.

To begin with, the quality of legislation could often be raised by consultations with outside people before Bills are presented to Parliament and during their passage through the two Houses. The memorandum listed various ways for carrying out pre-legislation consultation outside Parliament – Green Papers, White Papers, and the publication of draft clauses or draft Bills.

Within the House, the memorandum asked the Committee to consider a wider range of options for taking evidence, on both policy and implementation aspects, before the conventional standing committee stage of a Bill. These included pre-legislative inquiries, before a Bill's introduction; pre-Second Reading inquiries after its presentation to the Commons; and more use of Special Standing Committees, perhaps with more flexible powers. In view of the heavy workload of departmental Select Committees, the government suggested that the Committee might wish to consider an additional committee structure for improved scrutiny of legislation.

It would not be appropriate, the government argued, for all Bills to pass through all these suggested stages, but it was ready to use them more frequently in suitable cases. It asked the Committee to consider the relative merits of additional stages of scrutiny and the criteria by which they might be selected for different Bills.

The government said that the Committee might wish to consider ways in which the profile of Standing Committees could be raised and their proceedings made more focused and effective. The memorandum suggested that one possibility for the Committee to examine would be the holding of the general debate on the principle of each clause of a Bill, before the debate on amendments rather than after.

The memorandum also asked the Committee to consider possible variations from the standard division of work between the floor of the House and committees. For example, more use could be made of Second Reading committees for less important or controversial Bills, with some relaxation of the notice required for their reference to such a committee. The committee stage of Bills might be more frequently divided between a committee of the whole House and a Standing Committee (as with the Finance Bill at present). And the report stage might be replaced by re-committal to a committee of the whole House for major issues requiring debate on the floor, with the details being debated in a committee upstairs.

The government did not have a settled view on the treatment of important constitutional Bills. The convention that they should be taken at all stages on the floor of the House was of long standing and not to be lightly set aside, but experience showed that this did not always ensure that such Bills were properly scrutinised. The government saw a case for taking parts of such Bills in Standing Committees (a solution that had been favoured by both the Liberal Democrats and the Constitution Unit), and sought the Committee's views.

The programming (or timetabling) of legislation is a crucial factor. The familiar confrontational approach, leading to use of the guillotine, has been widely criticised. The memorandum suggested that if new ways of programming legislation effectively could be found then it might be possible for opposition members to be more constructive and for government ministers to be more receptive to constructive criticism. Voluntary agreements reached through the usual channels had generally been successful since the Jopling Report, but might not work if there were a heavy load of contentious legislation. The use of the guillotine inevitably involved some reduction in scrutiny. The government therefore asked the Committee to explore the possibility of programming legislation through arrangements which were more formal than usual channels agreements but more flexible than the guillotine. The government could assist by indicating at the outset for each Bill its preferred programme and the proposed balance between proceedings on and off the floor of the House.

The government asked the Committee to give its views on the merits or otherwise of allowing selected Bills to be carried over, from time to time, from one session to the next. However, only the government should be permitted to move such carry-over motions.

The memorandum also asked the Committee to consider whether departmental Select Committees should be encouraged to carry out post-legislative scrutiny in a more systematic way than they have in the past.

The government said it would welcome the early views of the Committee on all these matters, so that decisions could be taken as soon as possible.

The government's memorandum clearly indicated the general direction the government wished to take, but much more detail was required on how this was to be done. No doubt the Leader of the House, as Chairman of the Committee, had her own plans up her sleeve and would steer the Committee towards the solutions she had chosen. We had to wait and see.

The Committee's Report

The Select Committee reported to the House on *The Legislative Process* on 23 July, and the Report was published very shortly afterwards. Because of the need for a speedy conclusion and because so much relevant evidence had already been received by earlier Procedure Committees and by the Hansard Society Commission, the Committee did not hear oral evidence, but several helpful memoranda were received and the most significant were appended to the Report. The Report itself was a clear, concise and very well-argued presentation of the need for reform of the way primary legislation is scrutinised by the House of Commons, with an analysis of the essential requirements of a reformed system and of the options for improvement. It came up with specific and coherent recommendations. And – most importantly – it was totally unanimous.

The Committee concentrated on the procedures of the House itself. On these matters it followed remarkably closely the detailed recommendations of the Hansard Society Commission and the Liberal Democrat Party, and the more general priorities agreed by the Joint Consultative Committee on Constitutional Reform. And, with expansion and elaboration, but almost without change, it accepted the government's proposals as set out in its own chairman's memorandum.

At the heart of the government's approach, and of the Committee's report, was the belief that it would be wrong at that stage to propose major changes on a permanent basis. The Committee therefore preferred to recommend various options to be tried out on an experimental basis. These would be monitored and the views of members and others sought before further recommendations, on an ongoing basis, were made in the light of experience.

As so many of the proposed reforms have been canvassed elsewhere and described earlier in this chapter, and as (as the Committee emphasises) many improvements in parliamentary scrutiny of Bills could be achieved by more imaginative and effective use of present procedures and practices, it is not necessary to describe here in detail all the options advocated by the Committee. But the main recommendations of the Committee are set out below.

The Report rightly began with the central issue of programming of legislation, without which many of the optional improvements in legislative scrutiny would not work. It sought an approach which was more formal than simple agreement through the usual channels but more flexible than the guillotine. It recommended that, for a trial period, some Bills (including some of substance and at least one controversial Bill) should be selected by agreement between the parties and that discussions should be held between the parties and with backbenchers regarding the handling and programming of each of these Bills. In the light of these discussions the government would move, after Second Reading, an amendable programme motion which could cover the type of committee(s) to be used, the date by which the Bill should be reported from committee, the time to be provided for Report stage and

Third Reading and, in defined circumstances, provisions for carrying the Bill over into the subsequent session. The detailed programming within a Standing Committee or a Special Standing Committee would be drawn up by a programming sub-committee and agreed by the committee. Other procedural details were set out in the report.

The other principal recommendations of the Committee were as follows:

(1) It welcomed the government's intention to publish seven draft Bills in the current session; these might be given pre-legislative scrutiny by the House using either an ad hoc Select Committee or a Joint Select Committee (with the Lords) or the appropriate departmental Select Committee.

(2) The government should come up with proposals for better and fuller explanatory material when Bills are presented.

(3) The government should seek an opportunity to appoint an ad hoc First Reading Committee after the First Reading of a selected Bill.

(4) Greater use should be made of Second Reading Committees, with more flexible procedures, to consider non-controversial Bills.

(5) The committee stage of any Bill should be handled in whatever way is most appropriate for that Bill, but many options have long been ignored and greater use should be made of Special Standing Committees (with their procedures made more flexible) or of ad hoc Select Committees or of splitting the committee stage between a committee of the whole House and a Standing Committee.

(6) Reforms of Standing Committee procedures, including preliminary debates on the principle of clauses before debating amendments, more flexibility in sitting arrangements and time limits on speeches at the chairman's discretion.

(7) Earlier publication of notes on clauses.

(8) For certain Bills, the use of the original committee to consider uncontroversial amendments at Report stage.

(9) The similar use of committees for considering certain Lords amendments.

(10) Departmental Select Committees should be encouraged to monitor legislation after it comes into force, and ad hoc committees might also consider the operation of other legislation which causes concern.

(11) In defined circumstances it should be possible for government Bills to be carried over from one session to the next.

There were other legislative issues in respect of which the Committee made no recommendations in this Report, but to which they proposed to return. These included the procedures for Finance Bills, for consolidation, Law Commission and tax simplification Bills and for Private Members' Bills. The Committee did not examine European legislation or delegated legislation at that stage as the government proposed to make interim responses to both the Procedure Committee's and European Legislation Committee's reports on these matters and the Committee planned a separate report later in that session.

On one other important and potentially controversial issue the Committee was somewhat non-committal. The handling of constitutional Bills was clearly going to be a matter of prime political importance in the early sessions of the new Parliament. The government's memorandum to the Committee referred to the long standing convention that Bills 'of first class constitutional importance' should have all their stages on the floor of the House, but went on to say that overall a Bill might be better scrutinised if parts of it were considered by a Standing Committee. The Committee pointed out the difficulties in deciding which Bills are 'of first class constitutional importance' and summarised the opposing arguments, but concluded 'Whilst we see no reason why a programme for the passage of such a bill could not be agreed, if agreement were impossible the Government of the day would presumably feel obliged to fall back upon a traditional timetable motion.' The Committee produced an agreed report and, on this issue, donned a velvet glove, but the iron fist of the government's business managers was clearly exposed.

The First Report of the Select Committee on the Modernisation of the House of Commons constituted a major advance in the movement for reform of the legislative processes. But it was still not the end of the story. The Report had yet to be agreed to by the House, but, given the unanimity of the Committee and the position of the chairman, this was shortly achieved without qualification or dissent.

Finally the Committee's recommendations would have to be applied in practice. In view of the experimental nature of the proposals and the discretion left to the government and its business managers in selecting the Bills for novel procedures and the options for their scrutiny, this would be the crucial test of the government's commitment to reform of the House of Commons in this central area.

What has been done?

What significant changes have actually been made in the practices and procedures of the House of Commons since the Labour government came to power? The answer (at the time of writing in June 1998) is almost none.

Following the Fourth Report of the Modernisation Committee on Conduct in the Chamber, a number of relatively minor changes or reforms have been adopted. These include:

(1) giving the Speaker greater discretion on the time limiting of speeches, including injury time for interruptions;
(2) easing the convention that gave Privy Councillors priority in debate;
(3) permitting direct quotation in supplementary questions and from speeches in the House of Lords;

(4) displaying the constituency of a member on the annunciators in the Chamber;

(5) modifying the ancient practice of 'spying strangers' while still permitting the presence of a quorum to be tested;

(6) abolishing the old custom of having to wear a hat to raise a point of order during a division; and

(7) denying a member his or her salary during a period of suspension for misconduct.

Better behaviour and shorter speeches and questions have also been urged and the Speaker has been encouraged to take account of past failures in these matters when selecting speakers in debate. However, honourable members will still be required to refer to each other as 'honourable members'.

None of this is of great importance. More significant is the alteration in Prime Minister's Question Time. And, on the recommendations of the Modernisation Committee, useful improvements in the style and presentation of the Order Paper and other working papers of the House have been made. On the other hand, after extensive opinion polling within the House, the Committee decided not to recommend any form of electronic voting for divisions; the majority of members still prefer to walk through the lobbies.

However, it was in the area of the legislative process that major reforms were proposed and agreed to by the House on an experimental basis, and here almost nothing has been done.

Three slight advances have been agreed. The House has accepted the principle of carrying over Bills under certain conditions into a second session, following the Third Report of the Modernisation Committee. Parliamentary counsel have devised ways of publishing fuller and better explanatory material on Bills, on the lines of the notes on sections recommended by the Hansard Society Commission. And the practice of publishing some Bills in draft has been extended and some use of pre-legislative committees is planned. These are all useful steps forward, but are still to be tested in practice.

The other specific recommendations of the Modernisation Committee for improved scrutiny of Bills – which were agreed unanimously by the Committee and endorsed by the House – have so far been largely ignored. Eleven months after the Committee reported in July 1997, six Bills had been the subject of a programming order, but even these were not really the kind of carefully prepared and constructive programmes envisaged by the Committee. In effect they were guillotines of the old type applied by agreement, with the support of opposition parties. This agreement was a significant move forward, as was the fact that programmes were adopted at an early stage before any time had been wasted, but the programmes were not applied to all stages in some cases and no proceedings in Standing Committees were programmed.

Most surprising – and worrying for those anxious for reform – has been the failure of the government to try a single one of the options for improved scrutiny that could have been included, experimentally, in some programmes for Bills. Standing Orders have not been amended, even temporarily, so the carefully considered improvements, recommended by the Modernisation Committee and agreed by the House, have not (at the time of writing) been tried. In particular, no use has been made of Special Standing Committees or of other committees with power to take evidence – the crux of the reform proposals. Neither has any progress been made in the development of systematic committee scrutiny of recent Acts of Parliament.

CONCLUSION

Parliamentary reform is an ongoing, but never smooth and predictable, process. Usually there are long periods with little happening, during which new ideas slowly form and come together as the accepted wisdom, and then, when the men and moments are right, they are readily adopted and become the normal order of parliamentary life.

So it has been with the reform movement over the past 20 years. Nothing of major significance has changed since the acceptance of the departmental Select Committees in 1979, but over the intervening years there has been mounting dissatisfaction with the way the House of Commons has worked and with the conduct of its members. This has stimulated a growing desire for serious reforms, particularly regarding the rules applying to conflicts of interests, and the processes of legislation.

Before the change of government in 1997, significant steps had been taken to seek to eliminate undesirable financial practices on the part of some members, though these new rules have not yet been fully tested and the fundamental question of whether the House can regulate itself properly is not yet settled. If it fails in this task, the pressure for the regulation of parliamentary conduct to be handed over to the courts might become irresistible, with very serious constitutional implications and grave damage to the repute of Parliament. At present, however, the new rules must be given a chance to work – and new members may aid this process – and further reforms are not immediately needed. That aspect of reform of the Commons is therefore at present removed from the agenda, and the new government appears to have accepted this.

The reverse is true on almost all the other aspects of the practices, procedures and work of the House of Commons. Much thought has been given to procedural reform, especially for legislation, and the two main political parties on the Opposition side in the last Parliament committed themselves, before the election, to a major programme of reform if either of them came to power. However, in the past, parties which have been enthusiastic for change while in opposition have somehow lost their reforming zeal when in power, especially if they think that proposed changes might weaken their ability to get their own way in Parliament.

Sadly this appears to be the case once again today. The Labour government when it first came to power seemed to mean serious business and it started the reform programme without delay, with the Leader of the House fully committed and in charge. However, there were early signs that the advance could falter. Ann Taylor's decision to retain the government's power to decide the application of the proposed scrutiny procedures on a Bill by Bill basis was disappointing. It would have been clearer and more certain to provide that the Special Standing Committee procedure (at least) should be applied to all Bills unless the House otherwise ordered.

And reform has faltered. The experiments with the new procedures recommended by the Committee have not been given a fair wind and a fair trial. The government has defied the clearly expressed wishes of the House. It has also been selective in choosing what reforms to adopt, by making changes that secure for the government the advantages of programming its legislation but not giving the House or its members the opportunities for improved scrutiny that programming was designed to permit. The package deal has been broken.

It is not clear why this has happened. One day the official papers may tell the story. However the acceptance of reform appears to have been undermined by the stubbornness of the business managers who are reluctant to slacken the reins and allow true experiment. If this continues, not only will it result in inferior scrutiny and less acceptable legislation but it will also seriously damage the standing of politicians and Parliament by making procedural reform no more than a cynical charade.

This is the position at the time of writing in June 1998. However, the movement for reform started well and a new session will provide a new opportunity for the government to prove its good faith by allowing significant experiment – and even change – in 1999.

The proposed reforms of the legislative process are but the first stage of the programme. Further reports from the Modernisation Committee on many other aspects of parliamentary reform – including European legislation, delegated legislation, financial business (the new plans for three-year Public Spending Reviews and other changes will be relevant), scrutiny of policy and administration, accountability of ministers, research and information services – will be eagerly awaited. Further thought might also be given to the need for more systematic consultation with outside interests on proposed legislation and to the methods of monitoring this (as proposed by the Hansard Society Commission).

Further complications and challenges will be posed by the constitutional changes the government has initiated. Devolution, proportional representation and a reformed House of Lords would all affect the functions of the House of Commons, the way it does its work and the role of MPs.

So the central question remains: is the opportunity presented by this new Parliament and government to achieve real and thorough reform of the House of Commons going to be taken? The spadework has been done. The full programme of change, covering many aspects of the House, must now be carried through. A reformed and revitalised House of Commons is urgently needed to command the respect of the people. Such achievement would provide an ideal way for the House of Commons to celebrate the Millennium.

Valediction

I end on a personal note. For many years, as a Clerk in the House of Commons, I worked behind the scenes and through such bodies as the Study of Parliament Group to further the reform of the House. Since my retirement in 1989 I have been able to campaign more publicly, particularly as a member and Secretary of the Hansard Society Commission and as chair of the Working Group of the Liberal Democrat Party. Now at last there are signs of progress and some of the barriers to reform are coming down. However, I have had my say, and this chapter is my valedictory contribution. It is now up to the politicians to achieve real reform. We must wish them well.

Further reading

Reports of the Select Committee on Modernisation of the House of Commons, HC [1997–98]: 190 (*The Legislative Process*), 389 (*Explanatory Material for Bills*), 543 (*Carry-over of Public Bills*), 600 (*Conduct in the Chamber*), 699 and 779 (*Voting Methods*), 791 (*Scrutiny of European Business*)

Paul Silk and Rodri Walters, *How Parliament Works* (London: Longman, 3rd edn, 1995), especially Ch 12

J A G Griffith and Michael Ryle, *Parliament: Functions, Practice and Procedure* (London: Sweet & Maxwell, 1989)

Greg Power, *Reinventing Westminster: The MP's Role and Reform of the House of Commons* (Charter 88, 1996)

John Biffen, *Inside Westminster: Behind the Scenes at the House of Commons* (London: André Deutsch, 1996)

PART II

THE EXECUTIVE

CHAPTER 6

MONARCHY AND THE ROYAL PREROGATIVE

Professor Robert Blackburn (King's College, London) and
Professor Raymond Plant (Oxford University)

'Flummery is the farce that dances attendance on privilege. The monarchy breeds
both and, if it is to survive, it must consciously abandon the more blatant
manifestations of an ancient class division.'

(Roy Hattersley, Labour former Deputy Leader, 1992)

'It is where power is exercised by government under the cover of royal prerogative
that our concerns are greatest . . . Massive power is exercised by executive decree
without accountability to Parliament.'

(Labour Party, *New Agenda for Democracy*, 1993)

'The monarch now may be above reproach, but you can never tell what you are
going to get . . . The question needs to be posed again, in our time, whether the
mere accident of birth can ever now be expected to produce a man or woman fit
for the role that royalty requires.'

(Rev Canon James, Extra Chaplain to the Queen, 1998)

Within the Labour Party's 1997 general election manifesto, positioned at
the end of its section on 'A Modern House of Lords', was the one-sentence
paragraph: 'we have no plans to replace the monarchy'. This was a carefully
worded statement. As a public policy and expression of principle, it fell
considerably short of a ringing endorsement of the institution of monarchy in
new Labour's programme of constitutional modernisation. Yet any suggestion
of changes afoot would have aroused disproportionate attention being given
to the issue during the election campaign, particularly given the media and
public's obsession with all things royal. But on the other hand, the Labour
manifesto statement clearly does not rule out any changes or modifications to
the institution; indeed, it does not even preclude the adoption at some future
date of 'plans to replace the monarchy'.

Over the past ten years political and public attitudes towards the monarchy
have radically altered. This has taken place at the same time and as part of a
wider process in which fundamental changes have occurred within British

society itself. The British have become less deferential and more questioning of those in authority, especially those holding political office. Meanwhile, recent years have witnessed a growing chorus of critical remarks about members of the royal family and the institution of monarchy, which now flare up at regular intervals whenever some royal event or politician's comments serves to galvanise public and media attention. Within the Labour Party, there is almost certainly a majority now who favour a republic. Even prior to the last election a newspaper poll of Labour MPs indicated that 44 per cent wanted to replace the monarchy with a republic; and the vast majority of the others favoured sweeping changes to the institution and to its powers and style of public conduct.[1] Prominent members of the new Labour government are well known for having made controversial suggestions or stinging remarks about the monarchy or royal family before taking office, such as Home Secretary Jack Straw (calling for a slimmed-down Scandanavian style monarchy in a BBC Panorama programme), Northern Ireland Secretary Mo Mowlam (who suggested selling off Buckingham Palace to the National Trust in a press article), Welsh Secretary Ron Davies (who said Prince Charles was unfit to be King to a Welsh BBC televison audience) and Education Minister Kim Howells (who said during BBC's Question Time that the royal family had become 'a scandal-ridden anachronism').[2] So far as national opinion as a whole is concerned, a watershed was reached in 1997 when an opinion poll showed that support for the royal family had fallen below half of the adult population for the first time ever.[3]

Thus far into the life of the new Labour administration, Tony Blair has taken care to give his full endorsement to the Queen, personally and professionally. In his speech at the government banquet to celebrate her golden wedding anniversary, Tony Blair referred to Queen Elizabeth as 'simply the best of British'.[4] But if the Labour Cabinet, along with its shadow Conservative and Liberal Democrat counterparts, do not want any debate about the future of the monarchy, the reality is that the government will be powerless to prevent renewed political discussion of the institution over the next few years. Increasingly high-profile debates will continue as a media response to any newsworthy royal development that occurs. Furthermore, the constitutional reform programme of Labour and the Liberal Democrats carry unavoidable implications for the monarchy, despite the government expressing its support for the institution. Most obviously, the government's intention to remove the voting rights of hereditary peers in the House of Lords is bound

---

[1] *Independent on Sunday*, 23 October 1994. A later poll conducted for *The Independent* on 18 February 1996 showed that only 11 Labour MPs supported the monarchy 'without serious reservation'.

[2] Respectively: (J Straw) 5 December 1994 (see also *Tribune*, 5 February 1993); (M Mowlam) 7 August 1994; (R Davies) 1 March 1996, as reported in the *Daily Telegraph* the following day; (K Howells) 17 March 1994.

[3] ICM poll for *The Guardian*, 12 August 1997. To the question, 'Would we be better off or worse off without a royal family', 48 per cent replied 'better off', 30 per cent 'worse off'.

[4] 20 November 1997.

to be seen by opponents as a broader attack on the principle of hereditary power and status, including that of the monarchy. Ideas about making more accountable the powers of the royal prerogative exercised in the name of the Crown by the Prime Minister can quite easily be misrepresented as an attack on the monarchy itself. These questions will not go away just because it may not be politically convenient to address them in the view of party managers. Worse, it is likely to do great harm to the new Labour leadership if it seeks to stifle a debate on the issue, both within the party and outside, when it is likely to go on whether they like it or not. It would be better for Labour to have that debate out in the open sooner rather than later, with the initiative of the leadership behind it driving the agenda.

THE ELECTIVE VERSUS HEREDITARY PRINCIPLE

There is a perfectly defensible case to be made for constitutional monarchy in the context of a radical constitutional agenda, and this case needs to be made by those who want to stop short of republicanism. Of course, there is a principled case to be made for republicanism as part of this agenda, and indeed it has been made over the years by Tony Benn and others.[5]

The basic assumption of the Benn case is that political power should rest upon consent and that the elective principle is basic to securing such consent to the exercise of power. There is a great deal to be said for this approach, and this is why those who take this view see the new Labour government's present approach to Lords' reform as only an interim measure which should be completed by a further reform of the Lords to turn it into an elected Second Chamber. The idea that power should ultimately be exercised only by elective consent could lead to republicanism, but there is an alternative view which is perfectly plausible and which we suspect would command quite wide assent and which would preserve an hereditary but wholly constitutional monarchy. This would, however, entail removing from the monarchy its residual political power. In this view, an hereditary monarchy would still be defensible in the context of a more democratic constitution because the monarchy would not have political power and thus could be exempted from the claim that political power should only be exercised with consent.

If this is so, however, we have to be clear about the nature of heredity. At the moment, the debate about the succession mixes up two things: claims about the legitimacy of the hereditary principle, and claims about the character and virtues of the prospective monarch. People want two things which are not the same: an hereditary monarch, and a monarch who will, by his qualities of mind and character, symbolise something about the unity and the values of the nation. The point about hereditary monarchy is that you

---

[5] See Tony Benn, *Common Sense: A New Constitution for Britain* (London: Hutchinson, 1993).

have to put up with what the accidents of birth produce. It is quite another question as to whether the prospective monarch has the virtues necessary to symbolise something important about the life and values of the national community. No hereditary system can guarantee that the latter will be the case. The debate about the supposed virtues or otherwise of the Prince of Wales is only relevant if we believe that the monarch should be a symbol of national unity. So, for example, the Welsh Secretary Ron Davies' past complaints in 1994 about the Prince's predilection for hunting and other field sports is only relevant if we think that, as well as being an hereditary monarch, the future King Charles should represent the nation as a whole – a substantial number of whose citizens believe that these activities are wrong.

These are, however, two separate issues, and there is absolutely no guarantee that the hereditary principle will produce a monarch who is capable of symbolising the nation and its values. If we want a head of state who can symbolise the whole nation, or at least a majority in it, then this is probably a stronger argument in favour of an elected head of state than an hereditary one. It is only because of accident that the present Queen is able to do this, as well as being an hereditary monarch, that we think that both the hereditary principle and the symbolic one are the same. But they are distinct, and may not be easily united in the person of a future monarch. Indeed, looking at the history of the monarchy, there have been cases when the two features have been split apart – surely George IV would be a good example.

A genuine hereditary monarchy would, in the modern world, imply a rather limited role for the monarchy in both its political and symbolic forms. The monarch would have to abstain from political or near-political activities and retreat far more into a purely formal role as head of state just because the hereditary principle – for which there is something to be said as producing a head of state who is above politics – cannot ensure that it will produce a monarch who has the qualities to be more than this. Because the hereditary principle enshrines the accidental and the unpredictable, it would seem to be reasonable that the corollary of accepting the hereditary principle would be a monarchy with much more limited political and symbolic power in society. We could then get away from an embarrassing and sterile debate about the personal qualities of the Prince of Wales and into a much more productive and important debate about what sort of role an hereditary head of state might have, whatever his personal virtues.

MODERNISING THE CONDUCT OF MONARCHY

The processes required in moving towards this reduced and more limited form of monarchy will involve several inter-related initiatives on the part of the Palace and 10 Downing Street. They will include a winding down of the more antiquated social and ceremonial aspects of the institution as it at present operates, particularly those blatantly reminiscent of class or privilege. There will need to be a diminution of the public status of the royal family, as the institution of monarchy focuses more exclusively on its constitutional acts of state rather than any social functions it has assumed. And running throughout this whole process of reform will be the need for a sharp distinction to be drawn between the public and private aspects of monarchy, with clearly defined constitutional duties being attributed to the head of state.

Antiquarians and those sentimental of Britain's past derive pleasure from the fact that numerous ancient remnants of a royal and aristocratic method of ruling society are still with us today. But such enthusiasm, even where shared, must be tempered by the practical political and social requirements of the day, which include a head of state whose style and position reflects contemporary and forward-looking values, and whose public role is clearly intelligible and understood. Thus much of the regal pomp and ceremony accompanying state events such as the Opening of Parliament deserve to be stripped of those elements which are more in tune with a Victorian costume drama, and more emphasis should given to the primacy of Parliament by way of greater involvement of its principal officials including the Speaker of the Commons and of MPs or peers who chair major parliamentary committees.

Only one marginal revision of protocol surrounding the Opening of Parliament has been announced since Labour took office, to the effect that the Lord Chancellor who previously was prohibited from ever turning his back on the sovereign may now turn around to walk back to his seat after handing the Queen's Speech to the monarch in the chamber of the House of Lords. It is a matter for the Queen herself to determine whether she wishes to continue travelling to Westminster in a horse-drawn Royal Carriage, but others on public grounds of parliamentary procedure (especially at present when there is a political initiative aimed at modernising how Westminster works) might legitimately question the relevance or appropriateness of the manner in which the Queen proceeds to open a new parliamentary session's business, involving a long train of ladies-in-waiting dressed up mid-morning as if attending a charity ball accompanied by elderly aristocratic figures bearing swords. It is remarkable that Labour government whips are still prepared to tolerate being required to dress up in tights and garters for the occasion.

So too there is a great deal of fossilised legal verbiage and statements of outmoded royal etiquette still stamped on our common law and statute book, ripe for repeal or modernisation. The ancient law relating to who should be the monarch is itself out of date with current civic mores. There are signs that the Palace is ready to concur with the majority political and popular view that the succession to the throne rules should be changed so as to remove sex discrimination in favour of male primogeniture. Lord Williams of Mostyn, the Home Office Minister, stated in the House of Lords in 1998 that the government intends at some point in the future to bring forward legislation to introduce sexual equality into the line of succession, indicating that the

Queen had been consulted and 'had no objection'.[6] An Act of Parliament addressing this reform alone would need to refer to the 1701 Act of Settlement and expressly modify the application of the ancient common law rules of inheritance governing pre-Law of Property Act 1925 entailed interests in real property which recognise the right of male primogeniture.

If and when prospective legislation on this matter is prepared by the government, then the opportunity should be taken to rationalise a wider range of anachronistic special law which still operates with respect to the public and private affairs of the royal family. Currently, for example, under the Royal Marriages Act 1772 no descendant of King George II under the age of 25 years is capable of contracting matrimony without the previous consent of the Queen signified under the Great Seal and declared in Council; and every marriage or matrimonial contract entered into without such consent is null and void at law. Still today too, the common law and Treason Act 1351 extends the capital offence of treason to adulterous affairs of the wife of a King regnant and where the chastity of the wife of the heir apparent is violated during coverture. This process of modernising the law relating to the monarchy should be regarded as a tidying up exercise rather than any profound inquiry of weighty matters of state, and could be handled competently by the Law Commission.

By contrast, both a government inquiry and at least one House of Commons committee will need to be involved in a comprehensive review of the finances of the monarchy, an area of royal affairs which has raised the greatest degree of adverse political comment at Westminster in recent times, and where the line between the public and private faces of monarchy is regularly blurred. The Public Accounts Committee should be empowered to examine the expenditure and financial arrangements of the Royal Household in exactly the same way as other government departments; and in so doing it should establish the precise parameters of what is the nation's property (as opposed to the private property of the person who is monarch) where some measure of ambiguity exists or the the property in question was previously un-catalogued.[7] The vast royal art collection and extensive royal buildings belonging to the nation should be made more widely open to the public, except where they are maintained as government offices. The Queen's voluntary surrender of her immunity from payment of certain taxes (effective from 6 April 1993 and intended by Queen Elizabeth and Prince Charles to continue indefinitely) was universally welcomed at Westminster as a step in the right direction. She now pays income tax on all her personal income and on that part of the Privy

---

[6] HL Deb, 27 February 1998, col 916. The announcement was made when Lord Archer of Weston-super-Mare's *Succession to the Crown Bill*, HL [1997–98] 31, was due to be considered for a second reading (and subsequently was withdrawn).

[7] Parliamentary access to royal documents and information about such matters has not been straightforward: see Committee of Public Accounts, *Property Services in the English Occupied Royal Palaces: Responsibilities for Royal Household Remuneration and the Provision of Accommodation* (Ninth Report, 1997–98) 394.

Purse income which is used for her private purposes; she pays tax on any realised capital gains on her private investments and on the private proportion of assets in the Privy Purse; and inheritance tax will apply on bequests or gifts by the Queen other than transfers of assets from one monarch to his or her successor.[8] However, neither the constitutional office of head of state nor the financial position of the Queen can rationally justify the continuation of any existing tax immunities that do not apply to everyone else. In addition to the two royal palaces the Queen owns personally (Balmoral and Sandringham), the state makes available and maintains seven other buildings for royal purposes (Buckingham Palace, Windsor Palace, St James' Palace, Hampton Court Palace, Kensington Palace, Kew Palace and the Palace of Hollyroodhouse). The Civil List provides £7,900,000 towards office and staffing costs for the Queen, and the present rather grand travelling arrangements including the Royal Train (annual cost 1994–95, £2.5 million) and the Queen's Flight (annual cost 1994–95, £9 million) are underwritten by the Treasury. These sums and levels of subsidy are more than adequate to finance the work of the Queen, and hardly need to be buttressed by any further tax perks to the Queen in her personal capacity. Generally speaking, any modern head of state today – whether elective or hereditary – must emphasise its similarities to the people it represents if it is to retain their respect, and it must submit its governmental affairs to the normal scrutiny process of the constitution if it is to command the confidence of the country's elected politicians.

A new streamlined office of head of state that gels into the modern constitutional structure Labour is building will need to downsize substantially the social and philanthropic functions which the Palace and its associates have come to adopt for the royal family. As an entity the royal family has no constitutional or legal foundation; it simply emerged as a social and ceremonial phenomenon in the 19th century under Queen Victoria as a royal device to help promote and market popular acceptance of hereditary monarchy to the middle classes which had become increasingly sceptical of the utility of kingship due to social embarrassment caused by George III and George IV. By the turn of the century, Edward VII had come correctly to favour a royal function limited to the King's acts of state, but then under George V and to an even greater extent Queen Elizabeth II's father George VI, the family of the head of state were projected into the public eye as part of a distinct social function of the monarchy.

So today we have a wide number of wealthy and privileged relatives of the Queen being treated as VIPs not because of their own achievements or election to office but by virtue of their blood relationship to an hereditary monarch. The institution has sought to justify and compound this state of affairs by assuming for its members an obligation to carry out social, charitable and ceremonial functions, in return for which they are paid a sizeable

---

[8] For a Buckingham Palace explanation of the present arrangements, see *Royal Finances* (London: HM The Queen 2nd ed, 1995).

sum of money from the Civil List or else an allowance from the Queen.[9] This social aspect of monarchy has little or nothing to do with the constitution or the constitutional office of head of state.[10] Even within its own aims of gathering support for the monarchy by extending its personnel into the public sphere it has clearly proved counter-productive, since the dramatic decline in respect and support for the monarchy over the past decade is almost entirely due to the much publicised personal antics or problems of individual members of the royal family other than the Queen. The social public function that monarchy has assumed for itself over the past 100 or so years should be laid to rest as either irrelevant or inappropriate, and with its demise should go the concept of a royal family with which it is inextricably linked. Relatives of our future heads of state apart from their spouse and eldest child will best serve the country by carrying out careers and working lives in the manner of ordinary men and women, not in the fashion of wealthy and privileged aristocrats carrying out benign public acts of patronage, charity or ceremonial performance.

THE MONARCH'S PREROGATIVES AS CONSTITUTIONAL HEAD OF STATE

Thus redefined in terms of its public existence, reform of the monarchy will then entail a rationalisation of the royal prerogative which lies at the heart of its constitutional role as head of state. This will in itself prove a welcome opportunity for resolving some confusions and controversies that have existed up to now about the degree of personal discretion the monarch is permitted in the exercise of the royal prerogative powers – particularly those affecting the dissolution of Parliament, the appointment of a prime minister and the royal assent to legislation – and the precise parameters of the present rules which govern them. Generally, these residual political powers still retained by the monarch should be translated by way of statutory codification into closely defined and circumscribed constitutional duties of the head of state.

The royal power of dissolution of Parliament effectively determines the date of a general election.[11] As such, it represents the most central constitutional act in the life of our political democracy. This prerogative power, which is derived from medieval common law when Parliaments were treated as personal councils of the King to be summoned and dismissed at will, is normally exercised on the advice of the Prime Minister of the day. The political unfairness of this arrangement, as between the government and opposition, is a

---

[9] For details, see *Royal Finances*, p 28.

[10] But see Walter Bagehot, *The English Constitution* (1867, Penguin ed 1900) for his famous glorification of a family on the throne. Bagehot was an anti-democrat who opposed extending the franchise to the working classes and favoured monarchy and a leisured aristocracy in the House of Lords as devices to help sustain social deference to the ruling elite.

[11] Generally see R Blackburn, *The Meeting of Parliament* (Aldershot: Dartmouth 1990).

matter considered elsewhere in this book.[12] So far as the monarchy is concerned, there may well be circumstances in which a political dispute exists between politicians as to whether an immediate dissolution may take place or not. It arose as an issue in 1923, 1931, 1951 and 1974 – in each case where there was either a fragile or no overall majority in the House of Commons – and on all four occasions the monarch chose to follow whatever advice was tendered by the Prime Minister of the day. However, there is a long line of established constitutional theory which holds that a British monarch retains a reserve personal discretion over election timing, and even as recently as 1991 Lord Armstrong, the former Cabinet Secretary, publicly expressed the view that, 'It is not just theoretically correct, but common sense, that the sovereign should have the right to withhold consent to a request for a dissolution.'[13]

This particular royal prerogative is in any event likely to be superseded by Labour's eventual implementation of a four-year fixed-term Parliament. A proposal for fixed intervals between general elections was promised by Neil Kinnock as Labour leader and in Labour's 1992 manifesto (though it has not been mentioned in the party's documents since), and it may well become part of a package of electoral reforms arising out of the Jenkins Commission report to be published in 1998 and the forthcoming referendum on the voting system. A combination of persuasive factors, therefore, including the desirability of keeping the monarchy out of political involvement, now makes the case for a fixed Parliament very strong indeed. The statute providing for the new arrangements should lay down the precise circumstances in which an earlier election might be ever permitted within each four-year period, which might be a motion of no confidence in the government passed by the House of Commons.[14]

Also closely associated to the conduct of elections, is the royal prerogative of choosing and appointing the person who will be our head of government as Prime Minister. In practice prime ministerial appointment is straightforward so long as a general election produces an overall majority for one party, whose leader will automatically be legally endowed by the monarch with the seals of office. But problems arise if no such single party domination of the Commons exists. In hung Parliament situations, the royal practice this century has been to allow the incumbent Prime Minister the first claim on attempting to form a government, regardless of whether or not he polled a greater number of parliamentary seats than the opposition. Thus in February 1974 the then Prime Minister Edward Heath, whose Conservative Party polled 297 MPs to Labour's 301 under Harold Wilson, was not required to resign immediately following the election result, and over the next few days he proceeded to try and form a coalition in negotiations with the Liberal

---

[12] See Chapter 4, pp 83 ff.
[13] Interview with P Hennessy, 'The Back of the Envelope: Hung Parliaments, the Queen and the Constitution', Strathclyde Analysis Paper No 5, 1991.
[14] See further, p 86; and R Blackburn, *The Electoral System in Britain* (London: Macmillan, 1995) pp 61 ff.

Party. Only when it became clear that no pact with the Liberals was possible did Heath resign, thus allowing Wilson to be appointed Prime Minister. Far more controversial was King George V's endorsement of the former Labour leader Ramsay Macdonald staying on as Prime Minister over a National Government with the Conservatives in 1931, after his Labour government had collectively voted in Cabinet to resign office (an act of betrayal by Macdonald for which he was subsequently expelled from the Labour Party).[15]

For the future, the process of choosing a prime minister should be covered by a new system of parliamentary selection, involving the introduction of procedures for nomination and approval in the House of Commons, prior to the formal act of appointment being carried out by the head of state. This codification of the rules would have the additional advantage of providing an opportunity for Parliament to consider whether the person who has first claim on forming a government should be either (a) the incumbent Prime Minister (as at present), or else (b) the leader of the party which gains most MPs at the general election (a proposition almost certainly supported by the public at large).

A third royal power to be considered as part of a wider modernisation of the prerogatives of the Crown is the monarch's assent to legislation. This has proved far less of a political issue in modern times, and no royal veto of a government Bill has occurred in the period since 1707 when Queen Anne refused to approve the Scotch Militia Bill, though it was contemplated by George V in 1912 over the Irish Home Rule Bill. The fact remains, however, that the monarchy today still possesses this absolute legal power, the political parameters of which are not entirely clear. There are no real conventions on how this royal power of veto might ever be exercised. There could conceivably be occasions when a monarch personally regards the passage of some item of legislation as being morally reprehensible or of dubious constitutionality (particularly if it affected the vested interests of the monarchy) requiring a clearer mandate of the electorate. In all events, a preferable approach would be to remove any possibility of political involvement by making the head of state's signature an automatic certificate, simply indicating that the Bill had been properly passed through its required procedures in Parliament.

If the monarchy is to become a more formal head of state which abstains from political intervention, then this points to the desirability of codifying these royal powers of dissolution, prime ministerial appointment and royal assent by way of parliamentary statute, and establishing new procedures for settling any uncertainties or disputes which may arise in the future. From the Palace's own perspective such a development should be welcomed. For it will safeguard the monarch from becoming embroiled in politics in the event of a future controversy which existing conventions did not cover, from which it stands to gain only the hostility of whichever party against whose interests

---

[15] See R Bassett, *1931: Political Crisis* (London: Macmillan, 1958); and H J Laski, *The Crisis and the Constitution: 1931 and After* (London: Fabian Society, 1932).

the prerogative was used. The role of the monarch as head of state for the next century would become one of formalising the process whereby the government of the country was conducted in conformity with its constitutional law.

PARLIAMENT'S CONTROL OF THE EXECUTIVE'S PREROGATIVE POWERS

But the subject of the royal prerogative goes much further than just those powers which are vested solely in the person of the monarch him or herself, and is bound up with the legitimacy of all governmental activity which is carried on in the name of the Crown. By far the greater part of royal prerogative power that exists is exercised by the ministers and officials of Her Majesty's Government. The scope of executive action authorised by the royal prerogative at common law is very wide indeed and embraces some of the most basic and important tasks of government, extending across the whole terrain of foreign and international affairs, matters of national security, and into numerous matters at home such as the grant of royal charters, a multitude of public and political appointments, the honours system, and the nature and extent of our defence capability. The controversial feature of these prerogatives is that they are all extra-parliamentary powers. In other words, major policies and decisions may be adopted by the government under the prerogative without the need for any formal approval by either House of Parliament; indeed, such powers may be exercised without any form of parliamentary scrutiny or discussion at all.

If 'the less said the better' was the motto of the Labour leadership when drawing up its 1997 general election manifesto statements concerning the monarchy, it was equally so with respect to the prerogative powers generally. Indeed the election manifesto failed to mention the subject of the Crown prerogatives at all. This was somewhat surprising, given the strong emphasis on the need for its reform in the party's constitutional reform programme published in 1993, *New Agenda for Democracy: Labour's Proposals for Constitutional Reform*, drawn up under its then leader John Smith and its home affairs spokesperson at the time, Tony Blair. Under a separate section on 'Prerogative Powers', this Labour Policy Paper said, 'It is where power is exercised by government under the cover of royal prerogative that our concerns are greatest . . . Massive power is exercised by executive decree without accountability to Parliament and sometimes even without its knowledge.'[16] On military intervention abroad, it condemned the fact that there was no obligation upon governments to obtain the consent of the House of Commons before going to war and recommended formal ratification by Parliament as 'the absolute minimum that is acceptable in a democracy'.

---

[16] At p 33 and see Appendix 1 below.

The case for statutory codification of prerogative power is strongest in the field of treaty-making. Here the position of Parliament with respect to the approval and amendment of treaties negotiated abroad is clearly an anachronism.[17] We are now the only country in the European Union to have no formal procedures to guarantee parliamentary scrutiny for major foreign policy decisions such as treaty-making. As one peer remarked in a recent debate on the matter, 'We are talking about a remnant of the medieval or at least very early modern British monarchical constitution. It makes nonsense of the principle of the doctrine of parliamentary sovereignty that the Crown retains the right to sign and ratify treaties without having submitted them to Parliament.'[18] Treaties in the modern world deal with a proliferation of social and economic matters that affect our everyday working lives; they are no longer a matter simply of military or dynastic alliances. As recounted elsewhere,[19] the basic human rights agreements to which the UK became a party, the European Convention on Human Rights in 1951 and International Covenant on Civil and Political Rights in 1976 were negotiated and agreed without any parliamentary scrutiny, debate or approval. Similarly as argued elsewhere,[20] the 1924 Ponsonby Rule is clearly inadequate as a basis for scrutiny. In Lord Bridges' words, it 'is not really a rule at all; rather it is a unilateral statement of intention by a junior minister', involving the Foreign Office voluntarily laying a copy of negotiated treaties on the table of each House.[21] What is needed to redress the situation is a new statutory requirement whereby Parliament must approve negotiated treaties prior to formal ratification by the Lord Chancellor's office. This would be in line with Labour's own 1993 policy statement:[22]

'Labour's task is to expose how little actual power Parliament has in the face of government by executive decree . . . In certain areas of foreign policy these powers are in theory absolute. Agreeing treaties is currently a matter for prerogative power, not Parliament, as the current Maastricht debate has highlighted. Treaty after treaty is concluded without the formal consent of Parliament. Indeed, foreign policy as a whole is an area virtually free from democratic control and accountability; powers devolving from the Crown, free from parliamentary scrutiny, are vested in government ministers and go effectively unchallenged . . . Powers to ratify treaties should lie with our democratically-elected representatives.'

The present state of affairs serves to remind us that the principal beneficiary and custodian of Crown prerogative power is not so much the monarch as the government generally and the Prime Minister in particular. For, in

---

[17] See further Chapter 1, pp 32–4.
[18] HL Deb, 28 February 1996, col 1544.
[19] Chapter 18, p 376.
[20] Chapter 1, p. 33.
[21] HL Deb, 28 February 1996, col 1542.
[22] *New Agenda for Democracy: Labour's Proposals for Constitutional Reform*, p 33 and see Appendix 1. For a draft legislative proposal, see the Treaties (Parliamentary Approval) Bill, HL [1995–96] 27 (presented by Lord Lester QC).

addition to the prerogative powers already mentioned in the field of foreign affairs, at home it is under the authority of the Crown prerogative that prime ministers make all Cabinet, ministerial and senior civil service appointments; that Parliament is dissolved and a general election held when the Prime Minister wishes it; that knighthoods and other top honours are awarded at the recommendation of the Prime Minister twice a year; and numerous public appointments are made by the Prime Minister, even of bishops to the Church of England and of new members to the parliamentary Second Chamber. Tony Blair's declared crusade to strengthen our constitution by diffusing political power within and across its various components will therefore need to extend to his own individual position and powers in government.

TRANSFORMING THE 'PEOPLE'S MONARCHY'

All the signs are that Tony Blair enjoys an open and easy relationship with Queen Elizabeth, and so too Peter Mandelson with Prince Charles. This closeness and personal facility to communicate freely across the twin pillars of our executive structure, Crown and Cabinet, will be important if real progress is to be made under the new Labour government in translating our 19th century-based royal institutions into a convincing and effective 21st century constitutional structure. For such measures will most successfully come about from initiatives seen to be emanating from the Palace itself, rather than from 10 Downing Street, particularly if they are to avoid becoming embroiled in cross-party argument and opposition mischief-making.

On the part of Queen Elizabeth, she may welcome the assistance of government politicians she trusts in helping to create a more modern, forward-looking 'people's monarchy'. Six months after Labour took office, the Queen delivered a speech in Tony Blair's presence in which she made plain her willingness to co-operate and listen to government advice impinging on royal affairs.[23] 'It often falls to the prime minister and the government of the day to be the bearer of the messages sent from people to sovereign', she said. 'Prime minister, I know that you, like your predecessors, will always pass such messages, as you read them, without fear or favour.' It will be incumbent on Tony Blair, as the cypher of Labour and national opinion of changes now required to the conduct of monarchy, to exploit this receptiveness offered by the Queen and to give forthright guidance to our head of state. This is all the more important since the Queen and heir apparent are still to a large extent cocooned in a private working environment stiff with reactionary and subservient sycophancy to ancient tradition.

The new government will be sensitive to the public relations aspects of any royal reforms and how they might redound on Labour's ratings in the

[23] 20 November 1997.

public opinion polls. The tragedy of the Princess of Wales' death in August 1997 showed not only the great depth of popular personal feeling that can be invoked by royalty but a prime minister who was astute in giving vocal leadership and direction during the events that followed Diana's death to the satisfaction and approval of the country. Though the Prime Minister, through his official 10 Downing Street spokesperson, has declared himself to be 'a great fan of the monarchy',[24] it is well known that he is no admirer of any unnecessary or vacuous pomp and ceremony. Modernising the monarchy will certainly test the Blair administration's radicalism, but it is a project that is likely to involve a sustained effort of incremental change taking shape over a period of years, starting no doubt with matters of protocol to help shift the monarchy's aura of untouchability within the ruling establishment.

As a political reality, it is quite impractical in present circumstances to give serious consideration to abolishing the monarchy altogether. There has been no debate launched by any of the parliamentary parties and there is no strong majoritarian demand to be rid of the Queen.[25] Even if political leadership behind a republican programme of reform was to exist, the huge amount of administrative and legislative work involved for politicians and civil servants in its preparation would make the issue a low priority unless it was felt to be a genuinely vital reform because of some actual or pending crisis affecting government. A substantial body of opinion might well support a referendum on the continuation of the monarchy following the death of Queen Elizabeth,[26] and this might even carry the backing of Prince Charles himself as a means of seeking popular endorsement.

Nonetheless, we should keep in mind that in the longer term there is little doubt the monarchy is doomed. Monarchy is essentially a creature of the past and it is an historical certainty that at some point the institution will collapse, whether due to a crisis in its level of political and popular support, or else because the heir to the throne is unsuited to the job or unwilling to accept the responsibilities and constraints which the work of a head of state entail. Across the party political divide at Westminster, the real choice for the present is whether to leave the institution exactly as it is, and thereby contribute towards its present or impending crisis and collapse; or, as argued in this chapter, to seek to redefine the institution and its political powers suitable to its hereditary status so as to facilitate its continuity and working for as long as proves publicly acceptable.

---

[24] 10 Downing Street official spokesperson, 8 May 1998, as reported in the *Daily Telegraph* the following day.

[25] Only 7 per cent of people believe the monarchy should be replaced by a republic as soon as possible, according to an ICM poll for the *Observer*, 14 September 1997. 74 per cent believe the monarchy should continue but be modernised.

[26] 32 per cent of people think there should be a referendum to decide the future of the monarchy when the Queen dies or chooses to step down, according to a MORI poll published 24 December 1996. For a draft legislative proposal see the Elected Head of State (Referendum) Bill, HC [1995–96] 115 (presented by Paul Flynn).

This process of reform will involve codifying the prerogative powers of the Crown as much as reshaping the political and social institution of monarchy itself. And in so doing, its broader aim should be to settle the detailed constitutional and legal framework within which any British head of state – whether selected by hereditary or elective means – should be required to act in support of the new constitution Labour is now creating for the 21st century.

Further reading

Vernon Bogdanor, *The Monarchy and the Constitution* (Oxford University Press, 1995)

Anthony Barnett (ed), *Power and the Throne: The Monarchy Debate* (London: Vintage, 1994)

Ben Pimlott, *The Queen: A Biography of Elizabeth II* (London: HarperCollins, 1996)

Rodney Brazier, *Constitutional Practice* (Oxford University Press, 2nd edn, 1994), especially Chs 2–4, 9

Christopher Vincenzi, *Crown Powers, Subjects and Citizens* (London: Pinter, 1997)

Tony Benn, *Common Sense: A New Constitution for Britain* (London: Hutchinson, 1993)

CHAPTER 7

THE CIVIL SERVICE

Professor Gavin Drewry (Royal Holloway,
University of London)

'What [the Scott Report] illuminates, albeit indirectly and without comment, is the
shift from wait-a-minute to can-do. And can-do man is here to stay. Neither of the
two political parties wants to put the clock back, even if they could . . . Tony Blair
will not because, if he is elected, it will be to do things himself.'

(Peter Kemp, *The Independent*, 19 February 1996)

'What does Labour want Whitehall for? Does Mr Blair want power in order to do,
or power in order to be? Modern Whitehall is well fitted to give him the second.
For the first he would need to reform Whitehall far more radically than
Mrs Thatcher dreamt.'

(David Walker, *The Independent*, 14 January 1997)

The Labour government came to office in May 1997 having said little of
substance in the run-up to the election about the civil service that it was to
inherit from its predecessors. This near silence, punctuated by occasional
blandly emollient statements (such as the speech by then newly appointed
Chancellor of the Duchy of Lancaster, see p 168 below) was for the most
part maintained in the aftermath of the election. Yet it was an eloquent
silence, and one that was in marked contrast to the concern about the loyalty
and the elitist background of the higher civil service that had been evident
three decades previously, when a Labour government, then led by Harold
Wilson, took office after 13 years continuously in opposition. That period, inter-
minable though it must have felt at the time, was five years fewer than the
period spent on the opposition benches by Labour in the 1980s and 1990s.
On the face of it the contrast may seem particularly surprising given the
priority accorded by the new government to constitutional reform (and here
I am taking for granted that a civil service is an integral part of any state's
constitution, broadly defined). However, four points should be borne in
mind. The first is that the civil service had already been extensively refashioned
by the 'new public management' agenda of the Thatcher–Major years: the
'modernised' Labour Party had taken on board many aspects of that agenda;

154

it had, for instance, jettisoned clause 4 of its own constitution which had committed it to wholesale nationalisation, and it had broadly endorsed (albeit with some critical and cautionary reservations) such Conservative public sector reforms as Next Steps and the Citizen's Charter. On the basis of its own stance in opposition it is no surprise to find that Labour's approach to civil service related issues on taking office was to go with the flow of existing change rather than try to put the clock back or radically change direction.

Secondly, New Labour was a very different entity to its 'Old Labour' namesake of the 1960s – particularly in its absence of visible hang-ups about the social elitism of the Establishment and the enduring Oxbridge culture of the higher civil service. Thirdly, it had while in opposition been critical of the alleged 'politicisation' of the public service – especially of the partisan patronage that characterised appointments to quangos, but also of what it saw as a threat to the non-partisanship of the civil service itself posed, in particular, by Margaret Thatcher's unconcealed preference for 'can do' and 'one of us' people in top advisory positions. Having claimed the moral high ground over public appointments it was doubly necessary to keep its own hands clean in that area – though it has, as we shall see, run into some turbulent water over its early handling of the Government Information Service in Whitehall.

Fourthly, it may be argued in any case that the apparent absence of an agenda for civil service reform is in part illusory: changes such as devolution to Scotland and Wales; continuing developments in Northern Ireland (where there is already a separate civil service, a relic of a former era of devolved government in the Province); the possible further regionalisation of government in England; and promised moves towards more open government – not to mention further steps towards deeper European integration – are bound to have radical knock-on consequences for the structure and working culture of the civil service. By the next general election, early in the new Millennium the civil service will inevitably have undergone significant further changes – albeit, for the most part, consequential ones.

The main point to note is that whereas the previous Conservative administrations had given civil service reform a very high priority on their substantive policy agenda, the Blair government has had other fish to fry. To mix this culinary metaphor, from day one of her premiership, Mrs Thatcher had set about – in pursuance of her 'new right' ideological goals – to cook the goose of what she regarded as an over-privileged civil service, a popular objective in the eyes of an electorate that is chronically weary of what it sees as excessive red tape and for whom the word 'bureaucrat' is a pejorative epithet. For Tony Blair this was not really an issue, and his new government seemed to recognise the need quickly to harness the expertise and goodwill of the civil service to help shape and implement its programme.

The Thatcher years had left the impression – hardly a satisfactory one by any reasonable test of good governance – that the government and its civil service were somehow on different sides, which indeed they sometimes were. The restoration, soon after the election, of trade union rights at GCHQ, the removal of which by Margaret Thatcher in the early 1980s had caused great bitterness, can be seen as symbolic of the restoration of 'normal' relations between ministers and civil servants, as well as the righting of an injustice and an earnest of goodwill towards state employees, bruised by years of New Right battering.[1]

The early signs in the aftermath of the election were that the civil service, no doubt glad to see fresh ministerial faces, and having taken so much punishment over the years from the outgoing administration, was more than willing to respond positively to this approach. For the first time in years, civil servants found themselves re-cast in their traditional role as respected advisers and facilitators – rather than as the main targets – of the government's policy agenda. Professional neutrality meant that any celebrations had to be private and muted, but the sense of relief throughout Whitehall was almost palpable.

POLITICIANS AND CIVIL SERVANTS: SQUARING THE DEMOCRATIC CIRCLE

One of the most intriguing characteristics of modern democracies has been the growing dependence of elected politicians on the experience and expertise of non-elected officials as state functions have expanded both in scope and in complexity and have become to an increasing extent spatially dispersed. Individual ministers come and go, as do the governments in which they hold office. In a world of big government (recent attempts to roll back the state notwithstanding), politicians have to delegate extensively to their officials, while the latter serve as gatekeepers, protecting their ministerial masters from overload and prioritising their agendas.

In so do doing they are sometimes depicted as presumptuous usurpers of the electorally legitimated role of minister-politicians or even as malign saboteurs of the programmes of democratically elected governments. Ministers themselves sometimes believe – or purport to believe – such criticisms. Civil servants have sometimes been convenient scapegoats for ministerial failures and disappointments. In many countries bureaucrats are inhibited or even prevented from defending themselves publicly from such charges. This is particularly the case in Britain where a constitutional doctrine of ministerial responsibility, to which lip service is still paid but in which few people nowadays really believe, holds that ministers, and only ministers, are answerable for everything that happens in government departments.

Over the years political analysts and democratic theorists have wrestled with the logical and practical implications of this. The paradoxes and ironies

---

[1] However, there was some subsequent controversy about claims that the Blair government might be back-pedalling on its pledge to restore 'normal trade union rights': see the *Observer*, 17 August 1997.

inherent in a situation where the minister's constitutionally legitimated mastery of the policy agenda is so dependent on the support of a loyal civil service that sometimes has agendas of its own has spawned one of the most successful television comedies of recent years, *Yes, Minister* and its sequel *Yes, Prime Minister* (though the joke began to wear increasingly thin during the Thatcher–Major years).

It has increasingly been recognised that new forms of accountability have to be devised to bridge the gap between the fiction and the reality of ministerial responsibility in an age of big government, and the last 30 years or so have seen significant developments in that direction. For instance, in the 1960s a parliamentary ombudsman was established to investigate complaints of maladministration in government departments; in the 1980s the House of Commons acquired a stronger and more coherently organised system of Select Committees, to which civil servants frequently give evidence, in public and sometimes in front of TV cameras; the National Audit Act 1983 substantially extended the scope of public audit; there have been various moves towards greater openness and transparency in administration and policy-making (moves that the Blair government is committed to reinforcing, by way of a Freedom of Information initiative[2]).

The Thatcher government's most important civil service reform – the Next Steps initiative (discussed below) – sought to separate ministerial responsibility for policy from the 'operational' responsibility of senior civil service managers (agency chief executives) for the effective and efficient delivery of public services. Chief executives have become directly accountable to Parliament (eg as agency accounting officers, reporting to the Public Accounts Committee, and with their names being attached to written parliamentary answers in Hansard about agency matters).

However, as the furore over the Home Secretary, Michael Howard's, sacking of the Head of the Prison Service, Derek Lewis, made very clear, there remain some serious ambiguities about the demarcation line that purports to divide responsibility for 'policy' and responsibility for operational matters.[3] This was an area examined by the House of Commons Public Service Committee not long before the election (see below), and the Labour government, on the basis of its pre-election consultations with the Liberal Democrats, is committed to implementing the Committee's recommendation that the present non-statutory civil service code of conduct be given statutory force in a Civil Service Act.[4] It is in this and other areas relating to the accountability and professional conduct of civil servants in their relationship with ministers that the most interesting developments relating to the civil service seem likely to occur.

---

[2] See the White Paper, *Your Right to Know*, Cm 3818 (December 1997). The matter is still under consideration by the government at the time of writing.

[3] Derek Lewis tells his own side of this interesting story in his book, *Hidden Agendas* (London: Hamish Hamilton, 1997).

[4] See the *Report of the Joint Consultative Committee on Constitutional Reform* (1996) paras 83 and 84.

Before looking at some of those developments, consideration is given below to one of the main features of the UK civil service that always gives rise to speculative discussion whenever there is a prospective or an actual change of government from one party or another – its claims to political neutrality.

THE NEUTRALITY OF THE UK CIVIL SERVICE

It is a major distinguishing characteristic of the UK model of government that civil servants are politically neutral, and are expected to serve ministers of any government currently in office with non-partisan loyalty (not at all the same thing as *enthusiasm* for particular ministers and their policies – a quality which by definition is inconsistent with neutrality). This principle flowed from constitutional developments in the first half of the 19th century and has been accepted by all governments, of all political complexions, since then. It represents a sharp contrast with the civil services of many other European countries where the boundaries between political and civil service careers are much more permeable and where (in some countries) the minister is served by his or her own *cabinet* of hand-picked advisers, drawn both from the regular civil service and from outside; it contrasts also with the US's 'spoils system' in which many top officials are appointed by the incoming administration and relinquish their posts whenever there is a change of President.

Thus it has been noted that:

'When Attlee succeeded Churchill as Prime Minister in 1945, and returned to the Potsdam peace conference, he was accompanied by the same team of civil servants (including the same principal private secretary) that had made up his predecessor's delegation. This continuity surprised the Americans and the Russians, but the officials concerned made the transition without apparent difficulty and the Labour leader himself had no doubts about the impartiality of his staff. Out of office in the 1950s, Attlee would boast to international socialist conferences that the British career civil service was unequalled in the world, one of the strongest bulwarks of democracy, and that the same officials who had worked out the details of Labour's programme were now busy pulling it to pieces for their Conservative masters.'[5]

In similar vein, Tony Blair's first Chancellor of the Duchy of Lancaster (the minister[6] in charge of the Office of Public Service, which is part of the Cabinet Office), soon after the 1997 election, in a speech discussed below, recalled that he had talked recently to a number of Americans who:

[5] Kevin Theakston, *The Labour Party and Whitehall* (London: Routledge, 1992) p 1.
[6] There have been suggestions that the government might underline its 'modern' image by changing the title of this office to something less antique – perhaps Minister of Administrative Affairs.

'were staggered by what they had seen in Britain since the General Election. They couldn't understand how there had been this seamless change in the administration of Britain. They couldn't understand how the new Government had hit the ground running and was getting on with the new agenda right away. And, of course, that's one of the great traditions of the British permanent, professional Civil Service, dedicated to support the democratically elected Government of the day.'

Attlee apart, the most interesting Labour precedent for the purpose of the present discussion is the election of the first two Wilson administrations of 1964–66 and 1966–70. It is interesting for two main reasons. First, because this was an un-reconstructed 'Old Labour' administration, still substantially enmeshed with (and dependent on) a powerful, and similarly un-reconstructed, trade union movement, encumbered by a socialist party constitution, and carrying much of the historical anti-elitist baggage from the days – both real and imagined – of working class oppression. The Oxbridge-dominated higher civil service, with its image of exclusive London clubs, public school ties, bowler hats, and its conservative values, was an obvious target for left wing hostility. Secondly, because Labour came to power in 1964 after 13 continuous years of Conservative governments (albeit under four different prime ministers): and it must always be hard for any incoming government, after many years on the opposition benches, to accept, in its heart of hearts, that this neutral civil service really will transfer its undivided loyalty to its new masters.

Labour's reaction then to these perceived 'problems' was to set up a Committee of Inquiry into the civil service, under the chairmanship of Lord Fulton. The Fulton Report, which was published in 1968,[7] began by attacking, in ringing and provocative terms, the 'amateurism' of a civil service that was 'still fundamentally the product of the nineteenth-century philosophy of the Northcote–Trevelyan Report'.[8] The details of the Report's 158 recommendations lie outside the scope of this chapter. Many of those recommendations were not implemented – mainly because there was soon another change of government, following Mr Heath's election victory in 1970. The Heath government had its own agenda of public sector reform and, in the absence of continuing and sustained prime ministerial support, much of the Fulton Report – particularly those parts with which the senior civil servants charged with implementing the Report felt most uncomfortable – fell by the wayside. However, some of the Report's recommendations – particularly its call for the introduction of 'Management by Objectives', and its recommendation that there should be an inquiry into the desirability and the feasibility of 'hiving off' central departmental functions to specialist agencies – anticipated some of the reforms of the Thatcher years.

[7] Cmnd 3638.
[8] The reference here is to the Northcote–Trevelyan Report of 1854, which was the starting point for the gradual acceptance of the principle of a civil service recruited and promoted by merit, and so far as the higher civil service was concerned, a generalist tradition, and a culture based on university educated, gentleman, all-rounders. The origins of the civil service principle of political neutrality – a strict separation of civil service and political jobs – pre-date this.

When, in May 1997, Tony Blair became Prime Minister after his party had languished for 18 years in opposition, it apparently gave no thought at all to the possibility of a new inquiry comparable to that of the Fulton Committee, three decades earlier. There were good reasons for this, some of them already noted: Labour inherited a civil service that had already been reconstructed by its predecessors; the incoming administration was more empathetic towards Whitehall than its counterpart in 1964. The fact that there was to be no new Fulton – and indeed little restructuring of the configuration of Whitehall departments[9] – says a lot about both the style and the substance of New Labour's agenda – and in particular about its stance on public sector reform, in contrast to that of the previous administration.

This contrast emerges clearly when we look at the recent pre-history of the civil service inherited by Tony Blair – and in particular at some aspects of the 'New Public Management' revolution that took place under Margaret Thatcher and John Major.

THE PUBLIC SERVICES IN THE THATCHER–MAJOR YEARS: BLAIR'S INHERITANCE

The 18 years of Conservative government, preceding the advent of the Blair administration, was marked by radical changes throughout the public sector. Public service reform, rather than being seen as a *means* to enabling government to realise its key objectives with the minimum of cost and difficulty, was an *end* in its own right – at the very top of the government's substantive policy agenda. The reforms were driven in part by New Right ideas about the inherent inefficiencies and empire-building tendencies of public bureaucracies, contrasted with the benefits of providing public services through the play of market forces. They were manifested both in terms of numerous variations on the themes of privatisation and contracting out and in a crusade for greater efficiency, effectiveness and economy (the '3Es'). An efficiency unit, located initially in the Prime Minister's office, and later in the Cabinet Office (latterly as part of the Office of Public Service) played a major part in this pursuit of bureaucratic efficiency, both in the small scale but cumulatively significant sense of rooting out wasteful practices throughout Whitehall, and by developing new, across-the-board, management reforms – the best known of which were the Financial Management Initiative (FMI) and the Next Steps programme. The reform programme also gained impetus from the government's determination to diminish the power of the trade unions –

---

[9] The Wilson years (and the Heath years that followed) saw some radical re-drawing of departmental boundaries, perhaps the best known being Wilson's unsuccesful experiment with a new Department of Economic Affairs. Blair's most significant changes on first taking office were to re-merge the Departments of Environment and Transport and to separate International Development from the Foreign Office, under its own Secretary of State.

including of course the civil service unions, with which the Thatcher government came quickly into conflict, notably in the GCHQ case.[10]

The early phase of the reform programme featured Downing Street rhetoric about 'de-privileging' the civil service and plans to cut civil service numbers and peg back pay increases, themes which recurred throughout the 18-year Thatcher–Major period. In 1979 Mrs Thatcher inherited from the Callaghan administration a civil service of 732,000 staff. John Major's bequest to Tony Blair in 1997 was a streamlined service, of about 450,000. In total, the reforms transformed both the structure and the culture of the traditional civil service, and led to the development of a whole new vocabulary to go with it: in particular, 'agentification' (Next Steps), the 'contracting out', 'privatisation' and 'market testing' of departmental functions and the 'empowerment' of the consumer of public services (the Citizen's Charter – subsequently relaunched by the Blair government under the title 'Service First').

The Next Steps programme itself[11] – probably the most radical reform of the civil service this century – came from a report by the Efficiency Unit (then headed by Robin Ibbs) published in February 1988,[12] with a strong endorsement from Mrs Thatcher. The Ibbs Report found that the advantages traditionally claimed for having a unified civil service were outweighed by the practical disadvantages:

'the advantages of an all-embracing pay-structure are breaking down . . . the uniformity of grading frequently inhibits effective management and . . . the concept of a career in a unified Civil Service has little relevance for most civil servants.'

The Report concluded that:

'the aim should be to establish a quite different way of conducting the business of government. The central Civil Service should consist of a relatively small core engaged in the function of servicing Ministers and managing departments, who will be the 'sponsors' of particular government policies and services. Responding to these departments will be a range of agencies employing their own staff, who may or may not have the status of Crown servants, and concentrating on the delivery of their particular service, with clearly defined responsibilities between the Secretary of State and the Permanent Secretary on the one hand and the Chairmen or Chief Executives of the agencies on the other. Both departments and their agencies should have a more open and simplified structure.'

So far as ministerial responsibility is concerned, Parliament 'through ministers' should treat managers 'as directly responsible for operational matters'.

---

[10] The conflict gave rise to litigation that not only marked a low-water mark in relations between the Thatcher government and the civil service but was also a landmark in the modern development of judicial review. See *Council of Civil Service Unions v Minister for the Civil Service* [1985] AC 374.

[11] For an overview, see Philip Giddings (ed), *Parliamentary Accountability: A Study of Parliament and Executive Agencies* (London: Macmillan, 1995).

[12] *Improving Management in Government: The Next Steps* (HMSO, 1988).

In her Commons statement commending the Report, the Prime Minister made clear that there would be 'no change in the arrangements for accountability'; the work of Select Committees, the Public Accounts Committee and the Parliamentary Commissioner would not be affected.

And so it has come to pass. Agency chief executives are a very distinctive sub-species of senior civil servant – serving on short-term contracts and recruited in most cases by open competition, often from outside the civil service. From April 1991 departments and agencies became free to recruit their own staff for all posts except grades 1 to 7 (permanent secretary to principal)[13] and fast stream entrants. The Civil Service (Management Functions) Act 1992 removed legal impediments to the devolution to departments and agencies of many detailed aspects of staff management. By April 1994 the biggest agencies had taken responsibility for their own pay and grading structures. By April 1996 responsibility for pay and grading below senior levels had been delegated to all departments and agencies. All this meant a diminution of centralised Treasury control. By the time of Tony Blair's election victory, about three-quarters of all civil servants were working in a total of about 130 Next Steps agencies (ranging in size from about 30 staff in the Queen Elizabeth II Conference Centre to about 60,000 in the Benefits Agency).

Meanwhile, alongside and on top of the agency programme several other big initiatives had come on stream – notably the Citizen's Charter, launched in 1991. The White Paper, *Competing for Quality*, published in November 1991 heralded an extensive market testing programme; the Deregulation and Contracting Out Act 1994 removed legal obstacles to statutory functions being carried out in the private sector. In 1996 a new senior civil service came into being, embracing the top five senior policy grades, including all agency chief executives.

Compared with the situation when Labour had last held office, under Jim Callaghan, Mr Blair's inheritance was of a civil service greatly slimmed down, more managerial in its culture, more accustomed to working both with and in some contexts in competition with the private sector, and dispersed into semi-autonomous agencies – each responsible for its own staffing and headed by powerful chief executives.

At the same time, however, the civil service had retained many of its more traditional characteristics, and politicians had connived at this by keeping firmly in place the traditional doctrines of ministerial responsibility to Parliament, and by insisting upon the principle of a civil servant's undivided loyalty to the government of the day. It is arguable that the civil service inherited by Tony Blair and his colleagues in May 1997 was in a transitional state, between old and new – caught between 'continuity and change', an evocative phrase that appeared in the titles of two White Papers on civil service reform published in the mid-1990s.

---

[13] These former grade numbers have since disappeared with the creation of the senior civil service, covering former grades 1 to 5.

Sir Peter Kemp, former project manager of the Next Steps programme, has acknowledged that 'currently we are trying to build a 21st century system on top of a 19th century infrastructure', but claims that 'we are getting around to changing that':[14] he may be right. But during the pre-Blair years this interesting tension between the old and the new resulted in a certain amount of ambivalence in the reformist rhetoric adopted by Conservative ministers – bullish noises about the radicalism of the surgery, even a certain amount of gloating by politicians about the necessary pain being inflicted on greedy and inefficient bureaucrats, but combined with soothing noises that the best traditions of British public service would remain intact (and indeed better than ever) when the patient came out of hospital.

A side effect has been a degree of schizophrenia on the part of top civil service management, which contrived to advance a long way on some fronts (mainly those affecting the delivery of services) while moving somewhat more cautiously down the reformist road on others (especially those affecting the policy-making elite). More seriously, there are some continuing concerns about the fragmentation of the formerly unified service and about the possible blurring of lines of accountability in a civil service, three-quarters of whose staff now work in semi-detached Next Steps agencies.

AN AGENDA IN WAITING: KEY PRE-ELECTION REPORTS AND WHITE PAPERS ON CIVIL SERVICE REFORM

The continuing programme of radical public service reforms in the years preceding the arrival of the Blair government can conveniently be traced through a sequence of official/parliamentary reports and White Papers. Taken together these documents constitute both a valuable chronicle of an important era of change and an account of the state of the civil service and of the ongoing dynamics of reform inherited by the new government in May 1997. It is important to note that, although this material was the product of a period when the Conservatives were in office, much of it was founded upon an implicit consensus between the parties, and at the time of writing there is no sign that the Labour government is about to change direction in any radical way. However, a considerable corpus of unfinished business, carried over from the preceding administration, awaited the attention of the new government after the election.

Throughout the 1980s and early 1990s the House of Commons Treasury and Civil Service Committee (TCSC) (as it then was) tracked the unfolding of the government's public management reforms, including the Financial Management Initiative, the Next Steps and the Citizen's Charter. Its reports, apart from some marginal concerns, were generally very supportive of the

---

[14] Book review in *Public Administration*, 75(2), Summer 1997, at p 381.

reforms – underlining the fact that these were not matters that divided the parties in any substantial way. After John Major's 1992 election victory, the Committee embarked on a wide-ranging inquiry into the civil service. The inquiry stretched over two parliamentary sessions (and it is perhaps worth remarking en passant that the Labour Party did not give evidence to it).

The TCSC's Interim Report, published in July 1993 identified at least five separate elements of current concern about the civil service:

(1) concern about whether the management changes in the civil service in recent years, most notably the Next Steps initiative, have had fundamental implications which were not anticipated at the time the reforms were initiated;

(2) concern about the impact on the civil service of the market testing initiative and the possible privatisation of some civil service functions;

(3) concern about whether the formation of a higher civil service is suitable both for its management tasks and for the provision of good policy advice to ministers;

(4) concern about an alleged deterioration in standards of conduct in the civil service;

(5) concern about the implications for the civil service of a fourth successive election victory by the same political party.

In a White Paper, *The Civil Service: Continuity and Change*, published a year later, the government reaffirmed traditional civil service principles of integrity, impartiality and objectivity; non-politicisation; selection and promotion on merit; accountability through ministers to parliament. It signalled the establishment of a new senior civil service (see above) and said that every department would be required to review its senior management structure with a view to reducing layers of management where possible.

In November 1994, the TCSC produced its Final Report, *The Role of the Civil Service*, which endorsed the main elements of the White Paper, including the statement about 'key values'. However, it was critical of the way in which market testing had been conducted by the government, in particular the number of in-house bids that had been excluded; the Committee recommended that departments should report to Parliament any decisions to exclude such bids and that full details of all contracts awarded under the market testing programme should be reported to Parliament at the earliest opportunity. The Report proposed the promulgation of a new civil service code, and included its own draft text. It further recommended the introduction of a right of final appeal to an independent and strengthened body of Civil Service Commissioners to be given to aggrieved civil servants who have exhausted all internal grievance procedures. Regarding the Next Steps programme, the Committee recommended that there should be annual performance agreements between agencies and ministers, and that chief executives be 'directly and personally accountable to select committees' (ie not just on behalf of their ministers) in relation to such agreements.

Another White Paper, *The Civil Service: Taking Forward Continuity and Change* (January 1995) incorporated the government reply to the TCSC Report and restated much of *Continuity and Change*. The government accepted the TCSC's recommendation for a civil service code, with ultimate appeal to the Civil Service Commissioners. The Committee's draft was accepted, with significant amendments, as the basis of the new code, though it reserved its position on whether the code should have statutory status. In May 1995, the Nolan Committee's first report on *Standards of Conduct in Public Life* said that the new code should be implemented immediately, without recourse to legislation. It also recommended that departments and agencies should nominate one or more officials to investigate staff concerns raised confidentially, and the Major government agreed to this.

The White Paper promised the Civil Service Commissioners an enhanced role, including the auditing of departmental recruitment systems and monitoring of outside appointments to the senior civil service and, to underline his/her independence, the First Commissioner would no longer be a serving civil servant. The White Paper confirmed the plans for a new senior civil service, including senior management reviews, new pay arrangements for members of the senior civil service, and contracts for all senior civil servants. It rejected as unnecessary the TCSC's proposal for annual agency performance agreements. The White Paper emphatically reaffirmed that chief executives should be responsible to Parliament and its Select Committees, through ministers: 'the Chief Executive accounts to the Minister, from whom his or her authority is derived; and the Minister accounts to Parliament'. It rejected the TCSC's criticisms of the market testing process.

In the 1995–96 parliamentary session the Commons Public Service Committee launched an inquiry into Next Steps agencies, with particular reference to the relationship between ministers and chief executives, and the controversy surrounding the Home Secretary's dismissal of the Head of the Prison Service, Derek Lewis (see above). Following publication of and debate on the Scott Report early in 1996, the Committee widened the scope of its inquiry to cover broader issues of ministerial accountability to Parliament – with particular reference to the need to amend the document, 'Questions of Procedure for Ministers' (QPM), in the light of Scott's recommendations. This resulted, inter alia, in the Major government agreeing to make some important amendments to QPM, in particular to the section dealing with ministers' obligations not to mislead Parliament.

One controversial aspect of this was the fact that the proposed amendment told ministers that they must not 'knowingly' mislead Parliament and the public – a formulation that had featured in the government's defence of ministers' conduct during the Scott debates, and which had generated fury and cynicism in the ranks of opposition critics. In her evidence to the Public

Service Committee's inquiry into accountability, Ann Taylor, Labour's then Shadow Minister (later to become Leader of the House 1997–98), promised that a Labour government would rewrite QPM and that the offending word, 'knowingly' would be removed.[15]

In January 1997, the Committee produced a further report on the same subject, following the government's response to the earlier report.[16] The two reports were debated in the Commons a few weeks before the general election.[17]

In summary, radical public sector reform was a key element of government policy in the pre-Blair years, and there are many official documents and parliamentary debates through which these reforms can be traced. Labour, in opposition, did not, by and large, contest these changes in principle – and once in office showed no inclination to reverse them. Indeed, given the decision to adhere for the time being to the previous government's public spending targets, unravelling reforms that emphasised performance measurement and greater financial discipline would have made no sense. Programmes like the Private Finance Initiative, Fundamental Spending Reviews and the Citizen's Charter have been modified and relaunched. However, the shadow of Nolan, Scott and the Derek Lewis affair still hangs heavily over public life, and many of the issues of standards of conduct and public accountability that were highlighted by these events – and which featured prominently in Labour's attacks on the Major government – remain to be addressed.[18] The speed and method by which this will happen, remain somewhat uncertain at the time of writing. A new Civil Service Act is one promised aspect. The modernisation of accountability (along with the modernisation of Parliament, which has been addressed by a Select Committee established for the purpose soon after the 1997 election) is as much a part of the broader agenda of constitutional change as it is of 'civil service reform'.

LABOUR'S PRE-ELECTION THINKING ABOUT THE CIVIL SERVICE: THE MANDELSON–LIDDLE ANALYSIS

The incoming Labour government's careful and conciliatory approach to the civil service – harnessing the traditional strengths of the service to strong

---

[15] HC [1995–96] 313-III, Q 1055.

[16] HC [1996–97] 234.

[17] HC Deb, 12 February 1997, cols 273–293.

[18] Indeed, there have been some very faint echoes of Scott (and perhaps of the Westland saga in the 1980s) in the 'Sandline' affair, that was unfolding in the summer of 1998, as this chapter was being completed. This episode, involving alleged official complicity in the breaching of a UN arms embargo against a former illegal regime in Sierra Leone, and raising some questions about what if anything Foreign Office ministers knew about the matter, was referred to an independent inquiry (by Sir Thomas Legg) and was also being examined by the Commons Foreign Affairs Select Committee.

ministerial leadership – so evident in the weeks immediately following the election was foreshadowed in a chapter of a book co-authored by Peter Mandelson (then opposition frontbench spokesperson on the civil service and later to assume a key co-ordinating role as Minister without Portfolio in the Cabinet Office) and the Labour policy adviser, Roger Liddle.[19]

The authors began by acknowledging the professional neutrality of the civil service in general and of the Head of the Civil Service in particular: 'Never mind that Sir Robin [Butler] has already served Blair's two Conservative predecessors – he has also successfully served Labour administrations and, like the members of the private office whom the new prime minister will also inherit, his whole professional training requires him to transfer his loyalty and dedication to the new incumbent without pause.' We may note in passing – reinforcing the recurrent theme of continuity and neutrality – that Sir Robin Butler, remained in post until the end of 1997. It may also be noted that in appointing his successor, the Blair government did not (as it had been rumoured that they might) take the opportunity to split the posts of Cabinet Secretary and Head of the Civil Service; and that they selected someone in the traditional 'Oxbridge mandarin' mould.[20] Soundings for the appointment were taken by the new Minister without Portfolio, Peter Mandelson.

Mandelson and Liddle went on to warn incoming ministers against seeing the volume of work and paper as civil service obstruction, preventing ministers from doing the real job of running the country: on the contrary, they say, 'this paperwork is the real job.'

The authors looked at the vexed issue of politicisation, concluding that, having worked for ministers of the same party for so long, civil servants 'have been colonised rather than politicised'. Labour ministers should not resent robust, objective advice, honestly given: for many civil servants 'rediscovering their courage to speak up after years of keeping their heads down will be the chief challenge'. There was some ambivalence about the appointment of specialist political advisers – an issue that was to arouse some controversy in the aftermath of the election. The authors criticised Tory ministers for surrounding themselves with sycophantic sidekicks, on the lookout for seats at Westminster for themselves; advisers, they say, 'should work with, not against, the permanent staff.'

Traditional ministerial private offices, able to 'plug their minister fully into the Whitehall network' were preferred to the European model of ministerial *cabinets*. On the other hand, the authors did see the necessity of appointing some advisers from outside the service, at a senior level 'carrying sufficient weight to match those at under-secretary levels in key departments', and a Labour government should, they said, develop links with universities and

---

[19] Peter Mandelson and Roger Liddle, *The Blair Revolution: Can New Labour Deliver?* (Faber, 1996).
[20] Sir Richard Wilson, formerly Permanent Secretary to the Home Office – educated at Radley College and the University of Cambridge. See David Walker, 'Mandarin Charmer Takes Top Civil Service Posts', *The Independent*, 2 August 1997.

professional organisations. Recruitment of outsiders – both political and non-political – 'enriches the civil service' and enables the government to tap into resources that would not otherwise be accessible.

The civil service needs strong leadership, from the centre: 'the machinery will happily function in neutral when left to itself, but will not move forward without strong prime-ministerial direction'. Mrs Thatcher's capacity to win the attention of the civil service was acknowledged, but her regular disparagement of the civil service meant that civil servants' commitment to their jobs was 'poorly nurtured'. This message reappeared later in the chapter when the authors opined that:

> 'The government needs a permanent, professional core of officials, and ministers will not get the best out of the civil service by denigrating it. As prime minister, Tony Blair should be mean with, not to, the machine.'

This has proved – unsurprisingly, given the book's authorship – to be an accurate summary of the Blair approach to the civil service in the early months of the new administration.

'BETTER GOVERNMENT FROM THE BOTTOM UP': DAVID CLARK'S SPEECH

After the election, one early indication of the Blair government's (rather anodyne) thinking about the role of the civil service in carrying forward the new administration's agenda came in the form of a speech by Dr David Clark, soon after his appointment as Chancellor of the Duchy of Lancaster, to a well-attended gathering of civil servants and academic and media commentators on the civil service at the Queen Elizabeth II Conference Centre on 17 June 1997. His speech was entitled 'Delivering Better Government from the Bottom Up'.

The minister began by stressing the value he attached to the ethos and principles of public service and by promising that he and his colleagues would take every opportunity to reinforce such principle:

> 'Of selection and promotion on merit. Of accountability through ministers to a democratically elected Parliament. And of absolute integrity and incorruptibility which we accept are essentials and which we will underline by giving a legal force to the Civil Service Code of Ethics.'

Dr Clark went on to stress the need to deal with the problem of sleaze and start rebuilding public confidence 'not only in public servants but also in Ministers'; the government was reviewing QPM, and he hoped that this would now be published.

He noted that in recent years 'there have been momentous changes in your way of life and your way of work'. Three-quarters of civil servants now worked in agencies. The government was 'not planning to turn the clock back'. It wanted to build upon improvements in service delivery: 'delegation is here to stay' but at the same time, he said, 'we must ensure that central guidelines and common standards remain as important as ever.' The efforts to cut out waste would continue. 'Efficiency initiatives and benchmarking against other organisations are essential.' The emphasis given to the Citizen's Charter would continue, though with less of a 'top down approach': there was a need 'to reinvent the programme of charters so that we actually address the needs, the demands, the wishes, the wants of the ordinary man and woman'.[21]

What of the other big new public management reforms of the Major years? The message was that these, too, would be adapted to Labour's new strategy:

'when we come to market testing and contracting out then these will have a role to play, again not out of dogmatism but out of pragmatism, because we want the best value for money and the best way of delivering the public service to the individual'.

(Later, in response to a question, he said he hoped 'that we have been through the worst of what we have experienced [sic] in the downsizing of the Civil Service'.) The government had announced a review of the Private Finance Initiative. The promised moves towards greater transparency and accountability in government (he referred to the forthcoming White Paper on freedom of information) would 'change the culture of Whitehall'.

The speech concluded on the theme of collective decision-making, involving ministers and civil servants at all levels: civil servants, he said, 'provide the corporate oil . . . within which the wheels of Government will actually work'. Dr Clark promised the civil service 'open and fair dealings, recognition for work well done and terms and conditions in line with the most responsible and the best of the largest commercial employers'. He signalled his own belief in Investors in People. But he was, as ministers usually are, with the Chancellor breathing down their necks, cautious to the point of extreme vagueness on the subject of public service pay.

THE CIVIL SERVICE AND NEW LABOUR – THE 'SPIN' FACTOR

John Major gave opposition frontbenchers nearly 18 months access to senior civil servants to discuss the machinery for implementing Labour's objectives. In the weeks immediately before the election there were some heated but ephemeral controversies, mainly to do with the alleged use of civil servants to produce critiques of opposition plans for partisan electoral purposes.

[21] In June 1998 the Charter was relaunched as 'The Service First' programme.

Aspects of these controversies resurfaced after the election in relation to the Government Information Service, and the demarcation line between the respective roles of political advisers and 'spin-doctors', and those of civil service information officers employed by departments to explain government policies. The Labour Party had been particularly successful in its highly pro-active news management in the run-up to the election and, once elected, the continuing importance that it attached to communications and its relations with the media was clearly signalled by the appointment of Peter Mandelson, one of the Prime Minister's closest advisers, to a Cabinet post, with special responsibility for co-ordinating the presentation of government policy.

A few months after the general election, stories began to appear in the press about clashes between ministers and some of their departmental information officers, inherited from the previous administration. The Director of Information at the Ministry of Defence was 'moved to other duties'; in the Treasury, the Chancellor, Gordon Brown, dealt with the media mainly through a political adviser, Charlie Whelan, and the Information Officer, Jill Rutter, asked to be returned to policy duties. There was also a 'restructuring' of information services in the Northern Ireland Office and the Scottish Office. All this took place against the background of a more general review of departmental management of relationships with the media, set in train by Mike Granatt, the head of the Government Information Service, and Director of Communication at the Home Office – signalling what one newspaper account called 'a cultural revolution' in the Government Information Service.[22] The same article disclosed that a central media monitoring unit was being set up as a pilot project in the Central Office of Information. Shortly afterwards, press accounts appeared of a (leaked) memorandum circulated to information officers by Alistair Campbell, the Prime Minister's Press Officer, telling them that the change of government and the review of media relations gave the Government Information Service an opportunity 'to raise its game and be right at the heart of government'.[23]

A further episode was reported a few days later, when Jonathan Haslam, John Major's former press secretary, was said to have resigned his post as information officer at the Department for Education and Employment after a row with a minister, who had wanted to insert into a departmental press release a paragraph criticising aspects of the previous government's policies. The permanent secretary supported the information officer's contention that this would breach a recently published guidance note on the work of the Government Information Service[24] which says that information officers' actions 'should be objective and explanatory, not tendentious or polemical and should not be, or be liable to misrepresentation as being, party political'. This did

---

[22] Richard Norton-Taylor and Ian Black, 'The Ministry of Spin', *The Guardian*, 15 September 1997.

[23] 'Whitehall Press Officers get Lesson in Spin', *The Times*, 2 October 1997.

[24] Issued simultaneously with the new *Code of Conduct and Guidance on Procedures for Ministers*, Cabinet Office, July 1997.

not prevent Mr Haslam's resignation (he had in fact already been offered a job in the private sector), and the minister arranged for the paragraph to be released via Labour Party Central Office. A leading article in *The Times* on the same day suggested that, 'putting the Government's policies in the best light is one thing; putting the previous government's policies in the worst light is another' – which seems to sum up the position fairly enough. The same leading article went on to caution the government that using political spokespersons to brief the press, rather than civil service information officers, may backfire when a government runs into difficulty and needs the protection of a credibly neutral person rather than a partisan to present their case. A later article in the *Observer* quoted an unnamed civil servant as saying that, 'when Labour came in, I reckoned it would be three to six months before they appreciated that the virtues we have – civil service virtues – are in a sense protective ones: protecting ministers from dropping themselves in it'.[25]

The saga rumbles on, intermittently, during the summer of 1998. It is symptomatic really of two things. First, of the fact that the last months of the Major administration were particularly fraught ones in Whitehall, with ministers divided among themselves and acutely aware of the likelihood of their impending electoral defeat. Some of the consequent 'siege mentality' inevitably afflicted the civil service – and it bore particularly heavily upon the information officers, caught between, on the one side paranoid and frustrated ministers and, on the other, media people – most of whom, towards the end were making no secret of their belief, often tinged with ill-disguised glee, that the government was on the way out. It is perhaps unsurprising that some of these officials found difficulty after the election in adapting quickly to the new and much more bullish government mood and were loath to raise their heads above the parapet.

The other relevant factor is that the incoming government was in a hurry to make, and to be seen to make its mark on events. Moreover, skilful use of the media – and the spin-doctoring of policy messages – had played a crucial part in Labour's election victory, and was seen to be a key to consolidating that victory and establishing the government's credentials as a dynamic and decisive administration. The rather lumbering neutrality of the Government Information Service was bound to cut across the explicitly political mission of Peter Mandelson and the political advisers positioned strategically at the heart of the government machine.

This phenomenon is the product of a convergence of irreversible trends both in mass communications and in political behaviour. Future governments – of whatever party, or parties – are likely to behave similarly, and the official information services are learning to adapt to this.[26] Meanwhile, the episodes described here underline rather than contradict the continuing

---

[25] 'Is it all just spinning out of their control?', *The Observer*, 26 October 1997.
[26] Following recent controversies, the *Report of the Working Group on the Government Information Service* was published by the Office of Public Service, Cabinet Office, in November 1997.

commitment of the civil service to traditional norms of political neutrality, a commitment which quite comfortably survived the transition of power from a party that had been in office, for 18 years and that had, during that time, done so much to refashion the civil service. Those norms of neutrality may in fact be overdue for reappraisal – but that is another story, and one that lies far beyond the scope of this chapter.

Further reading

Gavin Drewry and Tony Butcher, *The Civil Service Today* (Oxford: Blackwell, 2nd edn, 1991)

Colin Campbell and Graham Wilson, *The End of Whitehall* (Oxford: Blackwell, 1995)

Peter Barberis (ed), *The Whitehall Reader* (Milton Keynes: Open University Press, 1996)

Dawn Oliver and Gavin Drewry, *Public Service Reforms: Issues of Accountability and Public Law* (London: Pinter, 1996)

Philip Giddings (ed), *Parliamentary Accountability: A Study of Parliament and Executive Agencies* (London: Macmillan, 1995)

Peter Mandelson and Roger Liddle, *The Blair Revolution: Can New Labour Deliver?* (London: Faber, 1996)

CHAPTER 8

FREEDOM OF INFORMATION

Professor Patrick Birkinshaw and Alan Parkin
(Institute of European Public Law, Hull)[1]

INTRODUCTION

In its manifesto for the 1997 general election the Labour Party committed itself to the introduction of a Freedom of Information Act (FOIA).[2] So too did the Liberal Democrats. The Conservatives had the most to say about open government in their manifesto, stating their achievements to date in making government in the UK more open. Such legislation, the then Opposition believed, would be a part of the constitution for the future and not the past. The Labour and Liberal Democrat parties in their Report of the Joint Consultative Committee on Constitutional Reform (1997, see Appendix 2 below), in outlining the pressing need to renew democracy in Britain, observed how government holds more information than ever before but the public lack a legal right to share information collected 'by their Government' (para 7). A statutory framework would establish independent machinery helping to shift the balance decisively in favour of the presumption that government information should be made publicly available unless there is a justifiable reason not to do so (para 27). The Committee, along with the Labour manifesto, further recommended the establishment of an independent National Statistics Service. On access to information, and on constitutional reform generally, there seemed to be clear space between the Conservative government and the Opposition.

On numerous occasions, not least at the Campaign for the Freedom of Information awards in 1996, Tony Blair had declared his support for a FOIA. Labour spokespersons had previously stated that a FOIA would be among the first passed by an incoming Labour administration because it would signal its renunciation of long-standing traditions of secrecy and that it would be cheap to operate. A Right to Information Bill presented by Robin

---

[1] The authors are grateful to Maurice Frankel of the Campaign for Freedom of Information for his helpful comments on an earlier draft of this chapter. The views expressed are those of the authors.

[2] Although Access to (or Right to) Official Information Act appears to be the more commonly used title, and one which is more accurate than the original US title.

Corbett MP in 1992 was supported by both the then Leader and Deputy Leader of the Labour Party. Tony Blair continued in 1996 by saying that a FOIA was 'not some isolated constitutional reform' but 'a change that is absolutely fundamental to how we see politics developing in this country'. It was a manifestation of the fact that government would regard itself 'as in some sense in a genuine partnership with people' and its presence would signal a 'culture change' in the way that Britain is governed. It would be a 'signal' of 'a new relationship'.

This is unmistakably the language of constitutional development and change. A FOIA would represent a significant constitutional reform in the culture of secrecy that has clothed the traditions of British government. We would therefore take issue with those who write that 'FOI' legislation is an administrative law reform, not linked to any wider constitutional change.'[3] On the contrary we believe it would be.

In December 1996, the Shadow Chancellor of the Duchy of Lancaster predicted FOI legislation within 12 months. By the early months of 1997, as the election loomed, there were rumours that Labour policy-makers were putting a FOIA on the back-burner in favour of legislation on devolution and other constitutional reforms. A proposal for a White Paper on FOI, but not a Bill, was included in the Queen's Speech in May 1997. This would allow time to study the options and to get it right. After all, the Labour Party had only been thinking about the subject for almost a quarter of a century (see below). Could it be that that great prize of successful UK general elections-parliamentary sovereignty, official secrecy and prerogative power was looking more and more appealing; too appealing to be disfigured by laws that might undermine executive prerogative? The size of the Labour majority gave the new government a mandate for constitutional change. Plans for such change are already well under way. New Labour, new constitution – and one that includes a FOIA. If such legislation were not forthcoming, it would have been a cause for condemnation in many quarters and it would have been seen as a blatant display of hypocrisy. More likely at this juncture is that legislation will be forthcoming. But legislation after one and a half to two years in office with a huge parliamentary majority is more likely to be executive minded.

Early indications appeared to suggest that independent enforcement by the courts of decisions allowing access to information against government wishes would not take place. More likely was the appointment of a special Information Commissioner who could make recommendations which could be 'backed up' by parliamentary pressure, presumably through the Select Committee on Public Service. This begged the question of the independence of committees, with in-built government majorities, from government whips.

---

[3] The Constitution Unit's primary concern was whether formerly a FOIA was a 'first class constitutional measure' requiring a Committee stage of the whole House in the Commons. Questions of parliamentary procedure ought not to blind us to questions of substance. Incidentally, reforming secrecy laws in 1989 involved a Committee on the floor of the House: The Constitution Unit, *Introducing Freedom of Information* (1996).

In December 1997, the White Paper on Freedom of Information, *Your Right to Know*,[4] was published and it appeared refreshingly radical in its content. There was to be an independent Commissioner who would have power to enforce decisions against recalcitrant departments or public bodies covered by the Act. In the case of persistent refusal, the Commissioner may refer the case to the High Court for it to punish as a contempt, rather like the situation where the Parliamentary Commissioner for Administration (the ombudsman) faces obstruction in the course of an investigation. However, unlike the ombudsman, the Information Commissioner would not rely upon the Public Administration Select Committee to 'enforce' decisions through that Committee. It was anticipated that a Bill would be enacted in the 1998–99 session. While there are some reservations about the contents of the White Paper, it does seem to fill the basic desiderata of an FOIA. What are these?

WHAT IS FOI?

Freedom of information (FOI) means that citizens have a presumptive legal right to documents held by public authorities which is enforceable, usually by an independent judicial body and which is subject to exclusions and exemptions, the latter of which are usually discretionary. The burden of proof is on the party seeking to rely on the exemption.[5] FOI legislation is a sign that democracy has come of age, that citizens have a right to participate in the decisions that shape their lives to the extent that they are entrusted as a legal right with information lying behind policy decisions, information about matters of concern to them or about themselves collected by government or other bodies and which might cover food production, nuclear experimentation, prison conditions, public health and safety, information about guidance or codes that government and administration use to determine citizens' rights or liabilities. In all regimes where a FOIA operates, its implementation has produced numerous examples of hidden fraud and waste of expenditure, and it has prevented further waste and promoted efficiency in public service and services, all for a relatively small amount of money.[6] FOI is a component of open government. Open government is an essential component of participation by the governed in the process of government; this latter aspect has been called one of the essential third generation of human rights.[7]

---

[4] Cm 3818, December 1997.

[5] See P Birkinshaw, *Freedom of Information: The Law, the Practice and the Ideal* (2nd ed, 1996).

[6] For some examples, see P Birkinshaw, *Freedom of Information*, pp 343–344. The Select Committee on the Parliamentary Commissioner for Administration saw the advantages as being: improved decision-making by ministers and civil servants; greater accuracy and objectivity of personal files; informed public debate on issues of the day; and a former Secretary to the Cabinet – Sir Douglas Wass – believed it would force departments to produce reliable indexes for departmental files.

[7] After civil and political rights (first generation) and economic and social rights (second generation).

On 14 December 1946, a Resolution of the United Nations General Assembly stated: 'Freedom of Information is a fundamental human right and is the touchstone for all freedoms to which the United Nations is consecrated' (65th plenary meeting). We would respectfully agree. As well as the right to obtain personal information about oneself held by government and other bodies, the right to obtain *reliable* information about government and its activities is the only sure basis on which government can be made properly accountable for the exercise of power on behalf of the public interest. The lesson here is not just for citizens or groups in their private capacities but also for Parliament in its stewardship of executive power and expenditure. Indeed, recent years have brought home the inadequate information base on which Parliament has to battle with the executive and FOI should further buttress the position of Parliament.

THE BACKGROUND

The Labour Party manifesto of 1974 contained suggestions for a possible FOIA. In 1979, Jim Callaghan's government was on the brink of seeing a Private Member's Bill become law which would have repealed the 'catch-all' s 2 of the Official Secrets Act 1911 and introduced a statutory right of access to official documents. The government had not objected to a Second Reading for the Bill – although its support was lukewarm. It had published a study on FOI by civil servants from the then Civil Service Department which stated that the government could not accept a statutory right of access to official information and that 'a gradual approach was required' which would not carry such a risk of 'damage'. A code of practice was more in line with UK tradition. Before the government could oppose the Bill, Gerry Fitt MP famously abstained in a vote of confidence on the government in the Commons and the Bill, along with the Labour government, fell. It was that close.

His successor's opposition as Prime Minister to FOI and her preoccupation with secrecy are well known. After an attempt at 'reform' of the secrecy laws in 1979 – a reform which fell in the wake of the Blunt affair and which would have presented a more restrictive secrecy regime than the notorious Official Secrets Acts 1911–39, Mrs Thatcher was forced into reform of s 2 of the Official Secrets Act 1911 by the unsuccessful prosecution of Clive Ponting and the Private Member's Bill reforming official secrecy. This Bill was presented by Richard Shepherd, a Conservative backbencher and was killed off by invoking the government payroll.[8] Official secrecy laws were reformed in 1989. The all inclusive sweep of s 2 has gone but the present laws are hardly liberal. They say nothing about access to information. Mrs Thatcher's own views, as expressed in 1984, were bitterly opposed to a FOIA:

---

[8] The first time this was invoked by a Conservative government against a member of its own party.

'Under our constitution, Ministers are accountable to Parliament for the work of their departments, and that includes the provision of information . . . Ministers' accountability to Parliament would be reduced, and Parliament itself diminished . . . In our view the right place for Ministers to answer for their decisions in the essentially 'political' area of information is in Parliament.'

This defensive posture was maintained by John Major's government but the growing emphasis on openness and information and consumerism in the Citizen's Charter[9] forced a rethink in government policy. Much of the impetus for the 1966 FOIA in the USA was consumer led and it was becoming difficult to intone about the merits of treating citizen/consumers well and providing information about comparative service and achievement levels under the Citizen's Charter when more general rights of access to information were not provided. In 1992, the government had introduced some open government measures which included the publication of the names of Cabinet Committees and their responsibilities, provision of more archive material, the revelation of the names of the heads of Intelligence and Security and the publication for the first time of Questions of Procedure for Ministers (QPM), ie the guidelines on responsible and acceptable ministerial behaviour.

THE 1994 CODE AND AMENDMENTS

The most important development came in 1993, when a White Paper was published under the Citizen's Charter initiative on the subject of open government. This announced a series of plans to enhance open government and to provide for access to official information. Access to information was to be allowed under an administrative code which covered all those departments and agencies and non-departmental bodies under the jurisdiction of the Parliamentary Commissioner for Administration (PCA), the ombudsman. The code took effect in April 1994 and was revised in January 1997 and it is accompanied by a much longer code on interpretation.[10] The government undertook to produce information of the following kinds: the facts and analysis of the facts which the government considers relevant and important in framing major policy proposals and decisions; explanatory material on departments' dealings with the public; reasons for decisions unless conventions or legal reasons limited this disclosure; full information, in accordance with the Citizen's Charter, about the running of public services and comparable information about performances. It would also produce information upon request, upon the terms laid down in the code as described below, relating to policies,

---

[9] Cabinet Office, Cm 1599 (1991).
[10] *Code of Practice on Access to Government Information* (2nd ed, 1997); *Guidance on Interpretation* (2nd ed, 1997).

actions and decisions and other matters touching upon the government's areas of responsibility.

Even though the code's future existence would appear to be short-lived, it is worthwhile dealing with this code in some detail because while it embraces some features of a FOI regime it also has unique aspects. First, it is an administrative code and not legislation so it does not create rights in law, not in private law at least.[11] Secondly, it does not provide a 'right' to documents but to information which will be collected, sifted and gleaned by civil servants before being handed on. Thirdly, it is not subject to an independent judicial body with power to enforce its decision against the executive, such as tribunals or courts.

All bodies covered by the code have to produce internal complaints procedures to deal with cases where there is a refusal to hand over information. Where this produces no satisfactory outcome for the complainant, the code is to be 'enforced' by the ombudsman who does not have powers of enforcement as such but who makes recommendations which are invariably negotiated to an acceptable conclusion. It has to be said that the ombudsman's record to date has been impressive and he has often adopted a combative stance on behalf of complainants and has managed to extract some important 'victories' from the departments under his control.[12] The ombudsman also has very wide powers to obtain documents from departments and agencies. But he has had his setbacks also and where an applicant is refused information when the ombudsman recommends disclosure there is little that the latter can do about it, short of flying in the face of the departmental decision. Prime Minister John Major himself stated that the ombudsman 'has it in his hands to hand on information' but this was an informal assurance which actually contradicts the legal position.[13] However, the Parliamentary Commissioner Act 1967 states that a minister has a power of veto over information which an ombudsman has collected in an investigation.[14]

A major problem about the code is that it sits somewhat uneasily with the Parliamentary Commissioner Act which contains significant exclusions from the information provisions – originally devised to define those bodies and matters outside the complaints jurisdiction of the ombudsman. These exclusions are in addition to exemptions contained in the code and may be relied upon to prevent access to information, usually on the grounds that access would be damaging to the interest being protected. In some cases, disclosure of certain items of information is deemed in itself to be 'damaging' to the public interest. Here the ombudsman has nevertheless won important

---

[11] Quaere public law, eg legitimate expectation?

[12] See Select Committee on the Parliamentary Commissioner for Administration, *Open Government* HC [1995–96] 84. Reference is to the ombudsman who retired in December 1996, Sir William Reid.

[13] ibid, p 9 (evidence of the then ombudsman, Sir William Reid).

[14] See Parliamentary Commissioner Act 1967, s 11(3) and also s 8(4) denying access to information about Cabinet or Cabinet Committee proceedings.

concessions because it has been accepted that in many cases he can balance the public interests involved in deciding where the public interest lies – in other words does the public interest in knowing outweigh the damage that may be done by disclosure? In this respect, the public interest test in the code is not unlike a court of law deciding where the balance lies in a public interest immunity claim – that is where government lawyers seek acceptance from the court not to disclose documents to the other litigant because it would be against the public interest. Government or other bodies may claim that it is not in the public interest for documents or evidence to be given because of the harm that disclosure would cause. However, following the Scott Report into the Matrix Churchill saga, the government announced that it would only claim the immunity where the *contents* of the documents needed to be protected, and not simply that the documents belonged to a *class* of document which had to be protected. The court has the final say on the question of immunity from production. In the case of the ombudsman, the concession is an extra statutory one because the government department etc could not only rely upon its veto powers (see above and s 11(3) of the Parliamentary Commissioner Act 1967), but it could additionally assert that the ombudsman is questioning the merits of a decision where there is no maladministration, which the ombudsman is not allowed to do.[15] It has been questioned whether refusing information on the grounds of the 'merits' of a decision is in fact likely, and that such a refusal would undermine any serious commitment to the code. The 'merits' argument may be legalistic, but it is a jurisdictional bar in a statute which cannot be overridden by a government undertaking.

This 'fudge' between the Parliamentary Commissioner Act 1967 and the code is also apparent in the government concession that a refusal to comply with the code will amount to maladministration causing injustice, difficult though it may be to locate 'injustice' in a refusal to supply publicly held information where there is no obvious loss, damage or insult.

Many parties agree that the operation of the code has been a significant improvement on the previous practice – which was basically secrecy in the absence of ad personam concessions.[16] As well as being more liberal, ie allowing greater access, than some UK statutory regimes – eg the Environmental Information Regulations 1992 (SI 1992 No 324) as amended[17] – while at the same time not being able to override other statutory exclusions or exemptions to access of which there are about 250, the code has been

---

[15] The courts have reminded the PCA and other ombudsmen that their powers are judicially reviewable: see in particular Sedley J in *R v Parliamentary Commissioner for Administration, ex parte Balchin* (unreported, 25 October 1996).

[16] There was the Croham Directive of the 1970s which exhorted departments to provide background information on government decisions but it faded from view in the beginning of Mrs Thatcher's office. The 1993 White Paper also promised liberalisation of the Public Records Acts and their 'closure' provisions.

[17] See House of Lords European Communities Select Committee, *Freedom of Access to Information on the Environment* HL [1996–97] 9.

used by government to be the guiding criterion on answering parliamentary questions (PQ). PQ practice has become more liberalised and PQs that have been blocked, and the reasons for doing so, have been published for the first time.[18] The ombudsman has decided to accept complaints from MPs where a PQ is refused but not from the MP who asked the question and only where the information requested is covered by the code; effectively, it becomes a code request. The Osmotherley rules which contain guidance to civil servants on giving evidence to Parliament have been redrafted to take account of the code.[19] So, one may ask, with all these improvements, why all the fuss about the absence of a FOIA?

First of all, because at the end of the day a code is simply that – an administrative code. The most dramatic illustration of the ease with which codes can be overlooked comes from the Matrix Churchill saga where the guidelines on arms exports were persistently misapplied or ignored.[20] One might cavil at using an example of guidelines which, though operational, were not originally presented to Parliament for almost a year and which were subsequently amended without notifying Parliament. However, the government has the final say on whether information is disclosed or not. Too often it is not in the government's interests to disclose information; its interests may not be the same as the real public interest.[21] This UK feature is unique in FOI regimes throughout the world. All the 'advances' in the operation of the code have been given by extra statutory concession. A change of government, a change of ombudsman and the concessions can be easily withdrawn or the code itself could be expunged or not so rigorously 'enforced'. No law would be broken. No less a body than the Select Committee on the Parliamentary Commissioner has recommended that the code be elevated to a statute, but the Major government did not accept this recommendation.[22]

The second concern relates to the lack of legal enforcement of the code. In the Select Committee Report, the Committee was content to leave enforcement to the ombudsman of the duties which the Committee recommended would be elevated to a statute; this would overcome any difficulties which might arise from the non-statutory nature of the code at present. Practices differ in different FOI regimes, but whether an ombudsman, a special commissioner

---

[18] See *Ministerial Accountability and Responsibility* HC [1996–97] 234. Not all refusals are recorded. Refusals are the consequence of ministerial convention not parliamentary convention; HC [1995–96] 313, para 38. Revisions on refusal to answer PQs so that, for instance, questions of their nature secret are no longer refused on that ground alone were introduced in 1993; see HC [1995–96] 313, para 39 for other changes. Dawn Oliver has questioned whether these changes have made much difference in practice: editor's comments (1996) *Public Law* at p 417. Tony Blair announced a reform of Prime Minister's Question Time to take place for 30 minutes on Wednesday afternoons instead of two 15-minute sessions.

[19] Cabinet Office, *Departmental Evidence and Response to Select Committees*, January 1997.

[20] HC [1995–96] 115, Vol I, section D.

[21] *R v Ponting* [1985] Crim LR 318 where the trial judge equiparated the interests of the state with the interests of the government of the day which on the basis of existing case law alone was a gross over-simplification. P Birkinshaw, *Freedom of Information*, pp 101–103.

[22] See *Open Government*, note 12 above and Government Reply, HC [1996–97] 75.

or a tribunal is chosen to make the initial decision, there is inevitably appeal to the courts where a final binding decision will be made. At present, the code lacks credibility because of the absence of this quality of enforcement. The answer given by Major's government that the minister is ultimately answerable to Parliament bears little substance when Parliament is dominated by a minister's party. Just think of the implications of a majority of 179 for instance.

Thirdly, there are too many omissions and exclusions from the code even were it raised to statute as the Select Committee has recommended. Excluded bodies include the Cabinet, the Bank of England (now with executive powers over interest rates), the Prime Minister's Office and the Securities and Investment Board. But a good many additional bodies are excluded from the ombudsman's jurisdiction. Some for very good reason, eg local government where there is already an access to information and open meetings law enforced through the courts or by way of the local government ombudsman. However, the 1993 White Paper on open government nonetheless stated that a similar code to that for central government would apply in local government without giving any attention to the relationship between this code and existing local government legislation. In fact local authorities were left to devise their own statements of practice.[23] The National Health Service has its own code supervised by the Health Services Commissioner. But many bodies escape any ombudsman or certainly any government endorsed scheme/code to provide information to the public.

Public bodies generally must comply with the principles laid down by the Nolan Committee on standards in public life, but how these principles are adopted and implemented, including openness, is largely up to the bodies themselves with advice from the relevant section of the Cabinet Office. A basic problem is that a good many bodies are on the fringe or interface of the public/private division and constitutionally are not state or public bodies and are therefore not covered. Furthermore, the ombudsman is excluded from examining Cabinet documents, added to which certain very important functions of government are excluded from the investigation of the ombudsman. Such exclusions cover commercial and contractual matters, personnel complaints, the Attorney General and Director of Public Prosecutions and so on. Therefore, it would seem that information covering these areas is also excluded because the ombudsman cannot investigate a complaint relating to them.

Fourthly, the exemptions are too broad, a point which is particularly true of the exemption concerning internal discussion and advice where disclosure would harm the 'frankness and candour of internal discussion' (see pp 184ff below).

---

[23] Association of Metropolitan Authorities, *Open Government. A Good Practice Note on Access to Information* (1995); see also *Local Government Ombudsman*, Issue 6, March 1996.

Last of all, the code does not provide specifically for access to personal information although access may be requested to such information and will be subject to the exemption covering personal information. The 1993 White Paper did suggest that legislation covering personal information – as well as health and safety legislation – would be forthcoming, the former possibly to be under the control of the Data Protection Registrar who currently only polices the area of computerised personal data. Such legislation has not been introduced. In 1995, however, an EC directive was agreed which will introduce a general right of access to personal records indifferent as to their format, ie data on a computer or paper. It has been seen as a Privacy Act and many of its provisions were vigorously resisted by the Conservative government. The directive has to be implemented by 1998. However, provisions under the Second and Third Pillars of the EU Treaty, which deal respectively with common foreign and security policy and policing and criminal justice, are not covered by the directive and there are various exclusions relating to policing and national security which in fact go further than the exemptions under the UK Data Protection Act 1984.

The above constitute the major weaknesses in the provisions of the code which in addition was poorly advertised, especially when compared with the publicity given to the Citizen's Charter.[24]

HOW TO PROCEED?

The frequency with which senior Labour Party spokespersons in opposition asserted that a FOIA would be introduced would have made it a cause of acute embarrassment and controversy were such an Act not forthcoming within the first year of office unless accompanied by the most unqualified promise of legislation in the second session. Such a failure would have been exacerbated by the nature of the revelations concerning the arrangements relating to tobacco advertising and Formula One racing when the latter was excluded from advertising bans on TV, an exclusion which appeared rather too close temporally to a gift of £1 million from Mr Bernie Ecclestone – Formula One's 'Boss' – to the Labour Party. Were legislation not forthcoming at that later stage, it would have amounted to an act of perfidy. An option for a Bill might have been something along the lines of the Labour MP Mark Fisher's (now Minister for the Arts) Private Member's Bill of 1993, the Right to Know Bill (No 18 1993) which had cross-party support in the form of Sir Teddy Taylor and Archy Kirkwood MPs. Options could include enacting the provisions of the 1994 code pro tem, pending an opportunity to introduce a fuller Bill, or some other simpler Bill, again as an interim

---

[24] See *Open Government*, note 12, at p 85: 'for example, £80,000 in total is being spent on advertising the Code, and in total since it began only £180,000 has been spent – half of a utility boss's salary . . .' which as an estimate has dated quickly!

measure. The new Labour government has in the event argued that the complexity of FOI in practice means that it will have to give further thought to the final version of the Bill.

It does seem, however, that to fulfil the Labour government's prior stated commitments nothing less than the Fisher Bill, which is a replica (with some additions) of the FOI Bill drafted by the Campaign for Freedom of Information, would be acceptable. The campaign was launched in 1984 to replace the Official Secrets Act 1911, s 2 and to introduce a FOIA. It has played a central role in successfully bringing a number of Access to Information Bills to the statute book. Various problems with the Bill which will need to be addressed and provided for are identified below. It does have some serious omissions in introducing an open government regime and many of the omissions are also a feature of the 1997 White Paper from the Labour government examined at p 189 below. The following text highlights the key provisions of the Fisher Bill.

Part I of the Bill provides for access 'by any person' to official records. Access is given to official records held by a public authority in connection with its functions as such, whether or not created by that authority, and whether or not it was created before the commencement of the Act. A record is held by an authority if it is in its possession, custody or power. The Bill seeks to define a public authority for the purposes of the Act and suffice to say while those who contract to perform functions on behalf of the Crown would be caught, it is unclear whether it would include bodies operating under the Private Finance Initiative for instance. Needless to say it seeks to capture the whole of the public sector as commonly understood plus a wide range of quasi governmental bodies. Doubtless many bodies will escape its net where they are privately established, not funded by public monies, but where they are used extensively by government to effect its purposes.[25]

An application has to be made in writing for access to an official record and public authorities have to assist applicants in their applications or where their applications are incomplete. 'Records' includes personal records and the right to access overrides any statutory or common law restriction – such as official secrecy – unless the information relates to the personal affairs of an individual or is contained in an order of the court.[26] The Bill has detailed provisions on procedural and administrative matters such as time limits and the form in which access is to be given. This is expressed in very comprehensive terms to include not only paper and computerised documents or those which are electronically stored but also sound records. Inaccurate personal information may be corrected and compensation may be awarded for inaccuracy.

---

[25] Bodies which have been subject to judicial review might be included but the approach of the courts has not been consistent, alternating between formalistic or pragmatic tests.

[26] Legal professional privilege is covered by the exemptions although the statutory exemptions appear to be narrower than the common law privilege. Under the 1997 White Paper, legal advice is excluded and the Select Committee on Public Administration believed that it should be exempt not excluded – see pp 194–5 below for a discussion of the Committee's Report.

Part II lists the exemptions from access. Reasons have to be given for withholding records under exemptions. The reasons have to state the ground of exemption, the identity of the person who claimed the exemption, procedures for claiming an internal review of the decision and for making complaint to the Information Commissioner (see p 187 below). Information is exempt if its disclosure would be likely to cause 'significant damage' to defence, security or international relations. Exemptions also cover law enforcement, legal professional privilege, invasion of personal privacy, health records, the economy and commercial affairs of authorities though there are qualifications to these exemptions.[27] Further exemptions cover the competitive position of third parties, or where applications substantially and unreasonably interfere with an authority's work or which would significantly damage the work of the authority 'by impairing its ability to obtain similar information in the future'. There are again some interesting qualifications to this exemption.[28] Where documents are already published they are exempt from the disclosure provisions. A ploy which has been used in Canada involves the statutory publication of official information which is available at costs far in excess of those under the FOIA regime. The most contested exemption covers internal advice and it merits a more extended analysis, especially as this exemption is also in the 1997 White Paper.

INTERNAL ADVICE

The Conservative government's Code of Practice on Access to Government Information (discussed at pp 177–82 above) exempts information relating to internal discussion and advice where disclosure would harm the 'frankness and candour of internal discussion'. This covers proceedings of Cabinet and Cabinet Committees; internal opinion, advice, recommendation, consultation and deliberation; projections and assumptions relating to internal policy analysis, analysis of alternative policy options and information relating to rejected policy options and confidential communications between departments, public bodies and regulatory bodies. The reasons for this exemption are founded on an unwillingness to conduct policy-making in a goldfish bowl and civil service apprehensions that if civil servants are identifiable from policy documents this would undermine their position both with ministers where they were seen by the press and public to disagree with ministers and with the

---

[27] So in the case of economic and commercial affairs where revealing information to a competitor of the authority would be likely to damage significantly the lawful commercial activities of the (exempt) authority it will not be exempt where the availability of information will lead to more informed choice by consumers of the authority's goods or services, or it relates to an investigation into a 'public safety hazard'.

[28] Similar provisions to those in the preceding note remove the third party exemption where the same factors apply, ie the damage is caused by informed consumer choice or relates to public safety hazard investigations.

Opposition where there would be hostility to the advice given by advisers and where it might be assumed that the adviser was not advising impartially but had an ideological commitment to a particular policy. Where this policy was anathema to the Opposition, revelation of an adviser's identity and advice would make use of that adviser when, or if, in office untenable.

Even accepting that it may not usually be in the public interest to disclose advice *before* a decision is made, this exemption is particularly broad and goes way beyond the legitimate protection of the policy process. For instance, analysis of alternative policy options and information relating to rejected policy options is exempted under the code, even *after* the decision. Surely this is the very information that would assist citizens to assess the strength of the case in favour of the preferred option; how strongly supported was the successful option? What was the degree of support compared with that for alternatives? Which choice was in the real public interest? The projections and assumptions relating to internal policy advice would appear to be more closely attached to factual matters or methodologies which ought not to be protected by exemptions. In the USA, for instance, agencies are placed under duties which are judicially enforced, and indeed often judicially expanded, to provide detailed reasons for decisions and policies adopted through rules, to provide alternatives to the adopted measures and policies and to be responsive to the public. Although internal advice is protected, factually based material is accessible under the FOIA in the USA and special advisory groups have to conduct open meetings and their records are available to the public under the Federal Advisory Committee Act. The special provisions of confidentiality which so protect the privileged insider consultation exercises in the UK are given no comparable protection in the USA.

The Bill supported by the Labour Party in opposition would still exempt advice, recommendations or opinions given by an official or a minister [sic]. But this would not include factual information, its analysis, interpretation or evaluation or projections based upon it. Nor would it cover expert advice on a scientific, technical, medical, financial, statistical, legal or other matter; it would not exempt guidelines used in taking decisions about the rights of persons, or the actual decisions and reasons for them. Information about the personal affairs of the applicant would not be protected as against that person, only as against third parties seeking the information.

This is a big improvement, but why should advice etc given by a minister or civil servant be protected after the decision is made unless it contains information exempt under another category? Why, furthermore, does a minister need the protection originally devised for civil servants? By all means, protect the decision-making process while it is still active and where exposure would inflict damage to that process itself. But where is the need to protect candour once the decision is made? Furthermore, the candour argument seems a little stretched given the undermining of the concept in the Matrix Churchill episode where the government eventually conceded that the class basis for claims of public interest immunity – one of which was internal candour of advice – would no longer be relied upon in litigation.[29] Only where it was in the public interest that the specific contents not be disclosed would the claim be made. When the policy is finalised why should advice not be disclosed? It should be noted that access would cover Cabinet papers, unless exempted on other grounds. If need be, and no one could reasonably object to this, the identity of any adviser – but not a minister – could be erased. The provisions of the Bill are not concerned with individual identity, but with the quality of decisions and the reasons for rejecting alternatives which may have been a better choice in the public interest and which were not based on a party political or other self-motivated interest.

The 'candour' and invidious position arguments would have no relevance to any special advisers outside the civil service structure who were appointed to assist ministers and their advice should only be exempted if it falls within another exemption.

PUBLIC INTEREST OVERRIDE, THIRD PARTIES AND CODES OF GUIDANCE

Crucially, clause 30 of the Bill is drafted to allow a public interest override for the exemptions where there is reasonable evidence that significant abuse of authority or neglect in the performance of an official duty, injustice to an individual, danger to the health or safety of an individual or of the public or unauthorised use of public funds has or is likely to have occurred 'and if in the circumstances giving access to the information is justified in the public interest having regard both to any benefit and to any damage that may arise from doing so'.[30] Where the balance is in favour of disclosure, access 'shall be given' where reasonable evidence supports one of the above findings. It is not a question of discretion.

Third parties who have given documents to public bodies as defined will be given a 'Third Party Notice' allowing them to challenge before the Information Commissioner or an Information Tribunal a decision to release the information and access will not be allowed pending a decision from the relevant body.

Authorities will have to make available codes of guidance explaining rights under the Act and also indexes of records to enable the public to identify records to which access may be requested. This will include references to exempt information, but there will be no requirement that the content of

---

[29] The statement was made on 18 December in the Lords and Commons: HC Deb, Vol 287, col 949 and HL Deb, Vol 576, col 1507. The Attorney General stated that real harm or damage meant 'substantial damage' quoting Lord Templeman in *R v Chief Constable of West Midlands Police, ex parte Wiley* [1994] 3 All ER 420, HL. Internal advice might be protected on a contents basis where the 'real harm' test was satisfied – the onus is on the body claiming the immunity.

[30] Clause 30(2) and cl 27.

any such information should be revealed. Any guidance affecting the rights, privileges, grants or benefits of individuals which the authorities may use to determine those rights etc must also be produced. Similar disclosures will have to be made of guidelines relating to obligations, penalties or any other 'detriments' affecting individuals. Where disclosures of these guidelines are not made and decisions detrimental to individuals are taken, orders of the court may set aside any adverse decision, may award compensation or do both of these.

ENFORCEMENT AND CHALLENGES

The Bill makes provision for an internal appeals/complaints procedure and this is a feature of the existing code. Internal redress of grievances within public bodies has, of course, become fashionable. But crucial differences are proposed by the introduction of an Information Commissioner – a sort of special ombudsman[31] – and an Information Tribunal. The Commissioner is not simply mandated to act as a grievance remedial device, but is charged with fostering the principles surrounding disclosure as well as facilitating and encouraging the latter promptly at the 'lowest reasonable cost'. The requester must invoke the internal procedures before taking his or her complaint to the Commissioner. Where third parties wish to challenge decisions to disclose their commercial or professional activities their challenge goes to the Tribunal, not the Commissioner.

The powers of the Commissioner are very broad. He (or she) may require any minister or other official/employee of the authority to produce relevant information and shall have the same power as the court to take oaths and examine witnesses and the same powers as the court in respect of the production of records. He may examine any record whether or not it contains exempt information and here one should note that the exclusions operating against the ombudsman under the Parliamentary Commissioner Act 1967 do not apply. There is no exclusion of Cabinet documents or areas of government activity. The Commissioner is not restricted by rules of admissibility governing courts[32] and he has power of entry on to property but legal professional privilege will protect documents.

At the end of the investigation the Commissioner makes his report, crucially to the applicant, which will contain his reasons, copies of any orders made by the Commissioner where an authority has failed to comply with any requirements under the Act or has exercised any discretion unreasonably and information on any rights of appeal to the Tribunal. The Commissioner may order an authority to give access to exempt information, but in the case of

---

[31] See Baxter 'Freedom of Information: Dispute Resolution Procedures' (1996) *European Public Law* 635.
[32] But little now effectively remains of the hearsay rule in civil litigation.

exempt information he has to make a decision on the public interest under clause 30. Access may be stayed pending appeal. Any failure to comply with the orders or any interference with a Commissioner's investigation may be certified for the court and if any such behaviour were to amount to a contempt of court may be punished as such by the court. Officials may not hide behind any laws enjoining secrecy in relation to the Commissioner's investigations, eg Official Secrecy Acts and it would appear rules of court relating to public interest immunity. The Commissioner would doubtless pay great respect to well-supported arguments that information should be exempt, just as a judge would balance the competing interests in claims for public interest immunity. Clause 55 seems to override Crown privilege, but this is anomalous because it has long been transmuted into public interest immunity. Clause 53(2) apparently affords absolute privilege to anything said or supplied in the course of the Commissioner's investigation. Detailed reports have to be provided to Parliament covering statistics under the Act.

Rights of appeal against adverse decisions are given to applicants, third parties and public authorities. The Tribunal can make binding orders, as indeed it would seem de facto could the Commissioner (note the latter's contempt powers for not following an order of the Commissioner) and the Tribunal may award costs against a successful public authority where an appeal has 'raised an important issue of principle'. Nothing is said about appeals from the Tribunal to the courts so judicial review would be the likely source of challenge. It is interesting to speculate on what line the courts might adopt in such challenges and whether the government might wish to preclude the opportunity for such judicial review.[33]

REFORMING SECRECY LAWS AND EMPLOYEE RIGHTS

Part V of the Bill reforms the official secrecy laws to make them far more liberal and to allow defences against criminal prosecution of prior publication and public interest disclosures where an employee or government contractor reveals abuse of authority or neglect in the performance of a public duty; injustice to an individual; danger to an individual's, or public, health and safety; unauthorised use of public funds; or other misconduct.[34] The Bill also provides that there shall be no dismissal or other disciplinary measure against an employee making such a public interest disclosure. These provisions only cover civil servants and government contractors and areas where there have

---

[33] Which may well be counter-productive given the reluctance of the courts to accept 'ouster' of jurisdiction clauses in statutes or instruments in the past: *Anisminic v FCC* [1969] 1 All ER 208, HL; *R v Secretary of State for the Home Department, ex parte Fayed* [1997] 1 All ER 228, CA.

[34] Scott VC has ruled that not disclosing information given to an employer by an informer or the informer's identity were breaches of natural justice: *The Times*, 1 May 1997.

been numerous scandals and whistle-blowing episodes have included the National Health Service, local government, universities and the private sector. An overpowering case can be made out for a general whistle-blower's charter. The previous attempt at introducing one was talked out of the Commons in 1996 by a Conservative government spokesperson.[35] In 1998, Richard Shepherd's Public Interest Disclosure Bill – a whistleblower's charter – was enacted.

Part VII provides rights of access to employment records by employees. At present, rights to electronically retrievable records are available under the Data Protection Act 1984. This right would be extended to paper records and the duties are enforceable through the High Court. Part VIII imposes duties on companies to disclose information under a variety of 'community responsibilities', eg health and safety and environmental laws. This would necessitate publication of information about breaches of legal duties and convictions, deaths and fatalities.

THE 1997 WHITE PAPER

The Labour government's proposals in the White Paper of December 1997 provide for a general statutory right of access to official records and information upon request and also to make certain information publicly available without any request. The first point to note is the extremely wide range of public bodies to be covered by the proposed legislation. These will range from the obvious departments and agencies of the Crown, to utility regulators, nationalised industries, public corporations, 1,200 non-departmental bodies, the National Health Service, administrative functions of courts, tribunals, police forces and authorities, armed forces, local authorities, local public bodies such as social landlords and technical colleges, schools, colleges and universities, public sector broadcasters, private bodies fulfilling statutory functions and privatised utilities. The fact that it is proposed that FOI will cover private sector bodies makes the White Paper a significant advance on existing FOI regimes. The proposal has been bitterly opposed by those bodies which will be covered. Will those bodies fulfilling statutory functions include those under contract to provide services to ministers and local authorities where the service is not itself a statutory function? The White Paper indicates 'Yes'.

The security and intelligence services will be totally excluded so that their organisations, the information they provide and information held about these organisations by other public authorities will not be available under the legislation. This is not entirely surprising, but it should be noted that even in the USA the security and investigation agencies are covered by the FOIA,

---

[35] This Bill sought to strike a balance between protection for a public spirited discloser and malicious or unmeritorious or unnecessary disclosures, the latter of which would not be protected.

albeit with wide exemptions. A blanket exclusion is not the most reassuring of approaches, especially in view of the fact that the security service has moved more and more into the realm of conventional police operations.[36] Where information is excluded it is outside the terms of the legislation completely so that the Commissioner will not have access to it and will not be able to pass any judgment on disclosure. Law enforcement and the criminal prosecution and investigation processes are excluded, although law enforcement is also an exemption covering information not included in the excluded categories. This is a little confounding. Legal advice protected by legal professional privilege will also be excluded, regardless of any public interest in its disclosure or whether litigation is likely or possible. There are in fact several areas where the White Paper proposals are more protective of secrecy than the 1994 code is.

The White Paper proposes that the Act would contain a list of those bodies covered by the Act, rather like the schedule of bodies within the ombudsman's jurisdiction. Like that model, it could be criticised for being too cumbersome. Why not simply list those bodies that are excluded? This is likely to be a much smaller list and will not be subject to constant amendment and updating.

The proposed legislation will allow any individual, company or other body to apply for information which includes records in whatever form – it will not be restricted to information as the 1994 code was. Access will cover records which were created prior to the Act coming into force; there are no time restrictions although some records will be caught by previous statutory restrictions affecting date of release. However, the new provisions will incorporate the existing public records legislation and will seek to ensure an increasing liberalisation, where possible, of access to such historical records within the 30-year period originally set out in the original statutory framework. The Act will cover records which the public body holds: personal and private records belonging to individuals, political party, constituency and other 'privately' owned papers will not be covered. There will be ample scope for disputes over proprietorship. Consider requests for minutes of the meeting between the Prime Minister and Bernie Ecclestone when tobacco advertising was famously discussed in close association with gifts by Ecclestone to the Labour Party.

The Act would not cover public sector employment records – employees would have to claim rights under the Data Protection Act 1984 which is about to be revamped in accordance with obligations under the 1995 EC Directive on Data Protection (see now the Data Protection Act 1998). There is considerable dispute as to the kind of paper documents covered by this proposed legislation. Nor will the Act cover records relating to criminal or civil legal enforcement including the investigation and prosecution functions of the police and other enforcement agencies. Legal professional privilege will be maintained as we have seen.

[36] Security Service Act 1996.

Applicants for information will have to pass various 'gateways' which seek to ensure that requests are reasonable and practicable for authorities to deal with and which also seek to achieve co-operation between the authority and requester in the application. These gateways will attempt to guarantee that requests are as clear and well-informed as possible and to prevent 'vexatious' requests. Examples are provided of where information would be denied at this point, eg it has already been published or will be published at a future date but there is a risk that vague claims to future publication could be abused. Authorities should be as helpful as possible in assisting requesters, and where access is denied, the latter may appeal to the Information Commissioner who may help to mediate the dispute.

While accepting that public authorities will pay for the 'bulk of the costs of FOI', authorities will be able to charge access fees of no more than £10 per request and there should be no charges for access to review and appeals procedures which could too easily encourage an 'irresponsible' attitude by officials forcing expenditure onto applicants. Charging schemes may be imposed for work done by officials which involve significant additional work and considerable costs. These would not allow a profit to be made by the authority and would not cover information which has to be made automatically available under the Act.[37] Consideration will be given to a two-tier system of costs to cater for additional charges for commercial requesters.

The decision on disclosure will be guided first of all by whether there will be the requisite degree of harm caused by disclosure and whether the public interest is best served by secrecy or disclosure. The government seeks to make these decisions as simple and as transparent as possible. It is planned to reduce the number of exemptions from the 15 contained in the 1994 code to seven protected 'interests' and the test of harm will be 'substantial harm' caused by disclosure. The interests are: national security, defence and international relations; law enforcement; personal privacy; commercial confidentiality – although this 'must not be used as a cloak to deny the public's right to know'; the safety of the individual, the public and the environment; and information supplied in confidence.

The last of the so-called protected interests or exemptions merits detailed consideration and concerns policy advice and policy formulation which has already been addressed above. Here a simple 'harm' test to the public interest will suffice to hold records or information back. '[N]ow more than ever government needs space and time in which to assess arguments and conduct its own debates with a degree of privacy.' Governments have made such claims throughout the centuries. In seeking to protect collective responsibility, political impartiality of public officials, free and frank discussion at

---

[37] Facts and analysis which the government considers important in framing major policy proposals; explanatory material on dealing with the public; reasons for administrative decisions to those affected; operational information on costs, standards, targets and complaints procedures on public services.

sensitive stages of decision-making, the reliance is to be placed upon a contents test in order to assess the degree of harm and not a class or 'nature' of documents argument, although the White Paper specifies various class documents which are likely to be exempt. Surely, exemption should be based on the contents alone? Factual information and 'raw data' used in the policy-making process should be disclosed. The White Paper's proposals are aimed at protecting opinion and 'analytical' information. But what if the analysis reveals that the wrong decision was arrived at? Interestingly, the White Paper announces that background papers to the White Paper itself will be published – a significant advance on the Conservative government's failure to publish such papers on, for example, the Citizen's Charter. The actual publication was not that enlightening.

It is acknowledged in the White Paper that although a framework in which public interest can be readily identified will be sought, the 'will-o'-the-wisp' quality of that concept will necessitate an incremental approach. Tests will include assurance that the original decision on disclosure or non-disclosure was not perverse, that decisions encourage the overall objective of the Act which is to promote greater openness, a point the Commissioner will seize upon or ought to in his or her interpretation of the legislation according to the guiding principles of openness. Tests will also include consistency with other legislation including EC requirements although it is fair to say that EC requirements on openness are rather jejune. Provisions in the Amsterdam Treaty (new Article 255) on access will have to wait almost four years for legislation.

Legislation which will have to be considered when dealing with FOI requests will include the Official Secrets Act 1989 and it is not clear how the less demanding tests of secrecy maintenance in that legislation ('damaging' not serious harm) will tie in with FOI provisions. It is unfortunate that any possibility of the Official Secrets Act influencing decisions on openness has been provisionally incorporated in such an open-ended fashion because the two regimes have different objectives: punishment of *unauthorised* leaks where some of the damage, possibly a great deal, relates to the fact that they are unauthorised, and creation of greater openness. The lack of detail on the relationship between the proposals of the White Paper and other legislation reveals the 'green edges' of the White Paper. Furthermore, the new Act will allow access to personal information by the subjects of that information as well as others (where not exempt) and such information will be covered by the FOIA although the Data Protection Registrar will have jurisdiction over subject access requests. It is to be hoped the FOIA will consolidate and replace as much of the existing legislation on personal records as possible. Co-operation between the Information Commissioner and Data Protection Registrar is encouraged and in the event of disputes between them the matter may need to be resolved in the courts. It is possible to predict a good degree of overlap and confusion where there is dual access under the FOIA and the Data Protection Act. This is certainly the view of the Data Protection Registrar.

On FOIA issues, the Information Commissioner will have jurisdiction. Unlike the Fisher Bill, there will be no tribunal to hear appeals from the Commissioner. The Commissioner will be an independent officer answerable to the courts and not Parliament and will not be subject to any political override. Before the Commissioner takes a complaint, there will be an internal formalised review which will usually be a prerequisite before an appeal can be made to the Commissioner except where, for instance, there is unreasonable delay by the authority in responding to a request. The Commissioner will publish an annual report for Parliament, and special reports if need be. He will publish reports on outcomes of investigations and 'best practice' guidance on the interpretation of the Act and will promote public awareness of the Act.

The Commissioner will have power to require disclosure of records, but not where they are excluded. The actual enforcement mechanism in the event of non-compliance will be via a 'court' – presumably the High Court – which will have power to treat any refusal to disclose or supply records as a contempt of court. The court's role will be limited to enforcing the Commissioner's decision. This builds partially on the ombudsman model; it is most likely that it will rarely be resorted to. The Commissioner will have a right of access to any documents covered by the Act. He will also have a right to review charges and charging systems under the Act and even to waive charges where there is a compelling public interest in disclosure. The Commissioner will be able to mediate disputes rather than formally determine them. He will also be given powers under warrant to enter premises and seize documents where relevant records are being withheld and a new criminal offence will be created of intentionally or recklessly destroying, altering or withholding records relevant to a Commissioner's investigation. He will have to work occasionally very closely with the ombudsman and Data Protection Registrar.

The Commissioner's decision is final with no further right of appeal, although it will be subject to the possibility of a judicial review. The arguments against appeal provisions, namely that they would have favoured the public authority, are no truer of that method of challenge than judicial review in so far as cost and delay are concerned. The Lord Chancellor has given his assurance that legal aid will be available in appropriate circumstances. A further remarkable and welcome departure from conventional British practice is that there will be no ultimate ministerial veto or certificate removing the appeal provisions or overriding the Commissioner's decisions.

'We have considered this possibility, but decided against it, believing that a government veto would undermine the authority of the Information Commissioner and erode public confidence in the Act.' (White Paper, para 5.18)

It is to be hoped that more secretive forces, forces present in any government, will not prevail in undermining this important provision as the Bill is steered through Cabinet Committees and then through Parliament. Such concerns may arise on the event of a reshuffle and it has yet to be seen what effect the replacement of Dr Clark by Jack Cunningham and the handing of the FOI brief to the Home Office will have on the progress of this legislation. We come back to these points in our conclusion.

The White Paper seeks views on the difficult question of third party rights where their information, possessed by public authorities, is sought by a requester. This is likely to lead to some third party notice procedure to protect commercial secrecy, confidential or sensitive 'personal privacy' information. It can raise very difficult issues.

In addition to the above provisions, the Labour manifesto referred to the need to introduce an independent National Statistics Office. It has been claimed, for instance, that Britain has the worst details on production statistics in the developed world and that information on school repairs and housing repairs has been stopped. The Royal Statistical Society has recommended an Independent Statistical Commission.[38] The case for such a body does seem to be well established and consultative proposals have been introduced on an independent National Statistics Office.

REPORT BY THE SELECT COMMITTEE ON PUBLIC ADMINISTRATION

Shortly before the 1997 White Paper was published, the Select Committee on Public Administration which took over the combined responsibilities of the Public Service Committee and the Select Committee on the Parliamentary Commissioner decided to review and take evidence on the White Paper and also the subsequent Bill that was to emerge on FOI.[39] This was an interesting development which would exist alongside any Standing Committee proceedings on the Bill. In the course of its examination, the Committee believed that various serious weaknesses had not been adequately provided for by government including the relationship between privacy protection and access. There was a concern that with the Data Protection Act 1998 which implemented the EC Directive on Data Protection, too much emphasis might be given to privacy protection of personal information even when there were compelling reasons for its disclosure. It was also felt that where two separate Commissioners were potentially covering the same area there would be a risk either of conflict or inconsistent approaches which might not easily be resolved by co-operation. The Committee made a series of recommendations on the relationship of the privacy and access regimes – and one has to bear in mind the incorporation of Articles 8 and 10 of the European Convention on Human Rights into UK law – in order to simplify the relationship and make its operation more harmonious.

[38] P Birkinshaw, *Freedom of Information*, pp 215–216.
[39] Select Committee on Public Administration, *Your Right to Know: The Government's Proposals for a Freedom of Information Act* HC [1997–98] 398-I & II.

The Committee regretted the extent of some of the exclusions of subjects and bodies from the White Paper and FOI regime, especially criminal investigation and law enforcement, which was also an exemption but without explanation as to how both exemption and exclusion could be operable at the same time. In addition, the Committee advocated a right of appeal to the Information Commissioner to establish whether an exclusion has been correctly claimed. Among numerous recommendations which sought to enhance the potential for greater openness in public life, the Committee recommended that the FOIA should become effective in Scotland without the necessity of waiting for a Scottish Assembly Bill, in case FOI is lost by default; that personnel information of bodies covered by the legislation should not be excluded; that the definition of utilities should be made clearer; and that public sector contracts with the private sector for the delivery of goods and services to the public should be covered by the regime. The Committee also wanted safeguards to ensure that commercial confidentiality was not abused by government, that there should be greater provision of indexes of government documents and that there should only be a one-tier system of charges under the legislation without any automatic access fee. It proposed various qualifications and clarifications to the policy advice exemption, that the Committee should examine the reports of the Commissioner who should be 'someone who has demonstrated the necessary toughness and independence' and that there should be a systematic legal requirement to remove all unnecessary impediments to openness in existing laws. Finally, the Committee urged various practices on government to further the spirit of openness fostered by the Act and to assist in its implementation.

A government spokesperson indicated in response to the Committee's report that utilities would only be covered in so far as they carried out statutory duties. It appeared that the call to remove security, intelligence and criminal investigation from the exclusions had not been accepted and nor had the Committee's recommendations on access fees and charges.[40]

IS THE WHITE PAPER THE BEST WAY FORWARD?

The 1997 White Paper offers an opportunity to break with past traditions excessive and unnecessary secrecy in British public life. The minister responsible, Dr David Clark, should be congratulated on a bold and imaginative initiative, especially as he seems to have been the recipient of a good deal of hostile reaction from within government. However, there are some omissions in the White Paper. It says nothing about reform of official secrecy laws. It says nothing about whistle-blowing provisions. The government has left this subject to a Private Member's Bill introduced by Richard Shepherd. Employees

---

[40] *Financial Times*, 20 June 1998, p 6.

in both the public and private sectors should be protected. Many of the most notorious cases of wronged whistle-blowers have concerned individuals in the private sector who have disclosed wrongdoing by their employers. This might involve disclosure of information about government contracts and over-pricing or anti-competitive behaviour or tax evasion for instance. Lord Nolan's (now Lord Neill QC's) Committee on Standards in Public Life has recommended that local spending bodies institute codes of practice on whistle-blowing, appropriate to their circumstances, which would enable concerns to be raised confidentially inside and, if necessary, outside the organisation. Nolan also recommended that confidentiality clauses in employment contracts in higher education be drafted to allow disclosure of information to relevant authorities. The authors endorse the view that disclosure to outside bodies should be allowed when this is in the general public interest, and not in the interest of the discloser because of some promise of financial reward, where internal channels are not satisfactory because they offer insufficient independence from the employer, or where they have been tried and found wanting. These provisions could usefully be in a FOIA with duties on all employers to produce codes to outline context specific details. We wait to see how the Shepherd Act will operate in practice.

Secondly, as Parts VII and VIII of the Fisher Bill suggest, there are many vital aspects of information held by private sector bodies which in the public interest should be disclosed. The extension over certain private bodies suggested in the White Paper has been noted. Private companies may wield economic power to rival that of governments. The Comptroller and Auditor General and Public Accounts Committee have been thwarted in their stewardship of public expenditure where monopoly industries are concerned. In all likelihood, there will be information held by these bodies which they will seek to protect by claims to commercial confidentiality. The exemption should be restricted to those aspects of commercial information that would seriously undermine the commercial competition of a trading body, noting of course that the public interest override will apply. Nonetheless, there was a good deal of special pleading from the privatised industries that they would now face unfair competition from those utilities which were not formerly in the public sector.

Lord Nolan's list of desiderata for standards of behaviour in public life have some application to the private sector – indeed many of them were necessitated because of the increasing influence of private sector techniques in public life (Cm 2850 I & II (1995)). These desiderata are: selflessness, integrity, objectivity, accountability, openness, honesty and leadership. Are these matters that are appropriate for legislation and if so what should be covered?

Before saying something about open government, a few points need to be addressed. First of all, if regional assemblies are created, how great a use of the FOIA will be made by such regional assemblies and their executives to get information from Whitehall, and vice versa assuming that the legislation will apply to regional bodies. This may well take place in what could become an increasingly constitutionally litigious context between assemblies and the centre. The White Paper makes provision for FOI for Scottish bodies which, unlike the Human Rights Bill which protects a threshold of basic rights, will be adapted to local circumstances under devolved legislative powers. There is no guarantee that such legislation will be forthcoming. This has caused concern north of the border and the recommendations of the Select Committee on Public Administration have been addressed.

Then there are the publicity and cost factors for the legislation. The 1994 code was poorly publicised and compared with the Citizen's Charter poorly resourced. The political correspondent of *The Times* has stated that of all the topics on which he receives correspondence, he has never received correspondence with regard to the code. There must be appropriate publicity for the FOIA. Such laws can operate effectively without draconian cost as experience from elsewhere testifies.[41] The White Paper contains important provisions detailing how the culture of openness can be encouraged by publishing internal manuals and user-friendly guides, giving reasons for decisions, providing professional training courses for officials, using central points for dissemination of guidance and assistance on best practice and regular monitoring of the Act. A central unit in the Cabinet Office for FOI has been established and it will form a focus for the generation of information and ideas on best practice and means of championing the Act together with the Office of the Information Commissioner, the Civil Service College and nominated contacts in departments and authorities. Its guidance, along with minutes of meetings, will be published.

The White Paper allows a right of access to personal information and the implementation of the EC Directive on Data Protection has been noted. This directive excluded Second and Third Pillar personal information and also personal files covering public security, defence, state security and the activities of authorities concerned with criminal law. The activities of MI5 have been extended to cover not only many policing functions but also the transfer to it of computer security functions in Whitehall. The Major government's 1993 White Paper on open goverment included a promise to legislate on access to personal records including police records so that by early 1997, the then government's commitment to do nothing in implementing the directive, that was not 'absolutely necessary', represented a worrying withdrawal from the 1993 position.[42] The subject of data protection was given widespread coverage with the provisions in the Social Security Administration (Fraud) Act 1997 allowing wholesale data matching and transfer between departments and agencies of personal data to help facilitate investigation of social security fraud. The Blair government seems to have given more sanguine support to necessary data protection laws than those envisaged in

---

[41] See P Birkinshaw, *Freedom of Information*, pp 56–57, 76–77.
[42] Home Office Consultation Paper on EC Data Protection Directive para 1.2. See now *Data Protection: The Government Proposals*, Cm 3725 (July 1997).

the EC or by previous governments and the Data Protection Act 1998 will not seek the exclusions that are present in the directive in relation to police and security, although these areas do enjoy very wide exemptions.[43] The May 1997 Queen's Speech outlined proposals for privacy legislation, and the incorporation of the European Convention on Human Rights will seem likely to generate considerable judicial developments in this field. There is certainly a feeling among the press and media that in any conflict between privacy and FOI, privacy will prevail forcing the government to introduce protection for 'genuine investigative journalism' in the Human Rights Bill, a concession which the government claims to have made.

Little has been said about open government. What for instance of the role of open meetings, open participation exercises in the formulation of government policy, open consultation exercises? OFTEL has conducted a series of more or less open meetings in its licence review responsibilities and information from these meetings is used to assist participating parties in their submissions. This has happened as the range of competitors has increased, as competition has developed and as the original duopoly of BT and Mercury has increasingly given way to a larger range of players. Here, information sharing has been seen as a way of facilitating ever increasingly difficult regulation. Not only business competitors but consumer bodies and environmental groups must be allowed greater access not only to information but to more open procedures for decision-making. What kinds of practices would we wish to see? The USA has provided some interesting examples: rule-making and accompanying participatory exercises; keeping a detailed record to facilitate the discovery of unlawful behaviour by officials and partial treatment; placing restrictions on what are known as ex parte hearings where exclusive meetings are conducted with interest lobbies in the legislative or policy-making process. The Federal Advisory Committee Act has long been an interesting example whereby not only are advisory committees opened up to the public and information made available on terms similar to the US FOIA, but a balance has to be maintained in the committee membership so that lop-sided domination by specific producers or interest groups cannot take place. People in the UK might care to ponder on the regulation and supervision of beef production for instance. There are doubtless practices operating informally along these lines in the UK now. What is needed are some hard legal duties. Once again Nolan's report on local trading bodies has interesting examples of best practice which could constitute the basis of legally enforceable duties.

What role could there be for pre-legislative hearings in Parliament? It has been suggested that interest groups and the public generally should be allowed to attend and participate in pre-legislative hearings. All evidence and documentation would be publicly available and opportunities for oral evidence and questioning of evidence submitted by participating parties. It

[43] *Data Protection: The Government's Proposals*, Cm 3725 (July 1997).

would be essential to have legislation like the Federal Advisory Committee Act so that the meetings and evidence of special advisory groups would be open and publicly available. To make participation an active and meaningful experience it would be essential that the internal advice/guidance exemption be least restrictive as possible. The May 1997 Queen's Speech announced that Bills for successive sessions would, where possible, be published for public consultation – the Human Rights Bill was one of various examples.

In Parliament itself the failure of ministers to announce either policy developments or amendments to existing policies led to the criticism of the Scott Report and the assertion in that Report that if ministerial responsibility were being replaced by ministerial accountability, then ministers were under a duty to provide Parliament with as full information as possible about the activities of government so that accountability is meaningful. The Vice Chancellor has subsequently become an advocate for FOI and he has suggested that there should be a commissioner appointed to adjudicate on those occasions when a minister would not disclose information in response to a parliamentary question.[44] If the government is serious about opening up government to the people, then it might not wish to overlook Parliament and the appointment of a commissioner in a FOIA to fulfil Scott's suggested role. Such a statutory appointment would give the Commissioner the necessary powers on a legal basis and the possibility exists to combine the Commissioner with the Commissioner for Standards who was established after the Cash for Questions saga.[45] A statutory existence would help to reinforce the seriousness of the government's commitment to an effective overseer of parliamentary practice and one which was not seen as an unsatisfactory and unconvincing exercise in self-regulation. Likewise, should the Commissioner on Appointments to Public Bodies not be made a statutory post with statutory powers of enforcement as well as report? One of Mr Blair's first acts in office was to announce that Lord Nolan would investigate the subject of the funding of political parties by private companies/bodies and individuals although it was subsequently reported that the Law Lord had some reservations about this task. Responsibilities have since been handed to Lord Neill QC who featured prominently in advising on the Ecclestone affair referred to above. Such as investigation would be a welcome development in open government. On what good reason should we not know who are the paymasters of political parties and politicians?

There are other important lessons that Mr Blair can attend to if his ideal of a new partnership between the people and their government is to become a reality as many hope and not a rhetorical fabrication.

---

[44] (1996) *Public Law* 410 at p 426.
[45] That Commissioner for Standards is established under internal Standing Orders of the House and reports to the Select Committee on Standards from whence the Commissioner's powers come. Committees are dominated by government MPs in proportion to their Commons majority! On events behind his 'sleaze' investigation into cash for questions, see D Leigh and E Vulliamy, *Sleaze: The Corruption of Parliament* (London: Fourth Estate 1996).

The EC/EU dimension to FOI and open government is assuming ever greater domestic significance. Decisions have been taken by the Council and Commission allowing access to EC documents and these are supported by a code of practice and followed a Declaration in the Maastricht Treaty on greater openness and access. However, these provisions are not convincing in their espousal of greater openness and many of the exemptions are in fact mandatory exclusions.[46] What is required is a binding provision allowing access to documents and open meetings for EC institutions in a revised Treaty. This has been a subject of discussion before the Inter-Governmental Conference and led to the inclusion of an Article 255 in the revised EC Treaty on access to documents. Furthermore, many bodies are not covered by the code of practice and the Council has denied that it has any relevance to the Second and Third Pillars – a denial which the EU ombudsman has challenged.[47]

In addition, the provision of information to national parliaments is often woefully inadequate. A Protocol in the Treaty of Amsterdam has improved the situation and has addressed the question of Third Pillar documents. Even when the Treaty of Amsterdam is ratified, however, and legally binding, it still leaves too much to national government discretion. Second and Third Pillar documents are given at government discretion at present. Second Pillar documents are not given in practice in the UK by the government to Select Committees. The Commons European Legislation Committee has a 'scrutiny reserve' over legislative documents, but even here the government undertaking not to approve a legislative document in the Council until scrutiny has been exercised has not always been met. Some of the government failures have bordered on the contumacious.[48] Both the subjects of access to EC and EU documents by citizens and national parliaments and their rights to EC/EU documents must be more satisfactorily resolved if the EC and EU are to become more than abstract and distant entities in the eyes of most EU citizens. These are subjects in which New Labour should set the lead in Europe.

---

[46] See P Birkinshaw (1997) *Government Information Quarterly* 27. The European Court of Justice has not accepted the existence of a rule of law providing for openness and access derived from the general principles of law informing the development of EC law and which leans on the traditions of member states although it has provided for some important technical victories for parties seeking access to Community documents: *Netherlands v Council* [1996] ECR-I 2169, *Carvel v Council* [1995] ECR II-2765, Case T-105/95 *WWF UK v Commission of the EC*, 5 March 1997, Case T-174/95 *Svenska Journalistförbundet v Council of the European Union*, 17 June 1998, CFI and note the judgment of the Advocate General in Case C-58/94 *Netherlands v Council*, 28 November 1995, paras 13 et seq. The Common Provisions of Title I state that decisions will now be taken 'as openly . . . as possible' in the EU as well as as closely as possible to the people.

[47] The EU ombudsman has also conducted an own initiative investigation into the access to information practices of the Treaty bodies and agencies not covered by the code (not including Second and Third Pillar bodies). The end result was an acceptance that they would be covered by rules similar to the Council and Commission code: see J Söderman (1997) *European Public Law* 351 and also his annual report for 1997 and his report as Rapporteur General at the 1998 FIDE conference in Stockholm: *The Citizen, the Administration and Community Law.*

[48] HC [1995–96] 51, paras 234 et seq.

CONCLUSION

It was stated at the beginning of this chapter that FOI is a constitutional issue – and so we believe. Devolution, reform of the House of Lords and other changes will have a more immediate and dramatic effect on the fabric of public life, but legally enforceable rights of access to official information will provide a ringing declaration that New Labour has introduced new government and one that is committed to openness, access and transparency. New Labour has been beset by its own problems concerning suppression of sensitive foreign affairs information, allegations of heavy handed use of government press officers to impose information control in and about government and the relationship of the Prime Minister with Rupert Murdoch. Any failure to promote suitable legislation will undermine the democratic credentials of both Mr Blair and New Labour. It is to be hoped that that will not be the case. The 1997 White Paper has many refreshing qualities, although it is still very green at the edges. The government reply to the Select Committee (HC [1997–98] 1020) did not accept some of the more ambitious recommendations of the Select Committee in its report, but it was still constructive and responsive in its content. FOI was a promise that many voted for. A significant contribution to the crushing defeat of the Major government was disquiet felt by the British people about the secrecy, hypocrisy, double standards and arrogance of a government which had too much of the night about it. In the absence of appropriate safeguards, all governments will have too much of the night about them. FOI is an instant panacea for nothing. But it makes such double-dealing and deceit by government all the more difficult to conceal. In the Cabinet reshuffle in July 1998, David Clark was replaced by Jack Cunningham as Chancellor of the Duchy of Lancaster, although it was rumoured that FOI was to be taken over by the Home Office – traditionally one of the most conservative of government departments. It appeared that 'difficulties' with the White Paper could delay the introduction of a bill in Parliament until 1999–2000. This would be unlikely to come into effect as law until 2001. It is to be hoped that Dr Clark's departure will not signal the end of more liberal policies on openness. The loser in the longer term, if such were to occur, will not only be the British public but also the new Labour government.

Further reading

Labour government White Paper, *Your Right to Know: Freedom of Information* (London: HMSO, Cm 3818, 1997)

House of Commons Committee on Public Administration, *Your Right to Know: The Government's Proposals for a Freedom of Information Act*, HC [1997–98] 398

Patrick Birkinshaw, *Freedom of Information: The Law, the Practice and the Ideal* (London: Butterworths, 2nd edn, 1996)

Constitution Unit, *Introducing Freedom of Information* (London, 1996)

Andrew McDonald and Grey Terrill (eds), *Open Government: Freedom of Information and Privacy* (London: Macmillan, 1998)

CHAPTER 9

NATIONAL SECURITY

Richard Norton-Taylor (*The Guardian*)

Hoisted by the executive whenever it wants to silence opposition and defend official secrecy, saluted by the judiciary, the flag of 'national security' is invariably honoured with unquestioning deference by Parliament. As two astute commentators have put it, 'Far too often, the cry of "security" functions in the political world as a sort of intellectual curare, inducing instant paralysis of thought'.[1] What may seem at first glance to be no more than an accepted, uncontroversial, totem is in reality a dangerous weapon.

'National security' has been deployed to deny natural justice. It was used by the Security Service, MI5, to recommend the detention without trial of over 100 people of Middle East origin in the 1990–91 Gulf War. One of them, Abbas Cheblak, a Palestinian writer who had lived in Britain for more than 15 years and a strong critic of Saddam Hussein, tried to appeal. 'National security', ruled Lord Donaldson, then Master of the Rolls, 'is the exclusive responsibility of the Executive and is par excellence a non-judiciable question'. With a flourish that would not have been out of place in totalitarian regimes, he added: 'Those who are able most effectively to undermine national security are those who least appear to constitute any risk to it'.[2]

Donaldson was merely echoing his predecessors. When the last Labour government decided to deport the American journalist, Mark Hosenball, in 1977, Lord Denning pronounced: 'This is no ordinary case. It is a case in which national security is involved, and our history shows that when the state is endangered, our cherished freedoms may have to take second place.'[3]

In the unanimous Law Lords' ruling upholding the Thatcher government's decision to ban trade unions at the GCHQ intelligence-gathering centre in 1984, Lord Fraser said: 'The decision on whether the requirements of national security outweigh the duty of fairness in any particular case is for the

---

[1] Laurence Lustgarten and Ian Leigh, *In From The Cold: National Security and Parliamentary Democracy* (Oxford University Press, 1994) p 20. Their book is a rare critical, in-depth, treatment of national security and the agencies involved in upholding the concept.
[2] *R v Secretary of State, ex parte Cheblak* [1991] 2 All ER 319.
[3] *R v Secretary of State for Home Affairs, ex parte Hosenball* [1977] 3 All ER 452.

government and not for the courts. The government alone has access to the necessary information, and in any event the judicial process is unsuitable for reaching decisions on national security.'[4] (Asked shortly after the union ban was imposed how national security had been threatened by the presence of trade union members at GCHQ, Sir Geoffrey Howe, the Foreign Secretary, replied: 'We cannot prove a single example.') The Law Lords returned to the theme when they upheld the government's argument that the *Sunday Times* was guilty of contempt of court for publishing extracts from *Spycatcher* – the memoirs of the former MI5 officer, Peter Wright – while a publication ban on *The Guardian* and *Observer* newspapers was still in force. 'The importance of a free press', said Lord Jauncey, 'cannot be overstated. Nevertheless, there are occasions where that importance must give way to other considerations. National security is one such consideration.'

Judges have rarely challenged public interest immunity (PII) claims made by ministers or the police. Upholding the Foreign Secretary's decision to sign a PII certificate suppressing evidence in a case taken to an industrial tribunal by Andrew Balfour, a former Foreign Office official in 1994, Russell LJ stated that 'the public interest in national security must prevail'. He went on: 'I am bound to tell you I know nothing about national security.'[5]

The Blair government has introduced a reform whereby appeals against deportation on national security grounds will in future be heard by judges rather than by a trio – the so-called 'the three wise men' – appointed by the executive. Under the Special Appeals Commission Act, the case for appellants will be made by a lawyer, albeit vetted and in camera, and the commission's decisions can be appealed further in the courts.

But 'national security' remains a catch-all exemption in every statute whose ostensible purpose is to promote civil liberties and protect the individual citizen against encroaching threats from state agencies buttressed by the development of ever-intrusive technology. The new Labour government's long-awaited White Paper on a Freedom of Information Act, published in December 1997, made it clear that documents relating to 'national security' would be exempt from disclosure. It was scarcely surprising. As Lustgarten has pointed out, 'Nowhere is . . . control over information more rigorously defended than in relation to foreign affairs, "defence", and "national security"'.[6]

The Data Protection Act 1984 allows Whitehall departments, the police, and the Security Service, MI5, to refuse on grounds of national security to disclose information to those on whom they hold computer files. Section 27 of the Act states that 'personal data are exempt . . . for the purpose of safeguarding national security'. National security exemptions are included in the

---

[4] *Council of Civil Service Unions v Minister for the Civil Service* [1984] 1 WLR 1174.
[5] Unreported.
[6] Laurence Lustgarten, Freedom of Expression and National Security in the UK, Address to Johannesburg Conference on National Security, Freedom of Expression, and Access to Information, convened by Article 19, the International Centre Against Censorship, September/October 1995.

Interception of Communications Act 1985, which covers the interception of telephone lines and the post.

The Public Records Act 1958 allows Whitehall departments to withhold documents, files, and archives indefinitely on grounds of 'national security' (or, indeed, for any 'special reason'). Section 10 of the Contempt of Court Act 1981 protects journalists and others to disclose their sources except when 'it is established to the satisfaction of the court that disclosure is necessary in the interests of justice or national security . . .' (The test of necessity, in effect, would be the executive's say-so.)

National security features as an exemption in key articles of the European Convention on Human Rights (ECHR), to be incorporated into British law by the Labour government's Human Rights Act 1998. Article 8 of the Convention states: 'Everyone has the right to respect for his private and family life, his home and his correspondence'. It adds that there shall be no interference by a public authority in this right 'except such as in accordance with the law and is necessary in a democratic society in the interests of national security, public safety or the economic well-being of the country, for the prevention of disorder or crime, for the protection of health or morals, or for the protection of the rights and freedoms of others'.

Article 10, which establishes the right to freedom of expression, states that this freedom carries with it duties and responsibilities and 'may be subject to such formalities, conditions, restrictions or penalties as are prescribed by law and are necessary in a democratic society, in the interests of national security . . .'

Cases where the European Court of Human Rights or Commission of Human Rights have upheld a government's claim based on national security include the GCHQ trade union ban, and attempts by journalists to lift a ban on interviews with members of listed organisations, including Sinn Fein.[7]

However, unlike courts in Britain, the European Court of Human Rights has not given governments carte blanche to suppress publication merely because they fly the national security flag. In the celebrated *Spycatcher* case, the European Court of Human Rights agreed that injunctions against the British media were 'prescribed by law' and their original purpose was legitimate. But the memoirs of the former MI5 agent, Peter Wright, had already been published in the USA. The main point at issue turned on whether the continuing injunctions were still 'necessary in a democratic society'. In an important judgment, the Court stated: '[Whilst] Article 10 . . . does not in terms prohibit the imposition of prior restraints on publication as such . . . the dangers inherent in prior restraints are such that they call for the most careful scrutiny on the part of the Court. This is especially so as far as the press is

---

[7] *Purcell and Others v Ireland*, Application No 15404/89, admissibility decision, 16 April 1991. The Commission stated that the order prohibited the use of the broadcast media 'for the purpose of advocating support for organisations which seek to undermine, by violence and other illegal means, the constitutional order and the fundamental rights it guarantees'.

concerned, for news is a perishable commodity and to delay its publication, even for a short period, may well deprive it of all value and interest.'[8]

As has been observed:

'European judicial supervision ensures that national security is not a blanket exemption from the rights set forth in paragraph 1 of Article 10 [covering freedom of expression] . . . It must be shown to the satisfaction of the Strasbourg enforcement bodies that the restriction is genuinely aimed, both in theory and in practice, at the protection of some aspect of the interests of national security and is not, for example, merely an excuse for saving the Government in power or the Civil Service from embarrassing revelations.'[9]

On the face of it, the Official Secrets Act 1989 – introduced by the Thatcher government after it failed to suppress *Spycatcher* – is in conflict with the ECHR, certainly with Strasbourg jurisprudence. Section 1 of the 1989 Act imposes an absolute, life-long, duty of confidence on serving and former members of the security and intelligence services. The Act also says that a minister can subject anyone to the same draconian constraints if, in his opinion, the individual's job is 'connected with the security and intelligence services and its nature is such that the interests of national security require' it to be so. There is no public interest defence – indeed, uniquely in British criminal law there is no defence at all. The prosecution does not have to prove any harm was caused by the disclosures.

The definition of 'national security' may, on the face of it, seem obvious – the physical security of the state, its inhabitants, its democratic institutions and their protection from outside threats. But it is not so simple. Asked in January 1988 by the Labour MP, Ken Livingstone, to define the term, the Prime Minister, Mrs Thatcher, replied that the term 'national security has been in general use for many years in a variety of contexts and is generally understood to refer to the safeguarding of the state and the community against threats to their survival or well-being'.

Lord Lloyd, the then Interception of Communications Commissioner, said in his annual report for 1989 that the term, 'national security', was 'narrower' than the term 'public interest' but it was 'obviously wider than the three heads of counter-terrorism, counter-espionage and counter-subversion'. The easiest example, he suggested, was defence: 'so if an interception (of communications) is judged necessary for the defence of the realm against a potential external aggressor, then clearly it is necessary in the interests of national security'.

---

[8] *The Observer and Guardian v UK and The Sunday Times v UK (No 2)*, both 26 November 1991, Series A, Vols 216 and 217.

[9] Lawrence Early and Paul Mahoney, *Freedom of Expression and National Security: Judicial and Policy Approaches under the European Convention on Human Rights and Other Council of Europe Instruments*. Paper to Article 19 conference in Johannesburg on National Security, Freedom of Expression, and Access to Information, September/October 1995.

That was as far as Lord Lloyd was prepared to go. It was neither wise nor possible, he said, to go further in attempting to define the term. Each case, he said, must be decided on its merits.

Two years later, Stuart Smith LJ, the Security Service Commissioner, noted in his annual report that 'the concept of national security . . . is not easily defined; indeed, it is probably undesirable that I attempt an all-embracing definition'. He added: 'In my opinion, it includes the defence of the realm and the Government's defence and foreign policies involving the protection of vital national interests in this country and abroad. In this regard, I would draw a distinction between national interest and the interests, which are not necessarily the same, of the Government of the day. What is a vital national interest is a question of fact and degree, more easily recognised when being considered than defined in advance.'

Yet it has been suggested that 'national security' is, indeed, synonymous with the the policies of the government of the day. The 1985 White Paper on Interception of Communications stated: 'The Secretary of State may issue warrants on grounds of national security if he considers that the information to be acquired under the warrant is necessary in the interests of national security either because of terrorist, espionage, or major subversive activity, or in support of the government's defence and foreign policies'.

Announcing that the security and intelligence agencies were to be subjected to a Whitehall-wide, root and branch, Comprehensive Spending Review, the Blair government in October 1997 said the exercise was designed to ensure that the activities of the agencies were consistent with the government's overall objectives. The suggestion is that any individual or group opposed to current government defence and foreign policies – its attitude towards nuclear weapons, for example, or the European Union – could be a legitimate target for surveillance or vetting by the security services.

The chief agency responsible for protecting national security is the Security Service, MI5. It was set up in 1909 as a result of paranoia about German spies in Britain. It was 80 years before it was brought within the framework of any law. The Security Service Act 1989 states that national security should be protected from espionage, terrorism, and from 'actions intended to overthrow or undermine parliamentary democracy by political, industrial, or violent, means'.

This is Whitehall's traditional, extraordinarily wide, definition of 'subversion', the enemy of national security. An all-party backbench attempt to introduce an amendment to the legislation, upholding the right of 'lawful dissent' in the Act, was rejected out of hand by the Thatcher government. Despite even MI5's claims that subversion is now a minimal threat, and its decision in 1992 to wind up its anti-subversion branch, the Act remains unamended. Asked on 12 December 1988, by the Labour MP, Stuart Randall, if he would publish the criteria he would use in assessing the extent to which, 'in given circumstances, national security will require the protection of the Security Service', Douglas Hurd, then Home Secretary replied: 'No'.

Far from being a clear concept, national security is an elusive one. It is also a movable feast. Sir Clive Whitmore, then permanent secretary at the Home Office, told a City University seminar in 1992 that 'national security', and threats to it, might involve quite different considerations in the 1990s to what they did in the 1950s. The elastic nature of the term gives the executive – and its security and intelligence services in particular – huge discretion to determine how national security should be interpreted. As one writer recently put it: 'No "objective" definition of national security exists; in its place are policy makers' views at any time as to what they perceive as threatening. Threat assessment is a subjective art.'[10]

Definition creep has gone hand in hand with mission creep. The role of MI5 – whose central function is to protect national security – has been expanded under the Security Service Act 1996 to cover 'serious crime', a concept which is also defined extremely broadly. It embraces an offence which 'involves the use of violence, results in substantial financial gain or is conduct by a large number of persons in pursuit of a common purpose', or 'for which a person who has attained the age of twenty-one and has no previous convictions could reasonably be expected to be sentenced to imprisonment for a term of three years or more'. This could cover offences ranging from a mugging to an anti-hunting or pro animal rights demonstration – anyway offences far broader than the phrases, such as 'organised crime' or 'international organised crime', used by ministers to defend the greater powers given to MI5.

To begin with, the targets have gone beyond the 'national' to include the 'international'. In one of her rare outings (her successor, Stephen Lander, has yet to speak in public) Stella Rimington, then Director General of MI5, said one of the agency's tasks was to counter the activities of groups and individuals based in Britain planning acts of violence abroad – she mentioned the Punjab and Kashmir. This task, she said, was 'one very important element of our wider obligations in the increasingly international context in which national security must now be seen'.[11]

Faced with common problems and targets – organised mafia-type gangs, drug traffickers, money-launderers, extreme religious or cult-based terrorism rather than state-sponsored terrorism – intelligence and security agencies of former cold war enemies are co-operating increasingly on a formal and structured basis. Increasingly close, yet very discreet, co-operation is taking place within the EU's so-called 'Third Pillar', a euphemism for issues and policies relating to 'law and order' and 'security' in a strictly inter-governmental framework where EU institutions, such as the European Commission, the European Parliament, or the European Court of Justice, have no role.

---

[10] Anne Rogers, *Secrecy and Power in the British State* (Pluto Press, 1997).
[11] Stella Rimington, National Security and International Understanding, Speech to English Speaking Union, 4 October 1995.

Decisions are increasingly being taken on matters which directly threaten civil liberties – law and order, asylum, immigration, cross-border links between national security agencies, telephone tapping – in a framework where the EU's democratic deficit is most prominent. The EU is also beginning to negotiate secret agreements with other law enforcement and security agencies, including the FBI, covering the interception of communications, extra parliamentary dissent, and demonstrations. Though the Labour government has negotiated an 'opt-out' allowing Britain to adapt its own measures on border controls, asylum, and so on, it has enthusiastically joined its EU partners in practical measures.

Meanwhile, the government has said it plans to introduce permanent anti-terrorism legislation. This will make it a criminal offence for individuals living in Britain to promote 'terrorist activities' abroad. It is an area fraught with difficulties, not least about what constitutes 'terrorism'. One man's terrorist is another's freedom fighter, a cliche whose significance Jack Straw has himself acknowledged. Would it catch a future Mandela? Would those encouraging the overthrow of Saddam Hussein be caught as well as those financing or promoting the overthrow of apparently popular, but unelected, governments? The new statute will reflect the 'globalisation' of 'national security' concerns.

The term, 'national security', has traditionally been and still is a signal to brush aside normal and central aspects of civil society, including democratic accountability. It remains an unthinking excuse for secrecy. The 'national security state' is divorced from the individual citizens which comprise it. Those ultimately responsible for defending this state are, according to the traditional approach, the security and intelligence establishment, and the armed forces, and no one else.

Labour governments have accepted this traditional, narrow, view in common with Conservative administrations. Perhaps, more so. Labour has been extraordinarily sensitive to any suggestion that it is 'soft' on 'security'. The security services attract and breed an essentially right-wing, illiberal, culture. Harold Wilson's reaction to MI5's hostility to his Labour administrations in the 1960s and 1970s was extraordinarily defensive. He harboured deep suspicions about MI5 but felt he could do nothing about the unaccountable agency even though it was responsible to him as Prime Minister. He always deferred to MI5, never daring to question its judgment.

There are signs that the Blair government will adopt a more sceptical approach. MI5, MI6, and GCHQ, as we have seen, are included in the Treasury-driven Comprehensive Spending Review scrutinised the activities of the agencies from a 'zero base' – the agencies will have to justify their existence as well as show they are spending their budgets efficiently. That is the theory. We shall never know if it has been put into practice because the analysis and the advice lying behind the decisions the government eventually takes will be secret. The government has suggested it is prepared to subject the agencies to more effective scrutiny by Parliament. Members of the existing, cross-party, parliamentarian Intelligence and Security Committee are appointed by the Prime Minister. It meets in secret, it is staffed by Cabinet Office officials, and its annual reports are sent to the Prime Minister who can censor them before they are published. Its current chairman, Tom King, the former Conservative defence secretary, was reappointed by Blair on the grounds that there were no Labour MPs with sufficient experience to take over the job when Labour gained power in the 1997 general election. Both Blair and Jack Straw, the Home Secretary, have, however, indicated they are prepared to introduce cautious reforms, by turning the Intelligence and Security Committee into a Select Committee answerable to the Commons. Straw did not object to newspapers publishing the views of the former MI5 agent, David Shayler, about his former employers. He said he was prepared to allow 'fair criticism' of MI5 so long as the agency's operational methods were not compromised. Strictly speaking, this was contrary to section 1 of the Official Secrets Act 1989.

It is time for MPs, as well as ministers and Whitehall, to adopt a more mature approach to 'national security' issues. It is also time that established democracies take the lead and break out of the straight-jacketed definition of the term. An attempt to define the traditional meaning of the term was made at the Article 19 Johannesburg conference, albeit in the specific context of freedom of expression and access to information:

> 'A restriction sought to be justified on the ground of national security is not legitimate unless its genuine purpose and demonstrable effect is to protect a country's existence or its territorial integrity against the use or threat of force, or its capacity to respond to the use or threat of force, whether from an external source, such as a military threat, or an internal source, such as incitement to violent overthrow of the Government.'

It added that restrictions sought to be justified on the ground of national security is not legitimate if its genuine purpose is unrelated to national security including 'to protect a Government from embarrassment or exposure of wrongdoing, or to conceal information about the functioning of its public institutions, or to entrench a particular ideology, or to suppress industrial unrest'.[12]

But the term, 'national security', should encompass political, economic, and social, considerations, not merely, the literal – physical – security of the nation. It is fallacy to argue that the twin concepts of national security and individual freedom are inherently in conflict with each other. Far from liberties being submerged by notions of 'security', the state – the nation – is more secure when society is more cohesive and therefore secure. As Lustgarten and Leigh put it: '. . . political and civil rights are major constituents of national security itself'.[13]

---

[12] Johannesburg conference, see note 9 above.
[13] Laurence Lustgarten and Ian Leigh, *In From the Cold*, p 5.

For the developing world, there are equally pressing, considerations. As a Washington-based think-tank has pointed out:

'During the 20th century, a growing reliance on military power has actually reduced national security as countries have accumulated unprecedented offensive potential. At the same time, this arms race has undermined the economies of rich and poor countries alike. Now, global environmental threats are forcing humanity to consider national security in far broader terms than that guaranteed solely by force of arms.

The profound transformations that our world is undergoing challenge the traditional conduct of diplomacy and the established forms of governance. Indeed, "national security" as such has become an outmoded concept: security is increasingly attained through the difficult process of global cooperation to create mechanisms for non-violent dispute settlement and establish environmental alliances. As they look back future generations may regard our recent obsession with national security maintained by force of arms as a curious historical diversion that distracted our energies from the most basic threats to human society.'[14]

The Blair government's programme of constitutional reform must embrace substance as well as structures. That means breaking the taboo surrounding 'national security'. The term is used far too freely, as an excuse to bypass normal tenets of accountability and participation in decision-making, depriving citizens of their basic rights and freedoms. Precisely because of this, issues and arguments about 'national security' must be matters not only for the courts, but for juries and Parliament. They cannot be left to the executive.

Meanwhile, the Blair government must take a lead in ensuring that security co-operation within the EU must be subjected to effective scrutiny by democratic institutions. That would truly be a significant legacy of its much-vaunted appeals for a 'people's Europe'.

Further reading

Laurence Lustgarten and Ian Leigh, *In From the Cold: National Security and Parliamentary Democracy* (Oxford University Press, 1994)
Anne Rogers, *Secrecy and Powers in the British State* (London: Pluto Press, 1997)
Adam Tomkins, *The Constitution After Scott* (Oxford University Press, 1998)

[14] Michael Renner, Worldwatch Paper 89, *National Security: The Economic and Environmental Dimensions* (Worldwatch Institute, Washington DC, May 1989).

CHAPTER 10

IMPLEMENTING CONSTITUTIONAL REFORM

Katy Donnelly and Nicole Smith
(formerly of The Constitution Unit)

In the run up to the 1997 general election the Leader of the Labour Party, Tony Blair, promised 'the most extensive package of constitutional change ever proposed'. The agenda set out in Labour Party Policy Papers in the years between 1992 and 1997, and summarised in the 1997 election manifesto, was long and daunting. Once elected the challenge facing the new Labour government, and those in other parties who supported the reform agenda, was no longer about whether to introduce these reforms, but how.

The history of previous attempts at reform suggested that regardless of public support and political will the implementation was unlikely to be straightforward. To take just two examples, House of Lords' reform has been under discussion since the 1920s; as has reform of the electoral system. But in neither case have attempts at fundamental reform succeeded. There has been no lack of blueprints; but very little focus on managing the process of change.

The failure of Dick Crossman's Bill to reform the Lords in the 1960s, and of the Callaghan government's attempt at devolution in the 1970s, provided sharp reminders for the Labour government of how easy it is for constitutional measures to absorb government time and energy with little reward. The Maastricht debates also offered a more recent reminder of the difficulties any government can face in tackling constitutional issues. Our unwritten constitution should make constitutional reform no more difficult to achieve than any other policy initiative; but politically it can make it harder. It is harder because there is no settled procedure for constitutional change; unlike under a written constitution, which prescribes the procedures for its own amendment. For example, there is no agreement about when a referendum might be required; nor about the appropriate parliamentary procedure for constitutional Bills. 'Unconstitutional' becomes a term of abuse: what is or is not constitutional is a matter for interpretation.

This chapter considers the obstacles to successful reform and reviews the way in which the Labour government has set about delivering its constitutional agenda. It focuses mainly on parliamentary procedure; but begins with some reflections on the earlier stages in the policy-making process.

WHITEHALL

Given the extent of the Labour Party's programme of reform a key priority was to ensure that the Whitehall machinery was geared up to deliver. Prior to the 1997 election there was no one part of the government machine which had overall responsibility for constitutional issues. The official guide to Whitehall, the Civil Service Yearbook, listed the Cabinet Office Machinery of Government Division which dealt with 'organisational functions including the allocation of functions between departments' and 'Questions on the relationship between Government and Parliament' and the Home Office Constitutional Unit, established in 1996, with an eclectic selection of responsibilities. At the time of the election, the Constitutional Unit covered elections and electoral law; relations between church and state; human rights; royal and ceremonial matters; and relations with the Channel Islands and the Isle of Man. In practice the constitution was the responsibility of half a dozen different Whitehall departments; and the responsibility of none. This absence of any central or co-ordinating resource to address constitutional issues needed to be remedied by a government intent on a wide-ranging programme of constitutional reform.

Steps were taken early on to tackle this weakness. In recognition of the capacity for internal tensions inherent in the spread of constitutional matters across different departments, and the need for coherence between measures that will be required for the reforms to be effective, the structure of Whitehall and the Cabinet Committees were reshaped to give effect to the reform programme. Lord Irvine of Lairg, Lord Chancellor and Lord Privy Seal, chairs a strategic Cabinet Committee covering the whole constitutional reform agenda and a Cabinet Committee dealing with devolution. The policy lead for many of the individual reforms has been left with departmental ministers; but the apparent intention is that Lord Irvine has an overall responsibility for the constitutional reform programme.

This approach should help to ensure consistency and coherence; the planning of a realistic legislative timetable; avoid overload on individual lead ministers; and ensure that one reform or set of reforms leads on to, rather than impedes the next. Lord Irvine's role as chairman of five major committees, including the key committees dealing with constitutional reform provides a link between measures and a view of the overall programme. As yet, however, it is difficult to assess whether one minister can maintain an effective oversight of all of these issues alongside their own departmental responsibilities.

A Constitution Secretariat was also set up within the Cabinet Office to support the Cabinet Committee dealing with constitutional issues. The Secretariat consists of two teams, one dealing with devolution and the other covering the rest of the reform programme. Its remit is to work alongside the departments with lead responsibility for each element within the reform programme and to drive forward progress, ensuring cohesion across the programme as a whole. On House of Lords' reform the Secretariat is also taking on a substantive

212

policy role, including writing the Green Paper and seeing the legisl
through Parliament. In addition there has been some reorganisation within
individual departments, including the creation of new units where necessary,
and the establishment of contact points across Whitehall on key issues which
affect all departments such as devolution and freedom of information.

In an unusual move, the pre-election discussions between the Labour
Party and the Liberal Democrats on the implementation of constitutional
reform (which resulted in a statement on key areas of agreement) led to the
creation of a joint Cabinet Committee, as mentioned in the Introduction.
There has been a high level of co-operation between the parties on constitutional issues. Whether this is a direct result of the work of the Committee, or
simply reflects common interests, is hard to judge.

CONSULTATION AND POLICY DEVELOPMENT

There is a strong expectation that constitutional reform should be based on
broad public and cross-party consultation. This was reaffirmed in speeches
from all the major political parties before the 1997 election. The use of commissions and consultation processes to develop policy is, of course, not exclusive to constitutional issues; but constitutional issues are different, because of
the perceived need for reforms to be built on political consensus rather than
derived from partisan policies. It also reflects an awareness that constitutional
reform is different from other policy changes, because it affects the rules of
the political game; and ideally should be agreed by the other players if it is to
endure beyond the lifetime of a particular government.

The nature of the consultation undertaken since the 1997 election on
constitutional issues has varied according to the state of policy development
in each area. In some areas a process of inquiry or consultation has been
undertaken as a precursor to final policy decision. Examples of this include,
cross-party consultation on House of Lords' reform; and the establishment
of an independent commission charged with identifying an alternative electoral
system for the House of Commons to be put forward in a referendum. In
other areas, policy was already well developed when the Labour government
took office – notably Scottish devolution which had been the subject of
considerable work through the Scottish Constitutional Convention and within
the Labour Party itself – it was clearly inappropriate for there to be any
extensive inquiry. But even on issues where the policy was clear and some
form of consultation had already been undertaken, the government took the
view that the reforms would be more effectively embedded if put to a referendum before legislation was introduced.

The ways in which these consultation processes have been used and in particular some of the ways in which past experience has informed the approach
taken by the government are considered below.

Cross-party talks

As already noted, the government initiated cross-party talks on reform of the House of Lords during the first parliamentary session of the new Parliament. By the summer of 1998 the talks were reported to have broken down without reaching agreement. This follows a long history of difficult negotiations about reform of the House of Lords.

Any reform of the Lords is likely to affect the party political balance as well as the balance of power between the two Houses. Largely for this reason formal cross-party talks have been initiated on three occasions this century: in 1910, during the constitutional crisis which led to the Parliament Act 1911; in 1948, when the Second Reading of the Parliament Act 1949 was adjourned for inter-party talks; and in 1968, prior to Dick Crossman's abortive Parliament No 2 Bill.[1] In each case the talks broke down and yielded only a limited outcome. The Parliament Acts of 1911 and 1949 were both government imposed; and Dick Crossman's Bill had to be withdrawn in the face of backbench opposition in the Commons.

It is obvious that, given the different constitutional views and political interests of the parties, it is never going to be easy to reach cross-party agreement on constitutional issues. Yet the success of such an approach requires the politics of consensus to prevail. If it does not, the consequential reforms are likely to be either piecemeal – introduced on the basis of whatever agreement was reached, not the comprehensive reforms originally intended – or rejected by the opposition parties. There is significant scope for tactical manoeuvring by the opposition parties during the talks, or even for frustrating the very establishment of talks by non-participation. There is also a danger that the party leaders may not be representative of the party at large (as happened in 1968), and may not be willing or able to whip their backbenchers into line during subsequent parliamentary proceedings.

One suggestion that has repeatedly been put forward is that a Joint Committee of both Houses should be established to consider reform of the House of Lords in detail. This was the recommendation of the Joint Consultative Committee established by Labour and the Liberal Democrats before the 1997 election. In some respects a Joint Committee has certain advantages as a vehicle for developing reform proposals. It can involve backbenchers (who in 1968 were not involved in policy development and eventually wrecked the proposals) as well as senior party figures; it engages both Houses, which is equally important, since in 1968 the Commons proved to be a greater obstacle than the Lords; and it can provide a forum for inter-party talks without the talks being directly between the parties. The concerns and preferences of the parties can be teased out without the parties being forced to take up positions or to abandon the talks if they fail to get their way.

---

[1] Further details of these can be found in The Constitution Unit, *Reform of the House of Lords* (1996) pp 77–78; *Delivering Constitutional Reform* (1996) pp 55–56.

A Joint Committee could also help to ensure a greater degree of openness, avoiding another of the difficulties of the 1960s, when the proposals were developed largely in secret, and might also go further than most parliamentary committees, commissioning research to assist in its deliberations and publishing consultative papers or using other mechanisms (eg polling) to sound out public opinion. If it is decided to proceed in this way, clear political direction in the terms of reference given to the Joint Committee will be crucial, not least because the answers given will depend upon the questions which it is set.

Expert Commissions of Inquiry

The need for clear political direction is also evident in the history of using expert commissions of inquiry to develop constitutional reforms. The Kilbrandon Commission on the Constitution, for example, complained that 'the width and diversity of our terms of reference . . . have made the mere identification of our task a major preoccupation'. In the end, the Commission's recommendations set out three or four different options for devolution, with a minority report tagged on for good measure.

The 'classic' means of involving experts in policy development has been to appoint a Royal Commission, but there are examples of other forums of inquiry which have tended to operate in a flexible way. The government's approach so far appears to recognise that Royal Commissions are unlikely to be effective vehicles for developing policy if used indiscriminately. They tend to be regarded, in particular by politicians, as an excuse for procrastination, and therefore require a short, tight timetable if they are to have credibility. Experience also suggests that they may produce findings which are not sufficiently policy oriented; or which fail to reflect the realities of the political environment into which they are delivered. A further disadvantage of Royal Commissions is the importance of engaging parliamentarians in the settlement of a constitutional issue, rather than collecting the views of external experts. All these issues need to be addressed if a Royal Commission is set up.

One field where there is a clear role for experts is electoral reform. It is estimated that there are at least 300 different electoral systems to choose from. For an effective decision on a new electoral system to be taken through a referendum – the government's stated intention – the range of options clearly needed to be narrowed down. Through the work of the pre-election Joint Consultative Committee, Labour and the Liberal Democrats agreed that an expert commission should be appointed early in the new Parliament, with a clear brief to recommend a single proportional alternative to the existing first past the post system. As discussed in Chapter 3, The Commission chaired by Lord Jenkins of Hillhead, with membership incorporating both expertise in electoral matters and political balance, was given terms of reference as follows:

'The Commission shall be free to consider and recommend any appropriate system or combination of systems in recommending an alternative to the present system for parliamentary elections to be put before the people in the Government referendum. The Commission shall observe the requirement for broad proportionality, the need for stable government, an extension of voter choice and the maintenance of a link between MPs and geographical constituencies.'

This has given the Commission (and all those campaigning around the issue) a fairly clear steer. There has however been some debate as to whether the Commission's terms of reference preclude it from examining systems which are held by some to be non-proportional. The Commission has invited submissions from the public and interested parties and has worked to encourage participation in the debate through roving consultation forums – although attendance at some events has been low. Such work should inform the Commission's view as to which option is likely to attract a broad consensus; and lay the foundations for the public education programme which will need to be undertaken prior to the referendum.

The Nolan Committee has shown that where there is a political imperative for results, it is possible for an advisory committee to work rapidly and to make clear and robust recommendations. The Jenkins Commission has yet to achieve such a high political and public profile, but the publication of its report may be the catalyst for wider debate.

Referendums

In some countries, referendums are required before changes to the constitution can go ahead, and many other countries have chosen to use referendums to settle constitutional issues. In the UK, the doctrines of ministerial responsibility and parliamentary government mean that the use of the referendum sits uneasily in our constitutional tradition. Prior to the 1997 general election, only four referendums had been held in Britain: one on EC membership, in 1975, and three others on the constitutional status of Northern Ireland (1973) and of Scotland and Wales (1979).

After the four referendums of the 1970s the argument that referendums have no place in the British constitutional tradition was hard to sustain. In 1997 the new Labour government clearly did not feel constrained by any reservations about the 'constitutionality' of using referendums. During its first year in office the government held referendums on Scottish and Welsh devolution, a strategic authority for London and the Northern Ireland agreement. All of which produced 'yes' votes, although on Welsh devolution by a very small margin and on the London authority on a very low turnout. Further referendums are promised on electoral reform and entry into the single European currency.

There are several arguments in favour of the continued use of referendums. Constitutional change is an issue in which the government and MPs have a vested interest and so arguably they should seek additional public approval. A referendum can also be a more precise and formal way of sounding out public opinion than a general election or opinion polls. This was well illustrated in Wales in 1979, where people voted four to one against the Welsh Assembly; even though polling had suggested opinion was evenly divided, and three out of the four political parties were in favour of devolution. Finally, referendums involve the electorate much more directly in public decision-making, and as a result can have an educational effect and increase voter participation in debate about public issues.

The ability of the referendum to settle issues once and for all should however be treated with caution. In the absence of a written constitution, the referendum can provide a limited means of entrenchment, but can also be seen as offering a snapshot of public opinion in respect of a specific issue. As the European question shows, a referendum cannot offer an authoritative answer for all time; and the sovereignty of Parliament means that the power to legislate against a referendum result, however recent or overwhelming, remains with Westminster.

Referendums are not therefore a panacea. Political expedience rather than democratic principle has been the dominant theme in UK referendums, especially on those issues which have caused party splits, such as Europe. There are no guarantees that a government will receive the referendum result it wants; nor can it be guaranteed that Parliament will pass legislation giving effect to policy agreed through a referendum.

Some also argue that referendums are a crude way to make decisions, simplifying issues by forcing a 'yes' or 'no' answer which is unable to reflect shades of opinion. This concern emerged in the debate around the referendum on a strategic authority for London where some felt that two questions should have put, separating the issue of a directly elected mayor from the establishment of an elected assembly. The choice and wording of the question can prove controversial as can the real, or perceived, unequal provision of information and resources. Unless rules or conventions are developed for the use of referendums such concerns are likely to remain. Some of these concerns could be addressed by the creation of an independent Referendum Commission, with statutory responsibility for supervising the conduct of referendums. Such a Commission could ensure that their administration is independent of government and party political interests, in order to ensure maximum confidence in the legitimacy of their results. But even with such safeguards, referendums should still be recognised as blunt instruments with which to *resolve* complex issues, although they can play an important role in engaging public opinion and entrenching significant reform.

HANDLING CONSTITUTIONAL MEASURES IN PARLIAMENT

The last attempts at constitutional reform by Labour governments in the 1960s and 1970s ended in failure, not least because of the obstacles presented by the legislative process. So far, the Labour government has not encountered significant difficulties in the parliamentary handling of its constitutional Bills. This may not be considered surprising given its overwhelming majority in the House of Commons, but even without powerful opposition the procedures for handling constitutional measures create their own pressures. In the House of Commons in particular, the time available for legislation imposes a major constraint on the government. The time taken by constitutional measures tends to be greater than for other Bills and can affect the introduction and passage of other legislation.

The struggle to get the Maastricht Bill through Parliament is a good example of the tactics which can be used to frustrate constitutional measures.[2] Although there was a clear majority in the House which supported the main substance of the Bill and the Bill itself was very short – three clauses amended to seven – its passage stretched over 15 months and inflicted considerable damage on the government. The government suffered one outright defeat and was forced to accept other amendments which it did not dare put to the vote.

Scrutiny

Unlike most public Bills which are automatically committed to a Standing Committee after Second Reading, by convention, 'first class constitutional issues' are committed to a committee of the whole House. This convention dates back to a Procedure Committee report in 1945 which recommended that Bills should, as a rule, be referred to Standing Committees, the exception being those concerned with 'first class constitutional issues'.[3] Prior to 1945 all Bills usually had their committee stage on the floor of the House.

Referring a Bill to a committee of the whole House is intended to allow for full debate of particularly significant Bills and a broader form of discussion than a Standing Committee is perceived to offer. In particular, taking the committee stage on the floor of the House provides an opportunity, in theory, for all MPs to take part in the debate. However, a committee of the whole House tends to bring out the confrontational and party political character-istics of parliamentary debate and any controversy surrounding a Bill will be exploited to the full. Controversy itself does not normally endanger govern-ment legislation, but it may nonetheless be damaging. The price extracted by opponents to a Bill is the loss of parliamentary time which the government could have used to get other legislation through. The main weapon of the

---

[2] For more detailed discussion of the passage of the Maastricht Bill, see D Baker, A Gamble and S Ludlam, 'The Parliamentary Siege of Maastricht 1993: Conservative Divisions and British Ratification' *Parliamentary Affairs* (1994) January and R Rawlings, 'Legal Politics: The United Kingdom and Ratification of the Treaty on European Union Part One and Two' (1994) *Public Law*.

[3] HC [1945–46] 9, *First Report of the Select Committee on Procedure*.

opponents of a Bill is to delay progress through raising points of order, making lengthy speeches, and tabling numerous amendments. The size of a committee of the whole House offers considerable potential for delay in this manner.

A further problem a government may face in a committee of the whole House is controlling opposition from its own backbenchers. The nature and significance of constitutional changes mean that the government may not be able to rely on the whips' normal powers of persuasion to keep its back-benchers in line. Even if some degree of cross-party consensus is achieved there is the danger that a cross-party alliance will be built amongst those backbenchers who oppose any constitutional change and possibly with those who see proposed changes as not going far enough (as happened with House of Lords' reform in 1968–69). The problems of containing backbench dissent are essentially political rather than procedural. In the 1997–98 session there has been little opposition to constitutional measures from the government's side and with such a large majority the government has little to fear.

The theoretical justification for taking a Bill in a committee of the whole House is that it allows all members to participate; thus it is a more appropri-ate forum in which to deal with particularly significant measures. It is debat-able how far this reflects reality. In practice, attention is focused on broader political questions (effectively providing a continuation of the Second Read-ing debate by other means) and there is little opportunity to consider details or more practical or technical questions. Debate tends to be dominated by a small minority of members, although the debate on the floor of the House ensures that a greater number of members become aware of the issues being debated. The proceedings have a high public profile, but the government is unlikely to make concessions unless there is a real possibility of defeat. The Opposition is left with the weapon of delay; but this is only really effective if the government is facing opposition from its own backbenchers. Faced with such opposition, the government is likely to impose a guillotine, possibly leaving large sections of the Bill undebated and further compounding the lack of scrutiny. Incomplete consideration of any Bill is clearly undesirable, but could be considered particularly unacceptable in respect of a major con-stitutional measure.

Time constraints

In any one session a government normally introduces between 50 and 60 measures of greatly varying complexity and length (constitutional and non-constitutional). The amount of time any government has to deal with these programme Bills on the floor of the House of Commons is limited to around 60 days in every session, given that time also has to be set aside for Opposition Days, Estimates Days, Service Debates, and so on. As the figures in

Table 10.1 Time spent on government Bills on the floor of the House of Commons

	1988–89	1989–90	1990–91	1991–92*	1992–93*
Total hours of sitting	1,582	1,468	1,374	696	1,934
% time on government Bills	29.4	25.4	24.6	27.1	31.7
Hours on government Bills	465	373	338	189	613

*1991–92 was a short session and 1992–93 a long session because of the election in April 1992.
Source: Sittings Reform and the Jopling Report, House of Commons Research Paper 94/96, 8 September 1994.

Table 10.1 show, this means that in each session the government has around 400 hours to get its main programme Bills through Second Reading, committee stages taken on the floor of the House, report and Lords amendments.

The estimate of parliamentary time is a crucial factor in determining the place of a measure in the legislative programme, but it is difficult to predict with any accuracy. The use of filibustering and delaying tactics mean that the length of time taken is not necessarily a useful indicator of the complexity of a measure, but rather of the extent of controversy surrounding an issue. The focus of controversy may not always be readily apparent to the Cabinet or to Whitehall in advance, and may also be instigated by the media rather than by parliamentarians. Analysis of the time taken to get major constitutional Bills through the House of Commons in the past (Table 10.2) illustrates how a major constitutional Bill can dominate a parliamentary session and severely limit the amount of other legislation the government can deal with. As is also clear from Table 10.2, in cases where the government believes progress on a major Bill is being unnecessarily delayed it may decide to introduce a 'guillotine motion' to curtail debate. Although there are clearly precedents for the use of the guillotine on constitutional Bills, opposition to a guillotine motion on an issue of constitutional importance will be particularly fierce. Indeed, the only occasion since the Second World War when a government has lost a guillotine motion was over a constitutional Bill.

In the 1997–98 session the government introduced eight bills which could be labelled 'constitutional'. Due to the timing of the election the government had the advantage of a particularly long session, but by summer 1998 there was a significant amount of legislation still to go through Parliament by the end of the session.

Table 10.2 Time spent in consideration of constitutional Bills on the floor of the House of Commons

Constitutional measure	Hours spent on the floor of the House
Parliament Act 1911	169 (guillotined)
Representation of the People Act 1918	220
Parliament Act 1949	20 in 1947; 11 in 1949 (passed under Parliament Act 1911)
Parliament (No 2) Bill 1968	85 (abandoned after 79 hours in committee)
European Communities Act 1972	223 (guillotined)
Scotland and Wales Bill 1976	124 (abandoned after 93 hours in committee)
Scotland Act 1978	158 (guillotined)
Wales Act 1978	107 (guillotined)
Local Government Act 1985	42 (176 hours in standing committee)
European Communities (Amendment) Act 1993	185

Source: Hansard.

Alternative procedures

There are essentially two different areas in which alternative procedures, or reform of existing procedures, for the handling of constitutional Bills, could ease the passage of such Bills whilst meeting demands for adequate scrutiny. The first is to take some stages of a Bill off the floor of the House by using another committee forum. The second is to alter the control of time, either by limiting the amount of time which can be spent on a Bill or by removing some of the constraints on time.[4]

Partial referral of Bills to a Standing Committee

This would reduce the time needed on the floor of the House by following the practice adopted for Finance Bills where most parts of the Bill are referred to a Standing Committee, leaving key issues to be debated in committee of the whole House. The question of whether it would be possible to treat constitutional Bills in this way was raised with the then Clerk of the House by the Procedure Committee in 1945.[5] In his view it was 'theoretically possible;

---

[4] See further The Constitution Unit, *Delivering Constitutional Reform* (1996).
[5] *First Report from the Select Committee on Procedure*, note 3 above.

the machinery part could go upstairs and questions of principle could remain on the floor of the House'.

This procedure has been adopted for legislation in the past, for example, the Sunday Trading Act 1994. The Local Government Act 1985, which abolished the GLC and the metropolitan counties, is the only example of a constitutional measure handled in this way. In this case, the first clause of the Bill was taken on the floor of the House, with the rest of the Bill being considered in a Standing Committee. This reduced the time spent on the Bill on the floor of the House considerably: 41 hours were spent on stages taken on the floor of the House and 176 hours were taken in Standing Committee.

With up to eight committees running at the same time, the use of Standing Committees saves parliamentary time and allows the government to deal with more legislation. Standing Committees also tend to attract less public and media attention than committees of the whole House – so defeats and concessions are perceived as less damaging to the government, and there is a greater willingness to meet critics half way. However, from a government point of view sending a controversial constitutional Bill to a Standing Committee will not necessarily be an easy option. Although the government continues to have a majority in a Standing Committee, because of the smaller numbers involved, the rebellion of a single member has greater significance. In addition, as in committees of the whole House, without timetabling, opponents will attempt to prolong debate as much as possible and the government is therefore just as likely to face a dilemma over guillotining the measure.

The Select Committee on Modernising the House, set up after the 1997 election, did consider this option, but expressed reservations and in the end its members could not agree. In the 1997–98 session the government did try to move the Government of Wales Bill into Standing Committee but the Opposition stood by the convention. Parliamentary reporters observed that during the subsequent committee stage there were sometimes fewer MPs in the chamber than would have been present on a standing committee.

Advance timetabling of all Bills

This would ensure that the government can plan its legislative programme with a degree of certainty by removing the possibility of filibuster and delay being used as tactics of opposition. Formal advance timetabling has been advocated by repeated Procedure Committee reports, opposition parties and external bodies as a means of enabling the provision of alternative, more constructive mechanisms for resistance (eg pre-legislative scrutiny and Special Standing Committees) providing more opportunities for amendment, at earlier stages; and preventing the situation where whole sections of Bills go unconsidered because a guillotine is imposed as the government's 'hidden' deadline nears.

Since December 1994 and the formal agreement to adopt voluntary time-tabling as a regular practice under the Jopling reforms, there have been no guillotine motions. However, the effectiveness of these voluntary arrangements is widely held to be the result of the uncontroversial legislation introduced during this period. In previous years, there has been a significant level of advance agreement through the 'usual channels', avoiding the situation in Australia where most Bills face a guillotine.

Advanced timetabling of all government Bills has, however, been repeatedly rejected by MPs. The most often voiced objection is a concern that more formal timetabling would tip the balance of power away from the Opposition, and in favour of the government. This objection takes two forms: first, concern that formal timetabling would remove opportunities for scrutiny and debate from the Opposition and especially from backbenchers on both sides of the House (which is in part a product of the negative associations of the word timetabling with regular guillotines and enhanced executive power). Secondly, concern that the Opposition's only means of forcing the government to accept changes to Bills is through filibustering, which would be impossible within the constraints of formal timetabling.

The first concern is perhaps easier to assuage than the second. Timetabling can facilitate improvements in the way legislation is considered – better use of committee time for proper scrutiny of Bills can be secured if there is agreement about what the main issues are and how time should be allocated to different parts of the Bill; deliberate time-wasting would no longer have tactical advantages for the Opposition (and government backbenchers who did so with government encouragement could more easily be condemned). As Philip Norton has argued, timetabling would 'allow for more balanced scrutiny of a bill, preventing undigested legislation flowing down the corridor from the Commons to the Lords. It would discourage opposition members from talking for the sake of it and may encourage more participation from government supporters, since the need for vows of silence would no longer be needed in order to get a bill through by a particular date.'[6] In addition, time that may be freed up by advance timetabling might be used to provide an extra day for private member's business or the debate of Select Committee reports.

As to the second concern, it is undeniable that one purpose of timetabling is to ensure that the government can plan its legislative programme with a degree of certainty by removing the possibility of filibuster and delay being used as tactics of opposition. So those who treasure the 'unpredictability of timing' as the key weapon in the Opposition's armoury will not be appeased. However, apart from absorbing parliamentary time which the government could be using for other legislation, there is little evidence that the power of delay is an effective weapon.[7]

The timetabling of certain categories of Bills may prove to be more acceptable than automatic timetabling of all Bills. For example, the Procedure

---

[6] Report of the Hansard Society Commission on the Legislative Process, *Making the Law* (1992).
[7] HC [1984–85] 49, Public Bill Procedure: Select Committee on Procedure.

Committee Report of 1985–86 recommended that Bills need only be subject to timetabling procedures where they were expected to take more than 25 hours in committee – and that timetabling for Report and Third Reading would take place only where the whips could not agree.

The Modernisation Committee has recommended that the House try on a trial basis a more formalised version of 'programming' Bills than set out by Jopling. This will work in conjunction with changes to the hours which the House sits and other (mostly minor) changes to conduct in the Chamber.

Allowing some Bills to be carried over from one session to the next

This is another means of reducing the pressure on the government's time-table (although it would not directly speed up the passage of individual Bills) and would prevent Bills being rushed through with inadequate scrutiny simply because the end of the session is approaching. The key argument in support of the carry-over of public Bills is that the constraints of time and congestion are inimical to the production of good legislation. Allowing for the carry-over of Bills from one session to another already happens in a number of other comparable parliamentary systems and in respect of private Bills in the UK Parliament. It would almost certainly be essential to allow for pre-legislative inquiries on published Bills or more regular use of Special Standing Committees. But it could also assist in securing the passage of potentially complex constitutional legislation.

The principal justifications for the present cut-off are: that it imposes a useful discipline on the government; that the Opposition can in extremis use delay to ensure bad legislation does not get to the statute book; and there are some parliamentary procedures designed on the basis of an annual session, eg the supply procedure. All of these points can, however, be addressed. Although a degree of discipline is certainly useful, the results of the present arrangements are to compress the opportunities for scrutiny and to produce flawed legislation. If more detailed timetabling were introduced, that would provide a substitute discipline. The discipline argument might also be met by ensuring that carry-over would only be permitted where certain criteria were fulfilled. The second point has less force, as history demonstrates that this does not happen; the guillotine is invariably imposed well before the possibility of delaying a Bill into oblivion is reached. Accommodating measures which assume an annual session would be a technical matter, which would have to be addressed, but it should not in itself represent an insuperable obstacle.

The Modernisation Committee did recommend that the use of carry-over should be extended beyond hybrid Bills, but it is not clear that this change will affect constitutional measures. The Committee recommended that to be eligible for carry-over, Bills should not have completed their passage through the House in which they originated, that the decision to carry over should take the form of a specific ad hoc motion; and that eligibility for carry-over should be agreed through the usual channels. This will in effect limit the use of carry-over to non-controversial measures.

Achieving change

It is possible to argue that it is precisely for significant constitutional Bills that alternative parliamentary procedures should be used. But in practice, the ability of a government to introduce new procedures (whether through changing conventions or Standing Orders) is circumscribed by the need to carry the opinion of the House with them, not least because of the desire to maintain goodwill on the merits of the Bill. In any case, reform of parliamentary procedure has a relevance which goes beyond constitutional Bills. The desire to secure the passage of a series of major constitutional measures should therefore be seen as part of a wider package of parliamentary reform.

Handling in the House of Lords

Although this chapter has concentrated on the House of Commons, the reaction of the House of Lords to constitutional reform has also proved to be a significant hurdle in the past. Before the 1997 general election, the extent to which the Second Chamber would oppose constitutional measures from a Labour government was unclear. Certainly, the possibility of hostility from the House of Lords to a Labour government had historical resonance. During the 1970s the House of Lords had showed confidence in exercising its delaying and amending powers, albeit in the context of a *minority* Labour government.

A further consideration prior to the 1997 General Election was how the reform of the Lords itself should be timetabled into the reform programme. Some argued that it was essential to remove the voting rights of (the overwhelmingly Conservative-supporting) hereditary peers before proceeding with other reforms, to avoid the House of Lords frustrating the government's wider plans. Others took the view that the threat of reform should be left hanging in the air, to encourage peers not to oppose constitutional (or indeed other) measures. This approach was not unprecedented. In 1910, after the Lords had refused to pass Lloyd George's budget, the government had threatened to use the royal prerogative to create enough sympathetic peers to pass the Finance Bill. Ultimately, this was not necessary to get the Bill through, but the threat had to be reiterated soon afterwards, in order to pass the Parliament Act 1911.

In 1997, the incoming Labour government was aware of one important factor which would influence the House of Lords' response to its constitutional programme – the 'Salisbury convention'. The convention had been introduced in 1945, and had been observed ever since. But as Lord Carrington, the Conservative peer, has explained, the convention was by no means definitive:

'Cranborne [Conservative Leader of the House of Lords, later Lord Salisbury] reckoned that it was not the duty of the House of Lords to make our system of government inoperable. Nor, he considered, was it justified that the opposition peers should use their voting strength to wreck any measure which the government had made plain at a General Election they proposed to introduce. He thus evolved guidelines, now unofficially known as the Salisbury Rules, which meant that the Lords should, if they saw fit, amend, but should not destroy or alter beyond recognition, any Bill on which the country had, by implication, given its verdict. The Lords in other words, should not frustrate the declared will of the people. I doubt if this amounted to a formal constitutional doctrine but as a way of behaving it seemed to be very sensible . . . by and large the Salisbury strategy worked.'[8]

The doctrine assumes that measures included in a government's manifesto are *de facto* supported by the public at large, and this support should trump the unelected peers' own views. The Salisbury convention does not, however, prevent the Lords from seeking to amend a Bill, and there is a delicate balance between members of an opposition party expressing their dissatisfaction and mounting a serious challenge to the government's legislative programme. For example, Labour governments suffered substantial amendments to some Bills which implemented manifesto commitments, including the Scotland and Wales Bills, and in total suffered some 355 defeats during the 1974–79 Parliament.[9]

In fact, during the first 12 months of the Labour government, the House of Lords has presented no serious opposition to the constitutional reform agenda. Of course, a range of significant amendments has been proposed to the constitutional Bills considered by the House and some have been accepted. Individual peers have spoken out against the policy objectives. But to date there has been no organised opposition, and no serious defeats for the government. The size of the government's majority has obviously been a key factor in this. The clarity of the manifesto commitments made in respect of constitutional matters has also contributed. On most Bills the government has also enjoyed the support of the Liberal Democrats and, on occasions, other key groupings – for example, a majority of Law Lords supported the Human Rights Bill.

Another important factor has been the extent of public consultation prior to legislating. The House of Lords tends to regard itself a guardian of constitutional propriety – peers are more likely to oppose the view of the House of Commons if they feel democratic principles have been ignored. For example, the House of Lords rejected interim arrangements ending elections to the GLC in the run-up to its abolition, on the basis that there was no guarantee that the abolition legislation would be passed. Conversely, evidence of particularly thorough consultation or a commitment to a referendum can reduce

---

[8] Lord Carrington, *Reflect on Things Past: The Memoirs of Lord Carrington* (London: Fontana 1988).
[9] B Hadfield, 'Whither or Whether the House of Lords?' (1984) *Northern Ireland Legal Quarterly*, Winter.

the potential for opposition from the House of Lords. This may well have influenced the Labour Party's decision to hold pre-legislative referendums on Scotland, Wales and the strategic authority for London.

At times during the first session, government ministers in the Lords have chosen to remind their colleagues of the intention to reform the House, but the threat of immediate reform has not been raised. But if peers have not proved to be a significant obstacle to the government's reform agenda so far, it remains to be seen how the House of Lords will respond to legislation which is directed at changing its own membership and role.

CONCLUSION

As this chapter has illustrated, in approaching the task of constitutional reform it is vital to understand the interplay between the political, practical and constitutional frameworks. Tackling the volume and complexity of the legislation whilst ensuring coherence and adequate consultation requires political will, but also careful planning and management of the process of reform.

Further reading

Reports of the Constitution Unit, especially *Delivering Constitutional Reform* (London, 1996)

Rodney Brazier, *Constitutional Reform* (Oxford University Press, 1991), especially Chs 1–2

PART III

EUROPEAN, REGIONAL AND
LOCAL GOVERNMENT

CHAPTER 11

THE EUROPEAN UNION

Professor Carol Harlow (London School of Economics)

New Labour came to power in 1997 as a 'party of the people'. It promised to replace a government described as 'unresponsive and heavily centralised' with one which is accountable and more democratic. In the UK, steps have been taken to make good this promise. A White Paper on freedom of information has been published and widely welcomed. A Human Rights Act has been enacted although is not yet in force. Scottish and Welsh Devolution Bills have been published. Representative government is to be restored in London, with an elected mayor and assembly. These developments, described in other chapters, are aimed at bringing government closer to the people. In the last three cases, the people have been consulted directly, through a referendum.

European union is an issue on which the public holds ambivalent and often incompatible views. The depth of the split on Europe within the Conservative Party has operated to disguise the degree of dissent within all British political parties on European issues. Only the Liberal Democrats have an apparently unbroken record of commitment to the European enterprise and this, cynics would say, is because their commitment has never been, and is not likely to be, put to the test. If it were, the Liberal Democrats would need to take more account of popular opinion and they too might quickly find themselves divided. Similarly, it would be unwise to assume that New Labour will have no further problems with Europe.

New Labour made a confident start in Europe. Signing up to the Social Charter and co-operation in the Treaty of Amsterdam brought its rewards in the shape of acquiescence in an opt out from unified border control and the common immigration and asylum policies. Some progress was also made with the thorny question of British beef exports. But New Labour had made the larger promise that it would 'start shaping Europe's future' and it had hoped to use the convenient UK Presidency to achieve this objective. By the end of the Presidency, when the government provided a balance sheet, there were some gains to report. The UK's reputation as the 'no man' of Europe had been salvaged – no mean achievement in the light of our unwillingness to sign up to the first round of monetary union. Some progress had been made with Europe's more intractable problems, such as the CAP and fishing quotas. But the most pressing issues in Europe are those of democracy and accountability. These are issues which will become still more pressing with the 'widening' to which the UK is deeply committed. Here there is very little progress to report.

Opinion polling had pointed to a widespread sentiment amongst the 'peoples of Europe' that Europe was somehow a 'good thing' and that European union, however imprecisely understood, was a desirable end. Now this may be changing. The Maastricht ratification process offered a warning of just how deep the divisions in public opinion really are over Europe. In Denmark, where anti-Maastricht parties won the 1992 ratification referendum, the 'Yes' vote just scraped home the next year[1]; in 1998 again, about 45 per cent of the electorate voted 'No' in the referendum to ratify the Treaty of Amsterdam. In the 1994 French European election, anti-Maastricht lists gained almost 40 per cent of the vote; the National Front, represented in the European Parliament, has caused headaches in every recent national election. A leaked Labour Party Policy Paper, prepared during the presidency, apparently reports declining support throughout Europe; only 46 per cent of those polled now see the EU as 'a good thing' against 70 per cent in 1990. Widening the frontiers of the EU is likely to deepen the divisions.

The problem is that the European institutions have never succeeded in capturing the public imagination nor in gaining solid public support. The European Union (EU) is managed in practice by an ill-assorted set of institutions,[2] under stress and liable to be sorely tested by further expansions of the EU. The rapid progression of negotiations for 'widening' the EU during the UK presidency has not been matched by reforms to enable the institutions to cope with expansion. Amsterdam rationalised legislative procedures and extended the scope of the co-decision procedure;[3] the European Parliament (EP) also gained powers of scrutiny and policy-making, especially in the area of the old Third Pillar (immigration, asylum and policing). There is little evidence, however, that the European electorate would see this as an advance in democracy nor that it shares the view of the Single European Act of the EP as 'an indispensable means of expression . . . for the democratic peoples of Europe'. To the contrary the leading commentators suggest that the EP:

---

[1] Siune and Svensson, 'The Danes and the Maastricht Treaty: The Danish EC Referendum of June 1992' (1993) 12 *Electoral Studies* 99.

[2] Deirdre Curtin, 'The Constitutional Structure of the Union: A Europe of Bits and Pieces' (1993) 30 CMLRev 17; Jean-Claude Piris, 'After Maastricht, Are the Community Institutions More Efficacious, More Democratic and More Transparent?' (1993) 19 ELRev 449.

[3] Co-decision procedure increases the influence of the EP by allowing an ultimate power of veto. For a concise explanation of the varying EC legislative methods see, Desmond Dinan, *Ever Closer Union? An Introduction to the European Community* (London: Macmillan, 1994) pp 273–281.

'... is not, as national parliaments are in many countries, the "meeting place" of the country, the centre of national debate and the hub of public life. It is often perceived as remote and its multi-lingual character reduces the opportunity for cut and thrust or drama in its debates.'[4]

Inside the UK, no Inter-Governmental Conference (IGC) has been accompanied by public debate about the appropriate structure for an enlarged EU comparable to that which introduced measures of national constitutional reform at the last election. In Europe, there is no appropriate structure for general consultation and no clearly legitimate representative structure.[5] Two non-voting MEPs represented public opinion at the 1996 IGC. Recently, the member state representatives who decide European agendas have been increasingly unwilling to take decisions which may involve consulting disenchanted and unpredictable electorates. So hard decisions are not taken and the EU continues to stagger from crisis to crisis.

The Commission warned that the 1996 IGC might be 'probably the last and only opportunity all 15 Member States will have to reflect together about how the Union is to function in a wider framework'. Not to put too fine a point on the matter, if the institutions are not to collapse into ineffectiveness, some hard and basic decisions needed to be taken at Amsterdam. In the event, little was achieved. Hard decisions on qualified majority and weighted voting in the Council and on representation and size in the Commission were all ducked and left to a new IGC to be held 'at least one year before the membership of the EU exceeds twenty'.

There are two hints in the Treaty of Amsterdam (ToA) that member states were concerned about the problems of 'widening'. The first and most direct was a new article (Treaty on European Union (TEU), Article F1) giving powers to the Council to discipline any member state found to be in 'serious and persistent breach' of the fundamental principles of the EU as expressed in TEU, Article F. This suggests concern about both democratic institutions and respect for human rights at national level. The second hint lies in the gradual emergence of the so-called 'Europe of many speeds'. On the one hand the ToA authorises 'closer cooperation' between groups of member states, such as will occur in the context of EMU; on the other it continues the practice of permitting assorted 'opt outs' tailored to the special needs or prejudices of particular countries, as has been done for Denmark, Ireland and the UK for the new policing and asylum competences. This development signals increasing divergence and breakdown in consensus, together with a hint of the probable outcome: retreat from the vision of European union and

---

[4] F Jacobs and P Corbett, *The European Parliament* (London: Longman, 3rd edn, 1995) pp 231–232.
[5] Sven Andersen and Kjell Eliassen, *The European Union: How Democratic Is It?* (London: Sage, 1996). The EP held public hearings before the IGC in which NGOs participated.

acceptance of divergence. The alternative of a European confederation rooted in the subsidiarity principle[6] is gaining ground.

A central effect of the European venture has been to move governance further and further from the people. This has been described in terms of a 'hollowing out' of the nation state,[7] whose powers have been, over the last two decades, transferred out of the public sector through privatisation, conveyed upwards through a process of globalisation, and devolved downwards through regionalisation. To many students of international affairs, the result has been an abdication of state responsibility and the substitution for democratic accountability of a triangular, corporatist elite, with states, international institutions and international business as the sole participants in governance.[8] Existing political arrangements have inexorably been redefined, as areas such as health, education, social welfare, environment, police and migration are sucked into the European orbit. As Muller and Wright observe,[9] these policy 'networks' are 'increasingly entangled in relationships at four territorial levels: the international, the European, the national and the local, and for some of these interests it is by no means clear that the national level is the most important'.

The consequence has been a yawning gap in accountability and control as power has been shifted from parliaments and vested in governments. For Juliet Lodge,[10] 'What was and remains ill-understood is the degree to which the European Parliament has not won powers forfeited to national governments by national parliaments: neither can exercise effective control over either what national governments do in the EU or what the EU executive does'. Lodge places the blame squarely on national governments, accusing them of deliberately engineering a situation whereby national parliaments were denied effective controls over national executives. If representative democracy is not to become meaningless, this is a trend which has to be reversed.

The theoretical underpinning for these transfers of power has traditionally lain in the so-called 'permissive consensus' which, at least in the initial stages of the European Community, allowed the legitimacy of European policy-making to be assumed. Policy-making developed as a series of bargains between Europe's governmental elites. The fiction of 'permissive consensus' was always dangerous; after Maastricht, it is revealed as a fiction and one which can no longer be taken for granted.

---

[6] Inserted as EC, Article 3(b) at Maastricht, after Amsterdam TEU Article G(5). See further, Alan Dashwood, 'Sates in the European Union' (1998) 23 ELRev 199.

[7] Robert Rhodes, 'The Hollowing Out of the State: The Changing Nature of the Public Service in Britain' (1994) 65 *Political Quarterly* 138.

[8] Susan Strange, *The Retreat of the State, The Diffusion of Power in the World Economy* (Cambridge: Cambridge University Press, 1996).

[9] Wolfgang Muller and Vincent Wright, 'Reshaping the State in Western Europe: The Limits to Retreat' (1994) 17 *West European Politics* 6.

[10] Juliet Lodge, 'The European Parliament', in S Andersen and K Eliassen (eds), *The European Union: How Democratic Is It?* (London: Sage, 1996) p 188.

A EUROPEAN STRUCTURE PLAN

It has been said, and is fast becoming the orthodoxy amongst academic commentators, that debate over the future of Europe has drifted into an impasse.[11] The underlying reason is political: uncertainty and lack of agreement over basic objectives. In the remainder of this chapter, I shall argue that efforts to construct a European community have been premised on a model which is beginning to look outdated. Having briefly considered alternatives, I shall suggest a number of incremental changes which might re-orient the European enterprise, making it more responsive to, and more representative of, the peoples of Europe.

Integration

Of the three models which might serve as a possible basis for the European enterprise, the most influential to date has undoubtedly been that of integrationism. The EU is seen as moving gradually into the role of federal government, while the member states gently decline into provinces. This model probably represents the preference of the 'founding fathers' and, for fairly obvious reasons, remains popular with the European elite. It is important to realise that the European Court of Justice (ECJ) has until recently been unashamedly integrationist. Integrationism, once described by one of the ECJ's most influential judges as a 'genetic code transmitted to the Court by the founding fathers',[12] is central to the concept of 'the New Legal Order' created by the Court.[13] It underlies the doctrine of 'direct effect', which allows EC law to be enforced by individuals in the national courts.[14] It is a thread running through the case law in the main areas of competition and the market. Given the role of case law in shaping the constitution of the EU, this is a point of some significance.[15] Since it is hard to see how the present EU legal order could survive the demise of integrationism, it is not surprising that the ECJ has not rushed to explore issues of subsidiarity.[16]

---

[11] Renaud Dehousse (ed), *Europe After Maastricht. An Ever Closer Union?* (Munich: Lawbooks in Europe, 1994).

[12] Federigo Mancini and David Keeling, 'Democracy and the European Court of Justice' (1994) 57 MLR 175.

[13] Case 26/62 *Van Gend en Loos* [1963] ECR 1.

[14] For explanation and comment, see Deirdre Curtin, 'The Province of Government: Delimiting the Direct Effect of Directives in the Common Law Context' (1990) 15 ELRev 195.

[15] Joseph Weiler, 'Journey to an Unknown Destination: A Retrospective and Prospective of the European Court of Justice in the Arena of Political Integration' (1993) 31 *Journal of Common Market Studies* 417; Takis Tridimas, 'The Court of Justice and Judicial Activism' (1996) 21 ELRev 199.

[16] Case C-84/94 *UK v Council (Working Time)* [1997] ECR I-5755. Article 2 of the Protocol on the Application of the Principle of Subsidiarity and Proportionality provides that the principles developed by the European Court of Justice regarding the relationship between national and EC law shall not be affected.

In some member states, though probably not the UK, integrationism still receives strong support. Supposedly, the process of EMU will give an additional fillip to this model by transferring to Union level the financial and economic powers which have proved so important in strengthening the central government in many federal systems, notably that of the USA. Creeping federalisation will, it is widely assumed, be the consequence. But the close results of the French and Danish referendums on Maastricht ratification spelt the end of the integrationist dream at the political level. In Germany, whose government is chief promoter of EMU and noted for its support of integrationist policies generally, the political crisis which followed on the disagreement between the German government and the Bundesbank over revaluation of gold reserves in the interest of attaining the EMU criteria conveyed a similar message. Since, prior to the General Election, all major British political parties were conceding a referendum on monetary union, this is an important political fact. For the moment, the issue of EMU, likely to have provoked popular revolt in a referendum, has been satisfactorily fudged. Perhaps it can be fudged again at the next election. Perhaps a manifesto commitment to entry can be substituted for the promised referendum. But it would be unwise to assume that the UK's problems with EMU are over.

Integrationism is the version of Europeanism most likely to provoke political backlash and which has always been successfully used to stir up hostility to the European enterprise. Governments play on the ambiguity of popular feeling every time they blame 'Brussels' for forcing them to adopt unpopular policies, while taking credit for more positive achievements brought about through the machinery of the Community. In the UK, European policy-making is usually managerial in style. The government may simply act, justifying its actions afterwards, unashamedly blaming 'Brussels' where necessary, a technique often used in Third Pillar matters. The government may temporise in Europe, running the risk of being labelled 'non communautaire', a necessary strategy for John Major which often left the UK isolated. National leaders can ignore popular opinion on Europe in a way impossible in national politics because of the weakness of Euro-politics. European issues are never properly put to the people. A study of the 1994 elections noted that the media had been blind to the 'continuous, close entanglement' between national and European politics and policy-making and had in consequence reduced the European elections to 'little more than national opinion polls'.[17]

For integrationists, the logical answer to a perceived 'democracy deficit' lies in the classic constitutional doctrine of separation of powers: a decrease in the powers of the Commission – seen, perhaps unjustly, as an unaccountable and elitist bureaucracy – and an increase in the powers of the EP. This nostrum is naturally deeply unpopular with national parliaments which see the EP as a competitor. Further democratisation of the European political

---

[17] Bridget Boyce, 'The June 1994 Elections and the Politics of the European Parliament' (1994) 47 *Parliamentary Affairs* 141, 156.

process would also be necessary. Voters seem to sense that political power is not really at stake; nation rather than party determines voters' policy preferences.[18] If voter apathy is blamed on the fact that European elections do not allow the people either to choose their rulers or to participate in policy-making, then (so the argument runs) voter allegiance can be secured by changing this position. The effect would be a to create a rival to the Council, a radical transfer of political power unlikely to be popular with national governments. Whether an upsurge of popular enthusiasm would ensue is, however, extremely doubtful.

The real barrier to such a development is the lack of political underpinning for European institutions. Government demands a measure of popular support which, in the European context, requires a partial transfer of loyalty. Everything points to the fact that in the EU this support has not so far been forthcoming. True, the right to vote is exercised, but the available statistical data consistently points to the low salience of EP elections. Thus average voter turnout across the EU in 1994 was 58.3 per cent, a fall from 63.8 per cent and 62.8 per cent in the two earlier elections. In the UK, only 36.4 per cent of the electorate voted in the 1994 Euro-election, a figure very close to local elections and far from the average of over 70 per cent in general elections. Typically, Euro-elections are treated as an opinion poll of national government performance. Writing before the advent of direct elections, David Marquand thought the chances of moving beyond a 'Europe of the nations' depended very much on the emergence of European political parties.[19] We are still awaiting this outcome nearly 20 years later. It has been said that[20] the position of European level political parties is still 'extremely weak in comparison to parties in most democratic systems' and that the crisis has actually deepened, with the election of the EP doing 'little to prevent the development of a new and much deeper wave of scepticism towards European integration'. What is the contribution of the present government? The new UK electoral scheme for European elections is a 'list system', largely incompatible with British electoral traditions. It will effectively transfer the choice of candidate from constituencies to national, political parties. Widely criticised as undemocratic, the change is likely to exacerbate problems of low turn-out.

A 'Europe of the Regions'

Given New Labour's attitude to devolution at national level, it might at first sight seem likely to be attracted by a regional solution to the problem of

---

[18] J Thomassen and H Schmitt, 'Policy representation' (1997) 32 *European Journal of Political Research* 165, 176.
[19] David Marquand, 'Towards a Europe of the Parties' (1978) 39 *Political Quarterly* 425.
[20] Simon Hix and Christopher Lord, *Political Parties in the European Union* (London: Macmillan, 1997) pp 198–199.

democratic deficit. This would also be compatible with the federal constitutions of some member states, especially Germany and Spain, models invoked during the Scotland referendum campaign.

The implications of a more regional structure for Europe are certainly significant for Scotland, where European affairs are to remain the responsibility of the UK government.[21] It is, however, envisaged that the UK could be represented both on committees and at the Council of Ministers by a Scottish minister.[22] This division of powers, likely in any event to prove problematic, would become still less acceptable in the context of a further dose of regionalism. There has been a substantial increase in direct regional representation in Brussels in recent years.[23] This too is likely to increase, creating further pressure inside the UK. Wales, where grants from structural funds were cleverly utilised in the early 1990s to draw the sting of right-wing dislike of state subsidy and development programmes, provides an example of the way in which Europe may foster policy differences inside the nation-state. Regionalism may operate to make such divisions more acceptable, or it may not. In Belgium, generally regarded as a failing federation, state responsibility for the enforcement of EC laws when enforcement is a matter for regional government has proved highly controversial.

The Commission, by definition integrationist, already had good relations with regional authorities through the regime of structural grants. The Commission may therefore have encouraged regionalist aspirations as a counterweight to the national interest representation in the Council. With Commission support, the Maastricht Treaty (EC Treaty 198a–198c, inserted by TEU, Article G(67)) introduced a Committee of the Regions to provide a voice for regional interests in EU decision-making, again a development consistent with bringing government closer to the people. The Committee of the Regions was granted no legislative role, its function being merely to advise and issue opinions. To date, powerful regions, such as the German Länder, prefer to negotiate for occasional seats on the Council of Ministers and on Commission committees. Both Council and EP are nonetheless inclined to see the new Committee as a potential rival. In consequence, the Commission's desire for regional democracy, namely, that *elected office* at local or regional level should be a criterion for appointment, has been resisted. Appointments remain firmly in the hands of the Council, which nominates solely on the recommendation of member states. Riven by faction, dissected by a north/south geographical division, and split again by a local/regional divide, the Committee has so far failed to provide a coherent sub-national voice.

---

[21] See the White Paper, *Scotland's Parliament*, Cm 3658 (1997–98). See also, Andrew Duff (ed), *Subsidiarity within the European Union* (London: Federal Trust, 1993) pp 87–106.

[22] *Scotland's Parliament*, Cm 3658 (1997–98). In fact, the proposal could be seen as a further decline in accountability, undercutting ministerial responsibility to the Westminster Parliament.

[23] Justin Greenwood, *Representing Interests in the European Union* (London: Macmillan, 1997) pp 218–241.

As presently emerging, the model of European regionalism has been described as one of 'contested hierarchy'.[24] It is not strong enough to do much damage but its existence generates confusion and creates the potential for a contradictory power structure. Should this so far weak and ineffectual voice be strengthened? There are two arguments against such a move. First, the inevitable result would be to reinforce the power of the unrepresentative Commission. Secondly, the Committee of the Regions stands as a pointer to a federal Europe in which the second (state or provincial) tier of government would be provided by the regions and member states might ultimately atrophy until, like the metropolitan boroughs under Thatcher, they were excised as unnecessary.

The challenge of post-modern governance, of which the EU is presently the most striking example, lies precisely in the fact that we cannot be certain that erosion or demolition of the sovereign national state will inevitably be a progression. As in post-colonial Africa or the post-Soviet Balkans, retrogression to less efficient and secure forms of pre-national governance is equally a possibility.[25] Some European federations, notably Belgium, already have to contend with dangerous tensions. For these, a 'Europe of the Regions' may seem capable of resolving some of their problems. Other tensions would, however, undoubtedly be created, particularly where peoples are seeking self-determination in an area which straddles national frontiers, notably in the Basque country. The 'Europe of the Regions' creates, in short, a very real and natural fear of Balkanisation. Progression to regional devolution in the UK, and the very real possibility of an independent Scotland, could encourage the break up of the UK within a 'Europe of the Regions'.

Plurality and Subsidiarity

It is the remaining option of a pluralist Europe committed to co-operation and co-ordination but firmly based on its national components and something less than federal in aspiration,[26] which seems to match the mood of the moment. This pattern, which began to emerge clearly in the Treaty of Maastricht, now finds a measure of confirmation in the Treaty of Amsterdam.

Maastricht retained the vision of 'ever closer union' but introduced the concept of 'subsidiarity', according to which 'decisions are to be taken as closely as possible to the citizen'. The Union was enjoined also to 'respect the identity of its Member States' (Article F(1), now TEU, Article 6(3)). A

---

[24] Lisbet Hooghe, 'Subnational Mobilisation in the European Union' (1995) 18 *West European Politics* 175.

[25] Robert Cooper, *The Post-Modern State and the World Order* (London: Demos, 1996).

[26] See Joseph Weiler, 'The Community System: The Dual Character of Supranationalism' (1981) 1 *Yearbook of European Law* 267; Marc Wilke and Helen Wallace, *Subsidiarity: Approaches to Power-sharing in the European Community* (London: Royal Institute of International Affairs, 1990).

new EC, Article 3b insisted that, except in matters where the EC possesses exclusive competence, the EC is to act 'within the limits of its powers' and 'in accordance with the principle of subsidiarity'. It should take action:

> '. . . *only if and in so far as* the objectives of the proposed action cannot be sufficiently achieved by the Member States and can therefore, by reason of the scale or effects of the proposed action, be better achieved by the Community.' (emphasis added)

The Article also contained the so-called 'necessity' or 'proportionality' test, whereby Community action 'shall not go beyond what is necessary to achieve the objectives' of the Treaty. Defective though it may be in terms of justiciability, the Article nonetheless stands as a symbol of intent. Later the same year it was fleshed out by the European Council during the UK presidency. Now the principles have been constitutionalised in a Protocol annexed to the Amsterdam Treaty.

Although the Protocol refers approvingly to institutional balance, the *acquis communautaire* and the relationship betweeen the EU and national legal orders, it places the onus on the former to justify new initiatives. Tests are imposed according to which action should be limited to the case where (1) issues possess transnational aspects and (2) cannot be adequately dealt with, or (3) would be resolved with markedly less effectiveness at national level. The EU should also be sparing with its legislation, favouring the more permissive directive and leaving form and methods of implementation to national authorities. In an implicit rebuke to the integrationist tendencies of the ECJ, the Treaty spells out that 'care shall be taken to respect well established national arrangements and the organisation and working of Member States' *legal systems*' (emphasis added).

There are further signals in the ToA of change of mood. The bare statement in the TEU that 'Citizenship of the Union is hereby established' is, for example, to be softened by insistence that 'Citizenship of the Union shall complement and not replace national citizenship' (EC, Article 8(1)). The authority in Article 128 of the EC Treaty, providing that the Community shall act in cultural matters and take account of cultural matters in general policy-making, is now modified by a requirement 'to respect and to promote the diversity of its cultures' (EC, Article 128(4)).

Given both the strength of its integrationist competitor and the integrationist thrust of EMU, such precepts are not in themselves enough to establish a model of subsidiarity. What is required is a cultural or mood change, to which the 'people's party' needs to contribute. A serious problem with modern government is that, unless it is *seen* to be busily governing, it may seem not to be worthy of its keep. As the Single Market nears completion, this is particularly true of the Commission, which administers virtually nothing and whose main output is regulatory. Unless Europe is seen to be taking on new competences, then the European enterprise may seem to lose its point.

The Edinburgh summit grudgingly accepted that less (and better) legislative output was desirable and a moratorium on new Community competences would be equally welcome. If subsidiarity is to be taken seriously, more needs to be left to national authorities. The role of the Commission must change. Harmonisation and integration will have to give way to co-ordination. Directives ought to return to being 'directive' in character.[27] A programme of rationalisation of existing legal instruments was authorised at Edinburgh.[28] Perhaps ironically, the highly inconvenient consolidation of the Treaties may be its first outcome.

This point is particularly relevant to policy-making in the area of Justice and Home Affairs. European politicians are prone to grandiose rhetoric, and in introducing the concept of the Union 'as an area of freedom, security and justice', the Treaty of Amsterdam (ToA) is no exception. Yet the ToA does go some way with its new Title IIIA on Free Movement of Persons, Asylum and Immigration to harmonise the old Third Pillar procedure with normal Community policy-making procedures. This is welcome, as was UK support for the change. The arbitrary, secretive and unaccountable nature of Third Pillar policy-making[29] can only be improved by greater openness and accountability: on one side to the EP, which gains *consultative* powers (TEU, Article 73o) and on the other to the ECJ, which gains at least limited jurisdiction (TEU, Article 73p). These changes will be welcomed by, and go some way towards satisfying the demands of, social action groups working in the field.[30] But it must not be forgotten that the UK has opted out and to maintain the opt out means that it will play no real part in future policy-making.

Thus the government is at a crossroads and needs to reflect very carefully. Improving the structure of EU policy-making should not create any assumption that policy-making at EU level is preferable. Transfers of policy-making to the European level tend to stifle debate, hamper public input and make participation by interest groups harder. A new Protocol was agreed at Amsterdam which seeks to limit asylum claims by treating EU countries as 'safe countries of origin'. There is provision too for closer co-operation and

---

[27] The extended status of directives derives from the doctrine of direct effect introduced by the ECJ in Case 43/75 *Defrenne v Sabena* [1976] ECR 455. See also, Deirdre Curtin, 'The Province of Government: Delimiting the Direct Effect of Directives in the Common Law Context' (1990) 15 ELRev 195.

[28] See Edinburgh Resolution (11–12 December 1992) and Council Resolution, 8 June 1993, OJ 1993 C166/1. And see, Tom Burns, 'Better Lawmaking? An Evaluation of Law Reform in the European Community', in Paul Craig and Carol Harlow (eds), *Lawmaking in the European Union* (Dordrecht: Kluwer, 1998).

[29] See Elspeth Guild, *The Developing Immigration and Asylum Policies of the European Union* (Dordrecht: Kluwer, 1996) and 'The Constitutional Consequences of Lawmaking in the Third Pillar of the European Union', in Paul Craig and Carol Harlow (eds), *Lawmaking in the European Union*, note 28 above.

[30] See especially, *The Union Divided, Race Discrimination and Third Country Nationals in the European Union* (London: Justice, 1997).

common action in the fields of policing, criminal proceedings, crime, drugs and terrorism. Could we be moving, as the Dutch fear, towards a 'Fortress Europe', with a single, illiberal policy on drugs, with no possibility of deviation or room for experimentation?[31]

Co-operation is one thing while harmonisation – the ultimate aim of the integrationist – quite another. So long as responsibility in international law rests with the member states, policy-making at national level has great advantages. Immigration control, terrorism, deportation and extradition are all, with policing, crime control and the security services, areas of traditional executive prerogative over which democratic control has never really been established at national level.[32] Behind Schengen, behind the machinery of the Third Pillar, there is a sense of wishing to keep it this way. So long as the undemocratic and illiberal *national* tradition in matters of immigration persists, it would be foolish to assume that the Amsterdam concessions will result in a rush of democracy!

The case against unification is a wider one. Transnational markets, postmodernity and telecommunications, have combined to persuade us that 'Big is Beautiful' and that uniformity and standardisation are desirable in themselves. To producers, administrative unification seems desirable because it cuts down on bureaucracy. A single European agency to regulate and process licences then becomes a desideratum. A genuinely pluralist Europe cannot emerge unless the fixation with the 'level playing field' is abandoned.

As the British public has begun to realise, regulation takes government out of the hands of the people, substituting an unelected body of experts.[33] It is of course essential to avoid dangerous products creeping through one country's laxity on to supermarket shelves throughout the Single Market. But conformity may equally be dangerous; this is the argument over genetic engineering. Harmonisation irons out alternatives and narrows the range of choice. Mistakes made at transnational level are harder and more expensive to repair. Conformity may often need to be subordinated to diversity.

TOWARDS A PARTICIPATORY EUROPE

It is one of the fundamental tenets of democratic societies that its citizens will actively participate in the process of governing. There is no point in bringing government to the people if people are not able or willing to participate. But translating this ambition into a reality in modern democracies is exceptionally difficult. 'For the ambition to be realised there needs to be a set of readily available opportunity structures for citizen participation, matched

---

[31] M Spenser, *States of Injustice* (London: Pluto Press, 1995).
[32] See *Council of Civil Service Unions v Minister for the Civil Service* [1985] AC 374.
[33] G Majone, *Regulating Europe* (London: Routledge, 1996).

by a set of citizen attitudes towards participation.'[34] In the European context, where *parliamentary* democracy has not had time to take root, the challenge becomes to fill the 'democratic deficit' by providing alternative 'opportunity structures'.

In describing a distinctive post-modern form of governance which is seen as emergent in the EU, more fluid and flexible in character, and different in form from those which operate in the member states, academics are using the image of 'networks'.[35] The imprecision of this imagery has its dangers. There are, however, two types of network installed at international and European levels, which may be looked at in seeking a basis for democratic development.

The first is a network of interest groups which come together as lobbyists. Far and away the most influential to date is the global commercial network, capable of manufacturing considerable political pressure and even of generating its own legal norms. (The arms lobby provides a good example.) The power of the commercial lobby is such as to endanger the autonomy of national government. At one and the same time it provides the main justification for and the most potent threat to the European enterprise.[36] Because the commercial lobby is able to operate through multi-national corporations at national, transnational and international levels, it creates a dangerous imbalance in political power and influence. It is, therefore, both essential for democracy and in the interest of national governments that alternative opportunity structures should be used to create a counterweight.

Machinery which can be used to level the policy playing field is already in being in Europe. Some is institutionalised, such as the Economic and Social Committee, comprising a mix of workers, employers, professionals and consumers, which exists 'to increase democratic accountability, make Community decision-making more transparent, and familiarise the economic and social sectors with the Council's legislative output'. This body is, however, in decline. The accession of the present government to the Social Charter by the Treaty of Amsterdam is undoubtedly a new start, presenting new opportunities. The European concept of 'social partnership' could represent a new departure in labour relations, inside the UK as in Europe.[37]

The Commission has drawn on the practice of international organisations to encourage interest representation by non-governmental organisations (NGOs), maintaining a register and making funds available. Commission support has helped to give social action groups a toehold in European public

---

[34] Jeremy Richardson, 'The Market for Political Activism: Interest Groups as a Challenge To Political Parties' (1995) 18 *West European Politics* 116.

[35] Karl-Heinz Ladeur, 'Towards a Legal Theory of Supranationality – The Validity of the Network Concept' (1997) 3 *European Law Journal* 33. See also Daniela Obradovic, 'Policy Legitimacy and the European Union' (1996) 34 *Journal of Common Market Studies* 191.

[36] Vivien Schmidt, 'The New World Order Inc: The Rise of Business and the Decline of the Nation-State' (1995) 124 *Daedalus* 75.

[37] For a fuller discussion of issues in this area, see Brian Bercusson and others, 'A Manifesto for Social Europe' (1997) 3 *European Law Journal* 189.

affairs. The Commission has a good record for seeking out the views of public-interest groups. Its practice receives encouragement from the Protocol on Subsidiarity and Proportionality, which exhorts it to 'consult widely before proposing legislation and, wherever appropriate, publish consultation documents' (Article 9). It has now published a code of practice[38] regulating dealings between the Commission and interest groups with a view to levelling the playing field, advancing transparency and maintaining standards in public life. These developments are important and deserve the full support of the Council and national governments.

Business, employers, unions and government, still form, however, a classic corporatist paradigm, whose monopoly of the policy-making process has long been a cause for concern. One way to ensure that neither commercial interests nor the 'social partners' dominate policy-making in Europe is to stimulate the growth of social action or public interest groups, encouraging them to create European networks. At home, the government-funded Equal Opportunities Commission has helped to stimulate consciousness of the European dimension to women's issues,[39] while Commission and EP have actively supported a European Women's Lobby to represent and defend women's interests at EU level. Recent research reveals that 62 per cent of women's groups surveyed were nonetheless pursuing such issues only at *national* level, proof either of substantial ignorance of EC competences or of reluctance to move into the European field.[40]

The ToA has made the great leap forward of bringing under the EC Treaty discrimination based on racial or ethnic origin. A new EC, Article 6(a) allows the Council, on a proposal from the Commission, to 'take appropriate action to combat discrimination based on sex, racial or ethnic origin, religion or belief, disability, age or sexual orientation'. The scope of the addition is debatable and it gives a relatively weak mandate, based on *unanimity* in the Council and on *consultation*, not co-decision, procedure in the EP. A new TEU, Article K.1 authorises 'common action' to combat racism and xenophobia. Less strong than their supporters would have liked, these provisions are nonetheless welcome, if long overdue. Issues of race and immigration are of great importance to our society, yet ethnic minorities are notably underrepresented at every level. Their interest groups too are conspicuously underfunded. The government has expressed the wish to revitalise the Commission for Racial Equality (CRE) 'and enhance its important role in promoting racial equality in Britain'. A strong national contribution from government and CRE and a European network with Commission support and funding could help to level this most unequal of playing fields.

---

[38] European Commission, *An Open and Structured Dialogue Between the Commission and Special Interest Groups*, SEC (92) 2272.

[39] As the government found to its cost in *R v Secretary of State for Employment, ex parte EOC* [1994] 1 All ER 910.

[40] Charlotte Bretherton and Liz Sperling, 'Women's Networking and the European Union' (1997) 3 *Newsletter of the ECPR Standing Group on European Level Interest Representation* 6.

The second type of network is the 'policy community'.[41] Policy communities are generally constituted on a sectoral basis. A specially well-developed network of this type exists in the environmental area. Originating at international level and clustered around the United Nations, the environmental lobby has positioned itself to make input at every level of global governance. EP committees and inter-groups,[42] which meet regularly, can serve as the focal point of a policy network. In this way, interest groups can help to close the gap between the electorate and the EP.

Agencies also serve an important function as the focal point of networks. The national experience of agencies is not particularly democratic. Agencies have tended to emerge as expert and autonomous bodies, relatively impervious to public opinion. This is the course they are beginning to take at EU level. They might, however, serve a different purpose.[43] Take the European Environmental Protection Agency (EPA), which at present acts merely as a conduit for information. There has been much talk of using it as an enforcement agency, again replicating a characteristic role for agencies at national level. The EPA could instead develop as a focal point for policy-making, producing policy documents to which national environmental agencies, citizens and NGOs could contribute; in other words, its primary role would not be that of policing but to stimulate a policy network whose work could be fed into the formal policy-making process through the Comitology (below). This would mean, however, distancing the EPA both from the Commission and member states, whose representatives at present tend to dominate the composition of agency boards of management, to make them more autonomous.

DEMOCRACY AND TRANSPARENCY

Without an adequate flow of information, even the first stages of democracy become meaningless. As Deirdre Curtin insists:

> 'It is regarded as essential to the democratic process that individuals are able to understand the decision-making process and the means by which the decision makers have reached their conclusions in order effectively to evaluate governmental policies and actions and to be able to choose their representative intelligently. An equally important objective of openness in democratic government is to enhance public confidence in government.'[44]

---

[41] Or 'chain of participants working in the same area who come to know and depend on each other over a long period': Greenwood, *Representing Interests in the European Union*, note 23 above, p 15.

[42] An inter-group is an unofficial grouping of MEPs interested in a specific area: Greenwood, *Representing Interests in the European Union*, note 23 above, pp 43–48.

[43] See Michelle Everson, 'Independent Agencies: Hierarchy Beaters' (1995) 1 *European Law Journal* 180.

[44] Deirdre Curtin, 'Betwixt and Between: Democracy and Transparency in the Governance of the European Union', in D Winter et al, *Reforming the Treaty on European Union – The Legal Debate* (Dordrecht: Kluwer, 1996) p 96.

Maastricht was a turning point when, for the first time, the Council admitted this point of principle. A Declaration on Transparency was annexed to the TEU and followed at the Edinburgh Summit by further resolutions. Subsequently, the Commission published a code of conduct on public access.[45] The requirements still fell well short of the practice in many member states, and Denmark and the Netherlands made the running in pressing for further openness. After Maastricht, battle was resumed in the Court and Tribunal of First Instance. Not surprisingly, these have so far responded half-heartedly[46] and this is too important a matter for incremental, judicial development.

The Treaty of Amsterdam does not make a great contribution in the area of transparency. True, a requirement has been added to TEU, Article A that decisions be taken 'as openly as possible'. A new Article 191a also gives citizens a right of access to EP, Council and Commission documents. The conditions, general principles and limitations are, however, left to be determined by the Council, while each institution retains control over its own rules of procedure. This is not likely to meet criticisms from Denmark and the Netherlands nor the complaint from Sweden that EU practice is forcing it to 'level down'. (Fortunately, matters have now been taken further by an 'own-initiative inquiry' of the European ombudsman (EO) opened in June 1996. To the EO, registers of documents seem the best way to secure consistent public access to EU documentation.) New Labour, committed in their 1997 election manifesto to the introduction of freedom of information legislation at national level ought to give its backing to the campaign for a more open Europe.

EUROPEAN RULE-MAKING

Arguments over democratic legitimacy in the EU have, at least until recently, focused either on election to the EP or to its limited law-making powers.[47] Joseph Weiler goes much further. He has proposed[48] a 'European public square'. This would enhance transparency by placing on the Internet full details of the decision-making process for every EU project. It could also include a 'Private Forum', which would allow meaningful exchanges between 'Community Institutions and certain private actors'; in other words, an

---

[45] European Commission, *An Open and Structured Dialogue Between the Commission and Special Interest Groups*, SEC (92) 2272.

[46] See Case T-194/94, *Carvel and Guardian Newspapers* [1995] ECR II-2769; Case C-68/94 *Netherlands v Council* [1996] ECR I-2169; Case T-105/95 *WWF (UK) v Commission* [1997] 2 CMLR 55; Case C-321/95 *Stichting Greenpeace Council (Greenpeace International) and others v Commission* (2 April 1998).

[47] Shirley Williams, 'Sovereignty and Accountability in the European Community' (1990) 61 *Political Quarterly* 299.

[48] Joseph Weiler, 'The European Union Belongs to its Citizens: Three Immodest Proposals' (1997) 22 ELRev 150.

extension of traditional consultation procedures. An 'Open Forum' would permit interested net-users to participate and to discuss EU policies amongst themselves and (implicitly) with the institutions. Weiler also suggests a European 'legislative ballot', to allow direct voting on certain citizen inspired legislative initiatives, at first at election time, later more generally. The novelty of this proposal is that it permits *direct* citizen input into rule-making, an option not always available at national level, especially in the case of legislation. Could this novel form of networking be the shape of direct democracy after the Millennium?

New Labour, enthusiastic for new technology, might show interest in this New Age proposal for a deepening of citizen interest and input into Europe. The Commission is already trying to take it further. But such a radical reform needs time for reflection. Moreover, in its more expansive forms, it may prove not to be technically feasible. In the meantime, two intermediate suggestions would help to alleviate the elitist nature of European rule-making processes.

Committees

The Comitology consists of a network of consultative and managerial committees established by the Council allegedly with a view to retaining control over delegated Commission powers of rule-making widely used to implement the Single Market and to deal with technical regulation.[49] Staffed largely by national civil servants, the committees are usually seen as impervious to public opinion and largely representative of national and Commission viewpoints; in other words, they are normally treated as a bureaucratic obstacle to democracy, badly in need of control. Some social action groups (eg environmentalists or consumer groups) have already been successful in inserting their own technical experts on to committees as members of national delegations. Groups also work their way into the Comitology by providing information and services which the Commission finds useful. With a little imagination, committees could become a channel for democratic participation in policy-making; just as EP inter-groups may form part of a policy network, so could the Comitology. The way forward is to take a close look at the composition of committees – an arduous task, since this information is not easily accessible. Not only should specific provision be made for representation through interest and pressure groups and perhaps MEPs but also (as is always done with Royal Commissions) for lay representation. By widening the numbers of people entitled to participate in rule-making, the basis of a European political process would begin to be laid as participants became more knowledgeable about and interested in European policy-making.

---

[49] See Ellen Vos, 'The Rise of Committees' (1997) 3 *European Law Journal* 210.

Negotiated rule-making

A second form of participation is borrowed from the Social Charter. Under EC, Article 118A, inserted at Amsterdam, management and labour must be consulted by the Commission on social policy. Moreover, agreements between the social partners can be implemented and brought into force either by the Council or at national level (Article 118B). This is a real if limited start to a form of participatory democracy which gives workers a voice in social policy-making. The procedure is a stronger variant of that envisaged by the American Negotiated Rulemaking Act,[50] designed to involve interested parties in the initial stages of rule-making prior to formalisation. Once an act is designated for negotiation, a 'convenor' is appointed to move to a negotiated outcome which is then referred back to the agency for consideration. Less open and less radical than Weiler's proposals, these compromises provide more realistic 'opportunity structures for citizen participation'.

NATIONAL PARLIAMENTS

Finding a role for national parliaments inside the European structure has not been, and is not likely to be, an easy task. Predictably, the British House of Commons maintains that national parliaments, 'with their diverse characters matched to their national cultures . . . are closer to the citizen, and are uniquely qualified to provide an element of responsiveness and democratic control that the Union needs'.[51] This is a position for which the UK would find allies in other member states with strong parliamentary traditions, notably Scandinavia and the Netherlands.

The leading academic commentator, Philip Norton, is ultimately pessimistic about an increased role in the law-making process for national parliaments, whether individually or through extension of existing procedures for inter-parliamentary co-operation.[52] It must be borne in mind, however, that, since the warning light of Maastricht, major reforms have been put in place in several national parliaments. Moreover, Norton wrote before the ToA which, responding to national concerns, contains a new Protocol on the role of national parliaments. Fears over erosion of national parliamentary democracy had been voiced at the IGC, though without much effect. A somewhat

---

[50] Pub Law No 101–648 (1990), No 104–320 (1996) 110 Stat 3870.
[51] HC [1994–95] 239-I, *The 1996 Inter-Governmental Conference: The Agenda; Democracy and Efficiency; The Role of National Parliaments*, para 107. See also HC [1995–96] 51, *The Role of the National Parliaments in the European Union*.
[52] P Norton, 'Introduction: Adapting to European Integration' (1995) 1 *Journal of Legislative Studies* 1. For the existing arrangements, see European Parliament, *The European Parliament and the Parliaments of the Member States, Parliamentary Scrutiny and Arrangements for Cooperation* (1994).

bland Protocol on the Role of National Parliaments in the European Union resulted. This aims to encourage 'greater involvement of national parliaments in the activities of the European Union and to enhance their ability to express their views on matters which may be of particular interest to them'. It strengthens their right to information, with the aim of providing a realistic chance of participation in decision-making. The COSAC, or Conference of the Committees of National Parliaments on European Affairs, is formally acknowledged for the first time. It receives powers to scrutinise legislative proposals and to address the EU institutions, with a particular mandate with respect to subsidiarity, human rights and the new area of 'freedom, security and justice'.

New Labour's initiatives to bring the UK Parliament closer to the people show little appreciation of the need to fill the European democracy deficit. Reform of the House of Lords, for which no blueprint is so far available, could even exacerbate the problem. The excellent reports of the Lords Select Committee on the European Communities are regarded with respect in Europe. The superior expertise of the House in European matters could easily be lost through reform without any corresponding gain in democracy.

Experience shows that the key to successful national parliament input lies in information. Those parliaments which have succeeded in establishing their right to see policy documents and legislative proposals at an early stage have been able to influence policy; late notification or post hoc scrutiny means no influence. The new Protocol provides for the prompt forwarding of information of all Commission consultation documents and proposals for legislation 'in good time'. Along with comment from the COSAC, comment from national parliaments is encouraged. This could be a big step forward. On the other hand, there is an obvious danger of building a further impotent consultative procedure into the over-complex EC law-making process.

In the UK, the procedures introduced by the Conservative government after consideration by the House of Commons Select Committee on Procedure[53] are beginning to shake down. There seems to be general agreement that they afford opportunities for stronger scrutiny of EC legislation than before, generating more interest in the Committees' work, thus lending them a more authoritative profile. But much remains to be done. The limited ambitions of the House of Commons, whose Select Committee on European Legislation concentrates on *scrutiny*, is astounding.[54] The Amsterdam Protocol should act as an incentive, if only by alleviating problems of access to EU documentation. A government with a strong majority has nothing to lose and everything to gain from parliamentary support and understanding of its European policies.

---

[53] HC [1989–90] 622-I, *European Community Legislation*, 4th Report of the Select Committee on Procedure. For the government response, see Cm 1081 (1990).
[54] David Judge, 'The Failure of National Parliaments?' (1995) 18 *West European Politics* 79, 85.

CONCLUSION

Unusually, New Labour came to power with a programme of constitutional reform, some inchoate, much quite carefully considered. Careful policy-making is often the fruit of intelligent opposition. Care had been taken with consensus-building, as the campaign for Scottish Devolution demonstrated. If no similar programme was in place for European affairs, this was largely due to the posturings of the 'Tory Rebels', which made goodwill seem the only requirement.

Like much else in the EU, representative democracy is attempting to straddle two incompatible strategies: integrationism and pluralism. The inevitable dilution of democratic institutions at national level has not been replaced by the democratisation of EU institutions designed for the limited purpose of a single market. The ensuing democratic deficit operates to the benefit of national executives, enabling them to escape control by representative assemblies, and of international business, accountable nowhere.

So is there a case for a written EU constitution? If we adopt the integrationist path, the answer is undoubtedly yes. The absence of any list of powers comparable to that found in modern federal constitutions makes the European enterprise frightening. We might on the other hand decide that democracy is possible only at national and sub-national levels, implying a real place in European policy-making for national institutions, more especially parliaments. It is time for Europeans to make up their minds.

It is time too for the British people to contribute to a debate from which they have so far been rigorously excluded. As Duff sees it,[55] 'chief players in the current and weighty system of the intergovernmental Conference are precisely those ministers, parliaments, parties and officials of the old, nation state Europe who, more or less wittingly, are obliged to concede powers that their predecessors once took for granted would be held inalienably'. But Duff's strictures could so easily be reversed to read: 'Chief players in the current and weighty system of the intergovernmental Conference are the very officials and elites of the new, corporatist Europe who are wittingly trying to take over powers that our predecessors once took for granted would be held inalienably'. Their powers are our democratic rights. Do we want them to be ceded?

Further reading

S Andersen and K Eliassen (eds), *The European Union: How Democratic Is It?* (London: Sage, 1996)

Paul Craig and Carol Harlow (eds), *The European Lawmaking Process* (The Hague: Kluwer, 1998)

[55] A Duff (ed), *The Treaty of Amsterdam: Text and Commentary* (London: Federal Trust, 1997) p xxxviii.

CHAPTER 12

SCOTTISH AND WELSH DEVOLUTION

Graham Leicester (Scottish Council Foundation)

Devolution to Scotland and Wales has led the way in the government's comprehensive programme of constitutional change. The Referendums (Scotland and Wales) Bill was the first constitutional measure introduced after the 1997 election, the referendums themselves the first practical expression of the government's commitment to change, and the elections to take place under a form of proportional representation in May 1999 will establish a Parliament and an Assembly which will change the face of the UK political system for good.

Both institutions will have been a very long time in the gestation and represent the triumph of a variety of political forces at work over many years, culminating in Labour's firm commitment to legislate for their establishment in the first year following the election. The size of Labour's parliamentary majority, and the collapse of the Conservative opposition in both Scotland and Wales, may lead us to underestimate how remarkable an achievement this will be. It may also obscure the fact that there are still tensions and inconsistencies in the devolution project which have not been overcome simply by force of numbers in the House of Commons. The following pages look back over the recent history of devolution – how the government came to develop the policy it has now passed into law – and offer some observations on the coherence, the durability and the possible longer-term consequences of the results.

HISTORY

The first serious attempt to legislate for devolution for both Scotland and Wales was made by a Labour government in a joint Scotland and Wales Bill in 1976. Even though the government were eventually forced to introduce two separate – and modified – Bills, the link between devolution to Scotland and to Wales has remained. It is present even now in the parallel progress the government has followed in implementing its commitment to legislate for devolution for both.

The recent parallel history hides very different pasts and very different motivations for devolution in the two countries. Scotland was a sovereign state until the Acts of Union of 1707 abolished the Scottish and English Parliaments and established in their place a Parliament of Great Britain. This was an 'incorporating union'. But the Acts nonetheless allowed Scotland to retain many of its distinctive features: the position of the Scottish established church, the continuing autonomy of Scots law and the legal system, organisation of local government (the Royal Burghs), and distinctive education system were all maintained.

Lindsay Paterson has argued the case for seeing the maintenance and development of such distinctive institutions over the years since 1707 as having secured for Scotland a considerable degree of 'autonomy' within the Union: 'not a fully independent state, of course, but far more than a mere province'.[1] He describes a managerial and technocratic response to perceived deficiencies in the treatment of Scottish public affairs by the Westminster government. He notes the establishment of the Scottish Office and a Scottish Secretary in the UK government in 1885 as typical of this approach: 'Repeatedly . . . nationalism was about the inadequate treatment of Scottish business by the state, not about imposed policies, far less about oppression. A nationalism of this sort is satisfied if it gets the instruments which it thinks it needs'.[2]

Many in the present Labour government would subscribe to that statement. They see the present move to devolution in practical terms as a way of reducing overload at the centre and often defend it in those terms. But whatever the motivation, the effect of this approach over the years in Scotland has been to feed a growing sense of political autonomy and distinctiveness. The building of the welfare state in the first half of this century increased the importance of the Scottish Office and made it the primary focus of government in Scotland even when technically responsibility lay with London departments.

Thus administrative devolution came to take on the impression of something far more substantial, so much so that James Kellas was able to identify the result by 1973 as a distinct 'Scottish political system'.[3] That sense of substantial political autonomy was bolstered, and still is, by a strong sense of nationhood. Tom Nairn disputes on those grounds Paterson's claim that effective treatment of Scottish business by the state is all that has been at stake in Scotland over the years. That, he says, is to take insufficient account of 'the illustrious cadaver of the seven-century-old Kingdom. In 1707 it was decreed undead, not dispatched to genuine oblivion. Embalmed by Union, it

[1] Lindsay Paterson, *The Autonomy of Modern Scotland* (Edinburgh: Edinburgh University Press, 1994).
[2] Ibid.
[3] James Kellas, *The Scottish Political System* (Cambridge: Cambridge University Press, 1973).

has not ceased to exert the most profound influence on each new generation'.[4] This is the tightrope that the government must tread in Scotland:
between Paterson's managerial decentralisation and Nairn's strong sense
of nationhood.

The history in Wales is much less complicated. England and Wales have
been a single unit for some 500 years. Gladstone was able to say that 'the
distinction between England and Wales . . . is totally unknown to our constitution'.[5] The pressure for devolution has been practical and managerial, as it
was in Scotland, but the sense of national identity has been less developed.
Hence claims have remained at the technical level. The Liberals' proposals
for home rule in the late 19th century were for a new top tier of local government rather than a law-making Parliament. That mood is still evident
today. Even when Plaid Cymru was created in 1925 as the political voice of
Welsh nationalism it concentrated more on preserving the Welsh sense of
identity – in particular the Welsh language – than on giving it recognition in
autonomous political structures.

Hence it was the rising electoral threat of Scottish Nationalism which
forced the government's hand in the late 1960s, even though by then Plaid
Cymru had won its first seat at Westminster. Wilson's Labour government
set up a Royal Commission on the Constitution in 1968 with a remit to
examine 'the present functions of the central legislature and government in
relation to the several countries and regions of the UK'. The Commission
failed to reach a consensus and came up with six alternative schemes for
devolution plus a minority Memorandum of Dissent.

That might have successfully buried the issue in practical politics, but by
the time the Commission reported in October 1973 the discovery of North
Sea oil and a sharp rise in oil prices had rekindled the SNP's appeal. They
gained six seats in the election in February 1974. Wilson hastily signed the
party up to legislative devolution for Scotland before going to the country
again in October. His sop to Wales was less impressive: executive devolution
with no powers to make primary legislation.

A weak government, soon in a minority, with no real commitment to
devolution struggled for the following four years to get devolution legislation on the statute book. The discrepancy between Scotland and Wales
caused confusion, especially when the two schemes were in the same Bill.
But Wales had to hang on to Scotland's coat-tails to have any chance of
gaining legislative time. In the event both Acts failed to win sufficient
support in post-legislative referendums forced on the government to secure
their passage.

The Wales Act was rejected by a majority of four to one. The Scotland Act
won a majority of the votes, but the low turnout denied the Scots victory on

---

[4] Tom Nairn, 'Upper and Lower Cases' (a review of Paterson's book), *London Review of Books*
(24 August 1995).
[5] Vernon Bogdanor, *Devolution* (Oxford: Oxford University Press, 1979).

a technicality.[6] The government fell as a result, ushering in a Conservative administration under Mrs Thatcher, who had opposed the government's plans from the start. Her administration fell back on the old practice of managerial rather than substantive change as a way to respond to political pressures in Scotland. The Scottish Grand Committee, for example, was shorn of all English MPs and given leave to meet in Edinburgh. Throughout their long period in office – and particularly once Michael Forsyth returned to the Scottish Office in 1995 – the government continued to invent more and more ingenious embellishments to the committee system, including latterly the Welsh Grand Committee. But this proved insufficient to close off pressure for more radical measures.

THE SCOTTISH CONSTITUTIONAL CONVENTION

A focus for such feelings emerged in Scotland in 1987, following a third successive general election in which Scotland had voted solidly for Labour – and against the poll tax – only to see a Conservative majority returned to Westminster. A small group was established to consider how Scotland could make progress on home rule in the face of a government adamantly opposed. In July 1988 it published 'A Claim of Right for Scotland'.[7] This was a well-argued plea for the people of Scotland to exercise sovereignty on their own behalf: to convene a constitutional convention to draw up a scheme for devolution and then to press for its adoption by the Westminster Parliament. The group elevated popular sovereignty over parliamentary sovereignty: one of the reasons why Tony Blair's vigorous assertion of the supremacy of the latter struck such a false note in Scotland during the 1997 general election campaign.

By contrast the demand for devolution in Wales remained subdued following the referendum defeat. Instead Wales began to carve out a more promising role for itself as a European region, linking with others to pursue co-operative projects and inward investment. This was a concept around which all Wales could rally. Government from London by a Conservative Party enjoying only minority support in Wales did not lead, as in Scotland, to passionate pleas for the right to self-government, but to a heightened concern with the growth of government by quango and Tory placepeople.

In Scotland a Constitutional Convention was established in March 1989. All the political parties in Scotland were invited to participate. The Conservative Party declined. The Scottish National Party attended the first meeting but then withdrew, afraid that Labour would operate an effective

---

[6] A backbench Labour MP had won an amendment to the Bill specifying that a majority vote in favour in the referendum had to comprise at least 40 per cent of the Scottish electorate for the Act to come into force. In the event the majority constituted only 32.8 per cent.

[7] Owen Dudley Edwards (ed), *A Claim of Right for Scotland* (Edinburgh: Polygon, 1989).

veto over all decisions in spite of the commitment to consensus. The Liberal Democrats were enthusiastic supporters. The Scottish Labour Party questioned for some time whether to become involved in a process it could not control, but eventually Donald Dewar, then shadow Scottish Secretary, took the momentous decision to participate.

The Convention rapidly developed a scheme for devolution to Scotland of all the then functions of the Scottish Office. This was little different from the scheme that had fallen in 1978. But there were two significant changes: a commitment to a form of proportional representation for the voting system, and a much more sophisticated system for financing the Parliament including limited devolved powers to alter the basic rate of income tax in Scotland by up to three pence in the pound. The first change was a critical demand from the Liberals and addressed the fear in the 1970s scheme that it would lead to domination of the Parliament by the Edinburgh–Glasgow central belt. The second change addressed the criticism that even the smallest parish council has some powers to raise its own revenue and the fact that there should be a link between the power to spend public resources and the responsibility to raise them.

This scheme was published on St Andrew's day 1990.[8] In the election of 1992 the partners in the Constitutional Convention campaigned for its implementation. The Labour leader Neil Kinnock had by then added a commitment to legislate for the scheme in the first year of a Labour government. This was an apparently spontaneous promise given in a television interview and was designed to bury any doubts about his commitment to devolution given his opposition in the past.

Labour did not win the election, and Neil Kinnock left the stage. John Smith, a long-standing supporter of devolution and the minister responsible for steering the ill-fated 1978 Act through Parliament, succeeded him as leader in the summer of 1992 – giving a much-needed boost to the home rule camp. The Convention regrouped and continued its work fleshing out the detail of its scheme, including choosing the additional member electoral system with 73 First Past the Post seats and 56 additional members taken from lists for the eight European Parliament constituencies.

In December 25,000 people demonstrated in Edinburgh in the margins of a European Council meeting largely devoted to shoring up the principle of subsidiarity – that decisions should be taken as close as possible to the people they affect – in an effort to save the Maastricht Treaty. At the same time the government were steadfastly resisting claims for greater autonomy within the UK. The irony was not lost on observers: the government's support for the principle of subsidiarity seemed to stop at the English channel.

Labour's commitment to devolution thus became a useful weapon in an increasingly bitter debate with the Conservatives, and within the Conservative Party itself, over the UK's relationship with Europe. What had tended to

---

[8] Scottish Constitutional Convention, *Towards Scotland's Parliament* (Edinburgh, 1990).

be seen up to then as a necessary political response to pressures in Scotland and Wales became a key element in a wider understanding linking the domestic and European agendas for institutional reform. The potency of that link was emphasised as the Conservative government fell apart over Europe: sterling's exit from the Exchange Rate Mechanism, the battle to ratify the Maastricht Treaty, the looming inevitability of Economic and Monetary Union. It was not difficult to appear more coherent on the subject of the European Union than the government at that time, but support for devolution and a more credible approach to subsidiarity certainly helped John Smith's Labour opposition to do so. The government's disarray also helped to convince Scotland once again that devolution required only the patience to wait for the next general election.

Labour entered that election with the same commitment to legislate for devolution in Scotland and Wales in the first year of government as in 1992. But there were three significant changes. First, devolution was by then only one element in a significant programme of constitutional reform – including the gradual establishment of regional assemblies in England – detailed elsewhere in this book. It was a programme which had explicit Liberal support, and on which the two parties had openly collaborated in the months leading up to the general election.

Secondly, there had been significant changes in the substance, reflecting the influence of Tony Blair's ascent to the leadership in 1994. In Scotland the powers of the Parliament were refined to meet the concerns of business that there should be a level economic playing field. Powers to 'initiate some form of public ownership', for example, which had found a place in the Convention's 1990 scheme, were omitted – along with much else in the economic and industrial sphere. The system for financing the devolved services was amended too, removing the element of assigned taxation (ie retaining a proportion of taxes paid by Scots in Scotland) in favour of adapting the existing method for funding the Scottish Office via a block grant from Westminster. A revised scheme reflecting such changes was adopted on St Andrew's day 1995.[9]

The most dramatic change was yet to come: a commitment to hold referendums in Scotland and Wales in advance of introducing legislation. In Scotland the referendum would include a separate question on whether the power to vary the basic rate of income tax, which had survived the Blair review and was an integral part of the Convention's scheme, should be implemented in practice. The decision to hold referendums was announced without warning in June 1996. It stunned Scotland in particular – angered by the thought that devolution might again be denied in spite of an election victory. The second question on tax was seen by many as a device to tame the Parliament before it was even established. It may well have been conceived as such – we may never know. Its more immediate effect was to plug the last gap in Labour's election platform as a party that would not raise taxes.

[9] Scottish Constitutional Convention, *Scotland's Parliament. Scotland's Right* (Edinburgh, 1995).

In Wales, the substance of the scheme of executive devolution put to the Welsh people in the 1997 election was little changed from that of 1992, or even of the 1970s. There had been no equivalent of the Constitutional Convention. The Campaign for a Welsh Assembly, dormant since 1979, was relaunched in November 1988 with support from Labour, Liberal Democrat and Plaid Cymru representatives. But the Welsh Labour Party resisted its calls for a cross-party convention and instead established its own policy commission. That commission published proposals in 1995, supplemented in 1996 and approved by the Welsh Labour Party conference, for an Assembly without primary legislative powers, without tax powers and elected under First Past the Post.[10]

Blair forced the Welsh Labour Party to look again at the electoral system for the Assembly at the same time as the decision to hold a referendum. In spite of some anxiety among Labour MPs about the consequences of a more proportional voting system, a special party conference in February 1997 agreed to fall into line with an additional member system as proposed in Scotland (40 First Past the Post members and 20 additional members). That was the least that could be done to try to bring the Welsh scheme into line with the rest of the constitutional reform programme. That no other part of the substance of the scheme was changed probably reflected a feeling in London that the Welsh Labour Party were in a better position to judge what the Welsh voters would support, rather than the constitutional theorists; and that in any event there was a strong possibility that the Welsh referendum, like the second vote in Scotland, might be lost.

To sum up, Labour went into the 1997 election with an ambitious programme of constitutional reform in prospect to be led by legislation on Scotland and Wales in its first year of office. But even at that stage there were three strong reasons to doubt Labour's genuine commitment to devolution: the late decision to hold pre-legislative referendums in both cases, the tight central control which had by then developed as Tony Blair's leadership style, and the suspicion that significant elements in the Shadow Cabinet would not shed too many tears if the Scottish Parliament were to lose its tax power and the Welsh referendum repeated the 1970s debacle and sent the party back to the drawing board.

POLICY INTO PRACTICE

There was no room for equivocation after the landslide victory on 1 May 1997, especially with the complete removal of all Conservative parliamentary opposition in Scotland and Wales. The Scottish and Welsh Offices rapidly got down to the business of implementing the government's manifesto. A

[10] Wales Labour Party, *Shaping the Vision* (May 1995) and *Preparing for a New Wales* (May 1996).

Referendums (Scotland and Wales) Act was rapidly passed committing the government to a referendum in Scotland on 11 September and in Wales a week later. Under intense time pressure to publish detailed proposals as the basis for those votes before the summer parliamentary recess, ministers and officials under the guidance of a Cabinet Committee chaired by the Lord Chancellor worked 'night and day' (in Donald Dewar's words) to formalise Labour's plans in government.

Two White Papers – *A Voice for Wales* and *Scotland's Parliament* – were published within days of each other in late July.[11] Confounding the doubters, these proposals were confirmed in the referendums which followed. In Scotland on a turnout of 60.2 per cent both questions were carried: 74.3 per cent in favour of the Parliament and 63.5 per cent in favour of the tax varying power. Support on both questions was almost unanimous: only two local authority areas returned small majorities against the tax power (Orkney and Dumfries and Galloway). This surprised even the most enthusiastic supporters who had worried up to the last minute about a poor turnout: it was a powerful demonstration of what the late John Smith had called the 'settled will' of the Scottish people. Tony Blair flew to Scotland to share in the victory.

In Wales a week later it was a very different story: only 50.3 per cent voted yes on a turnout of 50.1 per cent, representing a majority of less than 7,000 votes. Only with the last declaration of the night – Carmarthenshire with a 56.4 per cent turnout – was the result secured. Only one in four of the eligible electorate voted for an Assembly. Cardiff voted no.

It is not unreasonable to see these contrasting results as a consequence of the very different processes of policy development already described. The policy in Wales had been developed very much within the confines of the Welsh Labour Party with little effort to involve a wider constituency, a flaw compounded at the last by direct intervention from London on the crucial issue of the voting system and the decision to hold a referendum. Hence the White Paper when it appeared was more an act of advocacy for the principle of an assembly than a detailed constitutional blueprint. It laid great stress on the economic benefits of devolution, playing to the popular perception of Wales as a successful European region. It also clearly showed the guiding hand of London behind proposals for Welsh government, outlining reforms in other institutions (eg the Welsh Development Agency) to be made in advance of devolution and even specifying some of the policy priorities a Welsh Assembly would be expected to pursue (eg in relation to quangos).

That same equivocal, uncertain tone is reflected in the legislation to establish the Assembly. It is heavily prescriptive in insisting on checks and balances within the new Welsh political system: a statutory commitment for the Assembly to draw up a 'scheme' to 'sustain and promote local government in Wales', for example, a 'Partnership Council for Wales' consisting of

[11] *A Voice for Wales*, Cm 3718 (HMSO: July 1997); *Scotland's Parliament*, Cm 3658 (HMSO: July 1997).

Assembly members and local councillors, and Assembly committees for North Wales and for 'each of the other regions of Wales'. Largely as a result of this more prescriptive approach the legislation is longer and more detailed than its Scottish equivalent, in spite of the fact that it contains no provision for primary legislative powers and no tax power.

The Assembly will have no law-making powers, but will take over executive responsibilities currently exercised by the Secretary of State for Wales. The Assembly will operate in these areas within a legislative framework set by Westminster and will be able to make rules and regulations accordingly by secondary legislation. In practice therefore, the scope for Welsh autonomy in the administration of policy will depend on how sensitively and flexibly legislation is framed at Westminster.

Clearly that places a great and continuing burden on the Secretary of State for Wales to ensure that Welsh concerns are taken into account in making policy in Whitehall and Westminster. The Secretary of State is also given a prominent role as almost a 'virtual member' of the Assembly itself: able to attend Assembly meetings and participate in them, and with a right to receive all documents at the same time as they are made available to other members of the Assembly. There is even speculation that the Secretary of State and the head of the Welsh Executive might be one and the same person, at least in the early years – a constitutional nonsense that has been explicitly ruled out in Scotland.

One simply has to apply the reversibility test to the plans for the Assembly – would this work with governments of different political persuasion in Cardiff and London? – to see why the Constitution Unit has concluded that the legislation 'does not represent a properly thought out logical position, nor a particularly practical set of proposals. . . . Executive devolution is unlikely to be stable or long lasting'.[12] It is unfortunate, given that conclusion, that the legislation has no built-in flexibility for adjustment in future. The powers of the Scottish Parliament may be varied – to or from Westminster – by order subject to the approval of both Parliaments. Any such adjustment in Wales will require primary legislation.

Scotland's Parliament by contrast is a confident document, steady in tone, rational, conscious of speaking to a wide constituency of support. It is clearly a constitutional document and as such succeeded in silencing most potential critics of the detail of the settlement. The strong endorsement in the referendum also lends the resulting legislation a sense of permanence. The debate in Scotland rapidly moved on to the issue of who might be selected to stand for the Parliament and how competent they might be in using the powers at its disposal: it is taken as read that the scheme as agreed is a workable one.

The source of this confidence may well lie in the clarity of the legislation. In particular the government have learned the lessons of the 1970s and chosen to detail the powers reserved to Westminster rather than those

---

[12] Constitution Unit, *Commentary on the Welsh White Paper* (London, September 1997).

devolved to Edinburgh. Thus outside such areas as defence, foreign affairs, the constitution, fiscal, economic and monetary policy the Scottish Parliament will be free to exercise legislative autonomy, and to amend or repeal existing UK legislation as it sees fit. All Bills will be scrutinised by the Scottish Executive and the Presiding Officer (Speaker) of the Parliament to see that they fall within the Parliament's competence before they are introduced. There is also provision for the UK or Scots Law Officers to refer any question of vires or legislative competence to the Judicial Committee of the Privy Council for final adjudication in cases of doubt, after a Bill is passed but before it receives royal assent (a period of at least four weeks).

The tax power is also clarified in the legislation. It is made clear that the power to vary the rate of income tax applies only to income and not to dividends or savings, and that it is strictly limited in its effect to the equivalent of three pence on the basic rate. That would yield – or forego – about £450 million, 3 per cent of the Scottish Office's present budget. The figure of £450 million is preserved in the legislation as the upper limit of the Scottish Parliament's potential annual yield, regularly updated for inflation. If the UK Treasury were to alter the tax structure so that the Scottish tax power operated on a different range of incomes or taxpayers which made the £450 million no longer attainable, the onus in the legislation is on the Treasury to amend Scotland's powers accordingly. But the 'effect on the levels of after-tax income of Scottish tax payers' cannot by that means be made significantly different from the effect of the tax power as originally designed.

Having established these clear outlines, the legislation is remarkably permissive in allowing the Parliament freedom to develop and to regulate its operations as it sees fit. There is none of the heavy-handed exhortation of the Welsh scheme when it comes to local government of the regions. The bare bones of the Parliament's procedures are specified – stages for legislation, procedures for electing the First Minister – but in general such detail is left to the Parliament itself to determine. This is in keeping with the admirable constitutional principle stressed from the outset by Scottish Secretary Donald Dewar: 'Throughout the White Paper our guiding principle is to trust the Scottish people to make the right decisions on their own behalf'.[13]

It is in the area where this principle provides insufficient guidance that tensions in implementing the devolution legislation may arise in practice: managing the relationship between London and Edinburgh. This is precisely the area that the Scottish Constitutional Convention left untouched as outside their remit, and hence the area in which there remains a good deal of uncertainty and trepidation. There is very little detail in the legislation, for example, about the management of relations between the Scottish and British governments. This reflects the tone of the White Paper which suggested

---

[13] The Scottish Office, *Donald Dewar Delivers the Government's Promise for Scotland's Parliament*, news release (24 July 1997).

that problems between the two would 'usually be resolved quickly and amicably' and that arrangements for co-operation would be 'updated regularly to reflect the evolution of administrative conventions of cooperation and joint working'. There is nothing in the legislation to constrain that evolution in the future.

The Act, for example, simply prohibits the Scottish Parliament and executive from acting in contravention of EC law and gives the Secretary of State the right of veto if he fears that has happened or is in prospect. There is no attempt to reflect in legislation the White Paper's promise to involve the Scottish executive 'as directly and fully as possible in the Government's decision making on EU matters'. That commitment is a political rather than a legal one, and could not in practice be otherwise.

Other omissions give more cause for concern. The provisions on the calculation of the Parliament's grant are brief in the extreme, simply stating (as the 1978 Act did) that the Secretary of State shall from time to time make payments into a Scottish Consolidated Fund of such amounts as he may determine. This makes no reference to the existence of the Barnett formula by which the present Scottish budget is determined with respect to changes in English equivalent spending, even though the government is committed to preserving the system after devolution. It would be more reassuring, and more conducive to a stable long-term settlement, at least to have included a reference to the existence of an allocation formula based on the principles of equalisation according to need and relative population shares.

This is potentially a serious flaw. The Barnett formula was introduced in the wake of the 1970s devolution legislation, and specifically a Treasury needs assessment study[14] which showed that only 16 per cent of the 22 per cent discrepancy between Scottish and English per capita spending on the devolved services could be justified by Scotland's relatively greater need (dispersed population, poorer health etc). There is still a discrepancy in per capita spending of around 30 per cent on the services to be devolved this time around, but nobody can say for sure how much of this is now justified.

Sooner or later it seems inevitable that a new needs assessment will be commissioned – possibly in the face of pressure from the English regions. It would have been better to have made provision for the conduct of such an assessment – by an independent body – in the legislation. As things stand the decision to change Scotland's budget may be made unilaterally by the UK government, at best following a needs assessment exercise conducted by the Treasury. The White Paper's promise of 'full consultation between the Scottish Executive and the UK Government' may not survive a change in the political climate. In this respect the legislation establishing the Scottish Parliament fails the reversibility test earlier applied to Wales, detracting from an otherwise admirable constitutional Act.

---

[14] HM Treasury, *Needs Assessment Study Report* (December 1979).

CONCLUSION

It is commonplace to suggest in relation to constitutional reform that 'the devil is in the detail'. Some of those officials who contributed to the 60,000 person hours that went into drafting the Scotland Bill may be tempted to agree. But in terms of making that legislation work the general political climate in which the new institutions are established will be more important than the blackletter detail of the Act.

Labour's landslide, and the temptation to think as a result in terms of ten years in office, may have encouraged the feeling that devolution is an exercise in political management rather than in constitution building. Thus it has been agreed to review the number of Scottish MPs at Westminster following devolution in order to meet concerns that they might have a significant say on issues in England on which their English counterparts have no locus to speak in Scotland. But no commitment to review the number of Welsh MPs has been made, presumably on the grounds that their smaller numbers make this less of a political problem. A comparison of the schemes for Scotland and Wales is riddled with such inconsistencies.

Regarding devolution as practical political management is by no means a mistake – and may yet prove of some use in the context of Northern Ireland. Besides, a spirit of co-operation, of give and take, is undoubtedly going to be needed to make the devolution settlement work. But managing the politics offers only a partial view and underestimates the importance of the founding statutes in influencing the political context in which the new institutions will have to operate. It would have been better, for example, to include more incentives to practical co-operation and the free exchange of information in the legislation itself as guard against less propitious political circumstances in the future. In Wales the problem is compounded by the fact that even the legislation bears the hallmarks of political management and fails to establish anything like the clarity of purpose that the Scottish Parliament will enjoy.

In the end it will be the role of the centre that determines the success or otherwise of the project: central government and the political parties. Enoch Powell is renowned for his remark that power devolved is power retained. So it is, in the sense that Westminster may rescind its delegated authority at any time. But it is also power devolved. In Scotland in particular the government is establishing an autonomous source of democratic legitimacy, alternative government and potentially innovative policy.

If the Scottish experiment is successful, central government will itself be forced to adopt a more subtle, open and confident approach. No longer will it be possible to defend a policy simply with the claim that 'there is no alternative'. There might be – elsewhere in the Kingdom. No longer will it be sufficient to go to Brussels to 'defend the national interest'. That interest will increasingly be an amalgam of many different regional interests and possibly different political priorities.

It is important that the centre recognises these consequences of devolution and generates a sense of excitement about the possibilities they suggest for a more strategic approach. With its focus on reserved powers, the Scotland Act is as much about defining the role of central government as it is about the role of the devolved Parliament, perhaps more so. The success of the devolution project will depend on how readily that fact is accepted in the future: one suspects it was not openly acknowledged in the drafting.

Further reading

Labour government White Papers, *Scotland's Parliament* (London: HMSO, Cm 3658, 1997); *A Voice for Wales: The Government's Proposals for a Welsh Assembly* (London: HMSO, Cm 3718, 1997)

Constitution Unit, *Scotland's Parliament: Fundamentals for a New Scotland Act*; and *An Assembly for Wales* (London: 1996)

Lindsay Paterson, *The Autonomy of Modern Scotland* (Edinburgh: Edinburgh University Press, 1994)

Vernon Bogdanor, *Devolution* (Oxford University Press, 1979); *Power and the People* (London: Victor Gollancz, 1997) Ch 2

CHAPTER 13

ENGLISH REGIONAL GOVERNMENT

Paul McQuail and Katy Donnelly
(formerly of The Constitution Unit)

Liberate Catalonia!
(Written on a wall in Covent Garden, May 1997)

The most casual traveller through Europe is made aware of the pressure for separation, or at least a measure of independence, by certain regions from the central state. Signs on the wall make this evident: in the French-speaking Swiss Jura; in Savoie, a region attached to France as recently as 1860; in Galicia; not to mention the more widely known cases of Catalonia, the Basque country, Northern Italy and Wallonia. There are parallels between these, typically peripheral, regions and the cases of Scotland and Wales in the UK. But in England itself, evidence of this kind is sparse.[1] Why should this be?

History is part of the answer: there is no tradition of democratic regional government in England, perhaps because of the historic strength of local government. Even regional administration by central government has no great tradition. First tried by Cromwell, with the appointment of 11 Major Generals for divisions of England – highly unpopular in its day partly on the ground that it would lead to the break-up of the state – there was no further attempt until the First World War; but regional administration by central government has been found useful in some form since then.

The case for a democratic voice at regional level is of course not met by the representation of central government in the regions. There are three basic steps in the argument supporting democratic regional structures:

(1) that the UK is the most centralised state in Western Europe, and probably in the developed world;
(2) that this is damaging in terms both of democracy and efficiency;
(3) that there are functions that ought to be exercised and controlled at regional and not at local or central level.

---

[1] Cornwall perhaps being an exception.

264

The first point is undeniable (leaving aside the Republic of Ireland and Luxembourg), the second and third deserve further examination, together with consideration of possible remedies.

PRESSURE FOR CHANGE

The classic statement of the case for change in the arrangements for government in the English regions is still to be found in the Memorandum of Dissent to the Kilbrandon Commission, written by Lord Crowther-Hunt and Alan Peacock in 1973:

(1) local government is too closely controlled by the officials of central government;
(2) over-centralisation produces too much uniformity, whereas the needs of the different parts of the UK are obviously very varied;
(3) in the allocation of resources the special needs and wishes of the different parts of the UK are not properly appreciated;
(4) central government has now become so big and its attempts at administrative control so detailed that there is frequently a lack of co-ordination between the thousands of departmental officials;
(5) the centre is seriously overloaded. Ministers are overloaded and have little time for long-term or even short-term policy thinking.

By way of remedy, Peacock and Crowther-Hunt, against the background of a majority report recommending devolution for Scotland and Wales, produced a scheme for a degree of devolution to five English regions. Any scheme of devolution for England was pursued half-heartedly by the Old Labour government and ran into the sand with the collapse of that government in 1979.

Given the strength of the Peacock/Crowther-Hunt critique it is almost surprising to find it said in 1995 by the Commission on Local Democracy that 'Since the IMF crisis of 1976 a fundamental change has taken place in the power balance between local government and the centre in Britain'; and by the Audit Commission that 'in recent years the balance has been shifting towards national control of services as well as of expenditure'. How much further could there have been to go?

That further increase in centralisation was real enough – and became one of the main driving forces in the pressure for devolution or at least decentralisation in England during the 1980s and 1990s: the 1992 Labour Party manifesto had a proposal for a regional tier of government in England. Other pressures for change were:

(1) resentment in some regions, most strongly in the north, as the years of Conservative government went on, that there were substantial parts of

England, wider than counties, where the majority of the people were in permanent opposition to Westminster and Whitehall;

(2) the long-running debate about devolution for Scotland and Wales, with an increasing belief that something would come of it, and a fear that English regions would suffer (even more) in the resulting divvy-up of resources;

(3) European influences: not just the fact that even France, long famous as having the crown of the most centralised state in Europe, introduced directly elected regional government in the early 1980s; but pressure from the European Commission, using its financial muscle, to encourage – in the name of subsidiarity – the development of direct regional links by-passing central government.

LABOUR PARTY PROPOSALS

Renewed interest in the range of constitutional issues, inside and outside the Labour Party, in 1994, caused the party to produce substantive proposals, steered by Jack Straw as Shadow Home Secretary, for regional government in England. The proposals put forward in their consultative paper *A Choice for England* in 1995 were refined, but emerged substantially unchanged as a statement of policy in October 1996 as *A New Voice for England's Regions*. This was reflected in the 1997 manifesto as a commitment to 'build on these developments through the establishment of regional chambers to co-ordinate transport, planning, economic development, bids for European funding and land use planning'.

The underlying points of Labour's case for change echo those of Crowther-Hunt and Peacock. They focus most sharply on the further growth in the influence of unelected quangos (a term barely invented in 1973) and on the establishment of the integrated regional offices, set up by the Conservative government after the 1992 election as their sole nod in the direction of region-alism. These, with the other government-funded bodies, were identified as a layer of regional government which already existed, but without acknowledge-ment and without accountability.

To meet these criticisms, summed up in the idea of a 'democratic deficit' the Labour Party proposed a two-stage approach: first establishing indirectly elected Regional Chambers of local authority representatives in the regions which could move on where there is demand to directly elected Regional Assemblies. Arrangements would be made to represent business, community and trade union interests. Boundaries of the Chambers would be those of the Government Offices. Their functions would be strategic co-ordination of European funding bids; economic development; transport; and strategic land-use planning; and in addition democratic oversight of quangos and similar non-elected bodies. They would have no tax-raising powers. The

266

move to the Assembly stage would be by resolution of the Chamber, subject to the establishment of a predominantly unitary pattern of local government; parliamentary approval; and endorsement by a region-wide referendum. They too would have no power to raise taxes, and their functions would be wider, though not specified in detail.

OTHER PARTIES

As implied above, the Conservative position on regionalism in England has never been more than lukewarm. Having abolished the Economic Planning Councils established by the Labour government of 1964 as one of their first steps on taking office, the Conservatives' furthest advance – and that was largely a personal initiative of Michael Heseltine's – was the integration of the government offices in each region. They did, however, encourage the coming together of local authorities for certain defined purposes at the regional level, notably in the preparation of Regional Planning Guidance (RPG).

Decentralisation and subsidiarity have long been central themes of Liberal Democrat policy and a commitment to decentralisation is contained in the Preamble to the party's constitution: 'we aim to disperse power, to foster diversity and to nurture creativity . . . we stand for devolution of power to the nations and regions of the country within a federal framework'. This federalist approach was toned down in the run-up to the 1997 election as indicated in the report of the Labour/Liberal Democrat Joint Committee on Constitutional Reform in which both parties endorsed: 'a stage by stage approach which would first of all establish indirectly elected regional chambers based on the regional local authority associations which already exist. They would then allow directly elected regional assemblies to be established only where the proposal had been endorsed in a referendum in the region concerned.'

REGIONAL DEVELOPMENT AGENCIES

A separate strand of Labour Party policy derives from pressure in a number of regions for measures to reduce the very well-documented regional disparities in employment and life-chances. This has been reflected in the development of Regional Development Agencies (RDAs), a long-standing Labour commitment which appeared in the 1997 manifesto as in a number of previous ones. The proposal has its origins in the thinking which led to the creation in 1975 of the Scottish and Welsh Development Agencies as means by which regional imbalances could be reduced. Their immediate background lies in the Regional Policy Commission set up by the Labour

Party under the chairmanship of Bruce Millan, formerly the EU Regional Commissioner. The Commission's report, *Renewing the Regions*, July 1996, again recommended the establishment of RDAs. *A New Voice for England's Regions* mentions the relationship between the RDAs and the Regional Chambers in passing, noting that, 'By bringing together business, trade unions, professional, educational and training organisations the Regional Chambers will be able to develop an economic development strategy for each region; and to help establish Regional Development Agencies, some of whose board members they could appoint.'

MEANWHILE AT THE GRASS ROOTS

Regional government cannot be considered in abstraction from local government. It is potentially both a threat to local authorities and an opportunity for them to shape policy beyond the local level. Not without reservations, local government has on the whole responded positively to the emergence of regional government on the political agenda and indeed local government organisations have played a central role in driving the regional government debate forward over the last two years. But their support is qualified by the stipulation that powers of regional government should not take still more power away from local government. There are also strongly held reservations about a further round of local government reorganisation, and thus about a requirement for single-tier local government as a condition of progress towards regional government.

There is a wide variety of local government bodies which facilitate regional co-ordination and co-operation between local authorities. The status, activity level and relevance to regional government of these bodies vary considerably from region to region, but they illustrate both that local authorities can come together and effectively co-ordinate their efforts and that they perceive the need to do so.

The English Regional Associations of local authorities come the closest to the Regional Chamber model. They cover each of the standard regions coinciding in most regions with the boundaries of the Government Offices (the exceptions being Merseyside and the South East). As voluntary groupings of local authorities with no statutory recognition or powers they rely on the constituent local authorities (and in some cases other regional bodies) agreeing to co-operate and co-ordinate their actions. The main activities of the ERAs include regional planning, the environment, transport, waste and economic development issues. An important function is advising central government on Regional Planning Guidance. The size, status and level of activity of the ERAs vary from region to region and their current funding involves relatively small amounts of money and comes from local authority subscriptions or contributions.

Spurred on by Labour's proposals for regional government many of these bodies have been re-examining their role and structures and considering how they might best become shadow Regional Chambers. In Yorkshire and Humberside, for example, a new Regional Assembly was established in 1996. The merging of the three local government associations into the new Local Government Association has had its own regional dimension. One of the consequences of working in a single association is that its membership is too large to operate effectively in forums where each member authority has its own representative. As a result an electoral college system has been developed. This has been done at a regional level overlapping other regional groupings of local authorities.

INTERNATIONAL COMPARISONS

The degree of centralisation of power in the UK, mentioned above, is indeed a part of the case for considering regional government in England; it is further emphasised by the fact that England has a lower number of elected representatives (taking all levels into account) per head of population than other EU countries. On the other hand, the low turn-out for sub-national elections in the UK – also at the bottom of the range of international comparison – is a warning about the state of public demand for the redistribution of power from the centre. So too is the evidence, admittedly uncertain, of opinion polls about attitudes to regional government. That evidence suggests that demand is at best not overwhelming.

This is not very surprising for two reasons: lack of general knowledge about what regional government would do; and genuine difficulty in much of England in defining regions with which people can instinctively, and politically, identify. The example most commonly given is the North East, where there is a coherent regional sense for social, historical and geographical reasons; but even there, interest in regional government belongs to the political classes, not the public.

Neither of these reasons need be decisive; but the first underlines the need for a well-defined project, with a clear purpose and function, if regional government is to command popular support in England. The second can in principle be overcome, perhaps by following the French example. As in England, there are many parts of mainland France which do not fit into particularly coherent regional units; but a geographical pattern, by grouping Departments, was nevertheless imposed as the basis of elected regional government in 1981. However, as Andrew Adonis observed,[2] the regions 'are weak and have been taken over by the same politicians who run everything else . . . regional inequalities remain entrenched. Average income in the Paris

[2] *Observer*, 1 June 1997.

region is almost twice as high as in the east and south of France and ironing out territorial disparities is an issue of bitter controversy.'

It is debatable whether the reason for this is the lack of conviction about defining regions; or the lack of real will by the central government to decentralise control and (not at all the same thing) to redistribute resources. But the example of France needs to be remembered by advocates of regional government in England – and the pitfalls avoided.

The European Commission may, and its representatives do, encourage the idea of regional government in England; but they are in no position to demand it. Research at John Moores University for the Rowntree Foundation convincingly demonstrates that democratic regional government and organisation is not decisive in delivering better economic performance, or even success in attracting European funding. Effective regional co-ordination is of course shown to be a key factor.

Other features of international comparison are worth noting: while it is true that a pattern of elected regional government is almost universal in Europe, what is meant by a region in size, function, power and historical legitimacy varies almost to infinity. The term 'region' in this context is a loose concept.

Among the larger European countries, the examples most often cited as offering comparison with England are France (another highly centralised country where democratically elected regions were laid down uniformly from the centre – but see the comment above); and Spain, a country emerging from decades of civil war and dictatorship which has developed a highly diverse pattern of regions with different levels of decentralisation. The Spanish experience has been cited by Labour spokespeople as a precedent for a varied pattern of decentralisation. But this ignores history: if a parallel in the UK is to be found for Catalonia, the Basque Country and Galicia it is to be found not in England, but in Northern Ireland, Scotland and Wales, all with their claim to nationhood. And as Paul Preston, biographer of Franco points out, Franco's moderate followers who negotiated the transition to democracy

'could not escape from the centralist conditioning of their youth and saw the emergence of an autonomous Catalonia and Basque country with the greatest trepidation. Accordingly they came up with the cunning plan which they were convinced would dilute and render meaningless any concessions given to the Catalans and Basques. Their wheeze, known as 'café para todos' (coffee for everyone) divided all of Spain into regions and granted them all autonomy. They thereby began to dismantle the centralist state which was Spanish nationalism's proudest creation.'[3]

[3] 'Coffee for Everyone': review article, *Times Literary Supplement*, May, 2, 1997.

THE WILL TO DECENTRALISE

Unless there is a real will to decentralise away from central government, whether to local government or to a new regional tier, proposals for regional government will be neither here nor there: in that case, functions of such a tier could come only from local government. Labour Party statements have consistently maintained that functions would be devolved from the centre; this is an understandable position, but taken literally, always likely to be unrealistic. Some readjustment at both sides is likely to be needed to give coherence to a regional tier and this accounts for the Labour Party preference for single-tier local government as a precondition of elected regional government in any region. It would be possible to meet some of the objects of decentralising power by reversing the trend of reducing the independence of local government; the case for a regional tier depends also on establishing that there is a set of functions that requires democratic control at a regional level. How far does the two-stage approach advanced by Labour (indirectly elected chambers followed, in due course and if there is regional demand, by directly elected assemblies), meet these tests – particularly in a context in which Regional Development Agencies have been given priority for legislation in the government's first session, while giving statutory recognition to Chambers has been resisted?

THE TWO-STAGE APPROACH

In defiance of logic, it is helpful to consider Stage Two first, as set out in Labour's original Consultation Paper (the manifesto did not give detail). Stringent tests are proposed before Stage Two is reached: the Chamber, based on appointees of local government, must agree; there must be parliamentary approval; and in addition there must be a test of public opinion, probably by referendum. There must also be a 'generally unitary pattern of local government'. These are high hurdles, which may well in themselves be sufficient to keep Stage Two from being reached.

But there are substantive issues about a directly elected stage that are of more importance than the procedural matters, and to which not enough attention has been paid.

The starting point must be to define a set of functions that would be sufficient to justify setting up powerful new regional bodies, for the election of which people would be willing to turn out. The Constitution Unit report set out a 'Minimalist' model for the functions of assemblies:

271

Figure 13.1 'Minimalist model'

- the strategic responsibilities of Chambers:
  - strategic land-use planning
  - transport
  - economic development
  - co-ordination of European funding bids
- the voice of the region
- a statutory right of consultation on strategic or business plans for the Regional Development Agencies
- similar responsibilities for other key bodies (which would need to be given clear regional structures and budgets). For example:
  - regional arts associations
  - sports councils
  - health authorities
  - regional arms of Highways and other key Next Steps Agencies
  - English Partnerships
- consumer consultative arrangements for public utilities
- statutory right of consultation by Government on defined issues

---

Source: Constitution Unit, *Regional Government in England* (June 1996).

To go further than that almost necessarily requires taking on from the Government Offices some of the responsibilities that they have for distributing resources between local authorities. The Constitution Unit report has another model to illustrate a possible wider group of functions:

Figure 13.2 'Maximalist model'

- as for minimalist model
- assuming the functions of Government Offices in some or all of the following fields
  - education and training
  - industry
  - urban regeneration (including allocating SRB)
  - environment and transport
- responsibility for agencies, or regional arms of agencies, in above fields:
  - approval of strategic plan
  - Assembly being 'client' for the agency
  - appointment of all board members in the regions
  - formal transfer of some or all functions in the regions
- determining the allocation within the region of an allocated block of Lottery funding
- a block of expenditure allocated by Government to cover the above, with virement permitted

---

Source: Constitution Unit, *Regional Government in England* (June 1996).

While there are possible intermediate positions between these two models they illustrate the point that the 'minimalist' model produces bodies that would be unlikely to attract voters to turn out. And for directly elected regional bodies to have functions sufficient to command popular support, they would have to have responsibilities which local government would be bound to find unwelcome. The opinion of local authorities need not be decisive; but as they stand, they are the only elected bodies apart from central government that we have.

The proposal for local option could no doubt be made to work; but the complication and the financial and other consequences of it have not yet been thought through as they would need to be, particularly if the powers proposed for Regional Assemblies were extensive.

It would seem that there is not at present a convincing model for directly elected regional bodies in England. Whether there would be serious political support for such a project if it were defined in practical detail is an open question. It is of course possible that when the English public sees the development of proposals for devolution to Scotland and Wales, and particularly the terms of the financial settlement that will be needed, sentiment may change. No one wants to be left out of a good thing. The remainder of this chapter assumes however that – apart from in London – directly elected regional government is not a live part of the political agenda, for the time being at least. Nothing said since the election suggests otherwise.

LONDON

The strength of the case and support for establishing a strategic authority for London made it a priority in the government's programme. A Green Paper produced at the end of July 1997 proposed a small assembly together with a directly elected Mayor. The Mayor would have extensive executive powers, including responsibility for transport, economic development and a London police authority. The Mayor will also have a direct involvement in planning and environmental issues, setting a new planning strategy for London and having the power to tackle environmental issues.

A White Paper in March 1998 confirmed the main thrust of the Green Paper: the powerful executive Mayor will be held to account by a separately elected Assembly. The Assembly will be able to scrutinise all of the Mayor's activities and initiate other inquiries into issues which it considers to be of importance to London. The Assembly will also be involved in setting the authority's budget, working closely with the Mayor on the budget and strategic priorities. The Mayor will be obliged to consider the recommendations of the Assembly which will ultimately be able to agree or reject the Mayor's budget, subject to a two-thirds majority. The authority will formally be a local authority, but one of a very particular kind. Given its area, it will have some, but not all, of the characteristics of a regional government.

These proposals were put to a referendum which coincided with the London borough elections in May 1998. Having received the expected 'yes' vote (albeit on a low turnout) the legislation is expected to receive royal assent in summer 1999 with the first full elections for the strategic authority held in 2000.

REGIONAL CHAMBERS

In the run-up to the election Labour's policy on Regional Chambers – the first stage in moving to regional government – left a number of key issues to be settled. Some of these have been addressed – albeit indirectly – by moves since the election to establish Regional Development Agencies (a parallel policy initiative), but there remain areas and general principles which have not yet been tackled:

Functions

The functions usually, and understandably, identified as justifying treatment at regional level are:

(1) strategic land-use planning;
(2) transport;
(3) economic development, including inward investment;
(4) regional relations with the EU and its regions;
(5) providing a voice for the region.

These form a coherent group of linked functions which tally reasonably well with the functions of the Government Offices. They are strategic, not implying large staffs or expenditure. They also build on patterns already in place: as noted above, there are already regional associations of local authorities (some of these involving outside agencies) which deal with many of these matters at a regional level, and these associations are continually developing at varying speeds. These functions do however overlap with the role identified for the Regional Development Agencies. In addition, as local government itself is reformed (again a parallel policy initiative) there may follow the election of powerful executive mayors who may want to have influence over these issues themselves.

Legislation

It was recognised before the election that it would be possible to make progress with Regional Chambers without legislation. This would require agreement between the local authorities. It would also require commitment by central government to give the Chambers an enhanced role in agreeing regional strategies and priorities (for example, in criteria for the distribution of resources within the region; in preparing Regional Planning Guidance; and in the oversight of regional quangos). It would also be necessary, if the Chambers were to have an effective handle on quangos and related bodies, for the several government departments concerned to review the formal marching orders under which quangos operate in order to make them more responsive to the democratic voice expressed through the Chambers. To proceed in this way would need at least the force of a White Paper; and experience suggests the limits of the willingness of departments to put energy into an exercise on these lines.

A minimal legislative framework would demonstrate government commitment to the project and would certainly make the Chambers more effective bodies. Such legislation need not change the status of the Chambers in substance: they would still be joint committees of local authorities. The RDA legislation goes some way towards this by giving the Secretary of State the power to 'designate' regional bodies as the Regional Chamber providing the body satisfies basic criteria. The legislation does not however require a Chamber to be established for each region; specify objectives or functions; make provision about membership; or provide a funding mechanism. All this suggests lukewarm interest in the development of Chambers.

Boundaries

There is a case for adopting an existing set of boundaries in the interest of making progress and indeed the Government Office boundaries have been adopted by the government for the Regional Development Agencies. These offer a reasonable starting point and presumably the RDA boundaries will set the framework for the Regional Chambers.

It is sometimes argued[4] that the multiplicity of boundaries for central government purposes of various kinds – Hogwood has identified nearly 100 – points to the need for a wholly new set of boundaries for the purposes of regional government. For reasons set out in *Regional Government in England*, the pragmatic approach suggested above is to be preferred: total consistency of boundaries is unnecessary and in some cases undesirable. No doubt the boundaries of the principal services likely to be of concern to regional government should be examined and where necessary rationalised. But this can follow the main decisions about key structures.

There are nonetheless issues which have had to be settled about whether Merseyside should have a Chamber of its own; whether the South West region should be split to acknowledge its exceptional incoherence (Moreton-in-Marsh being nearer to Newcastle-upon-Tyne than to Lands End); and above all in the South-East. In the South-East there are two issues: first, the sheer size of the region: the territory of the South-East Regional Planning

---

[4] For example by Professor Brian Hogwood in *Mapping the Regions* (Bristol: Policy Press, 1996).

organisation (SERPLAN) includes 36 per cent of the population of England; secondly, what to do about London.

The strategic authority for London will follow the boundary of the former Greater London Council (GLC) and the definition of 'strategic' functions and their practical application will not be without difficulty: the history of the GLC and its relations with the boroughs, even those controlled by the same party, shows the problems clearly enough. The further commitment to an elected Mayor for London, welcomed by many, will no doubt complicate the division of functions. But however the new authority operates in practice, in economic, land-use and transport terms London is an inherent part of the functioning of the wider region. Any pattern of Chambers established for the region will have to acknowledge that; as the strategic authority for London will have to acknowledge that some decisions about land-use, and patterns of travel and employment will have to be made in a wider context than London itself. So far as they are political, such decisions will need to be taken by representatives of local authorities in the wider region, including London, or by central government.

Representation

Deriving membership of Regional Chambers from local authorities immediately raises issues of how the political make-up of the region should be reflected and how the interests of sub-regions, different types of local authorities and groups such as women and ethnic minorities should be safeguarded. With the emphasis on partnership there is also the issue of how partners outside local government are brought into the Chambers.

In terms of local authority representation, a starting point would be a representative from each member authority. This would in some regions produce very large Chambers and some form of weighted voting, possibly drawing on the LGA regional structures, is likely to prove necessary. Bringing in partners outside local government will be essential, but raises questions about which partners, how they should be identified and what powers they should have. There is a basic choice between having such representatives as members of the Chamber, whether by co-option or some other method; or whether a separate framework, drawing on existing models in some regions, is adopted. In either case, care will be needed in the balance of appointments (for example between 'environmental' and 'business' interests) and in ensuring that the partnership gives a well-defined role to its members.

Advantages and disadvantages

If it is accepted that, at least for the present, there is no realistic prospect of directly elected authorities outside London, the Chambers have some clear advantages: they are firmly grounded in local government, which is the only

276

elective system of government in the UK apart from Parliament; they are compatible with an increase in decentralisation of power to local authorities, if that is decided; their areas correspond to areas identified by the government (and widely accepted by others) as meaningful for many practical purposes.

There are certainly criticisms to be made of the Chamber proposals. The first is a point of principle: these are democratic bodies up to a point; but the concept of 'democratically appointed' bodies has, as one informed critic puts it, a rather Bulgarian sound. That is not simply a point of abstract principle: it is linked with the fact that Chambers will be essentially joint committees of local government, whether or not set up by legislation. The experience of such bodies is that they work best where their functions are well-defined, practical and not politically sensitive. The business of the Chambers will be complex and political to the core. The other experience of joint boards and committees is that they rarely attract the continued attention of the leading members of the parent local authorities. If Chambers are to do the work expected of them, including the development of partnerships with regional business, scrutinising the main regional quangos, and negotiating on a strategic level with the Government Office for the region, they will need the membership of talented and influential members of the component local authorities. These are just the members – in whom few authorities would claim to be rich – who are needed on their own frontbenches.

The Labour proposals point to the existing Regional Associations of local authorities as the basis of Regional Chambers and these seem likely to be the bodies 'designated' by the Secretary of State under the RDA legislation. However, few of the existing Regional Associations have an established track record or anything like the scale of resources needed to make an effective fist of the tasks proposed for Regional Chambers. Indeed it seems unrealistic to suppose that no additional resources will be required for the introduction of such Chambers.

Nevertheless, short of direct election, a version of the Chamber proposal continues to seem the most promising means of developing democratic institutions at the regional level. However, it is worth thinking more widely. One way of boosting the status of Regional Chambers would be to include a proportion of regional MPs and MEPs in their membership. This may be argued to be impractical in terms of time commitment (and members of the government would clearly be unlikely to be able to participate). However, arguably, as MPs and MEPs are at least notionally full-time politicians, whereas local authority members are still as a rule part-time, they might find it easier to make the time available. This may be particularly true at the moment given the large number of Labour MPs looking for a role on the backbenches.

NOT REGIONAL GOVERNMENT

It was clear in the period before the election that there were two very distinct strands of thought in the Labour Party about regional government, which were not being effectively brought together. While Jack Straw and his team, and the document they produced, homed in on the democratic deficit and the constitutional aspects of the case for change, John Prescott and Richard Caborn, by contrast, were focusing on the case for better co-ordination of regional economic development. Although there were cross-references between the two, these were slight and unconvincing. The Constitution Unit's report of April 1997, *Regional Chambers and Regional Development Agencies*, suggested means by which the two strands might be brought together, by developing a model of Development Agency which would not by the nature of its funding and accountability need to be established as a quango; and by proposing that legislation for the two strands should be brought together.

The Queen's Speech, decided within days of the election and delivered a week later, committed the government to legislating for Regional Development Agencies – a parallel Labour Party policy – but was silent about regional government in any other form. A consultation paper, issued at the beginning of June to initiate a rapid process of consultation, posed a large number of questions about every aspect of establishing RDAs, suggesting an open – indeed a vacant – mind on many key issues. This was followed in December 1997 by the White Paper, *Building Partnerships for Prosperity*, and the Regional Development Agencies Bill, with the RDAs expected to be established in April 1999.

The underlying question is the relative significance attached by the government to the twin forces behind the regional debate. Is the RDA proposal, with its emphasis on regional development, a deliberate down-playing of the democratic aspect to the debate? Or the result of an expedient decision to take the opportunity of a place in the legislative programme for a long-standing commitment to legislate on a limited proposal? (A traditional part of the bargaining for a place in the programme is the proposition that the particular proposal, apart from its merits and political attractiveness, is only a little one in terms of drafting and parliamentary time.)

We do not seek here (in the context of discussion of constitutional issues) to assess the value to the regions of RDAs. We have, however, argued elsewhere[5] that:

(1) RDAs that built on the strengths and experience of existing organisations concerned with regeneration in the regions would be preferable to a uniform model;

(2) effectively engaging business and other interests in the region in the process of regeneration requires a clear definition of tasks for Board members;

---

[5] Katy Donnelly and Paul McQuail, *Regional Chambers and Regional Development Agencies*, April 1997.

278

(3) Board membership is not the only means of engaging the energy of outside interests.

In addition to getting the organisation of the Agencies themselves right, the effectiveness of the RDAs will depend on the resources they have and on how their activity fits into the governance of the region as a whole. It is not wholly clear from the Secretary of State's statement of July 1998, following the comprehensive spending review, what resources the RDAs will have beyond those so far available to existing bodies and programmes including English Partnerships, the Single Regeneration Budget, the Rural Development Commission and others. At whatever level, a key policy question will be about distribution of resources, whatever the total and whatever the original source, between regions. To the extent that redressing imbalance between regions is an objective of the policy (this is not explicitly stated but has been frequently advanced by Labour spokespeople), some redistribution between regions must be implied. This will no doubt be more welcome in the regions who are favoured by the redistribution than by those who lose.

Even more significant than resource distribution, in practical as well as in 'constitutional' terms, is the question of accountability. The original consultation paper stated that 'Ministers do not want the RDAs to be simply creatures of government, central or local. They must be responsive to a wider coalition of local interests, including business and others, who make a key contribution to regional economic development, such as the higher education institutions.' (The omission of further education may be an accident.) The RDAs chairmen and members will be formally appointed by ministers and be formally accountable through ministers to Parliament. The Bill gives the Secretary of State the power to 'designate' a regional body as the Regional Chamber and to direct the RDA to 'have regard to . . . any views expressed by Chamber'. But exactly how this will operate in practice is unclear and RDAs will still be quangos. (One function they will certainly not be well equipped to carry out, among those proposed for Regional Chambers, is the democratic scrutiny of other quangos in the regions.)

The Local Government Association has actively campaigned for amendments to the Regional Development Agencies Bill in order to make RDAs more answerable to the Regional Chambers, though without success. The Environment, Transport and Regional Affairs Committee has also raised concerns about the accountability arrangements for the RDAs, recommending that 'the accountability of the RDAs to these chambers be more clearly specified. In particular, we recommend the chambers approve the corporate plans and budgets of the RDAs'.

In presentational terms, RDAs have slipped on to the constitutional reform agenda. Spoken of in the same breath as devolution to Scotland and Wales, the RDAs have been heralded by John Prescott as leading to 'significant devolution and decentralisation'. But the legacy of the pre-election separation of the regional governance and the regional development briefs is clearly evident. It is possible to imagine consultative bodies, perhaps even the non-statutory chamber, playing a useful role on appointments, policy and priorities; but a body appointed by ministers, receiving its funding from ministers, and acting under a corporate planning regime and output measures for which ministers will be answerable to Parliament, is a far cry from regional government. Proposals for democratic structures have come a poor second and the establishment of a new quango for each region is a striking departure from the claims and the intentions of the democratic tendency.

That RDAs will be quangos will matter less, the more the RDAs are set up primarily as delivery and perhaps co-ordinating bodies. However, some of the RDAs' functions amount to the strategic planning of the region – for example transport planning, promoting the environment and sustainable development, ensuring an appropriate spread of resources across the region. Functions at this end of the scale hardly seem suitable to be exercised by an appointed body. They are, however, functions that do need to be exercised at the regional level, and are part of the case for a democratic body at regional level charged with responsibility for developing a strategic framework for the region. The function is already in part exercised, so far as land-use is concerned by the Regional Conferences or Associations in preparing the Regional Planning Guidance (RPG), which is non-statutory but highly influential. But RPG needs to be related, at the political level, to strategies for transport, for economic development and regeneration; and for environmental improvement and sustainability.

The proposed Regional Chambers offer a possible mechanism for bringing these regional strategies together within a coherent, democratically controlled, framework of regional goals agreed with the Government Office for the region. We acknowledge some of the criticisms that may be made of the Chambers as at present proposed; but the Chambers are democratically based, they could have the right representation, and they were in the manifesto. There remains a case for enlarging their role; the case may well be strengthened by the operation of the RDAs.

A DEMOCRATIC OPPORTUNITY

Perhaps the analysis of ministers is that the real need of the regions is for economic development; and that RDAs will buy off pressure, particularly in the Northern Region, for a directly elected Assembly in the face of the proposed Parliament for Scotland, the Assembly for Wales, and the directly elected authority for London. They may be right about that. The passage of the Regional Development Agencies Bill offered the proponents of the argument about a democratic deficit the opportunity to make the case. Although many did take that opportunity, it was difficult to demonstrate significant demand for democratic regional government in England, certainly not demand strong enough for the government to concede a great deal.

DEVOLUTION

From an English point of view, the most important part of the regional debate is not what might happen in England (given that direct election is not on the cards), but what is likely to happen in Scotland and Wales. The consequentials for England need the closest possible scrutiny, inside and outside government. It is of course possible that implementing proposals for Scotland, Wales and London will renew pressure for regional government in England: it would be surprising if it did not, particularly when it comes to the revised allocation of resources that will be necessary. But reallocating resources will not be the only impact of devolution to Scotland that will require a watchful eye and an effective voice for the English, and the UK, interest in devolution. In the field of economic regeneration alone, there are English interests in the powers and policies of the Scottish Parliament, for example in the field of inward investment. Even within England, there will, following the establishment of RDAs, and the probable dismemberment of English Partnerships, be a need to pay attention to damaging competition between regions, and to manage some major issues. A central capacity will be needed to manage this; the creation of the new Department for Environment, Transport and the Regions, particularly while it is headed by the Deputy Prime Minister, will both assist in co-ordination and provide a – highly necessary – base for a strong voice for England.

There is no answer yet to the headline question whether the English regions want regional government. A year's experience suggests that the new government believes that they do not really want it; or at least that they do not want it enough. They may well be right. But the experience of Scotland, Wales and London will shift the balance of argument – though in unpredictable ways. In the meantime, those in the political classes who advocate a strong form of regional government in England would do well to devote time and thought to turning the idea into a practical set of propositions, facing up to the real difficulties involved. They should then seek support for it from the relevant constituencies; central government, local government, other organisations with a stake in the question; not least the people.

Further reading

Constitution Unit (Katy Donnelly and Paul McQuail), *Regional Government in England* (London, 1996); *Regional Chambers and Regional Development Agencies* (London, 1997)

Brian Hogwood, *Mapping the Regions* (Bristol: Policy Press, 1996); and with Michael Keating (eds), *Regional Government in England* (1982)

Report of the Royal Commission on the Constitution (London: HMSO, Cmnd 5460, 1973)

Labour Party, *A Choice for England* (Consultation Paper, 1995); *A New Voice for England's Regions* (Policy Paper, 1996)

CHAPTER 14

NORTHERN IRELAND

Professor Kevin Boyle (Human Rights Centre, Essex) and
Professor Tom Hadden (Queen's University, Belfast)

INTRODUCTION

A year is also a long time in politics. Few would have predicted that the
new Labour Government's most intractable inheritance from the long reign
of Conservative administrations, Northern Ireland, would be the site for its
most radical political and constitutional achievements within 12 months of
taking office. But the Good Friday Agreement of 10 April 1998 represents
just that.[1] Its endorsement in parallel referendums in both the Republic of
Ireland and Northern Ireland in May, and the subsequent elections to a
new Northern Ireland local assembly, which have produced majorities from
both Nationalist and Unionist communities committed to working the new
arrangements are historic events.

An equally important advance has been the recognition on all sides that
a settlement in Northern Ireland really does require a new approach to
relationships throughout the British–Irish Isles. For far too long the search
for a settlement was treated by most people in Great Britain and Ireland
as a distinct and separate issue which really had nothing to do with them.
But this was a false and ultimately dangerous conception. The Anglo-Irish
Agreement of 1985 and all subsequent inter-governmental documents have
accepted the principle that a solution to the Northern Ireland problem
requires a transformation of all the relationships between the peoples of
Great Britain and Ireland. But until recently the political and constitutional
flexibility which that required of all sides was not forthcoming. The new
Agreement achieved by the British and Irish governments and the parties in
Northern Ireland, if it proves durable, should be seen as a catalyst for deeper
constitutional reform in Great Britain and for a new relationship between the
two states.

---

[1] Cm 3883 (1998). The Northern Ireland Bill, published in July 1998, incorporates significant
parts of the Agreement by reference (as the text of this chapter was completed before the
Bill's publication, no discussion of its provisions is given below).

LABOUR PARTY POLICIES

The new possibilities in Northern Ireland are of course not due only to the energies of a new Labour government. While the commitment and skills of Tony Blair deserve recognition in coaxing the Northern Ireland parties to compromise, the path had already been prepared by successive British Conservative governments working in close partnership with successive Irish governments. A crucial difference however was that while Conservative governments sought to isolate any constitutional innovation in Northern Ireland from its policy of resisting talk of constitutional change in Great Britain, Labour has a constitutional reform agenda in which Northern Ireland is but a part.

Traditionally the Labour Party supported the reunification of Ireland. In addition it has had a formal relationship with the Social Democratic and Labour Party in Northern Ireland which has a similar commitment to reunification.[2] On that ground the Labour Party has consistently refused to organise in Northern Ireland or to permit anyone in Northern Ireland to become a member. The most recent Conference resolution on Northern Ireland in 1991 approved a policy document which committed the party to a policy of 'unification with consent'. This formulation appears to have been adopted to take account of the commitments made under the Anglo-Irish Agreement, which was formally approved by a huge majority of all major parties in the British Parliament. But the policy was widely interpreted as indicating that the Labour Party would actively promote Irish unification at least to the extent of seeking to persuade unionists in Northern Ireland to give their consent.

The advent of New Labour and the prospect and eventual achievement of a Labour government led to a distinct change in emphasis. Though the Conference policy document on Northern Ireland has not been withdrawn, its most prominent proponent, Kevin McNamara, was replaced as spokesperson on Northern Ireland when he failed to win a place in the Shadow Cabinet elections. His successor, Mo Mowlam, and Tony Blair repeatedly stressed the element of consent and played down any commitment to unification unless and until that is the clearly expressed wish of a majority of the people of Northern Ireland. They also gave strong support to the Downing Street Declaration and the Framework Documents agreed by the Conservative government and the Irish government. There is therefore no reason to doubt that the Labour government is as strongly committed as the previous administration to the underlying policies of communal accommodation within Northern Ireland as part of the UK and to co-operation with the Irish government on which the current settlement is based. The main difference is

---

[2] The SDLP, which was founded in 1970, takes the Labour whip in the House of Commons; both parties are members of the Socialist International and the European Socialist Group in the European Parliament.

that the Labour government is seeking to pursue these objectives within the framework of new constitutional arrangements for the UK as a whole. Unlike the Conservatives, Labour is committed to constitutional reform throughout the UK and to bringing power closer to the people. Northern Ireland cannot be exempt from this process. It is also, unlike the Conservatives, committed to the formal protection of individual and constitutional rights, for which the incorporation of the European Convention on Human Rights throughout the UK is only the first step.

THE CONTEXT OF THE GOOD FRIDAY AGREEMENT

The starting point for a constitutional analysis of the Good Friday Agreement must be the fact that in formal terms Northern Ireland, unlike any other part of the UK, has always had a written constitution, initially under the Government of Ireland Act 1920 and then under the Northern Ireland Constitution Act 1973. The 1920 Act made detailed provision for a regional Northern Ireland Parliament and government, both closely modelled on the Westminster Parliament, though its legislative powers were limited and subject to review in the courts.[3] This was supplemented under the Ireland Act 1949 by the grant of a limited right of self-determination to the people of Northern Ireland to remain – and thus by implication not to remain – part of the UK.[4] Under the 1973 Act the Parliament, which had been suspended in 1972, was replaced by an Assembly which was elected by proportional representation and which was granted similar legislative powers. Provision was also made for the appointment by the Secretary of State for Northern Ireland of a power-sharing executive. When the initial executive was brought down by a politically motivated strike in 1974, temporary provision was made under the Northern Ireland Act 1974 for what has become continuing 'direct rule' by the Secretary of State for Northern Ireland.[5] Under this regime legislation on previously devolved matters is made by Orders in Council, subject to affirmative resolutions by both Houses of Parliament.[6] Underlying this relatively straightforward structure for devolution, however, are the more fundamental provisions of the Acts of Union of 1800, which as will be seen must be taken into account. And from another very different perspective there are the provisions of the Irish Constitution of 1937 which asserted a

---

[3] The 1920 Act also provided for a similar Parliament for Southern Ireland, but this was never established, being overtaken by the Anglo-Irish Treaty of 1921 which made provision for a separate constitution for the Irish Free State.

[4] Section 1(2) provided that in no event would Northern Ireland, or any part thereof, cease to be part of His Majesty's dominions without the consent of the Parliament of Northern Ireland; this was amended under the Northern Ireland Constitution Act 1973 which provides for periodic referendums on the issue.

[5] The 1974 Act also established a Northern Ireland Convention which it was hoped would achieve agreement on a new constitution but which failed to do so.

[6] Northern Ireland Act 1974, s 1 and Sched 1.

right of self-determination for the people of Ireland as a whole and formally claim - and then in practice disclaim – jurisdiction over Northern Ireland.

It was the conflicting claims in these two separate constitutional frameworks which lay at the heart of the conflict within Northern Ireland. Any proposals for their reform and co-ordination, however, can in practice be considered only in the light of current political realities, including not only the commitments of the two main sections of the population in Northern Ireland but also the equally significant obligations of the British and Irish governments under the Anglo-Irish Agreement and subsequent inter-governmental declarations and under other international conventions.

These conflicting constitutional claims over Northern Ireland were not purely theoretical. They reflected real differences in the felt identities and aspirations of large sections of its population. Northern Ireland was created in the 1920s because a large majority of the people in that part of Ireland did not share the communal identity of most Irish Catholics or their aspirations for 'home rule' or independence. When the grant of home rule to the whole of Ireland became a distinct possibility in 1912 large numbers of Ulster Protestants were mobilised to prevent its imposition. But events in the southern part of Ireland, notably the Easter Rising of 1916, the general election of 1918 and the guerrilla war of 1919 to 1921, made it clear that the demands of Irish nationalists for self-government could not be effectively resisted. Faced with these conflicting communal and paramilitary pressures the British government decided that partition was the only solution to the problem.[7] Whether or not this was the best policy is a matter for historical judgment. But it created facts on the ground which cannot now be ignored. Partition established Northern Ireland as a unit of government whose status within the UK a clear majority of its people wished – and still wish – to retain. Partition however also entailed the incorporation within the UK of a substantial minority who did not wish to be separated from the people on the rest of the island.

That settlement delivered almost 50 years of relative stability. But it was achieved at the expense of the interests and aspirations of Northern nationalists.[8] Their economic and political interests were subordinated under the unionist regime to those of the Protestant/unionist community. But their aspiration to Irish unification was kept alive by a separate educational system and by continued support from fellow nationalists in what became the Irish Republic, not least in the formal claims in Articles 1 and 2 of the Irish Constitution of 1937.[9] At the time of partition the Catholic community represented about one-third of the population of the six counties of Northern Ireland. This relative balance was maintained under the Unionist regime

---

[7] This was implemented under the Irish Free State (Consequential Provisions) Act 1922.

[8] The factual information in this section is discussed in greater detail in Kevin Boyle and Tom Hadden, *Northern Ireland – The Choice* (Penguin Books, 1994), Ch 3.

[9] Article 1 asserts a right of self-determination for the Irish nation and Article 2 asserts that the national territory is the whole island of Ireland.

despite the higher Catholic birth rate by the twin mechanisms of internal job discrimination and external migration. As more equitable employment opportunities were eventually introduced under direct rule from Westminster, however, the proportion of Catholic/nationalists has gradually grown to a little over 40 per cent.

These population trends are directly reflected in recent voting figures. In the 1980s the main nationalist parties, the Social Democratic and Labour Party (SDLP) and Sinn Fein, regularly polled about 35 per cent of the total votes, the main unionist parties, the Ulster Unionists and the Democratic Unionists, about 55 per cent and cross-communal centre parties, notably the Alliance Party, about 10 per cent. In the 1990s the figure for the two nationalist parties has increased to almost 40 per cent while that for the main unionist parties has decreased to around 50 per cent. These figures indicate, if further evidence were needed, that the two main communities of nationalists and unionists remain firmly committed to their separate identities and aspirations and that the people in between with no strong communal affiliation are too few to be politically significant. During the past 30 years of communal strife and terrorism there has also been substantial population movement in urban areas towards greater residential segregation. And it is clear that paramilitaries on both sides retain the ability to escalate their activities and increase their membership in times of political or communal tension.

SEPARATION OR SHARING

One possible conclusion from these facts and figures is that the only practicable political solution for Northern Ireland is to recognise the separatist tendencies and divergent aspirations of the two main communities either by providing structures for government which allow each to manage its own affairs, as in Belgium, or by arranging for a formal repartition which would allow a smaller and more homogeneous Northern Ireland to remain within the UK and the remainder of its territory and people to join the Republic. A similar result could also be achieved by a precipitate British withdrawal or commitment to withdraw, leaving the main paramilitary bodies to fight it out for territory as in Bosnia.

There is clear evidence that this is not what the vast majority of the people in Northern Ireland want. A series of recent opinion polls which posed separation and sharing alternatives on a wide range of issues have indicated that almost everyone favoured greater sharing in education, in housing, in employment and in structures for local and regional government.[10] There was also general support for the policy of successive British governments

[10] See Tom Hadden, Colin Irwin and Fred Boal, *Separation or Sharing: The People's Choice*, published as a supplement to Fortnight Magazine in December 1996.

under the Fair Employment (Northern Ireland) Acts to foster fair participation by members of both communities in all major places of work in both the public and private sectors. The vote in the May referendum of 71 per cent in favour of the Good Friday Agreement has confirmed the findings of these polls and established beyond doubt that a substantial majority of the people in Northern Ireland want their politicians to share in a system of regional government.

THE GOOD FRIDAY AGREEMENT

The Agreement is the latest in a long line of proposed structures for power-sharing within a devolved government for Northern Ireland. The talks leading up to the Agreement were divided into three strands: Strand 1 dealing with the internal government of Northern Ireland; Strand 2 dealing with North/South relations; and Strand 3 dealing with relations between the UK and the Republic of Ireland. The Agreement itself reflects the commitment of all the parties to a broader agenda which interweaves the institutions designed to provide for each of these three strands with a number of more general principles: proportional participatory democracy and guarantees for a wide range of individual and communal rights within Northern Ireland; mutual recognition and provision for functional interdependence between Northern Ireland and the Republic; and acceptance that the long-standing inter-relationships between all the people of all the constituent parts of the British–Irish Isles also deserve some institutional recognition.

The key institution within Northern Ireland is to be a New Northern Ireland Assembly of 108 members elected on the established single transferable vote method of proportional representation. But proportionality is to be extended throughout the system of government. There are to be a series of Assembly committees to review the operation of each government department and their chairs and deputies are to be selected in proportion to party strength. The ministers in charge of departments will also be appointed on a strictly proportional basis, by the d'Hondt method. The effect of this will be to guarantee a share of government positions for all parties, including Sinn Fein, provided they remain committed to the principles of democracy and non-violence.

The principle of proportionality in the allocation of positions, however, is to be combined with more usual principles of democracy, since decisions on devolved legislation and other matters will require the support of a majority of members. But certain key decisions, such as the appointment of a chief minister and a deputy or the establishment of cross-border bodies or any other matter on the request of at least 30 members, will require cross-communal support, either by a majority of members representing each main community or by a weighted majority of 60 per cent including at least 40 per cent of members representing each community. These minority protection provisions, which are similar to those recently introduced in Belgium, clearly require members to identify their communal affiliation. The Agreement gives a choice between 'unionist', 'nationalist' or 'other', which will pose an awkward dilemma for the centre parties, since if they register as 'other' their votes will be effectively ignored on these crucial issues.

These complex structures will of course be dependent on the willingness of all the major parties to make them work. But they must also be seen as an integral part of the more general Labour programme for devolution throughout the UK. As in Scotland and Wales, many important decisions will be reserved for the Westminster Parliament and there will continue to be a Secretary of State for Northern Ireland in the British government. There will also be similar provisions to deal with any dispute on the respective powers of the central and devolved administrations.

The pragmatic approach of the Labour government to dealing with the special circumstances in each part of the UK is also apparent in the provisions of the Agreement in respect of fundamental human rights. The status of the Northern Ireland Assembly in relation to the European Convention on Human Rights will be identical to that of the Scottish and Welsh Assemblies. But the Agreement contains a number of additional provisions designed to 'reflect the principles of mutual respect for the identity and ethos of both communities and parity of esteem'. This will involve the development of a Northern Ireland Bill of Rights to give additional and more specific protection for individual and communal rights of special relevance to members of both communities and to members of neither community, the imposition on all government departments and public bodies of a duty to respect the identities and ethos of both communities and the establishment not only of a more powerful Northern Ireland Human Rights Commission but also of a new general Equality Commission to monitor the effective delivery of these rights. The Irish government has also undertaken to strengthen and underpin the constitutional protection of human rights in its own jurisdiction, to examine further the possible incorporation of the European Convention and to establish a Human Rights Commission with equivalent powers to those of the proposed Northern Ireland Commission. These commitments to a Bill of Rights and to the creation of effective human rights commissions should provide a useful incentive for the development of comparable protections in England, Scotland and Wales and in the UK as a whole.

The provisions for North/South relationships are designed to meet what initially appeared to be two incompatible positions: the demand from Sinn Fein and the IRA for 'North/South bodies with executive powers' as a first step towards unification and the insistence from unionists on full recognition of the legitimacy and equal status of Northern Ireland and full democratic accountability in any such cross-border co-operation. The Agreement clearly meets the unionist demand for the legitimacy of Northern Ireland to be fully recognised, both in its initial sentences and in the very clear acceptance of the principle of consent in the amendments to the Irish constitution. It also makes it clear that decisions within any cross-border bodies will require the agreement of both sides and will thus be at least indirectly accountable to the Northern Ireland Assembly and the Irish Parliament, Dail Eireann. Their formal structure is clearly modelled on those of the European Union: a joint North/South Ministerial Council which will meet at various levels with equal representation from the Northern Ireland Administration and the Irish government to agree on policies to be implemented either separately in each jurisdiction or by joint implementation bodies. But the decision on the precise areas for co-operation and the functions of the joint bodies has been left for the Northern Ireland Assembly to decide in consultation with the British and Irish governments during an initial 'shadow' period.[11] This will clearly be one of the most sensitive issues for the pro-Agreement parties in the Assembly to deal with. And if it is not dealt with effectively the whole process will be at risk, since the changes to the Irish constitution have been made conditional on its satisfactory resolution.

The final strand of the Agreement provides for a new set of institutions to deal with relationships between the UK and the Irish Republic. The Anglo-Irish Agreement of 1985 is to be replaced by a new British-Irish Agreement which binds the two governments to implement the terms of the Good Friday Agreement and to establish a new British–Irish Inter-governmental Conference which will take over the work of the Conference established under the 1985 Agreement in areas not devolved to the Northern Ireland Assembly and Administration, notably security and policing, though members of the Northern Ireland Administration are to be consulted. In addition, a new British–Irish Council, popularly known as the Council of the Isles, is to be established to bring together representatives from Scotland, Wales, Northern Ireland, the Isle of Man and the Channel Isles together with the two governments to discuss matters of mutual interest, such as transport, environmental protection, agriculture, education and health and where appropriate to agree on common policies or actions. Initially at least, however, there is to be no formal provision for decision-making. The closest model for this is perhaps the Nordic Council which was established in 1953 to promote co-operation between Denmark, Finland, Iceland, Norway and Sweden. But the impetus for the British–Irish Council stemmed largely from the desire of the Northern Ireland Unionists to balance the provisions for North/South institutions and it remains to be seen how seriously the Council will be taken by other participants. In principle the development of an institution for formalised co-operation of this kind makes good sense both in the context of Labour's programme for devolution throughout the UK and to reflect the long-established economic and cultural links and population movements within the British–Irish Isles.

---

[11] The Agreement requires the parties to agree by 31 October 1998 on 12 areas for co-operation of which six are to be delegated to joint implementation bodies on an all-Ireland basis.

BACKGROUND TO THE AGREEMENT:
MODELS FOR POWER-SHARING

The Good Friday Agreement is the culmination of efforts over 30 years to find a resolution of the conflict in Northern Ireland. Whether the new institutions can be made to work in the face of concerted opposition from a substantial section of the Protestant community and the members they have elected to the new Assembly remains to be seen. But many of its specific provisions can be related to difficulties which have been experienced during previous attempts to find a workable settlement.

Initially the British government sought to deal with the conflict on its own and focused exclusively on structures within Northern Ireland. The difficulty in establishing democratic arrangements on that basis and thereby to stem the escalating communal and paramilitary conflict eventually led to a recognition that any durable settlement would have to involve a wider approach which recognised the inter-relationships between the two parts of Ireland and also between Ireland and Great Britain.

The Sunningdale Agreement

The first attempt at a more general approach of this kind was the Sunningdale Agreement of 1973. The primary focus was on seeking a settlement within Ireland based on power-sharing between the two communities in the North and strong North/South institutions. But in hindsight insufficient attention was paid to balancing these objectives with measures to meet the concerns of unionists.

The process was initiated under the new Northern Ireland Constitution Act 1973 with a referendum to confirm the wish of a majority of the people of Northern Ireland to remain within the UK.[12] This was followed by an election on the single transferable vote system of proportional representation to a Northern Ireland Assembly and the appointment of a power-sharing executive from the Ulster Unionist Party, the SDLP and the centre parties, but excluding the Democratic Unionists and republicans. The formal basis for this was the power granted to the Secretary of State under the Act to appoint an executive if he was satisfied that it would 'command widespread support throughout the community' (s 2), a formula which was generally understood to mean representation from both major communities. The participating parties then agreed with the two governments at the Sunningdale Conference in December 1973 to establish a Council of Ireland with wide powers to develop North/South co-operation, not least in respect of policing. The power-sharing executive took office in January 1974. But the Irish government remained committed to its constitutional claim over Northern

---

[12] The referendum was held under s 1 of the 1973 Act and resulted in a 97 per cent majority in favour, since almost all nationalists boycotted the vote.

Ireland. This and the perception by a clear majority of unionists that the proposed Council of Ireland was a first step towards unification led to a political strike in May 1974 which toppled the executive.

The formula under the Northern Ireland Constitution Act 1973 clearly left a good deal to the discretion of the Secretary of State. But it has not proved possible to implement it since 1974. It was argued by nationalists that it did not provide a sufficient guarantee of participation at the highest level of government, and by unionists that it bound them to participate with whatever nationalist party had the ear of the British and Irish governments. In response the unionist parties regularly argued that power-sharing should be limited to the proportional allocation of chairmanships of parliamentary committees.[13] But that was always rejected by nationalists on the ground that it would not give them any share in executive power.

Weighted majorities

One possible alternative to a discretionary criterion for power-sharing is to rely on weighted majorities. When James Prior, as Secretary of State for Northern Ireland, was attempting to get agreement on what was called 'rolling devolution' – the gradual devolution of more powers to a newly elected Northern Ireland Assembly – he accepted a unionist amendment to the enabling legislation permitting a proposal for the devolution of specified powers to be made if it had the support of 70 per cent of members of the Assembly, though it remained subject to parliamentary approval at Westminster which could be granted only if both Houses were satisfied that the proposal would command widespread acceptance in Northern Ireland.[14] But the proposal could not in practice be implemented since both the SDLP and Sinn Fein refused to take their seats in the Assembly or to agree to any form of devolution which did not contain a substantial 'Irish dimension'.

During the extended talks process a rather more sophisticated approach to weighted majority voting has been developed, notably in the concepts of 'sufficient consensus' and 'communal veto' which have been derived from recent experience in other divided societies.

The concept of 'sufficient consensus' appears to have been borrowed from the peace process in South Africa, where it was used as a means of enabling progress to be made on contentious issues on which overall consensus could not be reached. In South Africa it meant agreement from the two main parties representing the Blacks and the Whites, the ANC and the Nationalists. In the procedural rules for the last stage in the talks process in Northern Ireland it meant the agreement of parties representing a majority of both unionists and nationalists.[15] And in the Good Friday Agreement it has been

---

[13] See, for example, *The Report of the Northern Ireland Constitutional Convention* (1976).
[14] Northern Ireland Act 1982, ss 1–2.
[15] *Northern Ireland: Ground Rules for Substantive All-Party Negotiations*, Cm 3232 (1996), para 24.

refined still further to mean a majority of members of the New Northern Ireland Assembly who have registered themselves as 'unionist' and as 'nationalist'. Though a parallel majority of this kind is specifically required only for the appointment of the chief and deputy chief ministers, the underlying concept is that in a divided society effective democracy requires the consent of a majority in both major communities.

The idea of a communal veto on contentious matters appears to have been borrowed from the mechanisms recently adopted in Belgium for the protection of the interests of the Flemish and Walloon communities. The new Belgian constitution provides not only that a 75 per cent majority of both French-speaking and Dutch-speaking members of the national Parliament is required to authorise relevant amendments to the constitution, but also that a 75 per cent majority of either group may temporarily block progress on any particular measure.[16] In the Good Friday Agreement, as explained above, the number of members required to trigger the communal voting mechanisms has been set at 30 and provision has also been made to permit 60 per cent of either communal group to veto specified Assembly decisions.

BACKGROUND TO THE AGREEMENT: THE CONCEPT OF JOINT AUTHORITY

Those who doubted the ability of politicians in Northern Ireland to make the essential compromises necessary for any system of power-sharing sought to develop alternative governmental structures which recognise the divergent aspirations and interests of the two main communities but are not ultimately dependent on continuing co-operation between them. The essential element in all these structures has been that the British and Irish governments should share authority over Northern Ireland on behalf of the unionist and nationalist communities respectively. But there has been considerable variation in the forms of joint authority that have been proposed.

The idea that this was the best way of dealing with the divergent identities and allegiances of the two communities in Northern Ireland was first raised by John Hume in the 1970s, using the analogy of the condominium by Britain and France over the Sudan and some other colonial territories. The concept was then developed and given some greater substance as one of the options proposed in the report of the New Ireland Forum in 1984.[17] It was described as a system of 'joint authority' under which 'the London and Dublin Governments would have equal responsibility for the government of

---

[16] Belgian Constitution 1994, Articles 4, 43 and 54; the provision for the registration of members' communal affiliation may also have provided the model for that aspect of the Good Friday Agreement.

[17] *Report of the New Ireland Forum* (Stationery Office, Dublin, 1984).

Northern Ireland' so as to accord equal validity to the two traditions there and thus to reflect the reality of their divided allegiances (para 8.1). The precise mechanisms by which joint authority might be exercised, however, were not discussed in any detail, though some possibilities had been explored in a number of preparatory studies commissioned for the Forum. What appears to have been envisaged was a more or less permanent system of joint direct rule with a number of ministers representing the British and Irish governments, though there was a suggestion that some powers might be devolved to an elected assembly. But this idea does not appear to have been seriously pursued during the negotiations leading up to the Anglo–Irish Agreement in the following year, though some commentators have argued that the right of consultation granted to the Irish government under the Agreement was in effect a first step towards a form of joint authority.

Since the New Ireland Forum Report a number of different models of joint authority designed to make it more democratic have been proposed. In 1984 the Kilbrandon Inquiry, an unofficial all-party body set up to make a considered British response to the Forum Report, suggested that Northern Ireland should be governed by a five-person executive composed of three ministers directly elected within Northern Ireland and two appointed by the British and Irish governments respectively.[18] It was argued that this would provide both the essential element of direct responsibility to the electorate and an effective guarantee against majority decisions either on legislation or executive action which would threaten the interests of either community. The two members who would be likely to be elected by unionists would require the support of at least one of the governmental appointees before they could push through any policy opposed by the representative of Northern Ireland nationalists and conversely the nationalist member and the Irish government's appointee would require the support of the British appointee before they could push through a policy opposed by the unionists. The Kilbrandon Report also suggested more tentatively that the power to legislate for Northern Ireland might likewise be shared by an inter-parliamentary body with representatives from the British House of Commons, the Irish Dail and from an elected Northern Ireland Assembly. The financial arrangements under which the structures might operate, however, were not discussed in any depth.

A further development of this model was proposed by the SDLP during the discussion of internal structures in 'Strand 1' of the talks process in 1992, apparently with some encouragement and assistance from the Irish Department of Foreign Affairs. This version envisaged that there would be a governing executive of six members, three elected in Northern Ireland, one each appointed by the British and Irish governments and a sixth member appointed by the European Commission. The direct involvement of a European representative was intended not only to reflect Northern Ireland's

---

[18] *Northern Ireland: Report of an Independent Inquiry* (London, 1984).

status as a distinctive region within an increasingly integrated Europe and the increasing shift of financial support for Northern Ireland from Britain to Europe, but also to defuse any strains which might arise within an exclusively British–Irish structure of the kind proposed by the Kilbrandon Commission. It is not known whether this idea was discussed with or encouraged by officials within the European Commission. But no European Union institution currently has the competence to undertake any direct role in the government of any part of the Union and there are too many other regions with similar problems to those in Northern Ireland for the member states to wish to create a precedent of this kind. French and Spanish concerns over the implications for Corsica and the Basque country, for example, would probably be sufficient to block any such proposal.

The most recent and fully developed version of this approach is the proposal for 'shared authority' developed by the Institute of Public Policy Research in close association with some members of the British Labour Party.[19] This envisaged that Northern Ireland would be governed by a five-member Shared Authority Council, similar to that proposed by the Kilbrandon Report, with both executive and legislative powers. In both respects its work would be subject to scrutiny by committees of an elected Northern Ireland Assembly which could also propose legislation. The Royal Ulster Constabulary would be absorbed into a new Northern Ireland Police Service with additional officers seconded from British police forces and the Irish Gardai. But any Irish financial contribution would be proportional to its population or gross national product in comparison with the UK. These new structures would then be entrenched into a constitution which could be amended only by a two-thirds majority in a referendum of all Northern Ireland voters, thus providing a stronger guarantee to either community than the current simple majority required for a change in constitutional status.

All these forms of externally shared authority would probably be workable if the co-operation of all concerned could be secured. They would provide clear institutional recognition of the dual identities and allegiances of the unionist and nationalist communities in relation to the UK and the Republic of Ireland. They would also provide some protection against breakdown in the not unlikely event of disagreement between elected unionist and nationalist representatives or a boycott by either, since the governmental representatives could maintain the processes of government without them. The major drawback is that they would be essentially undemocratic. One of the major advances made in the Good Friday Agreement is precisely that it has not been thought necessary to incorporate any elements of joint authority in the new structures for the government of Northern Ireland. In the event of a collapse of the structures which the Agreement provides for, however, these ideas will undoubtedly re-emerge.

---

[19] Brendan O'Leary et al, *Northern Ireland: Sharing Authority* (Institute of Public Policy Research, 1993).

BRITISH–IRISH CO-OPERATION ON COMMUNAL ACCOMMODATION

It is significant that none of these various forms of joint authority were seriously pursued in the succession of joint initiatives by the British and Irish governments since the early 1980s. Both governments have consistently rejected the concept and have sought instead to develop structures for inter-governmental co-operation within which representatives of both communities in Northern Ireland might be able to agree on some form of shared responsibility for their own affairs.

The shift in policy from a search for an essentially internal settlement to one which gave a direct role to the Irish government began in 1981 with a series of joint inter-governmental studies. It was apparently interrupted by the proceedings of the New Ireland Forum which was established in Dublin in 1983 by the main nationalist parties, excluding Sinn Fein, in both parts of Ireland. But though the Forum Report in 1984 analysed only three options – a united Ireland, a federal Ireland and joint authority over Northern Ireland by the Republic and the UK – the realities and requirements identified in it pointed to a less radical approach which eventually emerged as the Anglo-Irish Agreement of 1985.[20]

The Anglo-Irish Agreement

The Anglo-Irish Agreement as a formal international treaty provided the basic framework for both governments in respect of Northern Ireland throughout the lengthy talks process. It contained four principal elements. The first was a reiteration of the consent principle in a joint declaration that 'any change in the status of Northern Ireland would only come about with the consent of a majority of the people of Northern Ireland'; this was linked to an undertaking by the British government to give effect to the unification of Ireland if and when a majority of the people of Northern Ireland formally consent to it. The second was the creation of an inter-governmental ministerial conference, jointly chaired by British and Irish ministers and backed by a permanent secretariat at Maryfield in Belfast, with the primary task of seeking agreement on measures which would recognise and accommodate the interests of the two communities in Northern Ireland; the continuing sovereignty of each government within its sphere of responsibility was nonetheless reserved. The third was agreement on a policy of devolving power to a Northern Ireland administration provided it secured the co-operation of representatives of both communities. And the fourth was agreement that cross-border co-operation on security and economic and social matters should be continued and enhanced.

[20] For a detailed analysis, see Tom Hadden and Kevin Boyle, *The Anglo-Irish Agreement: A Commentary* (London: Sweet & Maxwell, 1989).

The Downing Street Declaration

These basic principles have been reiterated and developed in all subsequent joint policy statements by the two governments. In the Downing Street Declaration of December 1993 the main emphasis was on those aspects of the Agreement which might assist Sinn Fein and the IRA to agree a ceasefire. The British government therefore included a statement to the effect that it has 'no selfish strategic or economic interest in Northern Ireland' and that 'it is for the people of the island of Ireland alone, by agreement between the two parts respectively, to exercise their right to self-determination on the basis of consent, freely and concurrently given, North and South, to bring about a united Ireland, if that is their wish'. The Irish government reiterated the consent principle in a stronger form, namely that 'the democratic right of self-determination by the people of Ireland as a whole must be exercised subject to the agreement and consent of a majority of the people of Northern Ireland'.

The Framework Documents

The most detailed statement of the approach of the two governments was in the Joint Framework Documents finally agreed in February 1995, almost six months after the IRA and Loyalist ceasefires in the autumn of 1994. This reiterated the desire of both governments to promote the maximum measure of democratic self-government within Northern Ireland and to limit the extent of external joint authority to appropriate guarantees of the rights of members of both communities.

The proposed framework for internal government was an elected assembly to oversee the administration of Northern Ireland departments through a system of departmental committees, whose heads would be allocated on a proportional basis among all the parties. The assembly was also to have legislative powers on devolved matters, subject to a series of weighted majority requirements and blocking mechanisms in respect of controversial issues. The Framework Documents also included a proposal for the operations of the assembly and its committees to be overseen by a powerful triumvirate, a panel of three directly elected politicians with powers to nominate the committee heads, subject to approval by the assembly, to veto or refer for judicial consideration legislation which might be discriminatory or ultra vires, and to control the allocation of financial resources between departments. But in using these powers members of the panel, two of whom who would be likely to represent a unionist and one a nationalist perspective, would have to act by consensus. Finally there were to be continuing constitutional guarantees against discriminatory legislation or executive action.

The proposals for North/South relations were centred on a single North/South body, or council of ministers, composed of the heads of departmental committees from the Northern Ireland assembly and ministers from the

Irish government. This body was to have either consultative, harmonising or executive powers on a range of matters to be agreed and was to act either directly or by the creation of subordinate executive agencies. The areas in which it was suggested that the body might have executive powers included matters with a natural or physical all-Ireland framework such as transport, foreign promotional activities in tourism and industrial development and the administration of cross-border European Union programmes. The suggested areas for harmonisation included agriculture and fisheries, economic policy, education, energy, health and social services, industrial development and trade, though the examples given were of relatively non-controversial issues such as cross-border co-operation in accident and emergency services and the mutual recognition of teacher qualifications. There was also to be a parliamentary tier to oversee the operation of the new structures.

The constitutional proposals centred on the reformulation of Articles 2 and 3 of the Irish Constitution and of s 75 of the Government of Ireland Act 1920 to reflect the full acceptance of the principle of self-determination for the people of Northern Ireland and to withdraw any territorial claim by the Republic of Ireland over Northern Ireland, while preserving the existing birthright of all people in Ireland to be part of the Irish nation. It was also proposed that democratic representatives in both parts of Ireland should be encouraged to adopt a common charter or covenant which would protect the fundamental rights of everyone living in Ireland and of both main traditions in such a way that the guarantees would remain in force in the event of any future moves towards Irish unification.

The proposals for the relationship between the British and Irish governments envisaged the continuation and development of the arrangements under the Anglo-Irish Agreement of 1985, which was to be replaced by a new formal inter-governmental treaty. The Anglo-Irish Inter-governmental Conference was to continue its consultative role on all matters not devolved to the new Northern Ireland institutions; in addition it was to supervise the operation of these new institutions with power on either side to propose amendments or specific remedial action, subject to the continuing sovereignty of both the British and Irish governments over their respective jurisdictions.

WHAT REMAINS TO BE DONE

The Good Friday Agreement, as has been seen, follows closely many of the proposals in the Framework Documents. There are four major differences. The first is the addition of the proposed 'Council of the Isles' to balance the proposed North/South institutions and thus to emphasise the continuing inter-relationships of all the peoples of the British–Irish Isles. The second is the considerable extension of the provisions for the protection of individual and communal rights, which may be attributed to the fact that it was a

Conservative government strongly opposed to the entrenched protection of human rights which negotiated the Framework Documents. The third is the omission of the proposed triumvirate, which was in any event likely to prove unworkable: a provision to give a general power of veto to any one of three directly elected leaders, one of whom was almost certain to be an opponent of any settlement, was not a very sensible idea. The fourth is the omission of any explicit provision for direct intervention by the two governments to supplement or overrule the decisions of the new Northern Ireland Assembly or administration.

It does not follow that there is no continuing role for the British and Irish governments in implementing and protecting the Agreement. To begin with there is an obvious need to give political support to those parties in Northern Ireland which have committed themselves to making the Agreement work and to prevent a minority of opponents from making it unworkable. There is also an obligation on both governments to ensure that all aspects of the new constitutional regime in Northern Ireland meet the requirements imposed by international law on all state governments. The most significant of these is the protection of internationally recognised individual and communal rights and of the right of self-determination. Finally there is a need to ensure that the new structures provide a lasting constitutional settlement which can survive a gradual change in the balance between the two main communities in Northern Ireland. The risk of a resumption of communal conflict would be greatly increased if the carefully constructed package of measures contained in the Agreement had to be abandoned and replaced by a totally different set of arrangements if nationalists were to achieve a small majority over unionists in the foreseeable future. The underlying need for special constitutional arrangements for a place like Northern Ireland in which there are two roughly equal communities will remain whatever the precise balance in voting power between them.

INTERNATIONAL OBLIGATIONS

The primary duty on every state is to ensure the enjoyment of fundamental human rights to all those within its jurisdiction. The UK is already bound in respect of Northern Ireland, notably under the European Convention on Human Rights and the International Covenant on Civil and Political Rights. So too is the Republic of Ireland in respect of its territory. Though there is no formal bar on joint responsibility in this respect, the practical difficulties in isolating responsibility and ensuring compliance may be one of the factors which have discouraged the two governments from pursuing the joint authority option. A better method of proceeding in this respect is for both governments to incorporate the essential provisions of international human rights law into their respective domestic laws as a guarantee that these fundamental rights will be applied throughout the British–Irish Isles. The new Labour government is well on the way to achieving its commitment to incorporate the European Convention into British law. The Irish government has yet to make a parallel commitment. Though the report of an official review of the Irish Constitution[21] has recommended that the fundamental rights guaranteed in the Irish constitution should be rephrased where necessary to bring them into line with the Convention, there is no indication that this approach will be accepted or how long it would take to achieve. In the relevant section of the Good Friday Agreement the Irish government has undertaken only to reconsider the issue of incorporation. More resolute action on this issue is required. It would certainly be an inappropriate signal to those in Northern Ireland who fear that their fundamental rights might be adversely affected by any moves towards greater co-operation or ultimately unification with the rest of Ireland if the Republic were to be the only state in the European Union in which the rights guaranteed by the European Convention on Human Rights were not directly enforceable in national law.

Minority and communal rights

The incorporation of the European Convention is only an essential first step. The Good Friday Agreement recognises that in a divided society like Northern Ireland more will be required and that the first task of the new Northern Ireland Human Rights Commission will be to draw up a more comprehensive Bill of Rights for Northern Ireland. The basis for most of these 'add-on' individual and communal rights can be found in international instruments, such as the European Framework Convention on the Protection of National Minorities, the European Charter for Regional and Minority Languages and the United Nations Declaration on the Rights of Persons Belonging to National or Ethnic, Religious and Linguistic Minorities. But the choice of the precise form of words to be included in a new Northern Ireland Bill of Rights must be left for negotiation between the parties to the talks process. Only a few brief comments are required in this context. The first is that the Bill should contain an explicit right for all people in Northern Ireland to assert their Irish or British identity and citizenship without suffering any form of discrimination, so that the issue of national identity is clearly divorced from that of national territory. The second is that any formal protection of communal rights, notably in respect of state aid for Catholic, Protestant or Irish-speaking schools, should specifically protect the rights of those in either community or neither who prefer integration to separation, for example in the provision and funding of integrated schools. The third is that a new provision to guarantee parity of treatment or esteem for both main communities, and any extension of the existing prohibition of discrimination in

[21] *Report of the Constitution Review Group* (the Whitaker Report) (Stationery Office, Dublin, 1996).

legislation or other government action on the grounds of religious or political opinion, should expressly cover indirect as well as direct treatment or discrimination with appropriate exemptions for affirmative action programmes. The fourth is that any such constitutional protections should extend to Westminster legislation and governmental action as well as that of a Northern Ireland Assembly and government.

It must be remembered, however, that the primary obligation for the protection of individual and communal rights will remain with the British and Irish governments. Both the UK and the Republic of Ireland are already bound under the International Covenant on Civil and Political Rights to permit members of minorities to practise their religion, to speak their language and to enjoy their culture.[22] But this basic obligation has been greatly strengthened under the Copenhagen Document within the Organisation for Security and Co-operation in Europe (OSCE)[23] and the new European Framework Convention on the Protection of National Minorities, which impose an obligation on participating states to protect minorities from assimilation, to take positive measures to protect their languages and cultures and to grant them some measure of control over their own affairs. The UK has recently ratified the European Framework Convention, and the Irish Republic has undertaken to do so. Both must ensure that any new Bill of Rights for Northern Ireland, and any equivalent protections in the Irish Republic, comply fully with these international standards.

The Copenhagen Document and the European Framework Convention also give support to the protection of minorities through bilateral arrangements between neighbouring states. The Anglo-Irish Agreement of 1985 can be seen as a forerunner to these provisions in that it gave a significant role to the Irish government in the protection of the Catholic/nationalist minority in Northern Ireland. But it must be remembered that obligations of this kind are reciprocal and that in the event of any change in the constitutional status of Northern Ireland there would be corresponding obligations on the Irish government to accept continuing British involvement in the protection of the Protestant/British minority in a united Ireland, if that is their wish.

Self-determination

The second major obligation under international law which has a direct impact on the legitimacy of any settlement in Northern Ireland is the right of peoples to self-determination. As has been seen, conflicting interpretations of this concept were built into the Northern Ireland Constitution Act 1973, which granted the right to the people of Northern Ireland, and the Irish Constitution which granted it to the Irish nation. Since Sinn Fein and the

---

[22] Article 27.
[23] Document of the Copenhagen Meeting of the Conference on Security and Co-operation in Europe (1990), paras 30–40.

IRA based the legitimacy of their political and military campaigns on the claim that the right of self-determination by the Irish people was denied by partition, the issue is clearly of crucial significance and requires some further clarification.

In historical terms the principle of self-determination has long been accepted in both British and Irish law. The Anglo-Irish Treaty of 1921 made provision not only for the adoption of a new constitution for the Irish Free State by its elected representatives but also for the elected representatives of the six Northern counties in the newly created Northern Ireland Parliament to vote to remain in the UK. Self-determination for Northern Ireland was then given a formal statutory basis in British law in the Ireland Act 1949, when the Republic finally cut all ties with the UK. This formally 'declared and affirmed the constitutional position and the territorial integrity of Northern Ireland' and provided in s 1(2) that in no event would Northern Ireland, or any part thereof, cease to be part of his Majesty's dominions without the consent of the Parliament of Northern Ireland. When the Northern Ireland Parliament was abolished under the Northern Ireland Constitution Act 1973 this was replaced by an assertion of the right of the people of Northern Ireland to self-determination:

'It is hereby declared that Northern Ireland remains part of her Majesty's dominions and of the United Kingdom and it is affirmed that in no event will Northern Ireland or any part of it cease to be part of her Majesty's dominions and of the United Kingdom without the consent of the majority of the people of Northern Ireland voting in a poll held for the purposes of this section in accordance with Schedule 1 to this Act.' (s 1)

The Irish Constitution of 1937 also explicitly asserted a right of self-determination for the Irish nation:

'The Irish nation hereby affirms its inalienable, indefeasible and sovereign right to choose its own form of government, to determine its relations with other nations and to develop its life, political, economic and cultural, in accordance with its own genius and traditions.' (Article 1)

This was remarkably close to the formula eventually adopted in the United Nations Covenants in 1966. But the precise extent of the 'Irish nation' was unclear. If it is accepted that a right of self-determination can in practice only be exercised by the people of a defined territory, the meaning is dependent on the contentious provisions of Articles 2 and 3 which, as explained above, asserted and then in practice withdrew a claim that the national territory is the whole island of Ireland.

There is no clear definition in international law of what constitutes a people for this purpose and political considerations are clearly relevant to each individual case. But there is almost universal consensus that the right of self-determination can properly be granted only to the people of a well-defined territory. In Ireland the unresolved question was what was the relevant territory. The eventual resolution in the Good Friday Agreement began in the series of inter-governmental agreements and joint documents outlined above in which the British and Irish governments repeatedly stated that in practice it was the consent of the people of Northern Ireland that mattered. The formulation in the Downing Street Declaration was particularly to the point, though the precise form of words was clearly chosen to avoid any potential conflict with the provisions of the Irish Constitution: 'the democratic right of self-determination by the people of Ireland as a whole must be exercised subject to the agreement and consent of the people of Northern Ireland'.

It has been a major achievement of political debate and governmental negotiation over the years of the conflict that the consent principle, that Northern Ireland's population has a right to self-determination with respect to any change in its constitutional status, has at last been recognised, albeit on a conditional basis, under the Good Friday Agreement. The revised version of Articles 2 and 3 of the Irish Constitution, which will come into effect on the implementation of the remainder of the Agreement, clearly separate the right to be part of the Irish nation from the right of self-determination for both jurisdictions:

'It is the entitlement and birthright of every person born in the island of Ireland, which includes its islands and seas, to be part of the Irish nation . . .' (Article 2)

'It is the firm will of the Irish nation, in harmony and friendship, to unite all the people who share the territory of the island of Ireland, in all the diversity of their identities and traditions, recognising that a united Ireland shall be brought about only by peaceful means with the consent of a majority of the people, democratically expressed, in both jurisdictions in the island . . .' (Article 3)

It has also been a major achievement that the right of the population of the Republic to endorse in a referendum those parts of the Good Friday Agreement which involved a change in the Irish Constitution was recognised as an integral part of the approval of the Agreement.[24] There is little doubt that joint referendums of this kind would be accepted in international law as a legitimate exercise of the right of self-determination, if the issue were raised before the International Court of Justice.

One essential element in any new Northern Ireland constitution must therefore be a clear statement in identical terms in the fundamental laws of the UK of these principles of self-determination and consent. It would also be desirable for the terms of this new constitution and of a Northern Ireland Bill of Rights to be approved by a further referendum. This would fulfil

---

[24] The conditional amendments to the Irish Constitution were approved by a 95 per cent majority on the same day that the Agreement was approved by 71 per cent of those who voted in the referendum in Northern Ireland.

several important functions. It would finally remove the constitutional conflict which has bedevilled all attempts to reach a settlement in the past. It would emphasise the separate status of the new Northern Ireland constitution and protect it in legal theory from subsequent unilateral repeal by the British Parliament. And it would of course provide essential political legitimacy for the new arrangements. The idea that new constitutional arrangements must be approved by referendum of the people concerned has already been accepted for the UK as a whole in respect of membership of the European Union and also in respect of devolution for Scotland and Wales. This precedent should clearly be followed in respect of any new constitution for Northern Ireland.

A final and closely related consideration which deserves a brief mention in this context is the general principle of international law that no state may unilaterally exclude any of its citizens or any part of its territory without the consent of a majority of its people. Though there is no formal international convention to this effect, the principle has been given general international support in respect of South Africa's policy under the apartheid regime of disenfranchising large numbers of blacks by allocating them to supposedly independent homelands and the periodic attempts by Israel to exclude individual and groups of Palestinians from the Occupied Territories. It follows that it would be contrary to international law for any British government to attempt to hand over the territory of Northern Ireland to the Irish Republic, however awkward a problem its people may pose, without a valid act of self-determination by the people of Northern Ireland.

CREATING A LASTING CONSTITUTIONAL FRAMEWORK

The underlying objective of the Good Friday Agreement is to create a constitutional status and system of government for Northern Ireland which will recognise and accommodate the aspirations and identities of both major communities within these general principles of international law. To ensure lasting stability, however, it must provide assurance to both communities as the balance of population between them becomes more equal. A constitution which depends for its survival on one or two percentage points in voting power and is liable to be replaced by something completely different if nationalists become a majority is unlikely to provide the peace and stability which almost everyone in Northern Ireland wants. Experience in other divided societies suggests on the contrary that a transition of this kind might well lead to further conflict and violence. A change in the balance of voting power in Northern Ireland would not alter the fact that it is a territory in which there are two major communities in rough equality each of which must be recognised and accommodated under any constitutional regime. On this basis a new constitution for Northern Ireland as a distinctive unit of government should in so far as is possible provide for the same internal structures, the same fundamental guarantees to both communities and similar links with both the UK and the Republic of Ireland whether it remains part of the UK or becomes part of the Republic. In either case it might also be granted special regional status within the European Union.

The best starting point for a settlement of this kind would be a measure of separate constitutional status for Northern Ireland which would be protected within the UK from the supposedly absolute sovereignty of the Westminster Parliament and within the Republic of Ireland from constitutional amendment by a simple majority of the Irish people. In formal terms such a status might, as in Scotland, be derived from the Acts of Union.

The Scottish Acts of Union were passed in 1707 by both the Scottish and the English Parliaments and conferred their existing powers on the new joint Parliament at Westminster. But there were some important reservations, notably in respect of the Scottish legal system and the position of the Church of Scotland. The Scottish view of these guarantees, as explained in the case of *MacCormick v Lord Advocate*,[25] is that they are firmly entrenched by the constitutional settlement of 1707 and that any attempt by the Westminster Parliament to pass legislation which infringed them would be invalid and of no effect. Though the issue has never been openly tested, there can be little doubt that in the current political climate in Scotland any attempt by the Westminster Parliament to assert its absolute sovereignty by overriding the entrenched provisions of the Scottish Acts of Union would provoke a serious constitutional crisis. To that extent the Acts clearly form part of the UK's constitution and the doctrine of the absolute sovereignty of Parliament is unsound.

A similar argument can be based on the Irish Acts of Union of 1800. These also include some fundamental provisions, the most important of which is the union itself, which it is arguably beyond the powers of the UK Parliament to override. This issue was raised as one of the arguments against the validity of the Anglo-Irish Agreement in the proceedings for judicial review initiated by the Ulster Unionist Party in 1986.[26] Though the case was rejected on other grounds, the underlying argument as to the status of the guarantee under the Acts of Union was left open. The Good Friday Agreement likewise leaves the issue open. It explicitly commits the British government to the repeal of the remaining provisions of the Government of Ireland Act 1920, notably the provision of s 75 which states that 'notwithstanding anything contained in this Act, the supreme authority of the Parliament of the United Kingdom shall remain unaffected and undiminished over all persons, matters and things in [Northern Ireland] and every part thereof'.

[25] [1953] SC 396; the case was concerned with a challenge to the legitimacy of conferring the title 'Queen Elizabeth II' on the new Queen in 1952, but was decided on other grounds.
[26] *Ex parte Molyneaux* [1986] 1 WLR 331; for a more detailed analysis of the continuing impact of the Acts of Union see Brigid Hadfield, 'Learning From the Indians: The Constitutional Guarantee Revisited' (1983) *Public Law* 351–356.

But there is no mention of the Acts of Union and if the Scottish analogy is correct any purported repeal would in any event be invalid.

Though the formal legal validity of these arguments is clearly unresolved, they provide a useful reminder of the continuing separate status of Scotland and Northern Ireland, and perhaps also of Wales, in British constitutional law. This has clearly been given greater current legitimacy by the referendums of the Scottish and Welsh peoples on devolution and of the people of Northern Ireland on the Good Friday Agreement. It would be entirely appropriate for the same practice to be continued by a provision that any substantive amendment of a new Northern Ireland Constitution Act and a Northern Ireland Bill of Rights would also require the approval of the Northern Ireland people.

CONCLUSION

The purpose of this chapter has not been to discuss the very difficult problems which undoubtedly face the new Labour government in ensuring that the provisions of the Good Friday Agreement are fully implemented and protected against the kind of organised disruption which brought down the structures provided for in the Sunningdale Agreement in 1974. It has been to set out and discuss some of the underlying political realities and constitutional principles which must be faced in any lasting settlement in Northern Ireland.

The first of these is that the past 30 years of conflict in Northern Ireland have at huge cost clarified some fundamental issues. The most important is that the identities, interests and aspirations of both major communities must be accommodated and reflected in any lasting settlement. The Good Friday Agreement is a significant first step towards this objective. But it must also be stressed that any new structures for the government of Northern Ireland must be able to survive a gradual change towards greater equality in voting power between unionists and nationalists without triggering renewed violence on either side. There would be little point, as has been explained, in establishing the complex structures proposed in the Agreement only to abandon them for something completely different if nationalists were to become a majority, since that would in itself be likely to increase communal antagonism and set the scene for renewed paramilitary action. It would be a perverse interpretation of the Agreement, though it is one which has been adopted by some republicans, that it is merely a transitional stage to the transfer of exclusive state sovereignty over the territory and people of Northern Ireland from the UK to the Irish Republic. The implication of this is that any arrangements for co-operation between the two governments under the Agreement should be regarded as reciprocal in the sense that any role for the Irish government in protecting the interests of nationalists in Northern Ireland while it remains part of the UK should, if unionists so wish, be paralleled by an equivalent role for the British government in protecting the interests of unionists if Northern Ireland should become part of a united Ireland.

The second is that the Agreement has developed some novel and welcome principles of democracy – that structures designed on the basis of proportionality and consensus can be combined with those based on simple majority rule. It is ironic that these new ideas should have been developed in Northern Ireland with its long history of political intransigence and the abuse of majority power. And it remains to be seen whether they can be made to work in such an unpromising environment. Now that the idea that election systems should be based on some form of proportional representation is gaining ground in the rest of the UK, however, it may be that the structures negotiated in the Good Friday Agreement can provide useful food for thought on how the principle of proportionality can be extended to governmental decision-making. In that sense the Agreement is relevant not just for other deeply divided societies, but for all jurisdictions in which one party rule is either impractical or no longer acceptable.

The third and wider implication of the Agreement is in respect of the relationships between all the constituent parts of the UK and the Irish Republic. The establishment of the new British–Irish Council – the Council of the Isles – should not be regarded merely as a sop to unionists, but as a significant constitutional development within the UK as well as between the two parts of Ireland. The programme of constitutional reform which the new Labour government has embarked upon should not in its turn be regarded only as an exercise in administrative devolution, but as a long-overdue recognition of the need for new institutions, similar to those which are being developed in Europe as a whole, to reflect the diversity and traditions of all the peoples of the British–Irish Isles.

Further reading

The Good Friday Agreement (London: HMSO, Cm 3883, 1998)

Kevin Boyle and Tom Hadden, *Northern Ireland – The Choice* (London: Penguin, 1994)

Kevin Boyle, Colm Campbell and Tom Hadden, *The Protection of Human Rights in the Context of Peace and Reconciliation in Ireland*, Forum for Peace and Reconciliation, (Dublin: Stationery Office, 1996)

B Hadfield (ed), *Northern Ireland: Politics and the Constitution* (Milton Keynes: Open University Press, 1992)

Institute of Public Policy Research, *Northern Ireland: Sharing Authority* (London, 1993)

John McGarry and Brendan O'Leary, *Explaining Northern Ireland: Broken Images* (Oxford: Blackwell, 1995)

CHAPTER 15

LOCAL AUTHORITIES

Professor Ian Loveland (Brunel University)

In 1989, I addressed a conference in the USA on homelessness, then a very visible social problem on America's political landscape. My brief was to explain why, given that Britain had a national 'Homeless Persons Act', there were so many homeless people sleeping on the streets of our major cities. I began at what initially seemed something of a tangent:

'Suppose the Republicans win a bare Congressional majority in the 1990 mid-term elections. And suppose Mario Cuomo subsequently declares he will run for President in 1992. He campaigns on a New Deal ideology, implements such policies at State level and thereby advertises them to the entire country. Bush and the Republican Congress fear that Cuomo's plan may become sufficiently popular to win him the Presidency and gain the Democrats control of Congress. So Congress passes legislation cutting federal subsidies for New York's welfare programmes. But popular support for Cuomo's ideas remains firm. New Yorkers vote to fund the programme by increasing State taxes. Congress then passes an Act limiting the amount of tax New York's legislature can raise. Cuomo takes his ideas to the public through advertising campaigns and media appearances. Congress then tries to neuter his message by abolishing New York as a State. Cuomo is sacked; the State legislature disbanded. The task of governing New York is given to boards of Republican politicians appointed by the President. Congress tells New Yorkers to be grateful for this; they have been saved both from the horrors of social democratic government and from their own gullibility.'

This scenario would be a manifest impossibility in the USA. The USA's federal constitutional structure protects the existence and powers of the states, many of which have populations smaller than Greater London, from the ideological intolerance of whichever political party temporarily controls the Congress and/or the Presidency.[1] But the scenario was, I suggested, a fair if crude characterisation of the fate of sub-central government in Britain since

---

[1] James Madison's *Federalist No.10* remains the most eloquent and forceful exposition of the federal rationale.

1979. Britain's growing homeless population, I argued to my American audience, was in large part the consequence of the inability of our sub-central elected government to pursue economic policies which mitigated the nationwide rise in unemployment and to build new housing for the growing number of people who could not afford private sector accommodation.[2] This inability was in turn the result of the Thatcher governments' refusal to permit any governmental bodies in Britain to adopt Keynesian economic and social policies, a refusal to which, because of the unlimited sovereignty of Parliament, the government was able to give unlimited legal effect. In this constitutional context, the government's retention of what was initially conceived as a paradigmatically social democratic legislative initiative[3] was a profound deceit: the councils on whom the duty to house homeless people lay were denied the power to mobilise the economic resources necessary to discharge their responsibilities. That a local electorate might wish to shoulder the tax burden required to tackle homelessness effectively was an irrelevance; voters were simply not permitted to vote for higher taxes.

The sequence of Bills which the Thatcher and Major administrations were able to convince Parliament to enact to achieve this state of affairs is sufficiently familiar to require no more than the barest restatement here. The Local Government Planning and Land Act 1980 which clawed back central government subsidies from councils who overspent DoE imposed targets; the Housing Act 1980 which required the sale of council houses at absurdly low prices; the Rates Act 1984 which imposed ratecapping; the Local Government Act 1985 which abolished the Labour controlled GLC and metropolitan county councils; the Education Reform (sic) Acts which permitted schools to opt out of local authority control; the Housing Act 1988 which did the same in respect of council housing; and the Local Government Finance Act 1988 which introduced the poll tax. It is perhaps a pleasing irony that it was the grossly regressive nature of the poll tax that triggered Thatcher's own fall from power.[4] But her governments' onslaught on local political autonomy outlived her passing – and was indeed continued apace by the Major administrations.

From an American perspective, this constitutional context was at the very least bizarre. At most, it was a quintessentially anti-democratic phenomenon, particularly when one considered that voting patterns in the 1979, 1983 and 1987 general elections revealed that the Conservative, Labour and Liberal parties enjoyed markedly divergent levels of popular support in different parts of the country. As a matter of its people's political preferences, modern Britain was then (and remains) in geographical terms a constantly pluralist

---

[2] I Loveland, 'Governmental Responses to Homelesness in Britain: legal rights and political realities' (1991) *Law and Social Inquiry* 249–319.

[3] On the origins of the homelessness legislation see I Loveland, *Housing Homeless Persons* (London: Oxford University Press, 1995) Ch 3.

[4] See D Butler, A. Travers and A Adonis, *Failure in British Government: The Politics of the Poll Tax* (London: Oxford University Press, 1995).

society. But that pluralism is given only the most grudging and limited expression as a matter of constitutional law.

The core value of the US constitution – the geographical separation of powers inherent in a federalist societal structure in which sub-central, elected government bodies wield substantial political and economic authority – would of course permit such psephological diversity to be translated into an effective form of political pluralism. The election of Reagan and a Republican-controlled Congress were of far less import to the centre and centre-left of American politics than were the electoral successes of Thatcher and Major in Britain to the Labour and Liberal parties. In the USA, the proponents of such beliefs could still make a substantial difference to the laws under which they lived by winning power in their home states. In Britain, all they could do was hang on in the seemingly ever more desperate hope that a Labour or Liberal/Labour government might eventually win power at the national level.

That hope has now been realised. But it is not yet clear that this hope can sensibly be coupled with an expectation that the new government will invite Parliament to undo all of the many wrongs wrought on British local government by the Thatcher and Major administrations. Still less can we expect that the way in which governmental power is 'separated' on a geographical basis will be subjected to radical constitutional reform. This is not simply because in certain respects New Labour seems to have adopted policy positions towards local government which retain rather than reverse innovations implemented by its Conservative predecessors. It is also because, more fundamentally, New Labour, Old Labour and Conservatism of all tints and hues – indeed British political discourse in general – have been infected by a perniciously debilitating perception of the primary constitutional function that elected sub-central government should perform in a modern democratic country inhabited by 60 million people.

POLITICAL PLURALISM IN PRINCIPLE AND PRACTICE

'Over-centralisation of government and lack of accountability was a problem in governments of both left and right. Labour is committed to the democratic renewal of our country through decentralisation and the elimination of excessive government secrecy.'[5]

There are potentially two ways to view the role of elected sub-central government bodies in a unitary state. The first, which has enjoyed little currency in modern Britain, is to see them primarily as a counterweight to or restraint upon the power of central government. Canada between 1931 and 1980 offered the best example of this philosophy in practice. Canada was arguably

[5] Labour Party manifesto 1997, p 4 (see Appendix 3 below).

not in that period a federal state in the legal sense, but as a matter of convention its constitution recognised that the substantial legal powers wielded by its provincial governments could not be reduced without the consent of the provincial governments themselves.[6] This conventional underpinning of a federalist constitutional ethos had arisen not simply to accommodate the French-speaking Canadians concentrated in Quebec, but in recognition that the constant expression and implementation of divergent political philosophies on matters of substantial importance was per se an invaluable principle of constitutional morality.

The dominant British view of elected sub-central government has, in contrast, seen it as a vehicle for facilitating participation by the citizenry qua collectivity in small localities in the making of micro-level governmental decisions.[7] In more recent years, the thrust of Conservative government policy towards the decentralisation of political power has been to go far beyond reducing the first tier of sub-central government to the level of participatory micro-collectives. The structure of 'local' governance has been recast in a form which redefines 'collective' interests in two ways. First, collectivities are increasingly fashioned to address single issue rather than multi-functional policy questions: the school and public housing opt-out provisions are the clearest examples of this. Secondly, relatedly, the size of the collectivity is reduced almost to vanishing point: the parents at a single school, or the tenants of a single housing estate become the first tier of sub-central 'government'.[8]

As such, they lie in constitutional terms somewhere between an absurdity and an obscenity. They cannot possibly offer a vehicle for the mobilisation of a political ideology which can effectively question the policies pursued by central government through the simple but crucial device of offering citizens the opportunity to see alternative governmental programmes being put into practice. Every additional extension of this fragmentation and minimisation of the system of sub-central governance further insulates the party controlling central government from being held accountable to the informed consent of the electorate at large. To cast a vote for an opposition party in a national election increasingly becomes a speculative rather than deliberative venture; a leap into the political dark rather than another step along an already familiar governmental road; an article of faith rather than an exercise of judgment. Labour won the 1997 election not because the voters had a good idea of how it will govern in practice, but because they took a chance in believing that

---

[6] See C Turpin, *British Government and the Constitution* (London: Butterworths, 3rd ed, 1995) pp 25–29, 93–102; I Loveland, *Constitutional Law* (London: Butterworths, 1996) pp 377–384.

[7] See J Sharpe's classic article 'Theories and Values of Local Government' (1971) 18 *Political Studies* 154–169.

[8] The weight of academic analysis of the trend is now enormous. Among legal commentators, Martin Loughlin offers the most influential and stimulating critiques; see especially M Loughlin, 'The Restructuring of Central–Local Government Legal Relations' (1995) *Local Government Studies* 59–75; *Local Government in the Modern State* (London: Sweet & Maxwell, 1986); 'The Restructuring of Central–Local Government Relations', in J Jowell and D Oliver (eds), *The Changing Constitution* (London: Oxford University Press, 3rd ed, 1995).

– whatever Labour does – it could not possibly do any worse than a third Major government. The politics of hope have been intertwined with the politics of ignorance. This might be thought an unfortunate combination for the electorate of a supposedly mature democratic society.

One need not look very hard, nor very far, to find forceful illustrations of the principle that large and powerful units of sub-central government provide in some senses an effectively co-equal alternative to the national legislature and executive. The USA offers the most obvious example. Roosevelt, Carter, Reagan and Clinton all launched their successful campaigns for the Presidency from a base in state government; none of them had previously held or even sought national political office. Present day Germany provides a similar example: both Gerhard Schröder and Oskar Lafontaine emerged as powerful national figures after launching their political careers in their respective Länder rather than the Bundestag. But this geographical separation of powers need not be the exclusive preserve of a federal state. One need only glance across the channel to see that Jacques Chirac's official identity when he ran for the French Presidency was as Mayor of Paris. London, of course, does not yet have a Mayor. But Manchester does, as does Birmingham, Bristol, Portsmouth, Newcastle et al. But, who, outside of the particular Mayor's council chamber even knows who these people are? As repositories of potential national political power, the offices are meaningless.

Richard Nixon responded to his defeat by Kennedy in the 1960 US Presidential elections by seeking the Governorship of California, a sub-central office which (had he won it) would have given him both substantial governmental power and a national political profile. Similarly Jacques Chirac found the mayoralty of Paris a more than adequate political home following his failed candidature for the French Presidency in 1989. Observers of the French election in 1997 could not but have failed to notice how many members of Jospin's new Cabinet held local government posts.[9] But it is of course quite absurd to think that John Major could have seen the leadership of Cambridgeshire County Council as a viable power base from which to rebuild the shattered body of the Conservative Party; or that Michael Portillo would regard the leadership of Westminster Council as a route to regain national political prominence. It is equally preposterous to think that control of Camden or Sheffield Council would provide the Labour left with the governmental opportunity to re-establish a radical social democratic governmental presence in a Blairite Britain.

This is one of the greatest weaknesses of the British constitutional system; that leading positions in even the largest of local authorities do no more than provide a stepping stone from which ambitious politicians can jump towards the *bottom* rung of the national governmental ladder. One can count on the fingers of one hand the 20th century politicians whose prominence on

---

[9] Martine Aubry, deputy Mayor of Lille and Dominique Strauss-Kahn, Mayor of Sarcelles being the most high profile examples.

the national stage was the direct result of their eminence in local government – Joseph Chamberlain and Herbert Morrison are the only real political heavyweights whose careers have followed that path since 1900.[10] British councils are at most a training ground, an apprenticeship, a sparring ring for the people who will much later in life become our nation's senior politicians. For many, they are not even that. Neither Tony Blair nor Gordon Brown ever served on a local authority. Robin Cook passed but three years in the early 1970s as a junior member of Edinburgh City Council. With the exception of David Blunkett and Jack Straw, none of the present Cabinet have any substantial local authority experience. None have occupied any governmental post for over ten years. In effect, local government is an irrelevance to the pursuit of national political office. And it has – indeed has always had – that unfortunate status primarily because the elected bodies in the first tier of British sub-central government have invariably been far too *small*.

THE SIZE AND STRUCTURE OF THE
LOCAL GOVERNMENT SECTOR

The number of local authorities in Britain has shrunk markedly since 1972, but some 400 or so councils remain. Their populations varying appreciably in size, but the crude average of the first tier of Britain's sub-central government sector is around 140,000 people. This is rather smaller than the crowd at the first Wembley FA cup final in 1923. In the USA, that crude average is some 5.5 million; in Canada it is approximately 2.8 million. The Americans and Canadians have concluded the first tier of sub-central elected government in their respective countries must represent very substantially sized electorates. If it did not do so, there would be little justification for its possession of significant political powers: to grant such powers to inumerable local councils would more likely be a recipe for anarchism than pluralism. Nor could it serve as a potential source of opposition to – and hence restraint on – central government.

The only forceful advocacy of structural reform to British local government along such radical pluralist lines in the modern era was offered by the Redcliffe–Maud Commission in the early 1970s. Redcliffe-Maud had proposed that local government in England be reorganised into just 58 authorities, with an average population of some three-quarters of a million people.[11] The proposal was rejected by the Heath government (and would no doubt have met a similar fate under a Wilson administration) when it became clear that many backbench MPs had been 'persuaded' by the local councils in their constituencies that so radical a reform would be unwelcome. The Local Government Act 1972 did indeed reduce the number of local councils from

---

[10] George Lansbury does not count as a heavyweight in this sense, since the Labour Party he led had no realistic chance of gaining national power.
[11] See I Loveland, *Constitutional Law*, Ch 10.

the insane figure of some 1,500 then in existence. But the retention of over 400 councils automatically precluded the grant to them of any substantial political authority.

The structural weaknesses militating against the grant of substantial powers to British local authorities are not solely a matter of councils' miniscule size. They also derive from their bizarre jurisdictions. The council which has exclusive control over all local authority functions carried out within its boundaries remains the exception rather than the rule within the British constitution. District councils and county councils may share parts of the same geographical space, but their functional boundaries are quite different. This not only produces confusion and a lack of transparency in the allocation of responsibilities, but also prompts frequent squabbles when a particular policy question can raise two or more legal questions, each of which is formally the responsibility of different local government bodies. The question of homelessness has been, and remains, a powerful illustration of this problem. In so far as homelessness is seen as a housing issue, it is the responsibility of district councils. In so far as it is a social services or child welfare issue, it is a matter for county councils. Only in the few metropolitian borough councils were all local authority functions the responsibility of one elected body.

The Redcliffe-Maud Commission had also assumed that its 58 councils would be unitary authorities – their functional and geographical boundaries would coincide. The stuttering drift towards unitary authorities based on expanded and merged district councils that was initiated by Michael Heseltine on his return to the Cabinet in 1990 was eventually sabotaged by lobbying by county councils. A few new unitary authorities have been created, but their numbers remain small and their average size remains tiny.[12]

Beyond making a commitment to re-establishing an elected council performing some rather loosely defined strategic role in respect of the governance of Greater London, the Labour government seems most unlikely to embrace arguments in favour of larger units of local government. It remains wedded to the notion that the key word in the local government couplet is *local* rather than *government*. The unfortunate constitutional fact which seems most apparent on a review of events of the past 20 years is that the notion of local government is increasingly oxymoronic: the more localised the allocation of political power, the less plausible it beomes to view the exercise of that power as an element of *government*. Rather, the task performed by opted out schools or opted out housing estates is one of *administration*: and administration, moreover, of central government's political preferences.

The Major and Thatcher governments grasped that point very firmly. They grasped equally firmly the need to present the policy – quite dishonestly – solely in terms of an immediate transfer of power from councils to local people. That long-term power was really being transferred from local government to

---

[12] See G Filkin and C Moor, 'Reflections on the Local Government Review' (1997) *Public Administration* 131–143.

central government through the simple expedient of removing potential sources of opposition to the Conservative party was never acknowledged. The more interesting – and alarming – question now is whether the Blair government's evident disinclination to depart radically from previous central government policy and practice is simply a continuation of the Thatcherite agenda, namely an exercise in constitutional mendacity, or is it rather indicative of a failure to see through the fog of right wing rhetoric obscuring the local government landscape, namely an exercise in constitutional myopia? Neither prospect is attractive, but the second is distinctly less unpalatable than the first.

A radical Labour policy would disinter the Redcliffe-Maud Commission's Report from its Whitehall grave and breathe new life into its shrunken bones and wasted flesh. But it might readily be argued that even 58 first-tier sub-central elected government bodies is probably too many: 20 or 30 would be quite enough. The Labour proposal for directly elected Mayors – of little significance given the present proliferation of miniscule councils – could assume considerable importance in such a radically restructured sub-central government context. Political power – and more importantly potential political power – might then have a meaningful existence throughout the country rather than just in Westminster. A Conservative or Liberal Mayor of a Greater London Council exercising all the local authority powers in the capital would offer a constant threat to a Labour-controlled central government, as would a Labour Mayor to a Conservative government.

The argument in favour of greatly reducing the number of first-tier sub-central elected government bodies need not of course be an argument against the principle of having very small, highly localised elected authorities in towns or rural areas. The argument rather is that it is constitutionally indefensible to make such bodies the first (and only tier) of sub-central government. If a powerful unit of sub-central government wishes to further sub-divide its own legal powers on a geographical basis, there is no obvious reason to prevent it from so doing. Matters of community politics and the localised administration of government services can perfectly sensibly be decided at a sub-central level. This is not just because sub-central politicians are likely to respond more sensitively to localised concerns than their Westminster equivalents. It is also because we would then be spared the overbearing arrogance of national politicians who assume either that they have found the 'right' answer to the question of how best to structure governmental institutions and divide governmental powers, or who conclude – doubting the correctness of their own preferences – that their temporary possession of a Commons majority gives them a moral as well as a legal authority to impose those views on everyone else.

The structure of the local government sector is the most important facet of its constitutional identity. For while there are so many councils, it is so much easier for central government (be it Labour or Conservative) to resist the suggestion that local electorates be afforded the power to choose authorities which will wield significant powers. The Labour government's protestation to be the party of the radical centre has little cogency in respect of local government while our first tier of non-central government continues to be composed of a multiplicity of local authorities ranging in size from the small to the microscopic.

As suggested above, this trait is hardly a unique feature of New Labour thinking: Old Labour was equally lacking in this pluralist – in effect quasi-federalist – constitutional vision. What might be expected however is that New Labour would either reverse or mitigate some of the more egregiously intolerant policies inflicted upon the local government sector since 1979. Those policies were generally given legal effect through legislation, but were occasionally imposed through the courts. But even when measured against this really rather modest constitutional yardstick, Labour's local government programme appears to be a rather sickly and stunted creature.

FISCAL AUTONOMY

'Although crude and universal council tax capping should go, we will retain reserve powers to control excessive council tax rises.'[13]

'Crude council capping should go, though as any government must, we will retain reserve powers in extreme cases.'[14]

It seems clear that the Labour government will not engage in the kind of underhand manipulation of the rules regulating central government's contributions to local authority budgets that characterised the behaviour of the Department of the Environment in the Thatcher and Major years. One hopes that Gordon Brown's commitment not to raise income taxes will not be financed even in part by a reduction in local authorities' grant revenue, as was the Major government's last 'tax-cutting' budget. One would similarly hope that the Labour government will remove the warped allocation criteria that have permitted the Tory 'flagships' of Wandsworth and Westminster to finance virtually all of their expenditure from central funds. But reform of the DoE grant allocation mechanisms comprises only a part of the local authority sector's financial equation.

Local councils have no meaningful fiscal autonomy in modern Britain. Electorates cannot volunteer to pay high taxes in order to fund extensive services. The capping of rates, of the poll tax and now of the council tax represent perhaps the most graphic examples of central government intolerance of localised manifestations of democratic pluralism.

The Blair administration has made it clear that it may slightly loosen the financial stranglehold imposed on local electorates by the Thatcher and Major governments, although cynical observers of a literalist interpretive bent

[13] Labour Party manifesto 1997, p 34.
[14] Labour's *Contract for a New Britain* (1996) p 29.

might wonder why Labour suggests capping '*should*' go rather than '*must*' or '*will*' go. But as the quotations noted above suggest, local political choice will seemingly be kept on a DoE controlled taxation respirator rather than given a new set of fiscal lungs. In the first year of the Blair administration, both Oxfordshire and Avon county councils found themselves wheezing against the budgetary muffler wrapped around their electoral necks by John Prescott's newly enlarged Department for Environment, Transport and the Regions. For electors in those two counties, the significance of their right to vote in local elections has been markedly curtailed.

Quite why central government 'must' have such powers to cap local spending is unexplained. The truth is apparently as self-evident to New Labour as it was to Margaret Thatcher. But does it have any objective basis? Would Birmingham's hope to give free bus passes to pensioners and school children threaten our economy's international competitiveness? Would Lewisham's decision to spend a little extra money buying its fruit and vegetables only from countries whose regimes do not tyrannise their peoples fatally compromise the diplomatic manoeuvrings of the Foreign Office? Would Camden's wish to build 1,000 new houses for London's homeless people automatically mean the Chancellor of the Exchequer will have to raise interest rates? Would Tower Hamlets' wish to pay its dustmen more than they would get in the private sector send unemployment spiralling out of control?

Of course not. The consequences attached to the examples are extreme. But the policies are routine, even mundane. It is simply a nonsense to assume that the local government sector has ever possessed sufficient financial autonomy to make more than a marginal impact on central government macro-economic strategies. The Thatcher government's efforts to place an ever tighter grip on local government's fiscal freedom had little to do with economic rationality, and much to do with political authoritarianism. The purpose was to neuter social democracy as an ideology on the national political stage by denying it the space to breathe as a practical programme of government in the local political arena.

The basic point is a simple one. Local authorities cannot pursue social democratic political ends – and a fortiori local voters cannot choose councils which will do so – if they are denied the capacity to tax their residents as fully as local political opinion will allow. New Labour is no doubt correct in arguing that there is limited merit in looking to the past for precise rules with which to shape our future. But sometimes the past offers us principles which possess considerable longevity, and which should not lightly be cast aside. Sir Ivor Jennings made the crucial argument with admirable clarity some 40 years ago:

'Local authorities are elected by the people of the area not to carry out as agents of the central government the policy of that government, but to carry out the policy of the electors of the area. The furtherance of that policy needs expenditure, and for the expenditure and the means of meeting it the local authority is again responsible, not to the central government . . . but to the electors . . . The importance of this principle cannot be overestimated . . . so long as the rating power is independent of [central government] control, local government as a whole must be, to a large extent, independent.'[15]

To suggest that local councils in 1960 were 'independent' of central government rather overstates the case. Councils were then – as they are now and presumably always will be – substantially dependent on central subsidies to finance their activities. The independence of which Jennings spoke was really that of localised electoral communities from the national electoral community. In effect, he was urging, as a matter of convention, that central governments of either party accept that the legal regime controlling locally levied taxation be sufficiently loosely cast to guarantee a modest degree of intranational political pluralism. New Labour appears to be content to leave that principle in the constitutional dustbin into which the Thatcher governments cast it with such alacrity. And if this fundamental value is not to be retrieved, one might wonder if the election of a Labour government really will enhance the constitutional role of our elected local authorities.

LOCAL AUTHORITIES AS MORAL ACTORS

'Local decisionmaking should be less constrained by central government, and also more accountable to local people.'[16]

It would however be an over-simplification to suggest that restoring the council sector's tax-levying autonomy is the only worthwhile step a new government could take to reverse the anti-pluralist trends implemented by the Thatcher and Major administrations. There are few more notorious judicial decisions regulating local government behaviour than the 1925 judgment of the House of Lords in *Roberts v Hopwood*,[17] in which Poplar Council's attempt to pay its workers substantially more than they would receive for doing similar jobs in the private sector was declared unlawful. The case obviously has a fiscal dimension: the court held that all councils were subject to a 'fiduciary duty' which compelled them to structure their expenditure decisions in accordance with sound business principles. But the judgment is also recalled because of the court's remarkably stunted view of the local democratic process. This is best illustrated by Lord Atkinson's categorisation of the council's wish to pay its workers a decent wage as an indulgence of 'eccentric principles of socialist philanthropy'; by Lord Sumner's considered view that councillors could

---

[15] *Principles of Local Government Law* (London: University of London Press, 1960) pp 184–186.
[16] Labour Party manifesto 1997, p 34.
[17] [1925] AC 578. See H Laski, 'Judicial Review of Social Policy in England' (1925) *Harvard LR* 832–848; P Fennell, 'The Rule Against Socialism' (1986) 13 *Journal of Law and Society* 401–422.

not allow their 'personal opinions on political, economic or social questions' to influence their decisions; and by his extraordinary comment that the proper constitutional role of local government was to decide such matters as 'the need for a urinal, and the choice of its position'.

There would seem to have been little progress from this antiquated jurisprudential position. That is in part a consequence of legislative inaction. Parliament has yet to pass a statute which explicitly requires or even permits councils to base their decisions on avowedly moral or political grounds and releases them from their judicially created fiduciary duty. But the inertia also has a judicial dimension. The common law continues to reject the argument that local authorities should be assumed to have been granted such powers as a matter of necessary implication from their political status as locally elected, and thence locally accountable, government bodies.

Thus, in recent years there have been decisions such as *Wheeler v Leicester City Council*,[18] in which the House of Lords refused to permit a local authority to register its disapproval of apartheid by withdrawing access to council facilities from a rugby club that supported sporting links with South Africa. Similarly, in *R v Lewisham LBC, ex parte Shell*,[19] it was held that councils could not on political grounds decline to trade with companies that they considered to be supportive of the apartheid regime. That particular common law presumption was then extended by s 17 of the Local Government Act 1988, which expressly prevents councils from taking into account 'non-commercial' considerations when deciding how to spend their resources. Thus far, the government has expressed a willingness to replace provisions requiring compulsory competitive tendering with a new duty to achieve 'best value' – a concept which may be sufficiently elastic to permit councils to free themselves if only a little from the straitjacket of market forces.

More recently, the Court of Appeal chose to deny in *R v Somerset County Council, ex parte Fewings*[20] that an authority can invoke either its councillors' or its electors' distaste for what they consider the barbaric practice of stag hunting to prohibit such activities on its own land.

It seems unlikely that the courts will reverse this common law presumption in the immediate future. One might have hoped that the government could take the chance to marry principle with expediency and extricate itself from the difficulties created by its evident support for the private member's Bill to ban fox-hunting by passing legislation which empowers local authorities to permit or prohibit such activities throughout their areas. Such an initiative would offer the Blair government a simple (and fiscally neutral) opportunity to restore at least a little meaningful political power to the local political arena. Local government may now exist on the margins of political life, but that does not mean that a readjustment of those margins is a politically worthless

---

[18] [1984] AC 1054.
[19] [1988] 1 All ER 938.
[20] [1995] 3 All ER 20.

exercise. All that would be required is a one clause statute stating that Parliament intends local authorities to take 'moral' principles (even 'eccentric' moral principles) into account when exercising any of their powers unless the particular statute in issue explicitly declares that such considerations should be excluded from councillors' deliberations. It would be unfortunate if a fiscally conservative Labour government did not seize this opportunity, for every other worthwhile reform to the local government sector will cost at least a little bit of public money.

EDUCATION

'[Local education authorities] will be required to devolve power, and more of their budgets, to heads and governors. LEA performance will be inspected by Ofsted and the Audit Commission.'[21]

It is sometimes forgotten that one of the more egregiously intolerant central government intrusions into the local democratic process in the modern era was perpetrated by a Labour government. Tony Crosland's notorious, if candid, ambition to 'abolish every fucking grammar school in England and Wales' is hardly the mark of a democrat committed to a pluralist constitutional vision. The *Tameside*[22] litigation was prompted by the third Wilson government's attempt to attach an implausibly authoritarian meaning to the broadly pluralist and permissive terms of the Education Act 1944 by forbidding a local electorate to choose to retain grammar schools in its area. On this occasion, the House of Lords did seem (quite admirably) to discern a legitimate role for councillors' 'personal opinions on social and political questions' to influence their decision-making behaviour.

The denial of local choice which the Labour government could not achieve through executive action in 1975 has however been pursued through legislative means since 1979. The facility which permits a bare majority of parents of children at a given school to opt out of LEA control substantially disempowers local authorities. But it does not 'empower' parents, since their school will now implement a curriculum designed by the Department for Education and Employment, submit itself to inspection by a central government quango in the form of Ofsted, and have to go cap in hand to central government for its funding.

It also, by extension, disempowers local communities. This is a simple point. By removing schools from local authority control, Parliament reduces still further the political significance of local councils. They become even less a site for political contestation than they were before. It matters less and less which party controls them.

---

[21] Labour Party manifesto 1997, p 8.
[22] [1977] AC 1014.

The Labour government has no apparent plans to address this problem. The 11-plus (and thus presumably grammar schools) will be abolished. This is clearly grossly intolerant of the wishes of many local electorates to retain such schools. Grant maintained schools will nevertheless be retained, which presumably also means that local electorates that wish to place all their local schools under local political influence (control is too strong a word) are also denied the capacity to make that preference effective.

Furthermore, the 'comprehensive' schools that will remain must have streamed classes – irrespective of local political opinion. Primary school pupils will be subjected to compulsory assessment – according to standards set by central government. Ministers will be empowered to close 'failing' schools – with the criteria of failure being set by the Department for Education and Employment. In such circumstances, it is difficult to see what meaningful political role local authorities will retain in the education sector.

Labour's education policy also seems to have embraced two of the Thatcher/Major governments' strongly held but poorly founded ideological assumptions; first, that 'parents' form some kind of homogeneous bloc and, secondly, that they are invariably a source of wisdom and enlightenment. Given that parents are voters too, election results prove the first assumption to be a myth. The second is equally flawed: it is not so long ago that 'parent power' took the form of racist whites withdrawing their children from schools with a high proportion of non-white pupils.[23]

The incorporation of the European Convention on Human Rights into domestic law will prevent schools from indulging the more egregious manifestations of parental bigotry on matters of race, gender and sexual orientation, but it is a very strange kind of democracy which takes as its central premise the belief that the customer is always right. It is a strange kind of democracy indeed that regards citizens as customers.

Labour's retention of the Thatcherite ethos of competition and markets within the school sector is also poorly conceived from a constitutional perspective concerned primarily with fostering political pluralism. Parents can make only individuated decisions – which school to try to send their child to – or micro-political decisions – whether to choose grant maintained status for a given school. But what they are not being empowered to do is make or even influence macro-political decisions within their local authority boundaries. They cannot choose to pay high local taxes in order to employ many more teachers or refurbish school buildings. They cannot introduce innovative reforms to the curriculum. They cannot experiment with a selective school system. What they can do, in effect, is what David Blunkett tells them.

The Blair government has announced that education will be its highest priority. But the Labour Party manifesto does not make any clear commitment to central funding of the 'improvements' it identifies; any increase in education spending will be contingent on a reduction in unemployment which

---

[23] See C Vincent, 'Tolerating Intolerance' (1992) *Journal of Education Policy* 1–20.

will enable funds to be transferred to education from the social security budget. The first budget suggested that an additional £1 billion would be found for the education sector over the next five years, much of which will be presumably be directed to making good on the much heralded promise to reduce class sizes in primary schools to no more than 30. The promise could however be considered objectionable on two grounds. The first – the more prosaic – is the somewhat implausible suggestion that the initiative can be financed wholly by phasing out the assisted places scheme. This objection gains further force when one considers that it is likely that the two capped local authorities – Oxfordshire and Avon – will make good some of their budgetary shortfalls by not employing any more teachers. The second – and essentially constitutional reason – is that this is just not the type of decision that needs to be made by central government. If there is one lesson that can be drawn from the constant to-ing and fro-ing of education policy in the past 50 years, it is that there is no consensus on the 'best' way to school our children. If there is a second lesson to be learned, it is that a sensibly structured constitution would allow alternative policies to be pursued side by side over many years so that we can make informed decisions about which techniques and ideas best serve the goals we wish to set our schools. We may be in for a long wait.

HOUSING AND PERSONAL SOCIAL SERVICES

'We will place a new duty on local authorities to protect those who are homeless through no fault of their own and are in priority need.'[24]

'We aim to provide real security for families through a modern system of community care. . . . We believe that local authorities should be free to develop a mix of public and private care.'[25]

The Labour Party's promises about homelessness would seem to require a repeal of the homelessness provisions of the Housing Act 1996, and a re-enactment of the original 1977 homeless persons legislation. The new statute would also have to be framed in a way that reversed the decision of the House of Lords in *Awua*,[26] a decision which effectively repealed the main planks of the 1977 Act. This appears, on its face, to be an expensive commitment, and one moreover which absolutely reeks of orthodox Keynesianism. As such, it seems really rather unlikely that the commitment will be honoured. This becomes all the more apparent when one considers that enhancing the legal rights of homeless people against local authorities is of precious little use if councils have no housing to allocate.

[24] Labour Party manifesto 1997, p 26.
[25] ibid, p 27.
[26] [1995] 2 FLR 819. See D Cowan, 'Doing the Government's Work For It' (1996) 60 MLR 276–285.

Some 20 years ago, virtually a third of the British population lived in flats and houses owned by local authorities. It would be quite misleading to claim that all councils were model landlords, or that all council dwellings were of an adequate quality. The country nevertheless possessed an extensive supply of affordable housing, and had – compared to today – very few homeless people. Since 1980 the council housing sector has shrunk to but a shadow of its former self because of the interactive effect of the right to buy policy and the Thatcher/Major governments' refusal to allow receipts from sales to be used to build new housing. And, hardly coincidentally, we now have a large and growing homeless population.

The Labour government has indicated that it will permit local authorities to use funds they have received from the sale of council houses to build new homes and refurbish old ones. The 1997 manifesto was rather coy about whether this principle applies to accumulated receipts, or merely to the proceeds of future sales. Since more than 1.25 million properties have been sold since 1980, those accumulated receipts now amount to an extremely substantial sum, and could trigger an intensive and extensive Keynesian foray into depressed local economies. It seems that the Treasury and the DETR will however rein back any councils gripped by too much social democratic enthusiasm. The release of receipts will be 'phased to match the capacity of the building industry and to meet the requirements of prudent economic management.'[27] To quite what extent economic prudence will be allowed to prevent the housing of homeless people remains to be seen, but the cynical presumption would seem to be that local authorities will have to plead with the DETR for permission to spend even a small portion of their own capital revenues on new houses.

The decision of the House of Lords in *R v Gloucestershire County Council, ex parte Barry*[28] came too late to be addressed in the 1997 manifesto. But the judgment poses a potentially major obstacle for the Blair government to negotiate. In *Barry*, the House of Lords held that a council could rely on its lack of financial resources to justify a refusal to provide services (in this case under the Chronically Sick and Disabled Persons Act 1970) which it appeared to be legislatively required to offer.

The judgment has obvious and substantial implications for the provisions of care services in particular, and may potentially stretch to many other areas of council responsibility. Will a council be able to leave children untaught because it cannot afford to employ teachers? Will buildings be left to burn because fire engines are too expensive? Will homeless people be left on the streets because it costs too much to build new houses? *Barry* is an invitation to both local authorities and central government to evade responsibility for fulfilling commitments which the electorate might legitimately assume that Parliament has placed upon them. As such, one might expect a government

---

[27] Labour Party manifesto 1997, p 26.
[28] (1997) *The Times*, 21 March.

pledged to enhancing transparency and accountability in the provision of public services to promote legislation to reverse it. The Department of Social Security has however indicated that no such initiative will be forthcoming. The relevant minister, Paul Boateng, has commented that it would 'fly in the face of reason' to prevent local authorities from pleading an insufficiency of resources as a justification for not meeting statutory obligations.

TRANSPORT POLICY

'The key to efficient bus services is proper regulation at local level, with partner-ships between local councils and bus operators an essential requirement.'[29]

The stark contrast between Thatcherite and social democratic understandings of the appropriate limits of local government autonomy was nowhere better illustrated during the 1980s than in the House of Lords' judgment in *Bromley LBC v GLC*.[30] In *Bromley*, the court held that the GLC's statutory duty to run an 'economic, efficient and integrated' transport system for London did not empower it to levy taxes at a sufficient level to underwrite a long-term operating deficit. That such a fiscal subsidy might improve the quality and quantity of bus and tube services, that it might reduce traffic congestion on London's streets and pollution in its skies, that it might reduce the number of deaths from road accidents or entice more tourists to the city – all these factors were irrelevant if the GLC could not run London Transport according to private sector understandings of economic viability.

That London's transport system is now staggering towards gridlock on the roads and chaos on the trains is an indirect consequence of the GLC's ephemeral constitutional powers and existence. London's citizens have no direct electoral means to reach any alternative political end. Quite how much power the new strategic London council will possess remains to be seen. One cause for optimism is the Labour Party's manifesto suggestion that Parliament will be asked to subject all councils to a general duty 'to promote the economic, social and environmental well-being of their area' (p 34). This is a potentially significant power, but one which, if not carefully framed when enacted, could be effectively neutered by courts which remain in thrall to the *Roberts*[31]/*Bromley*[32] conception of the fiduciary duty. A radical measure would consist of legislation explicitly confirming that local authorities may conclude that they may offer long-term subsidies to loss-making transport services in their areas if they believe such services to be fulfilling a useful social or environmental purpose.

---

[29] Labour Party manifesto 1997, p 29.
[30] [1982] 1 AC 768.
[31] *Roberts v Hopwood* [1925] AC 578.
[32] *Bromley LBC v GLC* [1982] 1 AC 768.

The installation of John Prescott as Secretary of State of a new super-department embracing the responsibilities of the Department of the Environment and the Department of Transport may lend a further impetus to the argument that mass transit systems should be regarded as a social service rather than simply a commercial enterprise. Any such progress would of course be welcomed, whether in London or any other of the country's major conurbations. But while these might widely be desirable developments, they are hardly *constitutional* ones. They will simply reach as far and last as long as Parliament considers appropriate.

CONCLUSION – A MISSED (AND UNWANTED?) OPPORTUNITY

The constitutional status of local government will not be transformed by the Blair administration. Nor it seems will Parliament even be invited to restore the flawed status quo that regulated central-local government relations prior to 1979. Both omissions are much to be regretted.

A party of the 'radical centre' would seize upon local government as the means to achieve truly pluralist political ends. It would recognise that pluralism should enjoy both a *simultaneous* and a *sequential* dimension. It would accept that if a majority or even a substantial minority of the national electorate do not support the political party controlling the House of Commons, the constitution should guarantee that those people are afforded some means to see their political preferences given substantial practical effect. On the basis of the Labour administration's proposals so far, there is little indication that the outcome of a local election could make any substantial difference to the way in which particular areas are governed. To speak of local *government* will continue to be a contradiction in terms if the Blair administration does not invite Parliament to ensure that the Liberal Democrats and Conservatives are given the opportunity to *demonstrate* rather than simply *advocate* the claimed merits of their preferred policies on important political issues. Until that step is taken, the shine on new Labour's democratic credentials will retain a distinctly tarnished hue.

The obvious, cynical rebuttal to any such proposal is that a Labour government would be shooting itself in the foot by pursuing such a policy. Such decentralisation might enhance the Conservatives' prospects of success at the next general election. And one could be fairly sure that a new Conservative government could not be trusted to display the same degree of pluralist tolerance as its Labour predecessor. It would use a parliamentary majority to enact legislation denying Labour and Liberal controlled authorities the opportunities in opposition that it had itself enjoyed.

Such realism is less an excuse for inaction however, than a reason for appreciating the inter-connectedness of so many aspects of any programme of constitutional reform. Effective political pluralism does require a powerful first tier of sub-central government. And such independence can only be achieved if the boundaries, powers and fiscal autonomy of local authorities are placed in legal rather than just conventional terms beyond alteration by a central government commanding a bare parliamentary majority bestowed by the support of only a minority of the electorate.

The Labour Party has promised to tinker with the component parts of Parliament, but has not evinced any desire to curb its sovereign authority to legislate on all issues by a simple majority plus the royal assent. The Blair government evidently sees no need to explore ways to protect local political pluralism against the kind of sustained assault launched by the Thatcher and Major governments. It may be that the entrenchment of institutional pluralism – or indeed of any other supposedly 'fundamental' political value – is a constitutional impossibility. Perhaps the Diceyan orthodoxy as to the perpetual sovereignty of Parliament is an eternal truth. What is thus far rather disappointing is that the new government seems unwilling to look very hard for an alternative.

But that is perhaps unsurprising, given the insignificant, marginal role in which local authorities have been cast in the new Labour government's unfolding political drama. 'Power to the people' is a much circumscribed concept in the New Labour scheme of things. 'Empower' the people by all means – as long as they do not want to pay high local taxes to fund extensive welfare services, or to ensure that all local children have equal educational opportunities, or to provide affordable homes for those who are currently homeless or living in cramped, insanitary conditions. Despite what the Labour leadership seems currently to believe, a good many of the UK's 60 million people remain wedded to the principles of a social democractic ideology which is far more Keynesian in nature than the agenda promoted by the Blair government. It is also evident that many of them continue to adhere to a broadly Thatcherite political philosophy, located appreciably to the right of Blairite orthodoxies. Neither of those two factions of the population can realistically expect to see local authorities as a vehicle through which to express and evaluate their respective political preferences. Thus far, there is little reason to believe that the Blair Cabinet accepts that the *government* of England is a task that can appropriately be carried out at the sub-central level.

That New Labour seems to have imbibed the Thatcherite ethos that local authorities exist on the sufferance of central government is forcefully illustrated by the following extraordinary passage in the 1997 manifesto (at p 34):

'Every council will be required to publish a local performance plan with targets for service improvement, and be expected to achieve them. The Audit Commission will be given additional powers to monitor performance and promote efficiency. On its advice, [central] government will where necessary send in a management team with full powers to remedy failure.'

Can sub-central government exist in such a legal context? The only plausible answer would seem to be 'No'.

The great hope for the recognition of the decentralisation of government as an important constitutional principle in the next five years does not actually lie with local government at all. Paradoxically, perversely perhaps, it lies in the Blair administration's proposals for the devolution of substantial governmental powers to Scotland and to Wales and, in the longer term, to several English regions. Herein lies the potential, at least in Scotland, for the growth of a constantly pluralist political culture within the UK. One might readily expect Robin Cook to respond to a Conservative victory in the next British general election by deciding that the best position from which to defend social democratic political culture in the UK would be as First Minister of Scotland rather than as a member of the British Shadow Cabinet. And while that 'inter-national' pluralism may not be legally entrenched, it is difficult to envisage any circumstances in which even a Conservative controlled British Parliament would dare to revoke or curtail the powers granted to the Scots 'legislature'.

But two foci (two and a half if one includes the Welsh Assembly) of political power is hardly a sufficient number for a country the size of the UK. In recent years, British political discourse has confined the concept of 'federalism' largely to debates about the European Community and defined it in essentially negative terms. Perhaps the greatest contribution that the Blair government could make to the constitutional regeneration of sub-central government in Britain would be to stimulate discussion of federalism as a principle with which to reassess our country's internal political structure. And that contribution, of course, would initially at least entail no net addition to public expenditure at all.

Further reading

Tony Blair, *Leading the Way: A New Vision for Local Government* (London: Institute for Public Policy Research, 1998)

Paul Brindley, Wendy Hall and Gerald Holtham, *The Greater London Authority: Principles and Structure* (London: Institute for Public Policy Research, 1997)

J Stewart and G Stoker (eds), *The Future of Local Government* (London: Macmillan, 1989)

Martin Loughlin, *Local Government in the Modern State* (London: Sweet & Maxwell 1986)

D Butler, A Adonis and T Travers, *Failure in British Government: The Politics of the Poll Tax* (Oxford University Press, 1994)

PART IV

JUSTICE AND HUMAN RIGHTS

CHAPTER 16

THE JUDICIARY

Professor Rodney Brazier (Manchester University)

OLD LABOUR AND JUDICIAL SERVICES

The Labour Party's protracted and detailed policy review, conducted in the wake of successive defeats by Margaret Thatcher at the polls, culminated in 1989 in the publication of the comprehensive statement of policy entitled *Meet the Challenge: Make the Change.*[1] That radical paper was accepted at Labour's annual conference in the same year, and became part of its programme. Within the constitutional reform proposals which were envisaged in it were plans to make major changes in the administration of justice in England and Wales, a pivotal part of which affected the judiciary.[2] Indeed, had the Labour Party been able to implement that restructuring the justice system would have been the subject of the most radical changes of the 20th century.

At the core of the 1989 justice policy was the recognition that ministerial responsibility for the law was in a very unsatisfactory state, especially responsibility for judicial service matters.[3] So, for example, responsibility for them was spread around several ministers, whose duties had been acquired in a haphazard fashion; each minister had incompatible functions; the Lord Chancellor was beyond the reach of the House of Commons; and two ministers, the Lord Chancellor and the Prime Minister, appointed judges without adequate safeguards for the doctrine of the separation of powers. This problem would have been tackled by depriving the office of Lord Chancellor of major and historic duties. Over a period the Lord Chancellor would have become head of the judiciary only, the ministerial functions of the office

---

[1] Labour Party, 1989.
[2] *Meet the Challenge: Make the Change*, p 61.
[3] On this point see generally Tony Gifford, *Where's The Justice?* (1986) Ch 2; Carol Harlow (ed), *Public Law and Politics* (1986) Ch 10; Michael Zander, *A Question of Justice* (1988) pp 279–284; Peter Archer and Andrew Martin (eds), *More Law Reform Now* (1983) Ch 1; Rodney Brazier, 'Government and the Law: Ministerial Responsibility for Legal Affairs' [1989] *Public Law* 64.

being transferred elsewhere.[4] A Minister for Legal Administration, sitting in the House of Commons, would have become responsible for all courts and tribunals, court procedure, the magistracy,[5] legal aid, and the organisation, appointment and training of the judiciary. The obvious objection that an ordinary minister such as that, lacking the reassuring judicial robes of a Lord Chancellor, would constitute a real danger to judicial independence was countered by a proposal for a statutory and independent commission which would make recommendations on judicial appointments, thus reducing the power of politicians in those vital matters.[6] Once those changes had been phased in, the head of the new department would have taken the Lord Chancellor's place in the Cabinet. Under the same scheme the Home Secretary's role would have been altered as well, leaving him or her with responsibility for criminal justice, penal policy, and the criminal law. (Labour's earlier and provisional plan to merge the Lord Chancellor's Department (LCD) and the Home Office into a single Ministry of Justice was accordingly dropped. Any such proposal had been heavily criticised as being most unwise.[7]) Had the 1989 plans been implemented three highly desirable goals would have been achieved. First, the new Cabinet Minister for Legal Administration would have been fully accountable to the House of Commons, unlike the Lord Chancellor who (despite the changes which the Conservative government was to make after the 1992 general election[8]) cannot be called to account on the floor of the House of Commons. Secondly, the main responsibility for recommending judicial appointments would have been taken away from the Lord Chancellor and the Prime Minister and would have passed to an independent body. Thirdly, a more rational distribution of functions would have been achieved, with the Home Secretary's role being altered to that of a Minister of the Interior, and all administration of justice matters eventually being in the hands of the Minister for Legal Administration. As a result a modern and accountable system would have been created, ensuring (among other things) that ministerial and parliamentary influence in judicial service matters would be minimised.

The Labour Party put the essence of these plans for reforming the administration of justice before the electorate in its 1992 general election

---

[4] The Lord Chancellorship would have ceased to be a political appointment; it was unclear whether the holder might have remained Speaker of the House of Lords.

[5] The 1989 Policy Paper proposed a new selection system for lay magistrates, but no details were given in it.

[6] The precise relationship between the minister and the commission was not explained.

[7] The possibility of such a merger had been rejected some years earlier by the House of Commons Home Affairs Committee: see HC (1980–81) 92, para 114. The principal objection was that a unified Ministry of Justice would give a single minister wholly incompatible functions, such as responsibility for public order together with responsibility for furthering justice and civil rights matters.

[8] These included the appointment, for the first time, of a junior LCD minister in the House of Commons. The terms of reference of the House of Commons Home Affairs Committee were also widened to take in the LCD and the Law Officers' Department (subject to exceptions).

manifesto, as part of its constitutional reform package.[9] The manifesto indicated that the Minister for Legal Administration would be appointed initially as part of the Lord Chancellor's Department (LCD), but later would be the head of a separate department; and the manifesto promised an independent judicial appointments commission.[10] Labour's defeat by John Major was to set the scene for a further review of policy: and new Labour was to retreat from these administration of justice plans in at least one crucial respect.

NEW LABOUR: THE LORD CHANCELLOR REPRIEVED

When John Smith took over from Neil Kinnock the Labour Party had a lawyer as its leader for the first time since Clement Attlee. Under John Smith Labour's constitutional reform plans were recast in time for the 1993 conference, the new proposals being based on the paper *A New Agenda for Democracy*.[11] That paper restricted consideration of changes in the administration of justice to the vital issue of the judiciary,[12] and opened with the words 'It is hard to think of a more important issue than the selection of those who are to judge over their fellow citizens'.[13] It went on to say that judges must be people of integrity, independent of government, and free of any kind of social or political pressure.[14] According to the paper the system of selecting judges did not satisfy those considerations: in particular, there was no reason to continue with 'a patently anachronistic method' of appointing judges or to continue to fail 'to provide proper training and support for [judges]'.[15] So Labour reiterated its commitment to the creation of an independent commission, now to be styled a Judicial Appointments and Training Commission. The Commission would have as one of its first tasks the formulation of a 'more rational' career pattern for judges, so as to allow those lawyers who are suitable for judicial work to join the bench earlier in their careers than they do currently. How would that be achieved? A number of necessary changes were indicated in the paper. First, it would be necessary for the Commission to draw from a wider field of candidates for judicial office, so as to ensure that all the most able people were considered for appointment. In order to make certain that the whole field of possible candidates was considered, the paper said that qualified people would be expected to express interest in appointment and not just wait to be approached. As a small part of the

---

[9] *It's Time to get Britain Working Again* (Labour Party, 1992), p 24.
[10] Ibid.
[11] Labour Party, 1993.
[12] Ibid, pp 40–41; Appendix 1 below, p 462.
[13] Ibid.
[14] The dangers of political pressure on judges are easy enough to imagine: but what was the *social* pressure which worried the authors of the paper?
[15] What follows is drawn from *A New Agenda for Democracy* (1993) pp 40–41; see Appendix 1 below, pp 462–4.

process of extending the field of choice the door would be opened for the first time to academic lawyers to present themselves for appointment.[16] Secondly, the paper envisaged that a significant proportion of judges, including High Court judges, would be appointed at an earlier age than has happened before. If this were done judicial careers would develop (as the paper put it) properly; it would also make an earlier use on the bench of the talents of women and members of ethnic minorities, who are woefully under-represented amongst older lawyers from whom judges are now chosen. Thirdly, the Lord Chancellor's policy of starting lawyers off on judicial work in the Crown Court and county courts on part-time appointments would be continued: it would remain the case that judges would 'usually' start their judicial careers doing part-time work, so that their suitability could be assessed before permanent appointments were made. Lastly, the retiring age for judges would be reduced initially to 65, with discretion (exercised on the Commission's recommendation) to give limited extensions in special cases 'if requested'.

A New Agenda for Democracy was published in 1993. Some of those four specific policies have a familiar sound to them today, simply because the Conservative government had acted (or was soon to act) on two of them, and because another merely confirmed a long-standing practice. Thus in 1994 the Lord Chancellor, Lord Mackay of Clashfern, instituted a system of advertising for appointments up to the rank of circuit judge, and he published criteria for judicial appointments, and requiring formal applications to be made from those interested leading to formal interviews of short-listed candidates.[17] Those practices were adopted precisely to ensure that lawyers interested in judgeships would be fully aware of vacancies and of what was required for appointment, and thus in part in order to draw candidates from a bigger pool. Labour's 1993 paper did not indicate that any changes would be made in the procedures for appointment of judges at High Court rank and above, and none of substance were instituted by the Conservative government.[18] Again, the retirement age for judges was lowered under the Conservatives. Lord Mackay had caused Parliament to enact the Judicial Pensions and Retirement Act 1993, which, while not cutting the compulsory retirement age to 65 as the

---

[16] Academics have not been appointed as judges partly as a result of two inter-related considerations. It has been said that academics could not be made first instance judges because they would lack trial and other practical experience, and that their talents might be better used at appellate level; but that to appoint them direct to the appellate bench might cause resentment among trial judges who might be waiting for preferment. Hale J was the first High Court judge to be appointed other than from the ranks of practising lawyers: she had practised part-time but had mainly been an academic and a Law Commissioner.

[17] This was foreshadowed in the consultation paper *Developments in Judicial Appointments Procedures* (LCD, 1994), and is set out in detail in a revised version of *Judicial Appointments* (LCD, 1995). See also evidence from the LCD to the House of Commons Home Affairs Committee in its Third Report, *Judicial Appointments Procedures* (HC (1995–96) 52), Vol II, Appendix 1.

[18] The Lord Chancellor explained to the Home Affairs Committee that, for example, it would be pointless to advertise vacancies in the High Court and above because he, the heads of division, and LCD officials know all possible candidates well: see *Judicial Appointments Procedures*, Vol II, Q473.

Labour Party had advocated in *A New Agenda for Democracy*, did reduce it to 70 from 75.[19] That new retirement age has applied to all those appointed after the coming into force of the 1993 Act, although the Lord Chancellor can authorise a person to continue in office until the age of 75 if it is in the public interest to do so.[20] (The use of retired judges is a direct result of the volume of cases needed to be heard by an inadequate number of judges: Labour's proposal, on the other hand, read as though it would be for an individual judge to request an extension.[21]) The statement in *A New Agenda for Democracy* that judges under a Labour government would 'usually' start their judicial careers in the Crown Court and county courts mirrors the Lord Chancellor's practice, adopted as long ago as 1981, of requiring satisfactory performance in a part-time judicial capacity before anyone is appointed to a full-time judgeship. That policy has been applied to all judges, and no appointments have been made to permanent judgeships without a satisfactory part-time apprenticeship. As a result of the Conservative government's actions, the gap between the two parties' policies on judicial service matters was narrowed: but one very significant difference remained: the Labour Party wanted to take responsibility for recommending appointments to judgeships away from politicians, while the Conservatives did not.

A New Agenda for Democracy provides a sketch of the responsibilities and composition of the Judicial Appointments and Training Commission advocated by the Labour Party. The sketch set the scene for the Commission to monitor the careers of 'existing and aspirant judges'. To do so it would be required to seek a wide range of information and opinion on the aptitudes and abilities of candidates and of existing judges, and in every case the Commission would present a reasoned report on its findings. That would make the Commission a major source of information. The Policy Paper envisaged that only a small part of that information would remain confidential, and so (except for that) those seeking judicial appointments would be given full advice about their prospects, along with the reasons for decisions made about them, and advice about any further training or expertise that they might be thought to need. Oddly, the precise role of the Commission in the appointments process was left unclear: presumably it was thought that the Commission would recommend appointments, rather than itself actually making the substantive appointments: but if that was, indeed, intended the Commission's relationship with the appointing minister was left unclear. In one sense the calls for the creation of a judicial appointments commission are not such a radical summons to arms as once would have been the case, because the systematic and more objective methods of obtaining information about candidates which has been operated for some years by the LCD has

---

[19] Judicial Pensions and Retirement Act 1993, s 26 and Sched 5.
[20] ibid.
[21] According to *A New Agenda for Democracy*, limited extensions would be considered in 'special cases if requested' – which implied that the judge would make the request.

resulted in much more being known about potential candidates for judicial office.[22] Of course, the substantial difference under a Labour government would be that this gathering of information and advice about judicial appointments would be done by a new and independent commission, rather than by officials in the LCD, and the advice to ministers about judicial appointments and related matters, so it is argued, would be of a much higher quality. This important work would be carried out by full- and part-time commissioners, who (according to *A New Agenda for Democracy*) would be appointed from people having a range of legal and other expertise, including extensive experience of professional training and education. The chair of the Commission would be taken by 'a senior legal figure'. The Commission would consider general policy issues, review difficult or important cases, and formulate guidelines to be followed by its staff. It would be overseen by a new House of Commons Select Committee on Legal Affairs.[23]

A New Agenda for Democracy was notable for a major omission. Its consideration of reform of the judiciary was set out in the context of the party's other constitutional reform measures, but nowhere in the paper was anything said about Labour's 1989 plan for a Department for Legal Administration or about reform in the office of Lord Chancellor. That omission was remedied by the subsequent Policy Paper *Access to Justice*,[24] which was approved at the 1995 annual conference and which became the main law reform Policy Paper for Labour's 1997 general election campaign. That paper contained a comprehensive statement of the party's policy on civil justice in England and Wales.[25] It set out proposals for reform of court and legal services, encompassing a new community legal service, the development of alternative dispute resolution and of mediation, empowering the consumer of legal services, reforming court procedures and legal aid, and reform of the legal professions. But the document also marked a reprieve for the Lord Chancellor and the LCD – and by necessary implication the ditching of plans for any new ministry – and it gave more detail about the proposed Judicial Appointments and Training Commission.

There would be, according to *Access to Justice*, a new focus for the LCD.[26] Traditionally the LCD had concentrated on the judiciary and the legal professions, but its top priority under the Labour government would be the cause of the individual citizen and consumer of legal services. To that end the department would be restructured in such a way as to ensure that a dynamic and coherent approach to the delivery of legal services was pursued.[27] The

---

[22] Details of those methods are given by the Home Affairs Committee in its report (see note 17 above), Appendix 1, paras 2.3–2.4 (evidence from the LCD).

[23] Such a committee would presumably take over the Home Affairs Committee's duties in relation to the LCD and the Law Officers' Department.

[24] Labour Party, 1995.

[25] The wider implications of the Labour Party's policy on citizens' access to justice are considered by Alistair Hudson in Chapter 20 below.

[26] *Access to Justice*, 1995, p 7.

[27] ibid.

role, status and executive responsibilities of the LCD's minister in the House of Commons (since the creation of the post in 1992, a parliamentary secretary) would be enhanced.[28] In practice an enhanced status for a junior minister of parliamentary secretary rank could only mean appointment of a minister of State in the LCD. The Lord Chancellor, still sitting in the House of Lords, would remain head of the LCD and outside the regular exposure to House of Commons Question Time and to the more rigorous cut and thrust of that House. Such a change would not amount to much of an improvement in the ministerial disposition first made by John Major in 1992. While a Minister of State ranks above, and is paid more than, a parliamentary secretary, both ranks of junior minister have departmental responsibilities delegated to them by their ministerial chief and there is nothing else to distinguish the two ranks.[29] But the threat which had hung over the head of aspirant Labour Lord Chancellors since 1989 that the office might be abolished was removed in 1995 with the publication of *Access to Justice*. It cannot be a mere coincidence that the policy change was made soon after the appointment by the new Labour leader, Tony Blair, of Lord Irvine of Lairg as Shadow Lord Chancellor – the first person, by the way, to be recognised formally as holder of such a title in opposition.[30] That retreat was of a piece with the scrapping of other machinery of government changes which Old Labour had favoured: there would be no place in a Blair government for Ministries of Consumer Affairs, Women's Affairs, or of Race Relations.[31] With that step backwards was lost the opportunities for highly desirable recasting of ministerial dispositions for the law:[32] this was the contribution of Labour's legal policy-makers to New Labour's less challenging face. The only other commitment about the LCD in *Access to Justice* was a proposal to make the department accountable to the House of Commons through a new Select Committee on Justice and Legal Services;[33] no other information was given about such a committee, and without it no assessment could be made of whether such a committee would be an improvement on the Home Affairs Committee's work in relation to the LCD and the Law Officers' Department.

Access to Justice did, however, take forward the plans for a new Judicial Appointments and Training Commission.[34] The document took for granted

---

[28] ibid.

[29] See Rodney Brazier, *Ministers of the Crown* (1997), Ch 2.1, 2.2.

[30] Previously the spokesperson who shadowed the LCD in the House of Lords had formal responsibility for 'legal affairs', or some such formulation.

[31] *Meet the Challenge: Make the Change* had envisaged six new government departments. One of them (Arts) was given substance by John Major in 1992 when he created the Department of National Heritage. The Ministry of Legal Administration did not survive the writing of *Access to Justice*. The prospect of creating a Department of Environmental Protection was kept alive by Tony Blair appointing a Shadow Cabinet spokesperson (latterly Michael Meacher) on the subject: in government Mr Meacher became a Minister of State, Department of the Environment, Transport and the Regions.

[32] Such reforms were outlined earlier.

[33] *Access to Justice*, 1995, p 7.

[34] ibid., pp 12–14. What follows is drawn from those pages.

the existing defects in the system of appointing and training judges, and stated that the Commission's aim would be the development of a more rational training and career structure for the judiciary, together with a more open and objective selection process that would better identify judicial talent from sources other than the Bar (that is, from the ranks of solicitors, and academics).[35] The Commission would be independent of the LCD but would be answerable to the Lord Chancellor, and would advise him (dare I add 'or her'?) on all aspects of judicial appointments and training. In expressing things that way the document made explicit what was left implicit in *A New Agenda for Democracy*, namely, that the Commission's role would be an advisory, not an executive, one. The Lord Chancellor could decide not to act on a recommendation.[36] Commission members would be appointed from suitably-qualified lawyers, academics, and lay people with relevant experience. The Commission would have 'oversight of all judicial posts', although what such oversight would amount to was left unclear. Did it, for example, embrace a power to consider matters such as the demands of cases to be heard and to recommend the creation of any necessary additional judgeships? The Commission would be required to see that the appointment process was open, fair, and accessible to all. The development of a strong equal opportunities policy, and the encouragement of all those groups currently under-represented on the bench, would be important goals of the new Commission. The LCD's wide consultations on the suitability of candidates for judicial office would continue, but the secretive aspects would, the document stressed, give way to a new principle of openness, under which candidates would be able to comment in detail on the substance of any objections made to their possible appointment.[37] The functions of the Judicial Studies Board would be taken over by the Commission, which would then review the provision of judicial training and develop a more coherent and systematic approach, involving the establishment of closer links with academic research and teaching facilities. Judicial performance would be appraised by senior members of the judiciary under the supervision of the Judicial Appointments and Training Commission. For the first time judges would be provided with a comprehensive code of practice, produced by the new Commission, although no further explanation of that was given. Would such a code concern only the conduct of cases? Or might the code also prescribe for the first time how

---

[35] This attempt to widen the net to take in solicitors rather glosses over the fact that solicitors holding the appropriate advocacy qualifications have been capable of appointment to senior judgeships since the coming into force of the Courts and Legal Services Act 1990. So far only Sachs J has made it to the High Court as a former solicitor. Perhaps the paper meant that the *numbers* of solicitor-judges would be sought to be increased.

[36] The Lord Chancellor formally appoints all judicial office holders except High Court judges (the appointment of whom are recommended to the Queen by the Lord Chancellor), and Lords Justices of Appeal and Lords of Appeal in Ordinary (whose appointment is recommended to the Queen by the Prime Minister).

[37] A similar opportunity would be offered to unsuccessful applicants for silk.

judges should conduct themselves in their private lives?[38] *Access to Justice* also indicated that the Commission would 'monitor judicial discipline', although it was careful to add that the present formal machinery for removing judges of High Court rank and above would remain in place, namely by an address to the Queen agreed to by both Houses of Parliament. Clearly there was to be no question of a quango (however eminent) itself dismissing senior judges from office. The Commission would have an important part to play in ensuring that complaints about judges' conduct were taken seriously and were investigated properly, and that appropriate action was taken as a result. In my opinion inadequate and inappropriate machinery has existed for a long time to deal with alleged instances of judicial misconduct, and Labour's Commission could be the means of correcting that situation.

The magistracy received some attention in *Access to Justice*. The paper said that the Judicial Appointments and Training Commission would take over the function of advising the Lord Chancellor[39] on the appointment of stipendiary and lay magistrates, although whether this would lead to the dissolution of the existing local advisory committees was unclear. The Commission would try to increase the pool from which new lay magistrates could be chosen by meeting the CBI and local chambers of commerce in order to encourage employers to release more staff for magisterial duties. Transparency would be introduced into the selection process by ensuring that reasons were given to candidates who were not recommended for appointment. Vacancies for lay magistrates would be advertised as widely as possible.

It is not the usual practice of departmental Select Committees to invite the political parties to give evidence to them during their inquiries. The Home Affairs Committee was, however, supplied with the Labour Party's document *Access to Justice* during its investigation into judicial appointments procedures which was conducted during the 1995–96 session. When the Committee came to report[40] it was split on party lines on one major point, namely, whether there should be a recommendation in favour of creating a judicial appointments commission. Attempts by the Labour members of the Committee to alter the Committee's draft report were defeated by the Conservative majority.[41] Labour members wanted to adopt that proposal, being one which not only reflected party policy but also being one which had been

---

[38] Lord Irvine of Lairg said in a speech to the Bar's annual conference in 1996 that as Lord Chancellor he would be less easily embarrassed than his predecessors, and that, for example, he would not expect the mere fact of sexual orientation or cohabitation with a partner of the same sex to be disclosed by candidates for judicial office. See the report at (1996) 146 *New Law Journal*, 1414.

[39] And presumably the Chancellor of the Duchy of Lancaster, who currently advises the Queen about the appointment (but not the removal) of lay magistrates in the commission areas of Greater Manchester, Merseyside and Lancashire.

[40] Third Report from the Home Affairs Committee, *Judicial Appointments Procedures*, HC (1995–96) 52.

[41] ibid, pp lxxxvi–lxxxvii.

urged on the Committee by many witnesses who had given evidence. In the event the Committee rejected the idea that such a commission should take over the responsibility of recommending people for judicial posts.[42] The Committee's majority was not persuaded that the quality of people appointed would necessarily improve if there were to be such a commission,[43] a conclusion which can be said failed to give weight to several other reasons which would justify new machinery of that kind. While the Home Affairs Committee conceded that ministers should not be involved in judicial appointments (because that involvement breached the doctrine of the separation of powers) the Committee was sanguine about the matter. It felt that Lord Chancellors had prevented the danger arising that, for example, party-political appointments would be made, and the Committee was confident that future Lord Chancellors would continue to hold the ring. The Committee did recommend that the Prime Minister's role in the appointment of senior judges should end, on the ground that he or she was no better informed on the matter than the Lord Chancellor.[44] The Committee was also of the view that the value of the LCD's network of consultations (which ensured that information about possible candidates was collected systematically) might be diminished if a commission were to play a part in selecting judges.

In finding against a judicial appointments commission the Home Affairs Committee adopted the opposition to the concept which had been expressed by Conservative Lord Chancellors. Lord Mackay had set out his views before the Home Affairs Committee;[45] he had also done so in his Hamlyn Lectures.[46] In those lectures Lord Mackay conceded that, if the establishment of a completely new system for the judiciary were being considered, a judicial appointments commission might be regarded as appropriate.[47] But he rejected the idea on three grounds (presumably on the silent assumption that 'a completely new system' was not envisaged). First, Lord Chancellors had taken a strong personal interest in judicial appointments, which was underlined by their personal responsibility to Parliament for them. That position would be diffused among the members of a collective body. Secondly, no commission could have an intimate knowledge of candidates, and it would have to rely on references: the problem with that would be, he believed, that the more widely circulated references were, the less frank writers would be. Thirdly, Lord Mackay thought that a commission would split on predictable lines, although he did not indicate what those lines would be. The counters to that view can be sketched out.[48]

---

[42] ibid, Vol I, paras 130–142.
[43] ibid, Vol I, para 140.
[44] ibid, Vol I, para 128.
[45] ibid, Vol II, Q455.
[46] *The Administration of Justice* (1994), Ch 1.
[47] ibid, p 7.
[48] For a fuller rejoinder, see my evidence to the Home Affairs Committee published at HC (1995–96) 52, Vol II, pp 251–256, especially p 254.

The argument that there is, and must remain, direct ministerial accountability to Parliament for judicial service matters is an old one, and an unconvincing one at least in relation to judicial appointments. The Lord Chancellor
and his junior minister in the House of Commons have to defend the *system*
of appointments from time to time, and no one would deny that a close
personal interest has been taken by Lord Chancellors in creating judges. But
no Lord Chancellor has been called to account in Parliament for the actual
operation of his judicial appointments procedures. Indeed, had any questions
been put about individual appointments the LCD ministers might well have
refused to answer them, by analogy with the Home Affairs Committee's
terms of reference which rule out consideration by the Committee of such
questions. It is difficult to understand what exactly this 'direct ministerial
accountability' amounts to in practice, or how in reality it would be undermined if a commission were to take over primary responsibility for recommending new appointments. Indeed, such a development would improve the
separation of powers in the UK, which has for so long, and from a constitutional point of view so objectionably, been required to accommodate the
appointment of judges by two Cabinet Ministers, the Lord Chancellor and
the Prime Minister. Again, the writers of references would naturally have to
be reassured that their letters would remain confidential under any new
system, and provided that was done it is hard to see why a writer would be
deterred from writing frankly to a commission if he or she would have been
happy to write in that way to the LCD and its officials. As to Lord Mackay's
worry that a commission would split on predictable lines, it would be an
advantage if (for instance) the proper expectations of female candidates for
judgeships were vigorously pursued by Commission members who happened
to be women. Provided that, when final recommendations were being arrived
at in the Commission, every member acted and voted for the overall best
candidates, and did not press individual claims on what might be termed
'class' grounds, one of the main aims of the Commission might be achieved.
The late Conservative government's assertion that a commission would not
necessarily improve the quality of appointments is one which cannot be
proved or disproved short of adopting an alternative method and comparing
its results over time with what had been achieved before.

The Labour Party's novel publication of a draft manifesto in 1996, many
months before the last possible date for a general election, was matched by
the bold initiative of seeking the support of the party membership for it. *New
Labour: New Life for Britain*[49] was indeed approved by the membership.
Perhaps not surprisingly, no mention was made of plans to reform the judiciary in a document which represented a fairly compressed statement of the
whole of the party's then current policy: the wide-ranging constitutional
reform proposals were set out briefly, with the main detail being reserved for

[49] Labour Party, 1996.

the devolution plans.[50] Rather more surprisingly, no mention was made of the judiciary in the Labour/Liberal Democrat agreement on constitutional reform, which was concluded in March 1997.[51] Nor was it referred to in Labour's general election manifesto.

THE LABOUR GOVERNMENT'S UNFINISHED BUSINESS

When Lord Irvine of Lairg became Lord Chancellor in May 1997 he succeeded to a judicial service system which had already been altered in several respects by the Conservative government at the instance of Lord Mackay. Thus, as has been seen, Parliament had been brought somewhat closer to that system in two ways. The presence of the LCD had been made manifest in the House of Commons by the appointment of the first-ever junior minister, the Parliamentary Secretary, LCD, in 1992.[52] He was made the Lord Chancellor's spokesperson in the House of Commons, and was responsible for such matters as were delegated to him by the Lord Chancellor. That was a welcome development, because it gave MPs the ability to hold a minister – albeit a junior minister – to account for the LCD. The appointment represented an attempted compromise between those who, on the one hand, shared the Labour Party's former preference for a new and separate ministry for justice matters with its ministerial head in the House of Commons, and, on the other hand, those who (like the Conservative government) strongly favoured the retention of the LCD and the Lord Chancellor as the responsible minister. Alongside that ministerial appointment, the Conservative government had asked the House of Commons to widen the terms of reference of the Home Affairs Committee to enable it to oversee the policy, administration and expenditure of the LCD and the Law Officers' Department.[53] That change was made subject to the proviso that the Committee could not examine individual cases or appointments.[54] Lord Irvine of Lairg also succeeded to the judicial appointments and career progression established by his Conservative predecessors. That system is firmly entrenched. Under it, vacancies for circuit judgeships, district judgeships, and assistant recorderships are routinely advertised, although vacancies for Lords of Appeal in Ordinary, Lords Justices of Appeal, and High Court judges, are not.[55] The new Lord

---

[50] ibid, pp 28–31.

[51] Report of the Joint Consultative Committee on Constitutional Reform (Labour Party/Liberal Democrats, 1997).

[52] The Law Officers were never junior ministers to the Lord Chancellor.

[53] House of Commons Standing Order No 152. Those two departments had been excluded from the purview of the Committee from its creation in 1979 until 1992.

[54] House of Commons Standing Order No 152.

[55] Nor are, eg, vacancies for stipendiary magistrates and Masters of the Supreme Court: *Judicial Appointments Procedures*, Vol I, para 23.

Chancellor announced that, despite his predecessor's view that all possible candidates for the High Court bench will be known in the LCD, vacancies in that bench would henceforth be advertised. Lord Irvine also inherited a process under which applicants for judicial posts receive substantial job descriptions, a statement of the criteria for appointment, and an application form; and which results in short-listed applicants being interviewed by a panel which includes an official of the LCD and a lay interviewer.[56] Those panels make recommendations to the Lord Chancellor. The Home Affairs Committee unanimously commended those developments in 1996.[57] The system had already come a long way in the ten years after the arch-conservative Lord Chancellor, Lord Hailsham of St Marylebone, had left the woolsack to be succeeded (briefly) by Lord Havers and then by Lord Mackay.

What, then, is still to be done in order to deliver the Labour Party's commitments on the judiciary and judicial service matters? One change has just been made, thus fulfilling the commitment which had been given in *Access to Justice*. The Lord Chancellor's junior minister in the Commons was promoted, in the Labour government, to minister of state level in 1998, thus enhancing the junior minister's status. Obviously, however, the principal initiative would be the creation of the Judicial Appointments and Training Commission: it is at the core of Labour's plans for reform of the judiciary. Lord Irvine announced that a consultation paper would be issued about a possible judicial appointments commission in the autumn of 1997. The paper would examine the case from first principles for and against a change: clearly, the Lord Chancellor did not consider himself bound to make the change – which (to repeat the point) was not in Labour's manifesto. But the Lord Chancellor announced in the autumn of 1997 that the other burdens on his department meant that work on the consultation paper and a possible new commission would be suspended.[58] This was most disappointing. But all is not lost: it is quite possible that later in this Parliament, or perhaps in the next if Labour wins a second term, the LCD will return to the issue. For that reason it is important that the questions which would be involved in establishing such a commission be made as clear as possible. Those questions are set out in conclusion below.

A Judicial Appointments and Training Commission would have to be set up through legislation. It is true that, because the Commission's main role would be advisory, it could be set up as an act of prerogative, but a statutory basis would be essential, primarily so that the commissioners' independence could be enshrined in law beyond the whim of ministers. The Lord Chancellor and his Parliamentary Secretary would have much work to do in preparing the legislation necessary to establish a Judicial Appointments and Training

---

[56] The numbers of lay interviewers was being increased even at the time of the publication in 1996 of the Home Affairs Committee's Third Report, *Judicial Appointments Procedures*, Vol I, para 25.

[57] *Judicial Appointments Procedures*, para 45.

[58] Press Notice 220/97 (LCD, 9 October 1998).

Commission. The passage of any such Bill through the House of Commons would be helped by a Parliamentary Labour Party fully united on the policy, supported by the Liberal Democrats who have favoured the creation of such a commission for a long time.[59] The attitude of the House of Lords would be less easy to judge. The Conservative majority there (there at least until the government starts its reforms of that House) might share the Conservative government's view that an appointments commission is unnecessary. Because there was no reference in Labour's 1997 general election manifesto to the establishment of such a Commission, the Bill would not have the benefit of the Salisbury doctrine under which the House of Lords does not seek to vote down measures for which a government has unambiguous political authority derived from a clear manifesto commitment.[60] The Judges' Council and the heads of division are opposed to a new commission,[61] primarily on the ground that politics would be introduced into the appointments system, both in appointing the commissioners themselves and in its recommendations for appointments, which would (as the Council put it) be 'subjected to political scrutiny'. Senior judges, like Lord Bingham of Cornhill CJ, would no doubt express their opposition to the measure in the Chamber.

A wide range of questions would need to be settled in drafting a Bill to set up a Judicial Appointments and Training Commission. The main ones can be adumbrated now.

(1) It would be of central importance that a Judicial Appointments and Training Commission could be seen to be as independent as possible of government and of the legislature. Lord Chancellors have defended the status quo in relation to judicial service matters on the ground that the Lord Chancellor provides a barrier which protects the independence of the judiciary from MPs and others. A new commission would have to be seen to impose an additional (or, depending how you view that defence) better safeguard for the independence of the judiciary. For that reason the Commission's founding instrument should be a statute. The independence of the Commission should be enshrined in it by both general and particular words. It would be important that the Act states that the Commission is not subject to ministerial direction. Accordingly, as much detail as possible about the Commission must be included in the Act: there must be no room for lacunae to be filled by advice or suggestions from ministers. The terms of appointment for commissioners in the Act should incorporate a restrictive procedure for removal: it might be apt for the security of tenure for the commissioners to be the same as for Supreme Court judges, requiring the prior approval of

---

[59] For the current state of that policy, see *Here We Stand: Proposals for Modernising Britain's Democracy* (Liberal Democrat Federal White Paper No 6, 1993), p 49.

[60] For an explanation of that doctrine by a former Conservative Leader of the House of Lords, see Lord Carrington, *Reflect on Things Past* (1988), pp 77–78, 203–204.

[61] See their evidence to the Home Affairs Committee, reproduced in *Judicial Appointments Procedures*, Vol II, Appendix 16, especially p 224.

both Houses of Parliament before any commissioner were dismissed.[62] The Commission could be accountable to Parliament through a requirement that it submit an annual report to Parliament, and of course it would be dependent on Parliament for the resources to carry out its work. The exact relationship between the Commission and the Lord Chancellor would have to be explained in the legislation, especially by stating where final decisions about judicial appointments and other matters were to be taken. One model, which in opposition Labour seemed to favour, was to give the Commission advisory powers only, so that the Lord Chancellor would be free to accept or reject its advice. The advantages of that would be that the Lord Chancellor's ministerial responsibility (for what that may be worth) would be retained; perhaps more importantly such a model might reassure those who are a little nervous about the whole development by retaining some of the old structure in the form of the Lord Chancellor's powers to make appointments (and to recommend appointments). Caution might favour that approach, at least initially. But under another model the Commission could be given executive power, so that (for example) it actually took over the Lord Chancellor's role in making judicial appointments (or recommending them directly to the Queen). That approach has its supporters.[63] Such a scheme would break, at last, the power of politicians to appoint judges.

(2) The actual membership of the proposed Commission would exercise ministers, not least because those who (like Lord Mackay and the Judges' Council) oppose the development do so on the basis that it is the membership of a collegiate body which would necessarily cause divisions within the Commission, would diffuse ministerial responsibility for appointments, cause reference writers to be less than frank, and would be 'political'. Clearly, therefore, the members of a body with such important constitutional duties as recommending people to judgeships would have to be of the highest integrity, honesty and independence. So what should the Commission's membership be? Labour's proposal that the chair be taken by a senior legal figure would perhaps involve reliance on the well-known formula of someone who holds, or who has held, high judicial office. If that person were to be a serving judge (perhaps a Lord of Appeal in Ordinary) it is unlikely, at least in the early months and perhaps years, whether all the work necessary to establish the Commission would permit a part-time appointment. So the senior figure would have to be seconded from judicial work,[64] or a retired person would have to be drafted in to fill it. The other commissioners would be

---

[62] That is the position, for example, governing the removal of the Parliamentary Commissioner for Administration: he holds office during good behaviour, retires at 65, and otherwise is removable only on an address from both Houses to the Queen: Parliamentary Commissioner Act 1967, s 1(2), (3).

[63] See, eg, Carol Harlow, in Harlow (ed), *Public Law and Politics* (1986), Ch 10.

[64] For which there are many precedents, including the recent ones of Lord Nolan (seconded as the first Chairman of the Committee on Standards in Public Life) and of Lord Woolf (who conducted the civil justice review).

a blend of full- and part-timers. Would the commissioners be recruited from specified categories of people? It is vital to the scheme that a proportion of the body be lay people, and a fixed proportion of the total membership should be reserved for them. Ideally they would be not only representative of the great and the good (or at least the good), but at least some of them should have practical experience of selection and appointment processes. It might also be desirable to earmark other part-timer commissionerships for representatives of both the senior and lower judiciary, and of the legal professions. Given all that, the plan for the overall size of the Commission would have to be carefully designed so as to avoid the creation of an unwieldy body, albeit one in which some of the work was done by groups of commissioners.

When the question arises of selecting those commissioners who were to serve ad hominem rather than ex officio, clearly the Nolan principles would have to be followed, of which the overriding one is that appointments should be made on merit.[65] The Nolan principles are accepted by all the political parties, and it would be especially important that the process of selecting these commissioners was seen to comply fully with them. Candidates' politics would have to be declared during that process, in the same way that candidates for the lay magistracy are asked to declare any political allegiances, so that, so far as possible, no one political party were allowed to predominate on the Commission. This would be especially important given the view of the Judges' Council that the Commission (and especially the lay component) should not have a preponderance of members belonging to one party. Indeed, the political parties themselves must be seen to have no part whatever in the process. Accordingly, is there a case for a special appointment procedure? For example, it might be considered whether the Civil Service Commissioners should be pressed into service, or whether an appointing panel which included a judicial element should be set up. Perhaps there is a case for a parliamentary investigation into the qualities of candidates for the Commission. A parliamentary committee could inquire into candidates' political, legal, philosophical and social views. There is, of course, a risk that the use of a parliamentary committee might result in divisions in it on party lines over some appointments. But the tasks to be entrusted to the Commission would be so important that the best attainable method of achieving public confidence should be used.[66] Whatever method is devised, the initial appointments procedure must be manifestly seen to be beyond reproach.

(3) It might be thought that the working methods of the Commission would be for it to establish once its members were in office. There is, however, at least one important matter that should be considered at the legislation

---

[65] First Report of the Committee on Standards in Public Life, Cm 2850 (1995) Ch 4.

[66] It could be that Labour's proposed Select Committee on Justice and Legal Services might have a part to play in any parliamentary scrutiny of candidates.

stage, namely, the rules concerning the gathering of information about possible candidates for judicial appointments. The statute ought to include, as a minimum, safeguards for disappointed candidates – stating, for example, whether they were to be given reasons. In opposition the Labour Party (rightly) promised that reasons would be given in those circumstances. The Act should also include procedures which would permit people to see and comment on specified information held on them by the Commission: that should not be left to mere practice. Just as importantly, the structure of information-gathering might call for a statutory framework. If the Labour government is truly keen to devolve decision-making away from London, one way in which that could be done would be to take account of the legitimate expectations of localities. I have argued elsewhere that, in order to do this, and so as to reduce the central dominance of the LCD, a system of local committees, one in each circuit, should be set up under the aegis of the Commission.[67] A criticism of the present system is that all decisions on judicial matters are taken in London, regardless of the fact that much judicial work is undertaken throughout the country by judges who never come to London in the course of their official duties. There is a case for ensuring that, if not devolution of decision-making, at least a greater role for information-gathering and assessment be given to the circuits, with local recommendations being forwarded to the Commission. The composition of such local committees might include representatives of the local professions, local judges, as well as lay people. The committees might even be given the task of investigating complaints about the lower judiciary in their circuit areas, and recommending to the Judicial Appointments and Training Commission any action which should be taken; the committees might also be asked to make recommendations about the renewal of assistant recorderships and recorderships. Through such devolution the workload of the Commission should be reduced. The Commission might not itself be able adequately to discharge its functions if it had to deal centrally with all judicial service matters – especially given that some of its members would be part-time commissioners and some would be serving (and therefore very busy) judges.

(4) The legislation to establish the Commission would have to make clear whether it was to have any role in considering the appropriate levels of judge-power. Would the LCD retain all decision-making about the appropriate numbers of judges, as always fitting in any extra costs within its departmental budget? If that were so, the Commission would be left to fill vacancies. Alternatively, the Commission might be given a statutory right to express a view on the overall levels of judge-power, either based on information provided to it by the LCD, or even on the basis of its own research and its own ideas about how court services could best be supplied.

---

[67] See Rodney Brazier, *Constitutional Reform* (Oxford University Press, 2nd ed, 1998), pp 176–177.

(5)   The governing statute ought to charge the Commission with precise powers and duties in relation to complaints about judicial conduct. At present the best advice for many people who have a complaint about a judge is to appeal. But complaints are made to the LCD about judges' conduct, and if the complaint is substantiated after investigation the judge may receive either a private or a public rebuke.[68] In a serious case the Lord Chancellor may, where he has the power, dismiss the judge, or in theory (in the case of Supreme Court judges and Lords of Appeal in Ordinary) the address procedure could be activated. That system has been criticised as allowing the Lord Chancellor too much power over the lower judiciary, without unambiguous safeguards for an accused judge, and for relying on a parliamentary address system which is of little practical utility.[69] Assuming that the Commission were to be given responsibilities in relation to alleged judicial misbehaviour, a number of questions would have to be settled. To whom would an initial complaint be addressed? Who would investigate it? Would it be one commissioner, or a senior lawyer briefed by the Commission for the purpose? What rights would a complained-about judge have to be heard? If the complaint were to be upheld, would the Commission itself, or the Lord Chancellor on the Commission's recommendation, have the power to take action? If the present statutory provisions about removal of judges were to be kept broadly as they are now,[70] would it be desirable for the Commission to have the power to recommend, in any appropriate case, that a judge resign? In my view it should. Such a recommendation, from a body containing the judge's peers, would carry far more weight than, for instance, the early-day motions that are put down from time to time by angry MPs; the statutory machinery could remain in place as a long-stop.

(6)   Progress has been made in improving the quality of judicial work through the efforts of the Judicial Studies Board over almost 20 years. Labour's plans (formulated in opposition) envisage that the Judicial Appointments and Training Commission would replace the Judicial Studies Board. If the Commission carried out a review of judicial training (as Labour has suggested), several questions would need to be addressed. One would be whether the voluntary take-up of training after the initial compulsory segment has been completed is adequate. Should there be compulsory refresher training? Should there be compulsory instruction for the judiciary in new and important statute law? Few people object any more to judicial training on the lame ground that it somehow infringes the independence of the judiciary. Formal explanation of the policies and principles behind legislation, for example, in no sense impairs the ability of judges to apply the law in particular cases before them.

[68] See Rodney Brazier, *Constitutional Practice* (2nd ed, 1994), pp 288–296.
[69] See Brazier, *Constitutional Practice*, pp 296–299.
[70] Judges of the High Court and of the Court of Appeal, and Lords of Appeal in Ordinary, can be removed in practice only by the parliamentary address procedure; all other judges are removable by the Lord Chancellor on specified statutory grounds.

More fundamentally, is the judicial training system still geared to the notion of gifted amateurs being helped to make the best of things? Perhaps not: but the Commission should reassure itself that the best training schemes are indeed in place.

(7)   The Commission's expenses would be met from money provided by Parliament. The Commission would have to be funded adequately if it were to do its work properly, and the Government would have to accept that additional public expenditure would be needed. Even if some of the costs of the Commission would merely represent costs incurred already (for instance, in the civil service establishment within the LCD), new costs would be bound to be involved. Presumably some civil service support would be redeployed from the LCD.

(8)   Could a plea be entered on the small point of the Commission's title? 'The Judicial Appointments and Training Commission' is unnecessarily long-winded. Why could it not be called simply the Judicial Service Commission? That accurately describes its responsibilities, and is a title which is used for similar bodies in some other Commonwealth states.[71]

Further reading

Rodney Brazier, *Constitutional Reform* (Oxford University Press, 2nd edn, 1998) Ch 9

Carol Harlow (ed), *Public Law and Politics* (London: Sweet & Maxwell, 1986) Ch 10

House of Commons Home Affairs Committee, *Judicial Appointments Procedures*, HC (1995–96) 52

Labour Party, *Access to Justice* (1995)

Liberal Democrats, *Here We Stand: Proposals for Modernising Britain's Democracy* (Federal White Paper No 6, 1993)

---

[71] See generally S A de Smith, *The New Commonwealth and its Constitutions* (1964), pp 136 et seq.

CHAPTER 17

A BRITISH BILL OF RIGHTS

John Wadham (Liberty)[1]

For something like 800 years since the enactment of the Magna Carta in 1215, the UK has been something of a forcing ground for the theory, and to some extent the practice, of human rights and fundamental freedoms. The Magna Carta itself introduced the concepts of due process and trial by jury, Paine and Locke, amongst others, developed the philosophy of liberty and many other liberal innovations, for example freedom of the press, originated here. However, despite this laudable tradition, the UK's human rights record is not as one would expect from the world's oldest democracy. We may not witness the torture and extra-legal killings usually associated with human rights abuses overseas but nevertheless, not only has Amnesty International had cause to raise concerns about the UK's record with regard to Northern Ireland, criminal trials and the treatment of refugees and asylum seekers but the UK has one of the worst records of any country in Europe in the European Court of Human Rights.[2] The UK is also without a written constitution, highly unusual amongst modern democracies, and in addition, the legislature does not embrace the concept of 'rights'. In their place there are 'privileges', these being any actions not expressly proscribed by law. As such, there are no identifiable and enforceable positive human rights to protect the people of this country. At present, and until the Human Rights Act 1998 comes into legal effect, our rights exist only to the extent that they have not been taken away by the courts or, more frequently, by Parliament. They exist only 'in the silence of the law'.

The incorporation of the European Convention on Human Rights (ECHR) into domestic law will begin to redress this situation. However, both the Convention itself and its manner of incorporation are far from perfect solutions. The introduction of a full constitutional Bill of Rights would guarantee those rights which the UK has already agreed to uphold in international law and introduce a recognised culture of rights into society.

---

[1] Shennagh Simpson, Research Assistant at Liberty assisted with early drafts of this chapter.
[2] Up to the end of 1997 the Court had upheld violations in 50 cases against the UK.

Now that the Scottish people have opted in favour of devolution and the peace process in Northern Ireland has re-started there may be new Bills of Rights for both countries. The proposals in this chapter only apply to England and Wales however. There are difficult issues to be resolved as to how domestic Bills of Rights for all these different jurisdictions would relate to each other and to the Human Rights Act 1998 which incorporates the ECHR.[3]

It is perhaps worth drawing the distinction at this stage between the incorporation of the ECHR and the creation of a constitutional Bill of Rights. In fact in many other jurisdictions incorporation of international treaties is automatic on its ratification by that country. The incorporation of treaties can merely provide for their explicit judicial recognition in domestic law and the meaning of those treaty obligations may be subject to review by an international body, for instance, by the European Court of Human Rights. A Bill of Rights on the other hand is drafted for internal application, usually forms a body of fundamental law and usually there will be no external appeal.

In the current context of the UK the situation is slightly more complex because there is no tradition of incorporation for international treaties and the incorporation of the ECHR is de facto the first Bill of Rights for several hundred years. Although the method of its incorporation does not give it the status of fundamental law, it is given a higher status in domestic law than, say, the Bill of Rights in New Zealand was given. In those circumstances it is more difficult to draw a clear line between the two concepts and this chapter therefore will deal with incorporation as the springboard towards a Bill of Rights, not least because some in government and on the opposition benches will need to be convinced that any further steps need to be taken.

HISTORY[4]

Since the creation of the first Bill of Rights in 1688,[5] the subject came under little scrutiny in this country. More recently however, the publication of the Fabian pamphlet *Democracy and Individual Rights*[6] by Anthony (now Lord) Lester in 1968 effectively opened the debate in a contemporary context. He was particularly concerned with the role of government in passing a variety of xenophobic Acts[7] during the 20th century and how these had affected the rights of people fleeing persecution in their own country or had restricted the

---

[3] The Human Rights Act 1998, for instance, givs a lower status to legislation created by the Scottish Parliament that for the Westminster Parliament.

[4] For a more detailed account, see M Zander, *A Bill of Rights?* (London: Sweet & Maxwell, 4th edn, 1996) pp 1–39.

[5] Although this statute is referred to as a Bill of Rights, it essentially divided power between Parliament and the monarch.

[6] Fabian Tract No 390.

[7] Most notably Aliens Act 1905, Aliens Act 1914, Commonwealth Immigrants Act 1962, Commonwealth Immigrants Act 1968.

rights of New Commonwealth citizens legitimately settling in this country. Further to this, he was concerned with the power of individual officers of the state and the procedures, unavailable for scrutiny outside the government service, that informed their work and inadequate machinery for dealing with complaints against the police and other agencies of the state.

Lester proposed that as an initial step, to deflect any political reticence that a constitutional Bill of Rights may attract, a constitutional court should be established that would make recommendations for further action. This would allow the judiciary time to absorb the spirit of such a Bill before it became fully enforceable in the courts. The ECHR was suggested as a first step but this would be no more than an interim measure.

For the next few years the issue was batted around Parliament in a non-partisan way and was interpreted from both reactionary and liberal perspectives. Lord Lambton gave it a conservative slant, proposing a Bill that protected the individual from state intervention/interference. The baton was then passed to the liberal John Macdonald[8] and fellow liberals Lord Wade and Emlyn Hooson introduced motions in the Lords and Commons respectively. The power of the executive and burgeoning bureaucracy were once more cited as necessitating a Bill of Rights as well as the threat to privacy posed by new technology.

The debate crystallised in 1974 when Sir Leslie Scarman[9] delivered the first of his Hamlyn lectures.[10] He spoke of a need for an instrument to challenge the sovereignty of Parliament and protect basic human rights which were without representation in the legislature. Once more, contemporaneous events, in this case the dubious interrogation practices in use in Northern Ireland, were cited as evidence that such a law was needed. He was strongly in favour of entrenchment and believed that only by making a Bill of Rights superior to the machinations of Parliament could such fundamental rights be protected.

Two Conservatives supported a Bill of Rights in the mid-1970s. Sir Keith Joseph, concerned by events of the day such as industrial unrest and the introduction of a Labour Employment Bill, believed that a solution to protection of private property, corporate interests and the unfettered power of the executive was a Bill of Rights.[11] An interesting feature of his proposed Bill was a clause that would prevent government from introducing certain types of legislation unless they had a prescribed majority.

Lord Hailsham, a Conservative peer, previously in favour of incorporation, now advocated a new British constitution.[12] Subsequent to this an Ulster Unionist moved that the government establish a Royal Commission to investigate

---

[8] *A Bill of Rights* (Liberal Party Pamphlet).
[9] Now Lord Scarman.
[10] *English Law – The New Dimension* (1974).
[11] Talk to Conservative lawyers on 17 March 1975 and later in the pamphlet *Freedom Under Law* (Conservative Political Centre).
[12] *The Times*, 9 May 1975.

the UK Bill of Rights question[13] although it was withdrawn after being damned with faint praise by the Minister of State from the Home Office.[14] However, a Bill of Rights was introduced to the House of Commons by Alan Beith MP, a Liberal, under the Ten-Minute-Rule Bill the following week.[15]

In 1975, the Labour Party National Executive Committee introduced a paper effectively recommending incorporation. Their *Charter of Human Rights* advocated an unentrenched Human Rights Act that would protect the rights of 'ordinary' people who were frequently overlooked by those in power. Despite the Labour government's commitment to state ownership and control, it accepted that the balance was being tipped away from the individual and required some re-alignment. This did not placate those, however, who feared that such a charter would offer no protection against burgeoning state power, mostly Tories who preferred a Bill of Rights with entrenched clauses that would serve to reign in the executive.

In March 1976, Lord Wade moved a Bill in the Lords that in essence, would entrench the ECHR in all existing legislation and entrench, unless specified otherwise, in all subsequent enactments.[16] Hailsham argued that such a Bill would be no more than cosmetic as it contained escape clauses that would frequently be used. He favoured tackling parliamentary sovereignty by creating devolved assemblies and believed that a Bill of Rights alone would not be sufficiently comprehensive.

Lords Wade and Harris continued to be the chief advocates for a Bill of Rights in the Lords. However, they constantly faced constitutional conservatism, particularly with regard to the notion of judges being involved in deciding human rights cases. It was believed that this would remove the judiciary from its traditionally impartial role and involve it in the political process. There was also a fear of such a Bill attracting large volumes of possibly frivolous litigation and that, on the whole, the UK system as it stood was perfectly adequate and did not threaten human rights.[17]

In June 1976, the Home Office published a discussion document that favoured incorporation, drafted by Anthony Lester. This was followed by the Highgate House conference, attended by a number of experts[18] in the human rights field from the UK and abroad. The conference was opened by Roy Jenkins who delivered an address in favour of incorporation. Little publicity was given to the event to protect the views of certain individuals although a subsequent press release stated that the consensus was in favour of incorporation.

The position of the Conservative opposition had been unclear, although the Society of Conservative lawyers were on record as favouring incorporation,

---

[13] James Kilfedder MP – Hansard, HC Vol 894, col 32 (7 July 1975).
[14] Dr Shirley Summerskill.
[15] Hansard, HC Vol 895, cols 1270–1273 (15 July 1975).
[16] Hansard, HL Vol 369, cols 775 et seq (25 March 1976).
[17] See ibid, Lord Denning MR and Lord Lloyd of Hampstead.
[18] See Zander, *A Bill of Rights?*, p 21 for partial list of attendees.

if not a full Bill of Rights.[19] In January 1977, Leon Brittan, then opposition frontbench spokesperson on devolution, promised to table an amendment to the Scotland and Wales Bill that would incorporate the Convention in Scotland and Wales.[20] However, the Bill was eventually withdrawn and opposition amendments not heard. The issue was raised again by Brittan during the committee stage of the Scotland Bill a year later.[21] It was opposed by John Smith who stated that the governments position was outlined in the discussion paper of 1975 and the matter should go to a wider vote. The opposition were defeated by 25 in the Commons. This was the first occasion a Bill of Rights had been debated in the lower House and the subject has not subsequently been officially proposed by the Conservatives.

A few weeks after this, the subject was again raised by Lord Wade in the Lords.[22] Lord Hailsham moved that a Select Committee should be established and it subsequently elicited a wide range of views. The Committee eventually reported that whilst it agreed that the ECHR should be the basis for any domestic Bill of Rights, it could not reach agreement as to whether such a Bill on the statute book was, in fact, desirable. Further to that, it concluded that should such a Bill be deemed desirable, then it should not be imbued with too many expectations and that ultimately, the political climate and nature of the country were of greater importance.

Following the change of government in 1979, Lord Wade continued to move Bills through the Lords although they were always defeated in the Commons. The government took no action, despite their support when in opposition. In June 1984 however, 107 Tory backbenchers signed an Early Day motion calling for incorporation. The Thatcher Cabinet were unmoved.

In 1985, the Conservative peer Lord Broxbourne[23] introduced the Human Rights and Fundamental Freedoms Bill which called for incorporation. Having passed through the Lords, it reached the Commons a year later with cross-party support, although it was opposed by both frontbenches.[24] As had occurred before, the chief objection was that such a Bill would result in the politicisation of the judiciary.

In 1988, Charter 88, which started out as a document signed by 243 people, was established as a campaign for a Bill of Rights and wider constitutional reform. Despite the fact that the new campaign garnered support from a constituency considered to be of the centre-left, the Labour Party were still officially lacking in enthusiasm.[25] However, by 1991, their position appeared to be changing. In the interim, a number of influential think-tanks and pressure groups had published documents supporting a Bill of Rights,

---

[19] *Another Bill of Rights* (Society of Conservative Lawyers, November 1976).
[20] Speech reported in *The Times*, 15 January 1977.
[21] Hansard, HC Vol 943, col 491 (1 February 1978).
[22] Hansard, HL Vol 389, col 973 (3 February 1977).
[23] Formerly Derek Walker-Smith QC MP.
[24] Hansard, HC Vol 109, cols 1223 et seq (6 February 1987).
[25] See Roy Hattersley, then deputy leader, writing in *The Guardian*, 12 December 1988.

including Liberty's consultation document, *A People's Charter – Liberty's Bill of Rights*. Newspapers began to intimate that the Parliamentary Labour Party was ready to change its position on a Bill of Rights. The reality was not such a dramatic change of course; the Labour Party produced the *Charter of Rights* which listed 40 topics it wished to legislate on without mentioning a Bill of Rights.

It was not until 1993, when the Labour Party, by now under the leadership of John Smith voiced more enthusiastic support for a Bill of Rights.[26]

Although it was a Labour government who first signed and ratified the Convention in 1950[27] and granted individuals the right to complain to the Commission and Court,[28] it is only since the last election that Labour have been committed to incorporation.[29]

The recent history is that the Labour Party conference in October 1993 adopted a policy supporting a two-stage process to implement mechanisms to enforce rights.[30] The first included the incorporation of the ECHR, entrenching this set of rights by the use of a 'notwithstanding clause' procedure similar to the procedure used in Canada and setting up a Human Rights Commission to monitor and promote human rights. The second stage was for a Labour government to set up an all-party commission to consider and draft a homegrown Bill of Rights for future implementation. Graham Allen MP, who was then Shadow spokesperson on constitutional affairs, promoted a Bill which set out these aims in legislative form.[31] Tony Blair MP set out his views in July 1994 and reaffirmed the need for strengthened incorporation and the idea of a 'notwithstanding clause'.[32]

However, by December 1996 when Jack Straw MP and Paul Boateng MP published a consultation paper setting out the Labour Party's plans to incorporate the ECHR[33] the desire for a Bill of Rights seems to have waned somewhat. In this first consultation document the Labour Party has deferred the idea of a 'homegrown' Bill of Rights and the five key issues posed by the paper only concerned the incorporation of the ECHR. Interestingly some months before the Society of Labour Lawyers had published *Law Reform Now* which included a chapter written by Lord Irvine, the Lord Chancellor. The section of this chapter which concerned rights reproduced the 1993 policy but omitted completely any reference to a domestic Bill of Rights.

---

[26] See for instance, Francesca Klug, *A People's Charter: Liberty's Bill of Rights* (London: Liberty 1991); Zander, *A Bill of Rights?*.

[27] See A H Robertson and J G Merrils, *Human Rights in Europe* (Manchester University Press, 1993).

[28] On 14 January 1966 during the government of Harold Wilson.

[29] Michael Foot and others voted against Sir Edward Gardner's Bill to incorporate the ECHR, HC Deb, Vol 109, cols 1223–1289 (6 February 1987). The late John Smith gave his support to the incorporation of the ECHR in 1993 (*The Guardian*, 2 March 1993).

[30] For a complete history, see Zander, *A Bill of Rights?*

[31] Human Rights (No 3) Bill, 19 October 1993.

[32] *The Guardian*, 16 July 1994.

[33] *Bringing Rights Home: Labour's Plans to Incorporate the European Convention on Human Rights into UK Law.*

The Liberal Democrats and the Liberals before them have a much longer history of support for a Bill of Rights and the incorporation of the ECHR.[34] In the Report of the Joint Consultative Committee on Constitutional Reform, which reported on the joint agreement between the Labour Party and the Liberal Democrats, incorporation of the ECHR is a clear commitment but there is no mention of a Bill of Rights beyond the phrase:

'The Convention written in 1950, would need to be updated over time as a model for modern constitutional protection of basic human rights and responsibilities inherent in being a British citizen.'

The document is not as detailed as the Labour Party's consultation document but what details there are seem to follow the same pattern.

Many people will be disappointed that these documents do not recommend at the very least the setting up of mechanisms to consult on and develop a domestic Bill of Rights.

Nevertheless Labour has adopted at least the taste for a Bill of Rights. In a lecture[35] delivered under the auspices of Charter 88, Smith stated that a shift in the balance of power between the citizen and the state was required, that central government was remote and local government had been stripped of much of its autonomy following 14 years of interference from the Tories. He advocated devolution and regional assemblies as well as incorporation.

Smith supported a Human Rights Act and the establishment of a Human Rights Commission along the lines of the Equal Opportunities Commission. He was aware that such an Act should protect the rights of the individual and should not be available to protect large organisations or companies against the effects of social legislation. The substance of his lecture became Labour Party policy and led to a Human Rights Bill[36] being introduced to the Commons in January 1994 by Graham Allen, drafted by Liberty.

Anthony Lester, now a peer, continued his human rights work in the Lords by introducing a Bill in November 1994. It was criticised by the Law Lords but they supported incorporation in as far as it allowed UK judges to interpret human rights away from Strasbourg. The fact that a Human Rights Bill had received any support from the Law Lords was a significant development. However, the government continued to oppose any attempts to introduce such a Bill.

It is therefore clear that there has been a gradual shift in establishment opinion from resistance or apathy towards any type of human rights legislation to a situation where a Human Rights Act has been enacted which, when in force, will incorporate the ECHR into domestic law.

---

[34] See Zander, *A Bill of Rights?*
[35] 'A Citizen's Democracy' at Church House, Westminster.
[36] It received its First Reading with no debate and did not proceed further.

THE CASE IN FAVOUR

To the opposers of a Bill of Rights, the UK has an exemplary system that protects rights in its present form. However, even a cursory glance at the UK's record at the European Court of Human Rights quickly gives lie to this claim.

At present, Parliament has sovereignty in the UK giving a government elected even by a minority of the population a supposed mandate to do as it wishes. However, it is recognised that rights go beyond fulfilling what is believed to be the will of the people and are more often needed to protect minorities. Such minorities would include ethnic, sexuality and disability. There are also those on the fringes of society in some way and whose activities and chosen way of life do not attract wide public approval. Such minorities would include those suspected or convicted of crime.

The current system, where Parliament virtually has the power to legislate and therefore abolish and deny rights and freedoms, is all the more apparent in a situation where a government is seeking re-election. Whilst, to some extent, this is always the case, a pre-election period in particular tends to be a time when a government or the opposition is at its most populist and where reaction to moral panic, public outcry or other forms of engineered hysteria forms the basis for legislation that targets an individual and all too often erodes his or her rights, for example the Immigration Act 1968, Prevention of Terrorism (Temporary Provisions) Act 1974, the Criminal Justice and Public Order Act 1994, the Police Act 1997, amongst others. Where legislation is motivated by political expediency, human rights will inevitably take a back seat.

The balance, therefore, between the executive and the other branches of the administration needs to be redressed, with the courts providing a check on the excesses of Parliament driven by the executive. The judiciary, whilst hardly representative of the population as a whole, provides a degree of impartiality. Reform of the judiciary would go some way towards changing the composition of the bench (see below). Currently, judges 'make' law as their pronouncements on both statute and common law set precedents that others must follow and a Bill of Rights should act as a counterbalance to some of the more eccentric decisions. Any Bill of Rights would have to be aware of this proclivity; one does not have to stretch the imagination too far to conjure up a situation where a judge interprets the freedom of expression to make any ban on advertising, including tobacco advertising on Formula One racing cars, unlawful.[37]

From Liberty's point of view, the concept of the empowerment of the individual is one of the more important considerations. The current system

---

[37] In fact the authorities in Strasbourg do not regard commercial speech particularly highly (see D J Harris, M O'Boyle and C Warbrick, *Law of the European Convention on Human Rights* (London: Butterworths, 1995).

does not tell people explicitly what their rights are and in the highly arcane world of legislation, notions of 'proscription' and 'permission' do not encourage the layperson to challenge an abuse of rights. Taking cases to Strasbourg is a long and expensive process: a domestic Bill would make the legal process accessible to all. A Bill of Rights should become part of the National Curriculum, to be taught in schools as well as in further and higher education. This knowledge and subsequent level of popular consciousness should increase the level of informed debate around the subject. One can only speculate about the extent to which human rights in the UK would have been improved had a Bill of Rights been introduced years earlier.

The heightened awareness of human rights that should follow from the introduction of the Bill would place rights higher on the agenda of policy-makers and officials, making them mindful of the consequences of contravening the Bill when drafting legislation.

THE CASE AGAINST

In many ways, the UK is a conservative country and many believe that its constitution is not only perfectly adequate but superior to most others. Those who argue against a Bill of Rights believe it is a mature system that is flexible whilst simultaneously protecting rights. Parliamentary sovereignty, it is contested, allows the will of the majority to be represented in addition to protecting rights in partnership with the law. A Bill of Rights, however, would not be sufficiently flexible to accommodate individual circumstances and would tie Parliament to one set of standards.

A further objection to a Bill of Rights is the role the judiciary would play in interpreting principles enshrined in the Bill. This would apply particularly where the Bill is entrenched; in such circumstances, judges would be responsible for deciding current and future legislation that conflicted with the entrenched articles. There is concern that this situation gives an unacceptable level of power to an appointed rather than elected body. In addition, there is the practical problem that the judiciary's past record does not encourage confidence and places a question mark over whether or not judges should be charged with making decisions on fundamental rights. Some who would otherwise support a Bill of Rights oppose it on the judges' record alone.

For Liberty, at least, the decision is clear. Parliament is not, and perhaps never has been, a sufficiently robust guardian of the rights of the people. It has carefully created its own rights but its need for re-election makes it dangerous to leave the rights of the unpopular in its hands alone. Furthermore, a Bill of Rights will begin to create a culture of rights and gives those without influence in Parliament a fulcrum on which they can prise elected politicians away from riding roughshod over rights in the interests of popularity.

Judges and courts are of course not perfect either and they need to be improved but they make thousands of decisions affecting individuals every day. Liberty would prefer that the courts were given a set of principles to help them to respect fundamental rights rather than forcing them to patch and mend where they can.

THE OBJECTIVES OF A BILL OF RIGHTS

To increase public awareness of rights

Once it is fundamental law, the Bill and surrounding issues would be taught in schools, colleges and universities. It would attract publicity and produce its own case law, which would in turn attract further media attention. As it would introduce the concept of positive rights into this country, a Bill of Rights would help to stimulate a stronger sense of what these rights are and how they can be protected. It might also create a culture where individuals not only knew about their own rights but also respected those of others.

To empower people to challenge the actions of those who exercise power over them

This could be police officers, customs officials, secret service agents or any other local authority workers or civil servants. The majority of challenges brought under the Bill of Rights in the USA are against officials as opposed to the legislation itself. A Bill of Rights would ensure that the actions of thousands of officials could be called to account.

To act as a brake on government action

At present in the UK, the concentration of state power is with the executive, allowing laws that impact on people's rights, such as the Prevention of Terrorism (Temporary Provisions) Act, to be passed virtually overnight. An important function of a Bill of Rights would be either to prevent such laws from being passed or at least have a stalling effect that would allow for some measure of debate and scrutiny in the hope that they would emerge as better laws.

To force the government to legislate to protect specific rights

Successful challenges in the European Court of Human Rights have forced the government to change the law on issues such as homosexuality in Northern

Ireland and birching in the Isle of Man, bringing them into line with the rest of UK law. The principles enshrined in a Bill of Rights would provide leverage in areas where the law is silent or breaches fundamental rights.

To provide protection for minorities

Much of the worst discrimination in this country is suffered by minority communities, a situation exacerbated by a system of government that represents only the perceived will of the majority, heightened by their dependence on periodic election. This leads to a general reluctance to defend the rights of minorities. A Bill of Rights with a general anti-discrimination clause would provide some protection for vulnerable groups.

WHY THE ECHR PROVIDES AN INSUFFICIENT BASIS FOR A CONSTITUTIONAL BILL OF RIGHTS

The incorporation of the ECHR into domestic law is certainly an encouraging step but for a number of reasons, it fails to go far enough. The ECHR itself is 50 years old, was one of the first responses to calls for the establishment of international human rights law and was, in part, a reaction to the events in Nazi Germany. Its age, in common with any law that concerns the social world and its attitudes, means it no longer reflects society's view on a number of issues or the ways in which societal dynamics have shifted in a period of rapid change. The UK is one of the last states to incorporate and arguably, this should have been done 20 years ago. Whilst judges make efforts to interpret the ECHR in accordance with contemporaneous thinking, there are still areas that are wholly excluded from its scope that could not be remedied by any amount of creative case law. Such areas would need to be included in a domestic Bill of Rights.

The right to know

There is no right to information held by public bodies.[38] Although access to medical records and personal files held by local authorities is set out in statute,[39] there is no general right to the whole welter of information held by the government and its agencies. The Labour Party has, of course, given a commitment to open government and a Freedom of Information Act.

---

[38] Article 10 only protects the right to impart information.
[39] Access to Medical Reports Act 1988, Access to Health Records Act 1990 and Access to Personal Files Act 1987.

The rights of immigrants, asylum seekers and those being extradited

The ECHR places no obligation on the state to provide rights of due process or a fair trial to those facing extradition or deportation.[40] As there is a question over the deportee's entitlement to be in the country, they do not fall within the ambit of Article 6 – the right to a fair trial – which only applies where the individual concerned had a pre-existing civil right to be in the country. For those at risk of deportation, an important right would be a duty on the state seeking extradition to demonstrate a prima facie case in court prior to ordering the extradition.[41] This is particularly important where individuals are extradited to a country where they are away from their usual support network and are faced with a foreign legal system, conducted in a language they do not understand and are, therefore, at a considerable disadvantage. In such situations, the state wishing to extradite should, arguably, only have the power to do so where the charge is serious, where there is sufficient evidence to convict and where the country concerned operates a patently fair trial system.

Where an individual is held in detention pending deportation or extradition, he or she is not protected as detention in these circumstances is allowed under Article 5(1)(f). This also places no restriction on the length of detention or the merits of either the detention or the deportation.[42]

The ECHR does not include the right to enter a country as either a resident or an asylum seeker. Nor is there a right to due process for those who believe they have the right to enter and remain in a country. In fact, the rules governing the right to asylum enshrined in the United Nations Convention are not referred to in the ECHR.

Anti-discrimination provisions

Article 14 enshrines the right to be free from discrimination. However, due to the age of the Convention, it only deals with discrimination against certain groups and does not refer to discrimination on the grounds of sexuality or

---

[40] The right to submit reasons, the right to review (not necessarily before a court) and the right to representation, before an expulsion is effected are contained in Protocol 7, Article 1 but this has not been ratified by the UK. The article also permits expulsion without those protections where it 'is necessary in the interests of public order or is grounded on reasons of national security'.

[41] This was the position before the Criminal Justice Act 1988.

[42] Nevertheless in the case of *Chahal v UK* (27 June 1995) Application No 22414/93, the Commission found a violation on the basis of the length of time Mr Chahal was detained over pending deportation. This case is of particular interest because the applicant was detained for over five years pending deportation and the (then) government's argument for deportation was based on claims of national security which were not specified in detail before the domestic courts.

disability for example.[43] A further fault is that unlike equivalent provisions in the International Covenant on Civil and Political Rights,[44] Article 14 only applies where another article of the ECHR has been breached simultaneously. The result is inadequate treatment of the article by both the Commission and the Court, who tend to prefer the substantive article and hand down judgment accordingly.[45] As such, there is little guidance on the meaning of Article 14. Clearly, the ECHR does not provide an adequate basis to outlaw discrimination. However, it should be noted that the Council of Europe is considering whether there should be an additional Protocol to the ECHR modelled on Article 26 of the Covenant.

Criminal justice

The ECHR does not contain a provision outlining the minimum standards in the criminal justice system such as is present in Article 14(3)(g) of the International Covenant on Civil and Political Rights. The Covenant states that, in the determination of a criminal charge, a person shall not 'be compelled to testify against himself or confess guilt'.[46] The United Nations Human Rights Committee has already voiced concerns about the Criminal Justice and Public Order Act 1994 and its encroachment on the right to silence when it considered compliance with Article 14. The Committee was particularly concerned with the inferences that may be drawn from the silence of defendants.

The ECHR also fails to address the issue of the right to trial by jury in serious criminal cases.[47]

Detention

Although the ECHR contains restrictions on the legality of detention, no minimum standards are set for conditions of detention outside those contained in Article 3 – the provision against torture, inhuman and degrading treatment or punishment.[48] The conditions required to breach the rights contained in Article 3 would have to be particularly severe and this provision is not designed to deal with detention conditions that are 'merely inadequate'.

---

[43] However, it does make discrimination on the basis of 'other status' unlawful.
[44] See Article 26.
[45] There are some important judgments however. See, eg, the *Belgian Linguistic* case (1968) 1 EHRR 241.
[46] Although this may be partly protected and there are two cases from the UK being considered by the European Commission on Human Rights at the time of writing.
[47] Such a right is also not contained in any other international treaty of human rights but is contained in the Magna Carta.
[48] See, eg, the International Covenant on Civil and Political Rights, Article 10(1): 'All persons deprived of their liberty shall be treated with humanity and with respect for the inherent dignity of the human person'.

Other positive rights for those incarcerated are also missing – the ri
to a lawyer[49] and the right not to be held incommunicado in pa

Other rights

The ECHR, for instance, does not include any specific rights in respect of children.[50]

FURTHER WEAKNESSES IN THE EUROPEAN CONVENTION ON HUMAN RIGHTS

Some of the more important rights not addressed by, and wholesale omissions within, the ECHR that would hopefully be included in a domestic Bill of Rights have been outlined above. However, there are areas where the articles of the ECHR as they stand are subject to limitations. Some of these are illustrated below.

Article 2 enshrines the right to life, although this article has been drafted to contain the qualification that it can be breached where 'absolutely necessary' and that lethal force can be used where:

'(b) in order to effect a lawful arrest or to prevent the escape of a person lawfully detained;

(c) in action lawfully taken for the purpose of quelling a riot or insurrection.'

It is surely arguable that riot control or preventing escape from arrest is not, of itself and without there being any real threat to the safety of others, a situation sufficiently extreme to allow the use of lethal force.[51]

---

[49] The right to access to a lawyer has of course been litigated in Strasbourg but only as a consequential effect of the right to correspondence and right to access to courts, see, eg, *Silver v UK*, (25 March 1983) Series A, No 61 and *Golder v UK* (7 May 1974) Series A, No 18. These cases have not dealt with the right to see a solicitor on arrival at the police station as contained (in a less than perfect form) in s 56 of the Police and Criminal Evidence Act 1984. In *Murray v UK* (27 June 1994) No 18731/91 the Commission held that the failure to allow access within a reasonable period and the refusal to allow the lawyer to be present at police interviews breaches Article 6. This is not a right in itself but is dependent on the fact that the evidence (including 'evidence' from the adverse inference consequent on the suspect's silence) which led to the conviction may have resulted from the lawyer's absence.

[50] Such as that contained in the International Covenant on Civil and Political Rights, Article 24:
  '(1) Every child shall have, without any discrimination as to race, colour, sex, language, religion, national or social origin, property or birth, the right to such measures of protection as are required by his status as a minor, on the part of his family, society and the State.
  (2) Every child shall be registered immediately after birth and shall have a name.
  (3) Every child has the right to acquire a nationality.'

[51] In the case of the shooting by members of the SAS of three members of the IRA in Gibraltar, the European Court of Human Rights decided, by a majority of 10 to 9, that the preparations and briefing of the soldiers was sufficiently inadequate to make the government liable for a breach of their right to life, *McCann v UK* (27 September 1995) Series A, No 324.

Article 5(1)(e) sanctions:

'detention of persons for the prevention of the spreading of infectious diseases, of persons of unsound mind, alcoholics or drug addicts or vagrants.'

These are hopefully more enlightened times and society would not view the detention of those with an unconventional way of life as being acceptable where the detention is purely for that reason. It is unlikely that a Bill of Rights drafted today would contain such a clause.

The situation regarding infectious diseases is less clear but the epidemic diseases of the 1940s and 1950s are not as prevalent in Europe as they were when the ECHR was drafted.

Again the wider implications of public safety and the national interest are limiting factors in the scope of the rights of privacy and freedoms of religion, expression and assembly:

'except such as is in accordance with the law and is necessary in a democratic society in the interests of national security, public safety or the economic well-being of the country, for the prevention of disorder and crime, for the protection of health or morals, or for the protection of the rights and freedoms of others.'[52]

Expressions such as 'public safety' and 'national security' are arguably too vague to merit inclusion in a Bill of Rights. For example, Liberty's Bill of Rights replaces 'public safety' with the more specific 'imminent physical harm'. It is difficult to oppose provisions connected to the limitation of crime although Liberty feel that the 'protection of the rights and freedoms of others' is sufficient in these circumstances.

It can be argued that at least the absence of some rights in the ECHR can be cured by the incorporation of the additional provisions. Protocol 4 contains freedom from imprisonment for breach of contract, the right of freedom of movement within and from and to the country. Protocol 6 ensures that the death penalty is completely abolished and Protocol 7 rights of due process for aliens and those subject to deportation procedures. It also includes the right to appeal in criminal cases, compensation for miscarriages of justice, a ban on double jeopardy and equality between spouses. There are also other protocols being drafted by the Council of Europe which if ratified and incorporated by the UK would make a sufficient improvement on rights.[53]

---

[52] This is from Article 8(2), privacy and family life.
[53] The first of these concerns minority rights and the second a new improved anti-discrimination provision modelled on Article 26 of the International Covenant on Civil and Political Rights.

CONTENT

Despite the shortcomings in the ECHR mentioned above, Liberty has taken its style and form as a basis for developing a model for a domestic Bill of Rights.[54] It draws upon the 1966 United Nations International Covenant on Civil and Political Rights where this is stronger and less ambiguously drafted and where both the Convention and Covenant are silent, upon the relevant parts of other international, regional or domestic human rights instruments. In the absence of any suitable instrument Liberty has drawn upon broad principles set out in UK law.

These proposals restrict the content of the Bill of Rights to those rights traditionally included in such Bills. However some have suggested that any Bill of Rights for the 21st century not only should include socio-economic rights like the right to an adequate income and housing, but also the right to clean air and water and a healthy environment. For the purposes of this chapter it is assumed that any Bill of Rights will be restricted to civil and political rights.

Nevertheless for a Bill of Rights to obtain the aims set out above it will require the support of the courts, the government, Parliament and most importantly the people. It is therefore essential that the content, enforcement and methodology of any new Bill of Rights is subjected to the widest possible consultation process possible over a period of years. Graham Allen's Bill (see p 354 above) to incorporate the ECHR also proposed setting up a Bill of Rights Commission to consult widely and then to present recommendations to Parliament.

Such a commission would not need to be set up by legislation and could either be set up by creating an inquiry which would report to a particular minister or could be constituted by Royal Commission. Either way it would have to be composed of members of all political persuasions and of those who have experience of human rights issues and the consequences of violations of those rights. It should have sufficient resources to encourage responses and submissions not only from lawyers and human rights experts but from community groups and individuals. Its report should be available in sufficient time for the political parties to include the creation of a Bill of Rights in their next manifestos.

Obviously, the government's decision not to set up a Human Rights Commission at the same time as incorporating the ECHR is disappointing in many ways, not least because it could have acted as a focus for the development of this consultation process.

---

[54] See *A People's Charter: Liberty's Bill of Rights* (Liberty, 1991) and *Liberty Bill of Rights* (Liberty, 1995).

AN APPROACH TO ENFORCEMENT

It is fundamental to Liberty's proposals for a Bill of Rights that the Bill should be enforceable by individuals through the courts and be more than just a statement of intent. The Bill of Rights would have to include a right to redress and legal aid would have to be available for those taking cases. To implement a Bill in any other way would reduce its status to that of a rather toothless code of practice that would not adequately address the issues surrounding abuses of fundamental rights.

The Bill should be enforceable by individuals against the state and its agents, including the judiciary, the Crown, local government and quangos and would apply to all, including children, from the moment of birth. It would not be an appropriate instrument for protecting individuals against themselves nor could it be used to resolve disputes between individuals. A possible exception to this could be where the state has failed to provide adequate protection for human rights when this failure might constitute grounds for some kind of collateral challenge, something not available under the Human Rights Act 1998 (see s 6(6)). This procedure might for instance be used to ensure the state provides adequate remedies against abuse by third parties, eg violation of privacy by private security firms.

In the government's consideration of the incorporation of the ECHR it rejected the possibility of the rights in the Convention taking precedence over primary legislation. This overly-cautious approach cannot be justified as a part of the creation of a new constitutional Bill of Rights, particularly if the Bill followed a period of proper consultation.

Liberty would argue that where the courts have to resolve a conflict between the rights set out in a Bill of Rights and any other legislation, the Bill of Rights – which expresses the fundamental values of liberal democracy – should be given precedence. The Human Rights Act 1998 incorporating the ECHR means that where rights and statute conflict, statute will always prevail and the individual who is able to show to the satisfaction of the domestic court that his or her Convention rights had been violated will nevertheless lose the case. The 'loser' would then either have to petition the European Commission in Strasbourg for redress, or wait for Parliament to change the law. The 'loser' might be able to obtain compensation, but only several years later. They would not be able to obtain any other remedy such as an injunction, or any of the usual remedies in judicial review, such as certiorari, prohibition, mandamus or a declaration. These may often be the only true remedy for a person who has suffered a violation of the ECHR.

If the court is unable to construe a statute in a way which is compatible with the ECHR, the Human Rights Act 1998, when in force, will give it the power to expose the problem by making a declaration that there has been a violation of Convention rights. This is an improvement over some weaker models of incorporation, and clearly there would be pressure on the government to change the law where such a declaration was made.

More significantly, the government has suggested that although the court will not be able to set aside the statute there will be a 'fast track' procedure which will allow Parliament to amend the offending law and to bring it in line with human rights principles. However, problems arise when one starts to consider how such mechanisms might operate under a government which has no commitment to human rights.

Governments have a habit of ignoring individual rights when there is a need to be seen to be 'tough on crime', or where they perceive that public or media opinion, or other pressures, would not be in their favour, particularly in the run-up to a general election. It is precisely this that human rights legislation is designed to prevent. If a case concerned an unpopular group of people, like suspected terrorists, travellers or protesters, or was controversial in some other way, it is all too easy to imagine a future government's reluctance to change the law. Human rights cases are often, by definition, brought by people who are part of an 'unpopular' minority, or are controversial cases for some other reason.

Anxieties about the possible erosion of parliamentary sovereignty are misplaced. Other countries have identified systems which uphold both the importance of human rights and the sovereignty of Parliament, and there is no genuine obstacle to prevent the UK doing the same.

In Canada, for example, the courts either 'read in' the missing rights into the statute or alternatively make it clear that in the particular circumstances part of the statute no longer applies. Parliament then has the opportunity of either cleaning up the statute to comply with the ruling or re-enacting the statute and adding a clause stating that the provision applies 'notwithstanding' the Bill of Rights. This latter option then prevents the court from disapplying that provision of the statute even if it *does* conflict with human rights.

Parliamentary sovereignty is thus preserved and parliamentary accountability is enhanced by the need for the decision to override rights to be clearly argued and debated. But where Parliament has enacted legislation in a rush, which is all too often the case, any unintended consequences that might have resulted in violations of fundamental human rights can be put right by the courts.

Parliamentary sovereignty would not be compromised by allowing the courts to strike down legislation, as this very power would have been given to them by Parliament itself, in limited circumstances, to provide a human rights 'safety net'. The European Communities Act 1972 is an example of such an exercise of sovereignty which has worked successfully.

There is more at stake here than a theoretical debate for constitutional theorists and lawyers, as an example will show. Imagine that an ex-member of MI5, concerned about unnecessary invasions of privacy by the Secret Service believes that it is right to expose the details of this malpractice. This is a criminal offence under the Official Secrets Act 1989, and remains an offence however much the revelations are in the public interest. Article 10 of the ECHR provides a right of freedom of expression. If the ECHR is incorporated as the government intends, that right will not be available as a defence because the statute, the Official Secrets Act does not provide such a defence. If the ECHR is to make a difference in this case the MI5 officer – and the journalists that aided and abetted him or her – need to have a clear right to argue that the Official Secrets Act has been altered by incorporation of the Convention and freedom of expression is something the jury is entitled to consider when deciding whether or not to convict.

AGREEMENT AND AMENDMENT

A Bill of Rights should encourage a wider debate on civil liberties issues and, where views on fundamental rights conflict, should be open to scrutiny through the democratic process and not be the subject of discussions confined to the judiciary and the executive. Accordingly, the Bill should not be a blunt instrument but dynamic, protecting fundamental rights and embracing progress and shifts in society's attitudes. This may, in itself, involve debate as to what is and what is not a fundamental right. The terms of the Bill should therefore strike a balance between being sufficiently focused so as to leave no doubt as to what is expected and having enough flexibility to accommodate change without resorting to amendment.

As mentioned above, one of the chief failures of the ECHR is its inability to reflect changes in society. Although it would be hoped that a Bill of Rights would be able to accommodate some change without amendment, some formal mechanism for amendment would be required if a change became necessary. This method would preferably be distinct from the usual parliamentary process and allow some democratic participation.

Any amendment to a Bill of Rights would be have to be made through an Act of Parliament. However allowing any Bill of Rights to be amended as if it has the same status of any other legislation might result in the Bill of Rights being significantly changed every time a new political party took control of the government. This would considerably reduce the status of the rights in the Bill of Rights and it is likely to ensure that the rights become a political football.

The consultation process suggested above would, it is hoped, create sufficient consensus to allow the content of the Bill of Rights to be entrenched in some way. Methods for establishing the status of the Bill of Rights could include discussions and agreement by referendum, by a Speaker's conference of both Houses of Parliament or merely by the acceptance of the new constitutional status of the Bill by its passage through Parliament and supported by the public. Alternatively the matter could be dealt with by creating a special status in the constitution by amending the Parliament Acts.

Of course, if the establishment of a Bill of Rights coincided with the creation of a written constitution, then the constitution could ensure its status and the procedures for amendment.

366

Liberty has proposed that amendment of a Bill of Rights could not proceed unless a two-thirds majority in favour was obtained in both Houses on final reading. Should the Act be passed, the application of the amendment could be delayed by five years by the Second Chamber. This would not only give sufficient time to scrutinise the amendment for any potential reduction in rights but would also ensure that the change could become the subject of an election campaign. This would provide entrenchment through the democratic process.

Further work on such arrangements can of course be progressed if Parliament accepts the government's suggestion that a Human Rights Committee (or Committees) should be created in Parliament to monitor, promote and enforce human rights in Parliament.

Liberty proposes that a parliamentary committee be charged with supervising all human rights business and would play an advisory role during the amending process. This committee would be elected unlike Select Committees which are appointed, and its system of election would ensure that no individual party predominates. Liberty also proposes that this committee would be assisted by a new quango, established along the lines of the Equal Opportunities Commission or Commission for Racial Equality, which would also be responsible for monitoring and promoting human rights issues.

OTHER ISSUES

There are many other issues that will require considerable thought and resolution. Including of course the extent that private individuals and companies are liable for human rights violations. The current Human Rights Bill takes a middle line and has attempted to ensure that all those with public functions have to comply with the ECHR. At the time of writing there is considerable debate about the extent to which this Bill will impose duties on third parties, particularly newspapers.

REFORM OF THE JUDICIARY

As mentioned above, the introduction of a Bill of Rights would give considerable new powers to the judiciary which has given rise to concerns among some who would otherwise support a Bill. It is arguable therefore that a constitutional Bill of Rights should not be introduced without reform of judicial appointment that would address the unrepresentative nature of the present judiciary.

The constituency from which appointments are currently made should be broadened, allowing solicitors, barristers and academic lawyers to be appointed to all courts. A modern appointment and promotion system should be adopted, which would include public advertising of posts, shortlisting and interview. This would serve to create a more accountable system and allow for the implementation of an equal opportunities policy.

CONCLUSION

The incorporation of the ECHR will make a significant difference to human rights in the UK however weak the rights in the Convention are and however weakly it is incorporated. Incorporation is a necessary first step to a constitutional Bill of Rights. However, the difficulty that it creates for those of us who wish to move on to a second stage is one of delay. At the time of writing the Human Rights Act is not due to come into force before January 2000. It has been said by the government that a Bill of Rights will require further consideration. The government, having taken the step of incorporation, is going to require considerable persuasion that it should take any further steps until the results of incorporation are clear. Nevertheless to ensure that the UK gets a proper constitutional Bill of Rights the campaign must begin now.

Further reading

Robert Blackburn, *Towards a Constitutional Bill of Rights for the United Kingdom* (London: Pinter, 1999)

David Feldman, *Civil Liberties and Human Rights in England and Wales* (Oxford University Press, 1993)

Richard Gordon and Richard Wilmot-Smith (ed), *Human Rights in the United Kingdom* (Oxford: Clarendon Press, 1996)

D Harris, M O'Boyle and C Warbrick, *Law of the European Convention on Human Rights* (London: Butterworths, 1995)

Francesca Klug, *A People's Charter: Liberty's Bill of Rights* (Liberty, 1991)

Michael Zander, *A Bill of Rights?* (London: Sweet & Maxwell, 4th edn, 1996)

CHAPTER 18

A PARLIAMENTARY COMMITTEE ON HUMAN RIGHTS

Professor Robert Blackburn (King's College, London)

'Parliament itself should play a leading role in protecting the rights which are at the heart of a parliamentary democracy'
(Labour consultation paper, *Bringing Rights Home*, 1996)

The Labour leadership's policy statements over the period 1996–98 have indicated its firm support for the principle of establishing a parliamentary committee on human rights. No such parliamentary committee, expressly charged with a scrutiny function relating to civil liberties and human rights, has ever been established at Westminster. Neither has any existing Select Committee ever had incorporated into its terms of reference any statement of human rights, either of a domestic or international nature. Traditionally, this has rested upon the belief that Parliament conducts its legislative and administrative watchdog functions already with special reference to the implications of government business for the rights and freedoms of the individual, and consequently no special mechanism in either House of Parliament was necessary. In 1977, a House of Lords inquiry on incorporation of the European Convention on Human Rights (ECHR) declared itself sceptical of the utility of a special committee on human rights, believing that such a committee was no more likely to detect a breach of human rights standards than the House as a whole would be in its general conduct of scrutinising government Bills and administrative practices.[1]

Over the past 20 years, however, it has become increasingly evident that the UK government and Westminster Parliament are more than capable of carrying out administrative practices and enacting legislative measures that contradict internationally accepted standards of human rights. As is chronicled elsewhere, the UK has regularly been found to be in violation of the ECHR before the European Court of Human Rights.[2] Indeed it is precisely

---

[1] Report of the Select Committee on a Bill of Rights, HL [1977–78] 176, p 38.
[2] See eg S Farran, *The UK Before the European Court of Human Rights* (London: Blackstone Press, 1996).

in recognition of this fact that a substantial shift in political and legal opinion on the desirability of incorporating the ECHR into our own domestic law took place, leading to the enactment of the Human Rights Act 1998. But few would wish to rely upon the courts and legal litigation alone to protect our human rights. More than ever today, with a positive statement of human rights being implanted in our law for the first time under the Human Rights Act, it will be essential for Parliament to perform its proper role of scrutinising the conduct of government and legislative proposals for conformity with fundamental rights and freedoms.

This chapter examines the case for a parliamentary committee on human rights against the background of the Labour government's policy objectives in the fields of human rights reform and the modernisation of parliamentary procedure. It seeks to identify what the terms of reference of any such body should be, and the extent to which they should relate to general governmental business, both at home and also concerning international affairs, as well as to the scrutiny of legislative proposals. It considers whether more than one committee will necessarily be involved in any such initiative, and whether any pre-existing bodies might be able to carry out or contribute to the overall effort required. Finally, it addresses the question whether peers in the House of Lords or MPs in the House of Commons are best suited to the task of domestic and international human rights law scrutiny work, or whether perhaps some joint mechanism combining the talents and advantages of both groups of parliamentarians is the best way forward.

LABOUR POLICY OBJECTIVES

In its White Paper on incorporation of the ECHR, *Rights Brought Home*, which was published simultaneously with the Human Rights Bill in October 1997, the government emphasised that the question of any new parliamentary procedures regarding human rights, including the creation of a special committee and what its role and powers might be, 'is a matter for Parliament itself to decide'.[3] However, few will be in any doubt that the driving force behind a reform of this character, as with most all other matters of parliamentary organisation, will be the new Labour Cabinet and its members who are directly responsible for parliamentary affairs. In the House of Commons, the Leader of the House and President of the Council, formerly Ann Taylor, and now Margaret Beckett, is chairing a Select Committee to examine and report on the modernisation of the procedures of the House of Commons, and has behind her a commanding 177-seat overall Labour majority to ward off any difficulties posed by the opposition. In the House of Lords, there presides a particularly powerful Lord Chancellor, Lord Irvine, who has been

[3] White Paper, *Rights Brought Home: The Human Rights Bill*, 1997, at p 14.

appointed by the Prime Minister to chair the Cabinet Committee on Constitutional Reform Policy and also its sub-committees on incorporation of the European Convention on Human Rights and on House of Lords' reform.

The Labour leadership's general policy objective on the subject has crystallised into an endorsement in principle for the idea of a committee on human rights whilst reserving judgment on the details of any new parliamentary scheme of scrutiny pending the outcome and final shape of the legislation incorporating the ECHR. Consistent with Labour's readiness to consult widely with interested bodies over its reform programme generally, its Policy Papers in 1996–97 have tended to raise questions and options for others to comment on, rather than offer specific settled recommendations of its own. Thus the 1996 consultative document, *Bringing Rights Home: Labour's Plans to Incorporate the European Convention on Human Rights into UK Law*, issued by Jack Straw (then Shadow Home Secretary) and Paul Boateng (then Shadow Minister for the Lord Chancellor's Department) said that:[4]

'The passage of [the Human Rights Act] will provide an opportunity to strengthen parliamentary machinery on human rights. We also propose that a new Joint Committee on Human Rights of both Houses of Parliament should be established. This would have a continuing responsibility to monitor the operation of the new Act and other aspects of the UK's human rights obligations. It would have the powers of a select committee to compel witnesses to attend. Where new legislation was identified as having an impact on human rights issues it could be subject to scrutiny by the Joint Committee. The committee would be able to call on other bodies in discharging its responsibilities. More detailed work would need to be undertaken on how the Joint Committee would work in practice, should this proposal be adopted by Parliament.'

Ten months later, the new Labour government's declared views on the subject were expressed in its White Paper, *Rights Brought Home*, to be that:[5]

'The best course would be to establish a new Parliamentary Committee with functions relating to human rights. This would not require legislation or any change in parliamentary procedure. There could be a Joint Committee of both Houses of Parliament or each House could have its own Committee; or there could be a Committee which met jointly for some purposes and separately for others. The new Committee might conduct enquiries on a range of human rights issues relating to the Convention, and produce reports so as to assist the Government and Parliament in deciding what action to take. It might also want to range more widely, and examine issues relating to the other international obligations of the United Kingdom such as proposals to accept new rights under other human rights treaties.'

Then, during the passage of the Human Rights Act in the House of Lords, the Lord Chancellor, Lord Irvine, responded to amendments suggested by

---

[4] *Bringing Rights Home*, October 1996, at p 12.
[5] *Rights Brought Home*, 1997, at p 14.

Lord Meston QC and Baroness Williams that a human rights committee be installed straightaway, by saying:[6]

'The government favour a committee or committees. I did not say that there will be a committee. That is a matter for Parliament. I have a hesitation about an amendment which puts on the statute book the need for scrutiny and report by an appropriate committee of each House of Parliament in advance of knowing whether we shall have such a committee because that is dependent upon Parliament. I also have a concern that the very concept (even on the footing that we do have a committee) while good in terms of parliamentary scrutiny may be bad if it turned out to be an engine for delay in remedying human rights problems. One must balance all those points.'

Meanwhile, as a separate initiative in the House of Commons, one of the earliest acts of the new Labour government was to establish a Select Committee on the Modernisation of the House of Commons (MOHOC) on 4 June 1997. As already stated, this is chaired by the Cabinet minister and the Leader of the House, formerly Ann Taylor, now Margaret Beckett, and is very much in the business of seeing that what it recommends is actually carried out (unlike, it must be observed, the recommendations of most Select Committee reports). Two of the four priorities announced for top consideration by MOHOC are (1) the handling of legislative proposals, and (2) the means by which the House holds ministers to account.[7] Although, as yet, no mention of the subject has been made, nor any connection between the government's human rights and parliamentary modernisation programmes been publicly drawn, yet MOHOC's terms of reference are clearly wide enough to encompass the consideration of detailed proposals relating to one or more new committee charged with responsibilities with respect to human rights.

THE HUMAN RIGHTS ACT

A good case for establishing a parliamentary committee of human rights already existed before 1998.[8] But with the enactment of the Human Rights Act this year, there are even stronger grounds for setting up new parliamentary scrutiny procedures focused specifically upon human rights matters. The significance of the Human Rights Act is very great indeed and its effects will usher in what amounts to a new era in our legal and parliamentary systems.

---

[6] HL Deb, 27 November 1997, col 1150.

[7] See Government Submission to the Committee on Modernising the Procedures of the House of Commons, 1997, para 3.

[8] For earlier discussions of a human rights committee, see David Kinley, *The European Convention on Human Rights: Compliance without Incorporation* (Aldershot: Dartmouth, 1993); and Michael Ryle, 'Pre-legislative Scrutiny: A Prophylactic Approach to Protection of Human Rights' (1994) *Public Law* 192.

The individual rights and freedoms of the ECHR now represent an official code and moral yardstick against which to test not only the principles of the common law and parliamentary statutes but the legitimacy of government in general. This is further reinforced by the UK's membership of the European Union whose constituent treaties and institutions including the European Parliament and Court of Justice have given express recognition to the self-same human rights principles.

This major constitutional Act provides that all primary and subordinate legislation must as far as possible be read and given effect in a way which is compatible with the human rights articles of the ECHR. Section 4 of the Act authorises the judiciary to make a 'declaration of incompatibility' where it considers parliamentary legislation violates basic individual rights and freedoms. Section 19 requires government ministers when presenting any new Bill to Parliament to publish a written statement on the compatibility of the proposed legislation with the provisions of the ECHR. Section 10 establishes a new legislative procedure for enacting 'remedial orders' to rectify human rights violations following an adverse ruling in the European Court of Human Rights or in our domestic courts where a 'declaration of incompatibility' is made. In such circumstances, there can be no doubt that Parliament must respond by establishing the human rights of the ECHR expressly within its own terms of reference for the purposes of parliamentary scrutiny.

CREATION OF NEW PARLIAMENTARY FUNCTIONS

As is evident from the broad suggestions put forward in Labour's policy documents on the subject, there are a number of different types of function that a new parliamentary committee or committees on human rights might take responsibility for. These might be usefully categorised as being:

(1)   pre-legislative scrutiny;
(2)   monitoring the operation of the Human Rights Act;
(3)   international human rights treaty affairs; and
(4)   advisory reports and ad hoc inquiries.

These functions and the work they would entail will now be considered in turn.

Pre-legislative scrutiny

The most important function for any new procedures will be the scrutiny of legislative proposals for their compliance with the articles and jurisprudence of the ECHR. This is likely to be regarded as the highest priority for implementation, and will also be the most significant factor shaping the overall parliamentary scheme which emerges with respect to its new human rights work generally.

The work involved will be in the nature of a technical exercise, comparing and predicting the compatibility of the law proposed with the prospect of litigation under the ECHR, both in our domestic courts and before the European Court of Human Rights at Strasbourg. The type of scrutiny would not extend into the merits of whether the legislation in question was desirable or not in itself, upon which diverse interpretations and ideological points of view might be adopted. Only the two chambers of Parliament as a whole, assisted in the normal way through their existing committees, would be equipped to conduct policy debates and decision-making of that kind.

Several significantly different forms and processes of legislation will have to be accommodated by whatever committee scheme of parliamentary scrutiny is devised.

Government Bills

There will be government primary legislation to consider for compliance with human rights standards, which consists of about 40 public Bills each year.

Private members' Bills and private Bills

Private members' Bills and private Bills will need to be scrutinised separately, as the internal government audit procedures and the published ministerial human rights impact statement accompanying government Bills, as required under s 19 of the Human Rights Act, will not apply to these types of legislation.

Statutory instruments

There will be the very large quantity of secondary legislation to examine, which consists of at least 1,500 statutory instruments every year.

Remedial orders under the Human Rights Act

Of particular importance will be the special new category of remedial orders which may be enacted under s 10 of the Human Rights Act as a fast-track legislative process when the government wishes to respond swiftly to a declaration of incompatibility in UK domestic courts or an adverse ruling in the European Court of Human Rights.

European law-making

Some consideration of human rights implications might be thought necessary with regard to European law-making. Any such scrutiny arrangements, however, will be of a very different nature to the examination of domestic legislation, since the Westminster Parliament's role with respect to European legislation is limited to the expression of an opinion on Commission proposals in advance of the meeting of the Council of Ministers whic decides to adopt the legislation or not.

Precisely what would be involved in carrying out the functic particular types of legislation is considered further below (a with a discussion of related procedural matters.

Monitoring the operation of the Human Rights Act

Labour's 1996 consultation paper *Bringing Rights Home* proposed that a new parliamentary committee on human rights 'would have a continuing responsibility to monitor the operation of the Human Rights Act'.[9] The scope of a continuing function of this kind is less than clear, and could be drawn very widely. Such a function would include periodic general reviews of the Act, gauging the cumulative impact of incorporation of the ECHR upon the substance of British domestic law as well as upon the administration of the courts and litigation before the Court of Human Rights at Strasbourg. The Committee might consider it worthwhile to initiate separate special inquiries into aspects of particular importance or significance to the working of the Act, such as the courts' use of its powers under s 4 to make 'declarations of incompatibility' between statutory provisions and human rights, and questions of citizens' access to justice in the enforcement of their human rights. The committee would no doubt seek to identify areas for improvement, where the Act was perceived by members as working less effectively than it might, and bring forward recommendations for action.

There is also the question whether some form of parliamentary examination is necessary or desirable into the question of compatibility between the ECHR and all *pre-existing* measures of parliamentary legislation enacted prior to the Human Rights Act 1998. This would be a major function of its own, which otherwise would fall to the usual law reform bodies to perform, notably the Law Commission. Without some extra-judicial examination of this large subject, future complaints of human rights violation founded on laws prior to the Human Rights Act 1998 will still need to be resolved through the normal, costly process of litigation.

International human rights treaty affairs

Parliamentary scrutiny of governmental decision-making in the field of international human rights treaties would have two points of focus. The first would be to scrutinise whether the present obligations of the UK government under the terms of the international instruments to which it was a party were being properly carried out to the satisfaction of the Westminster Parliament.

[9] At p 12.

s would have a wider remit than simply the ECHR (a treaty enactment of members belonging to the Council of Europe) and most certainly include the International Covenant on Civil and Political Rights (ICCPR) and the International Covenant on Economic, Social and Cultural Rights (both being treaty enactments of the United Nations). One issue of recent controversy has been the failure of the UK government to consult Parliament prior to carrying out its reporting obligations to the United Nations Human Rights Committee as required under the terms of the ICCPR.[10] Similar reporting obligations are owed under a number of other international agreements to which the UK is a member, such as the International Labour Organisation and the Committee on the Elimination of Discrimination against Women. Any new human rights scrutiny procedures, therefore, might be expected to involve these draft reports being submitted to Parliament for debate, preceded by the examination and preparation of a report by a specialist committee on the subject.

An important second task for scrutiny procedures of treaty matters raises more fundamental issues governing the relationship between the executive and Parliament. To what extent should Parliament be consulted, and possibly control, the treaty-making powers in general which the government possesses under the royal prerogative?[11] For the purpose of this chapter which is concerned only with international human rights agreements, it is sufficient illustration to mention that in 1950 when the UK government agreed and ratified the ECHR itself, no parliamentary approval was sought or required, and no consultation or debate on the subject ever took place. This was similarly the case when the UK government ratified the ICCPR in 1976. More recently, Protocol 11 to the ECHR, reforming litigation procedures at Strasbourg and creating an enlarged Court of Human Rights, was ratified by the UK government in 1995 without any parliamentary scrutiny at all. There is now widespread agreement that Parliament should be involved in the process of human rights treaty-making and amendment, and any new scrutiny arrangements that emerge as a result are likely to involve a specialist committee for the purpose. Amendments to the articles of the ECHR will assume even greater significance after 1998, following our incorporation of the Convention under the terms of the Human Rights Act.

Inquiries and advisory reports

The Labour government's White Paper *Rights Brought Home* in October 1997 said that 'the new Committee might conduct enquiries on a range of

---

[10] Lord Lester, 'Taking Human Rights Seriously', in Robert Blackburn and James Busuttil (eds), *Human Rights for the 21st Century* (London: Pinter, 1997), Ch 4.

[11] The Labour Party in 1993 proposed that the power to ratify treaties should be transferred to Parliament: see *A New Agenda for Democracy: Labour's Proposals for Constitutional Reform*, p 33 (Appendix 1 below, pp 453–4).

human rights issues relating to the Convention, and produce reports so as to assist the Government and Parliament in deciding what action to take'. The following month, when presenting the Human Rights Bill to the House of Lords for Second Reading debate, the Lord Chancellor, Lord Irvine, further stated that:[12]

'It would be a natural focus for the increased interest in human rights issues which Parliament will inevitably take when we have brought rights home. It could, for example, not only keep the protection of human rights under review, but could also be in the forefront of public education and consultation on human rights. It could receive written submissions and hold public hearings at a number of locations across the country. It could be in the van [sic] of the promotion of a human rights culture across the country.'

As elaborated upon here by the Lord Chancellor, such a function would be unprecedented in Westminster terms. The public workload involved would be potentially vast, and the notion of a Westminster Select Committee travelling around the country holding public hearings seems rather unreal. These political utterances may be explicable in terms of the government trying to combat any disappointment that it failed to include the creation of a Human Rights Commission in its White Paper and Human Rights Bill. For as is discussed elsewhere, especially in Chapter 19, it is widely believed that a Human Rights Commission should be established to facilitate the working of the Human Rights Act and that among its most important functions would be the promotion of greater public awareness and education about human rights matters, undertaking inquiries into subjects of special concern, and constituting an expert independent advisory body for subjects referred to it by government and parliamentary bodies.

Nonetheless, with or without a Human Rights Commission, there would be advantages to including inquiries and advisory reports on human rights affairs within the terms of reference of a suitable parliamentary body. To some extent this would overlap with the work of the House of Commons Home Affairs Committee, particularly as (post-Human Rights Act) it is likely to adopt the human rights principles of the ECHR as a de facto set of principles by which to interpret aspects of its work and the criteria to be applied to government administration and policy, not only in relation to the Home Office but also the responsibilities covered by the Lord Chancellor's department. But the new committee entrusted with this wide-ranging role could be relied upon to proceed by way of complementing rather than duplicating other existing forms of parliamentary inquiry, and to undertake inquiries where it felt that other forms of parliamentary attention to some issues of human rights importance did not exist or else had failed.

---

[12] HL Deb, 3 November 1997, col 1234.

THE COMMITTEE STRUCTURE ON HUMAN RIGHTS AFFAIRS

Precisely how any or all of these new human rights functions might be carried out raises many practical issues, including questions of workload, compatibility of diverse forms of scrutiny or inquiry, and the pooling together of expertise for particular types of task. Whatever new form of human rights committee structure is adopted, it will have to take into account the organisation of other existing forms of parliamentary scrutiny.

Three options to consider

There are a number of ways in which the new human rights committee functions might be structured, most of which would work satisfactorily for immediate purposes. Three general approaches might be identified as follows.

Option One

The new human rights functions could be allocated among already existing parliamentary committees. This would be particularly feasible if, at least initially, the innovation concentrated on pre-legislative scrutiny for compliance with the ECHR.

The two principal contenders for taking on these new legislative responsibilities would be the Joint Committee on Statutory Instruments and the House of Lords Select Committee on Delegated Powers and Deregulation. Between them, these two bodies already sift through secondary and primary legislation respectively, and their terms of reference could be extended to include questions of human rights compliance. The enlarged workload for these committees would almost certainly involve the creation of one or more sub-committees to either or both of them. Additionally, with respect to the special category of remedial orders under the Human Rights Act 1998, responsibility for detailed scrutiny and report to the two Houses could be passed to the present committees that deal with deregulation orders under the Deregulation and Contracting Out Act 1994, namely the Select Committee on Delegated Powers and Deregulation in the House of Lords and the Deregulation Committee in the House of Commons.

The non-legislative functions mooted in Labour's policy documents could be allocated to the relevant departmentally related Select Committees in the House of Commons. Thus responsibility for monitoring the operation of the Act and undertaking inquiries and advisory reports might be undertaken by the Home Affairs Committee (having existing responsibility for administration and policy with respect to constitutional and judicial affairs), and scrutiny of international affairs could be taken on by the Foreign Affairs Committee or a new sub-committee specially created for the purpose.

Option Two

A second, more ambitious, option would be to conduct a wider reorganisation of pre-legislative Select Committees, integrating human rights into whatever new scheme of arrangements is adopted.

The two main existing bodies affected would, again, be the Joint Committee on Statutory Instruments and the House of Lords Select Committee on Delegated Powers and Deregulation. The most likely rationale for any such reorganisation would be a streamlining of the special pre-legislative scrutiny processes, distinguishing between primary and secondary legislation.

So, for example:

(1)   the Committee on Delegated Powers and Deregulation might be wound up (and so too the Deregulation Committee in the House of Commons),
(2)   a new Joint Committee on Primary Legislation created, to deal with human rights and delegated powers, and
(3)   the existing Joint Committee on Statutory Instruments could have its terms of reference extended to include human rights and deregulation orders.

The resulting two new joint committees would each need to establish a sub-committee structure to cope with their large overall workload.

Non-legislative human rights functions could be allocated either as in Option One, or alternatively a new Joint Committee on Human Rights, or separate committees in each House, might possibly be created for general monitoring and advisory purposes at home and with respect to international treaties.

Option Three

A more straightforward approach would be simply to establish a new Select Committee on Human Rights to discharge most or all of the functions currently being proposed by Labour.

This could be in the form of:

(a)   a single joint committee of both Houses,
(b)   two committees established in the Commons and Lords respectively, or
(c)   some structure combining both joint and independent elements for the purposes of carrying out functions of a different nature.

Thus if each House contributed 11 members to a joint committee, they could deliberate jointly for the purposes of reporting on technical matters (notably in offering expert advice on legislative compliance with the jurisprudence of the ECHR) and meet separately on matters of a political or policy-orientated nature (such as in offering opinions on the merits of government policy at home or internationally).

In order to evaluate these three different options, one needs to consider the existing work of the Joint Committee on Statutory Instruments and of the House of Lords Select Committee on Delegated Powers and Deregulation. This is because, first, they are the principal pre-legislative committees already existing at Westminster, and, secondly, they have some analogous procedures which will be of relevance to whatever scheme of parliamentary committee on human rights that is eventually adopted. Also worthy of consideration is whether any foreign legislatures can be a lesson in formulating the structure and working of a British parliamentary committee on human rights.

Joint Committee on Statutory Instruments

This parliamentary committee comprises seven members from each House, selected by their own respective Committees of Selection, with the chair being taken by an opposition MP. The Committee is empowered by each House to consider all statutory instruments (SIs) and draft SIs which are required to be presented to Parliament (as well as some which are not).

The Committee does not consider the merits of a SI per se; rather, its job is to check that the issue and drafting of the SI has conformed to certain procedures or principles. In other words, its scrutiny process is essentially a technical process, not a policy-orientated one. There are specific grounds in the Committee's terms of reference by which it may decide to draw an instrument to the special attention of Parliament.[13] These include, for example, 'unusual or unexpected' uses of a ministerial power, where the SI is beyond the scope originally envisaged in the Act conferring the power to make the order or regulations, where the effect of the SI is unclear, or where it has public revenue implications. Formally the committee lacks the power to send for persons, papers and records, but in practice it liaises closely with the government department responsible for preparing the SI. Before reporting to each House, the Committee invites the department to given an explanation on the matter of concern. As a joint committee, it was created in 1972 in substitution for two earlier separate committees, one in each House, which according to Erskine May it was felt had 'produced defects and anomalies in overall parliamentary control'.[14]

In the context of the proposal for new human rights scrutiny arrangements, therefore, it would be easy in theory to extend the grounds upon which this committee reviews all statutory instruments laid before Parliament to include reviewing such secondary legislation for compatibility with the articles and jurisprudence of the ECHR. This would undoubtedly add a major burden to the work of the Committee, but this might be supported by

---

[13] See Standing Order 151, HC [1997] 400; and generally J A G Griffith and Michael Ryle, *Parliament: Practice, Functions and Procedures* (London: Sweet & Maxwell, 1989), pp 444–445.

[14] Erskine May, *Parliamentary Practice* (London: Butterworths, 21st ed, 1989), p 551.

the appointment of an additional legal adviser to the Committee who was expert in human rights law. Another possibility is that the Committee establishes its own special sub-committee on human rights. The Joint Committee on Statutory Instruments already possesses the power to appoint its own sub-committees, and this would allow it to recruit other suitably-qualified MPs and peers who do not sit on the parent committee to be involved in the work. Certainly, if a distinction is to be drawn in scrutiny arrangements between primary and secondary legislation, then prima facie it would seem to make every sense to involve the Joint Committee on Statutory Instruments.

House of Lords Select Committee on Delegated Powers and Deregulation

A second existing committee which should be considered as a possible recipient of some human rights scrutiny function is the Delegated Powers Scrutiny Committee in the House of Lords. This body was set up by peers in 1992–93 in direct response to growing unease about a significant recent increase in use being made of delegated legislation by the government.[15]

The Committee's terms of reference are 'to report whether the provisions of any Bill inappropriately delegate legislative power; or whether they subject the exercise of legislative power to an inappropriate degree of Parliamentary scrutiny'.[16] It also has functions with respect to the scrutiny of deregulation orders, with some lessons for human rights scrutiny procedures, which are discussed separately below (at pp 386–7). It is the responsibility of the Committee to consider all Bills presented to the House of Lords and, where an enabling clause is found, to undertake an examination of the proposal and report on its desirability and drafting. The Lords have proceeded to select for this high-profile committee eight widely-respected parliamentarians, some with senior political or legal experience (currently, for example, Lords Merlyn-Rees, Dahrendorf and its chairman Lord Alexander of Weedon). Although it has only been in existence for five years, the Committee has already acquired considerable influence and is generally regarded as one of the most successful parliamentary innovations of the last two decades. Its views and recommendations are virtually always raised in the House and accepted by the government ministers concerned, leading to proposed amendments being carried. One significant example of its influence was in the case of the Education Bill in 1993–94, which as originally drafted allowed the Education Secretary to prescribe in the future by way of delegated legislation the kinds of activity upon which student unions could spend the financial support they received

---

[15] See the remarks of Lord Ripon who first put forward the proposal for this committee, HL Deb, 14 February 1990, col 1407f.

[16] *First Report of the Select Committee on the Procedure of the House*, HL [1992–93] 11; HL Deb, 10 November 1992, col 91. See also C Himsworth, 'The Delegated Powers Scrutiny Committee' (1995) *Public Law* 34.

from the state. This enabling clause was withdrawn altogether, following a report of the Committee that, 'The House may regard as inappropriate the delegation of legislative power to interfere with the freedom of association of students'.[17]

Significantly it was a question of human rights therefore that particularly served to sway the opinion of the Committee that the proposed statutory provision was 'inappropriate'. The quasi-constitutional purpose of the Delegated Powers Scrutiny Committee is clearly recognised in the Second Chamber and by the Committee itself. One of its earliest reports commenced with the words, 'Democracy is not only about the election of politicians; it is about setting limits to their powers'.[18] As a parliamentary body that already sifts through all primary legislative proposals, therefore, and one which already conducts lines of inquiry bearing some semblance to that of a constitutional watchdog, the Delegated Powers Scrutiny Committee – or some modified committee replacing it – would be well-placed to assume terms of reference with respect to pre-legislative scrutiny on grounds of compatibility with the ECHR.

Parliamentary human rights committees abroad

How other countries organise their parliamentary scrutiny arrangements with respect to human rights could be influential in shaping the eventual outcome of the new committee work at Westminster. A wide number of foreign legislatures now possess human rights committees of their own. A recent survey by the Inter-Parliamentary Union found that 52 countries have a committee or sub-committee expressly devoted to some aspect of human rights, with a further 44 addressing the subject within a different committee with broader remit such as constitutional or foreign affairs.[19] However, any clear lessons for the UK are obscured by the very wide diversity of arrangements to be found operating across these countries, with special human rights audit and scrutiny functions traversing the whole range of public institutions. Most pre-legislative scrutiny arrangements are undertaken by bodies operating outside Parliament, for example by the Attorney General's office, as in New Zealand; within government department human rights units, particularly justice ministries, as in Canada and the Netherlands; by some form of constitutional council, as in France; or by a government-funded human rights commission or institute, as in Australia, Norway and Denmark. The majority of countries also have significantly different indigenous political characteristics, rendering their own forms of scrutiny process less persuasive or compatible with Westminster traditions.

---

[17] *Twelfth Report of the Select Committee on the Scrutiny of Delegated Powers*, 1993–94, HL 90, para 13.

[18] Ibid, para 1.

[19] Inter-Parliamentary Union, *World Directory of Parliamentary Human Rights Bodies* (Geneva: IPU, 1993).

So far as parliamentary committees on human rights are concerned however, it is the Australian Parliament which is recognised as having pioneered scrutiny procedures and which provides us with the most advanced model for the UK. Australia has two important committees which address pre-legislative scrutiny on human rights grounds, being the Senate's Standing Committee for the Scrutiny of Bills (scrutiny of primary legislation) and its Standing Committee on Regulations and Ordinances (scrutiny of secondary legislation). The terms of reference of both committees are of a wider constitutional nature than human rights alone.

In the case of the Australian Committee for the Scrutiny of Bills, it is its responsibility to report on any provision in a Bill which affects any of the following principles:

(1) violation of personal rights and liberties;
(2) undue dependency on ill-defined administrative powers, or non-reviewable administrative decision; and
(3) inappropriately delegated legislative powers or removal of parliamentary scrutiny of such powers.

It was this committee, more than any other foreign model, that proved particularly influential in the House of Lords' decision to set up its own Select Committee on Delegated Powers and Deregulation in 1992, described above. This experiment having proved successful, the House of Lords might well be encouraged to follow the Australian pattern of this committee one step further by extending its terms of reference to embrace legislative compliance with the terms of the ECHR.

So far as the Australian Senate's Standing Committee on Regulations and Ordinances is concerned, four criteria exist against which it proceeds to scrutinise delegated legislation. These guiding principles are that:

(1) the order must be in accordance with the parent Act,
(2) it must not adversely affect personal rights and liberties,
(3) it must not oust the jurisdiction of the courts on administrative matters, and
(4) it should not contain matter more appropriate for parliamentary enactment.

Where any of these principles appear to have been infringed, it will present a report to the Senate.

The Australian Parliament has one further human rights committee of some importance, the Sub-Committee on Human Rights, which currently operates under the terms of the Joint Standing Committee on Foreign Affairs, Defence and Trade. This sub-committee has the large responsibility for reviewing Australia's entire human rights policy programme both at home and abroad, and not surprisingly some of the reports it has produced since its establishment in 1991 have been widely publicised and influential. Before long it is likely to emerge from out of the shadow of its existing parent committee into a separately organised Joint Committee on Human Rights, a parliamentary development it itself recommended in November 1994.

Conclusions and prospects for the form of the committee

The precise form of committee structure for carrying out the new human rights scrutiny functions could operate effectively in a number of different ways for immediate purposes. There are some practical considerations to take into account, however, before assessing the likely or best way in which to construct the new committee or committees. The end result is less likely to be determined by abstract logic than a mixture of the personal preferences of the government ministers involved, the degree of respect paid to existing traditions, a desire to minimise administrative inconvenience and financial cost, and the effectiveness with which the Cabinet harmonises its constitutional and parliamentary reform programme generally.

First, the initiation of new parliamentary procedures addressed at human rights could be incremental. In other words, the development of human rights scrutiny procedures at Westminster could be introduced as a building-block exercise. Parliamentary institutions in the UK tend to prefer a process of experiment and evolution before setting up for themselves any permanent major innovation. There is no necessity for all these human rights scrutiny functions to be introduced at Westminster simultaneously straightaway. The most immediate function to be addressed is that of pre-legislative scrutiny. Once such work had been seen to be carried out successfully, further functions with respect to reviewing the operation of the Human Rights Act, carrying out inquiries and advisory reports, and examining international and treaty obligations, could be added. However, it should be borne in mind that any ad hoc approach which failed to consider how the overall pattern of parliamentary scrutiny might best be developed in the future (and in the context of other actual or planned reforms) could end up as obstructionist to later developments.

Secondly, the Labour leadership in government is likely to become less enthusiastic about pursuing some of the human rights scrutiny functions it suggested in opposition or during its initial flush of holding office. Thus, the inquiry and advisory functions mentioned in its policy documents in 1996–97 are unlikely to be in the forefront of the coming reforms, as the Prime Minister, Lord Chancellor and Home Secretary come increasingly to value their own special policy units or departmental committees of inquiries. Furthermore, it might well be easier to construct any such functions as and when a Human Rights Commission is created since the Commission's functions can be expected to include a role with respect to policy and administrative inquiries. For example, the working of the Commission might be made accountable to a new committee set up specifically for the purpose of supervising and receiving reports from the Commission, analogous in some respects to the Public Services Committee with respect to the ombudsman, the Standards and Privileges Committee with respect to the Commissioner for Standards, and the Public Accounts Committee with respect to the National Audit Office. If the situation arises that Parliament believes it necessary to conduct an inquiry into some aspect of human rights, then mechanisms for this purpose already exist. In the House of Lords, peers may appoint an ad hoc Select Committee to investigate and report on any matter which it considers appropriate. In the House of Commons, the departmentally related Select Committees (particularly the Home Affairs Committee) will be able to interpret their existing terms of reference sufficiently broadly to undertake inquiries on matters of human rights as and when they felt it necessary.

Thirdly, the core work of the new human rights scrutiny procedures will almost certainly be undertaken by a joint committee of both Houses, at least initially. This will be so simply because the Labour leadership appears to have attached itself to the idea (see p 371 above). Joint committees, which in the past have been relatively rare creatures at Westminster, seem set to become a mechanism favoured by the new Labour administration. Since May 1997 the usual joint committees on statutory instruments and consolidation Bills have been established as well as the new ad hoc joint committee on parliamentary privilege and another promised next session as the means for examining long-term reform of the House of Lords. Although a reformed Second Chamber is likely to take on an elevated role with respect to human rights in the longer term (see Chapter 1), for the time being MPs are unlikely to want to abrogate their involvement in a parliamentary development widely perceived as being of major significance. Furthermore, an added advantage of MPs' participation in the scrutiny process, even if of a less independent and expert character than that of peers selected for the task, will help foster the Commons' application of human rights principles to be applied in their work generally. In terms of establishing the new scrutiny procedures, the Commons' shared ownership of the committee will undoubtedly add to the strength, public profile and credibility generally of the procedures themselves.

There are some practical advantages in a joint committee too. One is that a joint committee is able to provide one single source of authoritative advice, for example on whether proposed legislation does or does not comply with the jurisprudence of the ECHR. Conflicting expert advice from committees in each House would give rise to great confusion and loss of confidence among the ranks of ordinary MPs and peers. It was for these reasons that in 1973 the two earlier committees on statutory instruments which had existed separately in the Commons and Lords were merged into the present single joint committee. Another working advantage is that a joint committee on legislation can commence its work at an early stage, regardless of the House in which a Bill or draft SI is first introduced. If, for example, the House of Lords Delegated Powers Scrutiny Committee was enlarged and given responsibility for ensuring compatibility of domestic legislation with the ECHR, most measures would pass through all their stages in the House of Commons before being subjected to its expert examination and report.

THE HUMAN RIGHTS COMMITTEE AT WORK

Pre-legislative procedures

The most problematic issue in constructing the operation of the new scrutiny arrangements will be the effectiveness with which the new committees are permitted to examine legislative proposals and report on them to Parliament prior to final approval and enactment. However, in fact, many of the existing procedures and practices now operating with respect to the existing Delegated Powers Scrutiny Committee and the Joint Committee on Statutory Instruments can be adapted for use by the parliamentary committee (or committees) on human rights in their scrutiny of primary and secondary legislative proposals.

The committee with responsibility for primary legislation would need to examine all Bills and report to both Houses on matters of significance for compliance with the terms of the ECHR. The practice of the existing Delegated Powers Scrutiny Committee is that its legal adviser sifts through all Bills as they are presented to the House and a preliminary note is prepared on those measures to which she or he believes the committee's attention should be drawn. That committee then aims to conduct and complete its inquiry, usually between the Second Reading and committee stages of the Bill concerned, so that its report can instruct peers as it scrutinised the legislation clause by clause in the House. Before its report is prepared, the committee commonly contacts the government department concerned and offers an opportunity for the government to present its explanation or views on any matter of concern to the committee. These practices could also suitably be adopted in the committee work of the new human rights scrutiny arrangements.

With respect to government Bills, this scrutiny by the human rights committee would not be a mandatory part of the primary legislative process as such; rather, the committee should determine for itself which measures it should inquire into and report upon. Different considerations arise, however, with respect to private members' Bills and private Bills which, as already mentioned, will have been presented to Parliament without the benefit of the government's own internal human rights scrutiny process and without any consequential accompanying human rights impact assessment statement. Analogous to government Bills, it might come to be regarded as good practice for MPs to include some statement about human rights in the explanatory memorandum of the Bill, though without recourse to expert human rights law advice this is unlikely to be regarded as adequate. There is a case, therefore, for the proposed new committee to become a necessary part of the legislative process under Standing Orders of each House, to the effect that all private members' Bills and private Bills must, as a mandatory requirement after receiving a Second Reading, be examined for human rights implications and reported on by the human rights committee before proceeding further to the next stage of a Standing Committee.

With regard to the future scrutiny of normal SIs for human rights compliance, there is no reason for departing from the general present pattern of proceedings followed by the existing Committee on Statutory Instruments. The usual process could continue of, first, the Committee's legal adviser sifting through all SIs and draft SIs in order to draw the attention of the Committee to any significant matters; secondly, the Committee examining the issues raised and conducting an exchange of information or views with the government department concerned; and thirdly, preparing a report for both Houses. One procedural matter might be strengthened, however. Currently, it is a rule in the House of Lords, but not the Commons, that no debate should be held on an affirmative SI unless the Joint Committee on Statutory Instruments has reported on it.[20] With the enlarged powers of the new proposed committee on secondary legislation, a similar rule should apply to the House of Commons.

The question was raised earlier in this chapter whether European law-making should be made subject to any special procedures operating at Westminster. Since the Westminster Parliament is not the legislative body in question and its role is limited to advising the UK minister and issuing reports prior to external decision-making by the European Commission and Council of Ministers, the grounds for extending parliamentary scrutiny procedures in this respect are less pertinent than with respect to the other forms of legislation already considered. Furthermore, the existing Commons' Committee on European Legislation and Lords' Committee and Sub-Committees on the European Communities are already adequately equipped to take on board express human rights factors in their work, particularly Sub-Committee E of the Lords' Committee which deals with questions of law and institutions. Any problems picked up in proposed European directives or other measures with respect to human rights compliance could be reported upon to the House, and where necessary taken further by the UK minister or human rights committee(s) given responsibility for international human rights purposes.

Special procedures with respect to remedial orders under the Human Rights Act

Parliamentary scrutiny procedures with regard to remedial orders to be enacted under the Human Rights Act raise special factors for consideration.

---

[20] Standing Order 70, HL [1994] 15.

As already indicated, one distinctive feature of the Human Rights Act is to provide a fast-track procedure under s 10 for changing legislation in response to a 'declaration of incompatibility' by the UK courts or to an adverse ruling in the European Court of Human Rights. This fast-track procedure will be desirable when speedy action is necessary to redress some individual or minority grievance of a serious nature, though in some cases the existing prerogative powers at the disposal of the Home Secretary may be sufficient to provide an immediate remedy.

It is important to emphasise as a preliminary observation that this fast-track legislative procedure should be regarded by ministers and parliamentarians as an exception to the normal process by which rectification of UK law for compliance with the ECHR is made. It should not become simply a more administratively convenient and less time-consuming way of changing human rights law. The government should normally take positive action in response to adverse judicial rulings either at home or in Strasbourg by presenting a Bill to Parliament in the usual way, being subject to established parliamentary scrutiny arrangements.

The fast-track procedures in the Act provide for a draft statutory instrument (a 'remedial order') to be laid before Parliament 60 days prior to an affirmative resolution being voted upon in each House to bring the measure into effect. This single-stage of parliamentary approval is therefore substantially less extensive than the various stages and length of time devoted to government Bills. Yet the nature and importance of the legislation involved may be substantial in terms of our constitutional law and human rights. Furthermore, the Act contains a 'Henry VIII' clause under which it is possible for these orders to amend or repeal primary Acts of Parliament where the minister considers it appropriate.[21]

The architects of whatever new scrutiny arrangements are put in place will not need reminding that human rights law is concerned with striking an appropriate balance between conflicting individual rights or between particular rights and the national interest. This sometimes in practice involves the imposition of restrictions and the 'levelling-down' of individual rights. Emergency or urgent legislation in the past has not infrequently been concerned specifically with implementing such restrictions upon individual rights. It is therefore particularly important that parliamentary scrutiny procedures are effective in safeguarding against rushed legislation which may have wider implications for human rights beyond the different kinds of 'urgency' which might exist. If – as is the intention of the Human Rights Act – the courts are to refer matters of human rights violation to Parliament for legislative action, then the two Houses must have adequate procedures which provide for their in-depth consideration of the matter.

The way in which the House of Lords Delegated Powers Scrutiny Committee and the House of Commons Deregulation Committee presently conduct

---

[21] Schedule 2, para 1(2)(a).

their business with respect to the scrutiny of deregulation orders has some relevance to future parliamentary committee work in examining human rights remedial orders. This is particularly with regard to how special procedures can be evolved which *guarantee* that an effective scrutiny process has in fact been conducted prior to the enactment taking place. In 1994 the Deregulation and Contracting Out Act was passed which empowers ministers to make orders by way of SI amending or repealing any enactment which imposes unnecessary burdens on businesses or individuals in their commercial activities. An 'enactment' for this purpose was defined to include not only subordinate legislation but also Acts of Parliament. In other words, the 1994 Act contains a wide-ranging 'Henry VIII' clause, similar to the power to make remedial orders under the Human Rights Act, allowing statutory instruments to vary primary legislation. As a result, on the grounds that this power in the 1994 Act was contrary to normal constitutional wisdom, special consultation and scrutiny procedures were included in the Act over and above the normal process whereby an order or draft order is laid before each House for approval by means of a single resolution (as distinct from the various readings and stages through which primary legislation must pass).

Under the procedures contained in the 1994 Act with respect to deregulation orders, four mandatory stages are involved in the parliamentary process of scrutiny. These comprise:

(1) consultation with interested parties;
(2) preparation of explanatory memoranda;
(3) an extended period for parliamentary consideration; and
(4) an obligation to take any report of the Lords' Delegated Powers Scrutiny Committee and/or Commons' Deregulation Committee into account before a draft order is presented for approval in each House.

Section 3 of the 1994 Act specifies the process of consultation to be followed by the minister before presenting his draft order to Parliament, including that he 'consult such organisations as appear to him to be representative of interests substantially affected by his proposals'. The same section also specifies that when he presents the document containing his proposals to Parliament, he must accompany it with details relating to seven specified matters, including the rationale behind the proposal, its financial implications, and the nature of the representations he has received. Section 4 of the 1994 Act then lays down a period of 60 days in which Parliament has time in which to examine and scrutinise the minister's proposal. Finally, section 4 provides that 'the Minister concerned shall have regard to any representations made during the period for Parliamentary consideration and, in particular, to any resolution or report of, or of any committee of, either House of Parliament with regard to the document'. During the parliamentary passage of the Human Rights Bill, pressure from human rights groups and parliamentarians managed to secure some highly desirable amendments to the original form of the government's

Bill, which was assisted by the precedent of how deregulation orders are dealt with.[22] Thus under Sched 2 to the final version of the Bill, as enacted, there are now procedures for receiving representations, for explanatory memoranda accompanying draft orders, and for extended periods of time up to 120 days in which parliamentary scrutiny is to be conducted (rather than the 40 days which normally applies to SIs).

However, the Human Rights Act still fails to institutionalise any committee into its procedures for scrutinising remedial orders. Accordingly, when the new committee arrangements on human rights are established, some amendments to the Act will be needed, and also some changes in the Standing Orders of both Houses. With respect to scrutiny of deregulation orders, Standing Orders of both Houses serve to strengthen a 'scrutiny reserve' over deregulation orders. Thus in the House of Commons, SO 141 requires the Deregulation Committee to report on every draft order not more than 15 sitting days after the draft order was laid before the House, and where the Committee recommends that a draft order should not be approved, SO 18 provides that no motion to approve the draft order shall be made unless the House has previously resolved to disagree with the Committee's report. In the House of Lords, SO 70 prohibits any resolution to affirm a draft deregulation order until the Delegated Powers Scrutiny Committee has laid its report before the House, and SO 38 provides that any motion relating to a report from the committee will be given precedence in the day's order paper over a motion to approve the draft order.

Similar procedures to those which apply in the case of deregulation orders should be followed with respect to remedial orders enacted under the terms of the Human Rights Act. The new Standing Orders will need to ensure that the pre-legislative human rights committee has completed its work and presented a report to both Houses before the remedial order in question is debated and approved.

Composition and powers of the committee(s)

Less complex procedures to be settled will include matters of membership, support staff and the powers of the committee(s) to take evidence and appoint sub-committees. The importance of the legal adviser to any committee dealing with subject-matter of this nature cannot be overemphasised. His or

---

[22] An earlier draft of this chapter was circulated as a paper to MPs and ministers prior to the Committee Stage of the Human Rights Bill and formed the basis for representations by Liberty, Justice, Institute for Public Policy Research, Charter 88 and the Human Rights Incorporation Project on the need to extend substantially the remedial order procedure offered in the original Bill and to set up a human rights committee. Subsequently, virtually all of the scrutiny procedures proposed in that earlier paper (dealing with eg the consultation process, explanatory statements, and extended periods for consideration) were accepted, stopping short of creating a human rights committee simultaneously with enactment of the Bill. For the form of the original Bill, see R Blackburn, *Towards a Constitutional Bill of Rights for the United Kingdom* (London: Pinter, 1999), doc 40.

her role as a competent and reliable expert in human rights jurisprudence will be essential to the authoritative working of the committee(s), and the existing method of public appointment should be reviewed to see if any more professional or proactive procedures are desirable in order to ensure the recruitment of persons of first-rate ability for the job. Though the authorities in each House will handle personnel matters, the committee(s) in question should possess the power to remove, replace and appoint whomsoever they wish to work for them. The new committee(s) should be given the power to appoint sub-committees (as currently possessed by both the House of Lords Delegated Powers Scrutiny Committee and Joint Committee on Statutory Instruments), and in conducting inquiries it or they should be vested through Standing Orders with the power to send for persons, papers and records (currently possessed by the Delegated Powers Scrutiny Committee but not the Statutory Instruments Committee).

Some common characteristics of joint committees are worth citing if, as seems probable, this form of scrutiny does become the basis for some or all of the new human rights arrangements. Joint committees are composed of two groups, MPs and peers, each selected from the House from which they are drawn. A joint committee is in the nature of an inter-House conference, with each group being empowered to act according to the order and authority of their own House. One House cannot enlarge the powers of the joint committee unilaterally; to do so requires the agreement of both Houses. Depending on how the work of the committee is allocated, each of the two groups might meet independently, in advance of joint meetings or separately altogether for some purposes, and each group will possess its own clerk and have a de facto chairperson distinct from the joint committee chairperson.

PARLIAMENTARY IMPLEMENTATION

It seems clear that new parliamentary committee functions in the field of human rights will be implemented shortly, but what is less clear is from precisely where the initiative and blueprint for reform will come. The Lord Chancellor, Derry Irvine, the senior government member and speaker of the Upper House, the person who presented the Human Rights Bill to Parliament, and the chairman of the Cabinet sub-committees on incorporation of the ECHR and Lords reform, has as yet given no indication that he is taking charge of the matter. On the timing of the committee(s) being brought in, his view has been that it should await completion of the legislation incorporating the ECHR, and certainly not be included within the terms of the Human Rights Act itself.

As a mechanism for improving the legislative process and holding ministers to account for their proposals, the House of Commons Committee on the Modernisation of the House of Commons (MOHOC) could vest itself with the matter and come forward with proposals. Some of the questions to be addressed by MOHOC will certainly arise with respect to the scrutiny of legislation for ECHR compliance. For example, it has been suggested that new procedures should be implemented for conducting more pre-legislative consultation on draft Bills and that greater use should be made of Special Standing Committees where some specialised form of examination and evidence-taking is warranted in order to carry out the committee stage of a Bill.[23] In this context, a permanent committee on human rights could play an important role in any new pre-legislative processes which are initiated as a result of MOHOC's work. Being possessed of powers to take evidence and call witnesses, it could also operate as and when required by Parliament as a special body to be entrusted with the committee stage of Bills carrying special significance to human rights after Second Reading.

Parliamentarians, especially peers, have for several years now asserted themselves as being able and willing to assume the human rights scrutiny functions which are now being considered. Indeed, in July 1994 Lord Irvine himself whilst in opposition was a co-signatory to a Memorandum prepared by Lord Simon of Glaisdale, Lord Alexander of Weedon, Lord Lester of Herne Hill and himself entitled *Scrutiny of Legislation for Consistency with Obligations under the European Convention on Human Rights*. The document proposed to the Liaison Committee of the House of Lords 'a significant extension of the committee work of the House into an area where, we suggest, Parliament has an important scrutiny function to exercise, and where the House could bring to bear considerable expertise and experience'. If the Labour Cabinet waits too long in preparing its own proposals for a committee on human rights, then peers and MPs from all parties may take the initiative independently to unite around some well thought-out proposal presented to Parliament by a private member.

The implementation of the new committee(s) on human rights should take into account the desirability of harmonising arrangements with Labour's reform programme generally, both in its immediate and future objectives. So, for example, the ostensible long-term objective of both the Labour Party and the Liberal Democrats of a homegrown Bill of Rights should be borne in mind (see Chapter 17). In *A New Agenda for Democracy: Labour's Proposals for Constitutional Reform*, Labour publicly backed the development of a Bill of Rights once incorporation of the ECHR had taken place and been seen to operate effectively: 'The incorporation of the European Convention on Human Rights is a necessary first step, but it is not a substitute for our own written Bill of Rights.'[24] A Bill of Rights of this kind would carry major implications

---

[23] Generally see the parliamentary debates on the subject (especially HC Deb, 22 May 1997, cols 901f; and HC Deb, 4 June 1997, cols 500f); the first report of MOHOC, *The Legislative Process* (1997–98) HC 190; Charter 88/Greg Power, *Reinventing Westminster* (1996); Report of the Hansard Society Commission on the Legislative Process, *Making the Law* (1993); and Chapter 5 above.

[24] At p 31; and generally see R Blackburn, *Towards a Constitutional Bill of Rights for the United Kingdom*, Ch 6(c).

for Parliament, particularly since it is likely to involve some qualified form of entrenchment for the document in order to protect its articles from erosion by later ordinary statutes. Such entrenchment, in turn, would almost certainly mean that special legislative procedures and scrutiny arrangements would be desirable for the amendment or emergency derogation from its provisions. Whatever committee arrangements are put in place now should point in the direction of those which can be adapted for the purposes of a UK Bill of Rights.

The future role of a reformed House of Lords is another closely associated factor. The forthcoming changes to the Lords promised by the Labour government, discussed in Chapter 1, can only properly proceed upon the basis of some new statement or re-definition of the future work and functions of the reformed Second Chamber which are most likely to involve some elevated role with respect to constitutional and human rights affairs. This, therefore, makes it all the more important that the House of Lords plays an essential role in whatever scrutiny arrangements are now put in place. In this context, it is worth observing how the Memorandum cited above, co-authored by Lord Irvine, stressed that the Second Chamber should perform an essential role in any new human rights scrutiny procedures, as follows:

'We agree that it would be desirable for the House of Commons to devise procedures of its own or to join with our House in undertaking the work [of pre-legislative human rights scrutiny]. However, it seems to us to be work which is, in any event, well suited to the interests and concerns of the House of Lords and to its constitutional role.'[25]

Whatever final form of scrutiny procedures are devised and agreed by the new Labour government and Parliament, the novel institution of a parliamentary committee on human rights is to be warmly welcomed. It will help pre-empt administrative malpractice and minimise the prospect of poorly-drafted or misguided provisions reaching the statute book. Everyone agrees that the prevention of public activity and legislation likely to offend fundamental rights is preferable than relying alone upon the prospect of legal litigation under the Human Rights Act and a judicial ruling on the matter. This new development will also, particularly in the non-legislative functions to be performed, serve to imbue the working of Parliament with a sharper sense of respect for individual rights and freedoms. Baroness Williams, the former Education Secretary in the Labour government of the 1970s, put this point well during debates in the House of Lords on the Human Rights Bill:

'Involving Parliament more in issues of human rights, giving it clear responsibilities, is not only a way of ensuring that human rights are more generally understood in the country, but also of recognising that Parliament itself could usefully discharge many functions that it is not currently asked to do. There is a great deal of talent

---

[25] At para 9.

and ability in both Houses of Parliament which remain to be tapped in the interest of trying to ensure that human rights are properly upheld.'[26]

Further reading

Labour Party, Consultation Paper, *Bringing Rights Home: Labour's Plans to Incorporate the European Convention on Human Rights into UK Law* (1996); Government White Paper, *Rights Brought Home: The Human Rights Bill* (London: HMSO, Cm 3782, 1997), especially Ch 3

Constitution Unit (Nicole Smith), *Human Rights Legislation* (London, 1996)

David Kinley, *The European Convention on Human Rights: Compliance without Incorporation* (Aldershot: Dartmouth, 1993)

Michael Ryle, 'Pre-legislative Scrutiny: A Prophylactic Approach to Protection of Human Rights' (1994) *Public Law* 192

Robert Blackburn, *Towards a Constitutional Bill of Rights for the United Kingdom* (London: Pinter, 1999)

---

[26] HL Deb, 27 November 1997, col 1147.

CHAPTER 19

A HUMAN RIGHTS COMMISSION

Sarah Spencer (Institute for Public Policy Research)[1]

When incorporation of the European Convention on Human Rights (ECHR) was finally put onto the UK's political agenda by Labour's pre-election proposals, *Bringing Rights Home*,[2] a key issue was raised which has yet to be resolved. Will that change in the law prove adequate in itself or is it necessary for the government to establish a statutory body to promote and enforce the new law if it is to be effective?

This focus on the need for an institutional mechanism to complement the law, which mirrors the fruitful debates in the 1970s on the need for statutory bodies to ensure the effectiveness of the race and sex discrimination legislation, comes from a recognition that:

> 'The effective protection of human rights requires more than the acceptance of international standards and their incorporation into national law. The experience of many jurisdictions is that the formal acceptance of a bill of rights or constitutional guarantees of human rights may have little impact. . . . The creation of effective structures for monitoring and enforcement of any new fundamental rights . . . may therefore be as important as the enactment of the rights themselves.'[3]

Labour's view on whether a Human Rights Commission is necessary in Britain has oscillated. *Bringing Rights Home* suggested that a commission could fulfil some important functions in relation to the ECHR: providing advice and assistance to individuals, initiating or supporting public interest cases, conducting inquiries, monitoring the operation of the new Act, and

[1] I acknowledge with thanks the contribution which has been made by my colleague, Ian Bynoe, in the development of these ideas which draw on our report *A Human Rights Commission: The Options for Britain and Northern Ireland* (London: Institute for Public Policy Research, 1998).

[2] *Bringing Rights Home: Labour's Plans to Incorporate the European Convention on Human Rights into UK Law*, December 1996.

[3] K Boyle, C Campbell and T Hadden (1996) *The Protection of Human Rights in the Context of Peace and Reconciliation in Ireland*, Forum for Peace and Reconciliation Consultancy Study No 2, May 1996, pp 10–11.

scrutinising new legislation, including that emanating from the European Union, for conformity to the ECHR.

The Commission option became a firm commitment in a pre-election agreement with the Liberal Democrats on constitutional reform[4] but post-election it became once again only an option on which ministers were undecided. In a public lecture in July 1997, two months after the election, the Lord Chancellor said,

'This Government's commitment to promoting human rights is undoubted. A new Commission might be one way of assisting this process, acting as a driving force for change . . .'

but continued,

'We have to weigh up the potential benefits and decide whether these justify the creation of a new body with the expense that would entail, or to postpone that for future consideration until after a time in which the benefits from the new system can be evaluated.'[5]

When the Human Rights Bill was published in October 1997, it made no provision for a commission. The accompanying White Paper, *Rights Brought Home*,[6] argued that a commission was not central to achieving the objectives of incorporation but that the government retained an open mind on whether such a body might be established at a later date. It suggested that more consideration needed to be given to the form which the Commission might take, in particular its potential relationship with existing statutory bodies such as the Commission for Racial Equality and the Equal Opportunities Commission (and parallel bodies in Northern Ireland); and that the additional public expenditure needed to establish and run the Commission would need to be justified. The government maintained this position during the subsequent parliamentary debates on the Bill.

The government did reiterate a proposal first made in its pre-election consultation paper that Parliament should establish a Human Rights Committee and suggested that the Committee's first inquiry could examine the potential role and structure of a Human Rights Commission. It thus sought to defer a decision on the issue while opening the door to discussion, an invitation taken up by Labour, Liberal Democrat and crossbench peers in the House of Lords and by Labour and Liberal Democrat MPs in the Commons.[7]

---

[4] *Report of the Joint Consultative Committee on Constitutional Reform* (1997), para 22.
[5] Lord Irvine of Lairg QC speaking at the conference on 'A Bill of Rights for the United Kingdom' at University College London, 4 July 1997.
[6] *Rights Brought Home: The Human Rights Bill*, Cm 3782.
[7] See House of Lords Second Reading, 3 November 1997; Committee Stage, 24 November 1997; Third Reading, 5 February 1998; and House of Commons Second Reading, 16 February 1998.

NORTHERN IRELAND

In a very different political context, a proposal for a Northern Ireland Human Rights Commission was raised during the all-party talks in the spring of 1998 and a firm commitment to establish such a body was contained in the 'Good Friday Agreement'. The Agreement stated that the Commission should be established 'with membership from Northern Ireland reflecting the community balance' and that it would be independent of government. Its role, subsequently specified in the Northern Ireland Bill,[8] would include:

'• keeping under review the adequacy and effectiveness of laws and practices, making recommendations to Government as necessary;
• providing information and promoting awareness of human rights;
• considering draft legislation referred to them by the new Assembly;
• in appropriate cases, bringing court proceedings or providing assistance to individuals doing so;
• to consult and advise on the scope for defining in Westminster legislation, rights supplementary to those in the ECHR, to reflect the particular circumstances of Northern Ireland, drawing on international instruments and experience. These additional rights to reflect the principles of mutual respect for the identity and ethos of both communities and parity of esteem and – taken together with the ECHR – to constitute a Bill of Rights for Northern Ireland;
• to consider the formulation of a general obligation on government and public bodies fully to respect, on the basis of equality of treatment, the identity and ethos of both communities in Northern Ireland and a clear formulation of the rights not to be discriminated against and to equality of opportunity in both the public and private sectors.'

The Irish government undertook to establish a Human Rights Commission with a similar mandate and it was agreed that there would be a committee of representatives from each Commission to consider issues of mutual interest.

INTERNATIONAL CONTEXT

The UK is not alone in considering the merits of a national institution to promote and enforce human rights standards. Recognising the important but limited role which can be played by the international human rights enforcement machinery, the United Nations has in recent years placed considerable emphasis on the role of such institutions. The General Assembly approved a set of guidelines, the Paris Principles,[9] to ensure the independence and effectiveness of national human rights bodies and the centrality of their role was endorsed by the Vienna Declaration from the World Conference on Human

---

[8] At the time of writing, the Bill had not been published so that the specific functions and powers of the Commission are not discussed here.
[9] General Assembly Resolution 48/134 of 20 December 1993.

Rights in 1993. That Declaration committed member states to encouraging the establishment and strengthening of such bodies, recognising that it is the right of each state to determine what kind of institution is most appropriate to the circumstances of that particular country.

The rapid expansion in the number of national human rights institutions world-wide is one of the most significant developments in the protection of human rights since the war. Long established commissions, such as those in France and in Australia, New Zealand and Canada, have built up considerable experience which they are now sharing with the new commissions in Africa and South East Asia in particular. In Eastern Europe, the first national institution was established in Latvia in 1995 with considerable international support.

The UK has not been able to take a lead in advising on the establishment and strengthening of national institutions because it has not had any such body. On occasion, representatives of Northern Ireland's Standing Advisory Commission on Human Rights (SACHR) have been asked to attend international fora as the UK's only human rights public body with a broad remit. As an advisory body with no enforcement powers, funded directly by government and with only five staff, SACHR does not, however, comply with the Paris Principles and was therefore not always considered an appropriate body to fulfil that role. Were the UK to establish its own Human Rights Commission in accordance with those principles, it would undoubtedly strengthen the UK's standing when advocating respect for human rights standards abroad. The Northern Ireland Human Rights Commission could enhance the UK's credibility in this respect only if it is, in practice, given the mandate, powers and resources necessary to be an effective body.

THE ROLE OF A HUMAN RIGHTS COMMISSION

There are a number of roles which a British based, and a Northern Ireland Human Rights Commission could fulfil, although views differ on the priority which should be accorded to them. Whereas some have argued, in the British context, that pursuit of a test case strategy is of paramount importance, for instance, others put greater emphasis on its prevention role in scrutinising draft legislation for conformity to the ECHR, or on its promotion and training role. The three key roles which we have identified are enforcement, monitoring and scrutiny and promotion.

Enforcement

The Commission would advise individuals how they might obtain redress if they believe that their rights have been infringed. Depending on its level of resources, it would provide assistance in taking cases through the courts and develop a test case strategy, supporting and initiating cases to test and clarify the law. In so doing, the Commission would be providing a service to government as well as to individuals, helping to ensure the development of a coherent body of law under the ECHR – 'an expert body', in the words of Lord Lester QC,

> 'able to marshall the arguments and the evidence and have authority before the courts in enabling test cases to be properly mounted and argued'.[10]

Without it, law reform will be piecemeal, the outcome of random cases. Moreover, individuals may in practice find it difficult to get access to justice. Lord Goodhart QC:

> 'If there is no Human Rights Commission or Human Rights Commissioner, what is to happen to the lay person who believes that his or her Convention rights have been breached? They can go to their local Citizens' Advice Bureau but are unlikely to find anybody there who is sufficiently specialised to be able to give sensible advice. They may go to their local law centre, in the unlikely event that they can find one that operates in their area. They may go to a solicitor, but that will cost money for a totally uncertain future . . .
>
> It would be an enormous help if such a person could go to the Human Rights Commission or Commissioner for advice as to their Convention rights . . . for support in bringing the case before the court or tribunal which can give relief.'[11]

The standards set by the courts, on 'degrading treatment' in prisons, on the 'right to family life' in immigration cases or on the scope of the new right to privacy will be central to the long-term influence of incorporation on the individual and on society at large. But that impact could be enhanced by preventive and promotional measures which would avoid the need for cases ever to come to court, in particular by scrutiny of draft legislation and by promoting good practice.

One difficulty in this respect, presented by s 7 of the Human Rights Act 1998, is that it does not allow anyone other than victims and potential victims, albeit widely defined, to initiate cases under the Act. This restriction was forcefully contested during the passage of the Bill, without success. The Home Secretary did, however, write to the Institute for Public Policy Research (IPPR) that:

> 'I obviously agree that, if in due course there were to be legislation establishing a Commission with the role amongst others of initiating legislation in its own right, the legislation would need to re-visit Clause 7 of the current Bill.'[12]

---

[10] Committee Stage of the Human Rights Bill, 24 November 1997, col 841.
[11] Committee Stage of the Human Rights Bill, 24 November 1997, col 846.
[12] Letter from Rt Hon Jack Straw MP to the author, 17 November 1997.

Particularly in the early years after the Human Rights Act comes into force, the Commission could play a key role in enhancing the ability of advice agencies and legal advisers to provide an expert service. It would be a source of expertise on international human rights standards, and the case law under the ECHR, on which they could draw; a source of material and of training. This service would help to ensure that individuals received appropriate advice and thereby discourage weak litigation at public expense.

Investigation

It is vital that the commissions should be able to investigate serious incidents or apparent systematic abuse which cannot be addressed through taking individual cases through the courts, where appropriate by establishing a public inquiry. The Good Friday Agreement makes no mention of any such power although Northern Ireland's history is littered with incidents which remain the source of tension and distrust for lack of such an independent investigation.

In relation to systematic denial of human rights, the Australian Human Rights and Equal Opportunity Commission has found that its public inquiries have not only led to well-supported recommendations but raised the public profile and understanding of the issue and hence political support for reform. For an inquiry into homeless children, for instance, the Commission conducted hearings in 21 centres across the country and heard evidence from over 300 witnesses. Advertisements in newspapers solicited 160 additional written submissions. The inquiry commissioned its own research and visited refuges and youth centres. After 18 months it submitted a report which led most of the state governments to implement a major programme of reforms for which the federal government provided Australian $100 million.

Scrutiny of legislation and policy

A Commission in Britain could scrutinise, selectively, draft legislation in the UK and that emanating from the European Union. It should do so not only to assess conformity to the standards in the ECHR but to the wider standards in other key international instruments such as the UN Convention on the Rights of the Child or the Convention on the Elimination of Racial Discrimination.

In Northern Ireland, the Commission will be able to scrutinise draft legislation referred by the Assembly but should be able to scrutinise *any* draft legislation, from the Assembly or Westminster, on its own initiative. Moreover, the Assembly should be required to refer all draft legislation to the Commission to ensure that the Commission does not receive the draft only after it is too late for its advice to be adopted.

Government lawyers already conduct a limited exercise of this kind, following a procedure known as 'Strasbourg proofing'. Rather than ask whether the proposed measures meet the standards set in the international Conventions binding on the UK, it asks the narrower, defensive question: 'If the Government were to proceed with this measure, how great is the risk that it would subsequently be challenged successfully at the European Court of Human Rights?' The legal advice which ministers then receive is confidential so that MPs have no expert opinion on which to draw in challenging ministerial assurances that a measure fully complies with the ECHR.

Under the Human Rights Act, ministers will be required to make a statement to Parliament on whether the Bill which they are introducing is compatible with the rights in the ECHR. That requirement will undoubtedly encourage officials to consider very carefully whether any provision in the Bill could be in breach of the ECHR's provisions. The advice which they give will, however, continue to be privileged and the minister, in his statement, will not be required to throw any light on how the judgment on compatibility has been reached. In these circumstances, the statement may serve to curtail debate rather than, as the government hopes, to enhance parliamentary scrutiny of the human rights implications of proposed legislation.

In contrast, the opinion from the Human Rights Commission would be public information. It would strengthen the hand of parliamentarians when questioning ministers and could help to ensure that measures in breach of the ECHR do not reach the statute book. In practice, many issues would not be clear cut. Few proposals would be a clear breach where the advice would be unequivocal. Many would rest on judgment, in which knowledge of the international standards and the way in which they have been interpreted in the past would be a component of the debate. The expertise of the Commission could assist parliamentarians in that debate, enhancing their ability to fulfil their traditional perceived role as guardians of the liberty of the individual.

Parliamentarians in Scotland will have no less a need for expert advice as they consider draft legislation under their new powers, for instance on policing matters. The Scottish Human Rights Commissioner, proposed in our model (below) would give them systematic access to expertise on international standards and the applicability of those standards to domestic law and policy; advice which is unlikely to be available to them from any other source.

In recommending this role for the Commission we are not suggesting that it would replace the role of officials in any respect. To the extent that the Strasbourg proofing system were enhanced by government *and* the outcome of that process made available to parliamentarians, the need for the Commission to fulfil this role could be diminished. Equally, if the proposed Westminster Parliament's Committee on Human Rights is well resourced, with staff of sufficient expertise, there may be less need for the Commission to focus on this aspect of its work. There are doubts, however, that this will prove to be the case.

The government's legal advice will necessarily remain private. There are already concerns whether it will be possible to provide adequate resources for the Human Rights Committee and the role of a parliamentary committee will, in any event, always differ from that of an independent commission. The opinion of the Human Rights Committee will reflect a balance of political interests and, with a majority of members from the governing party, the Committee may not always find it easy to take an independent line. The Commission, in contrast, would be free from party political considerations and would look to international human rights standards and to experience of the interpretation of the law in real situations, for guidance on the view it should take.

The Commission could also scrutinise existing legislation and policy. In its early days, post incorporation, it might examine those pieces of legislation and regulations which may be most likely to give rise to challenge under the Convention in order to advise on early amendment. In examining policy and practice, it could provide expertise to an inquiry conducted by others, such as that of a Select Committee, or conduct its own inquiry for which it should have powers of access to public property, officials and documentation.

Adequacy of arrangements for protecting human rights
The Commission in Britain should have a duty to advise on the effectiveness of the arrangements for protecting rights in the UK. It might, for instance, consider the adequacy of protection of children's rights and recommend some legislative reform or that a Children's Rights Commissioner be appointed within the Commission. It could consider the discrepancies between the differing anti-discrimination statutes and advocate harmonisation or piecemeal reform. Were the Commission to bring the existing equality commissions within it at some stage (see below), it would facilitate reaching agreement on such issues and its authority in arguing for reforms would be considerably enhanced.

Promotion, education and training

The Commission should have the task of raising awareness of human rights principles and their implications. Depending on its level of resources, it could do this in a number of ways.

The media
The Commission could use the press and broadcasting media to ensure that the human rights dimension of public debates is brought to the fore. Often this will not be to assert the overriding importance of upholding a particular right but to reflect on the balance which needs to be struck between competing rights or between a human right and conflicting social policy objectives. In relation to CCTV, for instance, the Commission might focus attention on the need to find the right balance between protecting privacy and the need to prevent crime and suggest safeguards which would protect that balance.

402

It might comment on the implications of international rights standards for the resolution of a policy dilemma, such as any implications of 'the right to found a family' for policy on in-vitro fertilisation.

This approach would raise the profile of the Commission and awareness of the significance of human rights principles in everyday life. But it is an approach which would have to be used with care to ensure that the Commission's authority was enhanced and its political impartiality assured.

Promoting good practice

The existing equality commissions have sought to find the right balance between promoting good practice by employers and using the law to challenge discrimination. Where employers have been willing to adapt, they have found that more may be achieved through training and advice than through litigation. Government ministers have suggested that public bodies will equally have to adopt a human rights culture – but appear confident that, in Britain, this will happen without a Human Rights Commission to provide training and guidance:

> 'Every public authority will know that its behaviour, its structures, its conclusions and its executive actions will be subject to this culture. It is exactly the same as what necessarily occurred following the introduction of, for example, race relations legislation and equal opportunities legislation. Every significant body, public or private, thereafter had to ask itself with great seriousness and concern: "Have we equipped ourselves to meet our legal obligations?" That has caused . . . a transformation in certain areas of human rights. The same is likely to follow when this Bill becomes law.'[13]

It can be argued, however, that this cultural shift to prevent human rights infringements is only likely to take place if a statutory body gives priority to promoting good practice, particularly within those institutions which exercise control over people: the police, prison and immigration service, and those responsible for institutional care of the most vulnerable: children, the aged and the mentally and physically disabled. The Commission could be proactive in approaching those responsible for these services, co-operating on codes of practice or training manuals, providing advice on how to avoid 'degrading treatment' or the criteria for a 'fair hearing', working with the professionals to devise procedures which will both protect the vulnerable and protect them from challenge in the courts.

This role was advocated by some of the parliamentarians who spoke in the debates on the Bill. Baroness Williams:

> 'I believe the training and education of public bodies is just as important as the establishment of case law. . . .

[13] Lord Williams of Mostyn QC, Second Reading of the Human Rights Bill, 3 November 1997, col 1308.

I fear that, for failure to train them in what the Bill means, we shall see a great deal of litigation that is unnecessary, expensive, slow, tedious and repetitive.'[14]

Although the wider set of international conventions cannot be enforced in the UK courts, the Commission could promote those standards as ones which the government has undertaken will be met throughout the UK. It could advise local education authorities and residential homes on the implications of the UN Convention on the Rights of the Child or employers' representatives about the implications of the ECHR for surveillance of employees or any denial of religious freedom. As in all of its functions the Commission would need to use its resources strategically, working through other organisations to reach a wider audience.

Education

Incorporation of the ECHR could, at last, lead to discussion of human rights principles within schools. The principles in the ECHR – like freedom of speech or the right to respect for privacy – could be taught as a set of common values to which the nation subscribes, even if we may differ on the means to achieve them. In the same way that it is now commonplace for children to discuss 'saving the environment' as an accepted common good, despite the fact that views differ widely on how that should be achieved, human rights principles should be an integral part of each child's school life.

Baroness Williams, a former Secretary of State for Education, argued that the Commission:

'would, I hope, become the spark for a new attempt in our education system to introduce the concept of citizenship alongside that of religion and ethics. I can think of nothing more appropriate at the beginning of a new Government than to accept the need for a culture of human rights among our children and university and college students, because that is the bedrock upon which a culture of human rights will be built in this country.'[15]

A recent survey illustrates the extent of ignorance in the UK about human rights standards. Children aged 14–16 in Northern Ireland and in three developing countries were asked, inter alia, whether they had been told in school about the rights in the UN Convention on the Rights of the Child. Of the children in Botswana, 43.5 per cent said that they had been told. 68 per cent of children in India and 52 per cent of the children in Zimbabwe said the same. In Northern Ireland, it was only 6 per cent.[16]

The Human Rights Commissions could take the initiative to address this ignorance and to foster a cultural shift, promoting teaching materials which

---

[14] Committee Stage of the Human Rights Bill, 24 November 1997, cols 844 and 843.
[15] Second Reading of the Human Rights Bill, 3 November 1997, col 1301.
[16] Conducted by Richard Bourne for the London University Institute of Education with funding from the UK government and the Commonwealth Secretariat. To be published.

enable children to discuss the significance of each human right and its protection in law. Is free speech an absolute right and, if not, why not? In what circumstances is it legitimate for the government, or a parent or teacher, to restrict what an individual can say? If I infringe your right to privacy, can you infringe mine?

Through such discussions, children would gain an understanding of rights, and the responsibilities they entail, which they can apply not only to their daily lives but to their growing understanding of world events. The Human Rights Commission would not necessarily be involved in the production of teaching materials itself but provide the authority and expertise to shift these efforts from the margins to the centre of the education debate.

Research and information

Research would not be a function in itself but a means to an end, informing the Commission's monitoring and advice work and its inquiries. Depending on resources, research could be conducted in-house or commissioned from other bodies. It could be done in conjunction with others, including organisations with direct experience of the issue on the ground.

If the Commission is to speak with authority it will need accurate information and sound analysis. It will need to develop international research links to be able to draw on comparative material and could, over time, provide an invaluable research resource to other organisations in the field.

Were some existing public bodies eventually to become part of the Human Rights Commission, as proposed below, the scope for comprehensive research and data collection would clearly be greater. A database of discrimination cases, for instance, could be compiled and made available to legal practitioners for whom the absence of such a resource is cited as one of the disadvantages of the current fragmented approach to discrimination enforcement.

International role

While the focus of the Commission would be on human rights within the UK, it could contribute to the promotion of human rights abroad in two ways. It could participate in United Nations meetings to promote new standards, a convention on the rights of disabled people, for instance, and similarly those of the Council of Europe. Secondly, it could assist in establishing and building up national human rights bodies in other countries, perhaps particularly those within Commonwealth countries where the UK would be a natural source of assistance.

The UK Commission would also assist the UN supervisory bodies in their scrutiny of the UK's record in relation to particular conventions, for instance the Committee on the Elimination of Racial Discrimination. The Commission would not *represent* the UK but be present as an independent expert body, a role envisaged by the UN's Paris Principles and already familiar to bodies such as the Data Protection Registrar at a European level.

STRUCTURE OF THE COMMISSION

The UK has three separate jurisdictions, court and penal systems in England and Wales, Scotland and Northern Ireland. It has already been decided that Northern Ireland is to have its own, separate Human Rights Commission. Scotland will soon have a devolved Parliament which will take responsibility for wide areas of legislation affecting individual rights. Wales shares a legal system with England but has some particular human rights concerns, such as those relating to the Welsh minority, and is to have its own elected Assembly which will take decisions with human rights implications. There are significant numbers of people in Wales, Scotland and Northern Ireland who have reservations about decisions being taken in London which affect them. These considerations point to the need for separate bodies enforcing and promoting human rights in those parts of the UK.

On the other hand, some legislation is UK-wide and one of the bodies responsible for a key aspect of human rights protection, the Data Protection Registrar, has a UK-wide jurisdiction. Moreover, it is the UK government which is held responsible at the national level for meeting the UK's obligations under international human rights law. These considerations suggest the need for a body which, for some purposes, covers the UK as a whole.

The optimal arrangement may therefore be to have separate commissions, or commissioners, in Scotland, Wales, England and Northern Ireland which have formal links to a UK-wide body based in London. The UK body, chaired by the UK Human Rights Commissioner, would take responsibility for those (perhaps limited) functions of the Commission which need to be conducted at a UK level.

In Scotland, Wales, England and Northern Ireland there would thus be separate commissions or commissioners responsible for fulfilling the functions of a Human Rights Commission within their area. These 'regional' human rights bodies would be members of the UK-wide body and hence able to play a full part in its decision-making.

Relationship with existing public bodies

If the Commission in Britain had been established by the Human Rights Act, it is likely that it would, at least initially, have been a free-standing, separate body co-existing with those public bodies which already have some responsibility for enforcing human rights standards. Labour's 1996 consultation paper, *Bringing Rights Home*, noted that an important consideration in establishing a new commission would be the implications for bodies such as the Equal

Opportunities Commission (EOC) and the Commission for Racial Equality (CRE). Since the election, however, no formal proposals have been made to those bodies by the government setting out what those implications might be to which they could respond.

Free-standing Commission

The Human Rights Commission could remain a separate body, liaising with the equality commissions and the Data Protection Registrar, for instance, but leaving their structures intact. This would be simple, avoiding any amendment to the statutes of those bodies or complicated negotiations on how to bring the bodies together in any form.

This is the model to be adopted in Northern Ireland where a White Paper in March 1998, *Partnership for Equality*, proposed that Northern Ireland's equality bodies should be brought together to form a single Equality Commission, but the Good Friday Agreement decribed that body as being separate from the proposed Human Rights Commission.

The disadvantage of this model is that it would maintain the artificial institutional divisions between different human rights, leaving two major areas of human rights protection, discrimination and privacy, outside of its scope. It would thus allow cases, as they do now, to fall through the gaps between the separate bodies and prevent the Commission from promoting and enforcing human rights standards as a whole. The Royal National Institute for Deaf People (RNID) said, in its response to IPPR's consultation paper on the options for the Commission:

'In the absence of merger there will be a plethora of Commissions dealing with various aspects of human rights with different remits, functions, powers and procedures. This will be very confusing and frustrating for the potential complainants, especially considering that discrimination due to disability, age, gender and race frequently overlaps. . . . Having a single body responsible for dealing with all aspects of human rights will permit the development of a coherent strategy with a clear focus and priorities among competing objectives, despite its wide brief and diversity of functions.'[17]

Maintaining four separate bodies in Britain would prevent savings being made from the provision of common services, supporting four press offices, for instance, rather than one. Finally, the model may be politically unattractive to central government as it involves financing an additional public body.

For individuals seeking advice, who may not know on what grounds they have been discriminated against, and for employers seeking guidance on equality standards, a 'one-stop-shop' would be considerably more convenient. This points towards the second, long-term option which we considered

---

[17] Response to IPPR from the RNID, dated 28 February 1997.

– that of merging all of the existing bodies within one, undifferentiated Human Rights Commission.

Merger

The advantage of merging the bodies into one is that it would end the artificial division between human rights standards, enabling the Commission to take up the range of human rights issues which may be of concern within one case (eg an issue of race and sex discrimination or of privacy and of the right to family life). The inclusion of the EOC and CRE within the brief of the human rights enforcement body would help overcome the limits to their statutory role (although the limitation on their ability to handle ECHR discrimination cases could be rectified by amending the sex discrimination and race relations legislation respectively). A case such as that of race discrimination by an immigration officer which also amounted to an infringement of the right to family life, however, would still need the combined mandate and expertise of the CRE and the Human Rights Commission suggesting that some structural relationship will be necessary.

Merger would enable the greatest advantage to be made of cost savings achieved from the sharing of common services. It would permit resources to be allocated according to the severity of the issue rather than according to the historic allocation between existing bodies.

This fully-integrated model does, however, have disadvantages. As each existing body lost its identity within the Commission it could lose its focus and dynamism and no longer be able to attract as its most senior member of staff the kind of people who now run these public bodies. Members of the public, or of minority communities, would no longer be able to identify a particular body focusing on their particular concern and could feel that the priority accorded to that issue had been downgraded. This concern could be heightened if the resources from that body were quickly seen to be redistributed towards tackling other human rights problems, however meritorious.

There would be a further disadvantage should the government decide, at some time in the future that it wished to demonstrate that it was giving greater priority to the promotion and enforcement of a particular human right, for instance to the rights of children. Within a generic body, in which responsibility for different issues is undifferentiated, there is no visible way of demonstrating that additional priority has been accorded to one issue. Such a difficulty would not arise were the third model chosen.

Umbrella model

This model combines most of the advantages of integration yet has fewer disadvantages. It anticipates that in Britain, in the long term, the EOC, CRE and Data Protection Registrar, and potentially other bodies with a human rights remit, would be brought within the umbrella of the Human Rights Commission. This might be an arm's length arrangement initially – the heads of those bodies could be ex officio commissioners of the Human Rights Commission while continuing to run their separate bodies. At a later stage, the heads of those bodies – and potentially others – would become full commissioners of the Human Rights Commission – the Race Equality Commissioner, Gender Equality Commissioner and Privacy Commissioner. As such, together with the Scottish, Welsh, English and UK Human Rights commissioners, and the head of the Northern Ireland Commission, they would comprise its decision-making body.

Under this proposal, the new, free-standing Human Rights Commission would, in its first year, fulfil some or all of the range of functions the IPPR has proposed in relation to areas of human rights not covered by the existing bodies; and would conduct an extensive consultation exercise to establish with the existing bodies whether they could work most effectively as autonomous bodies or should come together in some form. The Northern Ireland Commission could equally have reviewed the roles of the existing equality bodies in Belfast, prior to any decision being taken to establish the Equality Commission.

The Human Rights Commission's yardstick in those discussions would be the institutional arrangements which would ensure the most effective promotion and enforcement of human rights standards. In practice, if the British bodies agreed that they should come together in some form they would need to resolve practical issues such as the location of the different commissioners (the EOC is currently based in Manchester and the Data Protection Registrar in Wilmslow) and whether the departments of the separate bodies, such as press or legal departments, could most effectively be merged or left to operate separately. Those services which it was agreed could most effectively be operated as one department could be accountable, through the Human Rights Commission's executive director, to the UK Human Rights Commissioner who would chair the Commission.

The umbrella model for the Human Rights Commission would have the following advantages:

(1) It would enhance the status of the existing bodies by locating them clearly within the framework of international human rights standards and by emphasising their independence from any interest group.

(2) It would enhance the effectiveness of the existing bodies (in addition to filling the gaps in the existing machinery of enforcement) by enabling them to work together on those issues and cases which concern more than one human rights principle – in taking test cases, in the remit of an inquiry, in training (eg on avoiding discrimination on grounds of race, sex, religion, age and disability) and in research.

(3) It would enhance the resources of the existing bodies by enabling them to save on common services (eg one finance department, not four) and by increasing their potential to raise funds from charitable and private finance because of the greater scope and status of the new body.

(4) It would facilitate the inclusion of new commissioners should the government decide that this would be appropriate.

(5) It would reduce the number of quangos without losing the separate focus and dynamism of the existing bodies.

Baroness Amos, a former chief executive of the Equal Opportunities Commission, endorsed this approach in the House of Lords:

'In my view the effectiveness of the Equal Opportunities Commission and the Commission for Racial Equality would be enhanced by becoming part of a Human Rights Commission. It would bring issues of race and sex discrimination from the margins to the mainstream; the two organisations would no longer be perceived as acting in the interests of a particular social group but would be seen as part of a body promoting and enforcing internationally recognised human rights. For the public, employers and other organisations seeking guidance, there would be a single body – a one-stop shop.

There will always be difficulties in changing the institutional structure of existing bodies. Reassurance will be needed that the intention is to strengthen each part of any new body and that neither race nor gender discrimination will be marginalised in any new structure. However, differences about optimal structures should not deter us from creating a body which will undoubtedly be needed if the Bill is to achieve its full potential in protecting the rights of people within the United Kingdom.'[18]

RELATIONSHIP WITH GOVERNMENT AND PARLIAMENT

The ground rules for the relationship between a national Human Rights Commission and the government are set down by the UN's Paris Principles. The central principle is that of independence from government – the Human Rights Commission should be free from government control and independent of party politics, must be able to act on its own initiative and subject to financial arrangements which give it the greatest possible freedom to determine its own priorities, subject to safeguards to ensure financial probity. The Principles and subsequent UN guidelines also provide that such bodies should be established by law; and that the procedures for appointment and dismissal of its staff should be such as

'to ensure that its members are, individually and collectively, capable of generating and sustaining independence of action'.

Appointments, the guidelines suggest, should be for a fixed term, not of short duration, and capable of reappointment for an additional term.

---

[18] Second Reading of the Human Rights Bill, 3 November 1997, col 1248.

The UK Human Rights Commission would probably be established by legislation introduced by the Home Office. It is our view, however, that the Human Rights Commission should not be accountable to that, or any other government department, except in relation to its financial arrangements. Rather, the Human Rights Commission should primarily be accountable to Parliament, in practice to the new parliamentary Human Rights Committee.

The Human Rights Commission should present an Annual Report to that committee and report to it from time to time on particular issues. Individual commissioners would also report directly to the Committee on the issues within their mandate, or indeed to other parliamentary committees considering issues of relevance to them. The appointment of the commissioners should be by the Crown but with the approval of the Human Rights Committee, an arrangement designed to ensure that these are neither solely government appointments lacking bi-partisan support, nor fall entirely within the control of Parliament with the danger that party politics could have an undue influence. Dismissal should, as with the Data Protection Registrar now, be only with the approval of both Houses of Parliament.

The Human Rights Commission should be subject to the provisions of any Freedom of Information Act and to the jurisdiction of the Parliamentary Commissioner for Administration.

RELATIONSHIP WITH OTHER ORGANISATIONS AND THE PUBLIC

It will be essential that the Human Rights Commission, and its individual commissioners, remain constantly aware of changing concerns about human rights issues on the ground and of the difficulties faced by the relevant public bodies in responding to those concerns. One solution to this might be for the Commission to have one or more statutory advisory bodies, meeting perhaps three to four times each year in different parts of the country. The Commission could decide whom to invite and whom to accept as members of the advisory bodies but in so doing should bear in mind the need for the Council to reflect views on the full range of human rights issues; the need to ensure that public bodies which may be the subject of those concerns are represented so that the Commission is, and is seen to be, in a position to take an informed view; and the need to reflect geographically the whole of the country.

The Commissions could learn from the experience of the South African Human Rights Commission which has established working groups of experts to work with its commissioners. This would be a practical way in which academics, practitioners and experts in non-governmental organisations could contribute to the work of the Commission, effectively extending its resource base.

THE COST OF THE UK HUMAN RIGHTS COMMISSION

The potential cost of establishing a *separate* body in Britain and of its operation in its first year has been calculated for IPPR by a recently retired senior civil servant. The estimate has been made for the first year of operation only as subsequent costs would depend on the outcome of any consultation with the existing bodies.

He concluded that the cost of establishing the Human Rights Commission would be in the region of £142,000 and the total cost of its operation in its first year (estimated to be 1999–2000) would be £2.8 million. This is a modest sum compared to the budgets of the existing commissions (the CRE budget for 1997 was in the order of £15 million; that for the EOC, £6 million). Nevertheless, public expenditure constraints mean that any new expenditure is problematic. Recourse might need to be made to charitable or even commercial sponsorship, albeit that care would have to be taken to avoid any potential conflict of interest in so doing.

CONCLUSION

The impact of the Human Rights Act incorporating the ECHR would be considerably greater were a Human Rights Commission established in Britain to promote and enforce the standards it requires. The mandate of the Commission should, however, extend beyond the narrow confines of the ECHR, promoting the wider range of human rights conventions binding on the UK.

In Northern Ireland, the jury is still out on whether the Commission will prove to be a credible body armed with the broad mandate, powers and resources it needs to be effective. Crucial will be the power to litigate on its own initiative and the power to investigate human rights abuses. As crucial will be the choice of commissioners. Their expertise, judgment and commitment to human rights protection could help in part to overcome an inadequate statutory remit.

In considering the establishment of a national institution for the protection of human rights, the UK is part of a worldwide initiative promoted by the United Nations to create and strengthen such bodies. Were the UK to have its own commission, including an effective commission in Northern Ireland, it would enhance its voice when advocating higher human rights standards abroad. It would be seen to be putting its own house in order and to have the relevant experience and expertise to advise states how to create effective institutions. This leadership could be particularly valuable within the Commonwealth where the number of such commissions is growing.

There are three key roles which a commission would need to fulfil: enforcement, monitoring and scrutiny of proposed legislation, and promotion. It should advise individuals, assist them to take cases through the courts and initiate its own litigation, focusing on a test-case strategy. Where a systemic problem could not be addressed through the resolution of individual cases, the Commission must be able to investigate, if necessary through a public inquiry, drawing on a wide range of evidence and presenting recommendations to government.

The Commission would scrutinise proposed and existing legislation and policy for conformity to international human rights standards binding on the UK; and would advise the government, Westminster or Scottish Parliament, Northern Ireland or Welsh Assembly, as appropriate, on the adequacy of the existing arrangements for protecting rights, advocating reform of the law where required. Finally, it would promote awareness of the relevance of human rights principles to decisions at every level, using the media and providing advice and training on good practice, particularly within those institutions exercising control over individuals or providing institutional care.

Recognising the separate jurisdictions in Scotland and Northern Ireland, and the realities of devolution, separate commissions or commissioners would be needed in Scotland, Wales and England, with formal links to a UK-wide body based in London. The Commission could initially be a separate, additional statutory body co-existing with public bodies which already have some responsibility for enforcing aspects of human rights – in particular the CRE, EOC and Data Protection Registrar.

In the long run, this would not be the most effective structure nor the most efficient use of public funds. I have set out the reasons why a complete merger of the existing bodies may not be the most attractive alternative, advocating instead an umbrella model in which the bodies would become part of the Human Rights Commission but retain individual commissioners with responsibility for specific areas of work. Wide consultation would be needed before such a proposal were implemented to ensure that the particular structure chosen would enhance the effectiveness of the existing bodies rather than dilute their impact as some fear.

The current model of commissions, in which decision-making responsibility is carried by around 15 commissioners appointed by the government, has not encouraged accountability either to Parliament nor to the communities and interest groups concerned. In the umbrella model, each area of policy, such as race equality, would be the responsibility of a single, professional commissioner rather than of a body of commissioners, taking key decisions collegiately with fellow commissioners of the Human Rights Commission – the Privacy Commissioner, Scottish Human Rights Commissioner and so forth.

That body would be accountable to Parliament, commissioners reporting individually on issues within their brief; a close relationship with frequent contact in contrast to the current rather distant relationship between the existing statutory human rights bodies and Parliament in which they lack adequate influence or accountability. Regular contact with interest groups through the advisory councils and working groups would ensure that commissioners were equally aware, and able to respond to, changing concerns on the ground.

A Human Rights Commission in Britain, as in Northern Ireland, is not an optional extra. The decision whether or not to establish such a body will determine whether incorporation of the ECHR does indeed lead to a sea-change in the level of human rights protection in the UK and a greater awareness of human rights and the responsibilities they entail, within the public at large. It may be felt that the existing public bodies with responsibility for aspects of human rights protection should remain autonomous. That debate should not stall indefinitely the establishment of a separate Human Rights Commission whose role will be crucial to the development of effective human rights protection throughout the UK.

Further reading

Labour Party, Consultation Paper: *Bringing Rights Home: Labour's Plans to Incorporate the European Convention on Human Rights into UK Law* (1996); Government White Paper, *Rights Brought Home: The Human Rights Bill* (London: HMSO, Cm 3782, 1997)

Sarah Spencer and Ian Bynoe, *A Human Rights Commission: The Options for Britain and Northern Ireland* (London: Institute for Public Policy Research, 1998)

Constitution Unit (Nicole Smith), *Human Rights Legislation* (London, 1996)

United Nations Centre for Human Rights, *National Human Rights Institutions – A Handbook on the Establishment and Strengthening of National Institutions for the Promotion and Protection of Human Rights* (Professional Training Series No 4, 1995)

Chapter 20

Citizens' Access to the Law

Alastair Hudson (Queen Mary College, London; former
Special Adviser, Labour Legal Affairs)

'It's the characteristic of our Western societies that the language of
power is law, not magic, religion, or anything else.'

(Michel Foucault)[1]

INTRODUCTION

The only two groups of people who are able to access our justice system are
the very wealthy or those who live on income support levels of income. The
majority of British citizens, typically those who are in work or who have only
modest savings, are unable to gain access to legal advice.

As Foucault maintains, the language of law is at the centre of the discourse
of power in Western society. For the individual, it is in the arena of law that
questions of rights and power are decided. Where there is no access to law,
there is no power. Without power there are no effective rights and no real
obligations. The issue of access is dominated by the lawyers themselves and
by political decisions as to the availability of public resources. As Foucault
said 'it is as if even the word of the law could no longer be authorised, in our
society, except by a discourse of truth'.[2]

The legal system does not operate effectively at any theoretical level. The
law does not work on the free market model which the Lord Chancellor's
Department[3] has long considered that it does, or ought to. There is no such
thing as a 'free market in legal services'. A free market requires a broad range
of suppliers who are able to offer comparable goods and services at a broad
range of prices. Typically that range of prices will include a range of qualities

---

[1] *Power/Knowledge: Selected Interviews and Other Writings 1972–1977*, Colin Gordon (ed) (London: Routledge, 1980) p 201.
[2] 'The Order of Discourse', 1971, in R Young (ed), *Untying the Text: A Post-Structuralist Reader* (London: Routledge, 1981) p 55.
[3] Under Conservative administrations, in any event.

415

of service, of back-up support, added extras on expensive models and budget features on the inexpensive.

A mature market in products like motor vehicles ensures that there are not only a broad range of vehicles used for a number of purposes (family saloons, long-distance cars for salespeople, executive cars for status, large vans for deliveries, lorries for road haulage) – such a market also enables a second-hand market so that most people in society are able to acquire some form of vehicle if they really require one. Even if they cannot afford such a vehicle, there is public transport (buses, trains and even taxis and ambulances).[4]

In the legal system there is no such market. There are publicly-funded legal services for those who are either very poor (legal aid) or those rich enough to appear very poor (legal aid for the apparently wealthy[5]). There is then legal service for those individuals rich enough to afford lawyers and for corporate entities wealthy enough to afford lawyers (large businesses, charities and so forth). For the rest of society there is no ability to access any other form of *legal* service.[6] There is no 'budget' form of legal advice. Some High Street solicitors are prepared to cut costs to bring in business. Fees are always open to negotiation or are left on a contingency basis. However, those fees are never open to negotiation in the same way that even non-NHS dentists are prepared to charge only £10 for a consultation and check-up.

There are a number of reasons why there is no free market in legal services. First, professional restrictive practices.[7] Secondly, over-complexity in the system's rules and practices.[8] Thirdly, the legal system operating as a closed system where lawyers dictate the substance and form of discourse.[9] Fourthly, a lack of alternative mechanisms of dispute resolution.[10]

Beyond law and politics: connexity and social justice

While the legal system remains inaccessible for most people, society is changing profoundly. One impact on the legal system in the changed world is the

---

[4] At the time of writing, in a coincidence of metaphor, the Lord Chancellor was reported (in *The Guardian*, *The Times* and the *Daily Telegraph*) as referring to sharp increases in court fees bemoaned by many lawyers, as like moaning about an increase in vehicle excise duty when compared to the price of cars. It was interesting to hear the Lord Chancellor, attacking 'fat cat lawyers' who earn enormous fees, when he himself was a recent alumnus of that feline club.

[5] See eg Lord Chancellor's Department consultation paper, *Legal Aid for the Apparently Wealthy*.

[6] Typically advice agencies do not have rights of audience before most courts and some tribunals – nor are their workers necessarily qualified to give legal advice.

[7] The nature of the professions is considered in more detail below.

[8] See the discussion of Lord Woolf's report into reform of the civil justice system below.

[9] See eg, the discussion of Teubner below and see Giddens, *Beyond Left and Right* (London: Polity Press, 1993).

[10] As set out below, there is a broad range of available dispute resolution but the discourse of substantive law remains the locus of political power.

growth of what Mulgan calls 'connexity'.[11] In his terms, despite this growing interdependence, institutions like the legal system are failing to connect with individuals by failing to provide them with access to remedies. As the world changes in this way, individuals are less able to protect their rights, to impose obligations on others or to forge new identities and connections.

The growth of inter-connectedness and the increased concentration on human rights raise the following sorts of problems:

'[T]he clearest sign of all of the heightening tension between freedom and inter-dependence is that in much of the world today the most pressing problems on the public agenda are not poverty or material shortage (although these remain acute for large minorities), but rather the disorders of freedom: the troubles that result directly from having too many freedoms that are abused rather than constructively used.'[12]

Having freedoms, but being unable to protect or advance them, is bound up with the growth of dispossession and disaffection in 1990s Britain. The modern legal system[13] makes little allowance for inequalities of bargaining power and the impossibility for most people of accessing legal advice. This is at root a political question, calling for a need to examine the possibility of social justice and equality without the possibility of recourse to law.

Law is, in theory, the great leveller. Only in the context of law is an individual equal in power to any other individual.[14] Where the legal system denies access, then that ability to be equal is lost. Therefore, access to justice is not simply about law or about legal procedural rules, it is about rectifying the denial of social justice. It is about the provision or denial of basic civil liberties.

In Mulgan's terms, a 'weakness infuses liberal politics which imagines the individual as a self-sufficient entity, not formed by society, and owing nothing to it, but rather heroic in his or her isolation, and defined by a series of claims that can be made on society'.[15] That is true of the legal system. Concentration is poured onto the creation of models for codes of rights and obligations with little attention being paid to the manner in which those rights can possibly be protected. The individual is not self-sufficient. Access to law or access to justice is necessary to achieve or create self-sufficiency.

---

[11] '*Connexity: How to Live in a Connected World*'; Geoff Mulgan (Chatto & Windus, 1997).

[12] Mulgan, *Connexity*, p 5.

[13] The better appellation is probably a 'postmodern legal system'. As with Jameson's definition of the term 'postmodern', our legal system is constantly self-referential, it pastiches old codes of dress and language constantly and draws for new ideas on old texts and habits of thought (see generally Frederic Jameson, *Postmodernism, or the Cultural Logic of Late Capitalism* (London: Verso, 1989)).

[14] See eg the recent McLibel litigation where two individuals were able to defend an action brought by the megalithic McDonalds corporation, converting it into the longest trial in English legal history.

[15] Mulgan, *Connexity*, p 9.

The further problem for the legal system is the extent to which it is a closed system. In the power equation quoted from Foucault at the beginning of this chapter, the individual who cannot enter the closed system of the law is denied power. Where power is discussed in the language of law, not being able to enter that discussion is a denial of power. In Teubner's terms:

> '"Legal reality" ... is a social, not a psychic construct ... it is the product of communications. And among social constructs, it is a highly selective one, since it has come into existence with an autonomous social system, the hypercyclically constituted legal system.'[16]

The law seals itself from other discourses about politics and constitution. Yet, it is through law that constitutional reform must be put into action.

LABOUR PARTY PROPOSALS

The political problem: rhetoric and resources

Before considering the detail of proposals to reform the legal system, it is worth considering the exigencies of day-to-day politics and the need to manage a public sector budget.

The problem of control of the costs of the legal system (let alone the need for radical alteration of that system) had been an intractable one for the Major administration and promises to be equally challenging for the new Labour administration. The issue of budgets and system management are the bane of modern government.

A statement made by Paul Boateng MP, when Shadow spokesperson for legal affairs is illuminating:

> 'The Labour Party's central aims and values focus on the need for strong communities which are able to sustain themselves as part of a successful society.'[17]

This attitude underlines the way in which politicians still want to *speak* about the aspects of government which they seek to *manage*: that is, they wish to conceptualise the problems rhetorically.[18] The political problem is one of

---

[16] Gunther Teubner, *Law as an Autopoietic System* (Oxford: Blackwell, 1993) p 45.

[17] Sometime Labour Party spokesperson on legal affairs, speech to the Labour Party Conference, Brighton, October 1995.

[18] As Robin Cook said: 'in opposition you wake up in the morning thinking about what you are going to say today; in government you wake in the morning thinking about what you are going to do'.

balancing ideological will with available resources. As will be considered later, the solution to balancing that equation may be to pursue bloody mindedly the logic of that political rhetoric.

The focus of the new Labour government's proposals[19] is on 'the consumer of legal services'.[20] This highlights another potential problem with the future of the legal system in political terms. As the problem is seen as one of consumption of legal services, the civil liberties aspect of access to the most mundane forms of legal advice and assistance is constantly downplayed. The legal system remains a system isolated within its own terms of reference – fenced off from the broader discussion of constitutional, political and national renewal.

The Labour Party's chief proposal to achieve this refocusing of resources is to create a Community Legal Service (CLS)[21] incorporating a radically reformed legal aid scheme and far greater provision for alternative dispute resolution. Coupled with this will be the reform of the franchising scheme, extended to control the cost of access to justice and to set high standards for the quality of services provided by franchise-holders. The renewed focus on the *consumer* of legal services must mean changes for the legal profession.[22] What it fails to hit upon is the need to focus on the end-goal of a just society and not on the trendy rhetoric of consumerism.

The heart of the political problem is that there is no new money to spend on publicly funded legal services and the maintenance of the court system. To manage the increase in demand and spiralling cost, there is therefore a need for a more fundamental refocusing of the structure of publicly funded legal services.

Labour Party policy in this context has undergone great change since 1992. It can be segregated into three distinct phases. The first phase is policy under John Smith, the second under the leadership of Tony Blair in opposition, and the third manifestation is policy under Lord Irvine as Lord Chancellor in the new Labour administration. It would be easy to overemphasise the differences in these drifts in policy. There are some differences in detail.

It is also important to understand the personnel involved. Under John Smith, the Constitution and Democracy Commission was chaired by Tony Blair: this was the body charged with the development of Labour Party policy in this (and other) areas. Under Tony Blair's leadership Jack Straw succeeded to this position. The current Lord Chancellor (at the time of writing) Lord Irvine sat on all manifestations of this commission. At the time of writing, Sir Peter Middleton is carrying out a review of civil justice and legal aid policy at the behest of the Lord Chancellor, Lord Irvine.

---

[19] As expressed while in opposition, it should be noted.
[20] As set out in numerous places in *Access to Justice* (Labour Party, July 1995).
[21] On the CLS, see below.
[22] See generally *Access to Justice*, July 1995.

What follows will concentrate on published Labour Party policy in advance of the 1997 general election, before considering the likely approach of the 1997–98 policy review.

Policy under John Smith

First, it is important to consider what was left out of the Smith era. Two important strands of policy were altered.

The first was the long-standing commitment to create a Ministry of Justice which would have its own Cabinet Minister and be accountable to a Select committee in the House of Commons. It was the aim of that policy that the Lord Chancellor's Department functions be subsumed into the Ministry of Justice. There were a number of reasons for this, but the core motivation was that, by creating a Ministry of Justice, justice policy would become the responsibility of an elected, Cabinet Minister who would be accountable directly to the House of Commons.

The creation of a central ministry would also recover the scraps of the justice system which are administered in other departments (such as some aspects of juvenile justice in the Home Office and Citizens' Advice Bureaux in the Department of Trade and Industry) and bring them under one roof. A number of savings to central spending budgets could be made by integrating many of the duplication of functions.

While the process of making legal affairs and citizens' rights reviewable in the House of Commons is important, policy concerning all the industrial, social security and other tribunals must be centred in one place so that efficient working practices, costs savings and better administration can be concentrated together. Binding these bodies together under one ministry should enable their independence to be enhanced in terms of industrial and social policy while their administration and support functions are improved.

The scope of the Ministry of Justice would be to look broadly at a number of issues concerning access to justice from the point of view of cost, standard of service and the organisation of the justice system.

The new ministry would be able to adopt the increased use of alternative methods of adjudication which are not as traumatic, expensive and prone to delay as courts for the user. A central ministry would ensure that the profession and the judiciary responded to the demands of the users of the system and of the new order of rights protection.

Most importantly, though, the justice function would be brought into the House of Commons for the first time, rather than being left to the Lord Chancellor in the House of Lords. With the creation of a new government ministry in the House of Commons, there would be a Select Committee which will enable MPs to oversee the running of the justice system.

The second change in Labour Party policy was the movement away from the consideration of bodies like a Law Foundation which would seek to bridge the gap between public and private partnership. A Law Foundation is an organisation which has been used to great effect in other jurisdictions as a non-governmental means of examining the way in which the justice system operates and of creating pilot projects for new techniques in dealing with disputes.

The justice system is currently riddled with examples of inefficiency and waste. Little work has been done to quantify the extent of this problem, but on a purely anecdotal level there is a very large amount of time wasted during litigation in preparing documents and waiting for the case to be listed. Court buildings are also under-used in many circumstances. Much of the work could be carried on in court buildings when the courts are not sitting or in areas where there is capacity which is surplus to court requirements. There are clearly efficiency savings to be made in this area. Similarly, the new technology available now would require testing in an advice centre environment and integration into the court building infrastructure in many places so that the court buildings and the advice agencies could continue to be brought closer together.

The co-ordination of research work in this area and the pilot schemes that would be necessary for the above proposals to cope with the implementation of the Civil Justice Review, would be the responsibility of the Law Foundation. By having the Law Foundation exist separately from the Ministry of Justice, it is possible for the profession, the advice agencies and consumer organisations to feed into the innovation process their individual concerns, and thus ensure that the justice system does not evolve in a way that is determined solely by civil servants or a central political agenda.

All of what follows under 'New Labour' proposals was in fact part of the proposals under John Smith. Separating the two, when one is really a sub-set of the other, is simply done to make it easier to see how policy developed.

New Labour proposals

'It is social justice which requires that there must be access to the law for all' – Tony Blair, speaking in Sedgefield, 28 January 1995.

The New Labour proposals, adopted by the Labour Party Conference in October 1995 as official party policy under Tony Blair's leadership, constituted the most detailed party political proposals available at that time. While the document that contained them (*Access to Justice*) was shorter than the document prepared under John Smith, the spread of proposals was still broad. There is only space here to consider the more important proposals relating to legal aid and the introduction of a community legal service, although something is said about attitudes towards the judiciary and the reform of the legal profession. The strength of the proposals lay primarily, in their scope and the recognition that reform of the legal system was a complicated undertaking.

The Community Legal Service ('CLS')

The CLS is the Labour administration's proposal for the reform of legal aid provision.[23] The problem with legal aid is simply stated. There was an increase in spending between 1979 and 1996 of 600 per cent in the Lord Chancellor's Department budget on legal aid with a corresponding reduction in the level of the population able to claim legal aid falling from 77 per cent to 47 per cent over the same period.

The CLS would not be an entirely new system in itself; instead it would be part of a restructuring of the legal aid system. Rather than set nationally applicable levels of income below which a person is entitled to receive legal aid, the aim is to give greater local control over the manner in which legal aid money is to be used. By creating distinct CLS boards, based on existing Legal Aid Boards, local budgets can be set to achieve locally prioritised objectives for legal services. Some areas have a need for representation in employment disputes, others see housing and social welfare as their most pressing needs. The CLS in conjunction with the Legal Aid Board and the Lord Chancellor's Department would set priorities for the expenditure of legal aid in those areas within budget constraints.

The extreme cultural shift this represents is the movement towards a system of *vertical* eligibility for legal aid, rather than *horizontal* eligibility on the basis of income.[24]

The question of a CLS is very much up in the air. At one level it operates as no more than a renamed version of Conservative proposals for block contracting and NHS-style trust reforms. A CLS will only work where there is flexibility in funding and a freedom to be bloody minded in the choice of priorities for which money will be applied. The most important point to note is that the creation of a CLS will create differences between the nature and composition of legal services delivery in different areas. The notion of equal rights for all citizens will therefore be made impossible. Some will be made more equal than others.

Ideologically this may be problematical and may create political problems of presentation. For example, the current system gives preferential treatment to those with matrimonial disputes. Where a particular community takes money away from matrimonial disputes and puts it towards those bringing industrial disputes, there is no longer horizontal equality.

The real difficulty will come with the body that makes the choices. Where bureaucrats make the choices bureaucratically, there will be talk of hidden agendas. It is only if the selection is seen to be the result of choice made

---

[23] The term 'community' is clearly a fashionable one. The Commission for Social Justice, set up by the late John Smith MP, indicated the need for an 'Investor's Britain' in which our institutions and citizens work together to enhance the growth of our communities: see *Strategies for National Renewal* (London: Vintage, 1994). The term community has been used more broadly under the influence of Amitai Etzioni by the New Labour administration.

[24] The vertical/horizontal distinction is considered at p 437 below.

by some body representative of local people, that this problem can be circumvented. There could be responsibility put onto local councillors, although local government might be loathe to assume this responsibility. Local magistrates' committees and local Legal Aid Boards carry the problem of being apolitical appointees who do not have any claim to be representative of their local communities. Perhaps local committees made up of people selected on a focus group basis would be a closer approximation – although educating them as to the complexities of legal aid budgeting would not be an easy task.

The strength of community-level selection of requisite spending priorities is that there can be a political discussion as to the needs and priorities that affect ordinary people. The presumption that this is a matter for expert decision-making (in the way that NHS trusts leave decisions about health-care treatment to the medical staff on the basis that they are 'clinical' decisions) masks the fact that it is a discussion about the entitlement to public resources. As in any other context, this is a straightforwardly political matter. Therefore, the solution to the operation of a CLS must be a political matter too.

The alternative is therefore to have centrally controlled delivery of legal services. All that the CLS will do at that stage is to channel funds. On that basis a CLS will not be responsive to local needs for justice provision.

Policy on the lawyers

The Labour Party's policy commitment in *Access to Justice* with reference to the judiciary was to create a Judicial Appointments and Training Commission, to carry out the functions of the Judicial Studies Board. The intention was that the Commission would be independent of the Lord Chancellor's Department and would have a strong lay presence. The primary role of this body would be to advise the Lord Chancellor on all aspects of judicial selection and the appointment of judges and magistrates. The requirement of such a body should, in this writer's opinion, be to make the selection of judges and QCs while publishing criteria for their choices – rather than referring the matter back to the Lord Chancellor for a final decision.

The often stressed pro-active role of this Commission would be to develop a strong equal opportunities policy and make every effort to encourage members of groups currently under-represented on the bench to apply for judicial and magisterial posts. What remains lacking is a thorough, formal procedure for both monitoring the performance of judges and for handling complaints from members of the public about judicial conduct. Judicial monitoring on this model was recommended by the Runciman Royal Commission on Criminal Justice.[25]

---

[25] Cmnd 2263 (London: HMSO, 1993).

Boateng was particularly damning of the legal professions. In his speech to Party Conference in 1995, introducing the *Access to Justice* document, he said: 'the gravy train must stop . . . there can be no more money for lawyers . . . to the lawyers the message is that the party is over – for the consumer, the message is that the party has only just begun'. This clear message was laid out as part of the reforms of legal aid and, later, in considering plans for compulsory pro bono work to be undertaken by lawyers as a condition of retaining their practising certificates.[26]

Reform of procedural rules: the Woolf Report

The archetypal lawyer's discourse about the reform of the system is set out in Lord Woolf's investigation into the civil justice system, culminating in another report called *Access to Justice*.[27] It is unfortunate that there has only recently been the political will to implement many or any of those proposals. 'Unfortunate' not in the sense that Lord Woolf's proposals offer a utopia (they simply do not) but rather that they move towards a form of legal system which is concerned with equality and fairness between citizens.

The three giants: cost, delay and complexity

Lord Woolf's fundamental aim is 'to improve access to justice by reducing inequalities, cost, delay, and complexity of civil litigation and to introduce greater certainty as to timescales and costs'.[28] There are also a tranche of specific objectives within that broader remit.

Lord Woolf has expressed his opinion that the system of civil justice ought to be: 'accessible, efficient and just'.[29] He described the current system as being 'expensive, slow, uncertain and unequal'.[30] The last identified problem is interesting. It has hints of the statement of aims of the Legal Action Group: that there be 'equal access to justice for all'. In Lord Woolf's opinion, people are not afforded an equal opportunity of justice if the system operates to deter them from seeking or obtaining access to justice.

The easy criticism of Woolf is that his strictly procedural reforms alone are unlikely to make any more litigants come to law. The problem for litigants is often not the concern about the delay involved in litigation, but rather the cost of paying for the first consultation with a lawyer at all.

---

[26] This initiative had the public backing of Tony Blair but has receded into the background under Lord Irvine's chancellorship. For more detail on these issues, see *Towards a Just Society* by Alastair Hudson to be published by Cassell in 1998.

[27] *Access to Justice: Final Report* (London: HMSO, July 1996).

[28] ibid.

[29] Speaking at the LSE on 30 January 1997.

[30] ibid.

The underpinnings of the Woolf Report

There are two key goals underpinning the Woolf reforms:

(1) Getting cases out of the system.
(2) Ensuring cases coming within the system are conducted in a 'proportionate' way.[31]

The draft Rules of the Supreme Court, prepared by Lord Woolf, will require that a case be dealt with 'justly'. The aim of case management is to achieve a just result where the rules do not otherwise provide for it. For example, if the rules do not provide for a set timescale or a set cost for the litigation, then the court will be given the discretion to impose such directions to ensure that the case is dealt with 'justly'. The rules should also have the effect that litigation is a last resort.

There will be three streams to the new system. Lord Woolf proposed to raise the limit (from £1,000 to £3,000) for claims to be taken into the 'lawyer-free zone' of the Small Claims Court. The proposed fast-track procedure will introduce a fixed fee for cases worth between £3,000 and £10,000. The aim is that the litigant will know: (a) the upside and downside of the cost; (b) the timescale for the litigation; and (c) the exact procedural requirements which the litigant must satisfy. It aims to introduce 'no frills litigation'.[32] The third limb of the new system, 'caseflow management', constitutes, in the terms that Woolf proposes, a radical alteration in civil procedure.

Lord Woolf identified the following as the core of his proposed reforms: '. . . a fundamental transfer in the responsibility for the management of civil litigation from the litigants and their legal advisors to the courts'.[33] Caseflow management in the civil courts is the linchpin of Lord Woolf's proposals.

The case against Woolf: is size important?

One regrettable feature of the Woolf Report[34] is that the importance of a case is not necessarily to be measured by reference to its significance to the parties but rather by reference to its cash value. Only cases with high cash value will qualify for the Rolls Royce system of caseflow management. A claim for payment of social security benefit will generally be small compared to a breach of contract claim between commercial parties. The potential impact of Lord Woolf's proposals would be that social welfare law claims would be de-prioritised at the expense of the interests of commercial parties. The notion of equal access to justice for all is an impossible goal to achieve if the system is ranking claims on the basis of cash sums.

---

[31] The proportion referred to is the ratio between size of damages sought, and size of legal costs.
[32] His Lordship's own expression.
[33] *Access to Justice: Interim Report* (HMSO: June 1995) p 52.
[34] It should be stressed that this is not one of Professor Zander's objections, but rather the author's own.

The very fact that a litigant will be required to rebut a presumption of lack of importance merely underlines the fact that those of restricted means are being relegated in the juridical scheme of things, at the expense of high-cash worth commercial litigation. Broadening the scope of access to justice will not be served by erecting barriers to entry in this way. It is the regulation of the mundane cases which are the measure of a legal system's egalitarianism, despite Lord Woolf's nod to the need to remove inequality.

Too much judicial control – justice or process?

The issue is between judicial control of litigation and party control of litigation. Is it an interference by the judges to set down timetables for the conduct of litigation? The answer to this question might depend on a more fundamental view of the role of the civil legal system in this regard.

There are two competing views. Lord Woolf considers that involving judges at an earlier stage will increase the likelihood of the issues being defined sooner and the parties reaching settlement. Zander's view is that involving judges at an earlier stage will increase the cost of litigation by requiring parties and lawyers to attend court sooner in cases which would probably settle in any event. He argues that at present more than 50 per cent of cases settle without court order.[35] Therefore, the introduction of judges into the decision of these cases is more likely to impede settlement than to hasten it.

The social role of law is the key question here. While there is no denying the extent of the crisis of feasibility facing the English legal process at present, there is a great danger of ignoring the purpose of that same system.

Personal injury claims: the case for disaggregation

Civil law is generally treated as being an homogeneous entity. The Woolf Report treats it in this way for the most part. For a lawyer, it is easier to think of one case as being the same as any other. It has the happy side effect, at least superficially, of removing any hint of bias. Unfortunately, as set out earlier, the current organisation of the legal system means that there is a power imbalance in the system at the moment. What is necessary is the disaggregation of types of case. Rather than seeing all litigation as being the same, it is only possible to remove imbalance by recognising the differences between cases.

One good example is the need to treat personal injury cases differently from other types of litigation. The problem with personal injury litigation is that most cases will settle. By requiring parties to go before a judge at an early stage in the proceedings will lead to a front-loading of costs and prevent early settlement in many cases. The way in which this form of litigation is necessarily conducted (relying on the production of expert evidence which frequently removes the need to go to court) marks personal injury cases out

---

[35] *Judicial Statistics*, 1994, p 30, Table 3.4. See, eg the *Report of the Personal Injuries Litigation Procedure Working Party* (the 'Cantley Committee'), Cmnd 7476 (1979) para 9.

as needing separate treatment. This is another example of the need to look at cases vertically and not horizontally.

Policy under Lord Irvine

There has been some rapid development of policy under Lord Irvine. The first notable factor is the determination of the new Lord Chancellor not to be bound by official party policy. The election manifesto was, necessarily, less detailed than *Access to Justice*, but in an interview with the *Observer* newspaper soon after the election,[36] he set out some policy stances which appeared to be in conflict with published party policy. Foremost amongst them was the abolition of plans to reform judicial appointments. Proposals to introduce a lay voice into appointments to the bench and to the creation of new Queen's Counsel, providing accountability in the selection process, are thus laid aside.

Indeed the position of the Lord Chancellor has become an interesting one since May 1997. His most famous public words, rather than constitutional or legal reforms, has been his announcement that he considers himself to be in similar mould to Wolsey – the chancellor at the time of Henry VIII who ran the Kafka-esque Star Chamber and was ultimately beheaded.[37]

The remit for the Middleton review bears indications of things to come.[38] The requirement to control the Lord Chancellor's Departmental budget, as well as the need to consider reform in itself, would seem to lie behind the appointment. As argued in this chapter, reform of either civil justice or legal aid must be carried out in the broader context of reform of the entire system of dispute resolution and advice throughout the UK.

The terms of reference of the Middleton review are important. In line with the intention to think the unthinkable, the task is one of getting back to basics but only in the context of cost-cutting. To quote from the terms of reference:[39]

'(3) In particular, the review is to consider: (a) whether the civil justice reforms can be implemented without imposing costs which outweigh savings both for potential litigants and the courts . . .'.

The review seeks change without increased cost – the issue is whether that can be achieved without a more fundamental restructuring of the system. For example, will the de-coupling of matrimonial legal aid be considered, given the fact that one-third of the total legal aid budget is spent on private matrimonial proceedings? The larger questions about use of rights and imposition of social responsibilities must be taken as part of policy-making in this context.

---

[36] The *Observer*, 27 July 1997.

[37] Lord Irvine's most infamous public spending decision is likely to prove to have been the decision to spend £59,211 on wallpaper for his official appartments; see, inter alia, *The Guardian*, 2 December 1997.

[38] *Review of Civil Justice and Legal Aid*. Report to the Lord Chancellor by Sir Peter Middleton GCB (Lord Chancellor's Department, September 1997). That Sir Peter is a former Treasury official is an interesting development in itself.

[39] Society of Labour Lawyers' newsletter, August 1997.

The terms of reference continued by setting down a second point for consideration:

'(b) the means by which the cost of legal aid can be kept within limits which society can afford and is willing to pay in the context of the overall public expenditure ceilings to which the Government is committed, while giving the fullest possible weight to the important values of legal aid as a rights-based entitlement equally available throughout the country'.

The expression 'limits which society can afford' raises the old question: what price justice? It is unfortunate the challenge needs to be couched in such starkly financial terms. However, simply to tinker with the system as it is currently organised would be to miss the opportunity to restructure the elements of the legal system which have caused so much of the rapid growth in the size of the legal aid bill.

Change can be achieved within existing spending limits only if there is a radical overhaul of the means of providing access to justice. Simply concentrating on the figures for legal aid, in a vacuum from dealing with the greater question of restructuring the system for providing access to social justice in the UK, will fail to cut costs while also failing to tackle the greater problems of breakdown in the social fabric and loss of communal identity. In the terms of what follows, it is possible to achieve the 'first political objective', cost-cutting, while also going some way to achieving the 'real objective' – movement towards a just society.[40]

Importantly, the New Labour proposal for a Community Legal Service (CLS) 'built on the existing plans for Regional Legal Services Committees' is supported by Middleton.[41] Further conditional fee arrangements were accepted by the Middleton review[42] and warmly embraced by Lord Irvine as a means of widening access to justice. The proposals have produced broad condemnation from civil liberties groups and the professions alike.

Common non-partisan reform proposals

There are a number of other proposals for reform to the system which have been made by other politicians or which have been considered, often informally, by the policy-making bodies. Due to lack of space, they are set up to be knocked down here. The common objection is a lack of focus on *producing* social justice.

---

[40] The principles identified in this submission, form the backbone of the forthcoming book by Alastair Hudson, *Towards a Just Society* (London: Pinter, 1999). The aim of that book is to reconcile three problems which are identified as the greatest problems currently facing the UK, with the question of how to provide something called 'justice' to UK citizens. Those themes are the breakdown of the social fabric, loss of communal and individual identity, and the weakening of democratic empowerment for UK citizens.

[41] *Review of Civil Justice and Legal Aid.* Report to the Lord Chancellor by Sir Peter Middleton GCB (Lord Chancellor's Department, September 1997) p 5.

[42] ibid.

Legal insurance

Rather than rely upon central legal aid funds, there may be circumstances in which it would be reasonable for some parties to take out insurance against successful litigation. The result would be that successful litigants would recover their costs from the insurance companies of those whom they have sued. One example of this would be potential polluters of water systems and air, as required in some jurisdictions in the USA.

This alternative would be of limited impact on the legal aid budget because it cannot be guaranteed that the bulk of litigants would fall within legal aid eligibility guidelines, but it would have the effect of increasing the ability of citizens to seek equal access to remedies against corporations.

Lord Irvine has supported the availability of insurance for use by practitioners entering into conditional fee arrangements in claims for money damages. The proposals suggest that litigants should pay the cost of the premium to acquire insurance to cover the legal adviser for the risk of losing the litigation. However, no pilot schemes have been set up, at the time of writing, and insurers have shown reluctance to support the scheme in public. Aside from this practical problem is the further issue of litigants finding the lump sum to pay for the premium when they are too straitened to afford legal fees in any event.

One alternative, insurance-based system would be similar to the Japanese system of compulsory insurance for healthcare, or the German system of legal insurance. Common to all such systems is the notion that the citizen pays for private insurance through taxation. That insurance will then pay for the whole of, or most of, the cost of any litigation undertaken by that citizen. The state is required to provide the funds for those citizens who are unable to afford the increased tax burden, or do not pay tax at all. Issues then arise whether the insurance should entitle the citizen to choose a lawyer themselves, or whether they are required to use a lawyer appointed for them by the state. This raises some of the arguments raised by a National Legal Service, which is considered immediately below.

It is submitted that this proposal would constitute a reversal of the core policy of the Legal Aid Act 1949 and the welfare state motivation that lay behind it:

> '...to make legal aid and advice more readily available for persons of small or moderate means, to enable the cost of legal aid or advice for such persons to be defrayed wholly or partly out of moneys provided by Parliament.'

Obtaining suitable insurance in the market would not guarantee that suitable advice could be obtained or paid for. It would rob the state of the ability to select priorities for state funding through the current legal aid system. The final objection is that legal aid is already paid for through central taxation, and therefore there is no need to increase the tax burden to pay for a new system. It would be better to make the current welfare state model (albeit a means-tested one) operate more effectively for the achievement of greater social justice.

National Legal Service

A regular proposal is that for a National Legal Service (NLS). There are a number of different approaches to this suggestion. At one level, it is little more than a Citizens' Advice Bureau (CAB) system where the advice workers are also empowered to appear in court. This model is extended in some cases to include a public defender function.

The CAB model would require the provision of representation as well as advice by the NLS for it to be more than simply a CAB or a Law Centre. At this level it is difficult to see what is achieved beyond the mass employment of lawyers by the state.

Once the NLS is expanded to mean the necessary availability of trained and qualified advocates on demand for any citizen for any type of case, then different arguments obtain. That all citizens are able to defend litigation without fear of cost would enfranchise many more citizens. It would remove many of the pressures to settle litigation. At that level the civil liberties aspects are compelling. However, where the NLS is extended to provide advice for anyone wanting to bring a claim (ie to act as plaintiff) without any concern as to the cost, the context changes slightly. Clearly, there is a public service available to all citizens which has great impact for the quality of citizenship.

The objections to an NLS are primarily twofold. First, there would a great increase in cost to the state of handling the increase in claims and paying salaries to all the lawyers involved and managing the system. Given the current strictures on legal aid spending, this would appear to dismiss this proposal in practical terms. Secondly, there is no guarantee of the quality of advice. The experience of some NLS-style programmes in the USA, for example, has been a haphazard ability to advise citizens effectively as to their rights because of a lack of time, because of a lack of expertise and because of bureaucratic inertia to bring the sort of seemingly speculative arguments which a privately paid lawyer would advance to protect a client. The 'dead hand' of the bureaucrats has been a great obstacle to such schemes in practice.

Contingency and conditional fees

The matter of contingency fees is often discussed in this area as a means of cutting the costs of legal aid. Contingency fees enable the litigant to meet the cost of legal fees entirely (in most cases) by paying a percentage of a damages award to the lawyers if successful, and paying nothing if unsuccessful. In personal injury cases, this enables many litigants to bring actions without worries as to meeting the legal bill. Alternatively, the 'conditional fee arrangement' has been proposed by the Middleton review under which parties would obtain insurance to cover the cost of fees if litigation is unsuccessful.

There are a number of objections, however. First, a court awards damages to a plaintiff on the basis of his or her loss. Therefore, if the damages are to compensate the wrong suffered by measuring the size of the loss, there is no calculation to take into account legal expenses – that is the purpose of the costs award. Therefore, to give away a part of the damages is to rob the plaintiff of a necessary part of the compensation for his or her loss. The result would be the alteration of the tone or manner in which litigation is conducted without a corresponding increase in the quality of justice received by the citizen, with the danger of it worsening.

Secondly, contingency fees open the client to bartering with lawyers from a position of weakness. Thirdly, contingency fees do not guarantee the increased representation of those whom the Labour Party would wish to see represented more. Indeed it is likely that only the high profile defamation cases would attract the interest of the lawyers, rather than the benefits of representing those who have suffered small industrial injuries which may yet affect their ability to work.

Fourthly, contingency fees only work in the case of claims for amounts of money. A claim to be housed on grounds of homelessness does not carry with it any award of money ordinarily. Therefore, there would be no possibility of contingency fees. Similarly, injunctive relief carries little likelihood of damages. Defending actions rarely carries any likelihood of damages awards, other than costs orders.

Contingency fees, therefore, cannot offer an entire answer. In many commercial cases, however, it is only the lawyers and the commercial litigants who stand to lose by the arrangement. In that context they should be permitted to enter into whatever arrangements they can negotiate between themselves.

As considered above, Lord Irvine has accepted the case for conditional fee arrangements to cut the legal aid budget. It remains to be seen how Lord Irvine intends, in the detail of his proposals, to replace the welfare state benefit, legal aid, with a partial system based on insurance-based conditional fees for money damages claims. It would appear that the up-front cost required from the litigant to enter into conditional fee arrangements will exclude those who are too poor to afford that cost. The solution would appear to be a concessionary, means-tested system as suggested by his Lordship before the Home Affairs Select Committee.[43] It is difficult to see how this proposal differs from the provision of legal aid.

THE IDEOLOGY BEHIND THE PRINCIPLES

The development of policies to deal with the reform or restructuring of the legal profession have suffered from under-theorisation. The legal system is only addressed as a political question usually when it has become too

---

[43] October 1997.

expensive. What is lacking is a way of looking at the legal system in a political context that links it to other problems of public policy. To increase access to law it is necessary to think differently about the larger system that gives us law, solves disputes and gives advice to citizens.

The following three conceptualisations are this author's own but draw on archetypes of three separate, established points of view: (1) the New Right, (2) the legal establishment, and (3) the social democratic left.

As discussed above, Labour's position has shifted since 1992 on the detail of this policy. There does appear to be some shift too in its intellectual underpinnings. At one level the party has moved from John Smith's humanist, ethical socialism to a 'democratic socialism' based on neo-Gramscian ideas of a new nation and the generation of community.[44] There was a production of something new in that shift from old style labourism which was inclusive of all churches on the electable left from trade unionists, welfare state social democrats and centre-left modernisers, to an ethos created out of American liberal ideals of a state which sought to create a context in which individuals were given the freedom to make their own lifechoices.

The following categorisations, then, see New Labour present in all of them in some context. The Old Labour affection for a Ministry of Justice and the generation of more human rights sits more clearly with the social democratic model.

Economic System Management Approach

The Economic System Management Approach is precisely that: the legal system is treated as a system which should be managed in the same way as any other system which makes demands on public funds. Its ideology is most clearly identified in the policies of the Major administration and could be rendered thus:

> '[To] introduce a system of block contracts covering the type, quality, volume and price of services to be provided . . . improve the targeting of funds towards areas of need, particularly where suppliers can provide high quality advice at less cost than the present court based approach . . .'[45]

The language used is the language of markets and of consumers. Rather than centralised, state provision of services, publicly funded legal services should be provided by providers holding block contracts. The traditional legal aid system operates in this way in any event. Private sector lawyers invoice central government or one of its agencies, and are paid for providing a service to the population.

---

[44] See generally Antonio Gramsci, *Selections from the Prison Notebook*, Quintin Hoare and Geoffrey Nowell Smith (eds) (London: Lawrence & Wishart, 1973) p 418; Roger Simon, *Gramsci's Political Thought* (London: Lawrence & Wishart, revised edition 1991) pp 43 et seq.

[45] Lord Chancellor's Department consultation paper, *Legal Aid – Targeting Need*, Cmnd 2854 (1995) p 21.

The goal of this first approach is to seek effective and economical solutions to problems in the interests of the litigant and the taxpayer. It requires centralised control to the extent necessary to create a discipline for setting priorities. Therefore, there would be regulation and controlled cost made possible by a system of block contracts operating within an overall predetermined budget. The role of the government agency would be that of an overseer concerned with targeting need and priorities.

The buzzwords are: 'effective', 'economical', 'discipline', 'block contract', and 'budgeting'. In line with the emphasis on the consumer is the need for these goals to be achieved for the benefit of the purchaser of the services. The emphasis is not primarily on civil liberties or a discourse of rights and obligations. Behind the economic system approach would typically be an idea of individual freedom on the Thatcherite model.

One of the great concerns about this means of providing the service is that it will develop monopoly providers in particular regions where some firms have block contracts and other firms do not. Large contract holders will tend to swallow the personnel, clients and business of smaller firms who do not hold contracts, and the availability of a market will shrink.[46]

However, the discussion of this model cannot be confined to the purely Thatcherite. The Community Legal Service (CLS) proposal under New Labour, for all the protestations that it will seek to do something other than create compulsory competitive tendering, sits very close to a supply-led attitude to public funding of legal services. Rather than provide a budget which meets demand for legal aid and the other services that come out of that one budget, the CLS would attempt to control the availability of funds, thus cutting supply and rationing the availability of service.

As discussed above, the political problem necessitates this new approach. Funds are limited in the politics of the 1990s and therefore service is limited. However, at least half of the problem is the reluctance to look at entirely new ways of providing the service. A legal system which focuses on the old-fashioned demands of the legal profession will fail to operate within the new strictures.

Legalistic approach

Within the legal system the lawyers will, of course, insist on having their say: despite the facts that it is the citizens' rights and not the lawyers' convenience that count. The study commissioned from Lord Woolf by Lord Mackay the Conservative Lord Chancellor produced the following analysis of the relevant goals:

---

[46] This approach grew out of the Conservative government's need to control spending on legal aid. The proposals made as to block contracting grew out of the reforms of the National Health Service and compulsory competitive tendering in local government.

'A civil justice system should: be just; be fair; at reasonable cost; at reasonable speed; be understandable; be responsive; provide certainty; be effective.'[47]

This approach is termed the legalistic approach because it does not seek to address any political or sociological considerations beyond the courtroom.[48] Typically the legalistic approach will look to timetables for litigation and the business of procedural justice. In assessing the merit of different cases, regard is given to the financial weight of the case and the complexity of the legal arguments. At the level of procedural justice, the solution is sought in combined sets of court rules rather than the restructuring of the profession or the opening up of alternative avenues of representation, advice and assistance. The salvation of the system is identified in the reform of court procedures in the same way that the problems are identified as being in those same procedures.

The use of the Woolf Report to cut costs is, as considered above, a potential poisoned chalice. Woolf is unlikely to make the legal system cost less. The fear is that it will actually cost more. More to the point, Woolf is unable to address head-on his own particular agenda of removing inequality. That is the business of a system which places movement towards social justice at its centre.

Social democratic approach

It is perhaps a little self-consciously that the third approach offers no more radical opposition to the technocratic precision of the New Right approach than 'social democracy'. There are two reasons why there is no 'socialist' alternative properly so-called. The first reason is that there is no political movement or party in the UK which approaches the question of law or, arguably, of human rights in a way which purports to do more than produce some 'fairness'.[49]

The Labour Party has never sought anything more radical than social democracy on a European model.[50] A truly Marxist organisation would seek to ignore law on the basis that it would wither away, or would at least be used as a part of the engine of revolutionary change in property relations. It is an unfortunate part of the internecine strife on the Left in Britain that the

---

[47] Lord Woolf, *Access to Justice: Interim Report* (June 1995).

[48] That is not to say that Woolf was content to operate within the remit assigned to him. The discussion below as to the detail of Woolf's Final Report indicates some of the desire to look beyond these legalistic confines.

[49] See eg Gordon Brown's tract 'Fair is Efficient – A Socialist Agenda for Fairness' which isolates 'fairness' as a suitable left-of-centre goal; Fabian Pamphlet 563.

[50] See on this Gregory Elliott, *Labourism and the English Genius* (London: Verso, 1995).

term 'socialist' is necessarily taken to be synonymous with 'Marxist', by both modernisers and traditionalists. The term 'social democratic' is advanced as meaning an approach concerned with 'social justice' and 'realising the potential of ordinary people'.[51]

The second reason is that much of the discussion of human rights among lawyers does not seek to redress any of these imbalances. As Professor Conor Gearty has explained:

'The [European Convention on Human Rights] contains no guarantee of equality. It accords the same "human rights" to corporations as to the rest of us. It largely accepts and protects the pre-ordained allocation of property in society by presuming that "[e]very natural or legal person" should be "entitled to the peaceful enjoyment of his [or her] legal possessions".'[52]

The concern of this social democratic model is to address the pre-Marxian socialist notions of social justice and equality of opportunity to achieve greater democratic empowerment. To that extent, the approach taken is a development of the 'social democratic approach'. However, its claim for socialism (properly so-called) is that a system of dispute resolution that removes power imbalances between litigants is, straightforwardly, an engine of equality. The law, and the systems that surround it, should seek *in their practice* to be transparent as between litigants. Once there are disaggregations of power between individuals at the level of *access* to justice, that is, in the context of procedural rules, the operation of substantive legal rules will necessarily be biased.

The social democratic approach is personified by policies such as the creation of a Community Legal Service which employs vertical eligibility criteria for access to resources; expansion of alternative dispute resolution; use of the information superhighway for advice and education; and the reform of the legal profession and the judiciary. The strength of the social democratic approach in this context is its unspoken determination to weaken the stark dividing line between the legal system and other social systems.[53]

The Labour Party's proposals should not be represented solely as a social democratic approach, any more than Lord Mackay's proposals should be considered to be solely based on the economic management approach. Rather, each takes some of the other.[54]

---

[51] John Smith, Preface to *Strategies for Renewal* (Vintage, 1994).

[52] 'The Cost of Human Rights: English Judges and the Northern Ireland Troubles' (1994) 47 *Current Legal Problems* 19, at p 21.

[53] See note 16 above and the text to it for a discussion of law as a closed social system.

[54] The Labour Party's proposals contain intentions to develop franchising of contracts and of community-based legal aid provisions which some have difficulty in distinguishing from the Conservative proposals.

FROM PRINCIPLES TO PRACTICE

The real problem with legal aid: a proposal

What is rarely acknowledged by lawyers in considering the legal aid bill is that legal aid is a payment of money from central taxation directly into lawyers' pockets. The matter is as simple as that. The question whether or not the legal aid bill is too high is really a question about whether or not too much money is being paid to lawyers. The point was made earlier that there is no market in legal services. Restrictive practices in the legal system, nothing less than an informal cartel formed by professional expectations, maintains standard fees at a high rate which leads to the current high level of the total legal aid bill.

The question therefore arises: why is legal aid to be provided in this way? Should legal aid seek to provide the whole of the fee to the lawyer as it does currently? An alternative system would be one which identifies the standard amount of money which would be required by a litigant to defray the cost of litigation. The Legal Aid Fund would provide payment for a standard amount of money which the Legal Aid Board considers appropriate for that type of case. By capping the amount of money available for particular types of case, lawyers would have to make the decision whether to offer their services for this amount or whether to price themselves out of the market for legal aid amounts. The litigant would then have greater scope to acquire representation in the legal marketplace. The litigant would be able to seek further amounts of legal aid where it could be demonstrated that the case contained complications which took it out of the ordinary run of cases.[55]

There is no reason why all of the cases which are currently paid for by legal aid and which are undertaken solely by barristers and solicitors should be able to continue. Voluntary agencies and advice agencies should be able to provide these services and make claims on the Legal Aid Fund where they can demonstrate the necessary competence.[56]

There is typically a distinction made between criminal legal aid and civil legal aid in this context. The constitutional argument is made that criminal legal aid concerns basic human rights, the right to freedom of the person and the right to a trial, whereas civil litigation concerns less precious subjects. That there is a possible conceptual distinction is beyond question. Whether the distinction is always real is another matter. The ability to defend yourself against an action to repossess your home is of more significance than the ability to defend a road traffic offence.

---

[55] This system has more in common with the German 'legal insurance' system. As discussed, it might be that control of fees through quality-assured franchising would reach the goals of increased access at lower cost.

[56] The competence referred to is considered at p 422 above in connection with the Community Legal Service and the quality of service provision.

Where the conceptual difficulty arises more significantly is not in this *horizontal* measurement of availability of legal aid into broad income categories. What appears to be more useful is to divide this issue into *vertical* differences between types of case. Where public resources are being used, there ought to be some public recognition that some types of case are of greater utility than others. Group actions for medical negligence are of greater social utility than the failure of City fraud trials.

The argument runs: why should a centre-left administration allow millions of pounds to be used by the apparently wealthy when other taxpaying individuals are not able to bring actions against their employers using legal aid? The solution would be to take the politically courageous decision to deny legal aid to the apparently wealthy (who receive it simply on the grounds that their lawyers and accountants can demonstrate that they have ostensibly no assets) and decide instead that other types of litigation are politically more important.

This approach has two immediate problems. First, it cuts against the principle of greater equality by introducing inequality in the form of bars to publicly funded legal services. Secondly, civil libertarians would be concerned that politics is being brought explicitly into the arena of justice. The answer to the first concern is the simple assertion that the current barriers to publicly funded legal services are hidden because they rely on the bulk of the population having income or capital above very parsimonious eligibility levels. That means the bulk of the population cannot afford to go to law. Making the law more equal means taking advantage away from those who are currently 'more equal' than the ordinary individual.

The response to the second concern is that the system currently advantages the well off to the detriment of the less well off: that is already a question of political power. Introducing politics to the situation expressly has the advantage of making legal aid provision more transparent and accountable. A political decision to focus resources in South Wales on housing disputes and social welfare claims would be unpopular with those who would seek to use the system to fund the whole of their defence in white-collar fraud trials – but that is in the nature of politics.

For example, one-third of the total legal aid budget (civil and criminal legal aid) is spent on matrimonial disputes. That is an annual amount of about £500 million paid to lawyers to conduct private divorce proceedings. This expenditure of legal aid on matrimonial disputes fails to recognise that in many situations the courts are not the best place to decide family disputes and that lawyers are not the best people to give advice or to reach these decisions. It also avoids the difficult question whether or not we wish to use large amounts of public money to fund private matrimonial disputes. Therefore, enormous sums of public money are being paid on translating ordinary family problems to legal disputes rather than investing in families by means of mediation or counselling services. Putting concern for social justice at the centre of policy is the only way to ensure that public money in the legal system is applied primarily to ends which are socially just.

Dealing with the lawyers

'Reform of the English legal system has failed up to now because of the entrenched power of the lawyers' guilds'. (Max Weber)

The lawyer often stands as gatekeeper to the acquisition of rights and obligations. Where the profession itself is distorted, there is a problem of acquiring entry to the availability of suitable legal remedies. There is as much a need for the lawyer to take up the cudgels as there is a need for a litigant prepared to fight it. The nature of the legal system is therefore an equally important part of the notion of access to law.

In 1995, of all QCs, women accounted for 6.6 per cent of the total, while in the population at large women accounted for 52 per cent of the total. As for members of ethnic minorities,[57] in 1989 less than 50 per cent of barristers' chambers had any ethnic minority members. While at the same time, more than 50 per cent of all black barristers practised from the same 16 chambers, indicating a concentration of the non-white Bar in particular chambers. By 1995 there were only six non-white QCs.

As the Bar continues to be so unrepresentative of the population, while retaining actual monopoly of advocacy in the higher courts and many of the courts of first instance, the issue for the operation of the British constitution must be: How can you *represent* the community if you are *not representative of* the community?

The nature of the professions is at the heart of the debate about the ability to access law. And yet, as Weber indicates, a great part of the political problem with reforming this system is the entrenched power of the lawyers' representative bodies. The Law Society and the Bar Council are vocal and significant players in the arguments about the reform of the system. Under their patronage, reform is generally piecemeal and technical – primarily because the lawyers abstract to themselves the authority to talk about the workings of the legal system. Again this becomes a discourse about power in which the lawyers are the only ones who are able to speak because they control the means of expression.[58]

CONCLUSION: THE CONTEXT OF CONSTITUTIONAL REFORM

The reader will be able to isolate some themes running through this discussion:

(1) The area of reform of the legal system has been considered to be a problem of practice rather than theory for too long.

[57] As defined by the Bar Council and identified in returns to Bar Council surveys.
[58] See Michel Foucault, *The Archaeology of Knowledge* (London: Routledge, 1989).

(2)   The principle of social justice is one which should lead this debate.

(3)   The solutions which may be required by the principle of social justice need not be jettisoned as part of a realpolitik assessment of available administrative resources.

(4)   The voguish and one-dimensional imperative of controlling public expenditure (which has become an article of faith in the administrative organs of the legal system) has ignored, for ill, the social need for complete access to justice in a society in which social relations are transforming rapidly.

The core objective of a restructuring of this system must be that access to justice is made as broad as possible. To work towards this end, it is necessary to make decisions about the allocation of resources. The difficulty is that the legal system in toto is not capable of sustaining this core objective of wider access to justice in the way that it is currently organised. The solution therefore requires a programme of policies which address the systemic problem and do not simply chip away at parts of it.

Unless you focus on the justice system as a means of generating a more just society, you will not get the priorities right. The call for reform is a call for justice; the call for access is a call for equality. To deny people the access to law is to deny them access to their rights. It is to deny them the access to the whole of their potential. In the words of the late John Smith, 'it is simply unacceptable to continue to waste our most precious resource – the extraordinary skills and talents of ordinary people'.[59]

Further reading

Alastair Hudson, *Towards a Just Society: Law, Labour and Legal Aid* (London: Cassell, to be published 1999)

Legal Action Group, *A Strategy for Justice* (London: LAG Publications, 1992)

Labour Party, *Access to Justice* (Policy document, London, 1995)

A A S Zuckerman and Ross Cranston, *Reform of Civil Procedure: Essays on 'Access to Justice'* (Oxford: Clarendon Press, 1995)

Lord Woolf, *Access to Justice: Final Report* (London: HMSO, 1996)

Legal Action Group, Roger Smith (ed), *Achieving Civil Justice – Appropriate Dispute Resolution for the 1990s* (London: LAG Publications, 1996)

---

[59] Preface to *Strategies for Renewal* (Vintage, 1994).

APPENDICES

APPENDIX 1

EXTRACT FROM LABOUR POLICY COMMISSION, *A NEW AGENDA FOR DEMOCRACY: LABOUR'S PROPOSALS FOR CONSTITUTIONAL REFORM* (1993)

EDITORS' NOTE: This Policy Commission Report was presented as an National Executive Committee Statement to the 1993 Labour Conference where it was introduced by Tony Blair MP, then home affairs spokesperson for the party.

FOREWORD

The key task of the policy commission has been to address the need for constitutional reform in the UK. We decided at the very beginning to focus specifically on that issue and not to attempt to re-write the Labour Party's entire policy in the area of democracy and the individual. This is in part through pressures of time, in part because we feel certain areas demand specific and separate consideration and in part because much of our policy in this area is both well established and strongly supported. We expect and want our commission to continue in existence to review those parts of the policy agenda not raised or completed in this report.

We have concentrated on the following principal issues: the adoption of a Bill of Rights; reform and change in local government and its relationship with central government; freedom of information and the removal of unacceptable secrecy in our society; relations between Westminster, local and regional government and the European Community; reform of Parliament; and reform of the judiciary.

We have not specifically reviewed policy areas such as commitments in respect of legislation on equality, discrimination on grounds of sex, race, disability or sexuality, or freedom of the press, as this document is concerned with constitutional rather than policy changes. It is fair to say, however, that though there may be necessary up-dating of policy in relation to these matters,

443

there was very broad support for existing policy, which stands unless and until changed by the party. In addition, the issue of crime and the criminal justice system is self-evidently a major topic in its own right and worthy of detailed consideration. We have also begun a consideration of the legal system. Further work will continue upon this in close consultation with our speakers on legal affairs.

After close consultation with our Scottish colleagues, we do not propose, at this stage, to review our policy in relation to Scotland. This will be a matter for the Scottish members of Parliament and Scottish party to develop in conjunction with our commission. This inevitably means that while the general principles are relevant and the Bill of Rights plainly applies, some parts of our proposals, for example those relating to the judiciary, cannot simply be translated to Scotland, where the procedures are entirely different. However, we do want to re-state our strong commitment to a Scottish parliament which will ultimately have responsibility for many of the issues raised in our report. We do not intend to change any of our commitments to Wales and Northern Ireland. The final topic where we wish work to continue is on the responsibilities and rights of the family – the family and children, the family and work and the family and carers.

INTRODUCTION

The issue of 'the constitution' is not an academic one. It is one in which all people have a direct interest. It is about power; where it is located and how it is made accountable. Unusually in the UK, we have no written or formal constitution. It is a series of conventions and doctrines established through practice and tradition alongside a patchwork of legislation. This is not in itself of vital significance, except that it has meant we have never had to confront the task of putting our constitution into words and therefore concentrating the national mind on the hard decisions of the distribution of power. The result is a constitution urgently in need of radical change and modernisation. We set out here the basis of a new constitutional settlement, a modern notion of citizenship that establishes new rules to govern the bargain between the individual and society. We recognise the importance of the community acting collectively, but to advance individual freedom, not at the expense of it. Our aim is to create a revitalised democracy which protects the fundamental rights of the citizen from the abuse of power, which proposes the substantial devolution of central government authority, and which insists that the legitimacy of government rests on it being both open and accountable to the people it serves.

Today, the executive is immensely powerful. Parliament is easily overwhelmed. The ability of the ordinary citizen to challenge the executive is tightly limited. The UK has one of the most centralised systems of government in

Europe. Under successive Conservative governments this process of centralisation has massively increased. Other institutions of government capable of exercising some restraining power over the centre – notably local government – have been hugely curtailed and undermined, often, unfortunately, as a result of deliberate policy. Unelected quangos, whose members are political appointees of government, now account for over £42 billion of public spending. We are a deeply secretive society, without even minimal legislation on freedom of information. The legal system – essential to any true implementation of the rule of law – is hopelessly out of date, dominated by vested interests and now seriously unravelling in the face of a massive restriction in legal aid.

In addition, the European Community now has a major impact on all our domestic institutions, including the executive. Its laws can have a direct effect and reach into almost all areas of national life. Yet the methods of holding to account decisions made in the European Community has not kept up with the pace and extent of change.

The result is that our democracy is profoundly flawed. If democracy is about content as well as form, the form of our constitution is imperfect and the content of our democracy even more seriously at fault. The case for change is clear.

It is also right that the Labour Party takes a leading role in making the case for change. The central belief of the Labour Party is that people do not live as isolated units but individuals within a society or community. Individual freedom to develop and prosper is held back by the absence of opportunity, particularly at work and in education – by the presence of powerful interests. The task of the Labour Party is to use the power of the community acting together to advance and liberate the individual.

The purpose of such action is not to give power to government but to give power to people. And it should not be merely through traditional forms of central government intervention that people are empowered. Government itself is a powerful interest that requires to be checked and controlled.

The failure of Conservative philosophy – even at its most elevated – is to believe that freedom is best secured through minimum intervention by government or community. The perception that has damaged the cause of socialism – often wrongly so far as democratic socialism is concerned – was that it put the interests of society or worse, the state, above those of the individual.

Precisely because we believe in using the power of the community, through government and in other ways, it is vital that we address the issue of its accountability. In particular, we should be seeking to re-shape the way government works. It is impossible to modernise Britain without modernising government.

We seek, therefore to retrieve the true ideological basis of democratic socialism – action by the community for the benefit of the individual – and set it to work for the modern age.

445

This requires, in turn, a new constitutional settlement for our country, one which establishes a just relationship between society and individual, one which above all, fundamentally redresses power in favour of the citizen from the state.

This new settlement should be effected in two ways: first it must grant individuals the rights needed to challenge arbitrary decisions and exercises of power that affect them, to guarantee equality of treatment without discrimination and the practical ability under the law to make these rights real. This is correct in itself but it also promotes much greater participation by people in the development of the country's democracy. The fairness of our society comes to be judged by the priority it gives to individual rights; and it encourages a more active idea of citizenship where rights are not simply a list of demands, but are accompanied by responsibilities as part of a contract between citizen and society.

Secondly, it should be based on the diversity of political institutions, each with their independence guaranteed, not on the belief that the government, once elected, should control – directly or indirectly – all other dependent political institutions. This means that the constitution should be subject to the necessary checks and balances, in order to hold the executive to proper account and to reflect the more pluralist, more decentralised, more devolved government which the people of our country want to see. The idea of a highly-centralised, paternalistic state handing out improvements to a dependent public belongs to a different age. We live in a society today whose culture, lifestyle and aspirations are much more diverse and varied than they ever have been. This must find an echo in our system of government.

This does not lessen our pride in past achievements. It is largely as a result of previous Labour governments that people have been able to achieve the greater material prosperity and quality of life that gives them the chance to take control of their own lives and shape their own future. These advances were not diminished through the existence of a strong community; on the contrary it was in part action by society as a whole that enabled individuals to gain that greater freedom. Such action, especially with millions in our country unemployed or in poverty and millions more blocked from reaching higher up the ladder of opportunity, is still vital. But the means of doing so and the terms of the bargain between individual and community will and should change constantly, with the changes in society itself.

So we put forward this programme of reform – which we believe is the most fundamental proposed by a major British political party – not simply as an itemised list of policies, but as part of a much bigger framework of ideas that define Labour's vision of the UK's future. Constitutional reform – alongside economic and social change – is one part of a different political agenda for our country. It is linked to the other parts. If the development of individual economic potential is essential both for personal and national economic success, then it can surely only benefit from a more active and developed notion of citizenship. And a more accountable public sector is likely also to produce more efficient public and social services.

We hope, too, that we can lay to rest the notion that this is just an issue for what are dismissively called 'the chattering classes'. It is real people who depend on local government services or suffer infringements through unreasonable executive action, or are held back through prejudice. It is to them that we must give the hope of change.

The following is a summary of our main proposals:

- support for a UK Bill of Rights;
- incorporation of the European Convention on Human Rights into UK law, with a provision that other laws are to be interpreted consistently with the Convention unless expressly provided;
- because it is recognised the convention is inadequate and outdated, we propose an all-party commission be appointed to draft our own Bill of Rights and consider a more permanent form of entrenchment;
- a strengthening and modernising of anti-discrimination law to provide equal treatment of every citizen;
- employee and trade union rights;
- a Freedom of Information Act;
- reform of the Official Secrets legislation and proper scrutiny of the security services; reform of the Royal Prerogative, with ratification by Parliament of both treaties and the declaration of war;
- a strengthened Data Protection Act;
- a recasting of the relationship between central and local government, with the Scottish Parliament, Welsh Assembly and regional councils in England replacing other tiers of administration, and the removal of capping restraints balanced by greater electoral accountability;
- reform of electoral law;
- reform of Parliament including the creation of an elected Second Chamber;
- reform of the judiciary and in particular a new system for the appointment of judges.

We do not claim this to be the final word on constitutional change. But it is a considerable start. We want it now to be the basis for the widest possible consultation in the Labour Party and beyond, involving those who are outside traditional party politics as well as colleagues in our own party. In this way we can prepare the ground for government and the creation of a modern democracy for the 21st century.

A BILL OF RIGHTS

The importance of human rights

The Labour Party's concern for the rights of the citizen is long-standing and deep-rooted. The party was founded to protect the oppressed and underprivileged against the powerful, whether the power of the state or the power of private organisations. Its traditions and attitudes make it proud to protect the rights and interests of individuals. That is why the Attlee government, in 1950, put the UK amongst the first countries to sign the European Convention on Human Rights. That is why the Wilson government in the 1960s and 1970s passed successive Race Relations Acts, and the Equal Pay and Sex Discrimination Acts.

However, in the last 13 years under the Tories, Britain has slipped behind the rest of Europe in the protection it gives to individual rights. The UK is virtually alone amongst major western European nations in not laying down in legislation the basic rights of its citizens, and in not giving those citizens a direct means of asserting those rights through the courts.

The European Convention on Human Rights

The quickest and simplest way of achieving democratic and legal recognition of a substantial package of human rights would be by incorporating into UK law the European Convention on Human Rights. That is now widely recognised, both within and outside the party, as a necessary and sensible step. Its implications, however, need to be carefully thought through.

The argument for incorporation

The essential effect of incorporating the convention as part of UK domestic law is that its protections can be relied on in the ordinary courts, and directly against the national government. At present, unlike the citizens of almost every other European country, citizens of the UK have no such rights. If they want to seek the protection of the convention, they must appeal to the Commission and Court in Strasbourg. That process is intolerably slow: three years at a minimum, and some have been known to take as long as nine years. Only the most determined people, or those who are supported by pressure groups, are likely to stay the course. And while the process grinds on, the abuse of rights at home continues.

The failure directly to incorporate the Convention into UK law has another unwelcome effect. Although, at the end of the day, the UK government is subject to the requirements of the Convention, the present set-up makes the protection of basic rights appear difficult and remote. It reinforces an atmosphere that suggests that basic rights are not of that much importance, and that the government regards them as a nuisance rather than, as it should, as a primary obligation. And that view is reinforced in the courts. The judges will take note of the requirements of the convention when interpreting legislation that is ambiguous or uncertain. But, in the absence of laws to the contrary, they have, perfectly properly, made it plain that, if a law exists that affects human rights in a way that clearly breaches the convention, that law, and not the requirements of the convention, that they will

The convention is not a vague, untested or uncertain code, but a statement of rights that has been interpreted and applied over many y ⌐y an expert court in Strasbourg. Our government is already, and has been since 1950, ultimately subject to the requirements of the convention. What is needed now is to make that protection for our citizens a real one, and not something that is available only after years of effort and litigation.

The legislative steps: protecting the Human Rights Act from judicial attack

Incorporation could be achieved fairly easily. Parliament should pass a Human Rights Act that incorporates the rules of the convention directly into UK law, and gives citizens the right to enforce those rules in the courts.

It is often argued that in technical terms a British Act of Parliament cannot be 'entrenched'. We propose to protect the Human Rights Act from being undermined by either Parliament or the courts by a clause that requires that any other Act that is intended to introduce laws inconsistent with the convention must do so specifically and in express terms.

That arrangement will have a number of benefits. First, if a government genuinely thought, say in a time of national crisis, that it must curtail basic individual rights, it can still do so. But it will have to do so openly and expressly, as in a democracy ought always to be the practice.

Second, however, it will in practice be almost impossible for existing or subsequent law to be interpreted as being inconsistent with the convention. Judges applying the present rules of interpretation will know that Parliament had to hand a means of making clear that it was derogating from the convention but did not use it. It would therefore be unlawful for them to interpret legislation in a way that is intended to breach the convention unless the legislation states that in express terms.

Third, the Human Rights Act will be expressly stated to apply to, and override, all legislation existing at the time at which it is passed. If the government wishes to exempt any law from the provisions of the Human Rights Act it will have to say so expressly, using the procedure just described. Parliament will have the final decision in any case where legislation is brought into question as a result of the application of the European Convention; but it will have to make that decision openly and expressly. Here again, therefore, government will have to be entirely open about what it is trying to achieve, and will have to justify what it is doing both to Parliament and to the public. In a democracy, Parliament decides what rights should apply, and should set them out in a manner that citizens can understand for themselves. Under these proposals, it will not be left to the discretion of the judges, or to archaeological investigations by legal and constitutional experts, to decide what protections citizens do and do not have.

The scope of protection: the rights of individuals, not of corporations

The rights that we seek to protect are those of the individual against the state. The Human Rights Act will therefore provide that its protections can be relied on only by individuals, and not by companies or by organisations. We do not want to repeat here the confusion and injustice that has occurred in some other countries, where companies and commercial organisations have tried to resist social legislation controlling their activities by claiming that it infringes their 'human' rights. And the Human Rights Act is not designed to alter existing legal relations between individuals, but to protect individuals from state power. So the bodies that will be subject to the Human Rights Act will be state and state-related ones: national and local government; the police; and any organisation that exercises state power. Individuals will be able to use the Human Rights Act to try to force the government to legislate to protect them against abuse of human rights by private bodies or individuals, for example, in relation to the use of surveillance techniques by private bodies. Subject to this, all governmental activity, and all the existing and future law, will be subject to the Human Rights legislation.

The enforcement of human rights

The rights that the legislation confers will be asserted in the first instance through the ordinary courts: either by applications for judicial review, to assert or confirm the existence and operation of a right in a particular case, or by way of defence in an ordinary action, should a state body try to use against a citizen a law that is inconsistent with the Human Rights Act.

This use of the ordinary courts is important in two ways. First, a special series of human rights tribunals, which dealt simply with human rights issues, would be vulnerable to incessant disputes between them and the ordinary courts as to which body should be hearing a particular case or complaint. The result would be delay and confusion and benefit only the lawyers. Second, and even more important, it is essential that regard for human rights pervades the work of all courts, and is recognised as an integral part of their work, for which they bear direct responsibility: whether they are, for instance, criminal courts dealing with claims of wrongful conviction or civil courts looking at government bans on free speech. That responsibility must be put on the regular courts: and the judges of those courts must be trained and be ready to respond to the challenge.

There should, however, be two further safeguards. First, at the final appellate level, where points of fundamental or wide-ranging importance about human rights may have to be decided, the final court should have added to its judges three further lay members, drawn from a panel of people with knowledge and understanding of society and of human rights in the broad sense. That will ensure that principles are not laid down from too narrow a legal perspective.

The lay members will be full members of the court, whose vote will rank equally with that of the judges. They will be appointed from a list to be drawn up, after wide consultation, by the Judicial Appointments Commission. Precedents for qualified laypersons being judges of a court already exist in the Employment Appeal Tribunal and the Restrictive Practices Court.

Second, to assist the courts, and also to assist individuals in asserting their rights, there should be established an independent Human Rights Commission, along the lines of the Equal Opportunities Commission and Commission for Racial Equality that were established by Labour governments. The commission would monitor the operation of the Human Rights Act, provide advice and support for those who wish to assert their rights and, where necessary, itself institute cases to confirm or clarify particularly important issues. The commission would thus act as a focus for human rights activities and ensure that the protection of the public was not left to the accident of individual enthusiasm or willingness to pursue cases.

Towards a UK Bill of Rights

The incorporation of the European Convention on Human Rights is a necessary first step, but it is not a substitute for our own written Bill of Rights. The European Convention is over 40 years old. It resulted from the excesses of Nazi Germany and was deliberately drawn with that in mind.

It does not cover freedom of information or data protection or the rights of disabled people and it is inadequate in its treatment of discrimination. It does not deal with economic or social rights.

In addition, some of the limitations in the convention relating to national security or disorder or the danger to morals go wider than we require in the UK. So there is a good case for drafting our own Bill of Rights. Its provisions would have to be carefully negotiated. There is also the immensely difficult issue of entrenchment. There are a range of different options that could be considered in more detail. There is the extreme form of entrenchment in the American system where judicial decisions can strike down any legislation and where judicial decisions are supreme, though this was not favoured by our commission. There is also the interesting idea put forward by Liberty of a hybrid system of democratic entrenchment which involves both the judiciary and Parliament in the enforcement process of a bill of rights. Another is the one that we are proposing for the European Convention, where Parliament retains the possibility of expressly opting out of the convention's provisions. Accompanying these forms of entrenchment are those constitutional arrangements where a special parliamentary majority, which is more than a mere majority, is required to alter the constitution or pass legislation inconsistent with it.

For these reasons the drafting of such a 'homegrown' Bill of Rights, together with its entrenchment, could not be done on a purely partisan basis. There would need to be a fairly wide consensus established in favour of its provisions for it to possess both credibility and durability. We therefore propose the establishment of an all-party commission that will be charged with drafting the Bill of Rights and considering a suitable method of entrenchment. This should report to Parliament within a specified and limited period of time.

Social and economic rights

The Universal Declaration of Human Rights and other international human rights legislation incorporate both civil and political and social and economic rights. In Britain, EC equality legislation has acted as entrenched legislation providing women a mechanism both for the defence as well as for the improvement, of their rights to equal pay and equal treatment. European health and safety legislation has acted in a similar way. And the European Acquired Rights Directive has provided protection for low-paid workers against the unacceptable face of unfair competition created by the government's refusal to accept that the Transfer of Undertakings (Protection of Employment) Regulations 1981 (TUPE) applies to non-commercial organisations. Social and economic rights are not covered by the European Convention of Human Rights. Labour has always recognised the mutual relationship between social and economic rights and civil and political rights on the other hand. Labour will explore how best a UK bill of rights can incorporate this view.

Labour endorsed the European Social Charter and will as a first and immediate move in this area opt into the Social Chapter. Labour remains committed to ensuring that every individual employee has the right to minimum terms and conditions of employment. Every individual employee should have rights – irrespective of working hours or whether they are employed on a temporary or casual basis: to protection against poverty pay; to safe working conditions and regular rest days, protection against discrimination, protection against unfair dismissal and rights related to family responsibilities. We must also give individuals rights through their unions, including the right to join, be represented and to participate in trade union activities. In addition, where there is substantial support amongst employees at the workplace for a union to be recognised there should be a legal right of recognition.

The ability to exercise a right is crucial to its existence. Equality of access to justice is essential to this. Labour has previously put forward proposals to review the industrial tribunal system to ensure that individuals have fair, fast, effective and collective remedies. We remain committed to this and shall review the practical enforcement of rights within the context of our overall review of the legal system.

A Bill of Rights to complement other legislation

The fact of incorporation of the European Convention on Human Rights or indeed the introduction of a UK Bill of Rights does not eliminate the need for legislation on human rights in specific areas. We intend to do further work in this area. The report which we wish to prepare on equality and discrimination will look at how we can build on existing policy and address issues of social and economic rights. But we remain of course committed to existing policy, to the extension of equalities legislation to protect individuals against discrimination on the grounds of gender, race, religion, disability, sexuality and age in employment and elsewhere. In particular, we remain committed to the consolidation, strengthening and extension of sex discrimination legislation to bring it into compliance with European community equality legislation, to construct a new Act which provides a right to equal treatment for women, and to shift the burden from individual women taking individual cases in order to ensure that organisations monitor, review and change their organisational practices to ensure that they are free from sex discrimination.

We will continue to press for a European-wide directive to protect people against race discrimination and remain firmly committed to the detailed proposals that we outlined in our document, *A Charter of Rights*, and our basic principles established in our policy document *Opportunities for all*. Legislation in these areas can then provide a basis for similar legislation in other areas where discrimination occurs.

PREROGATIVE POWERS

It is where power is exercised by government under the cover of royal prerogative that our concerns are greatest. We have concentrated our attention on two of the key areas of prerogative powers. Here massive power is exercised by executive decree without accountability to Parliament and sometimes even without its knowledge. Of course, in practice most governments recognise and accept the constraints of parliamentary approval. But, for example, in certain areas of foreign policy these powers are in theory absolute. Agreeing treaties is currently a matter for prerogative power, not Parliament, as the current Maastricht debate has highlighted. Treaty after treaty is concluded without the formal consent of Parliament. Indeed, foreign policy as a whole is an area virtually free from democratic control and accountability; powers devolving from the Crown, free from parliamentary scrutiny, are vested in government ministers and go effectively unchallenged. Whilst many on the right argue over whether or not the provisions of the Maastricht Treaty attack parliamentary sovereignty, Labour's task is to expose how little actual power Parliament has in the face of government by executive decree. The executive is generally free to bind this country under international law prior to, in the absence of, or in spite of the expressed wishes of Parliament. These powers to ratify treaties should lie with our democratically-elected representatives.

Going to war is again a matter, theoretically, for prerogative power and not Parliament. The Gulf War revealed deficiencies in the area of democratic scrutiny of executive action. Although eventually debated in the House, there is no duty for a government to obtain the consent of the House before going to war. Whilst accepting that in the case of national emergency the government may be forced to act without the immediate consent of the House, adequate safeguards should be put in place to ensure that if British servicemen and women are sent into battle, there will be adequate debate over the reasons for that decision. Formal ratification by Parliament of executive action in going to war is the absolute minimum that is acceptable in a democracy.

DEMOCRATISING EUROPE

There is justifiable anxiety about the power of European institutions. Popular distrust of the process of European integration is rooted in a lack of identification with what are often perceived as unresponsive, unaccountable, centralising European institutions. Labour's new constitutional settlement will help to remedy this using the concepts of subsidiarity, democracy and accountability.

Proposals for European legislation (directives, regulations and recommendations) currently come from the Commission. In future, we will seek to give powers for the Commission, Parliament or Council of Ministers to propose draft legislation to the European Parliament. This process would involve several democratic stages involving the national parliaments, the European Parliament, and the Council of Ministers.

European legislation can retain democratic respect only if it has the consent of the nation states and the legitimacy of democratic procedures in European institutions themselves. National parliaments should be consulted on any proposed legislation. In the UK we have already made proposals to strengthen scrutiny of EC legislation in Westminster. In particular our proposed European Grand Committee will be well placed to hear reports from ministers going to, or returning from Councils of Ministers as well as to consider draft legislation. Consideration should be given to whether membership could be open to British members of the European Parliament to participate as observers with speaking but not voting rights. To assist the more effective co-ordination between national parliaments and the European Parliament we will examine the possibility of joint committees of national and European MPs which could meet to discuss proposals for new European legislation.

Secondly, all proposed legislation should then be examined and voted upon by the European Parliament. Legislation must command the support of the majority of those directly elected by the people of Europe. Finally, the Council of Ministers, as now, would have to agree the proposal for it to become law.

We welcome the trend for other decisions taken by the European Community to be thoroughly debated by European MPs, and democratic scrutiny over the European Commissioners should be extended by making them more answerable to the European Parliament. Greater account needs to be taken of the work of other Community institutions. To this end there should be a biannual report from the Economic and Social Committee, and eventually from the Committee of the Regions, to the European Parliament.

Meetings of the Council of Ministers in turn should be much more open to public scrutiny when it is considering new legislation affecting Britain. There should be a published annual legislative programme so everybody can see the decisions the council has taken.

The Labour Party's Commission on European Policy is currently examining the wider context. However, in the field of constitutional reform we are clear that the European Community must develop as an open, democratic and accountable organisation. It must reflect the views and wishes of all the peoples of Europe.

REFORM OF PARLIAMENT

Parliament itself is hopelessly out of date in the way it works; its procedures are often arcane and irrelevant and Britain is the only democracy anywhere in the western world still to operate the hereditary principle in one half of its legislature.

A number of changes could be implemented immediately by administrative decision or changes to the Standing Orders of the House. Others will require legislation.

In relation to the House of Commons we have had detailed discussions in the Commission about the possible changes. We wish to propose significant changes to the scrutiny of Bills, in particular the taking of evidence on a Bill. We wish to strengthen departmental select committees to ensure their genuine independence from the whips, improve MPs' ability to communicate with and assist their constituents, to change the hours the Commons sits and the facilities and help available for members with family responsibilities.

However, we recognise that these changes must be made subject to detailed consultation with the PLP, the wider party and, of course, the public. We intend, therefore, to continue our deliberations upon the detail of reform and want to present a further report on this issue at a later stage, having had the chance to consult properly.

We also propose reducing the power of ministerial patronage by making all major public appointments subject to scrutiny by the relevant Parliamentary Select Committee and by ensuring that such appointments fully reflect the diversity of our society.

We do not believe there is any justifiable case for the Second Chamber in its present form. The sight of hereditary Tory peers wheeled out to vote through controversial legislation when entirely immune from electoral account, is a constitutional outrage. Of the 775 hereditary peers only 13 take the Labour whip. We believe the House of Lords in its present form should be abolished. Nevertheless, we still believe that there is a powerful case for a bi-cameral rather than uni-cameral legislature. The House of Lords, even in its current form, is a valuable revising chamber, its debates are often of high quality precisely because of the different experience of its members, and a second chamber is a necessary and important check on the power of the first. But it must be made democratically acceptable. We therefore propose replacing the House of Lords with an elected second chamber.

As a first step, the hereditary peers should not be able to sit and vote in the House of Lords. We should then begin the process of introducing proper democratic elections.

We have considered the question of changing the House of Lords' powers. The greater the degree of democracy, then obviously the stronger is the justification of power. However, we do not at present favour any substantial change to its position as a revising chamber. The prospect of a second chamber challenging or replicating the power of the first, would produce instability and inefficiency and is to be avoided. But this is again something that can be discussed further. Lord Dormand is presently chairing a committee of members of the House of Lords to examine reform of the Lords and he will report to our commission in due course.

LOCAL AND REGIONAL GOVERNMENT

We want to ensure that decisions are made as close as possible to the people electing them and that these bodies are representative of the diversity within our nation. Through giving people new rights to shape and alter decisions at a national and local level, we aim to ensure a more responsive and representative government.

We believe that it is essential that the formal political process is opened up to ensure a broader representation of people than we currently have either nationally or locally. Women and black and ethnic minorities are particularly under-represented. So too are young people. We believe that the differential age qualification between voting and standing as a Member of Parliament or local councillor should be removed. As a political party we aim to broaden the representation of our own representatives and aim to ensure that programmes of positive action are actively developed within all levels of government.

Creating vibrant regional and local government

Labour believes that strong local and regional government is an essential precondition for a properly functioning modern democracy. Active citizenship is about more than consumer rights; it requires vibrant local, regional and national democratic institutions. That is why we believe:

- power should be dispersed as widely as is possible, and should be exercised as locally as is practicable.
- public bodies which are responsible for the spending of public money, for the delivery of services, or, for making decisions affecting services should be locally accountable.
- local communities should, as far as is possible, be responsible for their own self government.
- information about government, administration and services should be freely available at a local level.
- national, regional and local identities should be respected and reflected in governmental structures.

Lack of proper accountability

As a result of central government policy there is now a growing democratic deficit at the heart of our system of government. Elected local authorities have lost major powers to the unelected state. Quangos are now responsible for spending £42 billion of public money, a larger sum than is spent by elected councils. The list of quangos which have taken functions away from local authorities now includes: health authorities, training and enterprise councils, governing bodies of grant maintained schools and FE colleges and housing action trusts. The services run by these quangos are no longer directly accountable to the public. Decisions on hospital closures and the future of schools and colleges are being taken behind closed doors by people who are accountable only to the minister who appointed them. The removal of powers from local authorities has undermined their legitimacy with their local electorate. It has also made it more difficult for all the main political parties to attract people of calibre to serve as local councillors.

The lack of democratic accountability is even more pronounced in regional administration. A whole tier of regional government has now grown up which is accountable only to Whitehall and to government ministers. A recent study (Local Government Chronicle 19.2.93) revealed that in the West Midlands there are at least 35 separate regional institutions through which central government influences the development of the region. The same study showed that about a third of the Department of Environment's total expenditure is subject to a high level of regional decision making through regional offices. Important responsibilities such as derelict land reclamation now come within the scope of regional DOE offices. Although these regional offices regularly consult with local authorities and businesses there is no formal process of accountability for them.

The introduction of universal capping of local authority budgets means that councils now have no real discretion over what they can raise in local taxation, whilst the Standard Spending Assessment has also left them with far less discretion over what they can spend. Through compulsory competitive tendering central government has also removed a considerable element of local choice about service delivery. And, of course, despite the efforts of many local authorities there has been a cumulative decline in the quality and range of services provided at a local level.

Labour's approach – a new settlement

Labour believes that there must be a new settlement between central government and the nations, regions and communities of Britain. The Conservative government is out of step with the trend in Europe, and in the rest of the advanced democratic world, which is towards greater decentralisation of power. We want to see the principle of subsidiarity apply, as it was intended to, not just between but also within nation states. Labour will set out a new constitutional framework which identifies the respective roles and responsibilities of each tier of government – national, regional and local.

As a first step, we repeat our pledge to sign the European Charter of Local Self Government, another charter which the government has opted out of. The charter is a major statement about the role, scope and powers of local authorities. By signing it Labour will send an important message that we believe in independent, adequately financed local government which has its rights enshrined in statute. We will also be putting Britain in the mainstream of Europe.

London is now the only European capital without the advantage of its own elected authority. Labour believes that Londoners must be given the right to elect a new Greater London Authority. This should be a new type of government designed for the new challenges that London faces. It should not be involved generally in running services directly but should be a strategic, co-ordinating and enabling body – working in partnership with the boroughs to promote and represent London and Londoners.

Devolution and regional government

Labour believes in the devolution of power to the nations of Scotland and Wales and to the regions of England. Our policy on devolution and regional government was set out in detail in Devolution and Democracy and in our 1992 manifesto. Labour is committed to establishing a separate parliament for Scotland, an assembly for Wales and regional councils in England. This new tier of government will allow people to take effective control over areas of policy like health, education, employment, transport, planning and industrial development. These are functions it will take from Whitehall and from the unaccountable regional state rather than from local government. A single, one-size-fits-all approach is not necessarily the answer. The new democratic structures must respect and reflect regional and community identities. The policy commission will look in more detail, over the next year, at what structures of government will be appropriate for the various regions of England, what functions they should perform and how they should be funded. It will also look at what system of consultation will be needed for the introduction of regional government and national parliaments.

The party already has a detailed programme for the devolution of power from Westminster to the new Scottish Parliament, whose powers will obviously be different and more extensive than those of the English regional assemblies. The power of the Welsh Assembly will clearly include those matters which will be subject to regional government in England, but there will be continuing discussion about the further powers that are appropriate for devolution.

A fair and stable system of local government finance

As part of the new settlement, Labour believes that a fair and stable system of finance should be established for local and regional government. The years of Conservative experimentation and centralisation have done much harm to local government. The poll tax not only caused personal misery to many thousands of people and wreaked havoc on local government financial systems, but it also cost the nation £14 billion. Its replacement, the council tax, may be property based but it still retains too much of the poll tax. The council tax is still not based on ability to pay, the disability discount is not extensive enough, and the second home discount is still automatic. Labour has proposed detailed amendments which would remove these problems and make the new tax fairer. Local authorities also suffer from an assessment system, the Standard Spending Assessment, which is rigged in favour of Conservative councils and which, in its first year of operation, has already been heavily criticised by the Audit Commission.

The policy commission will look in more detail, over the next year, at what should be the main features of a new system of local government finance. Labour is already committed to establishing a fair system of local taxation and to the restoration of the business rate to local control. The commission will look at how an independent assessment of council spending needs can be established, and examine the case for a greater proportion of revenue to be raised locally. Labour is also committed to removing the restrictions, which the government have imposed on councils, on the use of capital receipts, and to considering greater flexibility to raise money for capital programmes from capital markets.

We are committed to abolishing budget capping. The best check on the abuse of power is not Whitehall but the local electorate. Labour will replace capping with annual elections and a reformed local government finance system. The policy commission will look at giving local people more say over what their council spends by examining the idea of extending the budget period so that people can pass judgement on the financial policies of their authority when they vote for a councillor in the annual elections.

Labour believes in popular and accountable local government. We want to see councils which are small enough to relate to people's sense of community, but large enough to be able to deliver key services directly. That is why we are committed to the establishment of unitary authorities across the country. We shall monitor very carefully the government's proposals for Wales and Scotland to check that it is local needs and not party political considerations which determine their recommendations. The establishment of unitary authorities will further strengthen the case for regional government, as the need for co-ordination and planning will become still more apparent.

The commission will look at new forms of political management, leadership and accountability for local government. Our aim is not to provide a blueprint but rather to create an environment in which councils can innovate and experiment. The commission will look at ideas such as strengthening the role of council leaders, restructuring the committee system, establishing political executives balanced by scrutiny committees made up of backbench and opposition members, and the decentralisation of decision-making through neighbourhood forums, community councils or parish councils. It will also look at how the quality and calibre of councillors can be maintained through improving facilities and remuneration, through giving leading councillors the opportunity to be full-time councillors, and through examining whether there is a case to compensate employers for time lost, in order to encourage more private sector employees to become councillors.

Local government of quality

Labour believes that local authorities should be powerful enabling bodies instead of the enfeebled once-a-year committees which the government wants. That is why we are committed to introducing a new power of general competence for local councils. Local councils should be free to act as advocates for their communities and to control, set the standards for and hold accountable all major services delivered in their area. They should also be able to play the fullest possible role in economic development and job creation. Partnership with the private sector to rejuvenate inner city areas should be encouraged and not just tolerated.

Local authorities should be allowed once again to build homes for rent as well as to determine overall housing strategy. They should not be artificially excluded from direct service provision. There are a number of service areas where local authorities are and should remain the main providers, but there is an important role to be played by the voluntary sector and the private sector in service provision. The policy commission will look at how the terms of general competence should be defined and how it should be introduced.

Quality is top of Labour's agenda for local services. That is why it was Labour York City Council which first introduced the Citizens Charter, and Labour Lewisham which became the first council to achieve quality assurance from the British Standards Institute for its refuse collection and street cleaning services. Labour is committed to a quality programme for local authorities which includes: consultation with residents; customer contracts; quality audits; compensation if standards are not met; and the promotion of equality both for service users and providers. Labour also believes that there should be minimum standards set for quality which councils should be obliged to meet. In this context we will be considering how best to establish a Quality Commission in the light of the experience of Labour councils implementing our quality agenda and the changing role of the Audit Commission. We do not believe that compulsory competitive tendering is necessary to guarantee efficiency. The application of the Transfer of Undertakings (Protection of Employment) (TUPE) regulations to market testing and CCT has exposed how little these have to do with quality and efficiency and how much they have to do with cutting wages. The policy commission will look at how the legislation can be amended to guarantee quality and efficiency of service whilst protecting employment rights and local choice.

ELECTORAL LAW

Much of the work in this area has been done by the Plant Committee, which has considered the issues of electoral law in great detail. We have, however, considered certain aspects of it.

Several millions of those entitled to vote don't do so. There will always be those who choose not to vote. But there is growing evidence that a significant proportion of those who do not vote fail to do so, in part, because of the difficulties they face. It may be lack of knowledge and publicity about electoral registration or the cumbersome system of postal and proxy voting. There is often very limited geographical and physical access to polling stations, which particularly restricts the rights of disabled people to vote; and of course there are the complex and costly legal procedures for registration of complaints or challenges to malpractice.

The Labour Party is committed to examining all aspects of electoral law and administration and to ensuring that citizens are aware of their voting rights and responsibilities.

In particular, we fully support the proposal made by the Hansard Society amongst others and supported by the Plant committee, for an independent electoral commission which would be directly and solely responsible for all aspects of electoral administration and for ensuring freedom and fairness in all aspects of our electoral system. There is currently no single body that has overall responsibility for the administration of complaints relating to the electoral system.

In our evidence to the Home Office concerning electoral malpractice, the Labour Party drew attention to the increased incidence of candidates deliberately using descriptions that tend to confuse or mislead the public about party connections. For example, in Slough a so-called 'Independent Labour candidate' managed to secure enough votes to retain the seat for the Conservatives. This form of electoral deceipt should never be allowed to happen again.

We further believe that fundamental changes are required to the whole process of electoral registration and in particular to establish and maintain electoral registers as rolling registers so that names may be added as close to election day as reasonably practicable. Changes must be made to simplify the procedures for proxy and postal voting and determined efforts made to improve access to polling stations.

There is no justification for the continued discrepancy between the age of nomination and voting rights. We believe that it is right that the age of nomination which at present stands at 21 should be reduced to the age of 18.

THE JUDICIARY

It is hard to think of a more important issue than the selection of those who are to judge over their fellow citizens. Judges must not only be expert lawyers, but must also be men and women of integrity who are able to do justice in the extremely demanding circumstances of contested trials. They must also be people who are independent of government, and are not influenced by any kind of social or political pressure.

Those standards have not been assisted by the present secretive methods of selection and the restricted range of people from amongst whom judges are chosen. Labour is committed to establishing a proper Ministry of Justice. But even allowing for this, the system will remain fundamentally wrong. As public expectations of the judiciary increase, so does the public need to be reassured about the selection, and the training, of its judges. In particular there has been profound public concern about sentencing and the apparent insensitivity of some judges when dealing with offences of rape and violence. The independence of the judiciary must, of course, be sacrosanct. But that is no reason to continue with a patently anachronistic method of appointment or a failure to provide proper training and support for them.

A Judicial Appointments and Training Commission will be established to advise over the whole field.

One of the commission's first tasks will be to produce proposals for a more rational career pattern for judges, which will enable those who are suitable for judicial work to enter it earlier in their careers and to do the job more professionally. Elements in that policy would be:

- A wider field of choice, to ensure that all of the most able people are considered. Solicitors and academic lawyers, as well as practising barristers, will be encouraged to put themselves forward. And, more generally, qualified candidates will be expected to express interest in appointment and not await private invitation by government.
- A significant proportion of judges, including High Court judges, to be appointed at a significantly earlier age than at present. That would not exclude selection later. But for the majority it would enable the proper development of judicial careers. And it would make earlier use on the bench of the talents of women and of members of ethnic minorities, who are woefully under-represented amongst the older lawyers from whom judges are now chosen.
- Judges will usually start their careers in the crown and county courts. The new county courts, with their enhanced range of work, will be important tribunals in which it will be a challenging task for many judges to spend the whole of their career. And those who go on to the High Court will benefit from first acquiring full-time experience of judicial work.
- Judges will retire at an age closer to the retirement age of the rest of the working population. The retiring age would be initially 65, with discretion (to be exercised on the recommendation of the commission) to give limited extensions in special cases if requested.

The commission will have a special responsibility for judicial training. Training for judges was once regarded as unnecessary, or even as constitutionally improper. That absurd view is now exploded, with the recognition that litigants deserve to have their cases heard by a person who has a proper grounding in what may be new and complex issues, and sufficient understanding and experience of every aspect of his job. Proper training for judges does not in any way threaten their independence, but makes them more effective in their task of applying the law according to its rules.

The commission will be responsible for monitoring the careers of existing and aspirant judges, and for openly discussing with them their performance and the judicial work for which they are suitable. This will in no way affect judicial independence in decision making. The commission will seek a wide range of information and opinion on the aptitudes and abilities of candidates and of existing judges, and will in every case present a reasoned report. The commission will become a major source of information. A small part of this information may have to be obtained in confidence but, subject to that, all those seeking judicial appointments will be given full advice as to their prospects, the reasons for decisions made about them, and advice about any further training or experience that they are thought to need.

For the commission, this will be extremely challenging and important work. It will be necessary to have a blend of full-time and part-time appointments, and also a range of legal and other expertise. The chair and two vice-chairs will be full-time appointments. The chair will be a senior legal figure, and the vice-chairs lay persons of similar status. Other members, who will serve part-time but on the basis of a substantial commitment to the commission's work, will be drawn from a wide range within and outside the law, including members with extensive experience of professional training and education. The commission as a whole will consider general issues of policy, review difficult or important cases and formulate guidelines to be operated by its staff.

The commission will make a formal annual report. The commissioner's work can be scrutinised by a new Departmental Select Committee on Legal Affairs. This is a long overdue reform in the House of Commons in any event, but is given added justification with the establishment of the commission. We will also seek to broaden the representative nature of the magistrates' bench so that it reflects fully the diverse nature of our society and its people.

FREEDOM OF INFORMATION

Open government and freedom of information

'In the absence from English law of any freedom of information act . . . the public does not have any right to know.' (Mr Justice Rose explaining that he had no power to compel the Ministry of Defence to disclose a report into the accidental death of a young soldier, Kirk Sancto, to his parents.)

We live in a world of burgeoning information made possible because of new technologies, where organisations, including government, hold more information about us as individuals than ever before. Access to information is vital to us as individuals and citizens.

The Tory government holds and withholds information as it sees fit. John Major's open government initiative aims to remedy this. But its current proposals rely on voluntary disclosure with ministers free to block freedom of information should they wish. Even after the Matrix Churchill affair, ministers no longer argue that they are against the principle of freedom of information, merely that they can be trusted to be open without it. For example, the prison privatisation programme is proceeding without vital information being made public because it is said to be 'commercially confidential'. No wonder, when vested interests are protected in this way, we end up with the inefficiencies of Group 4.

The government argues against a specific Freedom of Information Bill on cost, yet in Australia, which has introduced a Freedom of Information Act, the Act cost only £5 million to administer – £2 million less than the amount the British government spent on promoting their Citizens' Charter. Other countries, such as the New Zealand, the US, Canada and Australia, as well as Denmark, Holland and France, provide their people with a statutory right to know. In this country there is strong support for such measures across party divides – a 1991 Mori poll found that 75 per cent of Tory voters supported such a measure.

Labour will give people the rights to information they need, because it is right to do so and because it will improve the efficiency of public services. We therefore propose a Freedom of Information Act which establishes a general right of access to official information held by national, regional and local government and by public and statutory bodies including the growing number of quangos. Information should be kept secret only in circumstances that should be tightly defined, for example if it can be proved that its disclosure would cause significant damage to defence, law enforcement, the work of the security and intelligence services and international relations.

Reform of the Official Secrets Act

The Tory government's 1989 Official Secrets Act imposes an absolute life long ban on former members and members of the security services speaking out about state wrongdoing. They have no public interest defence at all. What was presented by the Tories as a 'liberalising measure', in reality reinforces existing restrictions and means that potential evidence of government wrongdoings may never be reported.

New measures are necessary which balance the need to ensure the security of the country with the right for people to know about state corruption. Some material must, of course, remain protected information, for example, protected information relating to defence, international relations and the lawful activities of the security and intelligence services whose unauthorised disclosure would be likely to cause serious damage to the UK's interests.

In addition, information should also be protected if its unauthorised disclosure would be likely to result in an unlawful action, prevent detection or arrest of offenders or cause serious danger to safety or life.

There should however be a defence for individuals who disclose such information. It should be a defence to show that the protected material had already been made available or that the potential benefits of disclosing such material would outweigh the potential damage. In order to show the public interest defence it would be necessary to show that there was reasonable evidence that the disclosed material related to abuse of authority, official negligence, injustice to an individual, danger to health or safety, unauthorised use of public funds or other misconduct and that in the circumstances the disclosure was justified in the public interest having regard both to any benefit and or any damage that was likely to result. Civil servants and government contractors would generally have to show that they had taken reasonable steps to comply with the established procedures for drawing the abuse to the attention of the appropriate authorities without effect except in urgent matters.

The right to know about personal information

There are specific measures that could be taken to ensure that individuals have greater access to the personal information kept on them by other organisations. The Data Protection Act should be strengthened to improve individual access to files and to prevent abuse. People should have the right to see their employment records and records held by them on blacklisting bodies.

Accountability of the security services

The security services are set up to protect our democracy and democratic freedoms. They must not and should not invade individuals' privacy without justification. We believe it vital for the security services to be placed under the scrutiny of a parliamentary select committee.

Accountability of the private sector

We should improve the amount of information given by employers to employees and ensure that powerful institutions such as pension companies, building societies, financial institutions and others should provide better information to those directly affected by their decisions and financial standing. Labour also supports measures to require companies to disclose specific kinds of information relating to health and safety, the safety of products and damage to the environment, with limited exemptions.

CONCLUSION

The proposals in this statement constitute the most radical package of democratic reform ever presented to the British people by a major political party. Together they will open up our political system and make human rights and justice more readily available to all our citizens. We accept that this means that political action in future should be checked, negotiated and accountable – as it should be in a modern democracy. An open political system will be a catalyst for change – institutionalised, mediated and careful change no doubt – but change nevertheless.

The next Labour government will create a democracy which will no longer be confined by an over-powerful government, but where different institutions – each properly and legitimately established – can help to balance the executive power which has been so sorely abused in the eighties.

Having created clearly defined institutions and rights, the relationship which develops between those new features will be of great significance. There will undoubtedly be serious debate and even conflict between the different institutions – a reformed House of Commons will discomfort the executive;

an elected Second chamber will want to spread its wings; individuals using the Bill of Rights will expose the government to much greater accountability and influence the future development of the judiciary; European decisions will have to be debated in greater detail; and local government will be rejuvenated. Above all, individuals will not only feel greater ownership of the political system and be more demanding of it, they will also be less tolerant of the abuse of power and better equipped to put it right.

Though these reforms do not mean a formal written constitution, in which each aspect of government and citizens' rights is set out, they are nonetheless a significant step in that direction. Each part will require legislation which is carefully formulated and consistent with the others. We leave open the question of whether at a later stage we make progress to formal codification.

For the immediate future, and certainly for the duration of the first Labour term, our task is to bring life to the various elements that will form the basis of a new constitutional settlement for Britain to create a democracy for the 21st century.

APPENDIX 2

REPORT OF THE JOINT (LABOUR PARTY–LIBERAL DEMOCRATS) CONSULTATIVE COMMITTEE ON CONSTITUTIONAL REFORM (1997)

THE ESTABLISHMENT OF THE JOINT CONSULTATIVE COMMITTEE

1. In Summer 1996 Tony Blair and Paddy Ashdown asked Robin Cook and Robert Maclennan to explore the possibility of co-operation between the Labour and Liberal Democrat parties in relation to constitutional reform. Both parties had for some time been committed to a programme of constitutional change and shared a common view of the need to reform our democratic institutions and to renew the relationship between politics and the people. Following progress in the initial discussions the two parties agreed in October 1996 to establish a Joint Consultative Committee with the following terms of reference:

2. 'To examine the current proposals of the Labour and Liberal Democrat Parties for constitutional reform: to consider whether there might be sufficient common ground to enable the parties to reach agreement on a legislative programme for constitutional reform; to consider means by which such a programme might best be implemented and to make recommendations.'

This is the report of the Joint Consultative Committee's work.

MEMBERSHIP

3. The membership of the Committee was as follows:

Labour	*Liberal Democrat*
Robin Cook MP	Robert Maclennan MP
Donald Dewar MP	Jim Wallace MP

Jack Straw MP	Nick Harvey MP
Ann Taylor MP	Lord McNally
George Robertson MP	John Macdonald QC
Ron Davies MP	Professor Dawn Oliver
Baroness Symons	Michael Steed
Lord Plant	Lord Lester QC

The Committee also from time to time drew on the expertise of outside advisers. We would like to express our gratitude to all those who gave us their help and advice.

FOREWORD

4. The objectives of the British Constitution should be to secure a government that is democratic and a society that is open and free. Democratic Government should ensure that those who hold power in the name of the people are accountable to the collective wishes and interests of the people. Each individual citizen should have equal rights and responsibilities in an open society where the aim is to guarantee civil liberty, social cohesion and economic opportunity.

5. Democracy and freedom cannot be taken for granted. Every generation has a responsibility to ensure that these principles are given fresh meaning and defended against any tendency on the part of those in power to diminish their accountability to the people. There is today a pressing need to renew democracy in Britain.

6. There is too much power centralised in the hands of too few people and too little freedom for local communities to decide their own priorities.

7. Government holds more information than ever before, but the public still has no legal right to share information collected by their Government.

8. Parliament itself has probably not been held in lower esteem since the completion of the universal franchise. The passage of deeply unpopular and impractical measures such as the poll tax has raised doubts about both the accountability of MPs and the effectiveness of their scrutiny.

9. And Britain is alone in the Western world in allowing some people to take a seat in Parliament on the hereditary principle rather than by the democratic process.

10. Democracy cannot stay healthy if one party always stays in power. The defeat of the Conservative Government would in itself be an important demonstration that Government must be accountable to the people and cannot persistently ignore the wishes of the people.

11. However, a change of Government is not in itself sufficient. We believe we must also change our constitution in line with British traditions in order to renew democracy and to bring power closer to the people.

12. These objectives are not a minority concern. The accountability of power in our country determines how decisions are taken every day in ways which affect the lives of every citizen. The new system of local control of the NHS is only one of many recent examples of the manner in which public services have become more remote from local communities.

13. Nor is a modern and accountable constitution a more expensive constitution. On the contrary, we believe that local people often know better what will provide a more cost effective local use of public resources. A more open and devolved constitution will liberate talent, energy and initiative which at present does not find adequate outlet in our centralised state.

14. In the sections which follow we set out our priorities for reform. This programme represents a transfer of power to make political institutions more responsive to the people. It is a programme which offers Britain a constitution for the future, not the past. It will share power with the many, not preserve it in the hands of the few.

15. We have not attempted to spell out in detail the legislative programme for the next Parliament. The programme set out here will be implemented over a period of time. There are some agreed necessary priorities but it would be quite mistaken to suggest that measures of constitutional reform which are not to be implemented immediately, or in the first year of government, are somehow of lesser importance. A reform process must establish momentum and carry through a stage by stage programme of reform.

16. If this programme is enacted, Britain's democracy will have been transformed. We will enter the twenty first century a stronger, more democratic and more open society. It is a prize for which both our parties are determined to work.

Robin Cook   *Robert Maclennan*

BRINGING RIGHTS HOME

17. The provision in UK law of a code of human rights is essential to guarantee an open society and a modern democracy. The United Kingdom has been a signatory to the European Convention of Human Rights since 1951. People in this country are offered the protection and the guarantees of basic human rights that the Convention provides yet

to gain access to those rights, British citizens must appeal to the Commission and Court in Strasbourg.

18. Both parties agree that the rights and duties defined by the ECHR and its First Protocol should be incorporated by Act of Parliament into United Kingdom law. This Act would not affect the sovereign powers of Parliament.

19. When introducing Bills into Parliament, Ministers would be required to explain why any provision is, or appears to be, inconsistent with ECHR rights. This would strengthen Parliamentary scrutiny and aid the courts in interpreting Parliament's intentions in legislating.

20. The new Act would enable everyone to rely upon ECHR rights through the ordinary courts and tribunals.

21. A Joint Select Committee of both Houses of Parliament would monitor the operation of the new Act, scrutinise pending legislative measures in the light of ECHR rights, and advise Parliament about compliance with the UK's obligations under the international human rights codes to which it is party.

22. A Human Rights Commissioner or Commission, or similar public body, would provide advice and assistance to those seeking the protection of the rights enshrined in the Convention, and be itself able to bring proceedings to secure effective compliance with the ECHR, whether by judicial review or by representative proceedings on behalf of a number of people.

23. Incorporation of the ECHR would represent a very significant strengthening in practice of what amounts to the UK's fundamental law. The Convention, written in 1950, would need to be updated over time as a model for modern constitutional protection of basic human rights and responsibilities inherent in being a British citizen.

FREEDOM OF INFORMATION

24. The public have a right to know what government is doing in their name. Open and accountable government and freedom of information are essential to a modern democracy, yet the Government still continues to hide the workings of government behind a veil of secrecy.

25. Both parties are committed to a Freedom of Information Act. This would give the public proper confidence in matters of current public concern such as, for example, public health and food safety. It would also give proper access to information about the workings of government and allow individuals to see information held on them by government agencies.

26. Despite a promise to legislate on access to personal files, the present Government has failed to do so. The existing code of practice is welcome but does not go far enough in ensuring that people have proper rights of access to information. Freedom of information has been introduced in many Western democracies. Last year the House of Commons Select Committee on the Ombudsman added its weight to calls for a Freedom of Information Act.

27. There would of course be a need for exemptions in areas like national security, personal privacy and policy advice given by civil servants to Ministers, but the proposed legislation would establish independent machinery and procedures to achieve these purposes and shift the balance decisively in favour of the presumption that government information should be made publicly available unless there is a justifiable reason not to do so.

INDEPENDENT NATIONAL STATISTICAL SERVICE

28. Government is the most important source of statistical information about our society, but the integrity of that information has been brought into question by ministerial interference. Both parties agree that the National Statistical service should be made independent of Ministers, and answerable to Parliament, in a manner similar to the National Audit Office and the Comptroller and Auditor General.

BRINGING POWER CLOSER TO THE PEOPLE

29. Britain today is one of the most centralised countries in Europe. While other countries have successfully decentralised, the Conservative Government has continued to reject the case for passing power out of Whitehall and Westminster to the nations and regions of Britain. The results have been increased political disaffection, administrative inefficiency and strain on the Union.

30. The United Kingdom is a partnership of nations. England, Scotland, Wales and Northern Ireland have their own traditions. The value of the partnership between these nations is immense and makes each part stronger. Yet in recent years the demand for a new relationship has grown.

31. To ignore demands for greater decentralisation would be wrong and would allow resentment at our current system to grow. It is in the interests of Britain's future and of good government that there are

proper democratic arrangements in place throughout the country. There is already in Britain a system of administrative devolution, with powerful Scottish and Welsh Offices and now Government offices for the regions of England. In Scotland there is a distinct legal, education and local government system. Yet in all these places, decisions continue to be taken almost exclusively by the centre. Far from damaging the Union, devolving power will strengthen it by creating a new partnership between the nations and regions of Britain.

32. The principles on which devolution takes place should be popular consent, the maintenance of the Union, the preservation of local government, resources pooled and distributed on an agreed basis and proper constitutional provision for the resolution of disputes.

SCOTLAND

33. Demand has grown in Scotland in recent years for democratic control over Scotland's domestic affairs and for the Scottish Office to act according to the wishes of the people of Scotland. Both the Labour and Liberal Democrat parties have long standing support for devolution to Scotland.

34. Both parties, with other organisations in Scotland, took part in the Scottish Constitutional Convention which was established in 1989. The Convention has since published its final report, Scotland's Parliament, Scotland's Right. That report sets out in detail proposals for the Scottish Parliament.

35. It recommends a Parliament with legislative competence over those matters which are currently the responsibility of the Scottish Office. These matters include health, housing, education, local government and law and order. The Act would include provision for maintaining a strong and effective system of local government and would enable the Scottish Parliament to make accountable to the people the quangos and public bodies operating in Scotland.

36. The Parliament would be elected by the Additional Member System.

37. The principle of equalisation in finance would continue, with resources being pooled at the centre and allocated on an agreed basis. In addition there would be a power to vary revenue within a defined limit, providing the Scottish Parliament with a degree of autonomy over its budget.

38. In June last year the Labour Party announced its intention to hold a pre-legislative referendum and to seek specific endorsement for giving the parliament defined financial powers to vary revenue. Following the

election legislation to hold the referendum would be introduced as soon as possible and a White Paper would be produced detailing the devolution proposals.

39. Whilst Liberal Democrats have disagreed with this approach, in particular with the proposal for a second referendum question, they would not seek to frustrate or delay the referendum legislation, which could prejudice the achievement of our common goal – the enactment of the Bill to create a Scottish Parliament in the first session of the next parliament.

40. Both parties have endorsed the Convention's report as the basis for legislation to establish a Scottish Parliament. Both parties would campaign strongly for a positive outcome in that referendum. Following that outcome, both parties would support legislation to establish the Scottish Parliament within the first session of Parliament after the general election.

WALES

41. Both parties support the establishment of a directly elected Assembly providing democratic control over the functions currently devolved to the Welsh Office, being empowered to reform the quango state and providing a democratic forum for the development of policy.

42. Devolution would result in effective powers being transferred from central government to Wales. Those powers should be exercised in a way which provides maximum openness and accountability. The legislation shall place on the Assembly a responsibility to maintain a strong and effective system of local government.

43. There is deep public concern in Wales at the growing influence of quangos and other unelected bodies. The Assembly shall ensure maximum effectiveness and accountability in the operation of those quangos which remain.

44. The Wales Labour Party has decided that the Assembly should be elected by an Additional Member system. This development has been welcomed by the Liberal Democrats.

45. Following the election legislation to hold the referendum would be introduced as soon as possible and a White Paper produced detailing the devolution proposals. Both Parties agree that a short time should be allowed to lapse after the Scottish referendum in order to ensure the debate in Wales, with its distinctive form of devolution, is not overshadowed by the process in Scotland.

46. Both parties would campaign for a positive outcome to the referendum and would support legislation within the first session of Parliament after the general election to establish the Assembly.

THE REGIONS OF ENGLAND

47. The Conservatives have regional government in England through their establishment of government offices for the regions which now operate throughout England and which are responsible for the co-ordination of the work of the Departments of the Environment, Employment and Education, Trade and Industry and Transport. These co-ordinating offices, along with regional offices of other Government departments, and regional quangos operate without proper democratic scrutiny by the people of the regions concerned.

48. Both parties are committed to bringing power closer to the people in the regions of England and to ensuring greater co-ordination and proper scrutiny of the activities of quangos. The sense of regional identity and the demand for regional government in England varies considerably and it is no part of the parties' plans to impose elected regional assemblies on areas where there is no demand. Other European countries have devolved in a step by step manner which takes account of the differing degrees of national and regional identity which exist within them.

49. Both parties endorse a stage by stage approach which would first of all establish indirectly elected regional chambers based on the regional local authority associations which already exist. They would then allow directly elected regional assemblies to be established only where the proposal had been endorsed in a referendum in the region concerned.

LONDON

50. London is the only capital in Europe without an elected authority. The government's dogmatic refusal to allow Londoners a say in the running of their own city is a handicap to our world class capital. Some progress has been made in recent years with the establishment of a single body to represent London's local authorities, London First and the excellent work of the London Pride partnership. What is missing is a proper democratic voice to represent London as a whole.

51. Both parties endorse the establishment of an elected authority for London, with the consent of the people of London in a referendum, which would act as a powerful voice for the capital and work with the

boroughs and other organisations in London. The Labour Party have also proposed an elected Mayor for London.

QUANGOS

52. The power and influence of quangos has grown in recent years. They are now responsible for spending £60 billion a year, a fifth of all public expenditure. The decentralisation of power to Scotland and Wales, the establishment of an elected authority for London and the extension of democratic accountability in England's regions will help to bring the quango state under the proper level of scrutiny that a modern democracy demands.

53. Government will always have appointed bodies for some functions. Most people on such bodies carry out their duties diligently and with a deep commitment to public service. It is essential that the system of appointment and the practices of such bodies are beyond reproach. Both parties therefore endorse the principles of public appointment outlined in the Nolan report. They also firmly believe in greater openness in the operation of quangos and measures to extend scrutiny, and accountability at local, regional and national levels.

ELECTORAL SYSTEMS

54. There has, throughout this century, been debate about the use of the first past the post electoral system for elections. Liberal Democrats have long standing policy in favour of proportional representation. The Labour Party's Plant commission considered the electoral systems for elections to the House of Commons, devolved assemblies and the European Parliament.

55. Both parties are committed to the use of proportional electoral systems for the Scottish Parliament and the Welsh Assembly.

56. Both parties believe that a referendum on the system for elections to the House of Commons should be held within the first term of a new Parliament.

57. Both parties are also agreed that the referendum should be a single question offering a straight choice between first past the post and one specific proportional alternative.

58. A commission on voting systems for the Westminster Parliament should be appointed early in the next parliament to recommend the appropriate proportional alternative to the first past the post system. Among the

factors to be considered by the commission would be the likelihood that the system proposed would command broad consensus among proponents of proportional representation. The commission would be asked to report within twelve months of its establishment.

59. Legislation to hold the referendum would then be proposed and the choice placed before the people. This proposal would allow the crucial question of how our government is elected to be decided by the people themselves.

60. It is the purpose of both parties to improve the accountability of European institutions.

61. For elections to the European Parliament both parties have supported a proportional system based on regional lists. This system was considered in the 1970s during the passage of the European Assembly Elections Act. It was also recommended by the Plant Committee on electoral systems which reported in 1993 and was endorsed by Labour Party conference.

62. Both parties are therefore agreed that elections in Britain to the European Parliament should be on a regional list system.

63. Both parties are concerned about the lack of progress which has been made under the present administration in respect of reforms and improvements to the processes of electoral registration and voting procedures. The two parties shall consider further how these arrangements and those for referendums, can be improved and what further independent machinery may be desirable.

THE REFORM OF PARLIAMENT

64. Renewing Parliament is key to the wider modernisation of our country's system of government. No programme of reform could ignore the legislature itself. Parliament, for all its faults, remains central to national life. At times it can seem to embody the national spirit. It is precisely because of the importance of Parliament in our national life that it is right to consider whether it does its job well and to suggest improvements that can be made which will enable it to become a more effective legislature.

THE HOUSE OF COMMONS

65. The House of Commons no longer holds ministers to account and legislation is not given the scrutiny it requires. This country needs a

Parliament fit for the 21st century. Sensible reforms have been proposed by the House of Commons Procedure Committee, the Hansard Society and others. Both the Labour and Liberal Democrat parties are convinced of the need to re-establish confidence in the political process, politicians and Parliament itself. A more mature approach to the consideration of legislation is required.

66. The parties' priorities for modernising the House of Commons are:

67. • to programme parliamentary business to ensure fuller consultation, more effective scrutiny of bills and better use of MPs' time.

68. • to improve the quality of legislation by better pre-legislative consultation and the use of mechanisms such as the special standing committee procedure where evidence is taken before legislation is passed.

69. • to change Prime Minister's Question Time to make it a more genuine and serious means of holding the government to account.

70. • to overhaul the process for scrutinising European legislation so that decisions from the EU are more transparent and Parliament's role is more clearly defined.

71. • to strengthen the ability of MPs to make the government answerable for its actions.

72. • to enhance the role of Select Committees in ensuring the accountability of departments.

73. No one political party should dictate changes to parliamentary procedure: Parliament must own the process. Political parties must however take a lead. Early in a new Parliament a special Select Committee on Modernising the House of Commons should be established. Following the example of the select committee which examined the implementation of Lord Nolan's recommendations, the membership of this special Committee should reflect the full spectrum of interests and experience in the House and could include both the Leader and Shadow Leader of the House.

74. The review undertaken by the Special Committee should be open to the views of others, bringing in outside advisers where appropriate and canvassing the views of MPs, organisations involved in the work of Parliament and members of the public. It is hoped that the Special Committee could report swiftly on those matters requiring priority, especially legislation, so that it would be possible to implement its first recommendations early in a new Parliament.

THE HOUSE OF LORDS

75. There is an urgent need for radical reform of the Lords. Its current composition is indefensible, in particular the fact that the majority of its members are entitled to take part in the legislative process on a hereditary basis.

76. The two parties are therefore agreed that there must be legislation to remove the rights of hereditary peers to sit and vote in the House of Lords.

77. There is a valuable continuing role for some cross-bench or non-party element in a reformed House of Lords. The two parties believe the cross benchers should remain at their present proportion of around one fifth following the removal of the hereditary peers. An open and legitimate mechanism for appointing cross-bench peers should be developed and the cross benchers should be consulted about the mode of replenishing their members.

78. Some hereditary peers have also made useful contributions to the House. It should be made possible for a limited number of those who play an active part in the work of the Lords to become life peers.

79. Life peers should not be required to step down but there should be a procedure for voluntary retirement.

80. No one political party should seek a majority in the House of Lords.

81. The removal of the hereditary peers will still leave an imbalance in party representation in the Lords in the interim stage. Following their removal, we should move, over the course of the next parliament, to a House of Lords where those peers who take a party whip more accurately reflect the proportion of votes received by each party in the previous general election.

82. The removal of the hereditary peers' right to vote is the first stage in a process of reform. Following their removal a joint committee of both houses should be established to bring forward detailed proposals on structure and functions for the later stages of reform within a time limited period. This body should produce recommendations for a democratic and representative second chamber.

THE CIVIL SERVICE

83. The British Civil Service carries out its functions with professionalism and integrity. The ethics of public service, impartiality and political neutrality underpin and guide civil servants in carrying out their duties

and responsibilities and are important national assets. At present there is a code of conduct for the civil service which sets out those principles. The Public Services Committee of the House of Commons has recommended that the code be made statutory to ensure these principles have full legal backing.

84. Both parties agree that there should be a Civil Service Act to give legal force to the code which should be tightened up to underline the political neutrality of the civil service. It should also be reviewed in relation to other published authorities to clarify lines of civil service and ministerial accountability and responsibility.

CONCLUSION

85. The proposals set out in our report are presented as distinct measures yet they are closely related. Through them runs the common thread of empowering the people. To make this clear the new Government should make an early declaration setting out the principles behind its programme of constitutional reform and outlining the more open and modern democracy it seeks to create.

APPENDIX 3

EXTRACTS FROM THE PARTIES' GENERAL ELECTION MANIFESTOS (1997)

THE CONSERVATIVE PARTY

Foreword

The Conservative administrations elected since 1979 are among the most successful in British peacetime history. A country once the sick man of Europe has become its most successful economy. A country once brought to its knees by over-mighty trade unions now has industrial peace. Abroad, the cold war has been won; at home, the rule of law has been restored. The enterprising virtues of the British people have been liberated from the dead hand of the state. There can be no doubt that we have created a better Britain.

Why, then, do we still need a Conservative Government? Because resting on what we have achieved is not enough. To stand still is to fall back. *Our goal must be for Britain to be the best place in the world to live.*

We live in a tougher, more uncertain world. A fast-moving global free market is emerging. New economic powers are rising in the East. Family life and social attitudes are changing. Europe is adjusting to the end of communism. The European social model is failing. The nation state is under threat. We must respond to these challenges.

We have turned around our economic fortunes. We have fewer people out of work and more in work than any other major European economy. British people now have the opportunity of a prosperous future. But that prosperity cannot be taken for granted. We have to compete to win. That means a constant fight to keep tight control over public spending and enable Britain to remain the lowest taxed major economy in Europe. It means a continuing fight to keep burdens off business, maintaining our opt-out of the European Social Chapter. If we relax for one moment, our hard won success will slip away again.

We have strengthened choice and personal ownership for families, and rolled back the state from areas where it was interfering unnecessarily in our lives. But we now have the opportunity to achieve a massive expansion in wealth and

481

ownership so that more families can enjoy the self-respect and independence that comes with being self-sufficient from the state. Our far-reaching proposals for personal pension funds are central to achieving this – so too are our plans to increase support for the family in our tax system. Our aim is to spread opportunity for all to succeed, whoever they are and wherever they come from, provided they are prepared to work hard. To turn the 'have nots' into the 'haves'. To support the family in providing security and stability.

We have modernised and reformed many of the areas where the state still has a vital role. But we now have to build on these reforms to deliver even better services. We must continue providing the resources to invest in our modernised health service. We can now provide parents with a hard-edged guarantee of standards in schools. We need also to widen choice in areas where state bureaucracy has constrained it.

We have pioneered new ways of building partnerships that engage the private sector in areas previously dependent on the public purse. We now need to capture private sector investment on a massive scale to regenerate our cities, transform our crumbling local authority housing estates and modernise other public assets.

The only way to secure this future of opportunity is to stick with the Conservative programme of continuing reform. Now would be the worst possible moment to abandon the pathway to prosperity on which we are set. We must keep up the momentum.

At the same time we must maintain the security that a stable nation provides in an uncertain, fast-changing world. We must protect our constitution and unity as a nation from those who threaten it with unnecessary and dangerous change. And we must stand up for our interests in shaping a free-market Europe of sovereign nation states.

There is, of course, an alternative on offer: to load costs on business while calling it 'stakeholding'; to increase the role of the state, while calling it 'the community'; to succumb to a centralised Europe while calling it 'not being isolated'; to break up our country while calling it 'devolution'.

To risk this alternative would be a disaster for our country. We have come a very long way. We must be sure that we do not throw away what we have gained, or lose the opportunities we have earned.

You can only be sure with the Conservatives.

John Major

10. The Constitution

Alone in Europe, the history of the United Kingdom has been one of stability and security. We owe much of that to the strength and stability of our constitution – the institutions, laws and traditions that bind us together as a nation.

Our constitution has been stable, but not static. It has been woven over the centuries – the product of hundreds of years of knowledge, experience and history.

Radical changes that alter the whole character of our constitutional balance could unravel what generations of our predecessors have created. To preserve that stability in future – and the freedoms and rights of our citizens – we need to continue a process of evolution, not revolution.

Conservatives embrace evolutionary change that solves real problems and improves the way our constitution works. In recent years we have opened up government, devolved power and accountability, and introduced reforms to make parliament work more effectively. It is that evolutionary process that we are committed to continue.

Open, accountable government

In recent years we have taken significant steps to open up government to public scrutiny, and give individuals more information to hold government and public services to account.

We have introduced a code on access to government information, policed by the Ombudsman. We have published information on the workings of government previously held secret – including the composition of cabinet committees, and the structure of the security and intelligence services. We have introduced a new civil service code, and reformed the process for public appointments. We are pledged to legislate on the commitments in our 1993 White Paper on Open Government, including a statutory right of access by citizens to personal records held about them by the government and other public authorities. And we have set up the Nolan Committee and have implemented its proposals to ensure that the highest standards are maintained in public life.

But our reforms go even wider than that. We have transferred power from central bureaucracies to local organisations such as school governors and hospital trusts. We have introduced the Citizen's Charter. We have also required them to publish information on their performance – information which enables the local community to keep a check on standards and apply pressure where needed. Wherever possible, we are widening competition and choice in public services. We showed in Chapter 6 how we wished to push this agenda forward.

Regional government would be a dangerously centralising measure – taking power away from elected local authorities. We wish to go in the opposite direction, shifting power to the local neighbourhood – for example, by giving more power to parish councils.

Parliament

Parliament – alongside the Crown and our legal system – is one of the three key institutions that uphold our constitution. The supremacy of parliament is fundamental to our democracy, and the guarantee of our freedoms. The last 17 years have seen many changes to strengthen parliament and make it more effective – the flourishing of select committees, new procedures to scrutinise European legislation, reform of parliament's working day, and a budget that brings together tax and spending.

We have therefore already done much to improve the way parliament works and will do more. We have accepted the proposal from the Public Service Select Committee and put before the House of Commons a clear new statement of the principles underlying ministerial accountability to parliament.

All these developments have made parliament open to the citizen, and the government more accountable. In the next session of parliament we will continue this careful reform.

'To give parliament more time to consider legislation thoroughly we will extend the Queen's Speech to cover not only legislation for the immediate year but also provisional plans for legislation in the year after that.'

This will mean that more draft bills will be subject to public scrutiny before they reach the floor of the House of Commons. It will give select committees more time to take evidence and report. And this should also mean better legislation.

We do not believe there is a case for more radical reform that would undermine the House of Commons. A new Bill of Rights, for example, would risk transferring power away from parliament to legal courts – undermining the democratic supremacy of parliament as representatives of the people. Whilst this may be a necessary check in other countries which depend upon more formalised written constitutions, we do not believe it is appropriate to the UK.

Nor do we favour changes in the system of voting in parliamentary elections that would break the link between an individual member of parliament and his constituents. A system of proportional representation would be more likely to produce unstable, coalition governments that are unable to provide effective leadership – with crucial decisions being dependent on compromise deals hammered out behind closed doors. This is not the British way.

We have demonstrated we are not against change where it is practical and beneficial. But fundamental changes which have not been fully thought through – such as opposition proposals on the House of Lords – would be extremely damaging. We will oppose change for change's sake.

The Union

The Union between Scotland, Wales, Northern Ireland and England underpins our nation's stability. The Conservative commitment to the United Kingdom does not mean ignoring the distinctive individuality of the different nations. On the contrary, we have gone further in recognising that diversity than any previous government. We are publishing separate manifestos for Wales and Scotland.

While preserving the role of parliament at the centre of the Union, we have given new powers to the Scottish Grand Committee and Welsh Grand Committee – enabling Scottish and Welsh MPs to call Ministers to account and debate legislation which affects those countries – something that would be impossible with separate Assemblies. For the first time, Welsh members of parliament can ask their questions to Ministers in Welsh in Wales. Most recently we have similarly extended the basic powers of the Northern Ireland Grand Committee.

We believe this is the right way to go. By contrast, the development of new assemblies in Scotland and Wales would create strains which could well pull apart the Union. That would create a new layer of government which would be hungry for power. It would risk rivalry and conflict between these parliaments or assemblies and the parliament at Westminster. And it would raise serious questions about whether the representation of Scottish and Welsh MPs at Westminster – and their role in matters affecting English affairs – could remain unchanged.

Nor do we believe it would be in the interests of the Scottish or Welsh people. A Scottish tax-raising parliament, for example, could well affect the choice of where new investment locates in the United Kingdom.

In a world where people want security, nothing would be more dangerous than to unravel a constitution that binds our nation together and the institutions that bring us stability. We will continue to fight for the strength and diversity that benefits all of us as a proud union of nations.

Northern Ireland

While we cherish the Union and Northern Ireland's place within it, we recognise that there exist within the Province special circumstances which require further action to be taken.

After a quarter of a century we wish to see the unique and originally temporary system of direct rule ended and a successful restoration of local accountable democracy achieved. We want to see this brought about in a form which carries the broadest agreement possible. And we want to see the rights, traditions and interests of all parts of the community recognised within any such agreement.

We will accordingly continue to pursue a policy of dialogue and negotiation with and between the democratic Northern Ireland parties. We will continue to underpin such negotiations with the guarantee that the constitutional position of Northern Ireland cannot and will not be changed without the broad consent of the people of Northern Ireland. At the same time we will continue to take whatever security measures are required to protect the people of Northern Ireland from those who seek to achieve their political goals by violent means.

We seek peace. But we will never be swayed by terrorist violence nor will we ever compromise our principles with those who seek to overthrow the rule of law by force.

THE LIBERAL DEMOCRATS

Introduction

This will be the last election of this century. And one of its most important. We have ducked the challenges that confront our country for too long. It is time to face them. The choice you make will shape Britain's future for the next 50 years.

There are no quick fixes, no instant solutions. Eighteen years of Conservative government have left our society divided, our public services run down, our sense of community fractured and our economy under-performing. There is much to be done to prepare Britain for the next century and no time to waste in getting started.

Yet a terrible fatalism seems to grip politicians. Though the challenges are immense, the solutions we are offered are all too often puny. We are told we can't ask people to pay more for a better education. Or change the way we live to protect our environment. Or share more to give better opportunities to those who have less. Or modernise our politics to give people more say.

The Liberal Democrats reject this timidity.

We are in politics not just to manage things better, but to make things happen. To build a more prosperous, fair and open society. We believe in the market economy as the best way to deliver prosperity and distribute economic benefits. But we recognise that market mechanisms on their own are not enough; that the private sector alone cannot ensure that there are good services for everyone, or promote employment opportunities, or tackle economic inequality, or protect the environment for future generations.

We believe in a society in which every citizen shares rights and responsibilities. But, we recognise that a strong country is built from the bottom, not the top; that conformity quickly becomes the enemy of diversity. And that the imposition of social blueprints leads to authoritarian centralised government. Liberal Democrats believe that power and opportunity, like wealth, should be widely spread.

Above all, Liberal Democracy is about liberty. That does not just mean freedom from oppressive government. It means providing all citizens with the opportunity to build worthwhile lives for themselves and their families and helping them to recognise their responsibilities to the wider community.

Liberal Democrats believe the role of democratic government is to protect and strengthen liberty, to redress the balance between the powerful and the weak, between rich and poor and between immediate gains and long-term environmental costs.

That is the Liberal Democrat vision: of active government which invests in people, promotes their long-term prosperity and welfare, safeguards their security, and is answerable to them for its actions.

Much of what we propose here requires no money – only political will. But where extra investment is required we say where it will come from. This is a menu with prices.

The purpose of this manifesto is to widen opportunities for all.

And its aim is to build a nation of self-reliant individuals, living in strong communities, backed by an enabling government.

Rt Hon Paddy Ashdown

Which party will clean up the mess in our politics?

Our aim: To restore trust in British politics.

The problem: People know that British politics isn't working. Their politicians have lied to them, their Parliament has become tainted by sleaze and their government is out of touch and doesn't listen.

Our commitment: Liberal Democrats will modernise Britain's outdated institutions, rebuild trust, renew democracy and give Britain's nations, regions and local communities a greater say over their own affairs.

Reforming politics

Our priorities are to:
- *Restore trust between people and government*, by ending secrecy and guaranteeing peoples' rights and freedoms.
- *Renew Britain's democracy*, by creating a fair voting system, reforming Parliament and setting higher standards for politicians' conduct.
- *Give government back to the people*, by decentralising power to the nations, regions and communities of the United Kingdom.

Restoring trust in politics
British politics remains far too secretive. We cannot rebuild trust in politics without making government more open and accountable.

We will:

Safeguard individual liberties, by establishing a Bill of Rights. As a first step, we will incorporate the European Convention on Human Rights into UK law so that it is enforceable by the courts in the UK. We will set up a Human Rights Commission to strengthen the protection of individual rights. We will create a Ministry for Justice responsible for protecting human rights and overseeing the administration of the legal system, the courts and legal aid. We oppose the introduction of Identity Cards.

Break open the excessive secrecy of government, by passing a Freedom of Information Act establishing a citizens right to know.

Cut back the quango state. We will scrap unnecessary quangos, handing their functions over to elected bodies. We will require those that remain to meet in public and to list their members' interests. We will establish a fair, open and more representative appointment process for all quangos.

Give people more say in decision-making. We will make greater use of national referendums for constitutional issues, for example, changing the voting system or any further transfer of power to European institutions. We will enable referendums to be held on specific local issues where there is public demand.

Renewing democracy
Britain's political institutions are outdated and unrepresentative.

We will:

Modernise the House of Commons. We will reduce the number of MPs by 200 (one third) and introduce tougher rules for their conduct, behaviour and outside sources of income. We will improve drafting and consultation on legislation, and strengthen MPs' ability to hold the government to account.

Create an effective and democratic upper house. We will, over two Parliaments, transform the House of Lords into a predominantly elected second chamber capable of representing the nations and regions of the UK and of playing a key role in scrutinising European legislation.

Introduce a fair system of voting. We will introduce proportional representation for all elections, to put more power in the hands of voters and make government more representative.

Make politics more stable. We will establish a fixed Parliamentary term of four years.

Clean up party funding. We will reform the way political parties are funded and limit the amount they can spend on national election campaigns. We will make each party publish its accounts and list all large donors.

Giving government back to the people
Far too much power has been concentrated in Westminster and Whitehall. Democratic government should be as close to ordinary people as possible.

We will:

Introduce Home Rule for Scotland, with the creation of a Scottish Parliament, elected by proportional representation, and able to raise and reduce income tax.

Introduce Home Rule for Wales, with the creation of a Welsh Senedd, elected by proportional representation, and able to raise and reduce income tax.

Create the framework to make existing regional decision-making in England democratically accountable, and enable the establishment of elected regional assemblies, where there is demonstrated public demand. We will create a strategic authority for London.

Strengthen local government. We will establish a 'power of general competence', giving Councils wider scope for action. We will allow local authorities to raise more of their funds locally, give them greater discretion over spending and allow them, within strict limits, to go directly to the markets to raise finance for capital projects. We will, in the long-term replace Council Tax with a Local Income Tax, and replace the Uniform Business Rate with a fairer system of business rates, raised through local Councils and set in accordance with local priorities.

Northern Ireland
Peace in Northern Ireland depends on containing and ultimately removing the entrenched hostility between the two main communities in Northern Ireland.

We will:

Establish a power-sharing executive for Northern Ireland, elected under a fair and proportional system of voting. We will press for a new constitutional settlement based on the protection of individual rights through a Bill of Rights, incorporating the European Convention.

Give individuals more power and political responsibility. We will introduce a fair and proportional voting system for all elections, and reform and strengthen local government in the province.

Ensure respect for civil liberties. We will introduce an independent procedure for investigating complaints against the security forces, and reform the Diplock system so that three judges instead of one preside over non-jury trials. We will urgently implement the North Report's recommendations for an independent commission to supervise parades and marches.

Promote economic growth. We will strengthen the all-Ireland economy through the creation of effective cross-border agencies. We will invest in education and promote inward investment.

Build on the Joint Declaration and the Framework Document, by working with the Irish Government to create agreement between as many of the constitutional parties as possible. Sinn Fein can only be admitted to this process if, in accordance with the Mitchell principles, they and the IRA turn their backs on terrorism. Meanwhile, we must remain vigilant and keep in place the present means for countering terrorism.

THE LABOUR PARTY

Foreword by Tony Blair MP

I believe in Britain. It is a great country with a great history. The British people are a great people. But I believe Britain can and must be better: better schools, better hospitals, better ways of tackling crime, of building a modern welfare state, of equipping ourselves for a new world economy.

I want a Britain that is one nation, with shared values and purpose, where merit comes before privilege, run for the many not the few, strong and sure of itself at home and abroad.

I want a Britain that does not shuffle into the new millennium afraid of the future, but strides into it with confidence.

I want to renew our country's faith in the ability of its government and politics to deliver this new Britain. I want to do it by making a limited set of important promises and achieving them. This is the purpose of the bond of trust I set out at the end of this introduction, in which ten specific commitments are put before you. Hold us to them. They are our covenant with you.

I want to renew faith in politics by being honest about the last 18 years. Some things the Conservatives got right. We will not change them. It is where they got things wrong that we will make change. We have no intention or desire to replace one set of dogmas by another.

I want to renew faith in politics through a government that will govern in the interest of the many, the broad majority of people who work hard, play by the rules, pay their dues and feel let down by a political system that gives the breaks to the few, to an elite at the top increasingly out of touch with the rest of us.

And I want, above all, to govern in a way that brings our country together, that unites our nation in facing the tough and dangerous challenges of the new economy and changed society in which we must live. I want a Britain which we all feel part of, in whose future we all have a stake, in which what I want for my own children I want for yours.

A new politics

The reason for having created new Labour is to meet the challenges of a different world. The millennium symbolises a new era opening up for Britain. I am confident about our future prosperity, even optimistic, if we have the courage to change and use it to build a better Britain.

To accomplish this means more than just a change of government. Our aim is no less than to set British political life on a new course for the future.

People *are* cynical about politics and distrustful of political promises. That is hardly surprising. There have been few more gross breaches of faith than when the Conservatives under Mr Major promised, before the election of

1992, that they would not raise taxes, but would cut them every year; and then went on to raise them by the largest amount in peacetime history starting in the first Budget after the election. The Exchange Rate Mechanism as the cornerstone of economic policy, Europe, health, crime, schools, sleaze – the broken promises are strewn across the country's memory.

The Conservatives' broken promises taint all politics. That is why we have made it our guiding rule not to promise what we cannot deliver; and to deliver what we promise. What follows is not the politics of a 100 days that dazzles for a time, then fizzles out. It is not the politics of a revolution, but of a fresh start, the patient rebuilding and renewing of this country – renewal that can take root and build over time.

That is one way in which politics in Britain will gain a new lease of life. But there is another. We aim to put behind us the bitter political struggles of left and right that have torn our country apart for too many decades. Many of these conflicts have no relevance whatsoever to the modern world – public versus private, bosses versus workers, middle class versus working class. It is time for this country to move on and move forward. We are proud of our history, proud of what we have achieved – but we must learn from our history, not be chained to it.

The Conservatives seem opposed to the very idea of democracy. They support hereditary peers, unaccountable quangos and secretive government. They have debased democracy through their MPs who have taken cash for asking questions in the House of Commons. They are opposed to the development of decentralised government. The party which once opposed universal suffrage and votes for women now says our constitution is so perfect that it cannot be improved.

Our system of government is centralised, inefficient and bureaucratic. Our citizens cannot assert their basic rights in our own courts. The Conservatives are afflicted by sleaze and prosper from secret funds from foreign supporters. There is unquestionably a national crisis of confidence in our political system, to which Labour will respond in a measured and sensible way.

A modern House of Lords

The House of Lords must be reformed. As an initial, self-contained reform, not dependent on further reform in the future, the right of hereditary peers to sit and vote in the House of Lords will be ended by statute. This will be the first stage in a process of reform to make the House of Lords more democratic and representative. The legislative powers of the House of Lords will remain unaltered.

The system of appointment of life peers to the House of Lords will be reviewed. Our objective will be to ensure that over time party appointees as life peers more accurately reflect the proportion of votes cast at the previous general election. We are committed to maintaining an independent crossbench presence of life peers. No one political party should seek a majority in the House of Lords.

A committee of both Houses of Parliament will be appointed to undertake a wide-ranging review of possible further change and then to bring forward proposals for reform.

We have no plans to replace the monarchy.

An effective House of Commons

We believe the House of Commons is in need of modernisation and we will ask the House to establish a special Select Committee to review its procedures. Prime Minister's Questions will be made more effective. Ministerial accountability will be reviewed so as to remove recent abuses. The process for scrutinising European legislation will be overhauled.

The Nolan recommendations will be fully implemented and extended to all public bodies. We will oblige parties to declare the source of all donations above a minimum figure: Labour does this voluntarily and all parties should do so. Foreign funding will be banned. We will ask the Nolan Committee to consider how the funding of political parties should be regulated and reformed.

We are committed to a referendum on the voting system for the House of Commons. An independent commission on voting systems will be appointed early to recommend a proportional alternative to the first-past-the-post system.

At this election, Labour is proud to be making major strides to rectify the under-representation of women in public life.

Open government

Unnecessary secrecy in government leads to arrogance in government and defective policy decisions. The Scott Report on arms to Iraq revealed Conservative abuses of power. We are pledged to a Freedom of Information Act, leading to more open government, and an independent National Statistical Service.

Devolution: strengthening the Union

The United Kingdom is a partnership enriched by distinct national identities and traditions. Scotland has its own systems of education, law and local government. Wales has its language and cultural traditions. We will meet the demand for decentralisation of power to Scotland and Wales, once established in referendums.

Subsidiarity is as sound a principle in Britain as it is in Europe. Our proposal is for devolution not federation. A sovereign Westminster Parliament will devolve power to Scotland and Wales. The Union will be strengthened and the threat of separatism removed.

As soon as possible after the election, we will enact legislation to allow the people of Scotland and Wales to vote in separate referendums on our proposals, which will be set out in white papers. These referendums will take place not later than the autumn of 1997. A simple majority of those voting in each referendum will be the majority required. Popular endorsement will strengthen the legitimacy of our proposals and speed their passage through Parliament.

For Scotland we propose the creation of a parliament with law-making powers, firmly based on the agreement reached in the Scottish Constitutional Convention, including defined and limited financial powers to vary revenue and elected by an additional member system. In the Scottish referendum we will seek separate endorsement of the proposal to create a parliament, and of the proposal to give it defined and limited financial powers to vary revenue. The Scottish parliament will extend democratic control over the responsibilities currently exercised administratively by the Scottish Office. The responsibilities of the UK Parliament will remain unchanged over UK policy, for example economic, defence and foreign policy.

The Welsh assembly will provide democratic control of the existing Welsh Office functions. It will have secondary legislative powers and will be specifically empowered to reform and democratise the quango state. It will be elected by an additional member system.

Following majorities in the referendums, we will introduce in the first year of the Parliament legislation on the substantive devolution proposals outlined in our white papers.

Good local government

Local decision-making should be less constrained by central government, and also more accountable to local people. We will place on councils a new duty to promote the economic, social and environmental well-being of their area. They should work in partnership with local people, local business and local voluntary organisations. They will have the powers necessary to develop these partnerships. To ensure greater accountability, a proportion of councillors in each locality will be elected annually. We will encourage democratic innovations in local government, including pilots of the idea of elected mayors with executive powers in cities.

Although crude and universal council tax capping should go, we will retain reserve powers to control excessive council tax rises.

Local business concerns are critical to good local government. There are sound democratic reasons why, in principle, the business rate should be set locally, not nationally. But we will make no change to the present system for determining the business rate without full consultation with business.

The funnelling of government grant to Conservative-controlled Westminster speaks volumes about the unfairness of the current grant system. Labour is committed to a fair distribution of government grant. The basic framework; not every detail, of local service provision must be for central government. Councils should not be forced to put their services out to tender, but will be required to obtain best value. We reject the dogmatic view that services must be privatised to be of high quality, but equally we see no reason why a service should be delivered directly if other more efficient means are available. Cost counts but so does quality.

Every council will be required to publish a local performance plan with targets for service improvement, and be expected to achieve them. The Audit Commission will be given additional powers to monitor performance and promote efficiency. On its advice, government will where necessary send in a management team with full powers to remedy failure.

Labour councils have been at the forefront of environmental initiatives under Local Agenda 21, the international framework for local action arising from the 1992 Earth Summit. A Labour government will encourage all local authorities to adopt plans to protect and enhance their local environment.

Local government is at the sharp end of the fight against deprivation. Ten years after the Conservatives promised to improve the inner cities, poverty and social division afflict towns and outer estates alike. A Labour government will join with local government in a concerted attack against the multiple causes of social and economic decline – unemployment, bad housing, crime, poor health and a degraded environment.

London

London is the only Western capital without an elected city government. Following a referendum to confirm popular demand, there will be a new deal for London, with a strategic authority and a mayor, each directly elected. Both will speak up for the needs of the city and plan its future. They will not duplicate the work of the boroughs, but take responsibility for London-wide issues – economic regeneration, planning, policing, transport and environmental protection. London-wide responsibility for its own government is urgently required. We will make it happen.

The regions of England

The Conservatives have created a tier of regional government in England through quangos and government regional offices. Meanwhile local authorities have come together to create a more co-ordinated regional voice. Labour will build on these developments through the establishment of regional chambers to co-ordinate transport, planning, economic development, bids for European funding and land use planning.

Demand for directly elected regional government so varies across England that it would be wrong to impose a uniform system. In time we will introduce legislation to allow the people, region by region, to decide in a referendum whether they want directly elected regional government. Only where clear popular consent is established will arrangements be made for elected regional assemblies. This would require a predominantly unitary system of local government, as presently exists in Scotland and Wales, and confirmation by independent auditors that no additional public expenditure overall would be involved. Our plans will not mean adding a new tier of government to the existing English system.

Real rights for citizens

Citizens should have statutory rights to enforce their human rights in the UK courts. We will by statute incorporate the European Convention on Human Rights into UK law to bring these rights home and allow our people access to them in their national courts. The incorporation of the European Convention will establish a floor, not a ceiling, for human rights. Parliament will remain free to enhance these rights, for example by a Freedom of Information Act.

We will seek to end unjustifiable discrimination wherever it exists. For example, we support comprehensive, enforceable civil rights for disabled people against discrimination in society or at work, developed in partnership with all interested parties.

Labour will undertake a wide-ranging review both of the reform of the civil justice system and Legal Aid. We will achieve value for money for the taxpayer and the consumer. A community legal service will develop local, regional and national plans for the development of Legal Aid according to the needs and priorities of regions and areas. The key to success will be to promote a partnership between the voluntary sector, the legal profession and the Legal Aid Board.

Every country must have firm control over immigration and Britain is no exception. All applications, however, should be dealt with speedily and fairly. There are, rightly, criteria for those who want to enter this country to join husband or wife. We will ensure that these are properly enforced. We will, however, reform the system in current use to remove the arbitrary and unfair results that can follow from the existing 'primary purpose' rule. There will be a streamlined system of appeals for visitors denied a visa.

The system for dealing with asylum seekers is expensive and slow – there are many undecided cases dating back beyond 1993. We will ensure swift and fair decisions on whether someone can stay or go, control unscrupulous immigration advisors and crack down on the fraudulent use of birth certificates.

Northern Ireland

Labour's approach to the peace process has been bipartisan. We have supported the recent agreements between the two governments – the Anglo-Irish Agreement, the Downing Street Declaration and the Framework Document. The government has tabled proposals which include a new devolved legislative body, as well as cross-border co-operation and continued dialogue between the two governments.

There will be as great a priority attached to seeing that process through with Labour as under the Conservatives, in co-operation with the Irish government and the Northern Ireland parties. We will expect the same bipartisan approach from a Conservative opposition.

We will take effective measures to combat the terrorist threat.

There is now general acceptance that the future of Northern Ireland must be determined by the consent of the people as set out in the Downing Street Declaration. Labour recognises that the option of a united Ireland does not command the consent of the Unionist tradition, nor does the existing status of Northern Ireland command the consent of the Nationalist tradition. We are therefore committed to reconciliation between the two traditions and to a new political settlement which can command the support of both. Labour will help build trust and confidence among both Nationalist and Unionist traditions in Northern Ireland by acting to guarantee human rights, strengthen confidence in policing, combat discrimination at work and reduce tensions over parades. Labour will also foster economic progress and competitiveness in Northern Ireland, so as to reduce unemployment.

INDEX

The following abbreviations are used within entries:
ECHR for European Convention on Human Rights;
EU for European Union.

Geoffrey Belk

0134634S